Health Science for Teachers

Fifth Edition

Nathan Matza
MA, DrPH(c), CHES

Lecturer in Health Science
California State University
Long Beach, California

Reviewed and Edited by

Ricarda Benz, MD, OB/GYN, FACOG
Maria Matza, RNC, MSN, PhD
Professor of Nursing, School Nurse
Mary Margaret Popova, PhD,
Professor of English, University of Alabama

ISBN: 978-0-615-12320-2. Hygiapedo Publishing, Long Beach California.

Readers should be aware that Internet Websites offered as citations and/or sources for further information may have changed or disappeared between the time this was written and when it was read. It is highly recommended that readers use Google, or other search engines to quickly locate the latest source of information on relevant health topics and issues.

Health Science for Teachers originally printed in 1998, ISBN: 0-615-12320-1.

Revised edition, 2004, 3rd edition 2007, 4th edition 2010.

Printed in the United States of America. Hygiapedo Publishing, Long Beach California.

Health Science for Teachers Fifth Edition, (2013). ISBN: 978-0-615-12320-2.

Dedicated to my wife, Maria Matza.

To my children Eric, Jennifer, and Sara. To my grandchildren: Steven, Benjamin, Julia Rose, Elena, Sofia, Natalija, Liam, Isaiah, Jennevee and Steven J. Jr.

To Professor Julius Sumner Miller, Professor of Physics, who gave me passion and to my mentor, Bob De Wenter, Biology teacher, friend and confidant.

And a very special dedication to the memory of my esteemed friend and colleague, Professor Michael Smith, teacher, professor and passionate advocate for youth, who taught health education for over forty years in Long Beach, California.

Preface to the 5th Edition

Preface to the 5th Edition

Some things are getting better for teens, and others are not.

Behaviors that contribute to the leading causes of morbidity and mortality among youth and adults, often referred to as priority health-risk behaviors are usually established during childhood and adolescence, extend into adulthood, and are interrelated and preventable. The Centers for Disease Control and Prevention (CDC) has been monitoring risk behaviors in youth for several decades. The good news is that since the original publication of this text in the late 1990s, youth risk behaviors have changed for the better, i.e., kids are generally taking fewer risks and acting more responsibly, especially as it relates to reproductive behavior risks. Yet there are considerable areas of risk that need to be addressed.

The major behaviors, monitored by The Youth Risk Behavior Surveillance System (YRBSS), this author refers to as the **big six**. These big six issues among youth and young adults are: **1)** behaviors that contribute to unintentional injuries and violence; **2)** tobacco use; **3)** alcohol and other drug use; **4)** sexual behaviors that contribute to unintended pregnancy and sexually transmitted diseases (STDs), including human immunodeficiency virus (HIV) infection; **5)** unhealthy dietary behaviors; and **6)** physical inactivity. Nonetheless, we still need to teach our youth to make better choices because research indicates, for or example, that (1) almost half of 11th graders have been "high" on drugs or alcohol at least once, (2) the majority who drink are heavy drinkers; and (3) almost one quarter are binge drinkers. (Austin, Skager, 2004; YRBS, 2010a). One of the most significant findings since the 4th edition is that the annual deaths to all Americans from tobacco products now appear to have been eclipsed by annual deaths due to poor diet and lack of exercise. (Jia, Lubetkin, 2010). Dietary habits and lack of exercise now could lead to the conclusion that children born in the 1990s may not live as long as their parents! (Klich, 2008). The obesity epidemic in the U.S. is now so pervasive that many states have obesity levels greater than 30%. Kids today are more obese today than they have been in the last 30 years. (CDC. 2009a). Since 1991, the prevalence of many health-risk behaviors among high school students nationwide has decreased. However, many high school students continue to engage in behaviors that place them at risk for the leading causes of morbidity and mortality.

This 5th edition of *Health Science for Teachers* was written to help classroom teachers identify the health problems, issues and concerns of youth and to provide numerous solutions to help faculty guide youth to better lives. A significant change in the late 2000s among youth is the constant reliance on ever-present electronic devices such as smart phones, video games, electronic tablets, the old fashioned TV; and the explosion of social media websites such as Facebook, Twitter and others. While these devices and means of communication can serve as a rapid tool to connect to others; many kids get so wrapped up using these devices that they do not know how to interact with live people, face-to-face. Many young children do not even know how to listen for a dial tone on the phone because they only use mobile phones.

Educational leaders, parents, teachers and community advocates could help our kids stay healthy and lead productive lives by setting the stage for help. After nearly twenty years of advocacy from health education leaders, educators and concerned parents in March of 2008, The California Department of Education (CDE) finally adopted the Health Education Content Standards for California Public Schools, Kindergarten through Grade Twelve. (CDE, 2008). Chapter one and two will address the details of the new standards and teachers are encouraged to review them on the California Department of Education website. (Google Health Standards for California and CDE). Another significant document for teacher review is the *Health Framework for California Schools.* This document was last revised in 2003 and was scheduled to be rewritten in 2009; however the CDE suspended revisions due to the state budget crisis.

Finally, this edition of *Health Science for Teachers* is designed to help teachers with many of the everyday issues facing youth. Scientific information is presented to emphasize the problems and suggest solutions on a myriad of health topics; but the political implications at the local, state and national level will also be reviewed and discussed. Topics updated in the 5th edition include guidelines for nutrition, the obesity epidemic, inhalant abuse in young teens, updates on immunizations to prevent cervical cancer, reproductive health and family planning, and legal aspects for the classroom teacher including new health issues related to cyberbullying and violence prevention. Special focus will also discuss problems and solutions related to prevention of child abuse and neglect.

For updated information on many of these topics, students are encouraged to refer to the author's newly designed website: **nmatza.net** to locate many documents in the course documents section, and thousands of links to current health topics. While numerous websites will be referenced in the text, using **Google** as a search engine will serve as a very rapid way to locate specific content or resources. Readers are also encouraged to contact the author, Professor Nathan Matza by email anytime: **nmatza@csulb.edu.**

Table of Contents

Why Teaching? Giver of a Lifelong Gift

You are the giver of a lifelong gift. An impulse; an enduring tool; a prolific engine called learning. The infectious transfer of enthusiasm.

A glittering implosion...the exhilaration of thinking!

And because the price can be so very high, there are few who risk the full cost of caring, genuinely caring as you do.

It is your commitment, your sacrifice, your courage through which many ultimately realize the fruits of your sterling sheer goodness, and your talent for sharing.

So please know, and remember always, that in the giving of your priceless gift, boundless, limitless, you make their future...and ours.

It is for this that forever, always, the world will be in your debt. For you are the giver of a lifelong gift.

And we thank you; we salute you, Teacher.

Frank X. Trujillo, EdD

Chapter 1

Health Education: The School Setting

> *Nothing helps people stay healthy more than*
> *the power of real knowledge about health.*
> *... Dr. Roger Harms*

Introduction-Are we winning the battle to develop healthy kids?

Julia Rose was born in 2010. She probably will never see a cassette tape, an old cell phone without Internet service, and may never use a DVD. As she enters the world, technology is rapidly changing. Social networking seems to be the major form of communication of youth and schools of 2030 may only have computer tablet devices for kids (e.g. the iPad), or other devices not yet even invented, to use while old 'paper-type-documents,' those tools we use to call books, could collect dust on the old library shelves. And when Julia Rose goes home to relax, she will watch elaborate movies, and musical images displayed throughout her house filling up walls and will chat on a telephone device all streamed through a computer, or maybe just through the air! Many experts predict that by 2030 humans will be ready to receive brain implants of electronic gizmos to help us think, improve memory and whiz kids through school. Even the concept of teleportation posed by the scientific fiction of Star Trek may be beginning. "Beam me up Scotty! (Evans, 2009). While all these technologies develop, what will be happening to the health of humans, especial kids? Will they have necks at right angles to help them look down at electronic gadgets? Or will they be experimenting on drugs, foods or other devices to alter their state of minds. That is drugs and foods not yet even discovered, invented or synthesized in a future lab.

Perhaps the scene of 2020 will look like this: Dad is driving his new 2020 energy efficient, fuel cell or hydrogen fueled DXDZ2020 with three teenagers in the back seat, and nothing comes out of the exhaust but air and a little moisture. The three kids, aged 13, 15 and 17 are playing with their electronic games, watching a hologram 3D movie using their mini-laptop computers to communicate to their cyber-friends they never met, from various parts of the planet; all while chatting with friends on their 3D xyz phone device. Dad the driver, however, is talking to his GPS navigator to find a restaurant to go to and feed the ravenous kids some healthy food, while setting his vehicle on autopilot, and talking hands free to his wife who is in Italy on business. She should arrive home in about 2 hours by travelling on a supersonic plane. Suddenly all is quiet in the back seat. Dad looks in the rear view mirror and notices all three kids are now just sending text messages, and or just *think-sending* text messages. He asks, "OK kids, why do you have to send messages to each other when your family is in the back seat too?" Sofia, the young 13 year-old calmly responds, "Dad **we are talking to each other**, but we don't want you to know what we are saying." The 17-year-old Steven laughs loudly. This is the likely landscape of youth communication in the mid-21st century; the landscape in which future teachers must evolve into in order to thrive in this new world.

Classroom teachers today are keenly aware of the competition of multimedia, or 'electronic boxes,' portable players gadgets or other gizmos, that youth seem to dedicate so many viewing hours to every day. During the late 20th and early 21st century the big change with teen communication was the expanding Internet with names like You Tube, MyTube, MySpace, YourSpace, Twitter, HisSpace, HerSpace, FaceBook and InYourFace, along with numerous other websites which allow kids to take their classroom chatter and gossip and publish it world wide, **oftentimes before the lunch bell rings!** This posting, of course is followed by a quick online bargain purchase of clothes and electronics. What does all of this teen chatter have to do with health? Maybe the kids are telling each other something meaningful, significant, or even health promoting. Or, maybe they are just driving parents and school principals crazy.

A recent study presented at the 138th Annual Meeting of the American Public Health Association in 2010, brings up some major concerns. Some schools allow students to use cell phones as an alternative to laptop hardware during lessons. That could be a positive use of electronic gizmos, and a way to reduce school costs; but new research by Scott Frank reveals that excessive chatter may lead to poor health. Dr. Frank defines hyper-texting as more than 120 messages per day on school days. His data showed that teens who are **hyper-texters** were 40 percent more likely to have tried cigarettes, twice as likely to have tried alcohol, 43 percent more likely to binge drink, 41 percent more likely to have used illicit drugs, 55 percent more likely to have been in a physical altercation, nearly three-and-a-half times more likely to have had sex, and 90 percent more likely to report four or more sexual partners! This study stated that students were more likely to text if they were female, minorities, from low-income backgrounds and living in families without fathers. Frank further discovered that teens who face the greatest health risks are those who both hyper-text and **hyper-network** (spend more than three hours daily on social network sites). (APHA, 2011).

> *The academic success of America's youth is strongly linked with their health. Health-related factors such as hunger, physical and emotional abuse, and chronic illness can lead to poor school performance. Health-risk behaviors such as substance use, violence, and physical inactivity are consistently linked to academic failure and often affect students' school attendance, grades, test scores, and ability to pay attention in class…*
> **Centers for Disease Control & Prevention**

Throughout the 1980s, 1990s, and early 2000s, teen health was plagued with tobacco and drug abuse, disordered eating, and a myriad of sexually transmitted diseases (STDs). Expert research, however, has reported that we are making strides in lowering poor health behavior by youth. Various studies since 2002 indicate a definite decline in teen smoking, pregnancy and violent behaviors. By decades end, however, a previous decline in teen smoking rates leveled off. (CDC, 2010b). Lohrmann, and Wooley, speak optimistically about the role of comprehensive, and coordinated, school health. In their nationally recognized work, *Health is Academic*, they state, "Hundreds of thousands of children and adolescents across the United States are becoming health literate through regular participation in school-based comprehensive health education." They add, "...These young people know how to avoid both health problems...such as unintentional injury due to car crashes or HIV infection, and those that pose a greater threat during their adult life, such as cancer and heart disease." (Marx, Wooley, Northrop, 1998).

Update 2008: Whoops...maybe we are slipping again. Teen pregnancy rates were declining very well from the mid 1990s until about 2006, when the CDC reported that teen pregnancy rates rose for the first time in 14 years! Educators and researchers that **support comprehensive sexuality education (CSE)** agree that the increase seems to reflect abstinence only federally funded programs supported by the Bush administration that have been shown **not to work** in preventing teen pregnancy; do the math, abstinence only sexuality education fueled by federal funding from 1998 until 2008 and teen pregnancy rates go up! (Ventura, Albert, 2007) (Wire, 2008). Hmm…

The press often writes stories focusing on sex and sex education because it gets the attention of the reader and sells sodas, SUV's, hamburgers and a few newspapers. Arguments about pro-choice, anti-abortion, abstinence-only and methods of birth control have been debated for years. These arguments, however, too often are laced with political and social agendas. The decade from 1998 to 2008 saw overwhelming continuous support for sexuality education by parents, schools, and teachers, yet for a period of eight years the George W. Bush administration promoted, defended, funded and often erroneously published facts that would confuse the public and their children that want to live normal, healthy sexual lives. (Eisenberg, Bernat, Bearinger, 2008). Finally, in 2010 President Obama dramatically changed the sexuality education guidelines by providing federal funding in excess of $150 million to allow states to develop programs that include comprehensive sexuality education focusing on scientifically based evidence, and not just abstinence only education. A glimmer of hope was reported in 2011. Among teenagers aged 15 to 19 years, total births dropped 6%, from 42.5 births per 1000 teenagers in 2008 to 39.1 births per 1000 teenagers in 2009, reaching a record low, according to the US Centers for Disease Control and Prevention (CDC). Brady E. Hamilton, PhD, and colleagues with the CDC's National Center for Health Statistics in Hyattsville, Maryland, reported their findings in the December 21 issue of the National Vital Statistics Reports. (NVSR, 2010). These changes will be discussed in more detail later in this text.

Can a positive health educational program actually bring about health behavior change in kids? Recent studies do show that just **using positive messages** related to success, goals, self-esteem, without any formal sex education can decrease sexual acts by kids. (Hawkins, 2002). Details about teen pregnancy issues will be addressed in more detail later in chapters 8 and 10. While some subgroups in the south and Washington DC still have significant problems of teen pregnancy, data from the Alan Guttmacher Institute (AGI) indicate that pregnancy among teens and fewer abortions nationwide have continued to decline from 1988 until early 2005. (AGI, 2004, 2006).

The Youth Risk Behavior Surveillance System (YRBS)

The 2009 edition of the National Youth Risk Behavior Survey, (or Youth Risk Behavior Surveillance System (YRBSS), found that seatbelt use increased, fighting decreased, cigarette use decreased, spit tobacco use decreased, alcohol, marijuana, cocaine use decreased, sexual intercourse decreased, condom use increased **while participation in regular exercise decreased.** These trends seem to paint a better picture of the daily lives of kids, but one major problem still remaining since the 1980s is the overall increase of obesity in kids and the subsequent 25-30% rate of overweight prevalence in most adults throughout the entire U.S. (MMWR, 2006, CDC, 2009a). Data from the Center of Disease Control and Prevention (CDC) regularly measures behaviors that place youth at risk. These major health behaviors include what this author refers to as the **'big six.'** They are **(1) Behaviors that Contribute to Unintentional Injury and Violence, (2) Tobacco Use, (3) Alcohol and Other Drug Use, (4) Sexual Behaviors That Contribute to Unintended Pregnancy and STDs, Including HIV Infection, (5) Physical Activity; and (6) Dietary Behaviors and Obesity.** A brief summary of the YRBS 2009 data is listed below.

The Big Six

1.   **Behaviors that Contribute to Unintentional Injury and Violence**

- 9.7% of students had rarely or never wore a seat belt when riding in a car driven by someone else;
- Among the 69.5% of students who had ridden a bicycle during the 12 months before the survey, 84.7% had rarely or never worn a bicycle helmet;
- 28.3% of students rode in a car or other vehicle driven by someone who had been drinking alcohol one or more times during the 30 days before the survey;
- 9.7% of students had driven a car or other vehicle one or more times when they had been drinking alcohol during the 30 days before the survey;
- 17.5% of students had carried a weapon, (e.g., a gun, knife, or club) on at least 1 day during the 30 days before the survey;
- 5.9% of students had carried a gun on at least 1 day during the 30 days before the survey;
- 31.5% of students had been in a physical fight one or more times during the 12 months before the survey;
- 5.6% of students had carried a weapon (e.g., a gun, knife, or club) on school property on at least 1 day during the 30 days before the survey; and
- 13.8% of students had seriously considered attempting suicide and 6.3% of students had attempted suicide one or more times during the 12 months before the survey.

2.   **Tobacco Use**
- 46.3% of students had ever tried cigarette smoking (even one or two puffs);
- 19.5% of students smoked cigarettes on at least 1 day during the 30 days before the survey;
- 8.9% of students had used smokeless tobacco (e.g., chewing tobacco, snuff, or dip) on at least 1 day during the 30 days before the survey; and
- **Only 5.1% of students had smoked cigarettes on school property on at least 1 day during the 30 days before the survey.**

3.   **Alcohol and Other Drug Use**
- 72.5% of students had had at least one drink of alcohol on at least 1 day during their life and 41.8% of students had had at least one drink of alcohol on at least 1 day during the 30 days before the survey;
- 4.5% of students had drunk at least one drink of alcohol on school property on at least 1 day during the 30 days before the survey;
- 24.2% of students had had five or more drinks of alcohol in a row (i.e., within a couple of hours) on at least 1 day during the 30 days before the survey;
- 36.8% of students had used marijuana one or more times during their life;
- 20.8% of students had used marijuana one or more times during the 30 days before the survey;
- 2.8% of students had used any form of cocaine (e.g., powder, crack, or freebase) one or more times during the 30 days before the survey;
- 11.7% of students had ever sniffed glue, breathed the contents of aerosol spray cans, or inhaled any paints or sprays to get high one or more times during their life;
- 4.1% of students had used methamphetamines (also called "speed," "crystal", "crank," or "ice") one or more times during their life; and
- 3.3% of students had taken steroid pills or shots without a doctor's prescription one or more times during their life.

4.   **Sexual Behaviors That Contribute to Unintended Pregnancy and STDs, Including HIV Infection**
- 46.0% of students had ever had sexual intercourse;
- 13.8% of students had had sexual intercourse with four or more persons during their life;
- 34.2% of students had had sexual intercourse with at least one person during the 3 months before the survey;
- Among the 34.2% of currently sexually active students, 61.1% reported that either they or their partner had used a condom during last sexual intercourse; and
- Among the 34.2% of currently sexually active students, 22.9% reported that either they or their partner had used birth control pills or Depo-Provera to prevent pregnancy before last intercourse.

5.   **Physical Activity**
- 18.4% of students were physically active at least 60 minutes per day on each of the 7 days during the 7 days before the survey;
- 23.1% of students did not participate in at least 60 minutes of physical activity on at least 1day during the 7 days before the survey;
- 24.9% of students played video or computer games or used a computer for something that was not school work for 3 or more hours per day on an average school day;
- 32.8% of students watched television 3 or more hours per day on an average school day; and
- 56.4% of students attended physical education (PE) classes on 1 or more days in an average week when they were in school and 33.3% of students attended PE classes daily in an average week when they were in school.

6.   **Dietary Behaviors and Obesity**
- 33.9% of students had eaten fruit or drank 100% fruit juices two or more times per day during the 7 days before the survey;
- 13.8% of students ate vegetables three or more times per day during the 7 days before the survey;
- 22.3% of students had eaten fruits and vegetables five or more times per day during the 7 days before the survey;
- 29.2% of students had drunk a can, bottle, or glass of soda or pop (not including diet soda or diet pop) at least one time per day during the 7 days before the survey;
- 12.0% of students were obese and 15.8% of students were overweight. 10.6% of students went without eating for 24 or more hours to lose weight or to keep from gaining weight during the 30 days before the survey;
- 5.0% of students took diet pills, powders; and
- 4.0% of students vomited or took laxatives to lose weight or to keep from gaining weight during the 30 days before the survey.
- Other Health-Related Topics
- 22.0% of students had ever been told by a doctor or nurse that they had asthma and 10.8% of students still have asthma;
- 9.3% of students most of the time or always wore sunscreen with an SPF of 15 or higher when outside for more than 1 hour on a sunny day;
- 15.6% of students had used an indoor tanning device such as a sunlamp, sunbed, or tanning booth one or more times during the 12 months before the survey; and
- 30.9% of students had 8 or more hours of sleep on an average school night. (YRBS, 2010a).

As educators look ahead, however, we need to be cautious about the mere definition of sex as viewed by youth. The CDC reported on June 17, 2002 that middle school kids are starting to redefine "sex." Oral sex by many of these young teens is not "real sex." Teens text messages now include such terms as **'TVs'** or **technical virgins**, which means that the youth may have practiced oral, or anal sexual activity, but the girl is still a virgin since no vaginal intercourse occurred. Researchers stated, **"That girls choose oral sex first because they view it as something they control, whereas vaginal sex is seen as something boys control.** The result could be a generation that is increasingly promiscuous, startlingly frank and result in kids beginning to experiment with sex as young as ten." (CDC, 2002). This new attitude about oral sex often may produce embarrassing sessions in the pediatrician's office when the teen girl has to explain to her mom why her acute sore throat was diagnosed as gonococcal pharyngitis, or gonorrhea of the throat! While these data seem interesting, and often fill the pages of news media press releases, the actual sexual behaviors of teens is very difficult to measure since most data is self-reported. Moreover, data published from The Alan Guttmacher Institute indicate, "There is a widespread belief that teens engage in nonvaginal forms of sex, especially oral sex, as a way to be sexually active while still claiming that technically, they are virgins," and Lindberg states, "However, our research shows that this supposed substitution of oral sex for vaginal sex is largely a myth. There is no good evidence that teens who have not had intercourse engage in oral sex with a series of partners." (Lindberg, Jones, Santelli, 2008; Wind, 2008). Once again the media often loves to use sexual topics to promote products during the 2-3 second sound bites seen and heard throughout the news, and Internet.

One of the most challenging health problems that significantly impacts Americans in the last few years is obesity. **The obesity problem not only affects kids in the U.S but recent data has indicated that as many as 1 billion people of the world population are overweight.** This includes more than 30 million kids in China. Current obesity levels range from below 5% in China, Japan and certain African nations, to over 75% in urban Samoa. But even in relatively low prevalence countries like China, rates are nearly 20% in some cities. (WHO, 2005). Remember that in a typical city in China of about 1 million residents, 20% is equal to 200,000 people! The CDC now uses a new term to describe the problem i.e., the American society has become 'obesogenic,' characterized by environments that promote increased food intake, nonhealthful foods, and physical inactivity. Governmental policy and environmental change initiatives that make healthy choices in nutrition and physical activity available, affordable, and easy will likely prove most effective in combating obesity.

Childhood obesity is already epidemic in some areas and on the rise in others. The World Health Organization (WHO) estimates that 22 million children under five are estimated to be overweight worldwide. According to the U.S. Surgeon General, in the United States, the number of overweight children has doubled and the number of overweight adolescents has tripled since 1980. The prevalence of obese children aged 6-to-11 years has more than doubled since the 1960s. Obesity prevalence in youth's aged 12-17 has increased dramatically from 5% to 13% in boys and from 5% to 9% in girls between 1966-70 and 1988-91 in the U.S. The CDC reported that by the beginning of 2003 greater than 25% of Americans were overweight. (WHO, 2005), (Mokdad, Ford, Bowman, 2003). Additionally, **by 2009, nine U.S. States had obesity rates greater than thirty percent!** (CDC, 2009a). Obesity in childhood leads to a lifetime of coping problems for youth. Kids get embarrassed in PE classes, breathing becomes difficult, skeletal problems arise and the obese child that does little physical activity has a significantly higher risk of developing cardiovascular disease, metabolic syndrome (elevated cholesterol and triglycerides), stroke and type 2 diabetes. (AHA, 2005). Chapter 5 will address tobacco addiction and the 434,000 Americans that die from tobacco related diseases each year; but the CDC stated,

"Tobacco use and poor diet and physical inactivity contributed to the largest number of deaths, and the number of deaths related to poor diet and physical inactivity is increasing." In 2008 research from the CDC stated that the 434,000 annual deaths due to tobacco may soon be eclipsed by the greater than 300,000 annual deaths to Americans from obesity, poor nutrition and lack of exercise. Statisticians Jia and Lubetkin (2010) calculated that obesity related deaths from poor diet and inactivity **may now be equal to or greater than** tobacco related deaths. (Jia, Lubetkin, 2010).

Researcher Dr. William Klich of the The American Academy of Pediatrics and Baylor Medical School, puts the obesity epidemic in perspective by stating, "Because of the current overweight epidemic in children and teens, for the first time in over a century, **today's generation of kids will not live as long as their parents."** (Klich, 2008). The CDC published a very comprehensive document, related to adolescents in 2007, *Adolescent Health in the United States, 2007*. Readers are encouraged to review this document for current details of the health status of teenagers. (MacKay, Duran, 2007). The MacKay study reveals that the most costly and widespread adolescent health problems are often related to risky behaviors, as described in the 2009 YRBS study above, and are potentially preventable such as: unintended pregnancy, sexually-transmitted infections, violence, suicide, unintended injuries, and the use of alcohol, tobacco, and other drugs. Current indicators of adolescent health relayed in the report include:

- Approximately one-half of adolescents engage in some form of sexual contact. Sexually transmitted diseases (STDs) are the most commonly reported infectious diseases among sexually active adolescents;
- Pregnancy-related discharges accounted for almost one half of all hospital discharges among female adolescents in 2002-2004; nevertheless, birth rates among adolescents have declined markedly between 1991 and 2004;
- Motor vehicle traffic-related injuries and firearm-related injuries are the two leading causes of death among adolescents 10 to 19 years of age;
- Upper respiratory conditions, asthma, and abdominal or gastrointestinal conditions were among the leading diagnoses for adolescents' MD visits not related to an injury in 2002-2004;
- Alcohol is the most commonly used psychoactive substance during adolescence and marijuana is the most commonly used illicit drug among high school students; and
- A rapidly increasing percentage of the adolescent population is overweight. (MacKay, Duran, 2007).

Furthermore, the report shows that many health-risk behaviors are often established during youth and extend into adulthood. For instance, most adults who are addicted to tobacco began smoking as adolescents. Risk behaviors as well as other behaviors established during adolescence have been linked to subsequent morbidity and mortality. Additionally, the report emphasizes the need for intervention and prevention strategies to reduce such health-risk behaviors and promote a healthier transition from childhood to adulthood. To access the full report, please **Google** MacKay, Duran, 2007. (Note Google, now a verb, can quickly help readers locate original publications). ***The good news is that The California Department of Education (CDE) determined that about 65% of***

California high schools required students to receive instruction on health topics as part of a specific course.

Health Education and The School

Since the late 1990s health education programs have been developed to focus on all aspects of the lives of youth. This is referred to as **Coordinated School Health (CSH),** a CDC model (originated in1987), seeking to help youth realize and practice normative healthy behaviors with support of the school, parents, and the community at large. CSH may become the best way to help young people lead a positive healthy life, become health literate and avoid significant causes of disease and death. No single solution exists to improve the health status of children and adolescents in America. Individual families, local school boards, communities, health care professionals, governmental leaders and religious leaders must all work together to provide a continuously reinforced message to young people that will improve the state of health among youth. This is the basis of **Coordinated School Health.** It starts with a child as young as five years of age, and should continue throughout the entire K-12 curriculum.

Coordinated School Health for the 21st century must focus on such topics as mental and emotional health, use and abuse of tobacco, alcohol and other drugs, nutrition and exercise, disease, including sexually transmitted disease (STD), human sexuality, violence prevention, unintentional injury prevention, environmental and consumer health. Perhaps it took former Vice President Al Gore to earn both an Academy Award and a Nobel Prize to wake up the world about the environment. Hopefully this book will wake up teachers about the health of kids. **The purpose of this text is to provide ideas to help the classroom teacher become fully prepared to understand Coordinated School Health and utilize practical tools to enhance the teacher-learning environment. The ultimate goal of this work is to develop healthier kids.**

It is critical that Coordinated School Health must include much more than K-12 instruction. It must include other components such as health services from the nurse or medical staff and the mental and spiritual health support of the community from the clergy. CSH must also include school-based support including food services, psychological services, and adjunct support from physical education and school athletics. More than fifteen hundred schools nationwide now even include school-based clinics that serve specific needs of students at risk. These clinics provide services ranging from vision testing, hearing testing, dental exams, physical exams, immunizations, mental health counseling, services for reproductive care and prevention of STDs. Nonetheless, the school setting is very limited compared to the numerous outside influences youth face daily. A recent scholarly text from the Institute of Medicine, *Schools and Health: Our Nation's Investment,* succinctly clarifies this point:

Schools and Health: Our Nation's Investment

Schools should be held accountable for conveying health knowledge, providing a health-promoting environment, and ensuring access to high-quality services: these are the reasonable outcomes for judging the merit of a **Comprehensive School Health Program** (CSHP). Other outcomes-improved attendance, better cardiovascular fitness, less drug abuse, or fewer teen pregnancies, for example-may also be considered, but the committee believes that such measures must be interpreted with caution, since they are influenced by personal decision making and **factors beyond the control of the school.** In particular, null or negative outcomes for these measures should not necessarily lead to declaring the CSHP a failure; rather, they may imply that *'other sources'* of **influence on children and young people oppose and outweigh the influence of the Comprehensive School Health Program**. Allensworth, (1997).

The media, or as Professor Allensworth identifies it, "other sources," serves as one of the most powerful influences on young people today. Radio, TV, Internet sources, cell phones, and print media messages need to have a positive impression on youth. Too many times the school setting is totally negated by overwhelming media messages of sexuality, violence and dysfunctional family situations. In 1997 and again in 2002, the US Congress debated the issue of indecency on the Internet. This new explosive technology also should strive to promote positive health messages for youth. Minimally, parents, community agencies and school leaders should help students understand the new digital media messages related to their health.

Finally, California schools took action. During the 2004-2005 school year many districts and individual schools adopted new guidelines reflecting state laws limiting junk foods in the classroom and the sale of low nutritional value snacks. And, by the summer of 2007, The California *Education Code* (EC) 49430-49433 required all public schools to address, define or limit, 'junk foods,' 'fried foods,' 'snacks,' percentages of juices, and the sale of competitive foods on campus. This trend has now spread nationwide and numerous schools around the country have limited or eliminated unhealthy food choices, passed laws to reinforce healthier nutrition, and many even use chefs in the school cafeteria and serve fresh fruits and vegetables to kids everyday. The CDC publishes a website "Making it Happen," which can help schools, teachers and parents locate hundreds of programs, and plans to improve school nutrition for kids. (CDC, 2009b). Google CDC "Making it Happen" for details of this excellent program.

Students are taught how to prevent sexually transmitted diseases (STDs) in school and many schools even allow condom education; but the TV networks rarely advertise condoms for fear of offending a major segment of their viewers. This is ludicrous! Any child in America that stays home from school ill and watches an hour of soap opera programming, or views many current TV shows before 9 PM, will view far more sexual messages, without any reference to responsibility or sexual protection and with many negative messages as well. Many students continually receive mixed messages; teachers, schools and especially parents should help kids clarify the confusion.

The poet of rock and roll, Bob Dylan, once stated in musical lyric, '*The times, they are a changing.*' During the late 1990s, legislative changes and public outcries slowly started to bring about changes impacting the health of youth and adults as well. This author stood on the Las Vegas Strip and noticed two messages quite diametrically opposed. One read, "Flirt, Drink,

Smoke, Gamble and Play in Las Vegas." Directly across the street one of the newly designed billboards read, "Care if I smoke? Care if I die?" During 2000 the tobacco industry began to retreat, pay more fines for illness, and watch large icons literally fall. Not only did the tobacco industry agree to pay more than $234 billion for compensation from decades of deception about nicotine in December 1998, but also the famous 40-foot Marlboro Man advertisement was removed from Sunset Boulevard in Hollywood. This removal made national news in April of 1999. **Since the spring of 1999 all outdoor billboards and mobile ads for tobacco products have been banned throughout the U.S.** Studies from the Centers for Disease Control and Prevention (CDC) now indicate that tobacco use among all youth is declining (CDC, 2002). Amazingly, even China limited smoking in Beijing during the 2008 Olympics. Perhaps the largest smoking country in the world may start to save the lives of millions of Chinese citizens, or maybe not? And while it took over ten years (1999-2009), the federal courts ruled that the tobacco companies conspired for decades, much the same as racketeering gangsters, and allowed the FDA to control tobacco sales in the U.S. By 2012 new graphic images were required to be added to all cigarettes sold in the U.S. Chapter five will expand on the issues of tobacco, politics, and the impact on youth. (TobaccoFreeKids, 2010).

Violence Prevention.

Perhaps the tragedy at Columbine High School in Colorado during the spring of 1999, which caused the death of a teacher and injuries to several students, or the shooting deaths of 33 college students at Virginia Tech in 2007 will serve as a wake up call to Americans. Many youths of today are very troubled and need well-planned programs to help them lead stable and happy lives. Hopefully these national tragedies will help kids make positive decisions to improve their health and live happy lives.

Among adults, 65% of all deaths result from three causes: heart disease, cancer, and stroke. Most of the risk factors associated with these causes of death originate during adolescence. The phrase, **"pay me now or pay me later"** related to various other economic conditions in life, aptly applies to the risk behaviors practiced by teens and young adults. The research data stated above clearly defines the problems, yet many community leaders, parents, school systems and governmental administrators fail to place enough emphasis on prevention.

While research reports, opinion surveys and other documents may present the need for comprehensive health education in schools, political forces can affect behavior and result in changes. Tobacco initiatives and subsequent tax revenues have changed norms of tobacco use in many states. Mandated comprehensive school health curricula in grades K-12 must become the norm. Teachers should not have to spend excessive time to help kids "heal" from their unhealthy "injuries." Students must develop a self-sufficiency and coping skill behavior pattern while teachers, and parents, can serve to advise and recommend change. **Most importantly, secondary schools must require a health education course for graduation.** Less than two-thirds of California schools awarding diplomas actually require a health course to graduate. (Fisher, 1999). Due to financial constrains, however, health classes have not been a high priority for schools and even the state government. Many school districts are turning to online alternatives for health education of their youth.

The National Health Education Standards

The National Health Education Standards (NHES) were released in 2007 from the CDC and are very similar to those standards adopted in California during the same year. The National Health Education Standards (NHES) are written **expectations for what students should know and be able to do by grades 2, 5, 8, and 12 to promote personal, family, and community health.** The standards provide a framework for curriculum development and selection, instruction, and student assessment in health education. The NHES standards are listed below. Compare them to the California Health Standards below. NHES Standards and Performance Indicators state:

1. Students will comprehend concepts related to health promotion and disease prevention to enhance health;
2. Students will analyze the influence of family, peers, culture, media, technology and other factors on health behaviors;
3. Students will demonstrate the ability to access valid information, products, and services to enhance health;
4. Students will demonstrate the ability to use interpersonal communication skills to enhance health and avoid or reduce health risks;
5. Students will demonstrate the ability to use decision-making skills to enhance health;
6. Students will demonstrate the ability to use goal-setting skills to enhance health;
7. Students will demonstrate the ability to practice health-enhancing behaviors and avoid or reduce health risks; and
8. Students will demonstrate the ability to advocate for personal, family and community health. (ACS, 2007).

The California Health Standards Approved-Finally!

After about twenty years of suggestions, lobbying, recommendations and oral communications to the State Board of the California Department of Education, the health education standards were approved in March 2008! Once the standards became official, health education leaders, school administrators and input from parents, suggested that the legislature approve a course in health education for high school graduation. The framework recommendation below (not a mandate) was written by this author on the framework committee in 1994! That recommendation is also published in the 2003 modified framework and reads: **"This framework recommends that the kindergarten through grade twelve course of study in health be anchored by a full year's work at the middle school level and a second full year's work at the high school level."** The health framework provides guidelines for teachers to implement lessons to their students. The critical link between health and learning is a well-organized and implemented health education program for all students grades K-12. Risk factors that influence students' success in developing and maintaining a state of health include: (1) economic deprivation, (2) neighborhood disintegration, (3) poor family management practices,

(4) peer use of tobacco, alcohol, and other drugs, and (5) low expectations for children's success. Too often, these factors lead to academic failure. Chapters 2-4 will address these issues in detail.

All teachers should be aware of the process of implementing frameworks as they write lessons, follow standards for their subject matter areas, and teach students. In California the process of adoption for a state curriculum framework in the various subject matter content areas follows these steps: (1) The California Department of Education (CDE) organizes a committee of teachers and other educational leaders; (2) The committee is selected and meets in Sacramento for several months; (3) The committee writes and rewrites objectives and organizes the general direction for implementation in schools; (4) The final draft is sent to the State Board of Education for approval. After the State Board approves the framework the document is sent to each school district where the superintendent directs principals to have the local teachers write lessons based upon the framework. The **California Curriculum Frameworks** are: Career Technical Education, Foreign Language, **Health**, History-Social Science, Mathematics, Physical Education, Reading/Language Arts, Science, Visual and Performing Arts. Included in the frameworks are state standards, often adapted from national standards in all subject matter areas.

The Health Standards

As important as these statements and recommendations are to help kids lead a healthy life, still, there are many parents, students and even school administrators that do not see health education as important. During 2008 and 2009 some school districts were requiring students to take a health class for graduation, but were allowing their students to take a health education class online, without any direct human contact in a classroom setting. Ironically, **the 2008 newly approved standards for health require that the health instruction focus on a skills-based curriculum, and not just content.** For example, in a health class dealing with tobacco abuse, or prevention of STDs, teachers would utilize numerous group activities, such as practicing refusal skills to use drugs, or engage in sexual acts. *EC 51930* even requires refusal skills to prevent HIV/AIDS. As will be mentioned throughout this book, **"either we pay now or pay later."** We can invest in quality health education for our kids today, including refusal skills, etc., and prevent paying for it later, in the form of drug rehabilitation or welfare parents to an unmarried teen girl. Finally, health education that is both knowledge and skills base is important since many students with the knowledge, still practice risky behaviors. When skills are included within the curriculum, kids should be able to live a much healthier, and happier life.

State Curriculum Standards-Goals

The California State Board of Education approved the four goals from the standards: **Four characteristics are identified as essential to *health literacy*.** According to the goals of these state documents related to youth, health-literate individuals are:

1. Critical thinkers and problem solvers when confronting health problems and issues;
2. Self-directed learners who have the competence to use basic health information and services in health-enhancing ways;

3. Effective communicators who organize and convey beliefs, ideas, and information about health issues; and
4. Responsible and productive citizens who help ensure their community is kept healthy, safe, and secure. (CDE, 2008).

These four essential characteristics of health-literate individuals are woven throughout the health education standards.

The Overarching Content Standards by the California State Board of Education are, that all students will: (1) comprehend essential concepts related to enhancing health; (2) demonstrate the ability to analyze internal and external influences that affect health; (3) access and analyze health information, products, and services; (4) use interpersonal communication skills to enhance health; (5) use decision-making skills to enhance health; (6) use goal-setting skills to enhance health; (7) practice behaviors that reduce risk and promote health; and (8) promote and support personal, family, and community health. (CDE, 2008).

Advanced Placement Kids Not Receiving Health Education

As stated earlier, some school boards have allowed students to earn credit for a health education class using online sources, without attending any classroom sessions. Some of the reasons given are many students, especially advanced placement students, have impacted schedules and the health education requirement cannot fit into their high school schedule. Sometimes this alternative approach by school boards is done to appease anxious parents concerned that their child must earn high grades and can't be burdened with a health class. Sadly, many parents and school managers choose not to admit that these 'high achievers' may finish school, become doctors, lawyers or highly paid executives; but still have problems with alcohol, drug abuse and unprotected sex. **The State Standards for Health Education requires skills as well as intellectual achievement.** The following passage from the health standards clearly makes the point for **skills to prevent drug, use, etc.** If students are allowed to just take an online course, it will become very difficult to monitor, assess and evaluate any skills, such as refusal skills to use drugs, smoke cigarettes, or have unprotected sex. The following is excerpted from the California State Standards for Health Education:

> Health education has undergone a paradigm shift over the last 15 years. It has evolved from a primarily knowledge-based subject to a focused skills-based subject. This shift came about as data from national and state surveys, such as the California Healthy Kids Survey indicated that **although youth had knowledge of what was harmful to their health, they did not have the skills to keep from engaging in the risky behaviors. In other words, the students had the knowledge about why certain behaviors could and would cause harm; however, they were still engaging in these risky behaviors.** The focus in the health education standards is on teaching the skills that enable students to make healthy choices and avoid high-risk behaviors. Eight overarching standards describe essential concepts and skills; they are taught within the context of the six content areas. Each skill is learned and practiced specific to the content area and behavior. (CDE, 2008)

Online Health Education

As school districts and state budgets become scarcer, due to economic difficulties, many teachers will have to accept the online approach to teaching youth. When a classroom setting is not possible and online health education courses are established and utilized, it is imperative that the national standards be met. The International Association for K-12 Online Learning (iNACOL) established National Standards for Quality Online Teaching and Programs. These standards, while not allowing for much daily skills-based teaching, include the following:

- The teacher meets the professional teaching standards established by a state-licensing agency or the teacher has academic credentials in the field in which he or she is teaching;
- The teacher has the prerequisite technology skills to teach online;
- The teacher plans, designs, and incorporates strategies to encourage active learning, interaction, participation and collaboration in the online environment;
- The teacher provides online leadership in a manner that promotes student success through regular feedback, prompt response and clear expectations;
- The teacher models, guides, and encourages legal, ethical, safe and healthy behavior related to technology use;
- The teacher has experienced online learning from the perspective of a student;
- The teacher understands and is responsive to students with special needs in the online classroom;
- The teacher demonstrates competencies in creating and implementing assessments in online learning environments in ways that assure validity and reliability of instruments and procedures;
- The teacher develops and delivers assessments, projects, and assignments that meet standards-based learning goals and assesses learning progress by measuring student achievement of learning goals;
- The teacher demonstrates competencies in using data and findings from assessments and other data sources to modify instructional methods and content and to guide student learning;
- The teacher demonstrates frequent and effective strategies that enable both teacher and students to complete self and pre assessments;
- The teacher collaborates with colleagues; and
- The teacher arranges media and content to help students and teachers transfer knowledge most effectively in the online environment. (iNACOL, 2010).

Integrating Health Education Lessons

Secondary teachers can present many classroom health education lessons in an integrated fashion. **These lessons should support and not supplant health education instruction**. The *Health Framework for California Public Schools* (1994, 2003) addresses many approaches teachers could use to teach health topics on a daily basis. As previously stated, the framework also recommends a full year of health education to be taught at the middle school level, followed by an additional full year at the high school level. Lessons could include a biology teacher preparing labs on bacteriology while using prepared slides of syphilis or the bubonic plague. An English teacher could have students select topic sentences in a magazine article on methods of contraception. A social studies teacher might have students compare the impact of tobacco on American history during the 19th century. A teacher of government or earth science might have the students watch the 2006 Academy Awarded movie, An Inconvenient Truth, by Al Gore, and have the students debate the issues of global warming. Teachers could also have students read the classic articles on the Liggett Group **"surrendering secret memos"** to the courts stating that nicotine is addictive and **tobacco use does cause cancer**. (*Los Angeles Times*, 1997).

If a teacher allows students to select various reading materials and uses topics relevant to students' personal lives and health, educators can enhance a specific content lesson while not detracting from their teaching lessons and objectives within their subject matter specialty. Detailed reports relating the historical and political perspectives of the tobacco companies and their attempts to increase nicotine content or influence politicians can be accessed from the work of worldwide expert, and university professor, Dr. Stanton Glantz, author of *The Cigarette Papers,* and developer of the tobacco companies documents archive at **http://galen.library.ucsf.edu/tobacco/.** This website catalogs thousands of documents related to the deception and lies from the tobacco industry for the past five decades.

The school provides an excellent source to influence student health through instruction, clinical services, protective policies, and a health-enhancing environment. (Lovato, Allensworth, & Chan, 1989). Schools have the primary responsibility of educating and training children, but the school cannot address every aspect of the student's life. The school, the community, and the students themselves must address issues such as tobacco, alcohol, and drug use collaboratively. (CDE, 1991). As behavior changes develop in individuals, changes in norms will result. Today, young kids do not see tobacco use as an acceptable practice, despite the multi-billion dollar efforts of the tobacco companies.

Of utmost importance is the daily role-model parents play on student health behavior. The impact of parents profoundly affects student health practices. **What the parent or guardian does** is probably the most significant thing for the student to observe and emulate. If dad or mom smokes, so too will the child smoke. If dad or mom exercises daily, so too will the child exercise daily. If dad or mom drinks and abuses alcohol, ditch work, manipulate their friends and commit violence, so too will the child drink alcohol, ditch school, manipulate friends and commit violence.

The Harvard School Health Education Project, written in 1992, compiled a report on the current state of school health. The report summarized and synthesized 25 national studies to describe the **interconnectedness of children's health and education.** While it was written twenty years ago, the major ideas still hold today. Five major common themes emerged from this research. They are listed below:

1. **Education and health are interrelated.** Children whose lives are impeded by violence, hunger, substance abuse, early pregnancy, depression or hopelessness are not healthy children. Children who are unhealthy are children whose learning is impaired. *Not only can education contribute to improving health, but also conversely, a child's health status is a major determinant of educational achievement. In order to improve academic achievement, schools and other institutions must devote more attention to health concerns.*

2. **The biggest threats to health are "social morbidities."** National statistics reflect the increasing impact of health problems that are largely preventable. Many of these are strongly influenced by social environment and/or specific behaviors, which often are established during youth and extend into adulthood.

3. **A more comprehensive, integrated approach is needed.** Enough is known about what works and what does not work in addressing these problems in order to implement more effective programs. While there have been many successful programs, some have been too fragmented and have targeted categorical symptoms rather than their common antecedents. There need to be more collaborative programs and policies, which address the underlying causes of problems.

4. **Health promotion and education efforts should be centered in and around schools.** Most children are in school. In fact, elementary and secondary schools are the "workplace" for nearly one fifth of the U.S. population (children and adults). Schools have the unique capacity to affect the lives of students, staff, parents and entire communities. The components of comprehensive school health programs include health instruction at all grade levels; health services; a healthy, safe, and nurturing environment; physical education; food services; guidance and counseling; interaction with families and community organizations; and worksite wellness programs for school employees. In addition, school buildings can provide the sites for a broad range of community health promotion programs that need not be administered by the schools themselves. As community institutions, schools must play a larger role in addressing the health and social problems that limit not only academic achievement, but also our nation's public health and economic productivity.

5. **Prevention efforts are cost-effective and the social and economic costs of inaction are too high and still escalating.** School failure, under-achievement, and related health and social problems have serious repercussions not only for children and their families, but for their communities and ultimately for the overall benefit of our nation's economic and social systems as well. (Lavin, Shaprio, Weill, 1992).

This last point reported by Lavin, et al, related to economics and health is a simple one. *"Either pay now or pay later."* When a school district uses a fragmented health education curriculum with poorly trained staff, the impact on youth can be devastating. By avoiding well-planned health education now, schools and students will pay later. Children will pay the consequences by smoking, not exercising, eating poorly and failing to achieve academically. Schools will pay the consequences of students failing classes and repeating courses as a result of teachers using poorly prepared or outdated materials, schools may even need to pay large sums resulting from litigation against the governing board. This is especially true as it relates to controversial issues such as sex education and HIV education programs. *"Either pay now or pay later."* As school districts fail to help students with everyday health problems, local towns and communities produce students poorly prepared to deal with stress management, refusal skill techniques, and avoidance of pregnancy and STDs. As tax coffers support teenage pregnancy, welfare families, abused children, and babies suffering from fetal alcohol syndrome deformities, many students will become a burden to society. So much of this can be prevented by schools organizing well planned health education curricula, hiring and training well prepared professional health educators, and communicating regularly and consistently with parents and other community members to nurse children to a healthy, productive and positive life. *"Either pay now or pay later..."*

What is Health Education?

A simple dictionary definition of **health education** states, "Health Education comprises consciously constructed opportunities for learning involving some form of communication designed to improve health literacy, including improving knowledge, and developing life skills which are conducive to individual and community health." (Definitionofwellness, 2011). Since the early 2000s, however, a major focus regarding the health of youth has shifted from mere knowledge or information of health topics such as drug abuse, and nutrition; to the ability to **practice skills** to improve health. A health education program is the centerpiece of a comprehensive school health program. Support systems are critical to effect behavior change in children, but students must first develop concepts, skills and knowledge that will effect personal behaviors related to lifestyles. Health education must include:

- A planned, sequential pre-kindergarten through 12th grade curriculum, based on student needs and current health concepts and societal issues;
- Instruction designed to motivate health maintenance and **promote wellness**, not merely to prevent disease or disability;
- Activities to develop decision-making skills and individual responsibility for personal health;
- Opportunities for students to develop and demonstrate health-related knowledge, attitudes and practices; and
- Integration of the physical, mental, emotional and social dimensions of health as the basis for studying the ten essential content areas identified by the National Professional School Health Education Organizations (1984).

The **ten essential content areas** of health education in schools are as follow:

1. Community health;
2. Consumer health;
3. Environmental health;
4. Family life;
5. Growth and development;
6. Nutritional health;
7. Personal health;
8. Prevention and control of disease and mental disorders;
9. Safety and accident prevention; and
10. Substance use and abuse (Matza, English, & Lovato, 1993).

Health Framework

Curriculum Frameworks are the overarching documents that guide California schools in preparing curricula and implementing lesson plans in the classroom. Frameworks are written by committees of teachers and other educators for all K-12 subject matter areas. They are then approved by the State Board of Education and distributed to school districts, that in tern, provide them for teachers to write lessons plans. The California State Board of Education (CDE) revised the *Health Framework* in 1994 and published a supplemental version in 2003. State Frameworks are usually rewritten about every ten years; but the economic recession during the 2000s changed the sequence of events. During 2009 a committee was selected to rewrite the *Health Framework*. The CDE, however, under the influence of then-governor Schwarzenegger, postponed all curriculum framework committee revisions. Consequently, the 1994 major *Health Framework* document revision may not be completed until 2014 or 2015. That is a delay of thirty years from the original publication of the early 1990s! While the legislators struggle with financial difficulties, kids may suffer by not receiving the latest information and instructional materials to help improve their health. (Google: **http://www.cde.ca.gov/ci/cr/cf/** for the CDE explanation).

However, one of the most important statements related to health education, kids and school graduation requirements, can be found on **page 36** of the *Health Framework*. The section below was written by this author. The Framework states:

> Several national research studies suggest that significant changes in knowledge about health and attitudes toward health seem to occur after 50 hours of classroom instruction per school year or about one and one-half hours per week. **This framework recommends that the kindergarten through grade twelve course of study in health be anchored by a full year's work at the middle school level and a second full year's work at the high school level.** Various options exist for including health education in the curriculum at those levels, and decisions on how best to offer health education should be made locally. What is essential is that adequate amounts of time be allocated for such instruction. (California Department of Education, 1994, 2003).

A very large body of research on the importance of school health education that further reinforces the critical need for well-planned health education programs in schools was recently published by the Institute of Medicine. So often, by the time most students reach the high school level, they already have engaged in a multitude of risk behaviors or have formulated attitudes of acceptance for these behaviors. The Institute recommended that:

- All students receive sequential, age-appropriate health education every year during elementary and middle or junior high grades;
- **A one-semester health education course at the secondary level immediately become a minimum requirement for high school graduation.** Instruction should follow the National Health Education Standards, use effective up-to-date curricula, be provided by qualified health education teachers interested in teaching the subject, and emphasize the six priority behavioral areas identified by the CDC.
(Allensworth, Lawson, Nicholson, et al. (1997).

As schools adopt and implement these recommendations, students will achieve improved and healthy lives, be happy more, be able to resist pressure from peers, and avoid risky sexual behaviors, which can dramatically change their lives.

Coordinated School Health Programs (CSHP). What is a CSHP?

A coordinated school health program (CSHP) model consists of eight interactive components. Schools by themselves cannot, and should not be expected to, address the nation's most serious health and social problems. Families, health care workers, the media, religious organizations, community organizations that serve youth, and young people themselves also must be systematically involved. However, schools could provide a critical facility in which many agencies might work together to maintain the well being of young people. The following are descriptions of the eight components of a **coordinated school health program** from the Centers for Disease Control. **Coordinated School Health Model**: Health Education; Physical Education; Health Services; Nutrition Services; Counseling, Psychological, and Social Services; Healthy School Environment; Health Promotion for Staff; Family and Community Involvement.

1. Health Education: A planned, sequential, K-12 curriculum that addresses the physical, mental, emotional and social dimensions of health. The curriculum is designed to motivate and assist students to maintain and improve their health, prevent disease, and reduce health-related risk behaviors. It allows students to develop and demonstrate increasingly sophisticated health-related knowledge, attitudes, skills, and practices. The comprehensive health education curriculum includes a variety of topics such as personal health, family health, community health, consumer health, environmental health, sexuality education, mental and emotional health, injury prevention and safety, nutrition, prevention and control of disease, and substance use and abuse. Qualified, trained teachers provide health education.

2. Physical Education: A planned, sequential K-12 curriculum that provides cognitive content and learning experiences in a variety of activity areas such as basic movement skills; physical fitness; rhythms and dance; games; team, dual, and individual sports; tumbling and gymnastics; and aquatics. Quality physical education should promote, through a variety of planned physical activities, each student's optimum physical, mental, emotional, and social development, and should promote activities and sports that all students enjoy and can pursue throughout their lives. Qualified, trained teachers teach physical activity.

3. Health Services: Services provided for students to appraise, protect, and promote health. These services are designed to ensure access or referral to primary health care services or both, foster appropriate use of primary health care services, prevent and control communicable disease and other health problems, provide emergency care for illness or injury, promote and provide optimum sanitary conditions for a safe school facility and school environment, and provide educational and counseling opportunities for promoting and maintaining individual, family, and community health. Qualified professionals such as physicians, nurses, dentists, health educators, and other allied health personnel provide these services.

4. Nutrition Services: Access to a variety of nutritious and appealing meals that accommodate the health and nutrition needs of all students. School nutrition programs reflect the U.S. Dietary Guidelines for Americans and other criteria to achieve nutrition integrity. The school nutrition services offer students a learning laboratory for classroom nutrition and health education, and serve as a resource for linkages with nutrition-related community services. Qualified child nutrition professionals provide these services.

5. Health Promotion for Staff: Opportunities for school staff to improve their health status through activities such as health assessments, health education and health-related fitness activities. These opportunities encourage school staff to pursue a healthy lifestyle that contributes to their improved health status, improved morale, and a greater personal commitment to the school's overall coordinated health program. This personal commitment often transfers into greater commitment to the health of students and creates positive role modeling. Health promotion activities have improved productivity, decreased absenteeism, and reduced health insurance costs.

6. Counseling and Psychological Services: Services provided to improve students' mental, emotional, and social health. These services include individual and group assessments, interventions, and referrals. Organizational assessment and consultation skills of counselors and psychologists contribute not only to the health of students but also to the health of the school environment. Professionals such as certified school counselors, psychologists, and social workers provide these services.

7. Healthy School Environment: The physical and aesthetic surroundings and the psychosocial climate and culture of the school. Factors that influence the physical environment include the school building and the area surrounding it, any biological or chemical agents that are detrimental to health, and physical conditions such as temperature, noise, and lighting. The psychological environment includes the physical, emotional, and social conditions that affect the well being of students and staff.

8. Parent/Community Involvement: An integrated school, parent, and community approach for enhancing the health and well-being of students. School health advisory councils, coalitions, and broadly based constituencies for school health can build support for school health program efforts. Schools actively solicit parent involvement and engage community resources and services to respond more effectively to the health-related needs of students. (CDC, 2005).

Coordinated School Health Model

The Role of Teachers in School Health

Parents play the primary role of fostering positive health practices and lifestyles for their children. They can teach children communication skills, proper nutrition, disease prevention, how to deal with sexuality, and who to turn to for health support, such as child abuse prevention. Teachers see students several hours every day and can also reinforce positive behaviors in three ways:

1. **Direct instruction**, by organizing and presenting health topics in a health course;
2. **Integrated instruction** in social science, biology, art, English and home economics classes; and
3. **Incidental classroom health education** which is personalized and spontaneous teaching during "teachable moments." Often the most significant health education with young people occurs in the hallways, lunchrooms or school grounds.

Cultural Demographics and Health: Health and Cultural Sensitivity

Many California schools have registered 50-75 different languages spoken by students. Since the early 1990s the "majority" population of California students became the "minority population." By 2001, greater than fifty percent of the entire population of California consisted of non-whites, or more correctly, people of color. The white, Eurocentric foundation of the United States has changed significantly as schools entered the 21st century, **with people of color now representing greater than seventy percent of the entire student population in California.** The Golden State now has greater than six million kids enrolled in schools representing numerous ethnic groups. But, nearly fifty percent live in four counties: Los Angeles, Orange, San Diego and San Bernardino. (CBEDS, 2006). All students need to be treated with dignity, recognizing cultural, religious and familial values.

Many Asian cultures, for example, believe that health and illness are determined by the balance or imbalance of spiritual or supernatural forces, rather than by biological, behavioral or environmental factors. People following the Buddhist religion attach special religious significance to the head region, and American teachers should be cautious about touching the head or requiring kids to do a PE activity involving the head. Many Hispanics rely on faith healers or *curanderos* to solve various health problems instead of using traditional Western medical health services. Teachers should not be judgmental in viewing these health related cultural differences and should strive to increase student knowledge related to health education. Factors that influence how people identify with a particular culture include: their own historical, socioeconomic and political experience, education, family and peer influence, primary language, religion, age at time of immigration, where they lived and length of time in the U.S. citizenship status, and whether or not the individual resides in a culturally integrated community. For a detailed PowerPoint show on Hispanics and Cultural Awareness, contact nmatza@csulb.edu.

School Teachers Need to Know About Health Education and Culture

The majority of students in California schools by the end of the 20th century were significantly different than those that entered the U.S. at the beginning of the 20th century. Europeans from various countries came in large numbers in the early 1900s, but today families enter the U.S. from all over the world. Teachers must be prepared to help these students and teachers are also required to take teacher preparation courses reflecting the dynamic cultural changes that exist.

Hispanics, for example, represent a very diverse group. While Mexico is the nearest U.S. border for Latin American immigrants, many students now come from Cuba, Puerto Rico, El Salvador, and other Central and South American nations. Similarly, Asian students may come from Korea, China, Taiwan, Vietnam, Cambodia, the Philippines, or other countries. Each country has its own history, food, dance, music and beliefs. Each country also brings its own type of health practices. Most minority groups in the United States tend to use Western medical services less than the Euro-American population. **Up to two-thirds of minority populations still rely on traditional healers and treatment, instead of more commonly used Western medical care**. (Brainard, 1996).

In his book *Cultural Diversity in the Health Classroom,* Brainard clearly details the health differences and practices among Hispanics, Native Americans, Asians and other minority groups. Teachers should recognize the great diversity of students that come to their classes from families of many different nations. Many health problems and issues of minority students are similar to most other Americans, but the table below summarizes the major causes of death specific to U.S. minority populations, more generally called **people of color**. (Brainard, 1996).

Table 1.1
Major Causes of Death and Their Modifiable Risk Factors for U.S. Minority Populations

Disease	Modifiable Risk Factors
Cancer	Tobacco use, diet, alcohol abuse
Diabetes	Obesity, diet, alcohol abuse
Heart Disease/Stroke	High blood pressure, diet, lack of exercise, obesity, tobacco use
Homicide/Suicide	Alcohol or other drug abuse, poor conflict-resolution skills
Chemical Dependency	Alcohol or other drug abuse, tobacco use
Infant Mortality	Tobacco or alcohol use during pregnancy, late or no prenatal care, adolescent pregnancy, poor diet
Unintentional Injury (accidents)	Alcohol or other drug abuse, environmental hazards

(Brainard, 1996)

It is especially important to recognize that specific minority groups exhibit many of the same health problems and risk factors. Some groups have elevated risks for many chronic diseases. For example, compared to the majority population:

African Americans

- African American adults are 1.7 times as likely than their White adult counterparts to have a stroke;
- African American men are twice as likely to have new cases of stomach cancer as non-Hispanic white men;
- In 2005, African American women were 10% less likely to have been diagnosed with breast cancer, however, they were 34% more likely to die from breast cancer, compared to non-Hispanic white women;
- African American adults are twice as likely than non-Hispanic white adults to have been diagnosed with diabetes by a physician;
- Although African Americans make up only 13% of the total U.S. population, they accounted for 49% of HIV/AIDS cases in 2007;
- African American women were more than 20 times as likely to die from HIV/AIDS as non-Hispanic white women, in 2005.
- In 2006, African American adults aged 65 and older were 40% less likely to have ever received the pneumonia shot, compared to non-Hispanic white adults of the same age group;
- Women have death rates from heart disease higher than white women; and
- Have diabetes one-third more common than white men; (OMH, 2011).

Modifiable risk factors for African-Americans include drug use, high blood pressure, and obesity. Approximately 50 percent of African-American women are overweight compared to 25 percent of all women in the U.S.

Hispanic Americans

Hispanic Americans also experience the same kind of lifestyle and communicable diseases as the majority population, but the leading causes of death among Hispanics are unintentional injuries, homicide, chronic liver disease, cirrhosis and AIDS. Hispanics also have a three fold greater incidence of AIDS than the majority population. Puerto Rican born Hispanics have as much as **seven times the incidence of AIDS** compared to the majority population.

Recent reports indicate significant alcohol abuse among Mexican American men. In 1998 the federal government took a detailed look at alcohol abuse among ethnic groups. It found that Mexican-American men have the highest rate of heavy, problem drinking (i.e., consuming five or more drinks in one sitting at least five times a month). About 30% of California Mexican American men have major drinking problems, compared to 12% of white, 15% of black and 16% of Native-American men. Genetic research revealed that there does not seem to be a biological tendency toward alcohol abuse that is inherited specific to the Mexican population. On a nationwide basis, however, Mexican American men are twice as likely to be arrested for drunk driving as whites or blacks. In Los Angeles, the rate of cirrhosis of the liver for Mexican-American men is double that of white and black men. (Nazario, 1999). Additionally:

- In 2005, Hispanic men were 16% less likely to have prostate cancer as non-Hispanic white men;
- In 2005, Hispanic women were 33% less likely to have breast cancer as non-Hispanic white women;
- Hispanic men and women have higher incidence and mortality rates for stomach and liver cancer;
- Mexican American adults were 2 times more likely than non-Hispanic white adults to have been diagnosed with diabetes by a physician;
- Hispanics accounted for 17% of HIV/AIDS cases in 2007;
- Hispanic females have almost 5 times the AIDS rate as non-Hispanic white females;
- In 2007, Hispanics were 10% less likely to have heart disease, as compared to non-Hispanic whites;
- Mexican American women were 1.3 times more likely than non-Hispanic white women to be obese;
- In 2005, Hispanic men were 15% less likely to die from a stroke than non-Hispanic white men; and
- In 2005 Hispanic women were 25% less likely to die from a stroke than non-Hispanic white women.
  (OMH, 2011).

Asian Americans

Asian Americans residing in the U.S. include individuals from Indonesia, Vietnam, China, Korea, Thailand, Laos, Hawaii, Burma and the Philippines among others. This group is extremely diverse with a wide difference in cultural beliefs, education, socioeconomic status, income and degree of acculturation. Families of Asian descent pride themselves in being self sufficient, but often do not seek medical care or practice preventive health measures. In general, Asian Americans tend to have higher rates of tuberculosis, hepatitis B, anemia and hypertension compared to the majority population. Hepatitis B may progress to cirrhosis and liver cancer.

The most significant modifiable risk factor for Asian Americans is tobacco use.* It is estimated that since 2000 over four trillion cigarettes were sold to Asia each year. While the Ligget Group tobacco company made the historic public announcement that cigarettes cause cancer, since most of their products are exported (particularly to Asia), sales of many tobacco companies were not reduced immediately. (Los Angeles Times, 1997). Less than 30% of men in the U.S. smoke, 18% of men and women in California smoke, and only 13% of Orange County residents smoke, but smoking rates in certain Asian-American male populations are astounding: Laotians-92% of men smoke. Cambodians = 71% of men smoke. Vietnamese = 65% of men smoke. *As Asian Americans assimilate in the U.S, however, the above smoking rates often are reduced by <u>one half</u>. The World Health Association reported that many countries are showing an increase in smoking rates among both males and females. The American Cancer Society and the World Lung Foundation has an excellent, well documented website that serves as an ongoing tool to measure worldwide smoking rates by country.
(Google 'Tobacco Atlas,' or http://www.tobaccoatlas.org/).

Other Health Concerns in the Asian population:

- In 2007, tuberculosis was 24 times more common among Asians, with a case rate of 26.3 as compared to 1.1 for the White population;
- In 2006, Asian Americans were 1.2 times more likely to have Hepatitis B than Whites.
- Asian/Pacific Islander men were 40% less likely to have prostate cancer as non-Hispanic white men;
- Asian/Pacific Islander women were 30% less likely to have breast cancer as non-Hispanic white women;
- Both Asian/Pacific Islander men and women have three times the incidence of liver & IBD cancer as the non-Hispanic white population;
- In Hawaii, Native Hawaiians have more than twice the rate of diabetes as Whites;
- Asians are 30% less likely than non-Hispanic whites to die from diabetes.
- Filipinos living in Hawaii have more than 3 times the death rate as Whites living in Hawaii;
- Overall, Asian/Pacific Islander adults are less likely than white adults to have heart disease and they are less likely to die from heart disease compared to non-Hispanic whites.
- Asian/Pacific Islanders have lower AIDS rates than non-Hispanic white counterparts and they are less likely to die of HIV/AIDS.

- In 2007, however, Asian women had a higher case rate for AIDS than White women.
- In 2006, Asian/Pacific Islander children aged 19 to 35 months reached the Healthy The infant mortality rate for Asian/Pacific Islanders was 40% greater for mothers under 20 years old, as compared to mothers, ages 25-29 years old;
- In general, Asians/Pacific Islander adults are less likely to die from a stroke; and
- In general, Asian/Pacific Islander adults have lower rates of being overweight or obese, lower rates of hypertension, and they are less likely to be current cigarette smokers, as compared to white adults. (OMH, 2011).

Native Americans

Native Americans represent the smallest group of minorities but show significantly higher than average rates of morbidity and mortality related to lifestyles and poor health practices. Statistics presented in Healthy People 2000 list **alcohol abuse as the single most important modifiable risk factor for this group.** It is estimated that 75% of unintentional injuries in Native Americans are alcohol-related. Alcohol plays a factor in the homicide rate in this group that is 60% higher than that of the total population. Native-Americans have a higher rate of mortality than do members of the Euro-American population, a significant number of these Americans die before age 45. Most of the deaths can be traced to unintentional injury, cirrhosis, homicide, suicide, pneumonia and complications of diabetes. Native Americans also suffer higher rates of cardiovascular disease and diabetes. This is related to the risk factor of higher rates of obesity. (Brainard, 1996, Healthy People 2000, 1990). Additionally the 2010 **Leading Health Indicators** described by the Department of Health and Human Services were: physical activity, overweight and obesity, tobacco use, substance, abuse, responsible sexual, behavior, mental health, injury and violence, environmental quality, immunization, and access to health care. Furthermore:

- Native Hawaiians/Pacific Islanders (NHOPI) are 30% more likely to be diagnosed with cancer, as compared to non-Hispanic Whites;
- American Samoan men are eight times more likely to develop liver cancer, and Native Hawaiian men are 2.4 times more likely to be diagnosed with the same disease, as compared to non-Hispanic Whites In Hawaii, Native Hawaiians have more than twice the rate of diabetes as Whites;
- In Hawaii, Native Hawaiians are more than 5.7 times as likely as Whites living in Hawaii to die from diabetes.
- Filipinos living in Hawaii have more than 3 times the death rate of Whites living in Hawaii;
- Native Hawaiian/Pacific Islanders are 30% more likely to be diagnosed with high blood pressure as compared to Non-Hispanic Whites;
- While Native Hawaiians and Other Pacific Islanders (NHOPI) represent 0.3% of the total population in the United States, the AIDS case rate for NHOPI was twice that of the White population in 2007;

- The total number or reported AIDS cases has declined over the past five years for the White population, however it has continued to increase in the Native Hawaiian/Pacific Islander populations;
- The infant mortality rate for Native Hawaiians is 1.7 times greater than non-Hispanic Whites; and
- Native Hawaiian/Pacific Islanders are 30% more likely to be obese and to have high blood pressure, as compared to white adults.
  (OMH, 2011).

Teachers can contribute significantly to help minority students overcome health-related problems. Many of the children of families emigrating from other countries can serve as health educators for their own parents, cousins, relatives and friends. All teachers should be especially cautious when referring to their minority students, whether comments relate to their health status or other everyday issues. Educators and school leaders should avoid using derogatory terms such as "dysfunctional" or "broken" when referring to families. Other terms such as "culturally disadvantaged," "under-privileged," "deprived," "primitive," "backward," and "under-developed," should be avoided when referring to minority groups. All students should be treated the same and using terms as "non-white" when speaking of people of color implies that whiteness is the standard by which others are measured.

Health Risk Behavior and Academic Achievement

Does a healthy child do better in school? Can their health status improve grades? Will this translate to a healthier adult? These are some of the questions a school administrator may ask as he or she is disaggregating the annual Academic Performance Index (API) score for their school. The answers to theses questions seem to be yes, but it is often very difficult to measure change during one or two school years. The graph below illustrates how alcohol use, for example, can impact overall school knowledge and attendance, etc. That is, students who did not abuse alcohol did better in school and earned higher grades. (YRBS, 2009).

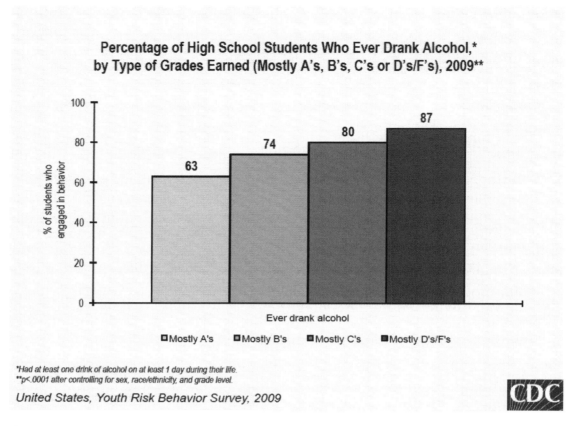

Percentage of High School Students Who Ever Drank Alcohol,*
by Type of Grades Earned (Mostly A's, B's, C's or D's/F's), 2009**

*Had at least one drink of alcohol on at least 1 day during their life.
**p<.0001 after controlling for sex, race/ethnicity, and grade level.

United States, Youth Risk Behavior Survey, 2009

In late 2009, Vinciullo and Bradley published a correlation study of Coordinated School Health Programs (CSHP) as a measure of School Achievement. Data were collected from all 50 states and the District of Columbia. Three reports were used to compile data and make comparisons of success in school and the use of the CSHP model. Documents reviewed were (1) The School Health Policies and Programs Survey (SHPPS), (2) the National Assessment of Educational Progress (NAEP), and the U.S. Census 2000 Profile. Three parameters studied were (a) The intervention called a CSHP: (b) Student achievement; and (c) Rate of poverty in each state. A stepwise regression analysis controlling for poverty using state-level data showed **statistically significant relationships with academic achievement. Students in states with health promoting programs (CSHP) demonstrated higher academic scores and higher rates of high school completion.** (Vinciullo, & Bradley, 2009). Thus health education is not only a key to producing healthy adults, health education will also allow kids to do better in school.

Health Education and the Impact of Family

Reports from the National Center for Health Statistics (NCHS) of the CDC, state that there is a significant relationship between health status and family characteristics. Traits such as income, education, martial status and the size of the family have a very important effect on all members of the family. People living with a spouse and children in two-parent households were the healthiest. Education and

family income also played a significant role.   The report, "The Health and Selected Socioeconomic Characteristics of the Family: United States, 1988-90," is a comprehensive analysis of eleven separate health variables.   These variables ranged from acute to chronic conditions and included the extent of disability. Highlights related to youth in the report include:

- Married men and women in all age groups are less likely to be limited in activity due to illness, than single, separated, divorced or widowed people;
- Children living with a single parent have higher rates of disability and suffer poorer health with a greater chance of being hospitalized;
- Children living in the poorest families report higher levels of poor or fair health, hospitalization and activity limitation, than those in families with higher income;
- Children under 18 years of age report higher rates of hospitalization where the responsible family members had less than 8 years of school, compared to those with more educational training; and
- Family members with higher levels of education and income and living with a spouse, are more likely to practice better eating habits, exercise regimens, and methods of prevention of STDs and pregnancy. (NCHS, 1990).

To view the full report, see the National Center for Health Statistics (NCHS) home page **at http://www.cdc.gov/nchs**. Numerous Internet websites will be referred to throughout this book and the reader is encouraged to read original reports as well. **The Internet "address," is the Universal Resource Locator (URL).** An extensive list of sites can be found in the reference section of this book and the reader is encouraged to regularly check the author's website: **www.nmatza.net,** and click on the pull down menu to locate numerous health resources. The search engine Google is also a quick way to locate numerous health related resources.

Health Education and the Impact of Women and Children's Health

The U.S. Department of Health and Human Services (USDHHS) has conducted research specific to women's health for many years. Children and adolescents from families with limited health care, poor role models for good health, and mothers suffering illness or disability may exhibit significantly reduced success in school. Lack of school success may range from poor diet leading to anemia that may result in poor grades, to alcohol or drug abuse leading to school absenteeism, or to low self-esteem. As was discussed earlier, even excessive use of text messaging or social networking can bring about poor health in kids. Lack of motivation related to marijuana use, and early pregnancy can also increase the risk of child abuse. Even vaccinations for controllable diseases such as hepatitis B, chickenpox, and the latest vaccine for genital warts (HPV), released in 2006, can promote life-long protection to all kids. The role of the teacher acting in place of a parent in the school setting, *in loco parentis*, is very apparent given the data listed above. This concept, *in loco parentis*, or the teacher as parent, will be addressed later in Chapter 11 within the context of the legal implications of teachers in public schools. Below are few of the issues related to health of women from the 2010 report "Women's Health 2010 USA."

- In 2008, females comprised 50.7 percent of the 304 million people residing in the United States;
- A baby girl born in the United States in 2007 could expect to live 80.4 years now, up from 48 years at the turn of the century and almost seven years longer than for men;
- In 2008, women aged 18 and older were more likely than men never to have smoked cigarettes in their lifetime (62.8 versus 52.4 percent);
- About 18% of women were current smokers in 2008;
- The frequency of alcohol consumption among women varies by age. Women aged 65 and older were most likely not to have consumed alcohol in the past year (62.5 percent), followed by women aged 18–24 and 45–64 years (42.0 and 38.9 percent, respectively).
- Women aged 18–24 years were, however, more likely than women of other ages to be heavy drinkers (8.2 percent;
- In 2008, an estimated 39.5 new cases of HIV per 100,000 males were reported in the United States;
- Among females aged 12 and older, nonfatal intimate partner violence (IPV) has decreased 53 percent from 9.2 per 1,000 females in 1993 to 4.3 per 1,000 females in 2008;
- Heart disease is the leading cause of death for all women, but for those aged 25-74 years cancer is the leading cause of death and lung cancer the leading cause of cancer mortality; and
- In 2008, fewer than 15 percent of women met the recommendations for adequate physical activity.
  (USDHHS, 2010b).

Women's Health and HIV Babies

The number of U.S. children born with HIV/AIDS has declined markedly since the mid-1990s in all demographic groups. Data reported from Women's Health USA, 2007, indicate the following: From 1994 to 2005, the number of non-Hispanic black infants born with HIV/AIDS has declined by 65.6 percent. The drop among non-Hispanic white infants born with HIV/AIDS was more than 80 percent during the same time, while the decline among Hispanic infants born with HIV/AIDS was 40.6 percent. Early prenatal care among racial and ethnic groups with historically low rates of utilization, including non-Hispanic Black, Hispanic, and American Indian/Alaska Native women, has increased by at least 20 percent since 1990. In 2004, 23.9 percent of women had untreated dental caries, with non-Hispanic Black and Hispanic women most likely to have untreated caries. Serious psychological distress occurs in almost 23 percent of women aged 18 to 25 years, compared to 9 percent of women over age 50. By 2005, 72.9 percent of mothers breastfed their infants, with Asian/Pacific Islanders most likely to breastfeed their infants (81.4 percent). And, by 2005, 71.8 percent of women aged 18 to 64 had private insurance, 14.6 had public insurance, and 17.8 percent were uninsured. (Women's Health USA, 2007). Chapter nine will address STDs and HIV/AIDS in detail with reference to these changes to pediatric AIDS cases. The Health Resources and Services Administration (HRSA), part of the U. S. Department of Health and Human Services, is the primary Federal agency for improving access to health care services for people who are uninsured, isolated, or medically vulnerable.

HRSA also is responsible for promoting and improving the health of our nation's women, children and families.

Teacher Training: Why Preservice Health Education?

The classroom teacher is the most significant adult person that impacts student health on a daily basis. For many students, the classroom teacher may also be the most significant adult role model in their daily life! Many research articles have reported the importance of health behaviors being influenced by health educators, but it does not have to be a health education teacher that will provide students with health knowledge. **All teachers serve as health educators.** Students may be drawn to a particular adult for help, guidance or friendship. While this relationship develops, health problems may surface and the classroom teacher can assist the student on a regular basis. This assistance might begin by taking the student by the hand (yes, actually touching the child!) to the nurse or psychologist to discuss a problem.

Preservice education is the term used to describe all of the training given to teachers while attending a college or university teacher education program. The college or school of education is directly responsible for preparing the teacher candidate to be sensitive and able to respond to student problems. While a new teacher may relish preparing lessons on factoring polynomials in a math class, or having the kids reconstruct the civil war using a computer model, health education problems also need to be addressed. Varnes (1994), lists four major areas of competencies for teacher training related to student health:

- recognition of common health problems;
- knowledge of appropriate referral procedures;
- basic health content information with methodology; and
- the teacher's place in the total school health program (Varnes, 1994).

Behaviorally stated objectives for health education for teachers are listed below. Teachers should be able to:

- explain contemporary concepts of health and health education;
- analyze factors influencing health attitudes;
- identify major causes of morbidity and mortality;
- cite factors improving comprehensive school health education;
- identify credible sources of information about new developments in health education and health promotion;
- compare growth and development in children;
- identify the role of community health agencies;
- administer first aid, emergency procedures and CPR;
- identify signs and symptoms of common student health problems;

- list nutritional needs for school-age children; and
- identify signs and symptoms and alternatives to student drug abuse.

Project Teach in California

California teacher education programs lead the nation in placing emphasis on preparing teachers to enter the classroom and help kids. All teachers are required to complete health education course standards as part of their teacher training. Since 1992, all K-12 teachers are also required to be CPR-certified before they are granted a credential and hired by public schools. In 1993, university professors assembled to discuss the problems related to the preservice training of teachers in California. The project examined current practices and collaboratively developed recommendations. This collaboration was called **Project Teach Health.** Project Teach Health reconvened in 1999 to follow up and revise previous programs established to help prepare California teachers. The committee represented the majority of university and state college professors that taught courses to prepare teachers to face health education topics with their students. Dr. Carolyn Fisher delivered a major presentation on the actual status of health education requirements in various school settings throughout the state and was able to conclude that, while most secondary schools do require health classes for graduation, many school boards and administrators do not place heavy emphasis on health instruction. (Fisher, 1999). Some of the Project Teach guidelines and recommendations are exemplary only and are as follow:

- The courses should each be three units with a minimum of 40-50 contact hours;
- Universities/colleges should offer two separate courses-one designed to prepare elementary teachers, and one for secondary teachers;
- Challenges to the courses should not be allowed (credit by examination);
- CPR certification must cover infant-child and adult CPR as well as choking emergencies;
- Instructors are expected to utilize the *Health Framework* and become familiarized with mandated areas of instruction and *Education Code* sections related to health education;
- The courses should deal with the health status of children and adolescents and not be a personal health class used in introductory college personal health courses;
- The course for the elementary teacher should include specific methods for developing lesson plans to be used with K-6 level students; and
- The courses should focus on common health problems of youth including: eating disorders, child abuse and neglect, acne, teenage pregnancy, tobacco, alcohol and other drug abuse, mental health, nutrition, and injury prevention and safety.
(Matza, Lovato & English, 1993). (Project Teach Health, 1999).

The Healthy Kids Resource Center was highlighted as a major resource addition to teacher preparation in California at the **Project Teach Health Conference of 1999.** Reference to this center and the extensive on-line resources will be used regularly throughout this course. Students should point their browsers to **www.hkresources.org** for a multitude of updated sources to assist them identifying numerous curriculum materials, laws, lesson plans, and other classroom resources.

Summary

Health education today is much more than hygiene and body systems. Coordinated health includes the impact of the school setting, the family, the clergy, community and peer based normative behavior. Society must play a positive role and not allow students to be unduly influenced by sensational messages promoted through the media. Parents, teachers and school staff should be especially concerned about student's health related to hyper-texting and excessive time spent on social networks and other electronic gadgets not yet even invented! School administrators must take an active role in educating themselves and others about the positive advantages of comprehensive health education included within a coordinated health program. School boards must be pro-active and not re-active, as in the case of the national incidents of violence committed in Colorado in 1999, and Virginia in 2007. The classroom teacher plays a critical role in teaching health education, either in a formalized setting or by using "hallway instruction." Professional educators need specific training in dealing with the health problems of students while they focus on their individual subject matter topics. Research utilizing the Internet should help all teachers become health literate. This training must be included in a carefully designed preservice program at the university or college level. The school community is the "workplace" for most of the children in the U.S. Unique changes can come about through a joint effort incorporating all these factors to help the child become an educated youth, make sensible and positive health lifestyle decisions, and ultimately become a health conscious adult. All teachers, regardless of subject matter specialty, need to be trained about the contemporary health problems facing their students and can serve as powerful role models positively impacting student behavior change.

Chapter 2

Health Education: and Teenagers

Schools could do more than perhaps any other single
institution in society to help young people,
and the adults they will become,
to live healthier, longer, more satisfying,
and more productive lives.
...Carnegie Council on Adolescent Development

Ah adolescence! Some of us remember it well, and others of us want to forget those difficult years. But adolescence includes that wonderful time of change, feelings, emotions, stress accompanied by lots of fun and games. Adolescence is certainly a time for the hormonal cascade that sometimes generates significant anxiety for many, especially to classroom teachers. Professor DiClemente states it clearly as he defines adolescence, **"Adolescence is a developmental period of accelerating, physical, psychological, social/cultural, and cognitive development, often characterized by confronting and surmounting a myriad of challenges and establishing a sense of self-identity and autonomy."** (DiClemente, (1996, 2009). Parents, school administrators and especially teachers are very aware of these factors as they perform their professional duties within the school. Most American teens today are intrinsically not much different than youth of past generations. Their emotional and physical health today may be more fragile and at risk because society during the 21st century is much harsher than society was in the 20th century. This is especially true during the high definition digital age when ideas, images, messages and entire daily conversations travel at lightning speed.

Generations born during the 1960s through the 1980s were in a transitional stage as communication methods changed in America. Teenagers during those three decades talked more face-to-face, had interactions with friends, families, and schools, mostly face-to-face, or via a telephone connected to a wire! Teens since the late 1990s and especially during the 2000s,

36

communicate via text messages, social networks and claim they have thousands of friends on some sort of Internet town, or community, someplace between cyberspace and the 'wall' of their FaceBook page! Tragically, however, many youth of today do not even know how to pick up a telephone and listen for a dial tone, since they only use mobile phones. This may be due to the loss of more personal and meaningful relationships. Thus it is often the role of the teacher to become an increasingly rare face-to-face interactive influence. Teachers today must be able to adjust, adapt and help these youth clarify their own goals, feelings and aspirations, and guide them to make healthy decisions-regardless of what subject matter they may teach.

Teenagers represent a very unique group of individuals. They really are not kids, nor quite yet adults during this unique time of life called adolescence. Adolescence is that special time when the child defines his or her place in the family, peer group and the community at large. Adolescence is the developmental period between childhood and adulthood. It is characterized by physical, psychological and sexual maturation. The behaviors, antics and silliness of teenagers make the job of the secondary teacher challenging; but often this challenge is made much easier by the joyous entertainment to the teacher by their clients-the wacky teens. One of the joys of being an adolescent is acting much like a child through a period of physical, emotional and intellectual development, while not being burdened with the daily struggles of adulthood. One of the joys of being a teacher in secondary schools is to watch these kids every day; even though the happy go lucky times of adolescence during the 1950s have changed profoundly for the teenager in the 21st century. No longer do kids just meet at the malt shop and hang out to interact. They interact by using the text message method. Maybe it will be a good idea for humans to evolve a neck that does bend at ninety degrees! Teaching adolescents is such a great job for many educators, because they also gain a sense of youth and energy working with their students. Some teachers, in fact, may sense that they are just older adolescents while enjoying the job of teaching. A retiring teacher of more than 30 years teaching recently received a best wishes card from colleagues that read, "Congratulations for finally graduating high school." Let us compare some of the acts of the 1950s to those of today. The scenarios below illustrate this point.

Adolescent Scenarios-1950s and 2000s.

Scenario 1 : Billy breaks a window in his neighbor's car and his Dad gives him a whipping with his belt.

1957: Billy is more careful next time, grows up normal, goes to college, and becomes a successful businessman.

2010: Billy's dad is arrested for child abuse. Billy is removed to foster care and joins a gang. State psychologist tells Billy's sister that she remembers being abused herself and their dad goes to prison. Billy's mom has affair with psychologist.

Scenario 2: Oscar falls while running during recess and scrapes his knee. He is found crying by his teacher, Mary. Mary hugs him to comfort him.

1957: In a short time, Oscar feels better and goes on playing.

2010: Mary is accused of being a sexual predator and loses her job. She faces 3 years in State Prison. Oscar undergoes 5 years of therapy. Oscar's parents sue the school for negligence and the teacher for emotional trauma and win both cases. Mary, jobless and indebted, commits suicide by jumping off of a tall building. When she lands, she hits a car and also damages a potted plant. The car's owner and the plant's owner sue Mary's estate for destruction of property. They both win.

Scenario 3: Johnny takes apart leftover firecrackers from 4th of July, puts them in a model airplane paint bottle, and blows up a red ant bed.

1957: Ants die.

2010: The Bureau of Alcohol Tobacco & Firearms (BATF), Homeland Security, FBI called. Johnny is charged with domestic terrorism, FBI investigates parents, siblings removed from home, computers confiscated, Johnny's Dad goes on a terror watch list and is never allowed to fly again.

Today, many teenagers face significant problems. Too many adults quickly discount the problems faced by teens reflecting upon their own experiences during adolescence. For many young people adolescence is a time of confusion, fear, anxiety, and danger often complicated by a very fragmented family. Too often parents leave teens unsupervised, allow them to take jobs too early, and think that they can fend for themselves. While simple tasks of eating and sleeping are completed by teens, the support needs and regularly monitored supervision of their lives are too frequently left unmet. Unfortunately, too many teens quickly assume adult responsibilities such as caring for sibling children, planning meals, or taking care of the elderly at an early age. One of the major problems associated with teen pregnancy, for example, is the lack of supervision on a daily basis. Many teen girls become pregnant between 3-6 in the afternoon while parents are not at home. Sometimes in their parent's bed! Chapters nine and ten will elaborate on these issues and offer solutions to help parents and teachers make life easier for themselves and youth.

But remember that not all teens are oversexed, overstressed or act crazy as is often depicted in the latest teen movies or TV shows. Despite the difficult times for some teens, many young people make the transition without any major trauma. Recent studies by sociologist Mike Males of the University of California Santa Cruz, and other experts, explain that this transition is related to the actual brain activity of the adolescent. Professor Males states:

> The latest discovery of adolescent biological deficiency follows a decade of blaming youths for virtually every social ill. The experts state, **"Adolescents are not in turmoil, not deeply disturbed, not at the mercy of their impulses, not resistant to parental values ... and not rebellious."** To test a theory, compare what it predicts to real life. Decades of psychological studies have exposed common typecasts of teens as "stubborn, fixed set of falsehoods," concluded University of Michigan psychologist Joseph B. Adelson. U.C. San Francisco medical-psychologist Nancy Adler's testing similarly found that "adolescents are no less rational than adults." A Carnegie Mellon University team reviewed 100 scholarly studies and reported the **"perception of relative invulnerability was no more pronounced for adolescents than for adults."** (Males, 2002).

Teenagers today are fundamentally not much different from youth of past decades. At times they act in strange ways, can become very emotional, act depressed, act happy or express a myriad of mood swings in a very short period of time. Their physical and emotional well being is becoming more fragile not because they are adolescents; but rather society has become a less-nurturing place in which they can develop and mature. The extreme fast pace of media images serves as an example. Watch any network type of television commercial or preview and notice that the sound bites of images rarely last more than 2 seconds. Perhaps this rapid flow of MTV-type media impacts the adolescent brain or subsequent behavior. Additionally, some teens frequently are victims of mental and emotional abuse, physical abuse, exploitation, including prostitution and pornography. Significant numbers of them consider suicide, suffer eating disorders and experiment with tobacco, alcohol and other drugs.

Teen Health, Race and Ethnicity

According to the CDC report *Adolescent Health in the United States,* significant changes in the racial and ethnic composition of the population have important consequences for the health of the adolescent population because many of the measures of risk behavior, health status, and disease differ significantly by race and ethnicity. In 2005, over 42 million residents of the United States were adolescents 10–19 years of age, constituting approximately 14 percent of the U.S. population. Three-fifths of the adolescent population was non-Hispanic white, and two-fifths consisted of other racial and ethnic groups. Since race and Hispanic origin distribution of the adolescent population, much like the general population has changed considerably since the late 1980s, it is projected that certain racial and ethnic groups will continue to grow. Black or African American, Hispanic, American Indian or Alaska Native, and Asian or Pacific Islander adolescents, as well as teens of two or more races, will constitute 56 percent of the adolescent population by the year 2050. (CDC, 2007e). In recent years, racial and ethnic diversity in the general population is reflected in changes in the adolescent population. Hispanic adolescents have recently surpassed black adolescents as the largest minority group of adolescents, and the proportion of adolescents who are Hispanic is expected to increase considerably by 2050. A large influx of immigrants has contributed to changes in the population distribution. In 1990, 19 percent of adolescents lived in immigrant families—that is, the adolescent was an immigrant or had immigrant parents. By 2004, the proportion of adolescents in immigrant families had increased to 22 percent. Most future growth in the U.S. population is expected to occur primarily through immigration and higher fertility rates among minority populations (CDC, 2007e). Additionally, the overall impact of the Hispanic population in California will be formidable:

- For the first time since the 19th century, Latinos account for a majority of births in California, a long-expected, yet still telling milestone in the state's demographics;
- Latinos make up about 37% of the state's population making them the largest minority group with a total population over 13 million;
- 50.2% of all births in 3rd quarter of 2001 were Latino;
- Young Hispanic females have the highest rates of teen parenthood of any major racial or ethnic group in the country;
- 50.6% of all births in 4th quarter were Latino compared to 30.4% White, 11.7% Asian or Pacific Islander and 6.1% Black;
- Nationally, census figures show the Latino population had reached about 37 million as of January 2004, making Latinos arguably, at least, the nation's largest minority;
- Latinos make up about 18% of all youths in the U.S. ages 16 to 25;
- More than two-thirds (68%) of young Latinos are of Mexican heritage; and
- Based of birthrates, Latinos constitute the:
  Majority of children that entered California kindergartens in 2006;

Majority entering high school in 2014;

Majority of workers entering the labor force in 2017, and,

Majority of young adults eligible to vote by 2019. (Rivera, 2005; National Campaign, 2011; Pew, 2011; CDC, 2007e).

The graph below illustrates the projected growth of adolescents in the U.S.

Race and Hispanic origin of adolescents 10–19 years United States, 1980–2050.

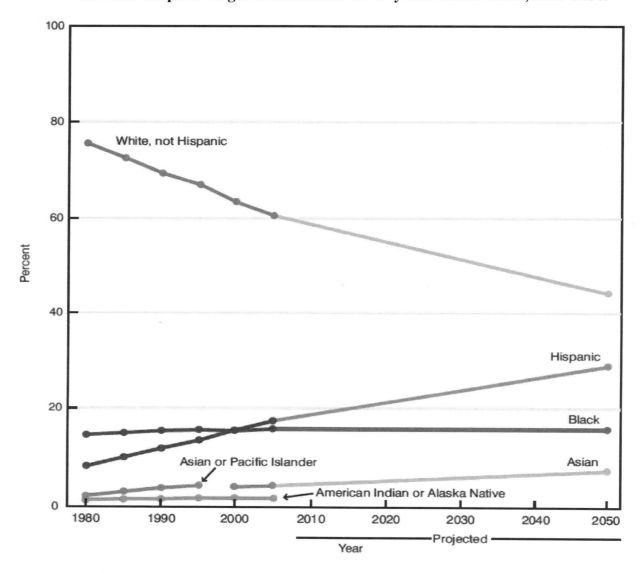

NOTES: Data for 1980–1995 are for Asian or Pacific Islander persons; data for 2000–2050 are for Asian person only. Population projections are not available for American Indian or Alaska Native persons. Persons of

Hispanic origin may be of any race. See data table for data points and additional notes.

SOURCE: U.S. Census Bureau.

A large influx of immigrants has contributed to changes in the population distribution. In 1990, 19 percent of adolescents lived in immigrant families—that is, the adolescent was an immigrant or had immigrant parents. By 2004, the proportion of adolescents in immigrant families had increased to 22 percent. Most future growth in the U.S. population is expected to occur primarily through immigration and higher fertility rates among minority populations, also referred to as people of color. (Adolescent Health, 2007).

Poverty during adolescence has immediate and lasting negative consequences. In 1998, 17 percent of all adolescents lived in families with incomes below the poverty level. One-parent households headed by women experience the highest rates of poverty. Forty percent of adolescents in female-headed families were living in poverty, compared with 8 percent of adolescents in two-parent families. Children represent 25 percent of the population. Yet, they comprise 36 percent of all people in poverty. Among children, 42 percent live in low-income families and 21 percent live in poor families. Employment during the adolescent years can have beneficial or negative effects on the health and well-being of youth. **In 1999 approximately two-fifths of adolescents 16–19 years of age were employed during the school year and over one-half worked during the summer months. While many teens enjoy the change over to work and school, many take on far too many tasks and suffer academic failure.** Among older children, i.e. adolescents aged 12 through 17, 38 percent live in low-income families and 17 percent live in poor families. The most significant factors are related to children's experiences with economic insecurity are race/ethnicity and parents' education and employment. (NCCP, 2009). Moreover, within the past decade, the low-income families (both poor and near poor) have been on the rise – increasing from 33 percent in 2000 to nearly 38 percent in 2009. During this same time period, the overall number of adolescent children ages 12 through 17 increased by three percent while the number who were low-income and poor increased by 19 percent and 29 percent, respectively. This upward trend in low-income and poor children follows on the heels of a decade of decline in the 1990s.

By 2009, however, the economic recession hit adolescent employment. The group of working-age teens with the largest relative decline in their employment rate over the past decade is high school students. During 2000, during an average month, close to 35 of every 100 high school students were working. By 2010, their employment rate had dropped to only slightly above 16 percent, a decline of more than half. Only 1 of every 6 high school students held a job in 2010, the lowest ratio in the near 30 year period for which such teen employment data are available. White high school students were more than twice as likely to work than Hispanic, Blacks and Asians. This dramatic decline in youth working certainly had an impact on their income. President Obama focused on increasing job opportunities during this time; but youth had a difficult time finding any employment, either during school or summer recess. With many Americans out of work, it is easy to conclude that job scarcity also affected adolescents. The impact of in-school work experience that increases annual earnings of high school graduates has been found to increase the likelihood of young adults obtaining apprenticeship and formal training from employers. (Chau, Kalyani, & Wright, 2010). Idle time for teens may cause an increase in health risk taking behaviors.

41

Adolescent Health Status

Indicators of adolescent health status include activity limitation; dental health, suicide ideation and attempts, as well as emergency department visit rates, hospital discharge rates, and death rates. The health of adolescents varies by age, gender, race and Hispanic origin. Suicidal ideation, or attempting suicide, is one indicator of mental or emotional health. In 1999, 25 percent of female adolescents and 14 percent of male adolescents in grades 9–12 reported seriously considering or attempting suicide. **Adolescent suicide has been the number three leading cause of death of youth for more than ten years.** Adolescents may be victims of violent crimes, including rape or sexual assault, aggravated and simple assault, and robbery. (CDC, 2007). Chapter 11 will address the legal aspects related to teen health and the impact of violence against adolescents.

In 1995–97 **pregnancy rates** increased with age from 67.8 per 1,000 for adolescents 15–17 years of age to 146.4 for adolescents 18–19 years. In 1997–98 there were approximately 493,600 births annually to adolescents 13–19 years of age, accounting for 13 percent of all births in each year. There was a consistent pattern of increasing birth rates by maternal age. Overall, 19-year-old adolescents were nearly seven times as likely to have a birth as their 15-year-old counterparts. Infants of adolescent mothers are more likely to be low birth weight than infants of mothers in their twenties and thirties. During 2000 France called a national emergency when teen pregnancy rates reached ten thousand. The U.S. teen population averages over a million pregnancies annually! (HBCC, 2002). The CDC reported an increase in teen birth rates in 2007. The birth rate for U.S. teens aged 15 to 19 increased by about 1 percent in 2007, from 41.9 births per 1,000 in 2006 to 42.5 in 2007. This was the second year in a row that teen births have gone up. They increased 3 percent in 2006 following a 14-year decline. Birth rates also increased for women in their 20s, 30s and early 40s, but remained unchanged for younger teens and pre-teens aged 10-14. Only Hispanic teens noted a decline in the birth rate, which fell 2 percent in 2007 to 81.7 births per 1,000. Unmarried childbearing increased to historic levels in 2007 for women aged 15-44. An estimated 1.7 million babies were born to unmarried women in 2007, accounting for 39.7 percent of all births in the United States-an increase of 4 percent from 2006. Unmarried childbearing in the U.S. has increased 26 percent since 2002 when the recent steep increases began. Other findings from the CDC research include:

- The cesarean delivery rate rose 2 percent in 2007, to 31.8 percent, marking the 11th consecutive year of increase and another record high for the United States;
- The percentage of low birth weight babies declined slightly between 2006 and 2007, from 8.3 percent to 8.2 percent. This is the first decline in the percentage of low birth weight babies since 1984;
- The preterm birth rate (infants delivered at less than 37 weeks of pregnancy) decreased 1 percent in 2007 to 12.7 percent. The decline was seen mostly among infants born late preterm (between 34 and 36 weeks) ; and
- Total U.S. births rose in 2007 to over 4, 317,119, the highest number of births ever registered in the United States. (CDC, 2007).

Health Practices and Teens

Throughout most of the 1990s smoking and the use of tobacco products accounted for the major cause of death to Americans. During 2004, however, data from the CDC has stated that **poor diet and lack of exercise may soon surpass the total deaths from tobacco.** More than 430,000 Americans die annually from tobacco, but recent reports indicate that deaths due to poor diet and lack of exercise cause nearly 400,000 annually. As was mentioned earlier, statisticians Jia and Lubetkin, (2010) calculated that the deaths due to lack of exercise and poor diet may now be **greater than deaths from smoking** in the U.S. (Jia, Lubetkin, 2010). The CDC stated: "The leading causes of death in 2009 were tobacco (435, 000 deaths; 18.1% of total US deaths), poor diet and physical inactivity (400,000 deaths; 16.6%), and alcohol consumption (85,000 deaths; 3.5%). Other actual causes of death were microbial agents (75,000), toxic agents (55,000), motor vehicle crashes (43,000), incidents involving firearms (29,000), sexual behaviors (20,000), and illicit use of drugs (17,000)." The data concluded that smoking still remains the leading cause of mortality. These findings, along with escalating health care costs and aging population, argue persuasively that the need to establish a more preventive orientation in the U.S. health care and public health systems has become more urgent. (Mokad, Marks, Stroup, et. al, 2004). **Either pay now or pay later.**

Table 2.1
The Ten Leading Causes Of Death, 1900　and Today
1900　　　　　　　　　　　　**Today**

All Ages	All Ages	Children 10-14	Youth 15-24
Pneumonia/flu	Heart Diseases	Accidents	**Accidents**
Tuberculosis	Cancer	Cancer	**Homicide**
Digestive tract inflammations	Stroke	Suicide	**Suicide**
Heart Disease	Lower Respiratory Disease (Asthma, Bronchitis)	Congenital anomalies	**Cancer**
Stroke	Accidents	Homicide	**Heart Diseases**
Kidney Diseases	Alzheimer's disease	Heart disease	**Congenital anomalies**
Accidents	Diabetes	Lower Respiratory Disease (Asthma, Bronchitis)	**Stroke**
Cancer	Pneumonia and influenza	Stroke	**Pneumonia and influenza**
Childhood Diseases	Kidney disease	Septicemia	**HIV**
Diphtheria	Septicemia	Pneumonia and influenza	**Lower Respiratory Disease (Asthma, Bronchitis)**

Source: National Center for Health Statistics (NCHS), (2007) Vol. 58# 19. May 7, 2010.

The National Center for Health Statistics (NCHS) developed an electronic database that is revised on a regular basis. These data can be accessed with the simple click of a mouse. Statistical data on nearly any health topic can be obtained by accessing the Internet web site at www.cdc.gov/nchs. The good news is that in 1998 deaths from HIV related illness dropped from number one for ages 25-44, to number five. The CDC reports that HIV cases in the U.S. have leveled off and during 2002 researchers were concerned that a rising trend may develop, especially in the young gay male population. This change may be associated with less public information about AIDS, less political and administrative support, due to newer protease inhibiting drugs, and an increase of unprotected sexual activity in both homosexual and heterosexual couples. However, in 2010 the CDC reported an increase in the gay population of HIV infection individuals. Gay and bisexual men-referred to in CDC surveillance systems as men who have sex with men (MSM)-of all race-continue to be the risk group most severely affected by HIV. This is the only risk group in the U.S. in which the annual number of new HIV infections is increasing. There is an urgent need to expand access to proven HIV prevention interventions for gay and bisexual men, as well as to develop new approaches to fight HIV in this population. (CDC, 2010c).

Chapter three will assist the teacher with many practical solutions in dealing with youth, Chapters four and seven will address issues of risk behaviors and substance abuse. Chapter five will focus solely on tobacco as it affects the lives of kids; and chapter six will discuss alcohol abuse. Chapter eight will focus on common selected topics related to teens including issues of gender and nutritional problems, especially the obesity epidemic. Chapter nine will clarify the impact of STDs on adolescent health. Chapter ten will present the reader with research on adolescent sexuality; and Chapter eleven will specify the legal factors associated with teen health within the school setting. Finally, Chapter twelve will describe common health problems affecting adolescents.

Healthy People 2020.

Goals and objectives specific to adolescents have recently been added to the governmental document Healthy People 2020. The major focus of this research is to improve the healthy development, health, safety, and well being of adolescents and young adults. Adolescents (ages 10 to 19) and young adults (ages 20 to 24) make up 21 percent of the population of the United States. The behavioral patterns established during these developmental periods help determine young people's current health status and their risk for developing chronic diseases in adulthood. While adolescent years and young adulthood are generally considered healthy times of life for youth, many social or health problems arise during these years. Significant examples as listed earlier in this text, include: homicide, suicide, motor vehicle crashes (especially caused by drinking and driving, substance use and abuse, smoking STDs including HIV, teen pregnancies and homelessness. As a result of being in this transitional stage, adolescents and young adults are especially sensitive to environmental influences and surroundings. Examples include peer group pressure, family practices and school policies, societal cues, and the neighborhood in where they live.

Adolescent Health is Very Important

Economics, social welfare and broad scale social issues seem to overshadow so many issues in the U.S. today; and issues affecting youth seem to be left behind. Kids go through the pubertal changes and look like adults; but often they may still be little kids behind their smiling faces. It is during this time that teens are seeking to become independent and may practice all types of experimentation. Numerous state and federal programs have been implemented in recent years to help address these issues. They include state graduated driver licensing programs, teen pregnancy prevention programs, violence prevention programs, delinquency prevention programs, mental health and substance abuse interventions, and HIV prevention interventions. (Healthy People 2020, 2011).

As was stated earlier, 'either pay now or pay later.' Financial burdens from adolescent problems can be very large and result in chronic diseases that are preventable. Adult health related problems from cigarette smoking alone, for example, which usually starts during teenage years, cost nearly $200 billion annually in the U.S. (Healthy People 2020, 2011). The leading cause of illness and death starting in adolescents are largely preventable as illustrated by the following examples:

Family

- Adolescents who perceive that they have good communication and are bonded with an adult are less likely to engage in risky behaviors;
- Parents who provide supervision and are involved with their adolescents' activities are promoting a safe environment in which to explore opportunities; and
- The children of families living in poverty are more likely to have health conditions and poorer health status, as well as less access to and utilization of health care.

School

- Academic success and achievement are strong predictors of overall adult health outcomes. Proficient academic skills are associated with lower rates of risky behaviors and higher rates of healthy behaviors;
- High school graduation leads to lower rates of health problem, risk for incarceration, and enhanced financial stability during adulthood;
- The school social environment affects students' attendance, academic achievement, and behavior; and
- A safe and healthy school environment promotes student engagement and protects against risky behaviors and dropping out.

Neighborhoods

- Adolescents growing up in distressed neighborhoods characterized by concentrated poverty are at risk for a variety of negative outcomes, including poor school performance; and
- Poor physical and mental health, delinquency, and risky sexual behavior.

Media Exposure

- Adolescents who are exposed to media portrayals of violence, sexual content, smoking, and drinking are at risk for adopting these behaviors.
  (Healthy People 2020, 2011).

Emerging Issues in Adolescent Health.

Healthy People 2020 projects that there are two important issues that influence how adolescent health will be approached in the coming decade. First, as the adolescent population becomes more ethnically diverse, with a rapid increase in Hispanic and Asian-American youth; this diversity will require culturally sensitive responses to help deal with these issues. This is especially important as it relates to adolescents living in poverty. Secondly, youth development interventions, which are defined as the intentional process of providing all youth with the support, relationships, experiences, resources, and opportunities needed to become successful and competent adults; must be implemented. Growing empirical evidence reveals that well-designed interventions that work can be successful in helping youth. (Healthy People 2020, 2011).

Teacher Concerns

Teachers often express so much energy, desire and concern for their potential students when given the chance to teach. One of the best ways for a teacher candidate to determine if teaching is a profession they choose to devote much of their lives, is to go and visit any local public school at about 3 PM. By watching teachers as they head for their cars at the end of a long day, dragging utility carts, or bags of ungraded papers, a major career decision can be made. What are the concerns of the teacher today? Dedicated teachers make up the majority of the teaching profession. Like any job, however, there are outstanding workers, poor workers, and the majority that represent the middle ground, or average group. But since dealing with children every day is significantly different than working in the retail trade, for example, the demands are very different, and involve complex human interaction.

Typical complaints of teachers related to students include that students, "don't listen," "talk too much," "waste time," "ditch class too often," or are just "too apathetic." The daily routine of a teacher is extremely complicated. If a worker in the retail trade sells a product to the public, they need only strive to be pleasant, and finalize a sale. The classroom teacher, however, must constantly monitor all aspects of the lesson, discipline students, communicate with parents, look for weapons, deal with cell phone and electronic gizmo interruptions, and conform to a myriad of administrative and legal mandates, while trying to maintain a calm, relaxed demeanor, and entertain their clients-the students.

Interactions in the world of business occur about 60-100 times each day. An interaction is defined as some brief comment, phone call or sales communication with another person. Teachers wrestle with greater than 1000 interactions every day! Everything from breaking up arguments, admonishing students to get to class on time, breaking up fights, responding to countless questions, and being especially observant to report any possible suspected child abuse or neglect as is mandated by state law. **Teachers are stressed!** What can the classroom teacher do? Several major areas of preparation will greatly enhance professional performance and worksite happiness. Most are related to communication. They include:

- Introspection and role modeling;
- Active listening techniques;
- Careful organization and planning;
- Assertion behavior training;
- Non-verbal communication;
- Classroom discipline; and

47

- Treating students with dignity.

Chapter 3 will explain these concepts in more detail.

Living in an industrialized society can be very unhealthy indeed. Doctor Richard Neal calls it "Modern Man."

Modern Man

Modern man in the industrial society is an animal which shortly after maturation is confined to a system of special cages, one of which, a mobile, steel and plastic cage, is exposed to one or two hours daily of high carbon monoxide gas while transporting to and from other cages with complex decisions, frustration, and danger. In other cages under constant temperature, the animal's physical activity is strictly constrained to hours of sitting, a few moments of standing, short walks and very low energy expenditure. Industrialized species of man are habitually overfed with salts, sucrose, animal and grain chow which usually includes 20 percent of calories in saturated fats, 20 percent in refined carbohydrates, 10 percent fermented spirits plus varying concentrations of herbicides, pesticides, hormones, antibiotics, antioxidants and radioactive isotopes. Man is often systematically conditioned to self-administer twenty potent doses of nicotine, four or five of caffeine daily. He is trained to lie motionless in a darkened cage for several hours and watch high definition digital images, which constantly present ambiguous information and suggestions for unhygienic and often very expensive purposeless activity. Man is rewarded to the degree which he pursues this goalless activity during the day. Exposed to such an environment for half his life span, nearly all animals develop irreparable lesions in the vascular system. Many suffer unregulated sugar concentrations in the blood. About half of the male animals experience severe damage to cardiac muscles. If the animal survives the dramatic onset of arterial insufficiency to the heart, he is returned as soon as possible to the same cages and systems.

Modified from: Richard Neal, MD, MPH. Professor-Loma Linda University. School of Public Health.

Poverty and Family Structure

Oftentimes, poverty plays a significant role in the health of people, and this is especially true of teenagers. Poverty during adolescence has immediate and lasting negative consequences. Adolescents in families who are poor are more likely than adolescents in other families to drop out of school to become teenage parents and to earn less and be unemployed more frequently as adults. Furthermore, poverty is strongly associated with reduced access to health care and poorer health status for adolescents. The structure of an adolescent's family is generally linked to the economic resources and support available to that adolescent. In 2005, almost 16 percent of all adolescents 10–17 years of age lived in families with incomes below the poverty threshold ($19,971 a year in 2005, for a family of four), whereas an additional 20 percent of adolescents lived in families near poverty (one to two times the poverty threshold). Adolescents who live in a household with one parent only are substantially more likely to have a family income near or below the poverty line than are adolescents living in a household with two parents. In many communities suffering extreme poverty, even with support of social welfare funding, both parents must arise at 4:30 AM travel on a bus for two hours, work 10-12 hours daily and return home on another two hour bus ride. Many times young children left alone to fend for themselves in these families may only receive one unhealthy meal a day. One-parent households headed by women experience the highest rates of poverty for a variety of reasons, including pay differentials and lack of paternal financial support. **In 2005, 36 percent of all adolescents in female head-of-household families were living in poverty, compared with 7 percent of**

adolescents in two-parent families. Non-Hispanic black and Hispanic adolescents in female head-of-household families were 1.7 times as likely to have a family income below the poverty line as their non-Hispanic white counterparts. Additionally, in 2005, 25 percent of non-Hispanic white adolescents lived with a single parent (mother or father), compared with 60 percent of non-Hispanic black adolescents and 35 percent of adolescents of Hispanic origin (Adolescent Health, 2007).

What Should Parents and Teachers Do?

Many of the topics addressed in this book should help parents, teachers and schools identify some of the significant problems related to the health of youth. Solutions are not easy, but suggestions such as those listed below will be given throughout this work to offer possible methods for adults to help the teenagers of the 21st century. Too often adults look for the magic bullet. Or they look for that special bag of tricks or quick solution to change. Young kids and teens rely more and more on peers for validation, friendship and, too often, guidance. While many parents are often busy with careers, leisure time etc., there are some sensible ways for parents and other adults to help the child make the transition from dependence to independence, i.e., young child, teen and young adult. Parents often are looking for solutions; and some of these rather simple suggestions or interventions are described below:

A Few Tips for Parenting when the Child Becomes an Adolescent

- **Listen more than talk;**
- Educate yourself about adolescent development;
- Remember **your own adolescence**: your changing feelings, anger at authority and fears and hopes;
- Take a course on good parenting;
- Teach the adolescent about the joys and troubles of life and ways to revel in the good times and cope with the bad;
- Use positive reinforcement for positive behavior whenever possible: it is far more effective than criticism or punishment for negative behavior;
- Teach the adolescent that rights and responsibilities go hand in hand, and give the child increasing responsibility for his or her personal well-being;
- Help the adolescent move toward independence;
- Offer the child chances to become involved in the community;
- Spend quality and quantity time with the adolescent;
- Encourage other caring adults, including friends and relatives to spend time with the adolescent;
- Accept that you have feelings too;
- Seek support and guidance for yourself in dealing with the changes in a child moving through adolescence;

- Remember that most youth have problems at some time; and
- Do not always push for drastic solutions; and continue to provide the adolescent with positive feedback and opportunities to grow. (Mc Carthy, 2000).

Interventions and Solutions

It must be emphasized that there is no magic trick, psychiatric tool, special method or secret family tradition that will help all kids. Each child is a product of his or her family and the unique values, cultural traditions and mores developed, demonstrated or implemented by their parents. A few additional suggestions below may help adults improve the health of their children.

Improve Knowledge, Attitudes and Behaviors of Young People

- Provide life skills and health education, including sexuality education in schools;
- Include peer educators in both formal and informal settings to provide role models;
- Promote radio, TV, and online public service campaigns including popular theater and culturally appropriate means that appeal to youth;
- Provide health services to young people such as subsidizing social marketing of condoms and other reproductive health products;
- Include voluntary counseling and testing for HIV/AIDS and other STDs; and
- Expand job opportunities for poor or under served youth.

Create a Positive Context for Adolescent Health Programs

- Develop national, state and local adolescent policies and standards;
- Promote anti-smoking policies such as taxes and advertising bans;
- Require K-12 schools to include coordinated health education at all grade levels and a culminating course as a high school graduation requirement;
- Develop a network of communication from local PTA meetings and include newsletters, websites, etc., distributed to school boards, state and national agencies;
- Change social norms for youth, especially related to tobacco, alcohol and other drug use;
- Create afterschool programs, mentors, and support from local business leaders to help develop a smooth transition from youth to adulthood;
- Provide job training for youth, especially those not going to college; and
- Insist that the schools, with family support, include healthy food choices and an emphasis on exercise throughout the daily school routine. (Adapted from, World Bank, 2003).

Summary

Students grind through the difficult times of adolescence. They may come from families that are fragmented, dysfunctional, poor or lacking in consistency. Many teenagers face violent times, abuse drugs and practice risky sexual behavior that puts them at risk for STDs and even death from HIV. Yet, a large part of the teen population moves into adulthood with minimal disruption. Lifestyles practiced during youth will profoundly influence quality of life, and may even extend longevity for students and their teachers alike. Adolescent health is significantly impacted by family, media, schools and peer pressure. Teachers as professionals face enormous tasks to help guide the youth of today. While some of these trends may seem very dismal, there appears to be a *light at the end of the tunnel*. Later chapters will describe a decrease in unhealthy behaviors of adolescence, especially related to abuse of drugs, school discipline and violence prevention and issues related to sexual activity. Communication and classroom planning and discipline are paramount to success. Keep smiling, don't give up, and do your best!

Chapter 3

Health Education: Practical Considerations for the Teacher

Children today are tyrants.
They contradict their parents,
gobble their food,
and tyrannize their <u>teachers</u>
… Socrates (420 BC)

Introspection and Role Modeling-But Who is Magic?

During the fall of 1991, Ervin "Magic" Johnson revealed his HIV positive status and shock waves were heard around the world. Kids all over the United States were asking questions. How could he have HIV? Is he going to die of AIDS soon? What does that have to do with me? Many children were very upset. Other kids in places like the neighborhoods of Cleveland, Ohio, Oakland, California, or Newark, New Jersey, echoed feelings that Magic was just some big 'high rolling rich guy' who slept with too many girls. They failed to see any personal connection. Other famous celebrities later went public with their HIV status, and many have died. Those that have died include author Isaac Asimov, entertainer Liberace, rapper Eazy-E, tennis star Arthur Ashe, and actor Rock Hudson. Current celebrities living with HIV include Olympic diver Greg Louganis, and heavyweight boxer Tommy Morrison.

But who is Magic Johnson? Teachers constantly strive to keep up to date on relevant issues, musical trends and the latest in adolescent lingo; but oftentimes, young teachers, even in their early twenties quickly get out of touch with the teen trends. Magic Johnson, former NBA all-star and Olympic gold medalist, may not even be recognized by many youth of today. By 2008, however, Earvin Magic Johnson became known not only for his HIV disclosure, but, more importantly, for much of the work he has done in business, volunteering, investing and especially focusing on communities of underserved people of color throughout the U.S. He even plays basketball occasionally at California State University Long Beach. For a detailed list of famous people that have succumbed to AIDS, including athletes, business executives, rap and hip hop stars, and hundreds of others, readers are encouraged to do a Google search for **celebrities with HIV.**

What about teachers? Are they role models for their students? Most certainly they are. The schoolteacher represents a very powerful role model for students, and in some cultures, next to the parents, the teacher is the most important person in their lives. That is why many students with English language difficulties refer to their instructor as "teacher." The term teacher is very endearing and respectful in many cultures around the world. Students will watch, emulate and always remember what they saw in the classroom. They may not remember much of the subject or content material, but they do remember the non-verbal or unspoken messages they see each and every day. **As nationally known motivational speaker, Dr. Steve Sroka says, "Kids may not remember everything you do or say, but they never forget the way you make them feel."** (Sroka, 2009). Teachers should be especially attentive to how they project themselves to impressionable youth. Students quickly judge the teacher that "espouses" good health, while a pack of cigarettes bulge from his shirt pocket. Or the teacher that yells at her students to remove the candies from their desks, while she continuously snacks on chips and sponsors an ASB club in selling many bags of candy for fund raising to purchase school supplies, despite the 2007 *California Education Code* mandate prohibiting candy sales during school hours. For a detailed review of food sales in schools see the *California Education Code* 49430-49436.

Communication

All teachers should strive to develop the very best in their communication skills when working with students. Even though many teens today spend countless hours 'talking' via text

messages on cell phones, real live reading and writing, especially within the school setting should be emphasized. Communication is much more than reading, writing and practicing speaking skills. While these skills are very important in relaying ideas and messages to students, the non-verbal component of communicating is of particular importance within the classroom setting.

Most credential training programs require students to become proficient in public speaking, and usually require courses in public speaking. It is crucial that teachers understand how many messages can be conveyed without ever saying one word. **Body language** is defined as any non-verbal message from one human to another. It can be expressed through eye contact, facial expression, hand movement, gestures or general body shape and posture. By examining details of the orbicularis oris, masseter muscle and other anatomical features of the human face, it has been estimated that the human face can generate in excess of 200,000 facial expressions. (Pease, 2004, Pease & Pease, 2006). The concept of non-verbal communication has a very pragmatic value for teachers. Teachers send very powerful messages on a regular basis and students receive messages and quickly interpret the feeling tone, mood, or environmental situation. **One of the most important aspects of body language is the impact on student discipline.** Classroom discipline is especially important nowadays with the often-sudden outbursts of violence in schools. Many new teachers are terrorized by the thought of disciplining kids. Oftentimes, school principals first step in evaluating their staff is to **observe classroom control**. Student discipline techniques will be discussed in more detail later in this chapter.

People constantly speak of their inability to communicate. Wives cannot communicate with husbands. Bosses cannot communicate with their assistants. Principals cannot communicate with their teachers. Large corporations have difficulties with the workers at the order desk; instead of sending 100 cases of merchandise to Oakland, (California) they send 1,000 cases to Auckland (New Zealand). A teacher cannot communicate with students, when they are asked to turn in two reports on Friday, and half the class asks how many reports are due and on which day!

Communication has always been and probably always will be a significant problem for humans. A worker at a fast food restaurant may struggle with English while taking an order. A computer data entry worker may have difficulty transferring telephone extensions. Or, a chemist cannot transmit the correct formula by using electronic mail. It becomes a wonder how teenagers can decipher their cryptic messages using text messaging on their cell phones. **Perhaps the**  **problem is so overwhelming today because too many Americans spend so much time communicating through remote control devices, gadgets and gizmos by altering visual images, and regulating auditory impulses, and not enough time just talking and relating to their friends, teachers, and loved ones face-to-face.** Long before the explosion of the Internet and electronic media, families would just tell stories. Much like the traditions of Native Americans, teachers can also be great storytellers and that can help students understand much more than the subject matter lesson of the day. Stories delivered by teachers can inspire students to read, make them want to learn, and hopefully influence students to practice health-enhancing behaviors.

Native-Americans have a long history of storytelling, as do so many other ethnic groups in America. There seems to be such a feeling of closeness when a child can sit down with an adult parent, or grandparent and just listen, and listen and listen. Teachers should also use some time just telling stories, not only to keep the child interested, but just to show a sense of caring and love while delivering detailed lessons. Students too can use storytelling at all levels K-12 to convey ideas.

It all began about 50, 000 years ago as humans struggled with vocal mechanisms and tried to speak. The vocal chords transmitted sounds that were different than primitive grunts, and speech was born. One could imagine with an eerie sense what that moment must have been like on earth when the first human being made some kind of primitive sound in the form of speech. From those early years, struggles existed as people began to convey ideas. Struggles occurred over territory in the cave of a Neanderthal, a segment of a town in the African desert, or whether or not a person of color could enter a country and attend school there. All of this is related to speech and communication. In many communities throughout the world today, not much of the above has changed.

A major reason that people have difficulty communicating, is that communication, and especially listening, is rarely taught. True, English teachers teach grammar, punctuation, syntax and writing skills, but where do people learn how to relate to each other? Unfortunately, for some, it only begins in the privacy of the psychotherapist's office. Today, so many kids spend an inordinate amount of time looking at a screen on a game, TV, text message or computer, that they do not learn how to interact with live people. **During 2004, many psychologists began recommending that parents should limit kids 'screen time' to no more than two hours daily, and that kids under two should have no screen time to allow normal neuron growth in the brain! (KidsHealth, 2008).** This task may be quite difficult for the modern day busy parent.

What can be done? First, one needs to recognize that there are specific techniques available to improve a person's listening and communicating abilities. Some of the original work related to listening and teaching children was proposed by communication expert psychologist Dr. Thomas Gordon in his books, *Parent Effectiveness Training* (PET) *Teacher Effectiveness Training* (TET) and *Leadership Effectiveness Training* LET). Gordon suggested that parents and teachers used "roadblocks to communication." Statements such as, "You've always been a student with lots of potential," or, "I know how you feel, but school will be better in your senior year," impede communication. Most teens are more concerned with what will happen in the next few hours, and not the next grade in school. Gordon called these kinds of responses **ordering, lecturing, praising, reassuring, and sympathizing.**

The respondent simply cannot speak in a meaningful, and engaging fashion.
(Gordon, 1973, 2001, 2006).

Active listening is a method where one uses many specific techniques to carefully focus on the speaker, and can greatly improve communication. By listening and watching body language, non-verbal clues, and subtle movements and by being sensitive to the emotional tone of a conversation, a truly interactive two-way dialog can result. For classroom teachers, active listening is one of the most significant elements of their job, and an element that is too often overlooked. Some specific examples and techniques of active listening are discussed below.

Passive listening-just say nothing. This can be extremely difficult for many because they are so desperate to "get in" what they want to say. This is much like two 15-year-old sophomores talking "at each other." Or like two flat screen TVs turned on and facing each other! But, in reality, if the conservation is two-way, and the information is important, the topic will eventually "get in." Passive listening includes watching body language, facial expression, gesticulation, body shifting, and especially eye contact, **while saying nothing!**

Simple acknowledgment-Just use simple statements or phrases, such as, "Oh!" "I see," and "Is that right," using well-focused eye contact, and leaning forward while the conversation continues, these short words show the speaker that the listener is *tuned in* to the speaker.

Door openers-Use verbal responses that invite the speaker to say more. "I'd like to hear more about that...Tell me what happened...Do you want to talk about it? " "What did you dad say then…"

Active listening-Use responses that convey back to the person empathic and accurate understandings of their communications. All of these techniques may not seem that important when taken individually, but taken together they are part of a repertoire of communication tools that will help improve feelings, attitudes and factual exchanges, especially between teachers and students. In addition, effective listening skills can profoundly impact discipline, especially in the classroom setting.

How to Improve Listening

The following techniques pioneered by Thomas Gordon can dramatically improve communication and listening techniques. Try to use these when working with students:

Open-ended questions. Use open-ended questions. By avoiding questions that end up with a **yes** or **no** response (closed-ended), communication can improve. For example, a potential question on a date might be, "Do you like to go to concerts?" (closed-ended). Instead, a more effective question might be, "Tell me about the kind of music you like." (open-ended). Or, a teacher having a private conference with a student might change, "Did you do your homework?" (closed-ended), to, "What were the problems you had while doing the assignment?" (open-ended).

56

Parroting. Just like a bird. Try to say the exact same words without any emotional content. Just repeat the words. This will signal to the listener that you are paying attention.

Paraphrasing. This technique just restates the message in your own words. Again, use little emotional content while the speaker is trying to relay a message. This is just a time to gather information.

Spend more time listening. This seems simple enough, but it is often very difficult for many to let other people finish. Resist the temptation to interrupt or anticipate what others will say. **Listen! Even if you do know what they will say!** Poor listeners talk too much. This is especially true of many teachers and parents as well. Active listening sends the important message to the other person that **they** are important.

Find interest in the other person. A basic roadblock to listening is labeling. Don't be too quick to label a person as boring, or a topic as uninteresting, or, worse yet, that the child is a known troublemaker.

Listen between the lines. A message has both content and emotion. A good listener watches both at the same time to interpret the entire message. Oftentimes, women have an intuitive way of understanding messages, while men may act too quickly without listening carefully.

Be aware of filters. All of us can filter out the portion of the message that we don't want to hear. This is also true between men and women. In general, women like more details in a conversation. Men usually want to get to the point and become irritated with too many details. This may be frustrating for both sexes, but people need to develop methods to compromise, provide better communication, and, hopefully, improve relationships. **Do Men and Women Communicate Differently?** Is there a real difference in the way men and women communicate? Evidence does exist.

Georgetown University expert linguist, and author, Dr. Deborah Tannen states that men and women communicate based upon societal roles. Men generally are problem solvers, seek independence and strive for status. (Tannen, 2001). Men want to "get to the point." Women, however, generally desire to seek a connection and focus on understanding with emphasis on intimacy, cooperation and developing relationships. Women enjoy talking for the joy of talking. Men can go to a store to buy a shirt, look for the shirt, pay for it, and find the quickest exit, sometimes actually timing themselves to see how fast they can return to their cars!

Women can spend hours relaxing, talking and enjoying "retail therapy" while visiting with friends, and buying nothing! For interesting updated research readers should also read her work,

He Said, She Said (2004). To learn more about the pioneering work on communication of Dr. Tannen, and review her excellent books, Google: Deborah Tannen or check her Internet link: **http://www9.georgetown.edu/faculty/tannend/.**

One of the best ways to practice communication techniques is just to watch people. Try standing around at a large shopping mall and watch and listen to the body language, voice tone, gestures and whatever methods people use to convey messages. Classes are often offered at community colleges or public community centers that teach public speaking, assertion training, non-verbal communication and even how to flirt! Consider exploring one of these options to improve your own communication style and abilities. This could not only improve your teaching skills, but could also improve your overall relationships with others.

Classroom Discipline

In 1987, psychologist Fred Jones published one of the best sources on classroom discipline based upon sound psychological and behavioral science research. Jones' book, *Positive Classroom Discipline,* clearly outlines a myriad of incentive systems and techniques

> *"The effective teacher spends the first two weeks adjusting students to routines, and the ineffective teacher starts the first day teaching and, spends the rest of the year chasing children."*
> **Fred Jones, PhD.**

to help the teacher eliminate behavioral problems develop a positive relationship with students, while lowering daily stress. The following ideas are based upon his research. (Jones, 1987, 2008). The problem that occurs in most classes relates to very small and trivial things. Horseplay, movement, paper tossing, text messaging or plain old rudeness! Teachers need to

place special emphasis on students not familiar with the American standards, customs and mores. But, at the same time, teachers should help guide students in developing American acculturation, while reminding them to keep their own beliefs and values. Simply stated, however, kids can be rude. As much as 20-25% of an excellent class may be off-task while a teacher is desperately trying to get them to complete a lesson. The term **on-task** merely refers to the fact that they are either doing or not doing the given assignment or activity. This can quickly amount to 24 students "goofing off."

What does all this cost the teacher? According to Jones (1987), it cost "flesh and blood." More than 50% of teachers will suffer dental grinding, insomnia, depression, exhaustion, and loss of enthusiasm, lower back pain, gastrointestinal problems, ulcers, or burnout in the first six to seven years. **Conclusion: Lack of discipline means zero learning!**

For recent information on Jones's original text, and his teacher manual *Tools for Teaching,* including numerous lessons, tips and simple ideas to deliver better discipline, see: **http://www.fredjones.com/.**

What can teachers do? Everyone remembers a certain adult such as a parent, uncle, or teacher that very quickly could control his or her kids. All it took was that one "look." That special look that was intimidating, and caring, yet loving and respectful. One of the best ways for teachers to develop a "look" or method of class control is to practice in front of a mirror. To control an entire class, often within 15-30 seconds, try to remember the following ideas. Most of the control is achieved through body language. Use a **cleansing breath** to totally relax the body and prepare to have students respond in a positive and meaningful way. (Remember they are all just kids, or big kids in the case of teenagers). And most importantly, according to Jones, all discipline should be self-eliminating and reinforced all of the time. The following description is modified from the Fred Jones Method.

Call the student by name and look them directly in the eyes. Take another cleansing breath and calmly ask them to change the behavior as you request. For example, "Ricki, it is time to finish the writing assignment." Use a low emotional tone and point your body to the problem student. Usually there are two students talking at one time. Pick the biggest *"mouth"* of the two! Point your body and feet to the problem and allow them time to move. If they do not respond, it is time to take action. Take another **cleansing breath**, slowly and calmly walk over to the noisy pair, face the noisiest student, and very quietly tell them to get to work. At all costs do not involve the rest of the class. As much as possible discipline should be personal and private. Remember all kids have a PhD in teacher management! They earned it in kindergarten!

Early in the semester, start by walking through the room and showing emergency plans, wastebaskets, pencil sharpeners, books, computer stations, cabinets and all the little details that students may need to use. Be clear on explaining what areas are off limits. An adjacent stockroom, or faculty office, for example, might have an "Employees Only" or "Off Limits to Students" sign. While this may seem limiting, students will clearly get the message that the teacher requires private office space to be away from student interaction. Other items like hall passes and security items should be kept out of student view and accessibility. The roll book should not be easily viewed by students. It usually contains confidential information such  as student phone numbers, identification numbers, or other pertinent data that are not for student reference.

Show them where assignments are to be turned in, or use a file folder, or cabinet with an "in and out" label. Also, laboratory classes are required to administer safety tests to protect students, faculty and staff. This will be discussed later under legal aspects in Chapter 11.

Develop methods that are smooth, quick and easy for students and faculty. Being organized is extremely important, not only to make life easier and efficient for the teacher; but also to portray a powerful message to kids about organization and study skills. Special concern items and teaching tips include:

Physical Arrangement

- Podium: Use wheels for easy mobility;
- Re-admit box: Have students drop off and pick up re-admits; (or convert to computerized attendance and eliminate re-admits)
- Seating chart: Be certain that it is clearly visible and readable, (especially for; substitute teachers);
- Audio-visual equipment: Be certain that it is out of reach of student tampering; and
- Use passwords on computers to avoid student access.

Positive Teaching Tips

- Talk to every student every day;
- Use quiet whispers and positive compliments regularly;
- Circulate throughout the class-even during lectures;
- Use positive praise, even for small improvements in student performance;
- Rearrange the seats every three to four weeks;
- Meet students at the door and say hello, or shake their hands;
- Use positive referrals, notes, or merit awards;
- Personally return students' papers using their names;
- Look students in the eye;
- Seek out the physically challenged, obese or disabled student;
- Tape yourself on video or audiotapes for later review (hide the microphone);
- Give the greatest responsibility to the most irresponsible student; and
- Most importantly, be honest. Tell them when you are ill or had a rotten night.

Matza's Tool Bag for the Classroom

The following items are usually not supplied by the school, but these little things can make life in the classroom go much smoother and help the teacher supervise children at the same time.

- Band-Aids
- Small flashlight
- Pen light to check out audio visual equipment in the dark
- Small screwdriver
- Clean erasers for white boards
- White board cleaning solutions
- Electric stapler
- Heavy duty 3 hole punch
- Extra batteries
- Locks to secure cabinets/drawers
- Headache meds/for teachers not students
- Emergency change of clothes
- Small clock or timer
- Comfortable shoes
- Extra reading glasses if needed

Professionalism

Teachers are professionals and should be treated as such. Sometimes, many teachers do not even look much like a professional and cannot understand why parents and others in the community may not give them the respect they deserve. Among the best ways to project a professional image is to prepare materials that look professional and arrive at work dressed professionally. Even smelling nice and clean can help. Carefully typed, spell-checked and easily read documents are critical for student success. **An excellent teacher is a lifetime student.** If the teacher expects the students to be able to enter the job market and work with professionally prepared materials, the assignments, worksheets, etc., should all look impeccable. Additionally, in order to stay current on the latest research, teaching ideas, and sample lessons, teachers should attend workshops, local and national conferences and maintain a continuous network system to keep in touch with colleagues. Professional educators should not only keep abreast with subject matter material related to their specialty, but they should also network with the business and community residents to bring together a coalition of efforts to help benefit their clients,-the students. Using the Internet and e-mail subscription lists (listservs) can quickly keep teachers abreast with current facts and trends related to their subject matter material. Educators should be certain that they and their students don't use all of their time using Google or Wikipedia as their sole reference sources.

The following list serves as a guideline to suggest ways in which teachers can improve their daily job and better serve students.

Professional Success without Stress

- Arrive early to class-prepare materials, review and finish details;
- Be overly prepared with lessons;
- Have backup systems in place, light bulbs, batteries, handouts, books and special lessons in case of a canceled guest speaker or other mishap;
- Exercise regularly, this builds energy, endurance, and strength, and lowers stress
- Model what you believe, body language speaks volumes;
- Use relaxation methods, like listening to music or meditating;
- Leave school problems at school;
- Play music during class;
- Laugh everyday;
- **Regularly back up all computer files on separate disks, or flash and external drives, keep copies at home**;
- Nurture positive relationships with loved ones; and
- Allow yourself time alone, a minimum of 20 minutes daily.

Summary

Teachers have a very complex job requiring careful organizing, planning and implementing of lessons for students. They must continuously study, prepare, and focus on communication skills to deliver messages to students in a professional manner. Students come to the classroom with many techniques that serve as attention-getting devices to place teachers in their service. The discipline of students is an art, which, when applied sensitively, can dramatically improve the classroom atmosphere and enhance learning. When students are treated like little adults and teachers approach them in a caring, yet firm manner, they will respond and participate in the lesson. Many methods exist to make teaching a better job. Each individual teacher should adapt their own personal style to enhance the learning environment; concentrate on positive discipline, and treat students like young adults. Hopefully, this will motivate students to participate in a positive and exciting classroom setting, and, of course, learn the subject matter at hand.

Used with permission of Teachers' Pocketbooks

Chapter 4

Risk Factors
for Drug Abuse

I touch the future,
I teach.
...Christa McAuliffe, Teacher/Astronaut

Red ribbon week, the DARE Program (Drug Awareness Resistance Education), the "Just Say No," slogan of President and Nancy Regan, and countless other programs, may bring up youthful memories of local police officers warning kids about drug abuse. Many of these programs, such as the DARE program, often showed detailed samples of actual drugs and drug paraphernalia, in an attempt to educate kids. The DARE program has been around for many years in attempting to keep kids drug free. This particular program, however does not seem to do much more than teach kids respect and appreciation for law enforcement-but does not deter youth from using drugs. Using available evaluation research on the DARE program including random assignment, true experimental design and quasi-experimental design, The Center for the Study of Prevention of Violence (CSPV) at the University of Colorado concluded the DARE program was not working. CSPV states,

> The available evaluation research on the DARE program includes both true experimental designs with random assignment and quasi-experimental design with good control groups. Overall, the research indicates that children who participate in the traditional D.A.R.E. curriculum (which is implemented in the fifth or sixth grades) are just as likely to use drugs, as are children who do not participate in the program. This same set of studies indicates there are some beneficial attitudinal outcomes of the D.A.R.E. program, which includes replacing negative stereotypes of police with positive attitudes toward police, as well as collective and unified support of and involvement in the program by parents, teachers and police. But, in general, participation in D.A.R.E. does not reduce the risk of future drug use." (CSPV, 1998).

Since the CSPV findings were published, however, DARE programs made many adjustments. As a result of numerous studies, DARE programs have improved. A recent report in 2004, from the University of Akron, The University of Akron Adolescent Substance Abuse Prevention Study, found some significant changes in attitudes and behaviors of young people regarding drug use. The newer program, focusing on 7th and 9th graders, "Taking Charge of Your Life," grew out of the DARE program and found:

- More students had better decision-making skills. The research found that decision making skills scores for those students receiving the New DARE curriculum were 6 percent higher than for control group schools;
- More students found drug use socially inappropriate and believed fewer peers used drugs. Results show the schools that received the New DARE curriculum documented as much as a 19 percent reduction in normative beliefs about the prevalence of substance use among their peers, demonstrating that more students receiving the new program perceive lower rates of substance use by their peers than students in the control schools;
- More students learned how to refuse alcohol, tobacco, and marijuana: Refusal skills were significantly higher -- 5 percent – among students who received the New DARE curriculum as compared to control group students; and
- Fewer students reported intent to use inhalants: Scores were significantly lower by as much as 4 percent with respect to intent to use inhalants for those students who received the New DARE curriculum. (Carnevale, 2004).

Additionally, another component was added in 2009 to DARE called *Keepin' it REAL* (kiR), has shown promise. "kiR" was developed by researchers at Pennsylvania State University and Arizona State University, with funding provided by the National Institute on Drug Abuse (NIDA). The curriculum represents over 20 years of research by the Drug Resistance Strategies Project about why our youth use drugs. The kiR curriculum is designated as an **evidence-based program** by the U.S. Department of Health and Human Services Substance Abuse & Mental Health Services Administration, and is listed on the National Registry of Evidence-based Programs and Practices (NREPP). The program uses the acronym REAL as its central message to help provide students with skills to refuse offers of drugs and other high-risk behaviors. In 2010 DARE added prevention of cyberbullying to the curriculum. Even though some of the evaluations of the DARE program are mixed, in 2009, President Obama supported the efforts of the revised DARE program. (Dare to Be More, 2011).

So-Why Use Drugs?

Risk taking is considered a normal part of development in the life of a teenager. These risks bring about much concern of parents, teachers, clinicians, researchers and schoolteachers because they endanger adolescents' health and well being. Unfortunately, many of the behaviors established during the teens often become part of regular behaviors expressed as adults. (Park, Mulye, Adams, Brindis & Irwin, 2006). Research has concluded that numerous factors bring about risk taking and are described with numerous theories. Four of these theories include **biologically based theories, psychologically based theories, social and environmental based theories, and biopsychosocial models of risk taking.** Biology is certainly a factor that parents cannot control, but biological factors are believed to result from four sources: (1) genetic predispositions, (2) "direct" hormonal influences, (3) the influence of asynchronous pubertal timing (early or late puberty compared to peers), and (4) brain and central nervous system development. Examples include a predisposition to alcohol abuse, the effect of drugs on neurotransmitters in the brain altering dopamine, and the later maturation of neurons in the brain associated with decision making which may not fully mature until the twenties for teenagers. (DiClemente, Santelli, Crosby, 2009).

Theories of risk-taking related to psychology examine the roles of cognition, personality traits, and dispositional characteristics such as self-esteem. Cognitive decision-making research suggests that adolescents give greater weight to proximal than distal consequences when making decisions. Numerous factors impact the **social and environmental** theories related to risk taking. Youth are certainly affected by the immediate family behaviors, role models, etc.; but they are also influenced by schools, churches and the working environment. The **biopsychosocial** factors of risk taking include the relationship of biological development to psychosocial processing during adolescence. Examples include egocentrism, future time perspective, self-esteem, and body image and peer behaviors. (DiClemente, Santelli, Crosby, 2009). So how do these theories relate to daily life of kids?

Many kids experiment with all kinds of activities while growing up. Drug abuse is just another one of those 'dares' that kids attempt. **The Federal Safe and Drug Free Schools** program state that kids use drugs to: relieve boredom, feel good, forget their troubles and relax, have fun, satisfy their curiosity, take risks, ease pain, feel grown-up, look cool, show their independence from adults or family; and belong to a specific group. Many times parents may think that drug dealers pressured their kids into taking drugs. This may be true sometimes, but children can find drugs easily in their own house. Parents should be very cautious to secure any drugs away from their kids, especially psychoactive drugs, or painkillers, such as Vicodin or codeine. (OSDFS, 2011).

Any athlete that has participated in a vigorous sport to the point of exhaustion has felt the numbness, relaxed state, and even the **euphoria** from the contest. While playing soccer, rugby, basketball, handball, or some other high-energy aerobic activity, the athlete may become injured, and not feel any pain. The reason for this is the release of naturally occurring **neurotransmitters** (opiate-like drugs), called **endorphins** that are produced in the brain to **prevent pain.** Athletes who enjoy this "second wind," as it is sometimes called, sense being "high" or getting a "rush" and only feel the pain of injury later in the locker room, while celebrating the victory or agonizing over the defeat. Is this drug abuse? A young mother feels relaxed and comfortable while watching a football game and rooting for her favorite team. She is sipping on a mug of beer and notices the calm, smooth relaxation and pleasure she feels, almost a sleepiness that she senses after completing two medium sized mugs. Is this drug abuse? A twelve-year-old boy, in a gang is known as a "Snakehomie-pee-wee-13" (or *Snake-13*, by his friends), in the world of methamphetamine, cocaine and other drug sales, decided he wanted to smoke some of the potent inventory he was distributing in the west coast inner city where he lives. Is this drug abuse? People have been using drugs for thousands of years throughout the world. In the U.S. most use is clearly legal, some use may have religious significance, and other use, which often may involve criminal activities, is clearly illegal. How does one define drug abuse? Is it simply by the volume, or frequency of use? Does it always have to be an illegal substance? **Drug abuse** is not an easy term to define. **This chapter will define and classify drugs, describe different types of drug use and abuse, differentiate between legal and illegal drugs. Teachers will also be presented with alternatives to excessive use, and locate referral sources for their students.**

What is a drug?

A simple basic definition of a **drug** is *any substance when taken into the body that alters cells.* Clearly, alcohol in a glass of wine and antibiotics injected to treat ear infections would both meet this definition. This physiological description merely states the ultimate fate of the chemical as it eventually meets the cell for absorption, pathophysiology, utilization and metabolism. Of course, the drugs that people abuse paint a much different picture of drug use than prescription medicines because they often affect the mind. **Drug abuse is persistent or excessive use of a drug without medical or health reasons.** A careful distinction should be made at this point between drugs and medicines. Many programs have been developed over the years to help kids and adults to stay away from drugs, but **most drugs are good.** This is a true statement since most drugs do have a medicinal value, and are used for some patient in a certain fashion, either by a doctor's prescription or purchased over the counter. The *Physicians Desk Reference (PDR)*, the basic reference for medical doctors, describes thousands of drugs. Some relieve pain, some help remove sores on the skin, some eliminate discharge from the eye or other orifice, and many destroy pathogenic bacteria, impede viral replication, or destroy other microbes. In actuality very few drugs have significant behavioral impact on individuals, and society at large.

Even though researchers studied the drug called nicotine for decades, it wasn't until April of 1997, that nicotine was officially declared an addictive drug, and as such, comes under the regulation and distribution laws. A Federal judged ruled, "tobacco products fit within the FDAs definitions of "drug" and "device," and that FDA can regulate cigarettes and smokeless tobacco products as drug delivery devices under the combination product and restricted device provisions of the **Family Smoking Prevention and Tobacco Control Act.** (HR.1256). (Coyne, 1997). Ten years later, The U.S. Congress, under the leadership of Senator Ted Kennedy and Representative

Henry Waxman, (S. 625, HR. 1108) again introduced legislation to allow the government, i.e., FDA to control tobacco as a drug. But not until 2010 did a federal judge finally rule that tobacco companies were acting much like gangsters and imposed Racketeering Influenced and Corrupt Organizations (RICO) rulings when they stated: "The major cigarette manufacturers are racketeers who carried out a decades-long conspiracy to deceive the American public and target children with their deadly and addictive products." (Campaign for Tobacco Free Kids-CTFK, 2010).

> *The tragic consequences of violence and the illegal use of alcohol and drugs by students are felt not only by students and such students' families, but by such students' communities and the nation, which can ill afford to lose such students' skills, talents, and vitality. (Title IV: Safe and Drug-Free Schools and Communities, 1998)*

Too often bureaucrats and other political leaders strive to bring about social and legal change to eliminate the 'drug problem,' but often forget to include tobacco and alcohol as drugs. Professor Goldstein (2001), in his book, *Addiction from Biology to Drug Policy,* addresses the drug problem as an issue that is very complex. According to Goldstein, addictive drugs fall into **seven families.** These families of drugs may be taken into the body via different routes: injection into a vein or muscle or under the skin, intranasal (snorting), or, inhalation (as by smoking), or by mouth. The seven families of drugs include **nicotine, alcohol, opiates, cocaine and amphetamines, cannabis products, caffeine,** and **hallucinogens.** (Goldstein, 2002).

Psychoactive or psychotogenic drugs are chemical substances that cause profound effects on the brain and behavior. These effects may include relaxation, severe hallucinations or dramatic mood swings. That is why people use them! Common examples include nicotine in tobacco, alcohol, cocaine, marijuana, amphetamines, depressants, designer drugs, and a wide variety of organic compounds called inhalants. For many years health educators have used such terms as "mood modifiers," "substances," and other terms to describe the kind of products people were smoking, chewing, injecting, ingesting or inhaling, and even eating. But, they all are basically chemicals. A teacher need not complete a college degree with a major in chemistry to understand and study drugs, but one can easily follow the media reports, and read the scientific evidence concerning the negative effects of these chemicals on individuals, families and society.

What is Intoxication?

Ronald Siegel, PhD, is a psychopharmacologist in the Department of Psychiatry and Biobehavioral Sciences at UCLA School of Medicine. In his controversial book *Intoxication: The Universal Drive for Mind Altering Substances,* (2005). Sigel believes that in addition to the three human drives of hunger, thirst and sex, there is a fourth drive in human behavior: that of intoxication. This fourth drive, according to his laboratory scientific research, is a natural part of human biology and accounts for our irrepressible demand for drugs. Hence, Siegel argues, that the so-called War on Drugs is as futile as it is pointless, since there will always be and always has been people who choose to subject their bodies and minds to different drugs. But the ruling class leaders such as politicians, police, legislators and judges decide that drugs should be illegal. His research also supports the idea that it is indeed possible to use narcotics and still be a very functioning member of society. Not all drug users end up as pathetic heroin junkies. The politics of drugs are extremely complicated, and doctor Siegel's research should be read by all responsible adults to at least think of possible perspectives as drugs impact the lives of children. (Siegel, 1989, 2005).

Why Use Drugs? Children at Risk

Some would argue that people should never use any drugs. They argue that we should allow the body to repair itself, or rely on various religious or spiritual approaches to overcome illness or disability. Most Americans, however, do see a need for the use of drugs for medical purposes under the direction of a medical expert, and even the use of over the counter (OTC) products, when properly explained. Unfortunately, too many individuals use a highly advertised product without reading the literature or labels carefully and rarely ask the available, and mostly underused, health professional, the pharmacist, for guidance and suggestions on how to use a particular drug. Studies by Hawkins and colleagues have painted a picture of an individual that may be at risk for the use of drugs. These include risks of the individual, the community, the family and the school. Teachers must be aware of these risks to assist their students in not developing abusive drug related habits. (Hawkins, Catalano & Lishner, 1985, 1991, 2000). As these factors are discussed, remember to include such legal products as tobacco and alcohol as drugs. Additionally, Hawkins, et al. stated, "The odds for violence of youths exposed to more than five risk factors compared to the odds for violence of youths exposed to fewer than two risk factors at each age were seven times greater at age 10 years, 10 times greater at age 14 years, and nearly 11 times greater at age 16 years. However, despite information gained from all significant risk factors, the overall accuracy in predicting youths who would go on to commit violent acts was limited." (Hawkins, Catalano, 2000). Tobacco is the most life-threatening chemical in America. Tobacco products and their medical risks will be discussed in much more detail in Chapter five.

Parents of kids in the forties, fifties or even the sixties knew that one of the best ways to keep their kids out of trouble was to keep them busy. Sign the kids up for clubs, sports, church activities, part-time jobs or whatever it would take to keep the idle mind engaged. Unfortunately, the fabric of family life in America has changed so dramatically that it is not as easy to supervise children with two working parents in a demanding economy. With less than ten percent of families operating as a **nuclear family** (mom, dad, with biological kids and maybe a dog named Rocky), the problem of drug abuse can arise. The following list, from the pioneering work of David Hawkins, et al., (2000), describes some of the major factors that put a child or young adult at risk for drug abuse. Perhaps you may recognize some of them from your own life? Teachers should remember that any one or two of the items from the list below does not mean the child is a drug addict.

Family Risk Factors

Family management

- Lack of supervision;
- Inconsistent or excessively severe discipline;
- Lack of caring;
- Parental modeling of unhealthy behavior;
- Lack of clear expectations for children's behavior;
- Low expectations for children's success, and
- Poor family health history, including alcoholism.

School Risk Factors

- Lack of clear school policy regarding the use of tobacco, alcohol, and drugs;
- Other health risk related behavior;
- Availability of drugs and unhealthy foods;
- Transient student population;
- Lack of student involvement in school activities, and
- Low student/family/community commitment to school.

Individual and Peer Risk Factors

- Early antisocial behavior;
- Alienation and rebelliousness;
- Antisocial behavior in late childhood and early adolescence;
- Poor attitude toward healthy behaviors;
- Early development of unhealthy behaviors;
- Greater influence by and reliance on peers than parents; and
- Friends who lead unhealthy lifestyles (Hawkins, Catalano, 1985, 2000).

What can an individual do to prevent problems related to tobacco, alcohol and drugs in their lives, in the lives of their families or close friends? In 1991, The California State Department of Education prepared a booklet, *Not Schools Alone*, which included **protective factors** that can help overcome the problem of drug abuse with children and young adults. If kids are given guidelines and powerful positive role models by their parents, the chances of them becoming associated with drug abuse can be dramatically limited. These protective factors include:

Protective Factors in Work, Play and Relationships

- Healthy friendships
- Goal-oriented

Healthy expectancies and positive outlooks

- A belief that effort and initiative will pay off
- Success-oriented attitude

Protective Factors of Self Esteem and Internal Locus of Control

- Feeling of competence
- Sense of personal power
- A belief that events can be controlled
- Self-discipline
- Ability to delay gratification and control impulsive drives
- Future oriented
- Humor-An ability to laugh at themselves and situations

Social Competence

- Responsiveness
- Flexibility
- Empathy/caring
- Sense of humor
- Problem-solving skills thinking critically, generating alternatives, planning produces change

Autonomy

- Self-esteem, self-efficiency
- Internal locus of control
- Independence
- Adaptive distancing

Sense of Purpose and Future

- Goal directedness with persistence
- Achievement motivation
- Educational aspirations
- Healthy expectancies
- Hopefulness for a compelling future (CDE, 1991).

This is a formidable list! This may seem like just a list of possible problems and solutions related to children and drugs, but this list can also be considered as a template for all kinds of healthy behavior changes. Go back and look at the protective factors. Are there some ideas that can serve to help you **alter your own health behaviors?** Think of ways to help your students. Could you develop a plan, write goals or lessons for students? How could the local school or community help? How could you develop creative lessons, within your subject matter area, to help kids resist tobacco, alcohol or other drugs?

What were you thinking? The Adolescent Brain and Substance Use

As children do many unpredictable acts, oftentimes teachers and parents ask the classic question to their kids, or students: **What were you thinking?** As teens exhibit often confusing or difficult behaviors, parents and other adults become very upset or confused as well. It may simply be the teenage brain. It does appear, however, that many of these strange behaviors of kids can be explained through brain physiology. Adolescent brain development has recently been defined as "a work in progress." According to a report by the California Department of Education, (2009), the brain continues to grow for many more years than previously thought. Contrary to earlier data, the brain continues to develop until we reach our early twenties. This is of particular importance for teachers that are trying to work with teens and have a difficult time understanding their behaviors in school. The areas of the brain last to develop are those important areas responsible for decision-making, learning, impulse control and memory. **Because teen brains are not yet mature, adolescents are especially vulnerable to specific consequences such as abuse of alcohol and other drugs.** (CDE, 2009).

A Brief Explanation of Brain Development

Many educators and researchers, until very recently, believed that the human brain develops by the age of three and matures around age ten. By using advanced brain imaging techniques, however, data now shows us that brain development is not completed until around age twenty-four. Between ages six and twelve, the brain's nerve cells responsible for thinking and the processing of information multiply and develop new communication pathways. When this growth is finished in nerve cells, a "pruning" process occurs in the early twenties, where connections between neurons unused die away, and those that are used remain. This is similar to the "use it or lose it" metaphor related to the body and exercise. During this time there occurs a thickening of the brain's myelin sheath (the white fatty material covering nerve cells and provides efficient transmission of nerve signals). The table below illustrates these functions and the ages of development. (CDE, 2009).

Brain Region	Function	Developmental Age
Frontal lobe	Self-control, judgment, emotional regulation	Restructured in teen years
Corpus callosum	Intelligence, consciousness, Self-awareness	Reaches full maturity in twenties
Parietal lobes	Integration of auditory, visual, and tactile signals	Immature until age sixteen
Temporal lobes	Emotional maturity	Still developing after age sixteen

(CDE, 2009).

Effects of Substance Use on a Developing Brain

Hormones produced during puberty (testosterone and estrogen) associated with risk taking and sensation seeking surge at a time when the brain is not yet fully developed, i.e., the teenage brain is still "cooking." This is evident in the teen's behavior to make decisions, weigh consequences, control impulses and accept responsibilities. Thus the "raging hormones" concept often portrayed and emphasized in media, movies, etc., coupled with the immature brain explains why teens are more vulnerable to abuse of illegal drugs, tobacco and alcohol. There are also biochemical reactions from these drugs that can have long-term impact on brain function later in life. For example, heavy alcohol use, which may start as young as twelve, can have a long-term impact on functions such as learning and memory. Brain scans of teens with alcohol problems had significantly smaller volume in the hippocampus (the brain structure of memory) than teens who did not use alcohol. Other studies also indicated lower scores on tests of learning and memory. (McNeely, Blanchard, 2010).

Tobacco use has also been shown to impact brain function from nicotine exposure. Teens with even low levels of nicotine exposure have shown substantial cell damage. Nicotine also changes the levels of brain chemical, or neurotransmitters, such as dopamine, norepinephrine and serotonin. These biochemicals, if improperly working, have been associated to alcohol and other drug use as well as mental disorders. When the chemical **dopamine** is released it produces feelings of pleasure, sometimes referred to as the "reward pathway." Hence drug abuse provides a shortcut to the reward pathway. Thus, without drugs, the user may feels angry, depressed, anxious or bored. (CDE, 2009). Besides, teenage smokers produce a terrible odor on their clothes, in their hair and in the classroom!

Implications for Prevention Education

It is very important for teachers to understand this picture of adolescent physical brain development, combined with the biological understanding of addiction. Adolescents are very complex children and this new understanding of their brain development can help teachers, parents and other adults that work with youth. Health education classes should also help students learn about their developing brains and explain why they feel and act the ways they do. "Why did you do that?" Parents often ask this of their kids and the teen my simply say, " I don't know." And chances are very likely that they do not know why. Therefore, information about brain chemistry can help them better understand and make proper adjustments in their lives.

How Can Parents and Teachers Tell if a Child is Using Drugs?

Teachers play a very important role in helping parents to keep their children away from drug use. American parents are very often busy with work, overtime, and more work, and more overtime. Sometimes, the teacher may spend more time with the child than the parents. Many times certain "acting out" behaviors in the classroom can be the key red flags to alert the professional educator that the child is using drugs. Parents and teachers should communicate together to prevent kids from using and abusing drugs. If a teacher or parent asks themselves the following questions, they may be able to help identify the onset of drug use in youth:

- Does the child seem withdrawn, depressed, tired and careless about grooming?
- Has the child suddenly become hostile and uncooperative?
- Has the child's relationships with other members of the family or friends deteriorated?
- Is the child no longer doing well in school? Are grades dropping or is attendance irregular?
- Has the child lost interest in sports, hobbies and other favorite activities?
- Has the child changed eating or sleeping patterns? (Kidsnet, 1997).

If most of the above questions are answered yes, there is a distinct possibility that drug or alcohol use may be occurring. There is also the possibility, however, that the child is ill, on special medication or suffering from other types of psychological problems. It is critical that the teacher and parent both monitor and carefully watch students for some of the above signs. If a student does exhibit problems, close communication should always continue between teacher, parent, administrator, counselor, and special education teacher, when appropriate. Sometimes a simple phone call from the teacher will alert the concerned adults involved to help the student.

Drug Prevention in Schools

Comprehensive prevention programs for the control of tobacco, alcohol and other drugs must focus on much more than health education and "Just don't do it," or "Just say No" campaigns. To be effective, programs must address curriculum, in-service for staff, parent education, intervention, community involvement and **positive alternatives for youth**.

Even though the items listed above will help change behavior of youth regarding drug use, the media delivers overpowering messages that counteract much of the efforts of teachers, government and health education researchers. Researchers report that from the fall of 1990 through the summer of 1992 more commercials appeared for alcohol products than for any other beverage. Beer commercials predominate television and include images in direct opposition of programs written by The U.S. Surgeon General and other agencies. The Center on Alcohol Marketing and Youth (CAMY) at Johns Hopkins School of Public Health, reported in 2010 that youth exposure to alcohol advertising increased 71% between 2001 and 2009! That amount of exposure is more than the exposure of either adults ages 21 and above or young adults ages 21 to 34. (CAMY, 2010b). The viewing audience is also exposed to alcohol advertising through the appearances of signs in large stadiums and the persistent sponsorship of sporting events. In contrast, messages about moderation and public service announcements are rare. (Madden, 1994). Since 1993, movies have directed excessive emphasis on smoking being depicted as a regular normative behavior for kids to see. And by 2005, smoking in movies became more prevalent than smoking during movies of the past thirty years. **Finally, thousands of tobacco signs were removed from billboards throughout the U.S. during the spring of 1999**, in hope of reducing use of cigarettes. Congress must now address the excessive advertising of alcohol, especially when targeted for youth, to prevent the development of youthful alcoholics evolving into the ten percent of the adult population that are often devastated by abuse of alcohol products.

Alcohol and Other Drug Policies

The Federal Drug-Free Workplace Regulations (DFWA) enacted in 1988, requires clearly defined anti-alcohol and anti-drug policies both in schools and the workplace. School districts and county offices of education that do not have a policy that includes each of the items are in **jeopardy of losing their DFWA funds**. References to legal mandates are included throughout this text and teachers can bring about many changes in their school setting by serving as activists to help enforce the laws. By becoming involved with the legal aspects of drug policies, teachers will help provide a safe working environment, and ultimately help students observe their teachers as powerful role models. Oftentimes, even school principals are unaware of many laws or regulations, and the teacher can serve as a collegial support professional to the school management team. The drug free regulations should include the following:

- Clear statements must prohibit unlawful possession, use, or distribution of illicit drugs or alcohol on school property or during part of any school-sponsored activity. **Compliance is mandatory for employees as well as students**;

- A description of the enforcement of this policy, provisions for due process, and the disciplinary sanctions must be consistent with local, state, and federal laws up to and including expulsion, referral for prosecution, and completion of a rehabilitation or cessation program;

- Procedures must be provided for informing students, parents, and employees of these sanctions and the services available. Procedures may need to be translated into appropriate languages; and

- Clear statements must be made about procedures for intervention that includes identification and referral of students and staff with drug, alcohol or tobacco abuse-related problems.

Tobacco-Free Policies

Assembly Bill 99 (AB 99), which authorized additional taxes of 25 cents per pack on cigarette sales in California, required policies to achieve tobacco-free school districts by 1996. Since the late 1980s many school districts have enacted such policies on a voluntary basis. And by 2010, many cities restricted smoking in parks, on beaches and California passed the "Smoke

Free Cars with Minors Law" restricting smoking in cars with minors present. School districts and county offices that do not have tobacco-free policies in place will not receive tobacco prevention funds and may jeopardize other federal funding as well. To view an outstanding website describing the trends and laws in California on smoking, consult the California Department of Health Services link: http://www.tobaccofreeca.com/. (Or Google Tobacco Free California). A fully implemented Tobacco Free Policy includes each of the following:

- **Prohibition of the use of tobacco products anywhere, anytime on district or county property and in district or county vehicles;**
- Procedures for the enforcement of this policy;
- Strategies or procedures for informing students, staff, parents and the community about the policy and its enforcement; and
- Required signs to be posted at each educational agency stating that tobacco use is strictly prohibited.

Smoking on the school campus still does take place. Not so much behind the gym, or in little pockets of the school, or student restrooms as in the past. Look around your campus and you may find a few smokers, especially the classified staff (non teachers), and even a few teachers and administrators, smoking in storage buildings, maintenance repair shops, or bus parking garages; and even a few still puffing behind the minimarket across the street, like they use to do when they were in school.

Curricula

Tobacco, alcohol and drug prevention should be taught at every grade, K-12. Ideally, a comprehensive health education coordinator, who can organize all of the mandated programs for students, should manage the curriculum. **Of paramount importance is the training of the teacher.** Elementary teachers need to be trained in developing lessons related to non-use of chemicals, tobacco, alcohol and other drugs during pre-service training at the university level. Secondary teachers should be fully credentialed to teach health science content courses, while other secondary educators can serve in supportive roles using integrated methods within their specific disciplines. **The curricula and activities should emphasize the following:** A clear no-use message; attention to the needs of special populations, e.g., disabled students and students with limited English language skills; focus on decision making, and not preaching; refusal skills instruction, including class role playing practice; and factual material based upon scientific data and not **"sensationalized media"** messages so frequently shown on radio and TV.

Parent Education and Involvement

Parent involvement is one of the most important yet difficult challenges of a comprehensive tobacco, alcohol and drug prevention program. Parents of high-risk youth need to be reached in whatever way possible, especially if language barriers exist. Newsletters, translation services or direct communication through phone calls could be used to reach them. Even providing childcare and organizing potluck meals can serve as a vehicle to involve parents to become part of the school "family." Sadly, however, when schools hold these meetings the parents that attend are not the ones most in need to help their children with drug related problems. However for many parents, "Feed them, watch their kids, and the parents will come." While parents are eating and their children are being supervised, the school can offer speakers or other forms of communication such as health fairs directed to the parent audience to assist them with drug prevention efforts for their families. This is of particular importance for families with limited English language skills. Parents of limited English speakers often are unclear about the policies and procedures in American schools. Since tobacco or alcohol use may be viewed differently in their homelands, the schools can clarify the specific rules, guidelines, etc., where their kids attend school. During the late 1990s some schools offered stop smoking classes on campus for students. These classes were usually funded by tobacco taxes and even included adults in attendance with the teens.

Parents guide on "How to Talk to Their Children about Drugs"

The old adage, "An ounce of prevention is worth a pound of cure," readily applies to the abuse of alcohol, tobacco and other drug use by children and teenagers. Research has shown that when children learn about the dangers of drug use from parents, they are half as likely to ever use drugs as those who do not. (U.S. Department of Education, 1994). Nonetheless, parents and teachers often find it difficult, or sometimes even intimidating, to discuss drug use with youth. The following guidelines are geared to specific ages and will open up lines of communication. Perhaps these guidelines may save a child's life.

Grades 4-6 (Ages 9-11)

- Set rules that alcohol and drug use will not be tolerated and are completely unacceptable;
- Be sure that the child can identify specific drugs and knows short and long term consequences;
- Encourage the child to participate in sports, youth groups, and community activities;
- Ask the child to explain how they would say "no" to drug use;
- Become friendly and communicate with the parents of the child's friends; and
- Insist that the school teaches refusal skills to all students.

Grades 7-9 (Ages 12-14)

- Explain to the child that young people, who use tobacco, alcohol and other drugs typically do so **before leaving the ninth grade** and peer pressure is very high;
- Discuss immediate side effects such as bad breath of smoking, burning of clothes and turn off from odors of drug use;
- Reinforce the idea that drinking and using tobacco or other drugs is unacceptable;
- Identify the impact of drugs on sports, behavior and school performance;
- Monitor the whereabouts of the child. Teach them to call home and check in at a very early age; and
- Talk to the child about any family history of alcoholism or drug addiction.

Grades 10-12 (Ages 15-17)

- Be very specific about possible fatal effects of drugs, fetal alcohol syndrome, and the relationship of drug use on pregnancy, and STDs;
- Focus on long term effects, such as loss of driver's license, jail, lack of college opportunities;
- **Limit unsupervised time for teenagers at home;**
- Cooperate with and talk to other parents on a regular basis about parties, and other alcohol/drug free events;
- Emphasize the goals, dreams and talents of teenagers. Spend time with them to review college bulletins and vocational plans; and
- Communicate with the school principal or governing school board regarding no tolerance polices of drug use by students at all school activities and school related functions. (U.S. Department of Education, 1994);
  For Additional Sources See: Partnership for a Drug-Free America, www.drugfreeamerica.org.

NIDA
NATIONAL INSTITUTE
ON DRUG ABUSE

The National Institute on Drug Addiction (NIDA), describes several principles for drug use prevention by addressing the family, the community and the school. Teachers should strive to follow these school preventative principles. (1) Prevention programs can be designed to intervene as early as preschool to address risk factors for drug abuse, such as aggressive behavior, poor social skills, and academic difficulties, (2) Prevention programs for elementary school children should target improving academic and social-emotional learning to address risk factors for drug abuse, such as early aggression, academic failure, and school dropout. Education should focus on the following skills, (3)

Education should focus on self-control, emotional awareness, communication, social problem solving, and academic support, especially in reading. Additionally, Prevention programs for middle or junior high and high school students should increase academic and social competence with the following skills: study habits, communication, peer relationships, self-efficacy, drug resistance skills, and reinforcement of anti-drug attitudes and policies. (NIDA, 2003).

Behaviors of Drug Abuse Observed by Teachers

T he classroom teacher plays a critical role in observing changes in students each and every day. Teachers are often too focused on classroom discipline, routines and lessons that they may miss some of the physical signs of drug abuse. A wide range of signs may be noticed depending on the drug being used. The teacher should observe with caution, since some students may simply be on medication, have diabetes or another medical condition, or suffer actual neurological dysfunction. The following list of *abnormal* or *unusual* student behavior may help teachers identify various commonly abused drugs and assist teachers to decide when it is appropriate to call for help or refer the student to other professional staff:

The section below describes common abused drugs by medical classification or use.

Stimulants-uncharacteristically energetic, loss of appetite, excitation, agitation, tremor of hands, licking of lips dilated pupils, irritability, hallucinations, and convulsions. **Alcohol**-swaying, our unsteadiness, slurred speech, nausea, vomiting, flushed face, alcohol odor, shaking hands, restlessness, confusion staggered walk. **Marijuana products**-forgetfulness, laughing tendencies, staring, relaxed inhibitions, increased appetite, red eyes, and odor of burnt leaves, apathy.

> For an excellent review of recent scientific data related to use and medical effects of marijuana, including a free guide for parents and their youth, Google *Marijuana Facts for Teens, Revised,* or:
> **http://www.nida.nih.gov/marijBroch/Marijteenstxt.html**

Narcotics-(Opiates)-euphoria, drowsiness, shallow breathing, constricted pupils, nausea or vomiting, slow thick speech, watery eyes, runny nose, loss of appetite, irritability, tremors, cramps, needle tracks or ulcerated sores near veins, itchy nose and skin. **LSD** illusions, hallucinations, bizarre behavior, poor perception of time and space, odd impulsive or dangerous behavior, lack of coordination, dilated pupils. **Barbiturates**-drunken behavior without the odor of alcohol, confusion, difficulty comprehending, lack of coordination, emotionally erratic behavior. **Inhalants**-euphoria, giddiness, confusion, watery eyes, loss of memory, depression, drowsiness, headache, nausea, and vomiting, lack of coordination, slurred speech. **Phencyclidine (PCP)**-exceptional strength, lack of pain from injury, paranoia, illusions, poor perception of time and space, impulsive dangerous behavior, unpredictable behavior, exceptional energy, staring (Peterson-Portis, Burhansstipanov, 1986, NIDA, 2008).

Intervention

Unfortunately, school-based counselors and psychologists are often the first groups or positions to be eliminated with districts facing tighter budgets; but hopefully, they will be employed at your school. These professionals can serve as excellent liaisons to get help for kids. Early intervention is critical in order to get young people on the right tract to overcome drug abuse. The suggestions below are offered from risk and protective factor research. They include:

- Planning for on-site delivery of intervention services such as counseling or support groups;
- Identifying and addressing risk factors in young children (e.g., aggressiveness, academic failure, or low bonding to school) and providing assistance to these children and parents;
- Refining and enhancing procedures for identification, assessment, referral, and aftercare of high-risk youth and organizing or using student assistance teams;
- Ensuring that districts use culturally based community agencies that have expertise and are prepared to meet specific needs of racial linguistic and ethnic groups within a community; (The American Cancer Society publishes documents in several languages); and
- Providing health education instruction for youth and parents about the impact of tobacco, alcohol and drugs on the fetus. (Project Teach, 1993, 1999).

Positive Alternatives

Positive alternatives to prevent drug abuse need to be in place, promoted through the school setting and offered as attractive alternatives for children to enjoy. Model programs such as **Friday Night Live, (fridaynightlive.org/)**, a California statewide program to promote drug free activities, community service events, parties and other recreation for youth, are excellent examples of programs that work. While non-smoking behaviors are slowly becoming the norm for adults and kids, youngsters need to find "other stuff" to do to avoid boredom and drug use. The Friday Night Live program allows kids to plan numerous activities such as dances, social activities, sporting events, community volunteer activities, all without the use of tobacco, alcohol or other drugs. Several factors need to be kept in mind when planning for such alternatives. They include:

- Methods to involve students in service projects;
- Activities that are planned, developed and led cooperatively by adults and students;
- After-school and summer programs;
- Community based programs;
- Involvement of parents in planning and developing alternatives (drug free "grad-night" programs have been very successful in many high schools);
- Cultural and language relevancy for all activities; and
- Activities that help children use up energy and are fun for them.

Summary

The real problem of drug abuse is not drugs. Drug abuse by kids is merely symptomatic behavior for underlying problems noted by many risk factors. Very powerful social systems exist that can dramatically impact the behavior of young people in the elementary or high school setting. Students without consistent guidelines, meaningful discipline and structure in their lives are often doomed for chemical abuse. Risk factors do exist and parents can help by enforcing family rules while offering a nurturing and loving place for a child to grow and develop. Schools and communities can change normative behavior, offer alternatives for kids, and decrease the tobacco, alcohol, and drug influence. Most importantly, the media should stop promoting products to youth, such as tobacco and alcohol, which are illegal for youth to purchase and use. Numerous websites provide excellent sources of current data on drug use and abuse. A few examples are: National Institute on Drug Abuse (NIDA)-www.nida.nih.gov, Food and Drug Administration (FDA)-www.fda.gov, Club drugs-www.clubdrugs.org and CDC Division of Adolescent and School Health - www.cdc.gov/DASH/.

> # This is a drug free,
> # alcohol free, tobacco free,
> # and weapons free school.

Chapter 5

Tobacco Use Prevention

Never regard study as a duty,
but as the enviable
opportunity to learn to know the
liberating influence of beauty in
the realm of the spirit for your own
personal joy and to the profit of the
community to which your
later work belongs.
... Einstein

Smoking Causes Kids to Get Fat?

This chapter will address the major problems related to tobacco use, adolescent use of tobacco products, the politics of tobacco, and the overall impact cigarettes and tobacco products have on mortality and morbidity of Americans. Can smoking cause kids to get fat? Of particular interest is a report in 2008 that discovered kids that use cigarettes may have a significant increased likelihood of becoming obese. Jasuja and colleagues examined body mass index (BMI), longitudinal relationships of cigarette use, continued use by teens, psychological distress, and physical activity relating to emerging adulthood with subjects from ages 11-34 years. **They found that cigarette use in early adolescence had direct paths to distress in the beginning of emerging adulthood, which in turn had significant relationships to cigarette use, physical activity, and subjective rating of health in mid-emerging adulthood.** These data suggest that prevention programs that have been previously applied to either cigarette use or distress prevention might also be applied to obesity risk in adulthood. (Jasuja, Chou, Riggs, et al., 2008).

Research reports, public health research and the popular press have portrayed the risks of cigarette smoking, that causes cancer of the mouth, tongue, face, lips, larynx, esophagus,

81

stomach, pancreas, bladder, cervix and kidney. Tobacco products are also responsible for chronic bronchitis, emphysema, chronic obstructive pulmonary disease, heart disease, strokes and even causing impotence and wrinkles. (Koop, 1991; USDHHS, 1986, 1988; CDC, 2002; Carmona, 2004). Cigarette smoking serves as a **gateway drug** for children and teenagers to experiment with other illegal drugs such as marijuana, cocaine and heroin. It does not take definitive scientific research to understand that it is much easier for a youngster to smoke marijuana or crack after having smoked cigarettes. (Jacobs, 1990).

The conclusion of the United States Surgeon General's Advisory Committee on Smoking and Health in 1964 that excessive cigarette smoking causes lung cancer is cited as the major turning point for public health action against cigarettes. But the Surgeon General and US Public Health Service (PHS) scientists had concluded as **early as 1957** that smoking was a cause of lung cancer, indeed, **"the principal etiologic factor in the increased incidence of lung cancer."** Throughout the 1950s, however, the PHS rejected further tobacco-related public health actions, such as placing warning labels on cigarettes or creating educational programs for schools. Instead, the agency continued to gather information and provided occasional assessments of the evidence as it came available. It was not until pressure mounted from outside the PHS in the early 1960s that more substantive action was taken. Earlier action was not taken because of the way in which PHS scientists, particularly those within the National Institutes of Health, and administrators viewed their roles in relation to science and public health. (Parascandola, 2001). **For most of the second half of the 20th century experts recognized tobacco and nicotine as a drug, but the consumer laws, and the rules related to drugs, always added the caveat, 'except tobacco.'** Even as recent as 2008, the U.S. Congress was still 'deciding' if the FDA can regulate tobacco, which in the minds of most experts, is definitely a drug. The tobacco companies have known about the effect of nicotine on addiction for decades and during 2006 increased nicotine concentrations in cigarettes. The Harvard School of Public reported in 2007 that the **tobacco companies raised nicotine levels in cigarettes by greater than 30%.** (Connolly, Alpert, & Ferris, 2007). In December 2010, the 30th edition Surgeon General's report revealed that the 7000 chemicals in cigarettes immediately affect the cells of the body, including the effects of secondhand smoke. This report submitted by Dr. Regina Benjamin will be explained in detail later in this chapter.

Other studies have linked cigarette and tobacco use with such dangers as addictiveness, drug interactions, tooth loss, poorer nutrition, infertility, osteoporosis and premature aging. Additional health problems now include low birth rate, ear infections, impaired back pain recovery (decrease of oxygen levels to lumbar disks), cervical cancer, diabetes (poor absorption of insulin), gastrointestinal cancer, leukemia (due to carcinogenic benzopyrene, polonium and over 7000 other chemicals), occupational lung cancer, and fires. (Bottom Line, 1992). To summarize, in 2004 Surgeon General Dr. Richard H Carmona stated, **"A new comprehensive report on smoking and health, revealed for the first time that smoking causes diseases in nearly every organ of the body.** Published 40 years after the Surgeon General's first report on smoking — which concluded that smoking was a definite cause of three serious diseases — this report found that **cigarette smoking is conclusively linked to diseases such as leukemia, cataracts, pneumonia and cancers of the cervix, kidney, pancreas and stomach."** Dr. Carmona also added, "We've known for decades that smoking is bad for your health, but this report shows that it's even worse. The toxins from cigarette smoke go everywhere the blood flows. I'm hoping this new information will help motivate people to quit smoking and convince young people not to start in the first place." (Carmona, 2004).

Other investigations have gone beyond the medical and health risks of tobacco products and have concentrated on the political and social ramifications. These include the effects of **environmental tobacco smoke (ETS)**, the targeting of women and minorities by tobacco advertising, and the special efforts of the tobacco industry to focus on sales to children and adolescents. (Glantz, 1987, 1998). Dr. Alan Blum, former editor of *The New York State Journal of Medicine*, reports such efforts in *The Journal of the American Medical Association*, and in The *New England Journal of Medicine*. Blum states it well, **"The leading cause of death in America is Marlboro."** (Blum, 1980, 1991). A brief history of ETS and tobacco related laws are summarized later in this chapter. The impact on second hand smoke is of particular concern to young children and teenagers. The tobacco companies settled with the U.S. Congress in 1998 and millions of dollars have been paid since to various parties from lawsuits related to tobacco addiction. The tobacco companies 'promised' they would shape up and change their advertising methods. Yet, ten years later by 2008, the companies still were targeting young kids and teens. Popular magazines with cigarettes and smokeless tobacco advertising reach a large number of adolescents through a combination of both youth-oriented and adult magazines. These exposure levels have generally increased since the Tobacco Master Settlement Agreement. (Morrison, Krugman, & Park, 2007). In 2009, current smoking prevalence was highest in Kentucky (25.6%), West Virginia (25.6%), and Oklahoma (25.5%), and lowest in Utah (9.8%), California (12.9%), and Washington (14.9%). Smoking prevalence was 6.4% in USVI, 10.6% in Puerto Rico, and 24.1% in Guam. Puerto Rico, and Guam, smoking prevalence was significantly higher among men than among women, and in no state was smoking prevalence significantly higher among women than men. (MMWR, 2010).

There is some good news related to tobacco. As states and other groups increase the taxes on cigarettes, the consumption of cigarette products is reduced. This is especially important in preventing youth from becoming addicted to tobacco. While cigarette tax increases are most powerful in reducing smoking among less-established smokers (who are less powerfully addicted), they have also helped to reduce smoking among the most heavy and habitual users. **Research in economic and medical journals shows that for every 10% increase in the overall price of cigarettes due to cigarette tax increases, adult smoking declines by about 4% and the number of youth who smoke drops by roughly 7%.** By the fall of 2008, because of local taxes on cigarettes, some retailers in New York City charged more than $10 a pack. New York Governor Patterson signed a bill in 2010 making a pack of cigarettes costing over $11 each. A one pack a day smoker in New York will have to pay over $3000 a year to maintain a nicotine addiction. While the cigarette companies promote the myth that cigarette taxes will not reduce smoking levels, cigarette company documents show that they know that cigarette tax increases reduce smoking among both adults and youth. The graph below from the **Coalition for Tobacco Free Kids (CTFK)**, illustrates the drop in U.S. consumption. (CTFK, 2008*)*. The medical and physiological effects of tobacco products are of particular concern. Kids have smaller lungs and thus receive a bigger impact on respiratory function and morbidity. Some conditions of concern are significantly related to youth.

Asthma

Secondhand smoke may make asthma attacks more frequent and severe in children who already have asthma--up to 1 million each year. Children with asthma who live with one smoker may be more than twice as likely to miss school because of a respiratory illness than are unexposed children without asthma. **And if children with asthma live with two or more smokers, they may be more than four times as likely to be absent with respiratory illness.** Other studies indicate that **even children without asthma are 40 percent more likely to miss school with a respiratory ailment if they live with at least two smokers.** Secondhand smoke is also associated with up to 300,000 cases of bronchitis and pneumonia in infants and toddlers each year. (Mayo, 2004).

Researcher and international expert on tobacco sales and marketing, Dr. Stanton Glantz, of the University of California San Francisco, in his book, *Tobacco, Biology and Politics,* summarizes key points related to tobacco use and children. They include: promotion and marketing of cigarettes, growth of the tobacco industry, addictive properties of nicotine, behavioral aspects, effects on nonsmokers (especially children), advertising and marketing targeted to youth, political ramifications between the medical community and the tobacco industry, and the emergence of the nonsmokers' rights movement. (Glantz, 1998). In 1996, professor Glantz researched and reviewed data, which was sent to the University of California San Francisco Medical Center by a former scientist (the "whistle-blower") Dr. Jeffery Wigand, from Brown and Williamson Tobacco Company.* This large volume of information was stored in the University library and Glantz completed a detailed scientifically researched book, *The Cigarette Papers,* which amplified the allegations against the tobacco companies. These documents explained that the tobacco companies knew for many years that cigarettes were addictive, and that they caused lung cancer and many other diseases. During the same year *The Cigarette Papers* was published. Interestingly, Dr. Glantz could not find a popular press publisher to publish this fine document since most popular magazines received tobacco ad revenue; but Glantz was finally able to use University of California Press to publish his book. Much of the data is posted on the Internet and numerous documents from his text can be accessed by the reader at: **http://galen.library.ucsf.edu/tobacco/.**

*In 1999 a movie, "The Insider," starring Russell Crow, the story about the Whistleblower, Dr. Jeffery Wigand, was released, and was nominated for seven Academy Awards.

> **"Every time the industry releases another movie**
> **that depicts smoking, it does so with full knowledge**
> **of the deadly harm it will bring to the children who watch it."**
> **…Letter to media CEOs…Vermont Attorney General William Sorrell, 2009.**

Jean Nicot, the French Ambassador to Portugal, popularized the 19th century use of tobacco (Nicotine was the drug later named after Nicot). Glantz states, "By the late 19th century, tobacco use was widespread, but only very small amounts were consumed in an occasional pipe or cigar, a wad of chewing tobacco, or a pinch of snuff. **Cigarettes were rare. So was lung cancer.** Had these tobacco-use patterns persisted, tobacco would not be the health problem it is today. It would, instead, be comparable to **illegal drugs,** which account for less than 2% of the number of deaths tobacco causes." (Glantz, 1992, 1998). Glantz attacks suggestions by the tobacco industry that the most important purpose of cigarette advertising is to recruit new smokers. He emphasizes that cigarette companies strive to provide youth with initiations into the adult world and present cigarettes as part of the illicit yet pleasurable category of products. He also points out that manufacturers do not communicate the health-related hazards. Finally, the death toll of cigarettes still lingers on…Smoking kills more than 430,000 people in the U.S. every year. **That is more than deaths from alcohol, suicide, homicide, car accidents, fires, heroin and cocaine combined!** A simple way to think of these numbers is that 430,000 deaths are the same as four jumbo jets crashing every day and having no one survive.

Secondhand Smoke

Secondhand smoke from cigarettes has also become a concern during recent years. Several thousand deaths annually can be attributed to environmental smoke, according to Glantz. (Glantz, 1992, Mayo, 2004). Doctor C. Everett Koop reported in his classic 1987 film for cable TV, "Smoking-A report from the Surgeon General," that a person in a smoke-filled room for eight hours a day will *smoke* the equivalent of one cigarette each hour just by being in the room; and that unborn fetuses take in the smoke their mothers consume. Children whose parents smoke have more respiratory infections, colds and general childhood illness as a result of their parents' smoking habits. (Koop, 1989). Many large cities like Los Angeles have banned smoking in all indoor places, including restaurants, bars, airports and entire shopping malls. In 1994, AB 13 was passed in California which restricts indoor smoking in most working areas; and on January 1, 1995, most indoor areas in California became smoke free! By January 1, 1998 even bars and gaming clubs became smoke free in the state of California. Since 2000, many states have followed the California model that has reduced the smoking rate of its citizens to less than eighteen percent. In 2002, as part of the rebuilding plan because of the September 11 tragedy, New York City increased taxes on cigarettes bringing the consumer price to eight dollars a pack! And as stated earlier, by 2011 a pack of smokes in New York City passed $11. Since the mid 2000s, many foreign countries passed smoking restrictions and by 2011 Ireland, Italy, Mexico, Spain, Wales, Scotland, Turkey and the 25 million smokers in India passed no smoking laws. With more than 350 million smokers and one million annual deaths from tobacco in China, shockwaves seemed to spread throughout the world media when China announced it would ban smoking in areas around Beijing during the 2008 Olympics! While different countries enforce various bans, the no smoking sign is now slowly popping up in dozens of countries throughout the world. The latest smoking bans worldwide can be found on a map by using Google: "smoking bans worldwide."

Public Response of Smoke Free California Since 1995 Law

Since the California Smoke-free Workplace Law went into effect in 1995, survey after survey has shown that Californians support the state's smoke-free law and have significantly benefited from it—even smokers. More than 90 percent of Californians surveyed in 2006, including the majority of smokers, said they approve of the smoke-free workplace law. And 52 percent of smokers who quit in the past 10 years said that having smoke-free public places made it easier for them to quit smoking. Revenue data from California's business, labor and hospitality industries confirm that smoke-free workplaces and bars have not hurt business because most Californians prefer eating at smoke-free restaurants. Many cities and counties throughout the state are adopting **smoke-free outdoor dining policies for areas such as cafes and patios.** As a result of California's strong public health protections, millions of Californians—young and old, smokers and nonsmokers—are living healthier lives, and a new generation of youth is growing up in a tobacco-free world. In fact, in 2006, 94 percent of Californians said they preferred dining in a smoke-free restaurant, including more than 80 percent of smokers (82 percent), which is a drastic increase from 1994, when only 43 percent of smokers preferred smoke-free restaurants. (CATS, 2006).

Indian (tribal) Casinos

The California Smoke-free Workplace Law (1995) makes it illegal to smoke in enclosed workspaces and that includes non-tribal gaming clubs. Tribal gaming clubs (casinos), however, are operated by sovereign governments; therefore they do not have to comply with California law unless stated in the "Compact" between state and local governments. As a result, employees of California Indian gaming facilities are still exposed to the dangers of toxic secondhand smoke.

While it is certain that smoke free environments, such as restaurants and bars will lower smoking in adults; it is less clear if a smoke free environment will prevent youth from smoking. Over the last several years, and especially since 2000, non-smoking is becoming normative behavior in children. In a four year, 2008, 3-wave study of youth in Massachusetts where participants ranged from 12 to 17 years, Siegel and colleagues measured youth overall progression to smoking, transition from nonsmoking to experimentation and transition from experimentation to established smoking. **The study found that local smoke-free laws might significantly lower youth smoking initiation by impeding the progression from cigarette experimentation to established smoking.** (Siegel, Albers, Cheng, et al., 2008).

The World Health Organization (WHO) issued a summary of the proven health effects of exposure to environmental tobacco smoke (ETS). They include:

- acute respiratory illness in early childhood;
- chronic cough, phlegm and wheeze in children;

- chronic middle ear effusions in children;
- reduced levels and growth of lung functions in children;
- increased bronchial hyper responsiveness in asthmatics;
- increased symptoms and decreased level of lung function in asthmatics;
- irritant effects on eye, nose, throat;
- malignancy--lung cancer;
- low birth weight;
- slowed lung maturation; and
- decreased attained weight.

The summary goes on to state:

> Furthermore, individuals with pre-existing health conditions, such as asthma, bronchitis, cardiovascular disease, rhinitis, colds, and allergies, often report more severe injuries due to secondhand smoke than do healthy adults. It should be remembered that nonsmokers are also exposed to the same occupational agents, as are smokers. Certain chemicals in ETS may interact with other workplace toxins such as asbestos, thereby further endangering the nonsmoker. ETS substantially augments already existing indoor air pollution concentrations of RSP, benzene, acrolein, N-nitrosamine, pyrene, nitrogen oxides and carbon monoxide. Thus, the effects of tobacco on health are often superimposed on the health effects of certain working conditions, making their cumulative effects even more dramatic. (World Health Organization, 1991, 2008).

In the American Heart Association's scientific journal, *Circulation*, Glantz and Parmley estimate that secondhand smoke is associated with 37,000 deaths related to heart and blood vessel diseases each year in the United States. (Glantz, Parmley, 1992, 2001). By 2010, the CDC reported that 46, 000 deaths from heart disease are a result of secondhand smoke exposure. The Department of Health and Human Services at the CDC estimates that nearly 4,000 nonsmokers each year die from lung cancer due to secondhand smoke. More than two million California nonsmokers were exposed to secondhand smoke in the workplace in 1990. As part of a California Tobacco Survey, Dr. Ron Borland, of the University of California, San Diego, reported on 7,162 adult nonsmoking, indoor workers. The rate of ETS exposure decreased with increasing education. Workers with less than a high school education reported higher levels of ETS exposure. The author concluded, "For industries and other institutions in which the employees are likely to be in these (high risk) demographic groups, high priority should be given to establishing ordinances mandating smoke free worksites." (American Heart Association, 1991). The U.S. Surgeon General further stated that 62,000 deaths occur in the U.S. annually from ischemic heart disease (IHD, narrowing of blood vessels to the heart). (Surgeon General, 1999, Mayo, 2005). **The World Health Organization stated that during the 20th century, tobacco killed 100 million people worldwide, and during the 21st century, the total deaths could reach one billion! (WHO, 2008.)**

Tobacco Legislation History and Indoor Smoking Ban:
We've come a long way, baby!

The major changes in smoking throughout the world have been very profound, especially during the years from 1975 to 2011. Below is a brief summary of various laws and edicts throughout the world with a special emphasis on the U.S.

1575	Mexican ecclesiastical council ban that forbade the use of tobacco in any church in Mexico and Spanish colonies in the Caribbean.
1600s	**The Pope bans smoking in holy places.**
1856	A debate about the health effects of tobacco begins in the British medical journal, *The Lancet.*
1939	Tax on tobacco products enacted (6% on retail price.
1954	The American Cancer Society (ACS) study shows the first link between smoking and lung cancer and *Reader's Digest* brings the information to the masses in an article titled "Cancer by the Carton."
1959	ACS Prevention Study connects cigarette smoking to early death from lung cancer.
1962	In Britain, the first Royal College of Physicians report, "Smoking and Health," recommends restrictions on tobacco advertising, increased taxation on cigarettes, and more restrictions on sales to minors and public smoking, causing cigarette sales to fall for the first time in a decade.
1964	**U.S. Surgeon General Luther L. Terry, MD, releases report concluding smoking causes lung cancer and other serious diseases.**
1965	Congress passes the Federal Cigarette Labeling and Advertising Act, requiring the following warning on all packages: "Caution: Cigarette Smoking May Be Hazardous to Your Health." Tax on tobacco amended to 40% of the wholesale price.
1970	President Nixon signs into law the Public Health Cigarette Smoking Act, banning television and radio broadcast advertising of tobacco products, and requiring each cigarette package to contain this cautionary label: "Warning: The Surgeon General Has Determined that Cigarette Smoking is Dangerous to Your Health."
1973	The U.S. Civil Aeronautics Board requires nonsmoking sections on all commercial airline flights. Arizona becomes the first state to restrict smoking in a number of public places and the first to do so explicitly because secondhand tobacco smoke is dangerous.
1975	Minnesota passes the landmark Clean Indoor Air Law to protect the public health and comfort and the environment by restricting smoking in public places and at public meetings, except in designated areas.
1976	The American Cancer Society's California Division gets nearly one million smokers to quit for the day, marking the first Smokeout event.
1979	Smoking restricted in federal government offices.
1980	Surgeon General issues report on smoking as a major threat to women's health.
1981	Insurers offer discounts on life insurance premiums to nonsmokers.
1982	The American Cancer Society Prevention Study II demonstrates that secondhand smoke increases mortality from lung cancer and heart disease.

1983	The San Francisco Board of Supervisors passes first workplace smoking restrictions, including bans on smoking in private workplaces.
1984	Congress enacts the Comprehensive Smoking Education Act, requiring a rotation of health warnings on cigarette packs and advertisements.
1986	The U.S. Surgeon General and the National Academy of Sciences declare secondhand smoke a cause of lung cancer in healthy nonsmokers.
1987	• Surgeon General announces that lung cancer surpassed breast cancer as the leading cause of cancer death among American women. • A Gallup poll finds the majority of U.S. adults (55 percent) favor a complete ban on smoking in public places.
1988	• The U.S. Surgeon General report classifies nicotine as an addictive drug. • Smoking ban on airline flights of two hours or less goes into effect. • New York City clean indoor air ordinance limits smoking in various public places. • California bans smoking aboard all intrastate airplanes, trains, and buses.
1990	Congress prohibits smoking on all interstate buses and domestic airline flights of six hours or less.
1991	• UCSF Professors Stanton Glantz and William Parmley publish a study that says secondhand smoke causes heart disease, and causes 53,000 deaths annually in U.S. • Several studies, including one funded by the ACS, finds that Joe Camel is as recognizable to young children as Mickey Mouse, and more successful at marketing cigarettes to children than adults. • The Food and Drug Administration (FDA) approves a nicotine patch as a prescription drug.
1992	Massachusetts voters increased the tobacco tax and establishing a large tobacco education and prevention program.
1993	• President Bill Clinton bans smoking in the White House. • **Vermont becomes the first state in the nation to ban indoor smoking in some public places.** • U.S. Environmental Protection Agency classifies secondhand smoke as a human carcinogen. • Los Angeles passes a ban on smoking in all restaurants. • The U.S. Postal Service eliminates smoking in all facilities.
1994	• McDonald's bans smoking in its restaurants, and the Defense Department restricts smoking on all U.S. military bases worldwide. • ACS launches the Campaign for a Million Lives to send one million letters to Congress supporting a $2 per pack increase in the federal cigarette excise tax. • **Tobacco companies' public image drops even lower when executives of the seven largest US tobacco companies swear in congressional testimony that nicotine is not addictive, and deny allegations that they manipulate nicotine levels in cigarettes.** • Amtrak bans smoking on short and medium distance trips. • Documents from Brown and Williamson, one of the largest manufacturers of cigarettes, show executives discovered smoking risks 30 years before the U.S. Surgeon General.

1995	• New York City passes legislation prohibiting smoking in most workplaces. • Maryland enacts a smoke-free policy for all workplaces except hotels, bars, restaurants, and private clubs. • Italy amends its 1975 smoking ban to include any places open to the public, such as post offices, banks and government offices. • **California passes legislation prohibiting smoking in most workplaces, including restaurants.** • "Marlboro Man" David McLean dies of lung cancer at 73. • Vermont's smoking ban is extended to include most restaurants, bars, hotels, and motels.
1996	• President Bill Clinton proposes FDA regulation of tobacco sales and marketing. • Implementation of the first part of the FDA tobacco rule requiring anyone appearing younger than 26 to show a picture ID to purchase tobacco.
1997	• The Federal Trade Commission files charges against RJ Reynolds Tobacco Company for unfair advertising practices, claiming that the Joe Camel advertising campaign encourages children to smoke. Shortly thereafter, RJR announces the elimination of the Joe Camel from their advertising campaign. **Joe Camel Died!** • Forty-eight million Americans have quit in the 21 years since the first Smokeout in 1976; 48 million still smoke; about 34 million say they want to quit. The average age of a first-time smoker is 13. • President Clinton issues an Executive Order prohibiting smoking in federal government offices and all recreational buildings on military bases worldwide. • **Direct medical costs associated with smoking surpass $50 billion, or about 7% of total health care costs in the U.S.**
1998	• Attorneys general representing 46 states, the District of Columbia, and five U.S. territories signed the Master Settlement Agreement with major cigarette companies to recover Medicaid costs of treating smokers. • **California bans smoking in bars.**
1999	The Master Settlement Agreement is approved in 45 states, releasing payments to the states from the tobacco companies. MSA provisions closing the Tobacco Institute and ending cartoon advertising and all tobacco billboards go into effect.
2000	The U.S. Department of Transportation bans smoking on all U.S. international flights.
2001	• The US Surgeon General issues Women and Smoking, which finds that 22 percent of women in the U.S. smoked cigarettes in 1998 and calls smoking-related disease among women "a full-blown epidemic." • Lung cancer accounts for 25% of all cancer deaths among women. • Canada mandates large, graphic cigarette pack labels, linking smoking with impotence, among other things. • In Lebanon, Senior Shiite Muslim cleric Grand Ayatollah Mohammed Hussein Fadlallah issues a religious edict (fatwa) ordering his followers to stop smoking. "A smoker is committing two crimes, one against himself and the other against the one inhaling next to him." • **News reports reveal that Philip Morris released a report to the Czech government which concluded that smokers save the state money -- by dying early.** • India's Supreme Court rules that smoking in public spaces must be banned countrywide.
2002	• The Centers for Disease Control and Prevention estimates smoking health and productivity costs reach $150 billion a year. • French health officials air advertisements warning about the ingredients in a "dangerous product." Half a million people call the hotline to learn what the product is: cigarettes.

2002	Thailand imposes countrywide indoor smoking ban.
2003	• **New York City's smoking ban goes into effect, forbidding smoking in all restaurants and bars, except for a few cigar lounges.** • In Illinois, a judge orders Philip Morris to pay $10.1 billion in damages for misleading smokers into believing that low-tar cigarettes are safer than regular varieties.
2004	• In Maine, bar, lounges, taverns, and pool halls are added to the states 1999 smoking ban. • A complete public smoking ban goes into effect in Connecticut – plus **Ireland. Norway, Sweden, and New Zealand** schedule public smoking bans. • Massachusetts and Rhode Island ban smoking in all public places, joining five other states: New York, Connecticut, Maine, Delaware, and California. • **On the one-year anniversary of New York City's smoking ban, studies find no adverse financial impact on bars and restaurants.** • In the United Kingdom, the British Heart Foundation launches massive anti-smoking campaign featuring a lard-type substance oozing from cigarettes, emphasizing what happens inside a smoker's arteries. • 400,000 Americans died from smoking, or, 440,000 if you count the 38,000 deaths a year from secondhand smoke and the more than 1,000 infants died because their mothers smoked during pregnancy. • **U.S. Surgeon General Richard H. Carmona releases a report that says smoking causes diseases in nearly every organ of the body.** "We've known for decades that smoking is bad for your health, but this report shows that it's even worse," Dr. Carmona says. "The toxins from cigarette smoke go everywhere the blood flows. I'm hoping this new information will help motivate people to quit smoking, and convince young people not to start in the first place."
2005	***Global Tobacco Treaty Takes Effect*** • The first global treaty on tobacco control goes into effect Sunday, Feb. 27. The Framework Convention on Tobacco Control (FCTC) requires member countries to take specific steps to stop people from using tobacco, and to put stronger tobacco control policies in place. • Countries that ratify the treaty must pass laws to limit smoking in indoor workplaces and take steps to fight tobacco smuggling. They are also urged to promote tobacco prevention and cessation programs. • **So far, 168 nations have signed the treaty and 57 have ratified the treaty.** • The United States has signed the treaty, but as of May 2008, has not yet ratified it. ACS and other groups sent a letter to President George W. Bush urging him to send the treaty to the Senate for approval.
2008	China, a country with > 350 million smokers, banned smoking at the Beijing Olympics
2009	**State of New York and the City of Chicago raised cigarette taxes that bring the total cost, including state and federal taxes in excess of $10 a pack!** Numerous states, counties, cities in the U.S. ban smoking in pubic parks, beaches and 20 ft. from doors and windows
2010	U.S. Federal Judge ruled tobacco companies are racketeers who carried out a decades long conspiracy to deceive the public and target children with their deadly and addictive products.
2010	Surgeon General Dr. Regina Benjamin releases 30th SG report on smoking: Smoking produces over 7000 chemicals, hundreds toxic and 70 cause cancer. Smoking damages DNA. Just one cigarette begins damaging the cells of the body.
2011	The FDA required tobacco packages to show graphic images and warnings of addiction on all tobacco products and advertisements by 2012.

Source: Modified from The American Cancer Society (ACS).

People of Color and ETS

A recent report describes an alarming lung disease disparity in Hispanic communities. According to the American Lung Association (ALA), the Hispanic community is disproportionately exposed to environmental hazards such as air pollution. The report, "Lung Disease Data in Culturally Diverse Communities," provides a definitive link between air pollution and lung disease prevalence in people of color. The researchers go on to state, "In many instances, Hispanic communities are disproportionately affected by environmental exposures, which can lead to a host of lung diseases." **This study showed that Hispanics and African-Americans together suffer disproportionately from asthma, compared to Whites, and provides important information about clean air and the long-term effects of exposure to tobacco smoke and air pollution.** The report calls attention to the health disparities and other socioeconomic factors that may account for the high prevalence rates within diverse communities. According to the report, lung disease affects people of all cultures, races, and ethnicities, but some groups have higher rates than others. **The study shows that Hispanics are more than twice as likely as either African-Americans or Whites to live near high traffic areas such as freeways and other areas with heavy diesel truck traffic.** A major area of concern in Southern California is the Long Beach Freeway (710) that is the route of thousands of trucks daily. The 710 freeway extends from the port of San Pedro to the San Gabriel Valley and thousands of people of color live in these communities. These areas have higher levels of air pollution and increase the risk of lung disease and premature death. Studies have also shown that Puerto Ricans may have higher asthma prevalence rates and higher death rates than other Hispanic subgroups and non-Hispanic Whites. (ALA, 2005).

Exposure to Second-Hand Smoke Widespread

According to a study conducted by HHS Centers for Disease Control and Prevention (CDC), nearly 9 out of 10 non-smoking Americans are exposed to environmental tobacco smoke (ETS, or second-hand smoke), as measured by the levels of cotinine in their blood. Fowler reported measurable levels of cotinine in the blood of 88% of all non-tobacco users. Cotinine, a chemical the body metabolizes from nicotine, is definitive documentation that a person has been exposed to tobacco smoke. (Fowler, 1996). Serum cotinine levels can be used to estimate nicotine exposure over the last two to three days. David Satcher, M.D., Ph.D., former U.S. Surgeon General stated, "This study documents for the first time the widespread exposure of people in the US to environmental tobacco smoke. This new information will be critical in estimating the extent of related disease and developing effective public health strategies."

While this research did not address the medical impact of ETS on health, a comprehensive analysis of many respiratory studies on the health effects of ETS concluded that ETS caused lung cancer in adult non-smokers and serious respiratory problems in children. Based on the health hazards of ETS, the **Environmental Protection Agency (EPA) has classified second-hand smoke as a Group A carcinogen (known to cause cancer in humans).** Both the number of smokers in the household and the hours exposed at work were associated with increased serum cotinine levels. Data from National Health and Nutrition Examination

Survey (NHANES III) also revealed that the cotinine levels and, therefore, exposure to second-hand smoke was higher among children, non-Hispanic blacks, and males. (CDC, 1996). In the summer of 2002, the United Nations, with data collected from the World Health Organization, also agreed that on a global level, second hand smoke is carcinogenic and that smoking related diseases are far more insidious than previously believed. (L.A. Times, 2002).

Mothers smoking, obesity and diabetes

Maternal smoking in pregnancy is linked to subsequent diabetes and obesity. Numerous studies indicate that smoking during pregnancy can harm the fetus. Another concern is the impact on the adult health of the fetus. Maternal smoking during pregnancy is a risk factor for the offspring developing early onset adult diabetes and obesity in later life. Cigarette smoking as a young adult has been independently associated with an increased risk of subsequent diabetes. Montgomery and Ekbom suggest that in utero exposure to smoking results in life long metabolic dysregulation, possibly owing to fetal malnutrition or toxicity. (Montgomery, Ekbom, 2002). The long-term effects of smoking on a fetus can be devastating to a child. Not only is there an increased risk of addiction later in life of the baby; but also research by Mamsen and colleagues indicate that prenatal exposure to maternal cigarette smoke reduces the number of germ and somatic cells in embryonic male and female gonads. This effect may have long-term consequences on the future fertility of exposed offspring and may provide one potential cause of the reduced fertility observed during recent years. Therefore parents trying to conceive a child may have difficulties all due to their mother's smoking before they were even born! (Mamsen, Lutterodt, Anderson, et al., 2010).

Low–tar 'safer cigarettes'

The tobacco industry has continued to try to promote the idea that a 'safer' cigarette can help prevent disease. Many consumers, including teens, may consider the safer cigarette as an alternative to smoke with less danger. This is a false assumption. Smokers inhale deeper and take longer drags to inhale the nicotine. Many studies conclude that "low-tar/low-nicotine cigarettes" are not safer. A National Cancer Institute monograph has concluded that cigarettes labeled as "low tar," "mild," or "light" are just as dangerous as other cigarettes. Switching to these cigarettes may provide smokers with a false sense of reduced risk, when the actual amount of tar and nicotine consumed may be the same as, or more than, the previously used higher yield brand. **Nicotine addiction results in smokers seeking a constant level of nicotine from smoking each day.** In 2010 President Obama signed into law a regulation allowing the FDA to ban the term "low tar," "light," "ultra light," "mild," and "natural," from cigarette labels. But the tobacco companies simply changed the color of many of their packages in 2010 to illustrate lighter faded colors without any of the above labels. (ALA, 2010). The FTCs tests used to measure tar and nicotine levels have provided numbers that have been used for promotional purposes. However, these numbers have been artificially low because the cigarette paper enables air to dilute the smoke during the FTCs machine tests, whereas real smokers maintain their nicotine levels by positioning the cigarettes differently. (NCI, 2001). The tobacco industry always seems to misrepresent the facts. During 2002 health education advocates continued to clarify the facts.

Tobacco, Education and Politics-It Finally Happened!

During the presidential election of 1996, much debate and discussion was presented regarding the tobacco industry, smoking laws, and kid's access of tobacco to kids President Clinton took an unheard of stance and aimed his efforts towards reducing tobacco use of kids. While the research from the CDC and other sources of the federal government made the claim of 1,000 deaths daily from tobacco induced addiction, it wasn't until 1996 that a politician took a very strong stand against tobacco. His name is Bill Clinton. Congressman Henry Waxman (D-California) brought virtually all CEOs of tobacco companies before a congressional hearing in 1994 and made them testify about the addictive potential and carcinogenicity of cigarettes. Doctor David Kessler (Kessler is both a doctor and a lawyer), Former Commissioner of the FDA during the 1990s, assisted the president and the congress in efforts to reduce tobacco related mortality and morbidity of Americans. Their main focus was on youth. An interesting sideline related to the CEOs testimony is that by April 1997, all but one of the CEOs resigned their positions, and one died.

President Clinton established the first-ever-comprehensive program to protect children from the health dangers of tobacco addiction. After much debate and study The Food and Drug Administration released the recommendations as their final rule on tobacco and children. The emphasis is on education and protection for children. This comprehensive and coordinated plan is intended to reduce tobacco use by children and adolescents by 50 percent in seven years. The conclusions were based upon recommendations of the American Medical Association and the National Academy of Science. If the U.S. Congress ever passes all of the proposals, the FDA rule will:

- Require age verification and face-to-face sale (except for mail orders), and eliminate free samples and the sale of single cigarettes and packages with fewer than 20 cigarettes;
- Ban vending machines and self-service displays except in facilities where only adults are permitted, such as certain nightclubs totally inaccessible to persons under 18;
- Ban outdoor advertising within 1000 feet of schools and publicly owned playgrounds. Permit black-and-white text-only advertising for all other outdoor advertising, including billboards, signs inside and outside of buses, and all point-of-sale advertising. Advertising inside "adult only" facilities like nightclubs can use color and imagery;
- Permit black-and-white text-only advertising in publications with significant youth readership (under 18). Significant readership means more than 15 percent or more than 2 million. There are no restrictions on print advertising below these thresholds;
- Prohibit sale or giveaway of products like caps or gym bags that carry cigarette or smokeless tobacco product brand names or logos;
- Prohibit brand-name sponsorship of sporting (including teams and entries) or entertainment events, but permit it in the corporate name;

- Vending machines and self-service displays will be allowed in facilities where only adults are permitted. By removing vending machines and self-service displays from sites accessible to children, the rule's goal will still be achieved, and the Agency will closely monitor the effectiveness of this provision for two years to determine if additional restrictions are necessary;
- Mail-order sales will be permitted. This provision will allow adults in rural or isolated areas to have access to these products. There was little evidence presented that children use mail order at the present time, but the Agency will monitor future trends;*
- Advertising using color and imagery will be permitted in "adult only" facilities totally inaccessible to persons under 18, provided that the advertising is not visible from the outside and is not removable; and
- In early 1997, several FDA regulations took effect, and retail vendors became more vigilant on checking identification of minors to reduce the sale of tobacco products to children. By the spring of 1999 all billboard and mobile advertisements were removed from the entire U.S. (The White House, 1996).

    * During March of 2005, tobacco companies agreed to no longer accept credit cards as payment for Internet sales of cigarettes.

See **http://www.cdc.gov/tobacco** for updated news about tobacco reform from the CDC and reports from the U.S. Surgeon General. The following sign is now posted in many stores:

To Our Valued Customers,

Effective February 28, 1997, we are required under Food and Drug Administration (FDA) regulations to verify age through a photo ID from any person buying cigarettes or smokeless tobacco who is under 27 years of age. If you have questions or comments, contact: Office of Policy (HF-26). Food and Drug Administration (FDA) 5600 Fishers Lane, Rockville, MD 20857. We regret any inconvenience.

Smoking Dads Risk Cancer in Kids

A new study revealed that fathers who smoke may damage their sperm and increase the risk of cancer in their children, later in life. Researchers say fathers' tobacco use might link as many as 15% of all childhood cancers to smoking, but no similar association was found for mothers who smoke. Dr. Thomas Sorahan, an epidemiologist at the University of Birmingham in England said, "Fathers who smoked 20 or more cigarettes a day had a 42% increased risk of having a child with cancer. Men who smoked between 10 and 20 cigarettes daily had a 31% increased cancer risk in their offspring, and the risk was 3% greater in children of those who smoked less than 10 cigarettes each day." These findings published in *The British Journal of Cancer*, were based on a review of the Oxford survey of Childhood Cancers, a collection of data begun in the 1950s, which has become the largest case study in the history of medicine. The researchers noted that other factors, such as social class, mother's exposure to x-rays during pregnancy, and parental age could not account for the increased cancer risk among children whose fathers smoked. The author said if the findings are valid, "cigarettes might soon carry the government health warning, **"Smoking can seriously damage your sperm! "** (Sorahan, 1997).

The American Medical Association (AMA) cited the report in its efforts to again try to persuade Congress to permit the Food and Drug Administration to continue to support the regulation of tobacco, and by 2011 new graphic warning labels were required. (AMA, 2007). President Obama signed HR 1256 bill into law in 2009. A brief summary of this law includes the following provisions:

- Grants the Food and Drug Administration (FDA) power to regulate tobacco products (Sec. 101);
- Requires tobacco product manufacturers to disclose all ingredients in its products, the form and delivery method of nicotine, and any research into the health, toxicological, behavioral, or physiologic effects of tobacco products to the FDA and notify the FDA of any future changes to any of the above (Sec. 101);
- Requires tobacco manufacturers to release all marketing research documents to the FDA (Sec. 101);
- Requires tobacco manufacturers to notify the FDA of any future changes to the ingredients of their products (Sec. 101);
- Requires all owners and operators of companies manufacturing or processing tobacco products to register with the Secretary of Health and Human Services and to be inspected once every two years (Sec. 101);
- Prohibits the FDA from banning existing tobacco products or requiring that they eliminate nicotine (Sec. 101);
- Requires FDA review of new tobacco products before they can go to market unless they are similar to products marketed before February 15, 2007 (Sec. 101);
- Bans companies from promoting products as lower-risk alternatives to traditional tobacco unless the FDA certifies that its sale is likely to improve public health (Sec. 101);
- Establishes a mechanism to assess fees on tobacco companies and traders to finance FDA oversight of the industry (Sec. 101);
- Orders a study on the public health implications of raising the minimum age to purchase tobacco products (Sec. 104);
- Requires the Secretary of Health and Human Services to create a plan relating to enforce restrictions on the advertising and promotion of menthol and other cigarettes to minors (Sec. 105); and
- Mandates larger, more varied, and more prominent warning labels on tobacco products (Secs. 201, 204).

Readers are encouraged to review the entire law proposed by Representative Waxman (D, California). Google the federal mandate, The Family Smoking Prevention and Tobacco Control Act, 2009 by using the term **HR 1256** for full details.

Benefits of Smoking Cessation

So many practical and healthful benefits result when people quit smoking. People who quit smoking live longer than those who continue to smoke. Quitting before age 50 will reduce the risk of dying in 15 years by one-half. Lung cancer risk is 22 times higher for smokers versus non-smokers. Smoking cessation reduces the risk of cancers of the larynx, oral cavity esophagus, pancreas, and urinary bladder. Quitting substantially reduces arterial disease that can lead to loss of limb. Maternal smoking cessation will reduce fetal abnormalities, bleeding, abruptio placentae, and pre-term delivery. Parental quitting reduces infections of the ear, and lung such as bronchitis and pneumonia. Women are especially worried about weight gain after quitting cigarettes. Cessation weight gain (average 4 pounds) far outweighs damage of smoking. With a determined effort, and support from friends and family nicotine withdrawal can be overcome within a few days.

The Good News about Quitting Smoking

The American Cancer Society (ACS) has developed a list of alternative activities that the ex-smoker might try as aids to get through the withdrawal period. When the craving for a cigarette arises, the smoker may engage in these behaviors: nibble on fruit, celery, or carrots; chew gum or spices such as ginger, cinnamon bark, or cloves; use replacements in conjunction

with quitting smoking, such as the nicotine patch or nicotine gum; perform moderately strenuous physical activity, such as bicycling, jogging or swimming; spend as much time as possible in places where smoking is prohibited; and associate with nonsmokers for long periods of time. **The economic savings after quitting can be significant. If an average smoker smokes one pack a day at a cost of $6 a pack retail, that would convert to nearly $2200 a year. Two pack a day habit would save over $4000.** New York City prices of $10 a pack retail, would cost more than $3600 and $7200 a year respectively.

The American Cancer Society also described the significant advantages to quitting over time. Even though many medical consequences could impair the health of a smoker, it is always a benefit to quit. Benefits of quitting start within 20 minutes of cessation.

When a smoker quits:

20 minutes later	• Blood pressure drops to normal • Pulse rate drops to normal • Body temperature of hands and feet increases to normal
8 hours later	• Carbon monoxide level in blood drops to normal • Oxygen level in blood increases to normal
24 hours later	• Chance of heart attack decreases
48 hours later	• Nerve endings start re-growing • Ability to smell and taste is enhanced
2 weeks to 3 months later	• Circulation improves • Walking becomes easier • Lung function increase up to 30%
1 to 9 months later	• Coughing, sinus congestion, fatigue, shortness of breath decreases • Cilia regrow in lungs, increasing ability to handle mucus, clean the lungs and reduce infection
1 year later	• **Excess risk of coronary heart disease is half that of a smoker**
5 years later	• Lung cancer death rate for average former smoker (one pack a day) decreases by almost half • Stroke risk is reduced to that of a nonsmoker 5-15 years after quitting • Risk of cancer of the mouth, throat and esophagus is half that of a smoker's
10 years later	• Lung cancer death rate similar to that of nonsmokers • Predaceous (cancer attacking) cells are replaced • Risk of cancer of the mouth, throat, esophagus, bladder, kidney and pancreas decreases
15 years later	• Risk of coronary heart disease is that of a nonsmoker

Source: American Cancer Society, (2008). Washington Division Centers for Disease Control.

Women frequently are greatly concerned about weight control and a significant number of female smokers continue to smoke to stay thin. The tobacco industry capitalized on this weight control issue as early as 1935. The theme of the day was: "Reach for a Lucky instead of a sweet." While it is true that smoking will suppress the appetite, the relative risk of breast cancer, for example, is much worse than a few extra pounds gained. Former Surgeon General Dr. Antonia Novello summarizes, "The health benefits of quitting smoking are immediate and substantial. They far exceed any risks from the average five pound weight gain or any adverse psychological effects that may follow those who are sick and to those who are well. **Smoking cessation represents the single most important step that smokers can take to enhance the length and quality of their lives.**" (Novello, 1993). Logically, would a woman enjoy fitting into a size five dress but have to face breast removal at age 41 from cancer?

Children's Risk Factors

Today, most of the American population acknowledges the health hazards of cigarettes and tobacco products, but few truly see the implications of tobacco's pervasiveness in our society for children, school settings, businesses, cities and states throughout the United States. Nicotine is an addictive drug. **Cigarette smokers are drug addicts**. As with any drug, children are at risk if they have a high number of the risk factors for drug use, which will be described in chapter six.

Children from Asian, Hispanic, Middle Eastern and other backgrounds may be at higher risk for tobacco use because smoking is not only accepted, but also promoted in their cultures. For example, Southeast Asian families often use cigarettes as a party favor at weddings. Many Hispanic cultures consider tobacco use a right of passage for the young macho male. Tobacco use may not be considered a health problem in these societies. China produces and uses more cigarettes than any other country in the world, and it is estimated that as many as 20-25% of Chinese 8 year-olds smoke cigarettes. The World Health Organization (WHO) estimated that **tobacco induced death was the number one cause of death worldwide during 2010.** For a detailed update on smoking in the Asian-American population see the CDC website: **http://www.cdc.gov/tobacco.**

The American Cancer Society is now providing health education materials in many languages to help recent arrivals to the United States learn more about smoking and health risks. Classroom teachers can convince preteen and high school immigrant students of the health risks, but their parents are not as easily won over.

Do smokers simulate smoking when they see someone else smoke? For regular smokers, smoking is such a highly practiced motor skill that it often occurs automatically, without conscious awareness. Research on the brain basis of action observation has delineated a frontoparietal network that is commonly recruited when people observe, plan, or imitate actions. researchers investigated whether this action observation network would be preferentially recruited in smokers when viewing complex smoking cues, such as those occurring in motion pictures. Seventeen right-handed smokers and 17 nonsmokers watched a popular movie while undergoing functional magnetic resonance imaging. Using a natural stimulus, such as a movie, experts kept both smoking and nonsmoking participants naive to the goals of the experiment. Brain activity evoked by movie scenes of smoking was contrasted with nonsmoking control scenes that were matched for frequency and duration. Compared with nonsmokers, smokers showed greater activity in left anterior intraparietal sulcus and inferior frontal gyrus, regions involved in the simulation of contralateral hand-based gestures, when viewing smoking versus control scenes. These results demonstrate that smokers spontaneously represent the action of smoking when viewing others smoke, the consequence of which may make it more difficult to abstain from smoking. (Brody, Mandelkern, London, et al., 2002).

> **"Cigarette smoking is the leading preventable cause of death in the United States. We have an enormous opportunity to reduce heart disease, cancer, stroke and respiratory disease among members of racial and ethnic minority groups, who make up a rapidly growing segment of the U.S. population."**
> **David Satcher, MD, PhD, Former U.S. Surgeon General**

The 2010 Conclusions from the Surgeon General

The Surgeon General prepares major reports on the health problems, risks and lifestyles of Americans, and reports directly to the President. The first report about cigarettes was published in 1964. The following summaries are from the 1990 report written by Antonia Novello, (the first female Surgeon General), who served from 1990-1993. The 1994 report by the Surgeon General focuses on the impact of tobacco products on young people. According to the report, despite the multitude of efforts in the early and mid 1980s, more than 3 million adolescents in the United States smoke cigarettes and 1 million-use smokeless tobacco. Even with three decades of health warnings, the tobacco industry has managed to slowly reduce the numbers of those that are quitting. Among seniors in high school by the year 2002, about 28% smoked cigarettes and 21% of males used smokeless tobacco.

In December 2010, Surgeon General Dr. Regina Benjamin released the 30th report from the U.S. Surgeon General's Office on smoking. Much has been discovered since 1964 and the Surgeon General recently produced an outstanding consumer friendly version for all to read. The new illustrated and understandable booklet, *A Report of the Surgeon General: How Tobacco Causes Disease,* is available for free download. Google Surgeon General's Reports for copies. A few of the new findings in the report now state that tobacco smoke is a deadly mix of more than 7000 chemicals; nicotine is powerfully addictive, smoking can start your body on a path toward cancer, smoking causes immediate damage to your arteries, smoking damages your lungs, smoking harms reproduction and your children's health, smoking makes diabetes harder to control, and secondhand smoke causes immediate harm to nonsmokers. (USDHHS, 2010a).

Of the 7000 chemicals from cigarettes, hundreds are toxic, and 70 or more are known to cause cancer. Here are some descriptions of just a few of these poisonous chemicals a smoker inhales each and every day they smoke. **Arsenic** - A silvery-white very poisonous chemical element. This deadly poison is used to make insecticides, and it is also used to kill gophers and rats. **Benzene** - A flammable liquid obtained from coal tar and used as a solvent. This cancer-causing chemical is used to make everything from pesticides to detergent to gasoline. **Cadmium** - A metallic chemical element used in alloys. This toxic metal causes damage to the liver, kidneys, and the brain; and stays in your body for years. **Formaldehyde** - A colorless pungent gas used in solution as a disinfectant and preservative. (Schools removed formaldehyde from preservatives over twenty years ago). It causes cancer; damages your lungs, skin and digestive system. Embalmers use it to preserve dead bodies. **Lead** - A heavy bluish-gray metallic chemical element. This toxic heavy metal causes lead poisoning, which stunts your growth, and damages your brain. It can easily kill you. **Propylene Glycol** - A sweet hygroscopic viscous liquid used as antifreeze and as a solvent in brake fluid. The tobacco industry claims they add it to keep cheap *reconstituted tobacco* from drying out, but scientists say it aids in the delivery of nicotine (tobaccos active drug) to the brain. **Turpentine** - A colorless volatile oil. Turpentine is very toxic and is commonly used as a paint thinner. When a person smokes, they draw these toxic chemicals into their lungs. The porous cells of the lungs then send the chemicals directly into the bloodstream where they are delivered to every cell in the human body. *Several types of cancer may result from inhaling some of the most carcinogenic chemicals compounds known to man.*

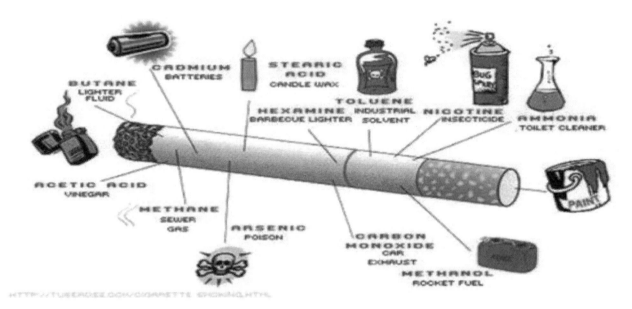

Nicotine is a highly addictive stimulant drug. In 2006 tobacco manufacturers boosted the nicotine content in cigarettes by 33%. Similar to heroin and cocaine, nicotine changes the way the brain works and causes people to crave more and more nicotine. Smoking causes both physical and mental addiction. Many smokers thought that 'low tar' cigarettes, or 'light' cigarettes or filtered cigarettes helped to prevent the toxins from entering their bodies. None of those marketing tools are true, and in 2010 the FDA banned tobacco companies from using those claims in trying to promote a 'safe' cigarette. There is no such thing as a safe cigarette for smokers. The financial cost of cigarettes to smokers is also astounding. Even without adding additional tobacco tax, as is being considered in many states, counties and cities, an average cost of $6 a pack for a one pack a day will cost about $186 a month, or over $2200 annually. If the smoker lives in New York or Chicago (at 2011 prices), the cost of a single pack is more than $10 which brings the monthly total to more than $300 or over $3100 annually. Many people could find lots of safer, non-life-threatening products to purchase for $200-300 a month! Additional findings form the Surgeon General Reports include:

- Spending time in a smoke filled room can trigger heart attacks;
- Secondhand smoke causes premature death and disease in children and in adults who do not smoke;
- Children exposed to secondhand smoke are at an increased risk for sudden infant death syndrome (SIDS), acute respiratory infections, ear problems and more severe asthma. Smoking by parents causes respiratory symptoms and slows lung growth in their children;
- Exposure of adults to secondhand smoke has immediate adverse effects on the cardiovascular system and causes coronary heart disease and lung cancer;
- The scientific evidence indicates that there is no risk-free level of exposure to secondhand smoke;
- Many millions of Americans, both children and adults, are still exposed to secondhand smoke in their homes and workplaces despite substantial progress in tobacco control;
- Eliminating smoking in indoor spaces fully protects nonsmokers from exposure to secondhand smoke.
- Separating smokers from nonsmokers, cleaning the air, and ventilating buildings cannot eliminate exposures of nonsmokers to secondhand smoke.
- Smoking can increase the risk for diabetes;
- Smoking causes bronchitis, emphysema, heart disease, cancer of the mouth, tongue, throat, pharynx;
- Nearly all-first use of tobacco occurs before high school graduation; this finding suggests that if adolescents can be kept tobacco free, most will never start using tobacco;
- Most adolescent smokers are addicted to nicotine and report that they want to quit but are unable to do so; they experience withdrawal symptoms and relapse rates similar to those reported by adults;
- Tobacco is often the first drug used by those young people who use alcohol, marijuana, and other drugs;
- Adolescents with lower levels of school achievement, fewer skills to resist pervasive influences to use tobacco, friends who use tobacco, and lower self-images are more likely than their peers to use tobacco;
- Cigarette advertising appears to increase young people's risk of smoking by affecting their perceptions of the persuasiveness, image, and function of smoking; and
- Community wide efforts, which include tobacco tax increases, enforcement of minor's access laws, youth-oriented mass media campaigns, and school-based tobacco use prevention programs, are successful in reducing adolescent use of tobacco. (Elders, 1994; SG, 2006, 2010).

Tobacco and Minorities: Conclusions of the Surgeon General's Report related to Minorities and tobacco use.

Data from the CDC focused on the health problems of tobacco use with specific ethnic groups: African-Americans, Hispanics, American Indians and Alaska Natives, Asian Americans and Pacific Islanders. The Surgeon General stated:

- Cigarette smoking is a major cause of disease and death in each of the four-population group studied in this report. African-Americans currently bear the greatest health burden. Differences in the magnitude of disease risk among racial and ethnic groups are directly related to differences in patterns of smoking.
- Tobacco use varies within and among racial/ethnic minority groups; among adults, American Indians and Alaska Natives have the highest prevalence of tobacco use, and African-American and Southeast Asian men also have a high prevalence of smoking. **Asian-American and Hispanic women have the lowest prevalence;**
- Among adolescents, cigarette smoking prevalence increased in the 1990s among African-Americans and Hispanics after several years of substantial decline among adolescents of all four identified racial/ethnic minority groups. This increase is particularly striking among African-American youths, which had the greatest decline of the four groups during the 1970s and 1980s;

- No single factor determines patterns of tobacco use among racial/ethnic minority groups; these patterns are the result of complex interactions of multiple factors, such as socioeconomic status, cultural characteristics, acculturation, stress, biological elements, targeted advertising, price of tobacco products, and varying capacities of communities to mount effective tobacco control initiatives; and
- Rigorous surveillance and prevention research are needed on the changing cultural, psychosocial, and environmental factors that influence tobacco use to improve our understanding of racial/ethnic smoking patterns and identify strategic tobacco control opportunities. The capacity of tobacco control efforts to keep pace with patterns of tobacco use and cessation depends on timely recognition of emerging prevalence and cessation patterns and the resulting development of appropriate community-based programs to address the factors involved.

African Americans

- In the 1970s and 1980s, death rates from respiratory cancers (mainly lung cancer) increased among African American men and women. In 1990–1995, these rates declined substantially among African-American men and leveled off in African American women;

- Middle-aged and older African Americans are far more likely than their counterparts in the other major racial/ethnic minority groups to die from coronary heart disease, stroke, or lung cancer;
- Smoking declined dramatically among African American youths during the 1970s and 1980s, but has increased substantially during the 1990s; and
- Declines in smoking have been greater among African American men with at least a high school education than among those with less education.

American Indians and Alaska Natives

- Nearly 40 percent of American Indian and Alaska Native adults smoke cigarettes, compared with 25 percent of adults in the overall U.S. (18 percent of Californians). They are more likely than any other racial/ethnic minority group to smoke tobacco or use smokeless tobacco;
- Since 1983, very little progress has been made in reducing tobacco use among American Indian and Alaska Native adults. The prevalence of smoking among American Indian and Alaska Native women of reproductive age has remained strikingly high since 19780; and
- American Indians and Alaska Natives were the only one of the four major U.S. racial/ethnic groups to experience an increase in respiratory cancer death rates in 1990–1995.

Asian Americans and Pacific Islanders

- Estimates of the smoking prevalence among Southeast Asian American men range from 34 percent to 43 percent—much higher than among other Asian-American and Pacific Islander groups. Smoking rates are much higher among Asian-American and Pacific Islander men than among women, regardless of country of origin;
- Asian-American and Pacific Islander women have the lowest rates of death from coronary heart disease among men or women in the four major U.S. racial/ethnic minority groups; and
- Factors associated with smoking among Asian Americans and Pacific Islanders include having recently moved to the United States, living in poverty, having limited English proficiency, and knowing little about the health effects of tobacco use.

Hispanics

It is estimated 40.4 million Americans (14.0%) are of Latin American or other Spanish descent, which makes Hispanic Americans the nation's second-largest racial/ethnic group. The number of Hispanics is projected to increase to 66 million by 2030 and to 97 million by 2050. Most Hispanic Americans are of Mexican, Puerto Rican, Cuban, or South/Central American ancestry. Although Hispanic Americans have settled across the United States, 77% reside in one of seven states: Arizona, California, Florida, Illinois, New Jersey, New York, and Texas. Some of the facts associated with this very large population related to tobacco include:

- Nationally, an estimated 16.2% of Hispanic adults smoke cigarettes, versus 13.3% of Asian Americans, 21.9% of whites, 21.5% of African Americans, and 32.0% of American Indians/ Alaska Natives;
- Among men, an estimated 21.1% of Hispanics are current cigarette smokers, versus 20.6% of Asian Americans, 24.0% of whites, 26.7% of African Americans, and 37.5% of American Indians/Alaska Natives;
- Among women, an estimated 11.1% of Hispanics are current smokers, versus 6.1% of Asian Americans, 20.0% of whites, 17.3% of African Americans, and 26.8% of American Indians/Alaska Natives;
- The estimate for current cigarette smoking among Hispanics in grades 9 through 12 is 22.0%, versus 12.9% for African Americans and 25.9% for whites;
- An estimated 24.8% of Hispanic males in grades 9 through 12 are current cigarette smokers, versus 14.0% of African American males and 24.9% of white males in these grades;
- An estimated 19.2% of Hispanic females in grades 9 through 12 are current cigarette smokers, compared with 11.9% of African American females and 27.0% of white females in these grades;
- An estimated 9.9% of Hispanic middle school students are current cigarette smokers, versus 8.5% of white, 7.6% of African American, and 2.7% of Asian American middle school students;
- Estimates among adults for current cigar smoking are 4.6% for Hispanics, 6.0% for whites, 6.9% for African Americans, 10.9% for American Indians/Alaska Natives, and 1.8% for Asian Americans;
- Estimates for current use of smokeless tobacco among adults are 1.1% for Hispanics, 0.6% for Asian Americans, 1.9% for African Americans, 4.0% for whites, and 8.6% for American Indians/Alaska Natives;
- Among students in grades 9–12, an estimated 14.9% of Hispanics, 10.3% of African Americans, and 14.6% of whites are current cigar smokers;
- Among male students in grades 9–12, an estimated 8.6% of Hispanics, 3.0% of African Americans, and 17.6% of whites are current users of smokeless tobacco.[8] Nationally, an estimated 13.6% of high school males are current users of smokeless tobacco;
- An estimated 3.8% of Hispanic middle school students are current users of smokeless tobacco, as are 3.0% of whites, 2.0% of African Americans, and 1.0% of Asian Americans in middle school.[9] Nationally, an estimated 2.8% of middle school students are users of smokeless tobacco;
- In general, smoking rates among Mexican American adults decrease as they learn and adopt the values, beliefs, and norms of American culture;
- Declines in the prevalence of smoking have been greater among Hispanic men with at least a high school education than among those with less education;
- Lung cancer is the leading cause of cancer deaths among Hispanics;

105

- For Hispanic American men, deaths rates for lung cancer are highest among Cuban-Americans, followed by Puerto Ricans and then Mexican-Americans; and
- An estimated 3.8% of Hispanic middle school students are current users of smokeless tobacco, as are 3.0% of whites, 2.0% of African-Americans, and 1.0% of Asian Americans in middle school. (CDC, 1998, 2007).
  For additional information see:
  http://www.cdc.gov/tobacco/data_statistics/Factsheets/hispanics_tobacco.htm.

How Can We Prevent Tobacco Use among Minority Youth?

The Truth Ad Campaign against smoking recommends a tobacco prevention model that comprises five settings: (1) home; (2) community; (3) classroom; (4) clinic; and (5) computer. At home, all tobacco use should be prohibited. Parents should role model tobacco abstinence and express strong disapproval as well as punishment for use. Researchers have found that parents can influence children by strongly disapproving of and using punishment for tobacco use. The public should advocate smoking control policies, including smoking prohibition in enclosed public places, restrictions on the sale of tobacco products (especially to minors), and appropriate taxation policies. Schools should use scientific and evidence based curricula to follow guidelines from the CDC. Most importantly, teachers must be properly trained to use the curricula and model non-tobacco use. Role models within the school setting must include all adults, including the secretarial, maintenance and other support staff. Kids watch adults very closely and emulate their behavior. Health care providers, doctors, nurses, etc., should reinforce a non-tobacco use with patients as a regular part of all treatment regimens. Preventing tobacco use among minority youth requires a multipronged and relentless approach, beginning in the home and extending to the community, classroom, clinic, computer, and counter advertisements. This kind of approach will be challenging, but well worth it to develop healthy children of the future.

Are teens smoking less?

During the month of October, 2001, **the number of new teen smokers fell by one-third.** Data reported from the U.S. government indicate that this drop may be due to higher prices and a cultural shift in tobacco use. From 1999-2001 the number of teen smokers fell by a third. Still there were over 783, 000 new smokers ages 12 to 17 in 1999. That means that 2,145 teens began smoking on the average day. In just two years, the number of new teen smokers fell by a third, according to government reports.

During 2005, Farrelly and colleagues, reporting in the *American Journal of Public Health,* announced significant drops in teens that smoke, especially in the state of California. Their research reported the impact of the "truth" campaign in a national sample of about 50,000 students in grades 8-12 surveyed each spring from 1997-2002. Their findings indicate that the campaign accounted for a significant portion of the recent decline in youth smoking prevalence and that smoking prevalence among all students declined from 25.3% to 18.0% between 1999 and 2002 and that the campaign accounted for approximately 22% of this decline. **In California** the prevalence of teens smoking has been reduced to about 13%, or the lowest in the nation! (Farrelly, et al., 2005).

Decline in U.S. Teen Smoking Stalls

Since 2000 there was a major decline in the number of U.S. high school students who smoke, and that statistic has been described as a result of increased taxes, non-smoking rules and health education awareness by youth. By 2004, however, the decline in teen smoking has slowed significantly compared to the dramatic drops seen in the late 1990s. Terry Pechacek, associate director for science at the CDC stated. "The only drop we have seen during this time is a decrease in African American female smoking, and we have taken our eye off the issue. Sometimes, we get complacent with our success and move on to other things." Additionally, states have cut budgets significantly for cessation and prevention programs while the tobacco industry aggressively targets teens with their $12 billion campaign. (Reinberg, 2010). Matthew L. Myers, president of the Campaign for Tobacco-Free Kids, said in a news release that "the good news in the CDC's 2009 Youth Risk Behavior Survey is that the high school smoking rate (the percentage who smoked in the past month) declined to 19.5 percent in 2009. This is the first time it has fallen below 20 percent and the lowest rate since this survey was started in 1991."The bad news," he added, "is that high school smoking declined by just 11 percent between 2003 and 2009, compared to a 40 percent decline between 1997 and 2003." Hence legislators, parents, teachers and school leaders must be vigilant and consistent with their messages to stop youth from starting to smoke as well as sending messages to have them quit smoking.

Smokeless or "Spit" Tobacco

Smokeless tobacco products include both snuff and chewing tobacco. The term smokeless is generally a tobacco company term that softens the description of the product. The CDC term of "spit tobacco" more aptly describes the use of small tobacco leaves. Snuff, which can be either dry or moist, is made from powdered or finely cut tobacco leaves. Both dry and moist snuff are used by placing a small amount (pinch) of snuff in the mouth between the lip or cheek and gum. This procedure is called **dipping**.

Effects of smokeless tobacco

Bad breath

Permanent teeth discoloration

Precancerous leukoplakia

Painful ulcers

In the U.S., it is estimated that there are 12 million people over the age of 12 using spit tobacco. Three million of these are under 21 years of age, and 1.7 million teenage users are between the ages of 12 and 17. The use of spit tobacco, particularly moist snuff, is increasing, especially among male adolescents and young male adults. As cigarette sales drop, spit tobacco sales increase. Studies have reported that many teenage users of spit tobacco believed that their habit was a safe alternative to cigarette smoking. They were able to purchase spit tobacco with little difficulty. The excess risk of cancer of the cheek and gum may increase nearly fifty fold among long-term snuff users. There is also a strong association between the use of snuff and cancer of the oral cavity. Spit tobacco products contain potent carcinogens. They include nitrosamines, polonium, and complex polycyclic hydrocarbons. Oral **leukoplakias** (white patches in the mouth or oral cavity) are related to the use of spit tobacco. Damaged tissues from the site of tobacco placement can lead to cancer of the tongue, lip and cheek. Chewing tobacco also causes gum recession. Chewing tobacco contains nicotine, a powerful stimulant drug. Much like the nicotine in cigarettes; smokeless tobacco can be addicting.

New Products and "New" Companies Enter the Smokeless Market

In April 2006, within two weeks of each other, both Philip Morris USA and Reynolds-American International (RAI) Tobacco Company (the two largest domestic cigarette manufacturers) announced plans to enter the smokeless tobacco market. First, RAI announced its acquisition of the Conwood Smokeless Tobacco Company (makers of Kodiak and Grizzly moist snuff and Levi Garrett chewing tobacco), the second largest moist snuff manufacturers in the U.S., and soon followed with an announcement that it will be test marketing (in Austin, TX and Portland, OR) a smokeless product called "Camel Snus" – a smokeless, pouch product using the traditional Camel cigarette brand name and logo. By August 2007, Camel Snus was test-marketed in half a dozen cities across the U.S. Also in the spring of 2006, Philip Morris USA announced plans to test market (in Indianapolis, IN) a smokeless, pouch product called "Taboka" beginning in July 2006. On June 8, 2007, Philip Morris USA announced plans to test market (in Dallas/Ft. Worth, TX) a smokeless, spitless, pouch product called "Marlboro Snus" beginning in August 2007. It is widely believed that Taboka was only introduced to provide test market data for Marlboro Snus. On August 21, 2007, PMUSA announced that it test marketed Marlboro Moist Smokeless Tobacco – a completely separate product from Marlboro Snus – in Smokeless Tobacco in the U.S.

These developments may lead to increased efforts by smokeless manufacturers to encourage adult smokers who are concerned about their health or who are interested in quitting to switch to smokeless tobacco. These developments could also lead to an increase in dual use of smokeless and combusted tobacco products in light of increasing limitations on public indoor and workplace smoking; and ultimately these changes could lead to increased youth experimentation with smokeless tobacco (due to the ability to use it discretely/secretly) and it could be a deterrent to youth tobacco use cessation efforts.

Tobacco Companies Still Targeting Women

As far back as the 1930s, tobacco companies have been targeting women to use cigarettes. The old message of "reach for a Lucky in stead of a sweet," aggravated the candy industry at that time; but today the purveyors of death still encourage women to smoke to be sexy, sophisticated and part of the in crowd. Phillip Morris' Virginia Slim brands have recently been designed to be smaller in diameter, suggesting a slim figure, and during 2010 the company introduced Virginia Slims as "purse packs." Purse packs are small rectangular packs that contain "superslim" cigarettes, are half the size of regular packs and come in mauve, and teal colors! R.J. Reynolds' Cameo brand are now packaged in shiny black boxes with hot pink and teal borders. Perhaps it is the teal color that attracts women to destroy their bronchioles? As mentioned earlier, smoking will deaden the nerve endings in the tongue which will curb the appetite; but the risk of disease and death far outweighs a few added pounds that could be worked off in the gym.

Cigars-the latest rage

Since 1993 the sales of cigars in the U.S. has been increasing. Cigar smoking is a known risk factor for certain types of cancers and chronic obstructive pulmonary disease (COPD). Researches discovered that cardiovascular disease, as with cigarette smoking, is a significant potential consequence associated with smoking cigars. Cigar smokers compared to non-smokers are at higher relative risk for coronary heart disease, upper aerodigestive cancers, lung disease and several cancers of the oral cavity. **There also appears to be a synergistic relation between cigar smoking and alcohol consumption with respect to the risk of oropharyngeal cancers and cancers of the upper aerodigestive tract.** While the cigar industry advertises the chic, status model of their tobacco product; recent research has established significant risk for potential fatal diseases. (Iribarren, Tekawa, Sidney, et al., 1999).

Throughout the 2000s there has been an increase in cigar smoking in America. Legislators often overlook cigar use among youth and often mistakenly believe that cigars are "not harmful" compared to cigarettes and deserve special treatment or consideration related to smoke free environments. Cigars are addictive, deadly and cause lung cancer, facial and tongue cancers, heart attacks and strokes as do cigarettes. Cigars produce more secondhand smoke than cigarettes and the smoke from cigars is even more harmful than cigarette smoke. Cigars contain the same toxic and carcinogenic compounds as cigarettes, and studies have shown that cigar smokers do actually inhale. Because cigars usually do not have filters, cigar smokers are exposed to more tobacco smoke and toxins. Other medical problems from cigar smoking include chronic obstructive pulmonary disease (COPD), oral and esophageal cancer and cancer of the larynx. One cigar smoked for up to one hour contains as much tobacco as a full pack of cigarettes. Each day, more than 3,500 additional kids under 18 years old try cigar smoking for the first time – almost as many as those who try cigarettes for the first time each day. (CTFK, 2009).

Tobacco and the Movies

Recent reports have shown that despite the 1998 tobacco company's financial settlement with the U.S. Congress, heavy emphasis on tobacco use in movies is still depicted. During the 1990s, 9 out of 10 Hollywood films dramatized the use of tobacco. Twenty-eight percent of the films — including one in five children's movies — showed cigarette brand logos. Do movies actually sell cigarettes and cigars? **Careful research has found that non-smoking teens whose favorite stars frequently smoke on screen are sixteen times more likely to have positive attitudes towards smoking in the future.**

Compare the 1993 blockbuster movie Jurassic Park and the 2010 successful movie Avatar. Both movies were box office smashes, both attracted a wide range of audiences, especially kids, and both movies had a major actor as a scientist (Samuel L. Jackson in Jurassic

Park and Sigourney Weaver, in Avatar) prominently smoking! But, more importantly, 31% of teens that saw more than 150 occurrences of smoking in movies (in theaters, on video, or TV) had tried smoking compared to only 4% among teens who had seen less than 50 occurrences. Even after controlling for the effects of parents smoking and other factors, seeing a lot of smoking in the movies tripled the odds that a teen would try smoking. **More smoking was depicted in movies during 2001 than the previous 30 years!** (L.A. Times, 2002). To see 'what is playing today' in the movies, including movies that promote smoking Google smokefreemovies.ucsf.edu.

Tobacco and Politics

Tobacco companies are businesses. As in any business, the ultimate goal is to earn a profit and stay in business. Tobacco companies spend in excess of **$13 million every day on advertising** and promotion in the U.S. alone. That means they spend more than $3 billion per year, $34 million daily, or almost **$400 every second!** For every one-dollar spent opposing tobacco use in America, the tobacco industry spends $4,000 to refute the warnings.

Most tobacco companies are huge international corporations. These companies have recently sought to obtain political and economic influence by acquiring subsidiaries of non-tobacco growing companies. While diversification of any business makes good sense, the political impact from tobacco companies' diversification can wield a powerful influence on other business, as well as governmental agencies. For example, if a publisher who is sensitive to tobacco-related health problems refuses to carry tobacco advertising in a magazine, the tobacco company can simply cancel advertising for other products in that publication.

Tobacco companies have even "infected" the professional literature. During the 1995 National Conference of the American Public Health Association in San Diego, researchers reported numerous occasions where tobacco company affiliated writers would write letters to the editors purporting to argue on various scientific points of view and research. The content of what they argued were of little importance, but these writers would later be quoted by tobacco company documents that a given author published in (prestigious journal) said . . .This method is used to attach official scientific creditability to their "source." **In essence, they were just quoting whatever they themselves said in a letter to the editor!**

California's Law for a Smoke-free Workplace

On January 1, 1995, the Smoke-free Workplace law (AB 13) took effect. By adding section *6404.5 to the Labor Code*, the bill protects employees throughout the state from the harmful effects of secondhand tobacco smoke. Secondhand smoke has been designated as a class A carcinogen by the Environmental Protection Agency (EPA), and the law is designed to

110

protect all employees in California. The law, with very few exceptions, prohibits smoking in nearly all-indoor enclosed places in California. For the purpose of this law, any enclosed workplace can be broadly defined as any place of employment, including offices and restaurants, which have four walls and a ceiling. The following places are **specifically excluded from *LC 6404.5***, but may be regulated by local governments through their own ordinances:

- Small Businesses with five or less employees: 1) when smoking area is not accessible to minors, 2) no employees are required to work in smoking areas, 3) the air from smoking is vented directly to the outside, 4) the employer complies with all state and federal ventilation standards;
- Gaming clubs and bars until January 1, 1998;
- Sixty-five percent of hotel and motel guest rooms;
- Designated portions of hotel and motel lobbies;
- Meeting and banquet rooms in hotels, motels, and restaurants, except when used for exhibit purposes or when food and beverage functions are being conducted; During these times, smoking may be permitted in corridors and pre-function areas near the meeting or banquet room if no employee is stationed there;
- Warehouses with more than 100, 000 square feet and 20 or fewer employees;
- Tobacco shops and attached private smokers' lounges;
- Employee break rooms designed by employers for smoking. The following conditions must be met: 1) the room is located in a non-work area where no one is required to enter as part of their work responsibilities, 2) the air from the smoking area is vented directly to the outside, 3) there are sufficient number of smoke free break rooms for non smokers, 4) the employer complies with all state and federal ventilation standards;
- Truck cabs or tractors, when a nonsmoking employee is not present;
- Private residences, except when used as a licensed child-care facility; and
- Theatrical uses, medical research, patient smoking areas of long-term care facilities.

In the event that employers do violate the law set forth in *LC 6404.5*, they may be subject to criminal penalties that are enforceable by local police or public health departments. Fines are as follows:

1. First violation fine not to exceed $100.
2. Second violation fine not to exceed $200.
3. Third and subsequent violations within one-year fine not to exceed $500.

After a third violation, employees may file a complaint with Cal-OSHA where **penalties are up to $7,000 per violation.** The legislation does allow additional restrictions by cities and municipalities. During the summer of 2004, many California beaches became smoke free and the State of California took action in outdoor areas as well. **Since January 1, 2004, all governmental buildings, including colleges and universities restricted outdoor smoking within 25 feet of doors and operable windows.**

Tobacco companies and tobacco vendors have feared that additional taxes to their products would lower business in such places as restaurants and especially bars and gaming clubs. Many shop owners and tobacco company interests lobbied against laws that banned smoking in most indoor areas. Researchers Glantz and Charlesworth, of the University of California, collected data from three states (California, Utah and Vermont) and 6 cities (Boulder Colorado, Flagstaff, Arizona, Los Angeles, California, Mesa, Arizona, New York, New York and San Francisco, California). Their findings not only showed no decline in revenues after the implementation of no smoking laws, but they were able to quantify an increase in sales in many locations. (Glantz, Charlesworth, 1999). By September 1998, three states and 212 communities had laws mandating smoke-free restaurants. The state of California and 31 communities had laws requiring smoke-free bars. Smoke-free restaurants are slowly becoming more common throughout the U.S. During 2002 several California businesses, hospitals etc. began to ban smoking even in outdoor areas, such as parking lots. By 2009, many cities also banned outdoor smoking in public parks and recreation areas.

The Youth Market

Tobacco companies constantly remind the public that their advertisements are merely designed to encourage adults to switch brands, and they flatly deny any targeted efforts towards youth. Doctors Ought to Care (DOC.), an anti smoking activist organization of physicians, has been countering this message throughout the United States and many foreign countries. To emphasize the pervasiveness of tobacco advertising, *The Journal of the American Medical Association,* (December 11, 1991) explains that not only have tobacco companies been targeting youth, but also some kids were able to recognize the Camel cigarette "Old Joe" logo more readily than the Disney's Mickey Mouse logo. (Fischer, Schwartz, 1991). When children played a game in which they were asked to place 22 product logos—(including products for adults)on a game board featuring twelve products—including: Mickey Mouse, pizza, hamburgers and automobiles, 30 percent of the three year-olds were able to match the Old Joe cartoon with Camel cigarettes. **Educators can use this booklet, or other tobacco company 'prevention' materials to illustrate to students the Institute's false and misleading message.**

Educating Our Youth

In 1989, 2.6 million children between twelve and seventeen years of age smoked cigarettes, and 1.5 million (57.5 percent) bought their own cigarettes; 85 percent of the purchases were from a small store. Tobacco-related diseases occur at higher rates for persons that start smoking at younger ages. As Altman states, "Access to tobacco is conducive to developing and maintaining a tobacco addiction. In field trials around the country, minors' attempts to purchase tobacco from stores and vending machines have been successful more than 50 percent of the time. Despite laws in 48 states and the District of Columbia that prohibit the sale of tobacco products to minors, under aged youth have been successful in 70 to 100 percent of attempts to purchase tobacco." (Altman, 1991).

As laws are passed and enforced, children who cannot purchase cigarettes will be much less at risk for the health problems related to tobacco use. Educational interventions directed at vendors to decrease or eliminate tobacco sales at the retail level have resulted in some temporary reduction, but the greatest decrease of sales to underage buyers has been documented in communities that have an active supervision or surveillance of retail stores accompanied with substantial penalties for noncompliance.(Feigheery, 1991). Law enforcement officers need to be as vigilant with tobacco sales and use by minors as they are with alcohol products.

From November 1990 until June 1991, the American Lung Association worked with the Latino Tobacco Free Coalition in the Los Angeles area to implement a student "sting" operation (with parental consent and approval) that was able to dramatically lower sales of tobacco to minors. The operation began by posting **California Penal Code 308** at locations where cigarettes were sold. Penal Code section 308 states: **"Unlawful to sell to persons under 18 years of age tobacco, cigarette or cigarette papers, or any preparation of tobacco, or any other instrument or paraphernalia that is designed for the smoking or ingestion of tobacco, products prepared from tobacco, or any controlled substance."** This law has been in effect in California for over 100 years!

Minors were then videotaped purchasing cigarettes. Later, vendors who had sold cigarettes to minors were visited by police officers and tactfully reminded about the law. Loya and Vitstrand completed a follow up study of 1400 vendors, and found that while 70% were selling to minors before the sting; only 30% sold to minors after the sting, a 40% reduction. At the end of one year the ratios were about 50% selling and 50% not selling to minors. (Loya, 1993). Sting operations have been repeated many times and recently, in Glendale California, youthful kids attempted to purchase tobacco products, while being under aged, and nearly 25% of the local markets still allowed purchases. (Gallegos, 2007).

Despite the continued efforts of health educators to help young people, many children and youth are not concerned with statistics about chronic problems such as cancer, emphysema and heart disease. **Information about other drawbacks of tobacco addiction, such as yellow and brown stains on teeth, bad breath, smelly hair, stinky clothes, wrinkles, a smelly house, may be more relevant, particularly if it's suggested that such effects are a turn off for most potential dating partners.**

Statistical data about deaths from tobacco use are often hard to visualize. A simple way to dramatize the greater than 400,000 deaths a year in the United States due to tobacco use is to ask a typical large middle or high school class of 38 students to gaze at the empty seats they leave in the classroom at the end of a one-hour session. Statistically speaking, everyone in that class will die as the bell rings. That number of deaths occurs twenty-four hours a day, seven days a week, just in the United States!

> **The tobacco industry spends $400 every second on advertising and promotion targeting youth!**

Smoking and Pregnancy. What we Know about Tobacco use and Pregnancy.

Women who quit smoking before or early in pregnancy significantly reduce the risk for several adverse outcomes. Compared with women who do not smoke. Data reported by the CDC also indicate that, women who smoke prior to pregnancy are about twice as likely to experience a delay in conception and have approximately 30% higher odds of being infertile. Women who smoke during pregnancy are about twice as likely to experience premature rupture of membranes, placental abruption, and placenta previa during pregnancy. Additionally, babies born to women who smoke during pregnancy compared to women that do not smoke while pregnant:

- Have about 30% higher odds of being born prematurely;
- Are more likely to be born with low birth weight (less than 5.5 pounds), increasing their risk for illness or death;
- Weigh an average of 200 grams less than infants born to women who do not smoke; and
- Are 1.4 to 3.0 times more likely to die of Sudden Infant Death Syndrome (SIDS) (CDC, 2008).

Approximately 13% of women reported smoking during the last three months of pregnancy. Younger, less educated, non-Hispanic, white women and American Indian women are more likely to smoke during pregnancy compared to their older, more educated, counterparts. Of women who smoked during the last three months of pregnancy, 52% reported smoking 5 or less cigarettes per day, 27% reported smoking 6 to 10 cigarettes per day, and 21% reported smoking 11 or more cigarettes per day. Exposure to secondhand smoke causes premature death and disease in children and adults who do not smoke. Between 1988 and 2002, cotinine levels, a biological indicator of tobacco smoke exposure, declined by approximately 70% among children and non-smoking adults. Despite this positive trend, in 2002 nearly half of all children and non-smoking adults still had detectable levels of cotinine. Pregnant women who are exposed to secondhand smoke have 20 percent higher odds of giving birth to a low birth weight baby than women who are not exposed to secondhand smoke during pregnancy. Children are at greater risk of being exposed to secondhand smoke than adults.

So significant is the effect of second hand smoke on children that lawyers have been able to get the courts to order parents not to smoke while visiting their children during custody situations. Cotinine levels in the children are used in court to prevent parents from smoking while their kids are present, even in their own homes! Children who are exposed to secondhand smoke are at increased risk for bronchitis, pneumonia, ear infections, more severe asthma, respiratory symptoms, and slowed lung growth. Additionally, cigarette smoking during pregnancy poses a wide variety of risks for a mother and baby, including miscarriage, stillbirth and potentially life-threatening pregnancy complications, such as abruptio placenta (premature separation of the placenta from the wall of the womb) and placenta previa (partial or complete blockage of the opening of the uterus by the placenta). The most common risk of smoking while pregnant is of having a low-birth weight baby. (CDC, 2008).

Long-term studies have suggested that smoking during pregnancy may be associated with subtle intellectual and behavioral problems in childhood. Children whose mothers smoked during pregnancy may have more problems learning to spell and read than those children whose mothers did not smoke and they also may be hyperactive. The dangerous effects of smoking are directly linked to the number of cigarettes smoked daily. Studies show that women who stop smoking before or early in pregnancy decrease their risk of having a low-birth weight baby to nearly that of women who have never smoked. Women who stop or cut back on smoking later in pregnancy can still significantly increase their chances of having a normal birth weight baby. (CDC, 2008).

Smokers Risk of Death

It is very important that we understand a little about statistical data. Many smokers will make statements about their grandfather, or their aunt that smoked well into their eighties and seemed "OK." While a very few people will suffer minimal problems related to tobacco, doctors estimate that greater than 50% of addicted smokers will suffer some serious medical problem, sometime during their life. What are the statistical risks of smoking? Many smokers are in a state of denial. Compare the chances from table 5.1

Table 5.1
Estimated Relative Risks of Various Activities

Activity or Cause	Annual Fatalities Per Million Persons
Active Smoking	**7,000**
Alcohol	541
Accident	275
Disease	266
Motor vehicles	187
alcohol-related	95
non-alcohol	92
Work	113
Swimming	22
All other pollutants	
	6
Football	6
Electrocution	2
Lightning	0.5
DES in cattle feed	0.3
Bee sting	0.2
Basketball	0.02

Source: Active smoking, CPS II; NHISs, 1965, 1985.
Bureau of the Census (1974, 1986) Document: Fact Sheet
on Smokeless Tobacco.

Students can be empowered to become activists in the crusade against tobacco use. In the summer of 1990, during a year-round school session at a predominately Hispanic Los Angeles middle school, the makers of Skoal chewing tobacco were advertising their deadly chew to sixth graders. A large sign, written in Spanish, was in direct view across the street from the school. The sign's ethnically related focus suggested that chewing tobacco gave men a macho image. Classroom teachers, along with the American Lung Association, American Cancer Society, The California Association of School Health Educators, and other anti smoking groups, called a press conference, attended by students at the school. The television cameras rolled and the sign was removed within five days.

During mid 1997, an organization was formed to serve as a central agency to help eliminate tobacco use in the adolescent population. The Center for Tobacco-Free Kids was formed to focus on the social and environmental issues and to influence public policies regarding the use of tobacco by teens. With funding in excess of $40 million from the Robert Wood Foundation, American Cancer Society and assistance from the American Lung and Heart Associations, this group has been very formidable, especially with continuous litigation, focusing on the tobacco industry at the national level.

Recommendation for Action

The following recommendations for interventions at all levels, from early childhood education to community action, including state and national political action, could help eliminate the problems of tobacco addiction.

Education

Provide **comprehensive health education** for grade kindergarten through six in all American schools. Include a full year of comprehensive health education in both the middle school and high school, as recommended by the *California Health Framework*. (CDE, 2003). Classes should be taught by fully credentialed health educators. Even preschool children benefit from comprehensive health education and anti smoking campaigns. Comprehensive health education addresses all health-comprising behaviors, including tobacco use. It helps foster health attitudes and behaviors about substance use, including tobacco, and promotes healthy lifestyles. In addition to offering information about the effects of tobacco and other substance use, a comprehensive health program helps students develop skills to avoid risky behaviors. (Fetro, 1991).

State-of-the-art classroom methods, such as computer-assisted interactive instruction and other technology teaching tools, may have additional impact on students. The role of the Internet with instant access to current data related to smoking and health topics will dramatically improve the public awareness of tobacco mortality and morbidity. Intensive prevention programs using role-playing and refusal skill techniques should start at grade four, if not sooner, and continue through grade twelve for all students. Imagine how quickly and easily a 10th grader could access health data and make decisions about his or her own behaviors from a cell phone in the class of 2020, even before ditching school or attending a wild house party!

Train students as health education peer-counselors to help classmates overcome smoking addiction. Offer smoking cessation programs for adults and students, funded by tobacco education taxes, at both business and school sites. As other states follow the California model, this concept will continue to spread nationwide.

Develop special classes in health education to promote health advocacy. Students could present data at city council meetings and school board meetings and advocate the elimination of smoking in all indoor settings, nationwide, from K-12 schools through universities and graduate schools.

Monitor and verify mail orders for sales of tobacco products to minors. This is especially important when minors purchase cigarettes through the Internet with little or no verification. Tobacco companies stopped accepting credit orders during 2005 ostensibly to avoid sales to minors; however, anyone can easily purchase cigarettes online by checking the box stating they are of age.

Involve high school students, civic leaders and community health agencies. Students could earn community service credits toward graduation. These groups could work with law enforcement to develop sting operations to eliminate tobacco sales to minors.

Promote a smoke free environment in all schools, not only for students but also for visitors, faculty and other staff. Use outreach programs to teach parents and other family members the importance of being role models for their children, especially in relation to tobacco use. Train students from families with limited English skills to act as health educators for their parents and family members, teaching them the health risks of smoking and tobacco products.

All individuals have the right to assemble in public and breath air free of toxic substances. People should be able to attend sporting events, restaurants and bars; use public transportation, such as buses, trains and airplanes; walk through a shopping mall; or visit virtually any public place, smoke free. Laws also should apply to the private sector where individual citizens are employed. The Nonsmokers' Bill of Right sates it well:

117

The Nonsmokers' Bill of Rights

Nonsmokers help protect the health, comfort and safety of everyone by insisting on the following rights:

The right to breath clean air. Nonsmokers have the right to breathe clean air, free from harmful and irritating tobacco smoke. This right supersedes the right to smoke when the two conflict.

The right to speak out. Nonsmokers have the right to express, firmly but politely, their discomfort and adverse reactions to tobacco smoke. They have the right to voice their objections when smokers light up without asking permission.

The right to act. Nonsmokers have the right to take action through legislative channels, social pressures or any other legitimate means, as individuals or in groups, to prevent or discourage smokers from polluting the atmosphere and to seek the restriction of smoking in public places. (Nonsmoker's Bill of Rights, 1992).

Legislation

The Former Secretary of Health and Human Services has made the following recommendations: Institute 19 years as the minimum age for legal tobacco sales; create a tobacco sales licensing system similar to that for alcoholic beverages; establish a graduated schedule of penalties for illegal sales, with separate penalties for failure to post a sign regarding legal age of purchase; place primary responsibility for enforcement with a designated state agency, with participation and input from local law enforcement and public health officials; and use civil penalties and local courts to assess fines. (USDHHS, 1990).

Legislation will effect many other changes in addition to banning the sale and distribution of tobacco products through vending machines, and outlawing the sale of single cigarettes from any location.

Pass and enforce laws that prohibit the purchase, distribution and use of tobacco by minors. Support laws such as those in California that discourage the use of tobacco products through taxation. Following the Canadian model, taxes could be raised to as much as 75 percent of the retail sales price of cigarettes.

Eliminate outdated tobacco subsidies while providing incentives for tobacco farmers to develop and produce other edible crops. Ban the exportation of tobacco products to other countries.

Ban smoking in all indoor public places nationwide such as restaurants, bars, shopping malls and sporting venues. Prohibit smoking on all public transit, including, but not limited to, taxis and buses as well as the ticket, boarding, and waiting areas of public transit depots.

Prohibit tobacco advertising and promotion in any facility owned by a city or any agency of a city, county or state government that hosts athletic events, as well as other government-owned premises, including facilities and parks. Prohibit all tobacco advertising and promotion within a two-mile radius of schools, community centers, churches and other places of worship.

Develop company or governmental policies to hire only nonsmokers, especially as police officers and firefighters, while offering nonsmoking employees lower rates on health insurance and life insurance. Insurance companies routinely run blood tests on life insurance applicants and some may not insure them at all if the test positive for smoking.

The Truth Campaign Against Smoking

Since 2000 the **Truth® Campaign** has actively developed numerous programs through the U.S. to help prevent youth from smoking and using tobacco products. The campaign is the largest national youth-focused program in the country. The primary focus is to prevent kids from smoking. Does it work? Yes, by using interactive media, video games, producing numerous videos and educational programs focused on young people, the Truth® campaign has lowered smoking rates in the youth population. Seventy-five percent of all 12 to 17 year-olds in the nation (21 million kids) can accurately describe one or more of the truth ads. Eighty-five percent (24 million) said the ad gave them good reasons not to smoke; and nearly ninety said the ads they saw were convincing. (Protect the Truth, 2010). Moreover, Farrelly, Davis, Haviland, et al., used a dose response relationship to determine youth smoking prevalence and found that the Truth® campaign accounted for a significant portion of the recent decline in youth smoking prevalence. They concluded that smoking prevalence among all students declined from 25.3% to 18.0% between 1999 and 2002 and that the Truth® campaign accounted for approximately 22% of this decline. (Farrelly, Davis, Lyndon, et al., 2009). The study concluded that the Truth® campaign was responsible for substantial declines in youth smoking.

Looking Forward

During the twenty-first century, we look forward to a time when the health objectives for the nation regarding tobacco use are met or exceeded. Children, teenagers and young adults will no longer accept cigarette and tobacco use as normal, sensible behavior. Tobacco companies will eliminate the glitzy advertising and promotion of tobacco products and concentrate on other products for which death is not the end result of product usage; and maybe cigarettes will even disappear from the movies. Our government will recognize and reinforce the scientific data related to complete freedom from tobacco use. Families will develop positive models for their children to emulate while living in a healthy environment. Newly arrived immigrants will adjust to American life without a cigarette attached to their hand. American homes, cars and hotel rooms will no longer be permeated with the smell of tobacco smoke. Businesses can take active roles in reducing smoking, and at the same time save substantial money. During 2007 Marriott Hotels went non-smoking worldwide! Americans will live longer, healthier lives--tobacco-free.

We are getting just a little closer. In November 1998 the U.S. government and the tobacco industry signed a settlement agreement, which assessed over $250 billion to be paid by the tobacco companies to cities and states throughout the nation. Part of that agreement, endorsed by 46 states, was related to tobacco advertising. The four major tobacco companies agreed to

119

remove all advertising from outdoor and transit billboards across the nation by April 23. The billboards were removed during April. The Marlboro man and his counterparts from other tobacco companies disappeared from thousands of billboards in the U.S. The very next day, numerous full-page tobacco ads appeared in major newspapers across the nation. The tobacco ads were replaced by anti-tobacco advertisements that are now **paid for by** the tobacco industry.

For a detailed and extensive list of references related to tobacco, ethnic implications, and other drug abuse by youth, consult the Healthy Kids Resource Center (HKRC) for science-validated studies. See: www.hkresources.org.

Good News about kids and smoking

During the summer of 2002, the CDC published a comprehensive analysis on the trends of smoking among adolescents. Cigarette smoking among adolescents is one of the 10 Leading Health Indicators that reflect the major health concerns in the United States. To examine changes in cigarette smoking among U.S. high school students during 1991--2001, the CDC analyzed data from the national Youth Risk Behavior Survey (YRBS). **This report summarizes the results of the analysis, which found that although cigarette-smoking rates increased during most of the 1990s, they have declined significantly since 1997.** Data was collected from sample sizes ranging from 10,000-16,000 in all 50 states and the District of Columbia. A few of the findings are listed below:

- Among female students, a significant trend was detected, indicating that the prevalence of current smoking peaked during 1997--1999 and then declined significantly by 2001;
- Similarly, among white female, black male, Hispanic, Hispanic female, Hispanic male, and 9th- and 11th-grade students, current smoking prevalence peaked by 1999 and then declined significantly by 2001; and
- During 2001, white and Hispanic students were significantly more likely than black students to report current smoking. Current smoking was significantly more likely to be reported by white and Hispanic female students than by black female students, by white and Hispanic male students than by black male students, and by 12th-grade students than by 9th- and 10th-grade students. (CDC, 2002).

The above recent report indicates that substantial progress is being made toward reducing cigarette-smoking rates among high school students. In spite of factors that might have promoted cigarette use, such as tobacco industry expenditures on advertising and promotion, which increased substantially during 1998--1999, and the frequency with which smoking was depicted in films; kids are now using tobacco much less. It is now very clear that smoking levels among high school kids have declined. Kids no longer think smoking is 'normal.' The adult population is still another matter. Even though an overall decline has taken place in America; even though places like tobacco growing Kentucky are passing indoor smoking bans; many adults that quit are readily replaced by youth smokers. (2004, Fiore, Croyle, Curry, et al.)

Cigarette Bootleggers, Internet Sales and New York City $10 a Pack

During the summer of 2008, New Yorkers started paying the highest cigarette taxes in the nation with the latest $1.25 tax that officials expect to bring in $265 million a year. Convenience stores across the state are definitely against the increase, as are their smoking customers; but health officials hailed the tax increase as a success. "This is a public health victory. We know one of the really effective tools to get people off of their nicotine addiction is to the raise the price." The commissioner also said, "Smokers will be paying $2.75 per pack in state taxes, a jump from the previous tax of $1.50. Before the new tax, the average price of a pack of cigarettes was $5.82 statewide, and about $8 a pack in New York City, which levies its own taxes." **Depending on the store the new retail price for a pack in the city now soared past $10!** It is estimated that 140,000 New Yorkers will stop smoking with this tax increase, and most importantly, youth are very sensitive to the price of cigarettes, and that could prevent over 200,000 youth from smoking. (Bauman, 2008). Bootlegged cigarettes have been brought in from Canada and other areas near U.S. borders. This coupled with the ease of purchasing cigarettes on the Internet could increase illegal sales in the U.S. Hundreds of websites promote the sale of cheap cigarettes and do not seem to require much more than a check box to determine if minors are buying the products. The important point is that the new taxes will help people quit.

You have come a long way baby,
all the way to cancer,
heart disease and emphysema.
Nathan Matza

Tobacco Summary

Appearance: Ground-up leaves, brown or black in color.

Also known as: Spit tobacco, snuff, chewing tobacco, smokeless tobacco.

Tobacco/nicotine products: Cigarettes, cigars, pipe tobacco, smokeless tobacco, nicotine chewing gum.

Short-term effects: Increased pulse rate; rise in blood pressure; drop in skin temperature; relaxation; increased stomach acid; reduced brain and nervous system activity; loss of appetite and physical endurance.

Short-term effects (nicotine): Vomiting, physical weakness, rapid but weak pulse, increased stomach acid, psychological dependence.

Long-term effects: Narrow, hardened blood vessels in brain; respiratory infection; cancer of the lungs, mouth, larynx, esophagus, bladder, kidney, and pancreas; ulcers; shortness in breath; emphysema; physical and psychological dependence; possible death.

Long-term effects (nicotine): Nausea, indigestion, high blood pressure, circulation disorders, ulcers, heart failure, possible death.

Withdrawal syndrome: Anxiety, nervousness, increase in appetite, nausea, headache, diarrhea, drowsiness, fatigue, insomnia.

Medical uses: None

Tobacco Graphic Illustration Summary

Figure 1.   The health consequences causally linked to smoking and exposure to secondhand smoke

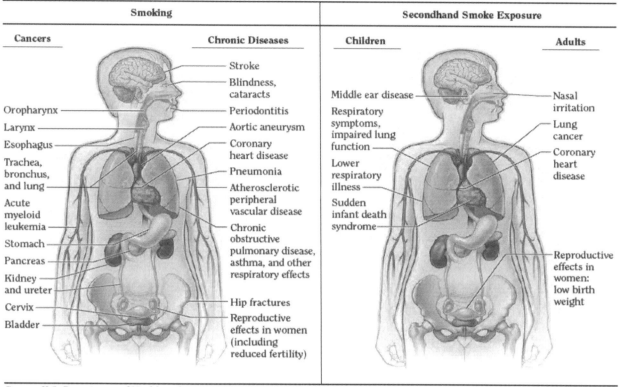

Source: U.S. Department of Health and Human Services 2004, 2006.

Summary

Tobacco users are drug addicts. They need help to overcome their addiction just like any other drug addict. Society needs to focus on prevention methods to not allow the tobacco companies to target kids and youth to purchase their toxic substance. The role that teachers and schools play is indeed, significant. People of different color, immigrants and those with tobacco related cultural beliefs can adjust to the American way of living a tobacco free life. Women need to be especially cautious not to use tobacco products, or to inhale chemicals from second hand smoke that can be very deleterious to their babies. Kids will listen, watch and emulate their teachers and parents. Administrators, teachers, and all support staff need to set an example for impressionable youth. Smoking kills and is a habit that should not be started by young people. Hopefully all of society will take the example planned for California schools. Ban all tobacco use indoors and provide a clean environment for everyone to breathe, especially the kids. California can serve as a powerful guide to other states and reduce all smoking of young people.

Chapter 6

Alcohol Prevention

*To teach is to touch the heart
and impel it to action.
...Louis H Sullivan, American Architect*

No one knows when beverage alcohol was first consumed, but it was probably the result of an accident that occurred more than ten thousand years ago. The discovery of beer jugs in late Stone Age has established the fact that intentionally fermented beverages existed at least as early as the Neolithic period, about 10,000 B.C. (Patrick, 1952). Wine clearly has been recorded as a finished product in Egyptian pictographs around 4,000 B.C. (Lucia, 1963). Hence, from the time an ancient Greek carried an animal skin sac filled with fermenting grape juice across the terrain, until today, alcohol has been enjoyed, abused and served as a source of entertainment to millions of humans throughout the world. European countries such as Italy and France, for example, routinely consume alcohol in religious ceremonies, and to accompany meals. American ships are christened with champagne, and even the president of the United States salutes the world with a champagne toast for various events. American sporting events, nationally televised programs and public meetings use alcohol as an every day form of enjoyment, recreation and socialization. Unfortunately, many alcoholics suffer chronic illness; many become addicted as teenagers, and have alcohol abuse distort their lives. Regardless of the age at the onset of the illness, millions of families are destroyed each year by alcohol abuse.

Historians Mark Lender and James Kirby (1982) report in *Drinking in America*, that most Americans have become ambivalent about alcohol. Some business workers still worry about the effect of the three-martini lunch, professional athletes feel they may not be able to compete, while drinking, and dieting women and men are worried about gaining weight. Alcohol consumption patterns, however, have changed in recent years with fewer people drinking heavily. In fact, most people do not have a drinking problem and can walk away from a restaurant or bar with their half-filled glass resting on the counter. In the 21st century many business professionals no longer consume large amounts of alcohol at lunch meetings, and would rather take a quick trip to the gym or a walk around the block. The problem arises with small children, some as young as 6-8 years of age, drinking to avoid the pain of a family fight; teenagers binge drinking for the sole purpose of getting drunk; college students over- drinking just to get accepted by the crowd; and mature adults developing lifelong addictions to alcohol which destroys their bodies, families, property financial securities, and communities. (Lender, Kirby, 1982).

Why Drink?

Relaxation is the most common reason to consume alcohol. Alcohol is classified as a central nervous system (CNS) **depressant** and acts to slow down most body functions such as respiration, circulation and nervous system activity. Other reasons people drink include: social ease, celebration, religious ceremony, friendship and romance. The advertising media heavily influences all of these reasons, and others. Similar to the tobacco companies, the alcohol advertisers promote the idea that everyone should drink. They should drink when they are happy, drink when they are sad, drink when they are sexy, drink when they are not sexy, and drink when they want to celebrate a job promotion. Many just drink to promote ethnic pride. Unfortunately, these highly glamorous ads do not properly explain, nor do they warn of the serious dangers of alcohol.

Alcohol: Just Another Drug

Every biologist understands that alcohol is basically the end product of fungi metabolism! Yeast and other organisms are added to grains, cactus, corn, grapes, and flowering hops to cause fermentation. Fermentation is the metabolism of sugar sources (usually glucose) by fungi for the purpose of deriving energy. The "wastes," which are toxic to the cells of these organisms (and all living cells), are collected and distilled in the form of **ethyl alcohol (or ethanol)**, the alcohol used in beverages. These beverages are commonly called whiskey, tequila, rye, wine, beer, wine coolers, and a broad selection of liqueurs of assorted fruity flavors. Ethyl alcohol is found in beer, wine and wine coolers, hard liquor (spirits), cough medicines, and certain other medications. It doesn't really matter how the alcohol is supplied, in a shot of tequila, a glass of wine or in a night time green colored cough syrup, (which often may have as much as 30% alcohol), but rather how it effects each individual user.

Alcohol in History

The Constitution of the United States banned alcohol use by passing the Eighteenth Amendment in 1919. Section 1 of this Amendment states, "After one year from the ratification of this article the manufacture, sale, or transportation of intoxicating liquors within, the importation thereof into, or the exportation thereof from, the United States and all territory subject to the jurisdiction thereof for beverage purposes, is hereby prohibited." The passage of this law opened up the era of organized crime related to the production/manufacture, sale and use of this simple organic compound, **ethyl alcohol.** Americans still found ways to drink, either by visiting back room "speak-easys," or by drinking home brewed concoctions, many of which were toxic and tasted terrible! Eventually, individuals did satisfy the need to relax and socialize with friends, but it wasn't until fifteen years later that alcohol consumption and production again became legal for all U.S. citizens. Prohibition ended in 1933 when the Constitution of the United States was amended with passage of the Twenty-First Amendment, Repeal of Prohibition, which dramatically changed the use of alcohol in America. This law

repealed the eighteenth amendment and again allowed alcohol to flow into bars, restaurants and the homes of adult American citizens. Prohibition was a great public health success during the 1940s and 1950s and did reduce alcohol use in America. (ABC, 1997). The per capita consumption of alcohol since prohibition has dropped throughout the U.S. The social and political problems of prohibition were, of course, a dismal failure resulting in an increase in organized crime and bootlegging.

Ingredients of Alcohol

What is in a drink? Ethyl alcohol is the same regardless of the kind of beverage served. A **drink** is defined as a can of beer (12 oz) a small glass of wine (5 oz) or one shot (1 1/2oz) of distilled spirits, such as vodka, tequila, or whiskey, with 50% alcohol (**100 proof**). Most beer has about 3-6% alcohol, wine 2-4 %, wine coolers 6%, table wines 10-14 % and fortified wines (sherry) 16-20% alcohol. Spirits (whiskey, rum, tequila, etc.), contain the highest amount at 40-60% alcohol. The term "proof" refers to **one-half the percentage** of alcohol in an alcoholic beverage. Thus vodka that is labeled 100 proof would contain 50% alcohol.

Alcohol and Wine Coolers

Recent sales of wine have targeted the youth market. Children and teenagers see commercials about wine coolers and often think of them as glorified soda. Some social scientists even classify wine coolers as 'gateway drugs to wine.' But the advertising does not say much about the addictiveness of wine, nor of the percentages of alcohol in many of the fruity products highly promoted to teens and college age students. Wine coolers became popular in the 1980s and are a combination of wine, fruit juice, and carbonation, and come in a variety of flavors, including strawberry, cherry, apple, and peach. People may think wine coolers are healthy because ads describe them as "light" and "natural," and they emphasize the fruit flavors. However, many **wine coolers actually contain more alcohol than beer** (6% versus 4%).

Alcohol Advertising and Youth-Do the Ads Work on Kids?

A large body of research clearly indicates that, in addition to parents and peers, alcohol advertising and marketing has a significant impact on youth decisions to drink. "While many factors may influence an underage person's drinking decisions, including among other things parents, peers and the media, there is reason to believe that advertising also plays a role." (ABC, 1997). Marketing and advertising methods for alcohol influences youth and adult expectations and attitudes, and helps to create an environment that promotes underage drinking. **Data from a long-term study in January 2006 concluded that greater exposure to alcohol advertising**

contributes to an increase in drinking among underage youth. Specifically, for each additional ad a young person saw (above the monthly youth average of 23), he or she drank 1% more. For each additional dollar per capita spent on alcohol advertising in a local market (above the national average of $6.80 per capita), young people drank 3% more. (CAMY, 2007).

Another study found that, among a group of 2,250 middle-school students in Los Angeles, those who viewed more television programs containing alcohol commercials while in the seventh grade were more likely in the eighth grade to drink beer, wine/liquor, or to drink three or more drinks on at least one occasion during the month prior to the follow-up survey. Additionally, researchers followed 3,111 students in South Dakota from seventh to ninth grade, and found that exposure to in-store beer displays in grade 7 predicted onset of drinking by grade 9, and exposure to magazine advertising for alcohol and to beer concessions at sports or music events predicted frequency of drinking in grade 9. They also found depictions of alcohol use in 92% of 601 contemporary movies, including in 52% of G-rated films. (CAMY, 2007).

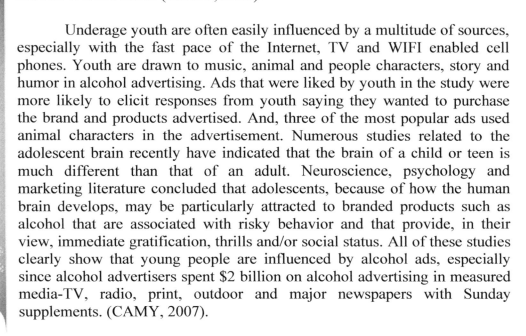

Underage youth are often easily influenced by a multitude of sources, especially with the fast pace of the Internet, TV and WIFI enabled cell phones. Youth are drawn to music, animal and people characters, story and humor in alcohol advertising. Ads that were liked by youth in the study were more likely to elicit responses from youth saying they wanted to purchase the brand and products advertised. And, three of the most popular ads used animal characters in the advertisement. Numerous studies related to the adolescent brain recently have indicated that the brain of a child or teen is much different than that of an adult. Neuroscience, psychology and marketing literature concluded that adolescents, because of how the human brain develops, may be particularly attracted to branded products such as alcohol that are associated with risky behavior and that provide, in their view, immediate gratification, thrills and/or social status. All of these studies clearly show that young people are influenced by alcohol ads, especially since alcohol advertisers spent $2 billion on alcohol advertising in measured media-TV, radio, print, outdoor and major newspapers with Sunday supplements. (CAMY, 2007).

Alcohol is the most commonly used psychoactive substance during adolescence, even though the minimum legal drinking age in the U.S. is 21 years. Alcohol use is associated with motor vehicle crashes, injuries, and deaths; problems in school and the workplace; and fighting, crime, and other activities with serious consequences. Binge alcohol use (binge drinking), in which five or more drinks are consumed on one occasion, and heavy drinking, in which binge drinking occurs on 5 or more days in the past month, increase the likelihood of negative outcomes. In 2005, 28 percent of adolescents 12-20 years of age reported drinking alcohol in the past month. Binge drinking was reported by 19 percent of adolescents and heavy alcohol use was reported by 6 percent. Alcohol use, binge alcohol use, and heavy alcohol use increased significantly between ages 12-13 years and 18-20 years. One-half of all persons 18-20 years of age had used alcohol in the past month and more than one-third reported binge drinking in the past month. Alcohol use varies by race and ethnicity. **In 2005, non-Hispanic white adolescents**

were significantly more likely to engage in alcohol use than were non-Hispanic black adolescents. Adolescents who combine drinking and driving are at an increased risk of injury or death. In 2005, 15 percent of students in the 11th and 12th grades reported driving after drinking alcohol. Adolescents who begin drinking before age 15 are four times as likely to be alcohol dependent as those who delay drinking until at least age 21. (CDC, 2006, 2007).

What Parents and Teens Should Know About Alcohol

The most widely used psychoactive drug in America is alcohol and more than eighty percent of men and women over the age of twelve have tried alcohol. That is nearly three times the number of those that experimented with marijuana. There are more than 18 million alcohol abusers in the U.S. and every year nearly 4 million Americans over the age of twelve undergo treatment for alcoholism and alcohol-related problems. Alcohol contributes to one hundred thousand deaths annually, including most fatal traffic fatalities. Drownings, boating deaths, fatal falls and fire-related deaths can also be traced to the abuse of alcohol. (Healthy Children, 2010). The real tragedy is when parents say, " My kid may be drinking, but at least he is not using drugs." This disconnect of alcohol from drugs brings about many contradictions with parents and their kids and can contribute to abuse of the drug alcohol and possibly lead to other drug abuse.

Kids and Alcohol Abuse

Young people who drink usually start with beer or highly advertised wine coolers that usually have a sweet taste and may be carbonated. Teenagers oftentimes think these drinks are "safer" than hard liquor but usually don't make the connection of alcohol volume and their own biochemical sensitivity to alcohol. A twelve-ounce can of beer and a four-ounce glass of wine both have the same amount of alcohol. Many wine coolers have the same amount of alcohol as beer, and a few have even more alcohol than beer. The alcohol in the wine or beer described is the same as a shot of eighty proof whiskey (40% alcohol) or vodka.

Signs of Alcohol Use for Parents, Teachers

Most adults are familiar with alcohol use but the following behaviors can serve as a reminder when observing students or kids within a given family. Alcohol use includes, slurred speech, impaired judgment, poor coordination, confusion, tremors, drowsiness (remember, alcohol is a depressant drug), agitation, combative behavior, weight gain, nausea, vomiting, smell of alcohol on the breath and the possession of a false I.D. card. Additionally,

- Alcohol is used by more young people in the United States than tobacco or illicit drugs;
- Excessive alcohol consumption is associated with approximately 75,000 deaths per year;
- Alcohol is a factor in approximately 41% of all deaths from motor vehicle crashes;
- Among youth, the use of alcohol and other drugs has been linked to unintentional injuries, physical fights, academic and occupational problems, and illegal behavior;

- Alcohol abuse is associated with liver disease, cancer, cardiovascular disease, and neurological damage as well as psychiatric problems such as depression, anxiety, and antisocial personality disorder; and
- Drug use contributes directly and indirectly to the HIV epidemic, and alcohol and drug use contribute markedly to infant morbidity and mortality. (CDC, 2009c).

Since 1988, all states prohibit the purchase of alcohol by youth under the age of 21 years. Consequently, underage drinking is defined as consuming alcohol prior to the minimum legal drinking age of 21 years. Current alcohol use among high school students remained steady from 1991 to 1999 and then decreased from 50% in 1999 to 42% in 2009. In 2009, 24% of high school students reported episodic heavy or binge drinking. Zero tolerance laws in all states make it illegal for youth under age 21 years to drive with any measurable amount of alcohol in their system (i.e., with a blood alcohol concentration (BAC) $\geq$0.02 g/dL). In 2009, 10% of high school students reported driving a car or other vehicle during the past 30 days when they had been drinking alcohol. In addition, 28% of students reported riding in a car or other vehicle during the past 30 days driven by someone who had been drinking alcohol. (CDC, 2009c)

Consequences of Underage Drinking

Youth who drink alcohol are more likely to experience

- School problems, such as higher absence and poor or failing grades;
- Social problems, such as fighting and lack of participation in youth activities;
- Legal problems, such as arrest for driving or physically hurting someone while drunk;
- Physical problems, such as hangovers or illnesses;
- Unwanted, unplanned, and unprotected sexual activity;
- Disruption of normal growth and sexual development;
- Physical and sexual assault;
- Higher risk for suicide and homicide;
- Alcohol-related car crashes and other unintentional injuries, such as burns, falls, and drowning;
- Memory problems;
- Abuse of other drugs;
- Changes in brain development that may have life-long effects; and
- Death from alcohol poisoning.
  (CDC, 2009c).

The Jellinek Curve

The Jellinek Curve below developed in the 1960s, illustrates specific behavioral changes during the progression of alcoholism. See if you recognize any of the signs in family members, students, friends or loved ones abusing alcohol. (Jellinek, 2010).

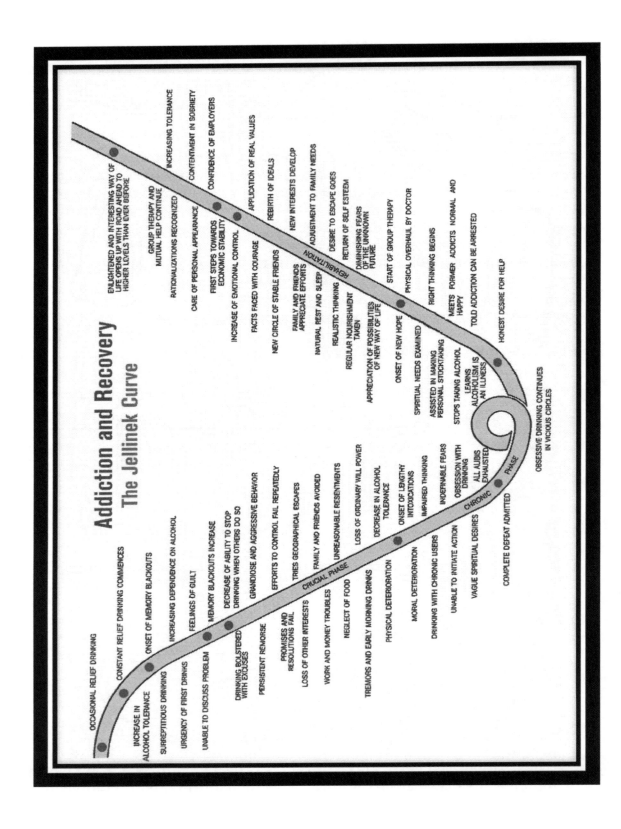

Women and Alcohol

Women's pattern of drinking are often quite different then men's, especially when considering the type of beverage, and frequency of consumption. Women's bodies react biochemically much differently than men in the metabolism of alcohol. Women have more body fat then men, slower metabolic rates and less of a stomach enzyme to metabolize alcohol. Since alcohol is stored in body fat, women burn off the alcohol more slowly and as a result are more susceptible to alcohol's health risks. Alcohol risks to women include a greater likelihood to alcoholic hepatitis (inflammation of the liver) heart disease among heavy drinkers, breast cancer and significant problems during pregnancy as described under Fetal Alcohol Spectrum Disorders (FASD) below. It is important to remember that when a woman is drinking a cocktail with fruit and other mixers, she is still consuming an ounce or more of liquor.

Physiology, Behavior, of Alcohol and Women

The comment of former First Lady Betty Ford, Rancho Mirage, CA, April 1995 stated, "Today we know that when a woman abuses alcohol or other drugs, the risk to her health is much greater than it is for a man. Yet there is not enough prevention, intervention, and treatment targeting women. It is still much harder for women to get help. That needs to change." **Women and teens have a greater percentage of body fat, less of a stomach enzyme to metabolize alcohol and have less water in their bodies.** These factors and several others increase the risk of alcohol abuse among women. Teen girls, as is true of all adolescents, do not have the same metabolic functioning systems or biochemical patterns as those of adults. That is why in many states, the blood alcohol content (BAC) for teens while driving is nearly zero (0.01 %). Drinking patterns in women start very early and place them at risk for:

- sexual assault;
- unprotected sex;
- breast cancer;
- violent victimization;
- traffic crashes;
- STDs, including HIV/AIDS;
- intravenous Drug Use (IVDU) use while under the influence of alcohol;
- lifetime alcohol dependence;
- domestic violence;
- cirrhosis of the liver;
- liver and brain damage;
- using cigarettes, cocaine, crack, inhalants; and
- menstrual irregularities. (USDHHS, 1993; NIAAA, 2008).

Fetal Alcohol Spectrum Disorders (FASD)

Since the 1970s, the effect of alcohol on the unborn has been widely publicized. Alcoholic beverages are so common in America, that ethyl alcohol (ethanol) is usually not thought of as a drug. Ethanol in drinks acts as a central nervous system depressant just as illegal depressant drugs do. Yet each year, women deliver babies who are addicted to alcohol and often suffer a myriad of birth related defects referred to as Fetal Alcohol Syndrome (FAS). Fortunately, FAS is **100% preventable.** Numerous studies indicate that alcohol acts as a toxic **teratogen** (chemical or substance that causes defects *in utereo*). (Jones, 1973, Carmona, 2005). When a woman drinks while she is pregnant, alcohol passes swiftly through the placenta to her unborn baby. The immature liver of a baby does not breakdown alcohol as adult liver cells would. **As a result, the alcohol level in the fetuses' blood can be higher than that in the mothers' blood -- and can remain for a longer period of time, causing the baby to suffer lifelong damage before it is born.** (Clarren, 1987).

Former U.S. Surgeon General Dr. Richard Carmona published new information related to alcohol and pregnancy in 2005 with a new medical classification, **Fetal Alcohol Spectrum Disorder (FASD).** FASD is the full spectrum of birth defects caused by prenatal alcohol exposure. The spectrum may include mild and subtle changes, such as a slight learning disability and/or physical abnormality, through full-blown **Fetal Alcohol Syndrome (FAS),** which can include severe learning disabilities, growth deficiencies, abnormal facial features, and central nervous system disorders. The 2005 press release updated a 1981 Surgeon General's Advisory that suggested that pregnant women limit the amount of alcohol they drink. "We must prevent all injury and illness that is preventable in society, and alcohol-related birth defects are completely preventable," Dr. Carmona said. "We do not know what, if any, amount of alcohol is safe. But we do know that the risk of a baby being born with any of the fetal alcohol spectrum disorders increases with the amount of alcohol a pregnant woman drinks, as does the likely severity of the condition. And when a pregnant woman drinks alcohol, so does her baby. **Therefore, it's in the child's best interest for a pregnant woman to simply not drink alcohol."** Additional studies indicate that a baby could be affected by alcohol consumption within the earliest weeks after conception, even before a woman knows that she is pregnant. For that reason, the Surgeon General is recommending that women who may become pregnant also abstain from alcohol. (Carmona, 2005).

Nearly forty years ago, U.S. researchers first recognized **fetal alcohol syndrome (FAS).** FAS is characterized by growth deficiencies (or decreased growth), abnormal facial features (specific facial features), and central nervous system (or brain) abnormalities. FAS falls under the spectrum of adverse outcomes caused by prenatal alcohol exposure called Fetal Alcohol Spectrum Disorders (FASD). The discovery of FAS led to considerable public education and awareness initiatives informing women to limit the amount of alcohol they consume while pregnant. But since the 1970s, much more has been learned about the effects of alcohol on a fetus. **It is now clear that no amount of alcohol can be considered safe.** The Surgeon General explains to prospective parents, healthcare practitioners, and all childbearing-aged women, especially those who are pregnant, the importance of not drinking alcohol if a woman is pregnant or considering becoming pregnant. The diagram on pages 135-136 illustrates a child with FAS. (Jones, 1973; Carmona, 2005).

Fetal alcohol syndrome (FAS) is one of the most common, preventable causes of mental retardation in the world today. It may occur as often as Down's syndrome and neural tube defects. FAS is estimated to occur in one to three cases per 1,000 individuals. **Research indicates that up to 50% of children born to chronic alcoholic mothers show some signs of fetal alcohol syndrome. (CDC, 2011b).** Although geographic and cultural differences affect the amount of alcohol a pregnant woman drinks, FAS occurs in all races and is more often a problem in developed countries.

Some common characteristics of FASD are:

- Facial abnormalities like telecanthus, where there is an increased distance between the inner corners of the eyes, and a thin upper lip;
- Mild to severe mental retardation resulting in learning difficulties;
- Low birth weight and height that persists through early childhood;
- Abnormalities of the heart and other organs. Abnormal facial features, such as a smooth ridge between the nose and upper lip (this ridge is called the philtrum);
- Small head size;
- Shorter-than-average height;
- Low body weight;
- Poor coordination;
- Hyperactive behavior;
- Difficulty paying attention;
- Poor memory;
- Difficulty in school (especially with math);
- Learning disabilities;
- Speech and language delays;
- Intellectual disability or low IQ;
- Poor reasoning and judgment skills;
- Sleep and sucking problems as a baby;
- Vision or hearing problems; and
- Problems with the heart, kidneys, or bones.
(CDC, 2011b).

Eye doctors are interested in FAS because of the frequent involvement of the eyes, which may cause significant visual impairment in children. The ability to see detail (visual acuity) is reduced in over 50 percent of children with FAS. Some problems such as near-or-farsightedness can be corrected with eyeglasses. Other problems that are caused by abnormal or incomplete development of the eye during pregnancy can result in a permanent reduction of vision. For example, the optic nerve may be small or abnormally developed, causing vision impairment. Strabismus (improper alignment or 'crossed eyes') is present in 25 to 50 percent of children with FAS. Some other possible problems include cataracts (clouding of the lens) and nystagmus (involuntary rapid movements of the eye).

There are also no lab tests to indicate FAS. Unlike cocaine, where tests can show whether the drug was taken in the past, the physician has no test to perform that would reveal a mother's drinking habits. Suspicions may be aroused if the mother was drunk at prenatal visits or when she delivered. The only way to diagnose FAS is to find the characteristic signs and symptoms and discover a history of drinking during pregnancy. Many women will not admit to excessive drinking while pregnant. Drinking six average drinks per day puts a fetus at definite risk to develop FAS. The amount of alcohol consumption that can lead to FAS cannot be anticipated; however, regular alcohol consumption is believed to cause an increase in fetal abnormalities. **Although an occasional drink has not been proven to have harmful effects on the fetus, most obstetricians advise no alcohol during pregnancy.** Based on the current, best science available we now know the following: (1) Alcohol consumed during pregnancy increases the risk of alcohol related birth defects, including growth deficiencies, facial abnormalities, central nervous system impairment, behavioral disorders, and impaired intellectual development. (2) **No amount of alcohol consumption can be considered safe during pregnancy.** (3) Alcohol can damage a fetus at any stage of pregnancy. Damage can occur in the earliest weeks of pregnancy, even before a woman knows that she is pregnant. (4) The cognitive deficits and behavioral problems resulting from prenatal alcohol exposure are lifelong, and most importantly (5) Alcohol-related birth defects are completely preventable. FAS is especially important to teen girls who may be experimenting with sex, have irregular menstrual periods and often are in total denial that they could be pregnant! For these reasons:

- **A pregnant woman should not drink alcohol during pregnancy**;
- A pregnant woman who has already consumed alcohol during her pregnancy should stop in order to minimize further risk;
- A woman who is considering becoming pregnant should abstain from alcohol;
- Recognizing that nearly half of all births in the United States are unplanned, women of child-bearing age should consult their physician and take steps to reduce the possibility of prenatal alcohol exposure; and
- Health professionals should inquire routinely about alcohol consumption by women of childbearing age, inform them of the risks of alcohol consumption during pregnancy, and advise them not to drink alcoholic beverages during pregnancy. (Carmona, 2005; CDC, 2011).

In the United States, FAS is the leading preventable birth defect with associated mental and behavioral impairment. There are many individuals exposed to prenatal alcohol who, while not exhibiting all of the characteristic features of FAS, do manifest lifelong neurocognitive and behavioral problems arising from this early alcohol exposure. In the United States, the prevalence of FAS is between 0.5 to 2 cases per 1,000 births. It is estimated that for every child born with FAS, three additional children are born who may not have the physical characteristics, such as facial abnormalities of FAS, but still experience neurobehavioral deficits resulting from prenatal alcohol exposure that affect learning and behavior. This is called the **Fetal Alcohol Effect (FAE).** Classroom teachers may have many hyperactive children in the class and have no idea that they may be FAE children.

The outcomes attributable to prenatal alcohol exposure for the children of **women whose alcohol consumption averages seven to 14 drinks per week** include deficits in growth, behavior, and neurocognition such as problems in arithmetic (sequencing ability), language and memory; visual-spatial abilities; attention; and deficits in speed of information processing. Patterns of exposure known to place a fetus at greatest risk include binge drinking, defined as having five or more drinks at one time, and drinking seven or more drinks per week, oftentimes a very common teenage alcohol abuse behavior. (Carmona, 2005).

Even though public health officials have been warning women about FAS for decades, recent data indicate that significant numbers of women continue to drink during pregnancy, many in a high-risk manner that places the fetus at risk for a broad range of problems arising from prenatal alcohol exposure including fetal alcohol syndrome. For example, data suggest that rates of binge drinking and drinking seven or more drinks per week among both pregnant women and non-pregnant women of childbearing age have not declined in recent years. Many women who know they are pregnant report drinking at these levels. Additionally, recent analysis of obstetrical textbooks suggests that physicians may not be receiving adequate instruction in the dangers of prenatal alcohol exposure. **The American College of Obstetricians and Gynecologists advises against drinking at all during pregnancy.** Nevertheless, **only 24 percent of obstetrical textbooks published since 1990 recommended abstinence during pregnancy, despite 30 years of research since the first publications proposed a link between alcohol exposure and birth defects.** Scientific evidence amassed in these decades has fortified the rationale for the original advisory against alcohol consumption during pregnancy. Continuing research has generated a wealth of new knowledge on the nature of fetal alcohol-induced injury, the underlying mechanisms of damage, concurrent risk factors, and the clinical distinction of alcohol-related deficits from other disorders. (Carmona, 2005).

FAS and FAE

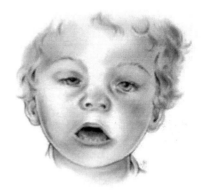

Babies born with FAS are abnormally small at birth and usually do not catch up as they get older. In most cases, they have small eyes, a short, upturned nose, and small flat cheeks. Many of their organs may not form properly, especially the heart. **Most babies with FAS have small brains and some degree of mental retardation.** Many babies are poorly coordinated, have short attention spans and exhibit behavioral problems. Mothers nursing babies with FAS have found it difficult to get them to feed because they were not able to concentrate on both the stimulus of the nipple and the eyes of the mother while she looked at the baby to form a mother-child bond. Drinking moderate amounts of alcohol (between two and five drinks daily) during pregnancy can also damage the fetus. These children are born with **fetal alcohol effects (FAE)**, which are characterized by some, but not all of the birth defects associated with FAS. It is estimated that nearly 50,000 babies are born each year with evidence of FAE. In addition to causing birth defects, drinking alcohol during pregnancy increases the risk of miscarriage, stillbirth and death in early infancy. Miscarriage in the fourth to sixth month of pregnancy is two to four times more likely among drinkers than in non-drinkers. **Babies of heavy drinkers also are two to three times more likely to die during the perinatal period (from the 28th week of**

gestation through the first week after birth) than babies of non-drinkers. (March of Dimes, 1990).

Teenagers are at particular risk. Adolescent females often have unprotected sex under the influence of alcohol, become pregnant, or become victims of sexual assault or STD, and may totally deny that they are pregnant during the first trimester. The fetal development of embryonic tissues, especially the central nervous system, can be profoundly affected by teenage binge drinking. Teenage girls frequently have irregular periods and may not even know they are pregnant! Continuous consumption of alcohol during this critical time can cause mental retardation. When FAS kids enroll in school, they become an additional burden on teachers, often require special educational support, and create a drain on the school budget and other resources, costing taxpayers millions of dollars-**just because a woman chose to drink alcohol while pregnant**. Finally, if a woman believes that her baby 'came out fine,' after delivery. Even though she drank 'just a little,' and later notices very slight behavioral problems, i.e., slower learning, or other subtle school related difficulties; her child may be suffering FAE. To learn more about FASDs as they relate to teachers, Google the CDC link "FASD."

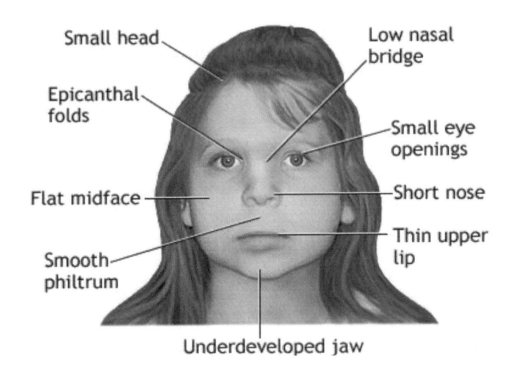

Alcohol and children

An estimated 6.6 million children under the age of 18 years live in households with at least one alcoholic parent. Current research findings suggest that these children are at risk for a range of cognitive, emotional, and behavioral problems. In addition, genetic studies indicate that alcoholism tends to run in families and that a genetic vulnerability for alcoholism exists. Yet, some investigators also report that many children from alcoholic homes develop neither psychopathology nor alcoholism. Many questions concerning children of alcoholics (COAs) still need to be addressed. They include: 1) What contributes to resilience in some COAs? 2) Do COAs differ from children of non-alcoholic (non-COAs)? 3) Are the differences specifically related to parental alcoholism, or are they similar to characteristics observed in children whose parents have other illnesses? School-aged children of alcoholic parents often have academic problems. School records indicate that COAs experience such academic difficulties as repeating grades, failing to graduate from high school, and requiring referrals to school psychologists. Although cognitive deficits in COAs may account, in part, for their poor academic performance, motivational difficulties or the stress of the home environment also may significantly contribute to their problems in school.

Studies comparing COAs with non-COAs also have found that parental alcoholism is linked to a number of psychological disorders in children. Divorce, parental anxiety or affective disorders, or undesirable changes in the family or in life situations, can add to the negative effect of parental alcoholism on children's emotional functioning. Children from alcoholic families report higher levels of depression and anxiety and exhibit more symptoms of low self-esteem, than do children from nonalcoholic families. Research on COAs is still in its infancy, but many studies suggest that a variety of differences exist between children of alcoholics and children of non-alcoholics and these differences occur at all ages. However, it is undeniable that the power of parental modeling profoundly influences the drinking behaviors of children. (NIAAA, 2007). Considerable research on COAs has been done in the recent past. Readers should contact the National Institute of Health website for current information related to COAs and schools. The URL link is: **http://pubs.niaaa.nih.gov.**

Alcohol Use is Down

According to Dr. David Hanson, teen drinking is on the decline in a number of categories. Hanson states, "government and university research repeatedly demonstrates dramatic declines in underage consumption rates." Additionally,

- The proportion of high school seniors who have ever consumed alcohol is down. The proportion of high school seniors who have consumed alcohol within previous year is down;
- The proportion of high school seniors who have consumed alcohol within previous 30 days is down;
- The proportion of high school seniors who have recently consumed alcohol daily is down;
- The proportion of high school seniors who have consumed 5 or more drinks on an occasion within the previous two weeks is down;

- Drinking among young people continues to drop. **For example, the proportion of young people aged 12 through 17 who have consumed any alcohol during the previous month has plummeted from 50% in 1979 to 17.6 in 2002,** according to the federal government's annual National Survey on Drug Use and Health. Thus, while one in two were drinkers in 1979, fewer than one in five were in 2006, the most recent year for which statistics are available; and
- College student drinking attracts much attention in the press. But the proportion of college freshmen that drink continues to decrease. Freshmen entering college in 2003 reported the lowest rates of drinking in the 38-year history of the national college Freshman Survey. The proportion reporting occasional or frequent beer drinking dropped to an historic low of 44.8%, down from 73.7% in 1982. Consumption of both wine and distilled spirits also dropped to a record low. (Hanson, 2005; CDC, 2009). The graph (Fig. 2) below compares binge drinking of youth and adults. (CDC, 2009).

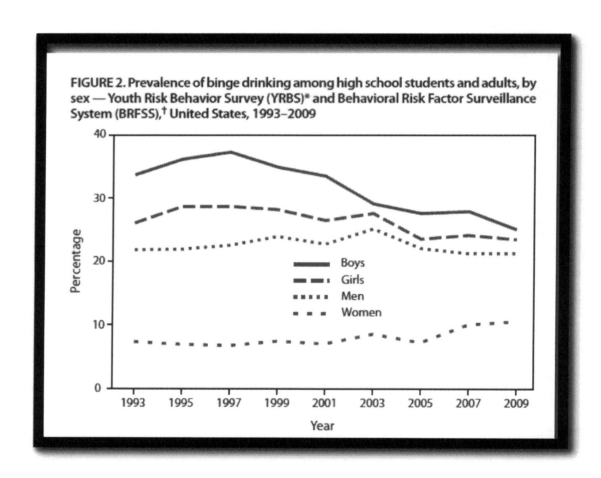

FIGURE 2. Prevalence of binge drinking among high school students and adults, by sex — Youth Risk Behavior Survey (YRBS)* and Behavioral Risk Factor Surveillance System (BRFSS),[†] United States, 1993–2009

Alcohol and the Body

Alcohol is a simple organic molecule that is readily absorbed in the mouth. Alcohol immediately goes to the brain and functions as a CNS depressant. It is wise for people serving alcohol to use food to absorb alcohol and slow down the time necessary to cause behavioral problems. After alcohol enters the stomach, it is metabolized by several body systems and excess alcohol may then appear in the blood. This volume of alcohol in the blood is measured as **blood alcohol content (BAC)**.

Effects of Blood Alcohol Content (BAC)

Some individuals may tolerate alcohol better than others as a result of individual physiology and the presence of specific enzymes. For most people, however, the levels of alcohol consumption as measured in the blood will have definite effects on the body and mind. At the **0.1% BAC** level, alcohol dulls intelligence, sensory perceptions and motor skills. It also encourages false confidence and bragging, increases talkativeness and activity, and lowers inhibitions. At **0.2% BAC,** alcohol inhibits clear thinking, impairs memory, slows movement, encourages bursts of anger, weeping, or excitement, inhibits balance, and walking a straight line becomes difficult. At **0.3% BAC,** alcohol impairs function of all sense organs, slurs speech, may cause double vision and staggering, inhibits judgment of distances, and encourages sudden and exaggerated mood shifts. At **0.4% BAC,** it may cause severe reduction in nervous and mental functions, greatly inhibit control of body movements, and stimulate uncontrollable vomiting and urination. This can lead to unconsciousness. At **0.5% BAC**, alcohol will bring on life threatening results affecting the medulla of the brain. It usually causes unconsciousness, or little or no reflexes, severely reduces blood pressure, breathing and heartbeat and inactivates brain function. **Over 0.5% usually causes death.** California law sets a BAC level of 0.08% for adults and 0.01% for minors. A measure of 0.01% is a very small amount of alcohol, perhaps one drink for an average to small teenager. **The biochemical systems of teenagers, especially in the brain, are not fully developed during adolescence and teens can become addicted to alcohol in a time span as short as 3 months to one year i.e., from Halloween in October to the Prom Dance in June!**

Other problems related to alcohol include:

- **Short-term effects.** Alcohol initially causes relaxation, loss of inhibitions, impaired coordination, slowed reflexes and mental capacity, attitude changes, poor judgment, respiratory suppression, and possible death;
- **Long-term effects.** Alcohol causes damaged liver, digestive disorders, brain and nerve damage, reduced sex hormone production (particularly in males), and physical and psychological dependence; and
- **Withdrawal syndrome.** Alcohol withdrawal includes shakiness, seizures, and hallucinations (usually occurring within 6 to 48 hours after the last drink), as well as delirium tremens (DTs). (NIAAA, 2008).

What about Red Wine and Health?

During the 1990s popular press magazines, especially those with ads from the wine industry, promoted the use of wine for good health. Is it true that a glass of Pinot Noir can make your heart work better, or lower your risk for heart disease? It remains unclear whether components in wine or the heart-healthy lifestyles of wine lovers are behind this boost in cardiac protection, according to researchers writing in the January 23, 2001 issue of *Circulation*, a journal of the American Heart Association (AHA).  Most medical doctors downplay the potential heart-healthy effects of red wine and encourage patients to exercise and eat more fruits and vegetables. **Wine drinkers, for example, tend to be thinner, non-smokers, educated, exercise more and drink with meals, all of which may help remove artery-clogging fats from their bloodstreams.** (Goldberg, Mosca, Piano, 2001).

And drinking too much wine-or any alcoholic beverage-has a definite down side. Numerous studies suggest that consuming more than two drinks a day over the long term can raise blood pressure in some people and increase the risk for stroke and other diseases. Goldberg and colleagues write, "Alcohol is an addictive substance and adverse effects of drinking occur at more moderate levels in some individuals," Goldberg serves on the American Health Association (AHA) nutrition committee. (Banks, 2000; Health Central, 2001). For most people, moderate drinking of wine or other alcoholic beverages may have some beneficial health effects. Studies have suggested that up to two drinks a day can raise levels of HDL ("good") cholesterol. Other research indicates that antioxidants, compounds in the blood that counteract cell-damaging free radicals, may protect against heart disease.

But exercise can boost HDL levels even more, and fruits and vegetables contain even greater amounts of antioxidants than a glass of red wine. What's more, the notion that antioxidants, such as vitamin E taken as supplements, can protect against heart disease has come under fire, as recent studies have failed to demonstrate these so-called protective effects. "We want to make clear that there are other risk-reduction options that are well-documented and free of the potential hazards associated with alcohol," Goldberg, from Columbia University in New York City, said in a statement from the AHA." "If you want to reduce your risk of heart disease, talk to your doctor about lowering your cholesterol and blood pressure, controlling you weight, getting enough exercise and following a healthy diet." **The panel concluded that while moderate drinking may not pose significant health risks to most people, there is no scientific basis on which to recommend that people consume red wine!**

Alcohol, Sex and Youth Under the Influence

Recent studies suggest a direct association between alcohol and other drug abuse and risky sexual behavior. The Tenth Special Report to the U.S. Congress on Alcohol and Health also determined that substance abuse may impair an adolescent's ability to make clear judgments about sexual activity and contraception. These factors place youth at greater risk for sexual assault, unplanned pregnancy and STDs, including HIV/AIDS. (Inspector General, 1992), (ABC, 2000). While researchers have been able to establish the link between injection drug use (IDU) and transmission of the AIDS virus, less is known about the role of alcohol abuse and sexual behavior that may lead to STDs and AIDS. The combination of alcohol and other drugs also weakens the immune system, thereby increasing susceptibility to infection and disease, especially viral infections such as HIV and Hepatitis B.

Alcohol and Adolescents

Morrison and colleagues researched the epidemiology and dangers of adolescent alcohol use, as well as society's attitudes toward underage drinking. Even though teen drinking has declined since 2000, **alcohol use is still the number one drug problem among youth in the U.S.**, and primary care physicians stated that the seriousness and prevalence of alcohol use by adolescents is underestimated. **While governmental leaders wage a "war on drugs," alcohol use has escaped the war entirely unscathed.** (Morrison, 1995).

Forney, and colleagues conducted a study on 3,017 students from grades 6, 8, 10 and 12, who completed a questionnaire about alcohol consumption. Two distinct attitudes of acceptable alcohol use emerged. One is the acceptance of alcohol and the other the rejection. Students, which used the school setting as a major source of alcohol information, were well informed and held the most conservative attitudes toward alcohol use. White students were more knowledgeable towards alcohol use; students of color, particularly males and older students had more liberal attitudes towards alcohol use. **It is strongly suggested that alcohol education for teens should also include information on acceptable use, as well as negative aspects of drinking.** (Forney, 1988). Tucker conducted research related to personality traits of adolescent drinkers. The students were enrolled in a health/physical education course with an average age of 15.8 years.

Several statistical tools were used to measure psychological, physical, social and lifestyle variables. Tucker states,

The study results indicate that those who drink are a well-defined subgroup that tends to be more neurotic, extroverted and less sensitive than the non-drinkers. While there were no differences in physical fitness between the groups, drinkers tend to be larger than nondrinkers. It is suggested that high school males who drink are similar in some ways to those who smoke cigarettes. Primary prevention and health promotion efforts should consider the many different aspects of the adolescent alcohol user. (Tucker, 1987).

Alcohol and the Teen Brain

Brain research using magnetic resonance imaging suggests that alcohol impacts the adolescent brain differently than adults. Or, a simply way to state it is the teenage brain is still cooking and not quite done. Thus a blood alcohol of 0.01 as state law requires for minors to be under the under the influence makes scientific sense. Young people are more vulnerable to the effects of alcohol on the part of the brain called the **hippocampus**. The hippocampus regulates working memory and learning. It is believed that heavy use of alcohol and other drugs during the adolescent years can actually lower scores on tests of memory and attention during the early or mid twenties. When youngsters begin drinking before age 15, they are four times more likely to become alcohol-dependent than those that wait until age 21 before drinking. Additionally, teens are more sensitive to the sedative qualities of alcohol (a depressant drug). Teenagers are able to stay awake longer with higher blood alcohol levels than older drinkers. This could explain how teens are exposing themselves to greater cognitive impairment and possible brain damage from the poisoning effect of binge drinking. (McNeely, Blanchard, 2010).

Alcohol and Minorities: "When in America, Do as Americans Do."

Interest in alcohol consumption among minorities has increased in recent years. As many newly immigrating citizens enter America, their behaviors related to the use of tobacco, alcohol and other drugs will be influenced by their acculturation. Researchers Black and Markides conclude that Hispanic women drink more simply by adopting the norms, practices, and values of the larger American society. (Black, Markides, 1993). **Similarly, Hispanic men have a much higher rate of alcoholism than most other ethnic groups in America.** (CDC, 2002).

Mixing Alcohol and Drugs

The combination of alcohol and other drugs can have a synergistic (combined effect of two drugs greater than each drug acting alone), individual allergic reaction, or other serious effect on behavior and physiology. The following list describes possible medical, or behavioral problems resulting from mixing drugs with alcohol.

Tranquilizer: E.g., Thorazine, Miltown, Valium, Librium, Ativan, Serax, Tranxene, Xanax, Equanil, etc., Plus **Alcohol:** causes decreased alertness and judgment can lead to household and auto accidents. An especially dangerous combination— even fatal.

Over-the-counter painkillers: Non-narcotic analgesics such as aspirin, ibuprofen, **Plus Alcohol:** Increases possible irritation and bleeding in the stomach and intestines. Possible liver damage.

Prescription painkillers: Narcotic analgesics such as Vicodin, Demerol, Darvon, codeine and codeine combinations, Dilaudid, Percodan, etc., **Plus Alcohol:** causes reduction of central nervous system functioning can lead to loss of effective breathing and death.

Time-release capsules & coated pills: E.g., Contac, some vitamin preparations, etc., **Plus Alcohol:** Alcohol dissolves the coating so the full dose may be felt immediately, instead of properly delayed.

CNS stimulants: Most diet pills, cocaine, methamphatamine, dexedrine, caffeine, Ritalin, benzedrine, etc., **Plus Alcohol:** The stimulant's effect may give the drinker a false sense of alertness. It does not help an intoxicated person gain control of his or her movements.

Alcohol and Physiology

A lcohol acts as a diuretic, a drug that increases the elimination of fluids from the body, just like drinking too much caffeine. For the average person, alcohol can be metabolized at the **rate of about 1 drink per hour**. However, there is individual variation due to gender and individual physiology. Because of a lower percentage of stomach enzymes, more body fat, and slower metabolism, women cannot tolerate alcohol the same as men. This is true even when adjusting the data for body weight. Certain racial groups such as Native Americans and Asians also do not tolerate alcohol as readily as most other groups. Some people cannot even tolerate one drink of alcohol and may have an allergic or respiratory reaction. This may produce skin rashes, or irregular breathing.

In the digestive tract, the liver must break down alcohol and thus becomes the organ of particular vulnerability from excessive drinking. Chronic drinkers suffer long-term effects such as **fatty liver**, which causes the liver to swell and produce abdominal distention. After many years of drinking, the liver starts to deteriorate and **cirrhosis** or scarring results. Alcohol causes the release of acids in the stomach that contributes to **gastritis**, (inflammation of the stomach), nausea and eventually peptic ulcers (breaks or tears in the stomach wall) and bleeding from the stomach lining. Alcohol abuse also contributes to **acute** and **chronic** gastritis and a severe form of heart disease called **alcoholic cardiomyopathy**, or heart muscle disease, which weakens the heart wall. The effect of alcohol on the heart is especially compounded with the combination of alcohol and smoking addiction. (Elders, 1994; Murkamal, 2008).

Alcohol also causes cancer of the esophagus, varicose veins of the esophagus, pancreatitis, hallucinations, and damage to brain cells. Brain scans have revealed tissue damage and neural function decreases as a result of excessive alcohol use. Alcohol causes weakening of the heart muscle, hypertension, and the inhibition of both white (leucocytes) and red (erythrocytes) blood cell production. (Elders, 1994; CDC. 2011).

Is Alcoholism Genetic?

Although the development of alcoholism seems to depend at least in part on the environment, research evidence reveals an inheritable tendency to develop alcoholism. A genetic predisposition to become addicted to other drugs may be likely, but it has not been as fully researched as the genetic factor in alcohol addiction. Although genetics probably is not related to a person's decision to begin alcohol or other drug use, individuals from families with a history of alcoholism or other drug addictions are now generally considered to be at higher risk. **Studies show that male offspring of parents with histories of alcohol addiction are one-and-a-half to two times more likely to develop alcoholism. Daughters of alcoholic mothers are up to three times more likely.** Recent studies conducted by the National Institute on Alcohol Abuse and Alcoholism (NIAAA) have been able to identify multiple genetic loci on the human genome, for alcohol dependence. As the scientific research gets more definitive, other problems may arise. Who is to decide how to target "genetic alcoholics?" What about the racial, ethnic and gender factors that may arise. Many more questions need to be answered, but the scientific evidence is mounting. (NIAAA, 1983, 1987, 1997,1999, 2007). For the latest details from NIAAA-Alcohol Alert see: **http://pubs.niaaa.nih.gov.**

143

Scientists have known for over three decades that alcoholism runs in families. Adopted children born to alcoholic parents are four times more likely to become alcoholic than those born to non-alcoholic parents, even when their adoptive parents don't drink. And by studying the inheritance of alcoholic traits in identical and non-identical twins, scientists have found genetic risk factors for many features of the disease, including the age when people begin to drink heavily and how much they will drink. Proving a genetic link, however, and distilling out the genes involved is not easy. Alcoholism is a complex disease that is influenced by many different factors. "Rather than there being one gene that makes somebody alcohol dependent, there are probably multiple genes interacting, with each other and environmental factors," says Dr. David Ball, a Senior Lecturer and honorary Consultant Psychiatrist at the Institute of Psychiatry in London. (Cross, 2004).

Alcohol and Crime

Does alcohol cause crime? The evidence is overwhelming. Every year thousands of people are victims of crimes associated with the abuse of alcohol. Alcohol related crimes include the following examples: 68 percent of manslaughter charges; 62 percent of assaults; 52 percent of rapes; 50 percent of spousal abuse cases; 49 percent of all murders; 38 percent of child abuse fatalities; and 20 to 35 percent of suicides.

There is also a correlation between **HIV infection and alcohol use**. Teenagers and young adults under the influence of alcohol, or other drugs, may make decisions related to unprotected sex, or participate in high-risk behavior such as anal sex while drinking. This can lead to unplanned pregnancies and even death from AIDS as a result of HIV infection.

Getting Help and Recovery

One of the best and most widely accepted alcohol treatment programs available throughout the world today is the basic 12-step program developed by **Alcoholics Anonymous (AA)** in 1935. This program has been copied and used by many other organizations as a source of help for millions of people from eating disorders (Overeaters Anonymous) to cocaine addiction (Cocaine Anonymous) and even addictive gambling (Gamblers Anonymous). For millions of people throughout the world, the 12-step program of AA becomes a daily-reinforced regimen to help them manage the disease of alcoholism. The URL for Alcoholics Anonymous (AA) is: http://www.aa.org. The twelve-step program below has been used successfully for more than seventy-five years.

Twelve Steps: Alcoholics Anonymous

1. We admitted we were powerless over alcohol-that our lives had become unmanageable.
2. Came to believe that a Power greater than ourselves could restore us to sanity.
3. Made a decision to turn our will and our lives over to the care of God,

AS WE UNDERSTOOD HIM.

4. Made a searching and fearless moral inventory of ourselves.
5. Admitted to God, to ourselves and to another human being the exact nature of our wrongs.
6. Were entirely ready to have God remove all these defects of character.
7. Humbly asked Him to remove our shortcomings.
8. Made a list of all persons we had harmed, and became willing to make amends to them all.
9. Made direct amends to such people wherever possible, except when to do so would injure them or others.
10. Continued to take personal inventory, and when we were wrong promptly admitted it.
11. Sought through prayer and meditation to improve our conscious contact with God, AS WE UNDERSTOOD HIM, praying only for knowledge of his will for us and the power to carry that out.
12. Having had a spiritual awakening as the result of these steps, we tried to carry this message to alcoholics, and to practice these principles in all our affairs.
    Source: Alcoholics Anonymous (AA).

What Can You Do For Your Loved Ones Who Have Problems With Alcohol?

Actually nothing! Many recovering alcoholics familiar with AA will immediately understand this concept. The only way an alcoholic can start on the road to recovery is to admit that a problem exists. If family members or loved ones try to coerce the addict to get help, it won't last nor will it intrinsically become part of the motivation of the addicted person. Nonetheless, you can try to offer some assistance. If a friend or family member confides in you about alcohol or any other drug problem: **Be understanding.** Listen to the reasons why that person uses drugs or alcohol. **Be firm.** Explain the harm drugs and alcohol can do to a person, and why the user should seek counseling and treatment. **Be supportive.** Help the user find assistance. Provide moral support through the hard times ahead. If a friend or family member confides in you about drug problem, try to avoid:

- Being sarcastic or accusatory;
- Being self-blaming, seeking sympathy for yourself;
- Covering up or make excuses for the person;
- Taking over the person's responsibilities, because that will leave the person with no sense of worth or importance;
- Making emotional appeals, which may increase a user's feelings of guilt; and
- Arguing with a person who is drunk.

Helping Yourself

These strategies can help you and others stay drug-and alcohol-free:

- Become informed about alcohol and other drugs;
- Become aware of the situations in which alcohol and other drug use can occur;
- Develop skills that build healthy relationships, including effective listening skills and skills for helping others feel good about themselves; and
- Become informed about prevention strategies to use at home, including role modeling, peer resistance techniques, and involvement in healthy activities.

Alcohol and Human Lives

Investigators have found that simply raising the price of alcoholic beverages reduces overall consumption. However, a policy to discourage alcohol problems through increased excise taxes on alcoholic beverages has seldom been used. Instead of rising with the rate of inflation, the federal tax on distilled spirits remained unchanged between 1951 and 1985, and the **tax on beer and wine has increased only once in 1993. The previous date for beer and wine excise tax was during the Truman Presidency in 1951**! Researchers have determined that if prices had risen with the rate of inflation, the number of youths who drink beer frequently might have been reduced by 24 percent. In addition, if the Federal beer tax had been adjusted with inflation since 1951, **the number of lives lost in fatal crashes might have been reduced by 15 percent.** The U.S. Congress (HR 1305), with pressure from the alcoholic beverage industry, is still debating about reducing the beer and wine tax to the 1951 levels, which, intern, will cause more deaths.

Problems with Booze?

How do you know if alcohol is a problem in your life? The best definition of an alcoholic is when alcohol becomes a major stumbling block in a person's life. This would include problems with school, work, family, the law or even sexual problems. Read the list below and see if any of these items describe how alcohol has taken over your life, the life of a student, friend or other loved one.

Physical Deterioration:

- Memory lapses, short attention span, difficulty in concentration;
- Poor physical coordination, slurred or incoherent speech;
- Unhealthy appearance, indifference to hygiene and grooming; and
- Bloodshot eyes, dilated pupils.

Dramatic Changes in School Performance:

- Assignments not completed;

- Grades dropping; and
- Increased absenteeism or tardiness.

Changes in Behavior:

- Withdrawal from the family;
- Changes in friends, evasiveness in talking about new ones;
- Increasing and inappropriate anger, hostility, irritability, secretiveness;
- Reduced motivation, energy, self- discipline, self-esteem;
- Diminished interest in extracurricular activities and hobbies;
- Chronic dishonesty (lying, stealing, cheating); and
- Sleeping more than usual and at unusual hours.

Readers should refer to chapter four on risk factors for generalized indicators related to tobacco, alcohol and drug abuse. The problems listed above are very similar and are related to addictive compulsive behavior patterns.

Surgeon General's Call to Action

The U.S. Surgeon General prepared a document, The Surgeon General's Call to Action to Prevent and Reduce Under Aged Drinking, with many specific details describing how to overcome problems with alcohol and especially the abuse of alcohol by young people. The six major goals from this well prepared and informative document include the following points:

- **Goal 1**: Foster changes in American society that facilitate healthy adolescent development and that help prevent and reduce underage drinking.
- **Goal 2:** Engage parents and other caregivers, schools, communities, all levels of government, all social systems that interface with youth, and youth themselves in a coordinated national effort to prevent and reduce underage drinking and its consequences.
- **Goal 3:** Promote an understanding of underage alcohol consumption in the context of human development and maturation that takes into account individual adolescent characteristics as well as environmental, ethnic, cultural, and gender differences.
- **Goal 4:** Conduct additional research on adolescent alcohol use and its relationship to development.
- **Goal 5:** Work to improve public health surveillance on underage drinking and on population based risk factors for this behavior.
- **Goal 6:** Work to ensure that policies at all levels are consistent with the national goal of preventing and reducing underage alcohol consumption.
  (To see the entire Surgeon General's document, Google: Surgeon General's Call to Action).

Where To Get Help

If you drink, use other drugs, or have any kind of chemical dependency, call for help. Do it today! If you or someone you know is having a problem with alcohol or other drugs, the number to call in **California** for referral to a helping agency is **(916) 445-0834.**

Other Resources: The National Every 15 Minutes Organization

> **"Dear Mom and Dad, every fifteen minutes someone in the United States dies from an alcohol related traffic collision, and today I died. I never had the chance to tell you…"**

The preceding statement represents one of the most powerful approaches to prevent youth alcohol abuse. *Every 15 Minutes* is a program presented to schools throughout the nation where students, parents, firefighters, police, and local hospitals role-play the death of a child due to alcohol and driving. This program is much more than a few smashed cars in front of the high school parking lot at winter break. The role-play often uses fire trucks, and even helicopters to dramatize the issue of drinking and driving for kids. Below is a brief summary of the program.

Excerpt from *Every 15 Minutes*:

> During the first day events the 'Grim Reaper' calls students who have been selected from a cross-section of the entire student body out of class. One student is removed from class every 15 minutes. A police officer will immediately enter the classroom to read an obituary which has been written by the 'dead' student's parent(s) - explaining the circumstances of their classmate's demise and the contributions the student has made to the school and the community. A few minutes later, the student will return to class as the 'living dead,' complete with white face make-up, a coroner's tag, and a black Every 15 Minutes T-shirt. From that point on 'victims' will not speak or interact with other students for the remainder of the school day. Simultaneously, uniformed officers will make mock death notifications to the parents of these children at their home, place of employment or business.

> After lunch, a simulated traffic collision will be viewable on the school grounds. Rescue workers will treat injured student participants. These students will experience first hand, the sensations of being involved in a tragic, alcohol-related collision. The coroner will handle fatalities on the scene, while the injured students will be extricated by the jaws-of-life manned by Fire Fighters and Paramedics. Police Officers will investigate, arrest, and book the student 'drunk driver.' Student participants will continue their experience by an actual trip to the morgue, the hospital emergency room, and to the police department jail for the purpose of being booked for 'drunk driving.' **See Every 15 Minutes: www.every15minutes.com.**

Resources for Alcohol Information

Al-Anon Group Family Headquarters: (800) 356-9996: http://www.al-anon.alateen.org/
Provides materials on alcoholism specifically aimed at helping families dealing
with problems of alcoholics (24hrs, 7 days a week).

National Council on Alcoholism: (800) NCA-CALL Provides referrals to local affiliates, and written information on alcoholism (24hrs, 7 days a week).

NIDA Help line: (800) 662-HELP Provides general information on drug abuse and on AIDS as it relates to intravenous users. Referrals offered.

Alcoholics Anonymous: Consult local phone directories or the yellow pages. **Many cities have thousands of meetings of AA almost 24 hours daily.**

As the Internet search functions get even more refined, using Google, or other search engines is a rapid method to locate many of the sources below. If the URLs change, Google the topic desired.

Electronic Sources Related to Substance Abuse:

The following links sources can serve as excellent resources to deal with alcohol abuse.

Alcohol Problems and Solutions: **http://www2.potsdam.edu/hansondj/**
Alcoholics Anonymous: **http://www.aa.org**
American Council on Drug Education **http://www.acde.org**
Campaign for Tobacco Free Kid **http://www.tobaccofreekids.org**
Canadian Centre on Substance Abuse: **http://www.ccsa.ca**
Centers for Disease Control **http://www.cdc.gov/**
Integrated Substance Abuse Program (UCLA): **http://www.uclaisap.org/**
Monitoring the Future Study **http://www.monitoringthefuture.org/**
Mothers Against Drunk Driving: **http://www.madd.org**
Narcotics Anonymous: **http://www.na.org/**
National Institute on Drug Abuse (NIDA): **http://www.nida.nih.gov/**
National Clearing House on Drug Abuse Prevention Research: **http://www.health.org**
National Council on Alcoholism and Drug Dependence: **http://www.ncadd.org/**
Partnership for a Drug Free America: **http://www.drugfree.org/**
US Food and Drug Administration (FDA): **http://www.fda.gov**
World Health Organization Programme
on Substance Abuse: **http://www.who.int/substance_abuse/en/.**

Summary

Since the days of Bacchus, the Greek God of wine, humans have consumed ethyl alcohol. Alcohol abuse has plagued families, cities and complete civilizations for centuries; but the reality today in the U.S. is that most people can consume alcohol products sensibly and carefully. The alcohol beverage industry is a huge organization and strives to promote sales as any business would; but about 10 percent of Americans are at risk for severe problems from alcohol abuse, especially children and ads should not be directed to children. Many national holidays are highly promoted through radio, TV, Internet websites and signs throughout the country. Too often, however, many of these holidays become drinking days and can lead to serious injury and even death, again, especially to children. Pregnant women or women who are planning to become pregnant, must be very cautious and refrain from alcohol use, especially during the entire gestational period. The first trimester is of special concern since that is the time that the developing fetus is vulnerable to the damaging effect of ethyl alcohol. The brain, digestive tract, reproductive organs and the heart can be seriously effected from alcohol absorption in the womb. During the last few decades, overall alcohol consumption has declined in young people, but there still is concern that kids and young adults today may become easily addicted to alcohol, especially if they see alcohol abuse in their families and inherit a genetic predisposition for alcoholism. Numerous organizations are available today, such as alcoholics anonymous, and many other state and national groups to assist the alcohol abuser and their families overcome the devastation caused by a simple organic compound, C_2H_5OH, or ethyl alcohol. Teachers should be especially watchful for signs of alcohol or other drug use within the school setting.

Sober
is
Sexy

Chapter 7

The Minor Players: Stimulants, Depressants, Psychedelics, and Inhalants

It takes a great deal of courage to stand up to your enemies, but even more to stand up to your friends.
...J.K. Rowling

Drug education programs start in the elementary school class, at about the fourth grade. This is the time for drug **prevention**, while the middle school and high school years are the time for drug **intervention**. If a child at the age of 9, 10 or 11 can develop protective factors to prevent the experimentation and ultimate addiction to drugs, the likelihood of abuse is significantly reduced by the time that child reaches 18 or 20. This prevention approach is especially important in kids using inhalants, marijuana and alcohol. But, if experimentation does begin, the younger child may choose to experiment with some type of inhalant. At the high school level, if a full year of health education is required for graduation (as is recommend in the *Health Instructional Framework,* 1994, 2003), the ideal curriculum would require students to enroll in a full semester in ninth and twelfth grades. The ninth grade curriculum reinforces the prevention mode related to drug use that was introduced in middle school. During the twelfth grade, instruction programs help students reinforce and develop refusal skills, and prepare them for an adult life practicing positive healthy behaviors. (CDE, 1994, 2003). This approach will help the teen practice skills as he or she enters adult life after graduation from high school and hopefully avoid drug abuse.

Overview: About Drugs

Drug routes of Administration and Types of Action. Drugs can be introduced into the body in a number of ways. The most common method is by oral ingestion swallowing a tablet, liquid or capsule. It may take up to 30 minutes for drugs to be absorbed by the bloodstream in this fashion. Abusers of drugs are impatient and exhibit addictive compulsive behaviors. Multiple use, especially during the early stage when kids star off by swallowing medications, greatly increases the chances of overdose and possible death. The child may inhale drugs through the nose or mouth, inject them subcutaneously into the skin, or inject them into the veins or muscles. Younger users may simply soak a rag with an inhalant, place it in a bag and draw up the chemical through the mouth and into the lungs. This method is often called '**huffing**.' It is also important for teachers and parents to remember that as kids take so many risks with life, they may just try any 'drug' that they get from a friend with no knowledge whatsoever what is in the pill or capsule.

A given drug may have a different effect with the same person for many reasons. Factors such as body chemistry, body weight, allergic response could dramatically alter the reaction to a given drug. Even identical twins may respond differently to the exact same drug taken the exact same way. Each individual human being has a unique physiology that will differ from any other person. **This is one of the reasons why it is not advised, nor legal, to use another person's prescription medications. Toxicity** is the level at which a drug becomes poisonous to the body. This may cause temporary or permanent damage. When a person drinks a large amount of alcohol, the depressant effects of this drug will induce sleep. But, when the blood alcohol level reaches levels beyond 0.4, death may result. The body eventually breaks down drugs in the liver through a process known as **detoxification**. Detoxification enzymes accomplish the breakdown. The body also can respond to drugs through a process called **tolerance**, which is the ability to withstand a given drug. Alcohol tolerance, for example can increase over time as the liver produces higher and higher levels of enzymes to metabolize **ethyl alcohol.** Over a period of years, however, the liver may become fat and eventually deteriorate as a result of a large volume consumption of alcohol. This condition is known as **cirrhosis** and is discussed in chapter 6. Thus a chronic alcoholic with liver disease will have less tolerance to alcohol after many years of drinking.

Drug interactions can occur with other drugs in four ways **additive, synergistic, potentiating and antagonistic.** (1) An **additive** interaction is one in which the resulting effect is equal to the sum of the effects of the drugs used. (2) **Synergistic interaction** is the result of two or more drugs combining where the total effect is greater than each of the drugs alone. Drinking alcohol and taking sleeping pills may produce a depressant effect four times greater than when pills are taken alone. (3) A drug can also be **potentiating,** that is, one drug will increase the effect of another. For example, alcohol may increase the depressive effect caused by antihistamines. (4) A drug may also be **antagonistic** a tranquilizer such as Valium, may overcome the stimulation from methamphetamine.

Sources of drugs are many. Alcohol can be extracted from grains, flowers and even cactus. Narcotics (opiates) are produced from the opium poppy, cocaine from coca leaves, caffeine from coffee leaves, nicotine from tobacco leaves, and marijuana from the leaves, and stems of the hemp plant, *Cannabis*. Hundreds of other drugs including LSD, PCP, amphetamines, sedatives and tranquilizers can be manufactured or synthesized in the laboratory.

Physical dependence occurs when physiological changes in the cells cause an overpowering and constant need for the drug. If the user does not get a shot, drink, or dose of the drug, the user may develop symptoms of withdrawal. These symptoms may be very severe, involving shaking, convulsions and even death. Alcohol, painkillers, barbiturates, cocaine and narcotics can result in physical dependence. Certain drugs may produce significant behavioral problems for users, but not necessarily cause physical dependence. This is called **psychological dependence,** or habituation that produces a strong craving for a drug because it produces euphoria or relief from stress. Marijuana and hallucinogenic drugs like LSD may not create physical dependence, but continued use can result in psychological dependence.

How do you know if you are "hooked," or addicted, to a drug? Many definitions have been proposed to describe the process of addiction. **One simplified version is, "you are addicted to drug *xyz* if its use becomes a major stumbling block in your life."** A more formalized definition of addiction is a "physiologic or psychological dependence on some chemical agent (e.g., alcohol, nicotine or other drug) with a tendency to increase its use."

Commonly Abused Drugs

Inhalants

An **inhalant** is any substance (not usually a drug) that can be ingested through the nose or mouth by drawing the chemical into the respiratory cavity (usually the lungs). Inhalants are volatile chemicals, i.e., usually organic chemicals that can be made into a gaseous state such as common rubbing alcohol, gasoline, turpentine, carbon tetrachloride, typing correction fluid, and glue. While an asthmatic may need to inhale medication, the drug abuser just wants to alter reality or get stoned. Why would a child want to inhale products such as gasoline fumes to get high? Some kids say for the "buzz," referring to the dizzy or euphoric state they feel when snorting this deadly hydrocarbon solvent. (NIDA, 2004, 2007).

Common Types of Inhalants

Most inhalants are common household products. They include paint thinner, fingernail polish remover, glue, gasoline, cigarette lighter fluid, and nitrous oxide. They also include fluorinated hydrocarbons that are found in aerosols, such as whipped cream, hairspray, spray paint, and computer cleaners. Used as intended, these household products are safe. When these products are sniffed, however, their toxic fumes can produce mind-altering effects. **Inhalants** usually act like depressants, (drugs that slow down the central nervous system (CNS), and act as

psychoactive gases and produce euphoria. Common names of these drugs include: **amyl nitrite** and **butyl nitrite** (rush, locker room, poppers) nitrous **oxide** (or laughing gas, the same gas used by dentists) plus **household products** such as model glue, paint thinner, aerosol sprays, and lighter fluid.

Younger Kids and Inhalants.

Inhalants are often among the first drugs that young children use. One national survey conducted in 2003-2004 found that 2.5 percent of 4th-graders had used inhalants at least once in the year prior to being surveyed. Inhalants also are one of the few substances used by younger children. Yet, inhalant abuse can become chronic and extend into adulthood. Data from national and state surveys suggest that **inhalant abuse is most common among 7th- through 9th-graders.** For example, in the Monitoring the Future study, an annual National Institute on Drug Abuse (NIDA)-supported survey of the Nation's secondary school students, 8th-graders regularly report the highest rate of current, past-year, and lifetime inhalant abuse; 10th- and 12th-graders report less abuse of inhalants. (NIDA, 2004, 2007). Other recent data indicate that adolescent inhalant use is stable overall but rising among girls. Almost 5 percent of girls between the ages of 12 and 17 used an inhalant to get high in 2005, an increase from 4.1 percent in 2002, according to a NIDA. Overall, inhalant use by boys and girls in this age group remained stable over the 4-year period, at an average annual rate of 4.5 percent, or an estimated 1.1 million adolescents. The report, "Patterns and Trends in Inhalant Use by Adolescent Males and Females: 2002-2005," is based on an analysis of the 2002-2005 National Household Survey on Drug Use and Health, an annual survey sponsored by the Substance Abuse and Mental Health Services Administration (SAMHSA). (NSDUH, 2007). "Young people who turn to inhalants may be completely unaware of the serious health risks," said NIDA Deputy Director Dr. Timothy P. Condon. "We know that inhalant abuse can start early, with research suggesting that even preadolescent children seek them out because they are easy to obtain. NIDA research also indicates that those who begin using inhalants at an early age are more likely to become dependent on them—and long-term inhalant abusers are among the most difficult drug abuse patients to treat." (NSDUH, 2007).

The big question is: Why Do Kids Use Inhalants? Many children think inhalants are a harmless, cheap, and quick way to "catch a buzz." The chemicals in the vapors change the way the brain works, making the user feel very good for a short time. While inhalants can be found around the house or purchased inexpensively at the local grocery or general store, kids often don't know that, in some cases, the harmful effects of inhalants can be irreversible. Regular abuse of inhalants can result in serious harm to vital organs in the body, including the brain, heart, kidneys, and liver. The vaporous fumes can change brain chemistry and may permanently damage the brain and central nervous system. They can cause abnormalities in brain areas that are involved in movement and high cognitive function. Frequent, long-term use can cause a permanent change or malfunction of nerves, called **polyneuropathy**. Other symptoms seen by long-term inhalant abusers include weight loss, muscle weakness, disorientation, inattentiveness, uncoordinated movement, irritability, and depression.

How Can Teachers and Parents Tell if Kids Are Abusing Inhalants?

Be observant and look for the following signs of inhalant use: chemical odors on breath or clothing; paint or other stains on face, hands, or clothing; hidden empty paint or solvent containers and chemical-soaked clothing or rags; drunk or disoriented appearance; slurred speech, nausea or loss of appetite, inattentiveness, lack of coordination, irritability, and depression.

Get Help as Soon as Possible if Someone is Using Inhalants

It may be difficult for someone to discover if a child is abusing inhalants; but if someone you know is using inhalants, encourage him or her to talk to a parent, school guidance counselor, or other trusted adult. Many local treatment agencies are available to kids in their school communities. In addition, the Substance Abuse and Mental Health Services Administration's Center for Substance Abuse Treatment (CSAT) has a National Drug and Alcohol Treatment Service that provides free and confidential information on hotlines and counseling services. CSATs toll-free phone number is 1-800-662-4357; treatment centers by state can also be located at **www.findtreatment.samhsa.gov.**

Stimulants

Stimulants represent a large group of chemicals. Some stimulants are found in common beverages like caffeine, others are chewed in certain cultures such as cocaine in the leaf form; and others are extremely addictive such as crack cocaine, and methamphetamine that produces a high within a matter of seconds. Nicotine, discussed in chapter five, is the worst stimulant when one considers that more than one thousand people die each day in the U.S. alone from their addiction to tobacco products. The effect of stimulants on the body is to speed up or "stimulate" nerve activity. Under the influence of stimulants blood pressure rises, heart rate accelerates, blood vessels constrict, the pupils of the eyes and bronchial tubes dilate, and adrenal and gastric secretions increase. Muscular tension increases and sometimes an increase in motor activity results. Anyone who has consumed several cans of soda, or cups of coffee which both contain caffeine, knows the beginning effects of a stimulant. The most commonly used CNS stimulants include **cocaine, amphetamine, caffeine** and **nicotine**, all of which affect the CNS (central nervous system, or the brain and the spinal cord).

Cocaine

Cocaine is derived from the leaves of the coca plant that grows high in the Andes mountains. Cocaine leaves are often chewed by many South Americans for pleasure and to increase endurance. In the 20th century Coca Cola® actually included cocaine as one of its ingredients. Physicians also once used cocaine as a cure for opiate addiction, but as side effects were discovered, this practice stopped. Some doctors still use cocaine as a local or topical anesthetic for various surgical procedures. Similarly, Coca Cola® no longer has cocaine as one of its ingredients because of the potential risk of addiction. During the 1970s and early 1980s cocaine was mostly abused by individuals with money. Today, the powder form of cocaine may cost up to $1000 an ounce, depending upon purity, and thus is usually not commonly used by kids. It was once glamorized as the "champagne" of "recreational drugs," often used by rock stars, gamblers, prostitutes, and even wealthy businessmen and women.

Method of Use: Cocaine can be swallowed and absorbed by the bloodstream, but this would take "too much time" for it to be absorbed. It is usually snorted, sniffed into the nose, or injected intravenously which will cause absorption, within minutes. The most common method for using cocaine for young people is either by "snorting" it in the nose, or by smoking it in the solid or "rock" form. These **rocks** are produced by changing the formulation of cocaine as a powder and then burning the rock. The term **crack** cocaine comes from the sounds made when the rocks are burned. Not only does this form of cocaine get rapidly absorbed into the bloodstream, often within 10 seconds; but it also can be made cheaply and purchased by kids for only a few dollars. A child need only a soda pop can with a hole punched to inhale this potent, highly addictive drug. Some users of crack cocaine become addicted in a matter of a few weeks.

Effects of Cocaine. Some of the physical and psychological effects of cocaine include:

- vasoconstriction (narrowing of the blood vessels);
- soaring overconfidence;
- euphoria, boundless energy, highly aroused state;
- hypertension;
- impaired judgment, hyperactivity, nonstop babbling;
- nausea, seizures, severe loss of appetite and malnutrition;
- impotence and loss of sex drive in men and women;
- suicidal thoughts;
- newborn birth defects, strokes, retardation and sudden infant deaths; and
- cardiac arrhythmias (irregular heart beat) and death from heart attack. (ABC, 1998; NIDA, 2007).

Cocaine Babies

How does cocaine hurt an unborn baby? Cocaine and crack can affect a pregnant woman and her unborn baby in many ways. During the early months of pregnancy it can cause a miscarriage. When the drug is used late in pregnancy, it may trigger labor, or can cause an unborn baby to die, or have a stroke that can cause irreversible brain damage. While the baby is in the womb, cocaine cuts the flow of nutrients and oxygen to the baby, so even if the baby is not premature, it may be much smaller than it would be otherwise. Cocaine use can also cause the placenta to pull away from the wall of the uterus before labor begins. This condition, known as *abruptio placentae,* can lead to extensive bleeding and can be fatal for both the mother and her child.

How does cocaine use during pregnancy affect newborns? Babies exposed to cocaine before birth may start life with serious health problems. Many prenatal and postnatal babies are born too small. Babies born prematurely often have low-birth weight (less than 5.5 pounds). Low-birth weight babies are **40 times more likely to die** in their first month than normal weight babies are. Some babies exposed to cocaine before birth have brain damage. Babies whose mothers used cocaine during pregnancy often score poorly on tests given at birth to assess the newborn's physical condition and overall responsiveness. Cocaine babies also may have neurological and respiratory problems. In some cases, the organs are malformed and many babies are born with missing limbs or suffer from **syndactyl**, a fusion of fingers or toes. (Webster, Brown-Woodman, 2005; NIDA, 2007).

Beginning at birth, these babies go through something similar to "withdrawal" from the drug. They are tremulous and irritable and they startle and cry at the gentlest touch or sound. Consequently, these babies are very difficult to comfort and often are described as withdrawn or unresponsive. Because these babies are so tremulous and hard to comfort, they often are not able to interact with others or to respond to their mothers. The baby's reaction to cocaine, frequently coupled with the mother's continued dependence on the drug, makes bonding between mother and baby difficult. Bonding is critical to a baby's emotional development. The mother has trouble coping with her crying baby and the baby is difficult to comfort. Babies born to women who used drugs during pregnancy are at increased risk for child abuse and neglect. **Cocaine actually destroys the maternal instinct** and mothers have abandoned their infants to get high on cocaine. (Chasnoff, Burns, Schnoll, et al., 1985).

Studies from Case Western University found that children exposed to cocaine before birth were twice as likely to have significant delays in mental skills by age 2, compared to toddlers with similar backgrounds, but whose mothers did not use cocaine. These children had an increased need for special education services when they reached school age. Dr. Glen R. Hanson, Acting NIDA Director, said, "This study adds important new evidence to a growing body of

157

knowledge. It is the first report of a clear-cut relationship between prenatal cocaine and mental test performance at age two. These findings remind us of the importance of continued efforts to determine which children and families are at risk because of exposure to cocaine, so we can prevent or ameliorate negative consequences of using this drug." (Hanson, 2005). Dr. Hanson added, "It is important that in this research process, we avoid inadvertently labeling or stigmatizing large numbers of toddlers because of drug use by their mothers during pregnancy. We want to use this type of research to help us be more effective in how we work with these children." (NIDA, 2002).

Additionally, almost 14 percent of the cocaine-exposed infants had scores in the mental retardation range, 4.89 times higher than expected in the general population. The percentage of children with mild or greater delays was 38 percent; almost double the rate of the non-cocaine-exposed group. Infants of mothers with evidence of higher and more frequent cocaine use during pregnancy fared the worst. Investigator, Dr. Lynn T. Singer said that there are several possible mechanisms by which cocaine exposure during pregnancy may affect infant outcome. "Developing neural systems of the fetal brain may be directly and adversely affected by cocaine exposure. Another possible explanation is that cocaine use during pregnancy may constrict the vascular system, subsequently decreasing blood flow through the placenta and resulting in low oxygen levels (hypoxemia) in the fetus." An estimated 1 million children have been born after fetal cocaine exposure since the mid-1980s, when the so-called crack epidemic emerged with the availability of a cheap, potent, smokable form of cocaine. (NIDA, 2002).

Classroom teachers need to recognize when a child enters school after being a victim of FAS, marijuana or cocaine abuse in utereo, the child will not always become part of the special education population. Many may only suffer mild CNS problems, limited behavioral difficulties or may not even be diagnosed by health professionals at all. Hence, many of these kids will end up in your regular classroom and could become a major disturbance to other children. The social implications of cocaine babies are multiple. There are many questions  that need to be addressed. Should a cocaine-addicted mother be separated from her baby? Should cocaine addicts be prosecuted for child abuse? Who will adopt the cocaine babies? What about the cost to taxpayers of cocaine babies? Will they have to be in special classes in school? Will teachers need special training on how to help children that have been subjected to cocaine? These are difficult questions and they raise many issues. English and social studies teachers may choose to have their students research these questions as a classroom project.

Amphetamines

Amphetamines were widely used in the 50s and 60s as appetite suppressants to help people control weight; but are no longer used for this purpose. Interestingly, the chemical structure of the "diet pills" marketed today has a remarkable similarity to amphetamines. Most of these OTC products for weight control are antihistamines. Common examples of amphetamines are benzedrine, dexedrine, methamphetamine, and others.

Effects of amphetamines are much the same as cocaine, but usually not as severe. They produce increased heartbeat, breathing and blood pressure. Users may also experience dry mouth. Larger doses over a longer period of time, especially with methamphetamine (often called "speed"), can lead to rapid or irregular heartbeat, tremors, and loss of coordination and extreme anxiety. Long-term effects of amphetamines include malnutrition, skin disorders (from injecting) ulcers, and lack of sleep and brain damage that may produce speech and thought disturbances. Very high dosages of amphetamines (100 mg daily or greater, for several weeks) may produce deep sleep. This can last for several days. A user may then become depressed, take more stimulants, "crash," and become depressed again in a viscous cycle of addiction.

Depressants

Depressants, or **hypnotics,** act in the opposite way of stimulants by slowing down the CNS. The most common depressant drug, alcohol, is discussed in chapter 6. Other products have genuine medical uses such as sedation for patients, or sleep inducement for medical reasons. Several kinds of depressants are discussed below. Three major groups of depressants include **(1) opiates (2) barbiturates and (3) tranquilizers.**

Opiates are drugs derived from the opium poppy. The term **narcotic** literally means "sleep inducing." Narcotic use, especially heroin, was the major type of drug abuse in the earlier part of the 20th century. Many other drugs have since been discovered, produced from mushrooms, manufactured in the laboratory, and artificially developed in the form of **designer drugs**. Narcotic drug use represents only a small portion of illegal drug use today since the majority of drug related problems result from tobacco, and alcohol abuse. Opiates are used to relieve pain and help serious coughing, but illegal use of opiates, such as heroin can be devastating to a child or young adult.. Most opiate drugs have beneficial uses in the medical profession. The most common opiate is **codeine** that many people have taken for pain or cough relief, as an **antitussive.** The major use of opiates is as an **analgesic** or pain relieving medicine. Other opiates include paregoric, used as an antidiarrheal, morphine and Demerol, both of which are used for extreme pain, or trauma from surgery and other pain relieving drugs such as oxycodone, and hydrocodone (Vicodin). **Methadone is an opiate used to treat heroin addiction.** Heroin has no medical use. Medical problems associated with the use of opiates include: addiction, secondary infection from contaminated needles, slurred speech, HIV infection, mental clouding, dizziness, nausea, vomiting, apathy, anxiety and fear. These symptoms may vary greatly among different individuals.

159

Barbiturates

Barbiturates, which are used medically for inducing sleep, relaxation, relieving tension and treating epileptic seizures, are usually taken by tablet or capsule. Used in low dosages, barbiturates act like alcohol to produce euphoria and mild intoxication. Excessive use can cause slurred speech, slow respiration, and cold skin, weak and rapid heartbeat. Side effects of barbiturate abuse include drowsiness and impaired judgment and performance. The withdrawal effects, which are similar to alcohol, may last for hours or even days. Many deaths result from the use of barbiturates combined with alcohol. This is an example of two drugs acting **synergistically,** as was discussed earlier in this chapter. Newborn babies of mothers that abused barbiturates may be physically dependent, may develop respiratory distress, have feeding difficulties, may sweat excessively, and act irritably.

Anti-anxiety Medicines

Anti-anxiety medicines have been used for decades in America. Their main purpose is for the relief of muscular strain, and tension. Several kinds are available for doctors to prescribe to their patients. Two of these **benzodiazepines**, Valium and Librium, are the most widely prescribed drugs in the United States. They are absorbed slowly into the bloodstream and take a while to reach the brain. Like barbiturates, high doses of **benzodiazepines** produce slurred speech, drowsiness, and stupor, and long-term use produces psychological and physical dependence. Withdrawal may include psychosis, coma and even death. A recent addition to the list of these abused drugs is a type of benzodiazepine called **Rohypnol or "Roofies."** Roofies are discussed in detail at the end of this chapter. Roofies and **GHB** cause memory loss and both drugs are often used as a date rape drug.

Part of the problem with the use of benzodiazepine is related to role modeling. As a parent forbids a child to use drugs, alcohol or other chemicals; they may also use them, in direct view of their kids, and display hypocritical behavior. **Children are much more impressed by parental behavior than parental words.** Parents that wish to keep their children drug free, should act as role models and remember to look in the mirror and evaluate their own personal practices.

Marijuana

Marijuana or pot as it is also called is the most commonly abused drug in America. Marijuana is a brown mix of flowers, stems, seeds, and leaves derived from the hemp plant *Cannabis sativa*, the botanical name for the weed. The main active chemical in marijuana is Δ 9-tetrahydrocannabinol, or THC for short. Marijuana is sometimes classified as a depressant drug, with mild alterations in perception. Some authors describe marijuana and other cannabis products as having hallucinogenic effects with regular use of three or more joints smoked each week. Most experts now use the NIDA classification of marijuana as a Cannabinoid. (See the

160

NIDA chart at the end of this chapter for detailed classification of commonly abused drugs). Either way, marijuana is a rather unique substance and is widely discussed for its medical applications as well as possible long-term effects. Hashish is an extract from the plant and is 2 to 10 times as concentrated as marijuana. (NIDA, 2010b).

How is Marijuana Abused?

Marijuana is usually smoked in a marijuana a cigarette (called a joint) or inhaled through a pipe or 'bong.' It is often smoked in blunts, which are cigars that have been emptied of tobacco and refilled with a mixture of marijuana and tobacco. This mode of delivery combines marijuana's active ingredients with nicotine and other harmful chemicals. Marijuana can also be mixed in food or brewed as a tea. As a more concentrated, resinous form, it is called hashish; and as a sticky black liquid, hash oil. Marijuana smoke has a pungent and distinctive, usually sweet-and-sour odor.

How Does Marijuana Affect the Brain?

THC in marijuana acts in the brain to produce many effects. When someone smokes marijuana, THC rapidly passes from the lungs into the bloodstream, which carries the chemical to the brain and other organs throughout the body. THC acts upon specific sites in the brain, or specific neurotransmitters called **cannabinoid receptors**, kicking off a series of cellular reactions that ultimately lead to the "high" that users experience when they smoke marijuana. Some brain areas have many cannabinoid receptors; others have few or none. The highest density of cannabinoid receptors are found in parts of the brain that influence pleasure, memory, thinking, concentrating, sensory and time perception, and coordinated movement. This change in the way the brain reacts is the reason that many young people experiment with marijuana for the 'buzz.' Marijuana intoxication can cause distorted perceptions, impaired coordination, difficulty with thinking and problem solving, and problems with learning and memory. Research has shown that, in chronic users, marijuana's adverse impact on learning and memory can last for days or weeks after the acute effects of the drug wear off. **As a result, someone who smokes marijuana every day may be functioning at a suboptimal intellectual level all of the time.** Research into the effects of long-term cannabis use on the structure of the brain has yielded inconsistent results. It may be that the effects are too subtle for reliable detection by current techniques. A similar challenge arises in studies of the effects of chronic marijuana use on brain function. Brain imaging studies in chronic users tend to show some consistent alterations, but their connection to impaired cognitive functioning is far from clear. This uncertainty may arise from other factors such as other drug use, residual drug effects, or withdrawal symptoms in long-term chronic users. (NIDA, 2010b).

Is Marijuana Addictive?

Long-term marijuana abuse can lead to addiction; that is, compulsive drug seeking and abuse despite the known harmful effects upon functioning in the context of family, school, work, and recreational activities. **Estimates from research suggest that about 9 percent of users**

become addicted to marijuana; this number increases among those who start young (to about 17 percent) and among daily users (25-50 percent). (NIDA, 2010b). A few of the problems of quitting marijuana from long term abusers include withdrawal symptoms including: irritability, sleeplessness, decreased appetite, anxiety, and drug craving, all of which can make it difficult to remain abstinent from smoking pot. These symptoms begin within about 1 day following abstinence, peak at 2-3 days, and subside within 1 or 2 weeks following drug cessation.

Marijuana and Mental Health

Many studies have shown an association between chronic marijuana use and increased rates of anxiety, depression, and schizophrenia. Some of these studies have shown age at first use to be an important risk factor, where early use is a marker of increased vulnerability to later problems. However, at this time, it is not clear whether marijuana use causes mental problems, exacerbates them, or reflects an attempt to self-medicate symptoms already in existence. **Chronic marijuana abuse may also be a marker of risk for mental illnesses, including-addiction, stemming from genetic or environmental vulnerabilities, such as early exposure to stress or violence.** Currently, the strongest evidence links marijuana use and schizophrenia and/or related disorders. High doses of marijuana can produce an acute psychotic reaction; in addition, use of the drug may trigger the onset or relapse of schizophrenia in vulnerable individuals. (NIDA, 2010).

Other Adverse Effect of Marijuana on Health?

Marijuana effects the heart by increasing heart rate by 20-100 percent shortly after smoking; this effect can last up to 3 hours. In one study, it was estimated that marijuana users have a 4.8-fold increase in the risk of heart attack in the first hour after smoking the drug. This may be due to increased heart rate as well as the effects of marijuana on heart rhythms, causing palpitations and arrhythmias. This risk may be greater in aging populations or in those with cardiac vulnerabilities. (Mittleman, Lewis, Maclure, et al., 2001).

Effects on the Lungs

Smoking tobacco products cause significant damage to the lungs as described in Chapter 5; and marijuana smoke also causes many of the same effects. Studies have shown marijuana smoke to contain carcinogens and to be an irritant to the lungs, much like tobacco. In fact, **marijuana smoke contains 50-70 percent more carcinogenic hydrocarbons than tobacco smoke.** Marijuana users usually inhale more deeply and hold their breath longer than tobacco smokers do, which further increase the lungs' exposure to carcinogenic smoke. (NIDA, 2010b). Marijuana smokers show dysregulated growth of epithelial cells in their lung tissue, which could lead to cancer; however, a recent case-controlled study found no positive associations between marijuana use and lung, upper respiratory, or upper digestive tract cancers. Thus, the link between marijuana smoking and these cancers remains unsubstantiated at this time. (Hashibe, Morgenstern, Cui, et al., 2006). Nonetheless, marijuana smokers can have many of the same respiratory problems as tobacco smokers, such as daily cough and phlegm production, more frequent acute chest illness, and a heightened risk of lung infections. A study of 450 individuals found that people who smoke marijuana frequently but do not smoke tobacco have more health problems and miss more days of work than nonsmokers. (Polen, Sidney, Tekawa, et al., 1993). Frequent marijuana smokers who do not smoke tobacco often miss more days at work. Respiratory illness accounted for many of the sick days of marijuana smokers. Research clearly demonstrates that marijuana has the potential to cause problems in daily life or make a person's existing problems worse. In one study, heavy marijuana abusers reported that the drug impaired several important measures of life achievement, including physical and mental health, cognitive abilities, social life, and career status. Many studies have associated workers' marijuana smoking with increased tardiness, accidents, and workers' compensation claims. (Gruber, Pope, Hudson, et al., 2003).

Medical Marijuana

The potential medicinal properties of marijuana have been the subject of considerable research and much heated debate. Scientists have confirmed that the cannabis plant contains active ingredients with therapeutic potential for relieving pain, controlling nausea, stimulating appetite, and decreasing ocular pressure. Cannabinoid-based medications include synthetic compounds, such as dronabinol (Marinol®) and nabilone (Cesamet®), which are FDA approved, and a new, chemically pure mixture of plant-derived THC and cannabidiol called Sativex®, formulated as a mouth spray and approved in Canada and parts of Europe for the relief of cancer-associated pain and spasticity and neuropathic pain in multiple sclerosis. Researchers continue to investigate the medicinal properties of THC and other cannabinoids to better evaluate and harness their ability to help patients suffering from a broad range of conditions, while avoiding the adverse effects of smoked marijuana. (NIDA, 2010b). Sadly, however, many cities such as Los Angeles have been plagued by illegal activities of selling marijuana to people without genuine medical needs. For additional **science based** information on marijuana, visit www.marijuana-info.org.

Experimental use of THC has been tried for the treatment of intraocular pressure for glaucoma, pain relief of cancer chemotherapy, insomnia, migraine, depression and epilepsy. Since early 1992, prescription marijuana (THC), has been banned for these medical treatments. By the fall of 1996, however, two states, Arizona and California passed statewide initiatives to legalize the use of marijuana for medical purposes. Since federal law supersedes state law, marijuana is illegal and the controversy and confusion about legalization of the drug for medical use continues to be discussed at state and federal levels. (L.A. Times, 1997). Even though during the late 2000s California and other states have reduced the penalties for possession of small amounts of marijuana, medical experts are warning parents and teachers of the medical problems and recent abrupt rise in marijuana use. Many kids now just think of marijuana as another medicine for people with cancer, or other problems. **Adolescents from eighth grade through the last year of high school are increasingly using marijuana**, according to the latest National Institute on Drug Abuse (NIDA) study of substance use rates. **To the surprise of many, nationwide, daily marijuana use increased from 5.2 percent in 2009 to 6.1 percent in**

163

2010 among high-school seniors, from 2.8 percent to 3.3 percent among 10th-grade students, and from 1 percent to 1.2 percent among eighth-grade students—the three grades surveyed by NIDAs 2010 Monitoring the Future Survey. (Psychiatric News, 2011). Reports in the psychological literature quote doctor Nora Volkow, director of NIDA, that clinicians should encourage parents to talk to their children about the dangers of substance use and counter societal messages that may be leading to increases in marijuana use Doctor Volkow stated, "Young people are particularly vulnerable because of serious short-term effects on developing brains, although its long-term impacts remain uncertain." The serious risk arises when focusing on marijuana abuse by youth with other preexisting psychiatric disorders and early interventions could be critical to disrupting long-term abuse. The 2010 MTF results are based on anonymous survey responses by 46,482 students in 396 public and private schools nationwide. (NIDA, 2010a).

What does "pot" do? One of the problems of marijuana use is the source of the product. Most users buy or obtain a sample of marijuana from another user, friend or drug dealer. Since there is little or no quality control, the user does not know "exactly" what ingredients are being smoked. Marijuana smoke contains more than 400 chemicals, including 61 cannabinoids. Marijuana also has been mixed with a wide variety of dangerous substances including the following: (1) *Aspergilus* fungus which can trigger allergic reactions (2) *Salmonella* bacteria which can cause intestinal infection, diarrhea and fever and (3) **Paraquat**, a herbicide sprayed to destroy pot fields, which may produce irreversible lung damage. Most of the research on THC has been done on Δ 9 THC. THC is only one of the 61 types of cannabinoids found in marijuana. Many of the products are **carcinogenic** (cancer causing), similar to tobacco products. Heavy long-term use leads to bronchitis, and emphysema much like tobacco use.

Marijuana and Babies-Is THC Dangerous?

Research by Hurd and colleagues determined that approximately 4% of women in the USA report using illicit drugs during pregnancy with marijuana (Cannabis sativa) being the most

common (75%) drug used among pregnant women. Hurd found that Δ9-tetrahydrocannabinol (THC, the major psychoactive component of cannabis) **readily crosses the placenta,** and maternal use can potentially affect healthy development in the fetus. **Human studies have in fact documented long-term disturbances in such behaviors as impulsivity, inattention and social disturbances; cognitive functions, e.g., poor visual reasoning and planning as well as verbal skills and memory in offspring of women who used marijuana during pregnancy.** Other accumulated evidence suggests that marijuana-exposed infants at birth have reduced weight and/or head circumference as well as decreased gestational length. Many advances through neuroimaging technologies have been able to disclose these changes in the CNS of the infant. (Hurd, Wang, Anderson, et al, 2006).

164

Does Heavy Pot Smoking Effect Youth? The Residual Cognitive Effects of Heavy Marijuana Use in College Students.

Yurgelun-Todd and colleagues studied 65 heavy users, who had smoked marijuana a median of 29 days in the past 30 days and who also excreted cannabinoids in their urine, and 64 light users, who only smoked a median of 1 day in the last 30 days, and who displayed no urinary cannabinoids. The Results of this research indicated that **heavy users displayed significantly greater impairment than light users** on attentional/executive functions, as evidenced particularly by greater reservations on card sorting and reduced learning of word lists. These differences remained after controlling for potential confounding variables, such as estimated levels of premorbid cognitive functioning, and for use of alcohol and other substances in the two groups.

A brief summary of their conclusions is as follows: According to researchers Yurgelun-Todd and Pope, **"Heavy marijuana use is associated with residual neuro-psychological effects even after a day of supervised abstinence from the drug. However, the question remains open as to whether this impairment is due to a residue of drug in the brain, a withdrawal effect from the drug, or a frank neurotoxic effect of the drug."** (Yurgelun-Todd, Pope, 1996).

Summary Effects of Marijuana. The immediate short-term effects of occasional use of marijuana do not seem to dramatically impact health. But, remember, during the mid-twentieth century cigarettes were considered just an annoying habit. The time factor must be considered related to marijuana research. Most of the extensive research began in the 1970s and the final evidence will not be clear until later in the 21st century, simply because genetic changes, birth defects, immunological effects and other medical problems may not be determined until long term use data analysis is completed. An analogy could be made of the smoker of cigarettes who started in 1930 and died of lung cancer in 1980, a mere 50 years. Nonetheless, the NIDA reports the following effects of THC, both short term and long-term effects. They include:

- memory loss, apathy, slowing of reaction time;
- sensory distortion, panic-anxiety feelings;
- euphoria, slowing down of the time scale;
- lung disorders, bronchitis; schizophrenia and/or related disorders in vulnerable populations;
- immuno-suppression, resistance to disease lowered (raising HIV risk);
- infertility, alters ovulation, sperm production;
- birth defects in babies, such as small head size, poor growth;
- serves as a "Gateway" substance to the use of other drugs;
- increases heart rate, blood pressure; and
- dysregulated growth of epithelial cells in their lung tissue, which could lead to cancer. (NIDA, 2006).

165

Teachers in the school setting should be alert and watch for specific **signs and symptoms** suggestive of marijuana use. Dr. Mark Gold, nationally known author on drug abuse, divides these into four groups: 1) behavioral signs, 2) social signs, 3) circumstantial evidence, and 4) medical symptoms.

Signs and Symptoms Suggestive of Marijuana Use

Behavioral signs

- memory problems
- chronic lying about whereabouts
- sudden disappearance of money or valuables from the home
- suspicious robbery or breaking and entering while family is away
- rapid mood changes
- abusive behavior toward self or others
- panic attacks
- frequent outbursts
- hostility with lack of insight or remorse
- increasing secretiveness

Social Signs

- loss of driver's license
- driving while impaired
- auto accidents
- frequent truancy
- loss of part-time job or problems at work
- under-achievement over the past 6-12 months
- definite deterioration of academic or job-related performance
- dropping out from rigorous sport or other activities
- legal problems, e.g. assaults, thefts, disorderly conduct

Circumstantial evidence

- smell of marijuana on clothes, change in hygiene or attire
- use of drug jargon
- drug or drug paraphernalia found in room, clothes, or vehicle
- whereabouts unknown for more than 36 hours
- drug terminology in school notebooks, or year book inscriptions
- change in friends
- definitive change in peer group to those unmotivated or known users of marijuana

166

Medical symptoms

- chronic fatigue and lethargy
- chronic nausea or vomiting
- chronic dry irritating cough
- chronic sore throat
- chronic unexplained conjunctivitis (pink eye)
- chronic bronchitis
- headaches
- impaired motor skill coordination
- trauma-especially repeated trauma
  (Gold, 1989, 1991, 1993, 1995).

The evidence is still mounting about the long-term effects of marijuana, and only time will answer all the questions. Is marijuana as addicting as other drugs? Will marijuana seriously impact fertility? Are sperm and egg cells altered? Will marijuana reduce the immune response to help one fight off disease? These questions, and numerous other, are still under investigation. Marijuana is still illegal in most states and can cause a user to be associated with the drug subculture, involved with criminal behaviors, and unsafe practices, such as unprotected sexual activity.

Hallucinogens

Hallucinogens include a variety of mind-altering drugs. Examples of hallucinogens include peyote, mescaline, LSD, PCP, and psilocybin. Many of them have been used for thousands of years and are associated with religious uses. Some hallucinogens such as PCP and LSD have only been around since the 1960s. LSD (lysergic acid diethylamide), or **acid**. was synthesized in 1938 and used in research for mental illness. It became popular as an "anti-establishment" drug during the time of the Beatles in the 1960s and 1970s. It is taken in very small amounts, usually on a sugar cube, or blotter paper and can be 1, 000 times more potent than most other abused drugs. This extreme difference can be confusing to drug users and often result in death. Hallucinogens cause alterations of sensory behaviors ranging from mild to very bizarre effects. One person may see double for a few seconds, then imagine the smell of flowers, while another user may suffer blackouts, "bad trips," and severe hallucinations. Some have jumped from buildings, freeway ramps or thrown themselves in front of cars. Flashbacks from LSD, often without any warning, may occur weeks, months or even years after use. In unstable persons that may be plagued with mental problems, severe psychotic episodes may be precipitated by the use of LSD. There is no evidence of physical dependence, but it may well create psychological dependence, with the user constantly seeking a new, better, more pronounced trip.

Psilocybin

Psilocybe stunzii, sometimes referred to as "magic mushrooms" is another hallucinogenic abused drug. It is not as potent as LSD, but can provide sensory distortions of time and space as well as hallucinations. It is popular in Central American Indian tribes. Psilocybin is sold on the street in America; but usually it is actually LSD or PCP that may be sprayed on ordinary mushrooms. The actual fungus, *Psilocybe* is native to California and is very difficult to identify without the expert help of a mycologist (fungus expert).

PCP

Phencyclidine, also known as PCP, "angel dust," "lovely," "green" or "peace pill," is no longer legally used, even in laboratory research. It was once used as an animal tranquilizer, to immobilize animals in transit; but the side effects were so severe, that it no longer is used for any medical purposes. It is manufactured as a white powder, capsule or liquid, and can be ingested, smoked, sniffed or snorted. It is often sprinkled on parsley or mint leaves and mixed with marijuana or crack. Since the late 1970s, PCP use has declined; but is still found on the streets in inner city and suburban schools. **This drug has been called the true "nightmare drug," because of its unpredictable, often bizarre, psychological effects on the user**. As a user smokes PCP, they may have immediate or delayed psychotic reactions and/or severe delusions. It may trigger very violent behavior, and the user may appear to have super-human strength because of the anesthetizing effect of the drug. Effects of PCP include: double vision, drowsiness, nausea and lack of muscular coordination. A stupor, lasting several days, may result from doses greater than 10 mg, and severe convulsions, respiratory or cardiac failure can lead to ruptured blood vessels and even death.

Designer Drugs

Designer drugs are illegally sold on the street and manufactured in clandestine labs. Many of these drugs are easily formulated with just a few chemical reagents. Prior to 1986, these drugs were legal because they were not the exact chemical compounds that were sold on the street. By changing a small portion of the molecular structure of products such as heroin, the chemist can produce a "new drug," or newly "designed" drug that may have very unusual and untested effects on the body. The Controlled Substance Analog Enforcement Act of 1986 (Public Law 99-570) has **banned all analogs or "cousins" of other street drugs.** Designer drugs include stimulants, depressants or hallucinogens that are altered and distributed illegally. **MDMA (methylene dioxymethamphetamine, or "ecstasy")** is similar to amphetamines, MPTP (similar to Demerol) and other analogs are extremely unpredictable because of the lack of quality control. Users have suffered brain damage, permanent paralysis and the inability to speak.

168

How long do Drugs stay in the Body?

Many people are concerned about casual drug use and the effect it may have on their bodies, or potential drug screening tests at work or school. The following table lists commonly abused drugs and the amount of time it takes for all of the chemicals to be metabolized in the body:

Alcohol	4-12 hours	
Amphetamines	2 days	
Barbiturates	1 day (short - acting)	2-3 weeks (long - acting)
Cocaine	2-4 days	
Darvon	6-48 hours	
Marijuana	5 days (moderate smoker: 4 times/week)	
	10 days (daily smoker)	
	20+ days (heavy smoker)	
Methaqualone	2 weeks	
Opiates	2-4 days	
Valium	1-5 days	

Variations are due to differences in an individual's physical condition, gender, metabolism and fluid intake, as well as the method and frequency of drug use.

Date Rape Drug—Roofies

One of the most recent drugs used by youth and young adults is called rohypnol or **'Roofies,' or the 'forget me' pill."** Rohypnol is the brand name of a sleeping pill, **flunitrazepam**, marketed in Mexico, South America, Europe and Asia. It is not marketed in the U.S. Rohypnol belongs to the group of medications called benzodiazepines which include Valium (diazepam), Librium (chlorodiazepoxide) and Xanax (alprazolam). There has been increasingly widespread use of Rohypnol, initially in Florida and Texas, but now use has become more widespread throughout the U.S. Most of the drugs are obtained by prescription in Mexico and transported across the border.

Abuse patterns of Roofies include: the drug taken alone as an intoxicant and abuse in school aged children as young as 8-10 years of age, and high school and college students using the drug to intoxicate a female, cause memory loss ending in sexual assault or rape. Rohypnol intoxication is generally associated with impaired judgment and impaired motor skills. The combination of alcohol and flunitrazepam is also particularly hazardous because together, their effects on memory and judgment are greater than the effects resulting from either taken alone. It is commonly reported that persons who become intoxicated on a combination of alcohol and flunitrazepam experience "blackouts" lasting 8 to 24 hours following ingestion. Disinhibition is another widely reported effect of Rohypnol, both when taken alone or in combination with alcohol. (Smith, Wesson, & Calhoun, 1997). During the late 1990s manufacturers of Rohypnol

169

added blue color to the chemical that makes the drug noticeable when poured in a beverage. Previously the drug was colorless and easily concealed.

GHB-As a date rape drug

As is often the case, drugs come and go on a regular basis. Rohypnol now has a competitor for its popularity, as a date rape medication i.e. **gamma hydroxy butyrate or GHB.** In 1996 GHB use was associated with 69 acute poisonings. A 17-year old girl with no previous history of drug, alcohol abuse died after drinking a soft drink at a party. This drug is the latest craze used to produce amnesia and eliminate any memory after a sexual assault incident. In the United States, GHB is under specific Food and Drug Administration exemptions for investigational research purposes for the treatment of narcolepsy. Although possession of GHB is not illegal under federal law, its manufacture and sale is prohibited under the Food, Drug, and Cosmetic Act. The Drug Enforcement Administration (DEA) is gathering information and considering a scheduling review for possible control of GHB under the Federal Controlled Substances Act.

GHB increases dopamine in the brain and is associated with coma, seizures, respiratory depression and vomiting. Coma and respiratory depression may be potentiated by concomitant use of alcohol. There is no known antidote for GHB overdose, and treatment is restricted to nonspecific supportive care. Many of those hospitalized have required ventilator support to breath and intensive care. GHB is produced in illegal labs and is also known as "Grievous Bodily Harm," "Georgia Home Boy," "Liquid Ecstasy," "Liquid X," "Liquid E," "GHB," "GBH," "Soap," "Scoop," "Easy Lay," "Salty Water," "G-Riffick," "Cherry Menth," and "Organic Quaalude." (CDC, 1999). **For an excellent detailed report on GHB and other date rape drugs see: clubdrugs.org.**

And then there was Ecstasy...

The intent of this text is to help teachers become generally familiar with drugs related to their students. Space does not allow for lengthy details about any specific drug, however, the recent popularity of ecstasy at "rave parties" by kids is addressed below by an expert, Dr. Nora Volkow, director of The National Institute of Drug Abuse (NIDA). In 2004 Dr. Volkow stated:

> The so-called "club drug" MDMA continues to be used by millions of Americans across the country despite growing evidence of its potential harmful effects. 3,4-Methylenedioxymethamphetamine (MDMA, or "Ecstasy") has gained a deceptive reputation as a "safe" drug among its users. This illegal drug, which has both stimulant and psychedelic properties, is often taken for the feelings of well-being, stimulation, as well as the distortions in time and sensory perceptions that it produces. MDMA first became popular in the "rave" and all-night party scene, but its use has now spread to a wide range of settings and demographic subgroups. According to the 2002 National Survey on Drug Use and Health, more than 10 million people have tried MDMA at least once.

Myths abound about both the acute effects and long-term consequences of this drug, often called "Ecstasy" or "X." Indeed, one reason for the rapid rise in the drug's popularity is that many young people believe that MDMA is a new safe drug. But MDMA is not new to the scientific community, with many laboratories beginning their investigations of this drug in the 1980s, and the picture emerging from their efforts is of a drug that is far from benign. For example, **MDMA can cause a dangerous increase in body temperature that can lead to cardiovascular failure. MDMA can also increase heart rate, blood pressure, and heart wall stress. Animal studies show that MDMA can damage specific neurons in the brain. In humans, the research is not conclusive at this time; however, a number of studies show that long-term heavy MDMA users suffer cognitive deficits, including problems with memory.**

What are the effects of MDMA?

MDMA has become a popular drug, in part because of the positive effects that a person experiences within an hour or so after taking a single dose. Those effects include feelings of mental stimulation, emotional warmth, empathy toward others, a general sense of well being, and decreased anxiety. In addition, users report enhanced sensory perception as a hallmark of the MDMA experience. Because of the drug's stimulant properties, when used in club or dance settings MDMA can also enable users to dance for extended periods. However, there are some users who report undesirable effects immediately, including anxiety, agitation, and recklessness.

As noted, MDMA is not a benign drug. MDMA can produce a variety of adverse health effects, including nausea, chills, sweating, involuntary teeth clenching, muscle cramping, and blurred vision. MDMA overdose can also occur - the symptoms can include high blood pressure, faintness, panic attacks, and in severe cases, a loss of consciousness, and seizures.

Because of its stimulant properties and the environment in which it is often taken, MDMA is associated with vigorous physical activity for extended periods. This can lead to one of the most significant, although rare, acute adverse effects -- a marked rise in body temperature (hyperthermia). Treatment of hyperthermia requires prompt medical attention, as it can rapidly lead to muscle breakdown, which can in turn result in kidney failure. In addition, dehydration, hypertension, and heart failure may occur in susceptible individuals. MDMA can also reduce the pumping efficiency of the heart, of particular concern during periods of increased physical activity, thereby further complicating these problems.

MDMA is rapidly absorbed into the human blood stream, but once in the body MDMA interferes with the body's ability to metabolize, or break down, the drug. As a result, additional doses of MDMA can produce unexpectedly high blood levels, which could worsen the cardiovascular and other toxic effects of this drug. MDMA also interferes with the metabolism of other drugs, including some of the adulterants that may be found in MDMA tablets.

In the hours after taking the drug, MDMA produces significant reductions in mental abilities. These changes, particularly those affecting memory, can last for up to a week, and possibly longer in regular users. The fact that MDMA markedly impairs information processing emphasizes the potential dangers of performing complex or even skilled activities, such as driving a car, while under the influence of this drug.

Over the course of the week following moderate use of the drug, many MDMA users report feeling a range of emotions, including anxiety, restlessness, irritability, and sadness that in some individuals can be as severe as true clinical depression. Similarly, elevated anxiety, impulsiveness, and aggression, as well as sleep disturbances, lack of appetite and reduced interest in and pleasure from sex have been observed in regular MDMA users. Some of these disturbances may not be directly attributable to MDMA, but may be related to some of the other drugs often used in

171

combination with MDMA, such as cocaine or marijuana, or to potential adulterants found in MDMA tablets. (Volkow, 2004).

NIDA Prevention Principles

The National Institute on Drug Abuse (NIDA) has prepared a guide to help parents, teachers and community leaders develop programs to prevent youth from becoming entangled in the world of drugs. These prevention principles have emerged from research studies funded by NIDA on the origins of drug abuse behaviors and the common elements found in research on effective prevention programs. Parents, educators, and community leaders can use these principles to help guide their thinking, planning, selection, and delivery of drug abuse prevention programs at the community level. Highlights of the document are: (1) Prevention programs should enhance protective factors and reverse or reduce risk factors; (2) Prevention programs should address all forms of drug abuse, alone or in combination, including the underage use of legal drugs (e.g., tobacco or alcohol); the use of illegal drugs (e.g., marijuana or heroin); and the inappropriate use of legally obtained substances (e.g., inhalants), prescription medications, or over-the-counter drugs; (3) Prevention programs should address the type of drug abuse problem in the local community, target modifiable risk factors, and strengthen identified protective factors (4) Prevention programs should be tailored to address risks specific to population or audience characteristics, such as age, gender, and ethnicity, to improve program effectiveness; (5) Family-based prevention programs should enhance family bonding and relationships and include parenting skills; practice in developing, discussing, and enforcing family policies on substance abuse; and training in drug education and information; (6) Prevention programs can be designed to intervene as early as preschool to address risk factors for drug abuse, such as aggressive behavior, poor social skills, and academic difficulties; (7) Prevention programs for elementary school children should target improving academic and social-emotional learning to address risk factors for drug abuse, such as early aggression, academic failure, and school dropout. Education should focus on the following skills-self-control, emotional awareness, communication, social problem solving, and academic support, especially in reading. (NIDA, 2003).

Other suggestions from the NIDA report include (8) Prevention programs aimed at general populations at key transition points, such as the transition to middle school, can produce beneficial effects even among high-risk families and children. (9) Community prevention programs that combine two or more effective programs, such as family-based and school-based programs, can be more effective than a single program alone; (10) Community prevention programs reaching populations in multiple settings—for example, schools, clubs, faith-based organizations, and the media—are most effective when they present consistent, community-wide messages in each setting; (11) Research-based prevention programs can be cost-effective. Similar to earlier research, recent research shows that for each dollar invested in prevention, a savings of up to $10 in treatment for alcohol or other substance abuse can be seen. (NIDA, 2003). **Pay now or pay later!**

Everyday, Practical Ideas for Preventing Alcohol and Other Drug Use

The U.S. Department of Health and Human Services (USDHHS), has provided a guide to help communities develop programs to reduce and or eliminate drug abuse in American communities. These programs/initiatives should be broad based and seek to focus on families, communities, schools, governmental agencies and the media. Prevention methods suggested are:

Individual

- Provide factual information about alcohol and other drugs;
- Address beliefs about alcohol and other drugs;
- Meet social or psychological needs of young people;
- Address early antisocial behavior;
- Reduce the feeling that "It can't happen to me;"
- Help young people cope with emotions; and
- Improve poor life skills.

Parental Approaches

- Provide information on alcohol and other drugs;
- Teach and encourage prevention strategies at home;
- Help develop skills for building strong family bonds; and
- Form parent support groups.
- School-Based Strategies
- Involve parents or other caretakers
- Establish and enforce no use policies;
- Monitor alcohol and other drug use and evaluate efforts;
- Involve the community;
- Incorporate a comprehensive tobacco, alcohol, drug curriculum;
- Establish policies for seeking help for students and faculty;
- Consider uniforms/dress codes for students; and
- Establish student and employee assistance programs.

Peer Group

- Support non using groups and clubs;
- Create peer education programs and peer leadership programs;
- Provide opportunities to observe non using role models; and
- Teach peer-resistance strategies.

Teacher's Programs

- Provide training about alcohol and other drugs and about prevention;
- Help teachers explore their own attitudes and beliefs about alcohol and other drug use;
- Train teachers to recognize signs of trouble; and
- Develop referral skills.

Mass Media Approaches

- Ask radio stations to eliminate humor and irresponsible commentary about alcohol and other drugs;
- Involve local sports stars and celebrities in prevention efforts;
- Make TV, radio, and print commercials to raise awareness and reinforce prevention and intervention efforts;
- Provide news or new angles for journalists and broadcasters;
- **Ask for equal coverage for celebrations that don't include alcohol;**
- Educate college and university newspaper editors about alcohol advertising; and
- Reinforce media prevention effort with long-term community programs.

Regulatory and Legal Action

- Increase sales tax on alcohol;
- Support adherence to rules and laws and raise awareness of consequences of breaking laws;
- Enforce minimum drinking age of 21; and
- Educate advocacy groups about how laws, ordinances, polices, etc., impact behavior (e.g., zoning laws regulating the number of alcohol; distributors within zones) (USDHHS, 1989; Volkow, 2003).

Summary

The checklist above represents only a sample of the strategies being used or piloted in communities throughout the United States. To be truly successful, people should try to involve many additional segments of the community to establish, nurture, and sustain a long-term commitment to prevention. Classroom teachers and parents can often serve as the first source in the identification of drug and other health problems of youth. They can dramatically enhance drug use prevention efforts. Increased prevention efforts generally lead to an increased need for intervention and treatment services, and it is important not to stimulate a need that cannot be fulfilled. Prevention planning should be mindful of this situation. Another social problem, however, is that tobacco, and alcohol are both legal, and society often does not look upon tobacco and alcohol as a "real drug" problem. Many parents today still make ridiculous and irresponsible statements like, "It's only beer that my son used, I'm so glad it wasn't "real drugs." Teachers can help communicate the notion to kids and their parents that alcohol is also a drug, sometimes a very deadly one. Remember that alcohol related accidents are the number one cause of death to youth.

While reasonable or responsible use of a drug such as alcohol can be addressed, educators must be cautious to advise minors about the short and long term effects of many of these products.

Summary of Major Abused Drugs

Teachers should review the following lists in Table 7.1 of commonly abused drugs. Look for similarities and differences. Do you think you may be experiencing any of the problems listed? What about your students, friends and family members? What about the parents of your students? Denial is the first sign of chemical addiction. Educators should keep this data available at school as a reference source to help them identify potential problems with students.

Drug Abuse 101 for Teachers and Parents

For many decades kids have been using drugs to alter their state of mind and just to experiment with their friend. The street names change often, newer drugs are discovered, or adapted from approved pharmaceuticals and parents and teachers often become confused while observing the behavior of adolescents. The information below should help readers identify specific drug use behaviors. Table 7.1 below is modified from the National Institute on Drug Abuse (NIDA), a division of the federal National Institute of Health (NIH). The details are purely for reference and teachers are not expected to memorize all of the data. This information will help parents and classroom teachers better understand the common types of abused drugs by youth. Many more details can be found using the Google search engine for NIDA and commonly abused drugs. (NIDA, 2010).

175

Table 7.1 Commonly Abused Drugs (Modified from NIDA-Commonly Abused Drugs).

Substances: Category & Name	Common Examples & Street Names	DEA Schedule & How Administered	Intoxication Effects & Potential Health Consequences
Tobacco	Cigarettes, cigars, bidis & smokeless tobacco (snuff, spit & chew)	Not scheduled, smoked, chewed or snorted	*Increased blood pressure & heart rate, chronic lung disease, cancer throughout the body*
Alcohol	Liquor, beer & wine	Not scheduled/swallowed	*Low doses: euphoria, mild relaxation lowered inhibition; higher doses slurred speech, nausea, emotional volatility, impaired memory and sexual function, FAS, depression & heart disease*
Cannabinoids			
Hashish Marijuana	Boom, gangster, hash Blunt, dope, ganja, grass, herb, joint, weed skunk, grass	Swallowed, smoked Swallowed, smoked	*Euphoria, relaxation, slowed reaction time, impaired balance & coordination, increased heart rate and appetite, impaired learning, memory, anxiety, panic attacks, respiratory infection & addiction*
Opioids			
Heroin	Diacetylmorphine: smack, horse, brown sugar, dope, H, junk, skag, skunk, white horse, China white	I*, Injected, smoked, snorted	*Euphoria, drowsiness, impaired coordination, dizziness, nausea, sedation, feeling of heaviness in the body, slow breathing, constipation, endocarditis, hepatitis, HIV, addiction, death*
Opium	Laudanum, paregork, big O, black stuff, block, gum, hop	II, II, V, swallowed, smoked	
Stimulants			
Cocaine	Cocaine hydrochloride, blow, bump, C, candy, Charlie, coke, crack, flake, rock, snow, toot	II, snorted smoked & injected	*Increased heart rate, blood pressure, body temperature, metabolism; feelings of exhilaration, increased energy mental alertness, tremors, anxiety, panic, violent behavior, cardiovascular problems, seizures, addiction*
Amphetamine	Biphetamine, Dexedrine, bennies, black beauties, crosses, hearts LA turnaround, speed, uppers, truck drivers	II, snorted smoked & injected	**Also for cocaine**: nasal damage and methamphetamine-severe dental problems
Methamphetamine	Desoxyn, meth, ice, crank, chalk, crystal, speed, glass, go fast	II, snorted smoked & injected	

Club Drugs			
MDMA, methylendioxy-methamphetamine Flunitrazepam	Ecstasy, Adam, clarity, Eve, lover's speed, peace, X, uppers Rohypnol, forget-me pill, Mexican Valium, R2, roach, roofies, roofinol, rope, rophies	I, swallowed, snorted & injected IV swallowed, snorted	**MDMA-** mild hallucinogenic effects, increased tactile sensitivity, empathetic feelings, lowered inhibition, anxiety, chills sweating, teeth clenching, muscle cramping, sleep disturbances, depression impaired memory, hyperthermia, addiction **Flunitrazepam** sedation, muscle relaxation, confusion, memory loss, dizziness, impaired coordination, addiction **GHB**-drowsiness, nausea, headache, loss of coordination, memory loss, unconscious, seizures, comma
GHB	Gammahydroxybutyrate, G, Georgia home boy, grievous bodily harm, liquid ecstasy, soap, scoop, goop, liquid X	I, swallowed	
Dissociative Drugs			
Ketamine	Ketalar SV, cat Valium K, Special K, vitamin K	III, injected snorted, smoked	*Feelings of being separate from one's body & environment, impaired motor function, anxiety, tremors, numbness, memory loss, nausea* **Also for ketamine-** analgesia, impaired memory, delirium, respiratory depression and arrest, death
PCP & analogs	Phencyclidine, angel dust, boat, hog, love boat, peace pill	I, II, swallowed, smoked, injected	**Also for PCP & analogs:** analgesia, psychosis, aggression, violence, slurred speech, loss of coordination, hallucinations, extreme strength from numbness

177

Salvia divinorum	Salvia, Shepherdess's, Herb, Maria Pastora, magic mint, Sally-D	Not scheduled Chewed, swallowed, smoked	
Dextromethorphan (DXM)	Found in cough, cold medications, Robotripping, Robo, Triple C	Not scheduled Swallowed	**Also for DXM:** euphoria, slurred speech, confusion, dizziness, distorted visual perceptions
Hallucinogens			
LSD	Lysergic acid diethylamide, acid, blotter, cubes, microdot yellow sunshine, blue heaven	I, swallowed, absorbed through mouth tissues	*Altered states of perception and feeling, hallucinations, nausea*
Mescaline	Buttons, cactus, mesc, peyote	I, swallowed, smoked	**Also LSD & Mescaline-** increased body temperature, heart rate, blood pressure, loss of appetite, sweating, sleeplessness, numbness, dizziness, weakness, tremors, impulsive behavior, rapid shifts in emotion **Also for LSD-** Flashbacks, Hallucinogen Persisting Perception Disorder
Psilocybin	Magic mushrooms, purple passion, shrooms, little smoke	I, swallowed	**Also for psilocybin-** nervousness paranoia, panic
Other compounds			
Anabolic steroids	Anadrol, Oxandrin, Durabolin, Depo-Testerone, Equipoise: roids, juice, gym candy, pumpers	III, injected, swallowed, applied to the skin	**Steroids-** no intoxication, effects hypertension, blood clotting, cholesterol changes, liver cysts, hostility & aggression, acne in adolescents, premature stoppage of growth in males, prostate cancer, reduced sperm production, shrunken testicles, breast enlargement, menstrual irregularities, facial hair in females
Inhalants	Solvents (paint thinners, gasoline, glues, gases, (butane, propane, aerosol propellants, nitrous oxide, nitrites, laughing gas, poppers, snappers, whippets	Not scheduled, inhaled through nose or mouth	**Inhalants-** varies by chemical used-loss of inhibition, headache, nausea, vomiting, slurred speech, loss of coordination, unconsciousness, memory impairment, sudden death

* **The U.S. Controlled Substance Act (CSA)** classified drugs on different levels of medical use. Schedule I and II drugs have a high potential for abuse. They require greater storage security and have a quota on manufacturing, among other restrictions. Schedule I drugs are available for research only and have no approved medical use; Schedule II drugs are available only by prescription (unrefillable) and require a form for ordering. Schedule III and IV drugs are available by prescription, may have five refills in 6 months, and may be ordered orally. Some Schedule V drugs are available over the counter.

What About Treating Drug Addiction?

After more than thirty years of scientific research, experts were able to determine numerous ways to stop drug abuse, avoid relapse by users and help addicts lead more successful lives. NIDA has developed these fundamental principles to help individuals, mental health staff and educators interested in helping youth. (NIDA, 2010). The research-based data is listed below.

1. Addiction is a complex but treatable disease that affects brain function and behavior. Drugs alter the brain's structure and how it functions, resulting in changes that persist long after drug use has ceased. This may help explain why abusers are at risk for relapse even after long periods of abstinence.

2. **No single treatment is appropriate for everyone.** Matching treatment settings, interventions, and services to an individual's particular problems and needs is critical to his or her ultimate success.

3. Treatment needs to be readily available. Because drug-addicted individuals may be uncertain about entering treatment, taking advantage of available services the moment people are ready for treatment is critical. Potential patients can be lost if treatment is not immediately available or readily accessible.

4. Effective treatment attends to multiple needs of the individual, not just his or her drug abuse. To be effective, treatment must address the individual's drug abuse and any associated medical, psychological, social, vocational, and legal problems.

5. Remaining in treatment for an adequate period of time is critical. The appropriate duration for an individual depends on the type and degree of his or her problems and needs. Research indicates that most addicted individuals need at least 3 months in treatment to significantly reduce or stop their drug use and that the best outcomes occur with longer durations of treatment.

6. Counseling—individual and/or group—and other behavioral therapies are the most commonly used forms of drug abuse treatment. Behavioral therapies vary in there focus and may involve addressing a patient's motivations to change, building skills to resist drug use, replacing drug-using activities with constructive and rewarding activities, improving problem-solving skills, and facilitating better interpersonal relationships.

7. Medications are an important element of treatment for many patients, especially when combined with counseling and other behavioral therapies. For example, methadone and buprenorphine are effective in helping individuals addicted to heroin or other opioids stabilize their lives and reduce their illicit drug use. Also, for persons addicted to nicotine, a nicotine replacement product (nicotine patches or gum) or an oral medication (bupropion or varenicline), can be an effective component of treatment when part of a comprehensive behavioral treatment program.

8. An individual's treatment and services plan must be assessed continually and modified as necessary to ensure it meets his or her changing needs. A patient may require varying combinations of services and treatment components during the course of treatment and recovery. In addition to counseling or psychotherapy, a patient may require medication, medical services, family therapy, parenting instruction, vocational rehabilitation and/or social and legal services. For many patients, a continuing care approach provides the best results, with treatment intensity varying according to a person's changing needs.

9. Many drug-addicted individuals also have other mental disorders. Because drug abuse and addiction—both of which are mental disorders—often co-occur with other mental illnesses, patients presenting with one condition should be assessed for the other(s). And when these problems co-occur, treatment should address both (or all), including the use of medications as appropriate.

10. Medically assisted detoxification is only the first stage of addiction treatment and by itself does little to change long-term drug abuse. Although medically assisted detoxification can safely manage the acute physical symptoms of withdrawal, detoxification alone is rarely sufficient to help addicted individuals achieve long-term abstinence. Thus, patients should be encouraged to continue drug treatment following detoxification.

11. Treatment does not need to be voluntary to be effective. Sanctions or enticements from family, employment settings, and/or the criminal justice system can significantly increase treatment entry, retention rates, and the ultimate success of drug treatment interventions.

12. Drug use during treatment must be monitored continuously, as lapses during treatment do occur. Knowing their drug use is being monitored can be a powerful incentive for patients and can help them withstand urges to use drugs. Monitoring also provides an early indication of a return to drug use, signaling a possible need to adjust an individual's treatment plan to better meet his or her needs.

13. Treatment programs should assess patients for the presence of HIV/AIDS, hepatitis B and C, tuberculosis, and other infectious diseases, as well as provide targeted

risk-reduction counseling to help patients modify or change behaviors that place them at risk of contracting or spreading infectious diseases. Targeted counseling specifically focused on reducing infectious disease risk can help patients further reduce or avoid substance-related and other high-risk behaviors. Treatment providers should encourage and support HIV screening and inform patients that highly active antiretroviral therapy (HAART) has proven effective in combating HIV, including among drug abusing populations. (NIDA, 2010)

Chapter 8

School Health: Selected Topics

> *Because of the current overweight*
> *epidemic in children and teens,*
> *for the first time in over a century,*
> *today's generation of kids will not*
> *live as long as their parents.*
> *...William Klich, MD*
> *American Academy of Pediatrics*

A dolescents have very unique health problems. Unfortunately, these problems also seem to evolve into adult problems later in life. Many teens often have a very difficult time seeing past their own "circle of friends," and will frequently make exaggerated and grandiose statements such as, "everyone I know is smoking pot," or "all of my friends are having sex." Tragically, many can't seem to look ahead and consider future consequences of how the high-risk behaviors they practice in the present will alter their health later in life. This may be simply because 'later in life,' for many teens is just the next day or weekend, or even after school at 4 PM. Social scientist DiClemente, and colleagues, describing adolescent risk taking, state it very clearly:

Adolescence is a developmental period of rapid physical, psychological, sociocultural and cognitive changes characterized by efforts to confront and surmount challenges and to establish a sense of identity and autonomy. While many adolescents navigate the sometimes-turbulent course from childhood to adulthood to become productive and healthy adults, there is growing concern that **far too many others may not achieve their full potential as workers, parents, and individuals**. Unfortunately, adolescence is also a period fraught with many threats to the health and well being of adolescents, many of whom suffer substantial impairment and disability. Much of the adverse health consequences experienced by adolescents are, to a large extent, the result of risk behaviors. (DiClemente, Hansen, & Ponton, 1996, 2008, Ginzberg, 1991).

Earlier chapters listed the various risk factors that put students in situations that may negatively impact their health. Examples included lack of consistent discipline, caring and clearly defined limits for developing youth. Other factors, such as the use of alcohol, can cloud sensible decision-making and can lead to unprotected sexual activity, STD infection and sometimes HIV. (Chapter nine will expand on STDs, HIV and youth). This chapter focuses on several selected topics related to adolescents and their development. While there exists dozens of health related problems in schools; only a few important ones will be reviewed. The concept of a school health program is reviewed and explained. **The main focus of this chapter will address: teenage suicide, unplanned pregnancy, adolescent nutrition, eating disorders, the obesity epidemic, issues of confidentiality, and students with special health needs.** Solutions for prevention and intervention for teachers, parents and school leaders will also be identified. A special emphasis will address **gender issues** and help guide teachers to understand students dealing with sexual orientation.

The School Health Program

Students spend most of their "working day" at school. Unfortunately, however, too many students also spend their "school day" at work. Social interaction is very important for kids, but the business of schoolwork often gets distracted during their "working day." This type of behavior has a direct effect on academic learning and success in school. It is true that some children may work to help with family expenses; but frequently many kids may be working to buy the latest electronic, gadget, game, gizmo, handbag or jewelry. The school is a microcosm of daily life for children and developing adolescents. It serves as a central focus for their social life, and also creates an atmosphere for learning, interacting, and practicing healthy lifestyles. The teacher serves as one of the most important contacts with the student in observing, recognizing, and identifying health problems, because in many situations, kids spend more time with their teachers than working parents. The school health program in the 21st century includes much more than the presence of a school nurse, school counselor, and a few health teachers.

During 2010 and 2011 much debate occurred with the U.S. Congress and President Obama on Health Care. This book will not address the political implications of the health care issue in America because that is the subject for another entire text. The focus for teachers in this section is the health of kids in the school setting. As described earlier, healthier kids will do better academically in school than kids suffering poorer health.

183

School Health Clinics

One of the more recent forms of health care in the school setting is the **school-based clinic.** The school-based clinic is a local medical facility usually closely housed near the school building. Since the early 1980s, many schools have linked up with local health care services, hospitals and other providers to serve students in the school environment. Despite national negative attention, and undue emphasis on birth control services and condom distribution, school-based clinics have become a crucial part of many school settings and have helped thousands of students nationwide with various health care needs. Los Angeles Unified Schools (LAUSD), for example, offers the following services: families for medical enrollment, individual or family counseling, parent in control classes, parent support groups, domestic violence prevention information, substance abuse information, medical services including immunizations, physical exams and treatment of minor illnesses, food, shelter and clothing assistance, ESL and adult education classes or referrals, parenting assistance, tattoo removal referrals, and numerous hotline numbers. For details about this unique school based clinic approach in LAUSD Google: LAUSD School Based Health Clinics.

By 1994, several hundred school based clinics served children in schools nationwide. Most of these are located in the east and Midwest and the far West. Some are fully operational on campus, while others are linked to a local medical facility and help students with a wide variety of medical problems. By 2010, more than 1900 such clinics were operational in the U.S. and over 120 in California. Since many families do not have any health care, the school-based clinic can serve many health related needs. This arrangement, **usually not funded directly by the school**, can help students with the following: primary care, routine and sports physicals, laboratory tests, chronic illness management, immunization, pregnancy tests, pediatric care of infants of adolescents, HIV testing, screening for vision and hearing problems, gynecological exams and diagnosis and treatment for STDs. Counseling services at school-based clinics include: health education, nutrition education, mental health counseling, job counseling, weight reduction, HIV counseling, medical screening and support group treatment for substance abuse. School Based Health Clinics have even been shown to improve student's grades. See the website describing many school health centers in California: **www.schoolhealthcenters.org.**

A recent statewide program in California, Healthy Start, is a grant-funded program that seeks to address many health problems of kids within an academic setting. Each local Healthy Start initiative provides comprehensive school-integrated services and activities which may include: 1) Academic/Education, 2) Youth Development Services, 3) Family Support, 4) Basic Needs, 5) Medical/Health Care, 6) Mental Health Care and Counseling, and 7) Employment Services. Some of these programs may have well trained experts such as psychologists, registered dieticians, and other health care workers within a well planned program, right on the school campus. From 1992 until 2007, over 1 million students were served in California with Healthy Start Grants. During 2007, however, the CDE stopped funding the program, but requests are being resubmitted to the governor to revise the plan as state funds become available. A detailed description of this innovative program can be found at: **http://www.cde.ca.gov/.**

School Health and Confidentiality

Kids in school are minor children. They have the right to keep their personal medical records, psychological problems and family situations kept private. Teachers should exercise professional standards in keeping this information private and confidential. The health office may only notify certain teachers in a confidential memo about a particular health problem of one student. **Teachers should not discuss this information with colleagues in the lunchroom or during faculty meetings. Disclosure of personal information could impair the health and safety of a child and possibly lead to criminal prosecution of teachers.**

The faculty mailbox should be confidential and inaccessible to students. Memos may be marked "confidential" or "for your eyes only," and should not be shared with non-essential parties, especially other students. **Parents have the legal right to keep personal and family topics out of the school setting, and are not required to disclose any medical information to teachers or schools.** Teachers are not allowed to release the students' names or phone numbers, e-mail addresses, etc., to anyone not associated with the school staff. Vendors and sales persons typically try to access student records to sell products, or arrange trips for graduating seniors. Regardless of the seemingly harmless intent of these solicitors, the school administrators and faculty must maintain confidentiality. This confidentiality is not only mandated by law, but the school district and its employees could be found liable should criminal acts be perpetrated against minor students.

Additionally, teachers need to respect the rights of privacy of colleagues by not circulating any faculty handbooks or other documents, which may have names, addresses and phone numbers of all employees. Curious students may call teachers at home, which can be an annoying invasion of privacy, but safety and security issues for staff members must also be considered. This information should not be left on counters, or in any place open for student viewing. Perhaps the most likely negative consequence of releasing faculty directories is the impact it may have on teachers' home mailboxes when they are entered in "junk mail" databases! It is also recommended that confidential memos be kept under lock and key.

Mental Health and Suicide Prevention

Suicide in America is not a new problem. From 1950 to 1980 suicide rates among persons 35 and older have decreased, but during the same period the suicide rate tripled in persons 15-24 years of age. While the 15-24 year age group has the highest suicide rate of children and young adults, marked increases have been reported for those 10-14 years of age. (Saltzman, 1992). From 1960 to 1987 the suicide rate doubled for males and tripled for females. From 1997 through 2010 suicide has been in the top four leading causes of death for persons 15-24 years of age. (CDC, 2010d). Violence in America is now considered a public health issue, and the topic of death to youth is so significant that since 2004 the CDC set up a new surveillance system called the National Violent Death Reporting System (NVDRS), that monitors suicide and other violent forms of death in the U.S. (CDC, 2010d).

Why would so many young people want to take their own lives? Many adults growing up during the 1950s through the late 1980s remember the stress, pain and difficulty of adolescence, but few have a real sense of how many teens are overly stressed today. America is a complex society with gangs, crime, drug abuse and high rates of teenage pregnancy. The reasons for attempting suicide are very complex, and include physiological and psychological etiologies, varying from individual to individual. These may include the following: psychiatric illness, clinical depression, alcoholism, neurotransmitter imbalance (serotonin in cerebrospinal fluid), suicidal contagion influence (copy-cat suicides), loss of job, or loved one, heavy use of drugs, movement from city to city, and loss or disruption of social support system, or **even excessive use of the Internet.** (CDC, 2010d).

In recent years, the CDC and other governmental agencies related to mental health reported the following data related to suicide ideation, attempts and the impact on special populations.

- Suicide took the lives of 30,622 people in 2001;
- Suicide rates are generally higher than the national average in the western states and lower in the eastern and Midwestern states;
- In 2002, 132,353 individuals were hospitalized following suicide attempts;
- In 2001, 55% of suicides were committed with a firearm;
- Suicide is the eighth leading cause of death for all U.S. men;
- Males are four times more likely to die from suicide than females;
- Suicide rates are highest among Whites and second highest among American Indian and Native Alaskan men;
- Of the 24,672 suicide deaths reported among men in 2001, 60% involved the use of a firearm;
- Women report attempting suicide during their lifetime about three times as often as men;
- The overall rate of suicide among youth has declined slowly since 1992. However, rates remain unacceptably high. Adolescents and young adults often experience stress, confusion, and depression from

186

situations occurring in their families, schools, and communities. Such feelings can overwhelm young people and lead them to consider suicide as a "solution." **Few schools and communities have suicide prevention plans that include screening, referral, and crisis intervention programs for youth;**

- YRBS reported that suicide was the third leading cause of death for youth in 2004-2008; and
- American Indian and Alaskan Natives have the highest rate of suicide in the 15 to 24 age group; and
  (CDC 2004, 2007b, 2010d).

Suicide Ideation and Attempts

As difficult as it may be to think about, teachers must be prepared that, after teaching a few years, some of their students will die! Most deaths from children and teens are a result of accidents, or as the CDC describes, unintended injuries, but a few students will take their own lives. During 2009, suicide was the third leading cause of death among adolescents 13–19 years of age. (CDC, 2010d). Many adolescents seriously consider suicide without attempting it, or they attempt but do not complete suicide. It is not just one or two experiences that may push the child to consider suicide. Suicide attempts are caused by many influences. Some of the factors include: (1) feelings of hopelessness, worthlessness and a preoccupation with death; (2) abuse of drugs, alcohol, or tobacco; (3) history of suicide attempts, or a family history of suicide; and (4) a very stressful life event or loss of a loved one.

In 2005, about one-fifth of all high school students reported seriously considering suicide or attempting suicide during the previous 12 months. About one-half of all students who seriously considered suicide actually attempted suicide (8 percent of all students). About 2 percent of all students reported having an injurious suicide attempt that resulted in an injury, poisoning, or overdose that was treated by a doctor or nurse. In general, **female students were substantially more likely to consider suicide than male students in all racial or ethnic and grade level subgroups.** Among students in grades 9–11, female students were significantly more likely to attempt suicide than male students were by the 12th grade. **In contrast, the rate of completed suicides was significantly higher for male adolescents than for female adolescents.** This is likely due to the fact that males may use more violent means, guns, etc., and females may attempt less violent means such as drug overdose. (Behman,

187

Kliegman, Arvin, 1996; CDC, 2007b).

Among female students, Hispanic students were significantly more likely to report a suicide attempt than non-Hispanic white or black students were. No difference by race and ethnicity was present among male students. In 2005, 20 percent of male students and 37 percent of female students reported feeling so sad or hopeless almost every day for two or more consecutive weeks during the past 12 months that they stopped doing some usual activities. (Gould, 1998; CDC, 2007b).

Suicide Signs

Suicide can be a tragic act of severely depressed individuals. **It is estimated that more than 6,000 adolescents kill themselves every year.** (CDC, 2010d). With estimated attempts of the general population greater than one-half million. Why**? How bad can life be that a young person decides to take his or her own life?** Many adults that have graduated from high school even as recently as ten years ago, have a difficult time understanding how stressful life is for many teenagers today. Adolescents are constantly inundated with messages about violence, sexuality, depressing topics and many spend countless hours at video arcades or on the Internet simulating more violence, sexuality and high erratic activity. Consider the earthquake and Tsunami that devastated Japan in 2011 and the overwhelming images displayed. **The most frequently reported warning signs of potential suicide in teens and young adults are:**

- withdrawal from friends;
- feelings of hopelessness;
- changes in eating, sleeping habits;
- dramatic mood swings, without any explanation;
- decrease in academic performances;
- previous suicide attempts, or attempts by other family members;
- increased use of tobacco, alcohol or other drugs;
- persistent boredom;
- withdrawal from family events;
- isolation;
- dropping out of teams, jobs, or group activities;
- preoccupation with death in written themes, school work or art work;
- loss of romantic relationships;
- giving away prized possessions;
- threatening suicide, saying "**I could always kill myself**;" and
- sudden violent, hostile behavior changes.
  (LA Suicide Prevention Center, CASHE, 1986; Peck, 1987; CDC, 2004, 2007b).

188

How does a teacher know if these signs are serious enough to take any specific action? The Los Angeles Suicide Prevention Center recommends asking four questions. (1) Are you thinking about suicide? (2) Do you have a plan? (3) Do you have the means? (4) When will you do it? If you have a thorough conversation with a close friend, student or loved one and you determine that the answers to these questions **are definitely "yes"** and you do nothing...it is estimated that 98% will be dead within 48 hours! (Peck, 1987).

Suicide Prevention

What can be done? Be there as a friend. A truly dedicated and empathetic friend is worth a million dollars. Listen carefully, and listen attentively. Look them in the eyes and try to identify any sense of urgency. Are they really seriously considering suicide, or are they just having a bad day? **Ask them if they are thinking about suicide!** Give them a hug and provide a nurturing closeness. Human touch is one of the most powerful emotional contacts. Keep them active with other people, activities or friends. Seek professional help. Go with them and help them make a connection with a mental health professional. Sometimes just a gentle touch of the shoulder while directing them to a counselor can mean much more than many words. Most of all, don't play psychotherapist. Just love them! By being available with a telephone number, message service, or other close friend as a support figure, you may prevent a needless suicide and waste of a young life.

Too often everyone is wrapped up in his or her own lives. Parents work too many hours, students are very egocentric, and they often take on too many activities, and spend inordinate amounts of time with their friends. Teachers are especially busy with paperwork and lesson planning. Take the time. Watch out for friends and students or loved ones. You may save someone's life! Although the messages that they are sending may be very subtle, they could be calling out for help. Four major steps should be taken to prevent suicide (1) recognize the signs and symptoms, (2) listen carefully to verbal and non-verbal messages, (3) act quickly, and (4) locate a support and referral system. The Los Angeles Suicide prevention center developed an acronym to help professionals remember how to intervene. The key word is **APPROACH.** Approach means:

189

A-P-P-R-O-A-C-H

A =   ask questions
P =   pursue intentions
P =   provide support
R =   reach out
O =   offer help
A =   act quickly
C =   communicate concern
H =   hold out hope
(Hirsch, 2011).

The teacher may be the only significant adult that the student feels they can turn to in time of need. The most important role of the teacher is to serve as a role model and be a positive individual, friend and even confidant, while recognizing signs of suicide. This can be especially helpful if teachers also talk to their colleagues about troubled students. Sometimes a quick phone call to the school psychologist may actually save a student life that very day! Teachers often enjoy a quasi-confidential relationship with students. When it comes to topics like pregnancy or information about birth control, teachers must honor this confidentiality as students can access these services without parental consent. When it comes to a possible suicide attempt, however, teachers have a legal requirement of notifying parents, or school officials of any eminent danger. It must be emphasized that classroom teachers primary role is to teach their specific content such as English, art, history or math, etc.; but they should also be watchful while working with youth should any serious signs arise, such as suicide or abuse.

Unplanned Pregnancy

During the 1970s and 1980s, rapid changes in coital activity were documented in teenagers. Between 1971 and 1979 there was a 50% increase in sexual intercourse in young girls by age 15. By the end of the 1990s, many reports indicated that greater than 70% of high school students have had intercourse at least once before they graduated in the senior year. Only as recently as 1997 and 1998 have a few experts reported that the tide slowly changed related to teens and sex and many have reported more conservative attitudes. The

190

National Center for Health Statistics (NCHS) has documented a significant reduction in the births of babies to teen-age girls in America.

Every year in America almost 500, 000 teenagers give birth. Most are unmarried and many are not ready for the emotional, psychological, and financial responsibilities and challenges of parenthood. Teenage childbearing has important health and social consequences for these young women, their babies, and their families. Recently, the teenage birth rate has declined in all states. Rates for black teenagers have dropped more than for any other population group. Contributing to this decline are indications that teenagers today are less likely to be sexually active, and sexually active teenagers are more likely to use contraception. (NCHS, 2004).

Birth rates have fallen for teens overall in the 1990s and 2000s, as well as for unmarried teens since mid-decade; however, the proportion of births to unmarried teens has continued to rise, from 14 percent in 1940 to 67 percent in 1990 and 79 percent in 2000. This is because very few teens are marrying today. It is interesting to also note that the birth rate for married teens has dropped substantially. Nevertheless, teens do not account for the majority of births to unmarried women, which were only 28 percent in 2000. However, the U.S. teen birth rate remains the highest among developed countries (54.7 births per 1,000). According to the latest data available, the rate is lowest in Japan at about 4 births per 1,000 teens and is below 10 per 1,000 in a number of countries, including Denmark, Finland, France, Germany, Italy, the Netherlands, Spain, Sweden, and Switzerland. (NCHS, 2004). To view the full report on teen pregnancy rates throughout the world, see the NCHS website at: **http://www.cdc.gov/nchs/products/pubs/pubd/hestats/teenpreg1990-2002/teenpreg1990-2002.htm.**

Sexuality Activity Among Teens

The Alan Guttmacher Institute (AGI), recently reported sexual activity during the teen years in the U.S. It is estimated that although only 13% of teens have ever had vaginal sex by age 15, sexual activity is common by the late teen years. By their 19th birthday, seven in 10 teens of both sexes have had intercourse.   And, on average, young people have sex for the first time at about age 17, but they do not marry until their mid-20s if at all! **This means that young adults are at increased risk of unwanted pregnancy and sexually transmitted disease (STDs) for nearly ten years!** Teens have been waiting longer to have sex than they did in the recent past. In 2006–2008, some 11% of never-married females aged 15–19 and 14% of never-married males that age had had sex before age 15, compared with 19% and 21%, respectively, in 1995. During 2006–2008, the most common reason that sexually inexperienced teens gave for not having had sex was that it was "against religion or morals" (42% among females and 35% among males). The second and third most common reasons for females were "don't want to get

191

pregnant" and "haven't found the right person yet." Between sexually experienced teens, 72% of females and 56% of males report that their first sexual experience was with a steady partner, while 14% of females and 25% of males report a first sexual experience with someone whom they had just met or who was just a friend. Many teens don't realize that the 'very close friend' in their life may quickly become a sexual partner with little or no warning. Teens in the United States and European teens have similar levels of sexual activity. However, the teens from Europe are more likely to use contraceptives and to use effective contraceptive methods. Therefore, European teenagers usually have substantially lower pregnancy rates than American teens. (AGI, 2011).

Contraceptive Use

A sexually active teen **who does not use a contraceptive** has a 90% chance of becoming pregnant within a year. The majority of sexually experienced teens (79% of females and 87% of males) used contraceptives the first time they had sex. Contraceptive use at first premarital sex has been increasing. Fifty-six percent of women whose first premarital sex occurred before 1985 used a method, compared with 76% in 2000–2004 and 84% in 2005–2008. (AGI, 2011).

Some suggest that the role of the media, with thousands of sexual messages impacting youth, may contribute to increase teen sexual activity that results in unplanned pregnancy. Others see the lowering of the **menarche** (first menstrual period) as another factor. This reduction in menarchal age has changed in American females in the last 100 years to a low of about 12.8 years. Lack of supervision of young teens also contributes to the increase of teen sexual activity. **Many students have sex in the afternoon between 3 and 6 PM in their parents' bed while both parents are working!** In addition, alcohol and other drugs cloud decision-making processes for kids, and they may spontaneously have sexual relations. Perhaps Americans need to look more closely to European teen sexual behavior.

The Washington Times reported that European teenagers lose their virginity later, have fewer sexual partners, and have lower birth rates and abortions compared to American teens. Studies suggest that the European teens are seeing a consistent message about sex that focuses on safe practices, as well as abstinence, while the U.S. policy calls primarily for promotion of abstinence before marriage. **Many European nations approach teenage sexual topics as health issues, not moral issues. Additionally, Europeans use media campaigns and family life education in schools to promote the use of contraceptives.** Americans lose their virginity at an average age of 15.8, while Germans lose their virginity at an average of 16.2, French at 16.8 years, and Dutch at 17.7 years. Dutch and German teens have an average of 1.7 and 1.9 sexual partners in their teen years, respectively, compared to American teens average of 3.05 partners. However, a recent survey in the United States of over 275,000 high school freshmen found that teens are becoming less accepting of casual sex, possibly due to fear of contracting sexually transmitted diseases. (Weitzen, 1999). Perhaps much of the emphasis of HIV and STD

192

prevention education during the late 1990s and early 2000s has brought this about.

American teens had a birth rate of **54.7 births per 1,000** in 1999, while Germany and the Netherlands had rates of only 13 births per 1,000 girls and seven per 1,000 girls, respectively during the same period. Furthermore, the Netherlands has a significantly lower rate of abortions, as does France. AIDS is less prevalent among teenagers in France, Germany, and the Netherlands as well. (Mann, 1999). James Wagoner, the president of Advocates for Youth, a social science research group, stated that the **United States "is the only industrialized country in the Western world with an official government abstinence program,"** (Stobbe, 2010). Yet America has "the highest rates of teenage pregnancy, HIV, and sexually transmitted diseases." The Netherlands has the most liberal approach, yet teens in Holland start having sex later in life and have fewer partners. Finally, in 2009 the U.S. teen birthrate (39.1 births per thousand teen girls) was surpassed by Bulgaria (42.2 births per thousand teen girls). Some reports indicate the lack of regular use of contraceptives, high rates of abortion and HIV may account for the higher rates in Bulgaria. The following graph lists births per 1,000 teens from 1940 to 2009. (Stobbe, 2010).

A major factor involved in sexual activity is that developmental processes in adolescents move along separate tracks compared to adults. Adolescence is a time for change. Teens will begin to assert their feelings, react to authority, and protest rules and regulations during this maturational process. But this process varies considerably. One young girl may be advanced intellectually and can solve complex mathematical equations, while being physically underdeveloped and socially unsophisticated. In contrast, another young teenage girl, may develop breasts at a very early age, become involved with dating too early, and participate in sexual activity even before entering high school. This discontinuity presents a definite challenge to teachers, health workers, and especially parents.

Sex education programs in the school setting can be very beneficial to students if developed with board approval, parental involvement, and student lessons based on assertion

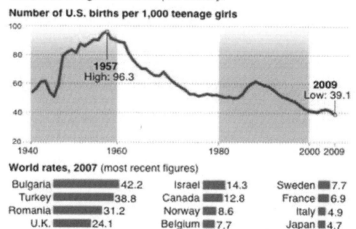

US teen births high comparatively

The birth rate last year for U.S. girls ages 15 to 19 was the lowest since the government began tracking the statistic in 1940. However, it is still high for a developed country.

Number of U.S. births per 1,000 teenage girls

1957
High: 96.3

2009
Low: 39.1

World rates, 2007 (most recent figures)

Bulgaria	42.2	Israel	14.3	Sweden	7.7
Turkey	38.8	Canada	12.8	France	6.9
Romania	31.2	Norway	8.6	Italy	4.9
U.K.	24.1	Belgium	7.7	Japan	4.7
Ireland	15.9	Germany	7.7	Netherlands	3.8

SOURCES: Centers for Disease Control and Prevention; World Bank   AP

training, refusal skills and abstinence. This comprehensive approach emphasizing skills is part of the core values of the 2008 California Health Content Standards. The mere presentation of facts on contraception will not work alone in changing or influencing sexual behaviors. Nonetheless, there are parents that insist that if schools offer condom education, kids will engage in early sexual experimentation. The research data does not support this notion. **Providing contraception knowledge in a school setting, when presented by professionally trained health educators, will delay the time of first intercourse in teens, and those that do choose to have intercourse will use some form of birth control.** (Zabin, 1986; Kirby, 1994, 2007).

The **"Life Options"** approach is another attempt to prevent teenage pregnancy. In addition to using educational intervention, and medical service support; students are given an opportunity to develop options for life, such as jobs, internships, mentoring programs, college scholarships and a variety of incentives to keep them busy and focused on specific goals. This, coupled with psychological support and community activity support, such as volunteer service, can significantly reduce the problem of teen pregnancy.

Gender roles are changing and children, growing up in a very rapid pace electronic data access society, are experiencing social changes regarding attitudes about sexuality. They see mixed messages everyday about sex, condom use and the consumption of beer and wine coolers. Kirby and Haffner comment on this quite well:

> As young people attain puberty, many of them feel anxiety about their changing bodies and their changing relationships with members of the opposite sex and with their families. Youth often feel vulnerable and succumb to peer pressure or exploitation. Many young people become involved in intimate sexual relationships before they leave junior high school; more than half of all teenagers do so before they leave high school. Some of these teenagers experience dissatisfaction and guilt; about a million become pregnant each year; many contract a sexually transmitted disease; and a small but increasing number become infected with HIV. Many youth are unclear whether to have children or to pursue education or careers. (Kirby, 1992).

The National Campaign to Prevent Teen Pregnancy (NCPTP) in Washington, DC recently documented significant evidence to indicate that the education community does care about preventing teen pregnancy. In their *Notes From the Field* they report that educational success is significantly impacted by teenage pregnancy, both for the teen and their child. They also report that the problem of teen pregnancy is greater than most people often think; and, most importantly that the education community can make a big difference in reducing teen pregnancy. Further research from NCPTP concludes what should be obvious to any observer that works directly with youth: **The education community can make a big difference in reducing teen pregnancy.** The following points help to reinforce these concepts:

- **Less than one-third of teens who begin families before age 18 ever complete high school;**
- Parenthood is a leading cause of high school drop out among teen girls;
- Children of teen parents often do worse in school and are 50 percent more likely to repeat a grade;
- Educational failure is a key predictor of teen pregnancy;
- Nearly one million girls get pregnant each year in the United States;
- More than 4 out of 10 young women become pregnant at least once before age 20;
- Nearly 80 percent of these pregnancies are to unmarried teens;
- Over one-half of teen pregnancies end in birth and fewer and fewer teens choose abortion or adoption;
- Fourteen percent of high school-aged males report causing at least one pregnancy. (NCPTP, 1998);
- The United States has one of the highest rates of teen pregnancy and births in the industrialized world. (NCPTP, 1997);
- Teen pregnancy costs the United States at least $7 billion annually. (NCPTP, 1997);
- **Students who feel a strong connection to their school and have a higher grade point average are more likely to postpone sexual activity. (Blum, Reinehart, 1998);**
- **Students cite teachers and counselors as second only to their families as the most reliable sources of sexuality related information. (NCPTP, et al, 1997, 1998);**
- Youth development programs i.e., school-to-work activities, community service activities, mentoring, tutoring and other activities that foster a sense of self in youth, are proving promising in lowering rates of early pregnancy. (Kirby, 1997); and
- Female athletes are less likely to get pregnant, begin having sex later, have sex less often, have fewer partners, and are more likely to use contraception than non-athletes. (Women's Sports Foundation, 1998). (Kirby, 2007).

Teens and Sex Since 2000

The numbers reflected in this section are summarized from **teenpregnancy.org,** an advocacy group seeking to reduce the prevalence of teen-age mothers. The most currently available data is quoted below. **How bad is the problem?** The United States has one of the highest rates of teen pregnancy and births in the western industrialized world. As discussed earlier, **teen pregnancy costs the United States at least $7 billion annually.** Additionally,

- Thirty-four percent of young women become pregnant at least once before they reach the age of 20 -- about 820,000 a year;
- Eight in ten of these pregnancies are unintended and 79 percent are to unmarried teens;
- The teen birth rate has declined slowly but steadily from 1991 to 2002 with an overall decline of 30 percent for those aged 15 to 19. These recent declines reverse the 23-percent rise in the teenage birth rate from 1986 to 1991. **The largest decline since 1991 by race was for black women.** The birth rate for black teens aged 15 to 19 fell 42 percent between 1991 to 2002;
- Hispanic teen birth rates declined 20 percent between 1991 and 2002. The rates of both Hispanics and blacks, however, remain higher than for other groups. **Hispanic teens now have the highest teenage birth rates.** Most teenagers giving birth before 1980 were married whereas most teens giving birth today are unmarried;
- The younger a teenaged girl is when she has sex for the first time, the more likely she is to have had an unwanted or non-voluntary sex; and
- Nearly four in ten girls who had first intercourse at 13 or 14 report it was either non-voluntary or unwanted. (teenpregnancy.org, 2005).

Nationally known researcher, Dr. Douglas Kirby has been studying issues related to teenage pregnancy and STDs for decades. The good news is that schools, intervention programs, and perhaps even parents, have made some changes related to the sexual behaviors of kids. Some of the changes during this decade are small, or subtle, but things are improving in the prevention of sexual risk-taking behaviors of youth. The following section will describe some of the major trends Kirby and colleagues discovered related to teen sexuality during the decade 1997-2007.

- Teen pregnancy and birth rates have declined by about one-third since the early 1990s;
- **These declines are being driven by decreased sexual intercourse and increased use of contraceptives;**
- Despite the declines, teen pregnancy and birth rates in the U.S. remain far higher than those in other fully industrialized countries;
- Teen mothers are less likely to complete high school, less likely to attend college, and more likely to be single parents than women who delay childbearing just a few years;
- Children of teen mothers often suffer the most serious consequences of teen childbearing-they tend to grow up in less supportive and stimulating home environments, have lower cognitive development, worse educational

outcomes, higher rates of behavior problems, higher rates of incarceration (sons) and higher rates of adolescent childbearing themselves than children born to older mothers;

- Teen childbearing costs taxpayers $9.1 billion in 2004;
- Young people (age 15 to 24) represent 25 percent of the sexually active population but account for about half of all new cases of STD;
- About one-third of all sexually active young people become infected with an STD by age 24;
- Teens still have some of the highest rates of STD infection;
- To reduce unintended teen pregnancy and STD, including HIV, communities must address and change behavior that leads to these outcomes;
- Teens can avoid pregnancy by abstaining from sex and can reduce their risk of becoming pregnant by using effective contraception. Programs for teens should and do address both types of behavior; and
- **Teens can reduce their risk of STD by abstaining from sex, limiting the number of sexual partners, increasing the amount of time between sexual partners, reducing the frequency of sex, using condoms, and being tested and treated for STDs.** Teens can also be vaccinated against hepatitis B and HPV (human papillomavirus), and boys can be circumcised. (Kirby, 2007).

Who suffers the consequences?

Teen mothers are less likely to complete high school (only one-third receive a high school diploma) and only 1.5% has a college degree by age 30. **Studies have shown that nearly 80 percent of unmarried teen mothers end up on welfare.** The children of teenage mothers have lower birth weights, are more likely to perform poorly in school, and are at greater risk of abuse and neglect, and the sons of teen mothers are 13 percent more likely to end up in prison while teen daughters are 22 percent more likely to become teen mothers themselves. (Teenpregnancy.org, 2005).

Preventing Teen Pregnancy: Progress has stalled.

The 2009 YRBS Youth Risk Behavior Survey (YRBS) addressing teen pregnancy came to a dramatic conclusion: **progress has stalled!** This survey administered through the CDC every two years in grades 9-12 in 42 states and 20 local education and health agencies, and includes a variety of questions about risky behavior including questions about sex, drug and

197

alcohol use, physical fitness, seatbelt use, and other issues. Approximately 16,000 students completed the questionnaire in 2009. The YRBS has been used since 1991 and has provided interesting data about the behavior of high school students over time. It is important, however, to recognize one major limitation of the data. The research is limited to youth enrolled in high school and does not include those teens that have dropped out or were absent the day the of survey, or data does not reflect older teens who have graduated from high school. (CDC, 2010a). Some of the 2009 YRBS survey findings include:

Teen Sexual Experience

- In 2009, 46% of all high school students reported ever having had sexual intercourse-46% of girls and 46% of boys;

- Between 2007 and 2009 the proportion of students who ever had sex essentially remained unchanged; and

- **The proportion of high school students who have ever had sexual intercourse declined from 54% in 1991 to 46% in 2009;**

Sexually Active Teens

- In 2009, more than one-third (34%) of all high school students reported being sexually active-that is, they had sex in the previous three months. Thirty-six percent of girls and 33% of boys reported being sexually active;

- In 2009, 48% of non-Hispanic black students, 35% of Hispanic students, and 32% of non-Hispanic white students reported being sexually active;

- Nearly half (49%) of all 12th grade students reported being sexually active compared to 21% of 9th grade students; and

- Between 2007 and 2009 the proportion of students who were sexually active remained unchanged (35% in 2007 vs. 34% in 2009). Between 1991 and 2009 there was a slight decrease in the proportion of sexually active high school students from 38% in 1991 to 34% in 2009.

Contraceptive Use

- In 2009, 61% of sexually active students reported using a condom the last time they had sex, and 20% of sexually active students reported using birth control pills the last time they had sex;

- Non-Hispanic white students were three times (27%) more likely to report using birth control pills before last sex compared to non-Hispanic black students (8%);

- Eleven percent of Hispanic students reported using birth control pills sex;

198

- Among all high school students, those in 12th grade were most likely to report using birth control pills before last sex, and least likely to report using a condom the last time they had sex; and

- Condom use at last sex has increased from 1991 to 2009 (from 46% to 61%). However, birth control pill use at last sex has remained essentially unchanged from 1991 (21%) to 2009 (20%).

Sex Before Age 13

- In 2009, 6% of high school students reported that they first had sex before age 13 compared to 7% in 2007; and

- Between 1991 and 2009, the percentage of teens who reported having had sex before the age of 13 decreased from 10% to 6%.

Multiple Partners

- In 2009, 14% of high school students reported having already had four or more sexual partners-essentially unchanged from 2007 (15%);

- Boys (16%) are more likely than girls (11%) to report that they have had four or more partners;

- The number of sexual partners also differs according to race/ ethnicity. Non-Hispanic black students (28%) are more likely than their Hispanic (14%) and non-Hispanic white peers (11%) to report that they have had four or more sexual partners in 2009; and

- The proportion of students who have had four or more sexual partners decreased from 19% in 1991 to 14% in 2009. (CDC, 2010a).

National Campaign New Data (NCPTP) Below are a few of the new attitudes and practices of young people reported in the 2010 NCPTP research:

- The overwhelming majority of teens (87%) and adults (93%) agree that it is important for teens to be given a strong message that they should not have sex until they are at least out of high school;

- **Most teens (46%) and adults (73%) wish young people were getting information about both abstinence and contraception rather than either/or;**

- Most teens (65% of girls and 57% of boys) who have had sex say they wish they had waited;

199

- About nine in ten teens (91% of girls and 87% of boys) and two-thirds of adults (66%) say that teen pregnancy is a "very important" problem in the United States;

- Significant percentages of teens (63%) and adults (72%) agree that "teen boys often receive the message that they are expected to have sex;"

- **Most teens (71%) and adults (77%) also agree that "teen girls often receive the message that attracting boys and looking sexy is one of the most important things they can do;"**

- About nine in ten teens (95% of girls and 93% of boys) say it is important for them right now to avoid getting pregnant or causing a pregnancy;

- Most teens (93% of girls and 88% of boys) say they would rather have a boyfriend/girlfriend and not have sex rather than have sex but not have a boyfriend or girlfriend;

- **Most teens (71%) and adults (81%) agree that sharing nude or semi-nude images of themselves or other teens electronically (through cell phones, websites, and/or social media networks) leads to more sex in real life;**

- About nine in ten teens (87%) and adults (90%) believe reducing teen pregnancy is a very effective way to reduce the high school dropout rate and improve academic achievement; and

- Most teens (73%) and adults (70%) believe religious leaders and groups should be doing more to help prevent teen pregnancy.

(NCPTP, 2011).

Common Sense: Family Planning for Prevention

Contraceptive use. The Alan Guttmacher report states, "A sexually active teen who does not use a contraceptive has a 90% chance of becoming pregnant within a year. The majority of sexually experienced teens (79% of females and 87% of males) used contraceptives the first time they had sex. Contraceptive use at first premarital sex has been increasing. Fifty-six percent of women whose first premarital sex occurred before 1985 used a method, compared with 76% in 2000–2004 and 84% in 2005–2008." (AGI, 2011). Chapter 10 will describe the medical and behavioral aspects of contraceptive use in detail.

University of Washington Researchers determined that a comprehensive sexuality education program will reduce teen pregnancies. In addition to teaching about HIV/AIDS, and STD prevention, a well organized and planned curriculum that includes methods of birth control, family planning, setting goals, planning careers and methods to practice refusal skills will assist teens in making sensible decisions about their sexual life. The University of Washington (UW) researchers concluded. **"Adolescents who received comprehensive sex education had a lower risk of pregnancy than adolescents who received abstinence-only or no sex education."** (AGI, 2011). The authors analyzed records of 1,719 straight teens ages 15 to 19 taken from the 2002 National Survey of Family Growth. After demographic differences were considered, students who had taken comprehensive sex education classes (67% of students) were 60 percent less likely to report a pregnancy than those without any sex education (9% of students) and 50% less likely than teens that received abstinence-only education (24 %of students). Moreover, they were no more likely to have intercourse or get an STD than their peers who received abstinence education. The federal government has endorsed abstinence-only programs for more than a decade, and the **Title V Abstinence Education Program was not renewed as of the fall of 2007.** Some abstinence programs discuss contraceptives but emphasize their failure, not success, rates. Nonetheless, many schools through the U.S. were still using the abstinence only curricula in 2011.

Compared with other developed nations, Americans have higher rates of teen pregnancy, abortion, and STDs. Groups that support abstinence programs, such as Spokane-based Teen-AID, question the conclusions of the study because even abstinence-only students are exposed to messages in society that premarital sex is acceptable as long as it is done safely. According to Pamela Kohler, program manager of UWs Center for AIDS and STD, "We're building more and more evidence that [abstinence-only] education isn't having much effect." Kohler concluded, "Teaching about contraception was not associated with increased risk of adolescent sexual activity or STD. Adolescents who received comprehensive sex education had a lower risk of pregnancy than adolescents who received abstinence-only or no sex education." (Kohler, 2008).

What helps prevent teen pregnancy? The primary reason teenage girls that are virgins give for abstaining from sex is that having sex would be against their religious or moral values. They also give other reasons including a desire to avoid pregnancy, fear of contracting a sexually transmitted disease (STD), and not having met the appropriate partner. Additional research data also reveals: Three of four girls and over half of boys report that girls who have sex do so because their boyfriends want them to. **Teenagers who have strong emotional attachments to their parents are much less likely to become sexually active at an early age.** A significant number, ninety-four percent, of adults in the U.S., and 91 percent of teenagers-think it important that school-aged children and teenagers be given a strong message from society that they should abstain from sex until they are out of high school. **Seventy-eight percent of adults also think that sexually active teenagers should have access to contraception.** While there has been an increase in contraceptive use among teens, behavioral use of birth control products, etc., remains inconsistent. Three-quarters of teens use some method of contraception (usually a condom) the first time they have sex. **A sexually active teen that does not use contraception has a 90 percent chance of pregnancy within one year.** Teens who have been raised by both parents (biological or adoptive) from birth, have lower probabilities of having sex than teens who grew up in any other family situation. (NCPTP, 2011).

When should I talk to my child about sex? The earlier, the better. One of every 3 girls has had sex by age 16, 2 out of 3 by age 18. Two of three boys have had sex by age 18. Surprise: Teens do want to hear from their parents. Seven of ten teens interviewed said that they were ready to listen to things parents thought they were not ready to hear. **Do teens wish they had waited to have sex?** Yes. A majority of both girls and boys who are sexually active wish they had waited. Eight in ten girls and six in ten boys say they wish they had waited until they were older to have sex. (Teenpregnancy.org, 2005).

The events leading up to a teen pregnancy are not random events. Research shows that youth at greatest risk are more likely to live in high poverty areas with low education levels, to be poor, to have experienced a divorce, separation or their parents never have married, and their mothers or sisters are more likely to have given birth as adolescents. Additionally, these youth invest little time in school, have low expectations for their futures and may be more aggressive during elementary school. They are more likely to use alcohol and other drugs and engage in unhealthful or risky behavior. Males have higher levels of testosterone and males and females both experience early puberty. They are more likely to have experienced abuse or sexual pressure and hold more permissive sexual attitudes. Females often begin dating at an early age and are more likely to date older males. (Kirby, 1997, 2007).

Teen Age Pregnancy and Abstinence

Throughout the 1980s, school districts, educators and policy makers in the U.S. launched many campaigns to overcome the problem of pregnancy with adolescent girls. Some "abstinence only" programs around the country have even claimed significant success in lowering the pregnancy rate in communities. While abstinence as part of a comprehensive family life program is very important; many scare tactics and lack of education on condoms and birth control methods, do not effect change in sexual behaviors. Some studies have actually falsified data to support their cause. (Dryfoos, 1985, Roosa, 1990). The few studies that have shown successful changes were compiled with data that (a) relied on self-reporting measures of sexual behavior, (large discrepancy between reported behavior and true behaviors is often found) and (b) short-term, small scale, and/or non-replicated outcomes. The final outcome is that while nationwide programs were expanded in the mid and late 1980s, birth rates among school-age mothers increased 20 percent, reversing 25 years of previous decline. (USPHS, 1988).

The California Vital Statistics Section for 1990 shows **that adults, not peers, are fathers in most "school-age" childbirths.** Among students in grades K-8 (ages 11-14) more than half the fathers are post-high school adult men. When the youngest and oldest 5% of fathers are adjusted for 95% of them are between the ages of 17-31. Furthermore, the younger the teenager girls' age, the older the male father. Thus the omission of the predominant role of adult-teen intercourse tends to obscure research literature. Teen boys do cause pregnancies, but at a much smaller percentage than do adult men over age 18. (Males, 1993).

The Federal Abstinence Only Curricula Not Working and Has Errors

A significant report to congress prepared for Representative Henry Waxman published in December 2004, clearly identified that the federally funded **abstinence-only program was ineffective and even stated false and misleading information to the public.** This report included much carefully documented research from the CDC, National Center for Health Statistics, and numerous peer reviewed sources. **The report reinforced that abstinence-only curricula does not work to prevent pregnancy and risky sexual behaviors in youth.** The report found that over 80% of the abstinence-only curricula, used by over two thirds of grantees in 2003, contain false, misleading, or distorted information about reproductive health. Specifically, the report found: (1) false information about the effectiveness of contraceptives. (2) many of the curricula misrepresent the effectiveness of condoms in preventing sexually transmitted diseases and pregnancy. (3) One curriculum says that "the popular claim that 'condoms help prevent the spread of STDs,' is not supported by the data"; (4) another states that "[i]n heterosexual sex, condoms fail to prevent HIV approximately 31% of the time"; (5) and another teaches that a pregnancy occurs one out of every seven times that couples use condoms. Shockingly, these erroneous statements are presented as proven scientific facts. (Waxman, 2004).

Additional information from Abstinence-Only Curricula contains false information about the risks of abortion. (1) One curriculum states that 5% to 10% of women who have legal abortions will become sterile; (2) that "premature birth, a major cause of mental retardation, is increased following the abortion of a first pregnancy"; (3) and that "tubal and cervical pregnancies are increased following abortions." **This is not true; these risks do not rise after the procedure used in most abortions in the United States.** Abstinence-Only Curricula treat stereotypes about girls and boys as scientific fact. One curriculum teaches that women need "financial support," while men need "admiration." Another instructs: "Women gauge their happiness and judge their success on their relationships. Men's happiness and success hinge on their accomplishments." (Waxman, 2004).

Abstinence-Only Curricula Contain scientific errors. In numerous instances, the abstinence-only curricula teach erroneous scientific information. One curriculum incorrectly lists exposure to sweat and tears as risk factors for HIV transmission. Another curriculum states that "twenty-four chromosomes from the mother and twenty-four chromosomes from the father join to create this new individual;" every high school sophomore learns the correct number is 23.

203

Finally, Abstinence-Only Curricula blur religion and science. Many of the curricula present as scientific fact the religious view that life begins at conception. For example, one lesson states: "Conception, also known as fertilization, occurs when one sperm unites with one egg in the upper third of the fallopian tube. This is when life begins." Another curriculum calls a 43-day-old fetus a "thinking person." (Waxman, 2004). During 2010 The Obama Administration approved additional funding for comprehensive sexuality education including methods of abstinence. California law does not allow school districts to offer abstinence only curricula in public schools. To read the entire federal report, use the URL:
http://oversight.house.gov/Documents/20041201102153-50247.pdf.

AIDS Education Requirement

Since 1992 HIV Education is required for all students in California at least once in the middle school and once in the high school setting. While many groups and political activists are against any form of sexuality education for young people, the law is very clear as to what material should be addressed related to HIV/AIDS prevention education. The *Education Code* states that HIV prevention instruction **shall be taught both in the middle and high school class curriculum.** Instructional materials about AIDS must reflect research from **scientific sources** such as the following: (1) The Surgeon General of the United States, (2) The Centers for Disease Control and Prevention (CDC), (3) The National Academy of Sciences, and (4) Peer reviewed scientific research. (*E.C.* 51934).

Revised Sexuality Education Laws: The California Comprehensive Sexual Health and HIV/AIDS Prevention Education Act (Effective January 1, 2004. - *EC 51934*)

During 2003, the California Legislature revised, and organized the numerous laws related to sexuality education for K-12 children. This law, *EC 51934*, is very important, not only to prevent the spread of the virus that causes AIDS, but also to specifically identify scientific sources which schools must use to teach kids about AIDS prevention. Chapter nine will review HIV/AIDS transmission in detail, and chapter eleven will address the legal implications of teaching about AIDS in schools.

Homosexuality

Oftentimes, when a teenager comes out of the closet,
the parents go into the closet.
...Mike Henigan,
PFLAG parent advocate.

California Joins Massachusetts to legalize Gay Marriage

On Thursday May 14, 2008   The California Supreme Court made history and struck down two state laws that had limited marriages to unions between a man and a woman, ruled that same-sex couples have a constitutional right to marry. The 4-to-3 decision, drew on a ruling more than 60 years ago that struck down a state ban on interracial marriage, and made California the second state, after Massachusetts, to allow same-sex marriages. Hundreds of people celebrated in San Francisco, where thousands of same-sex marriages were thrown out by the courts four years earlier. This decision by the state court was denounced by religious and conservative groups that support an initiative that would amend the California Constitution to ban same-sex marriages and overturn the decision. In the decision, Chief Justice George wrote, "The California Constitution properly must be interpreted to guarantee this basic civil right to all Californians, whether gay or heterosexual, and to same-sex couples as well as to opposite-sex couples." By 2011 the U.S. Supreme Court has not yet acted on the constitutionality of the Proposition 8 in California that will allow gay couples to marry.

Most often, the topics of homosexuality and bisexuality are not adequately addressed in the school setting. While experts argue that the estimated percentage of gay and lesbian students may range from 5-10% of the general population; the actual numbers could range between 100-300 students at a large high school campus. Many of these students frequently are in much emotional pain, suffer significant depression, and feel very isolated and ostracized from the general student body. How can a gay or lesbian student talk to their friends about a same sex "partner" comfortably; while their peers rave about their own romances with a boy or girl of the opposite sex?   A few of the problems of gay and lesbian students are discussed below.

Issues Facing Gay and Lesbian Students-Issues of Prejudice

Lesbian, gay, bisexual, and transgender (LGBTQ) youth and those who are questioning (sometimes added to the acronym as Q) their sexual orientation are happy and thrive during their teen years. When they attend a school that has created a safe and supportive learning environment for all students and have caring and accepting parents, they fit in with the rest of the students with minimal problems. This helps all youth achieve good grades and maintain good mental and physical health. Some LGBT youth however, face greater difficulties in their lives and school environments compared to their heterosexual peers, such as experiencing violence.

205

Experiences with Violence. Negative attitudes toward gays, lesbians, bisexuals, and transgender people put LGBT youth at increased risk for violence compared to other students Violence can include behaviors such as bullying, teasing, harassment, physical assault, and suicide-related behaviors. CDC reported a 2009 survey of more than 7,000 LGBT middle and high school students (aged 13-21) and that in the past year, because of their sexual orientation: eight in ten had been verbally harassed at school; four in ten had been physically harassed at school; six in ten felt unsafe at school, and, one in five had been the victim of a physical assault at school. Tragically these types of experiences with violence also occur outside of school and may continue into young adulthood. A study published in 2004 looked at discrimination and violence among young gay and bisexual men between the ages of 18 and 27 and found that 37% had been harassed and 5% had experienced physical violence in the past six months because of their sexual orientation. (CDC, 2009d).

Effects on Education and Health OF LGBT Youth. Violence experienced by LGBT youth has negative effects on their education and on their health. In 2009, almost 1 in 3 LGBT students ages 13 to 21 responding to a survey reported that they had missed at least one day of school in the past month because they were concerned about their safety. LGBT youth who experience more frequent harassment perform lower in school by almost half a grade point compared to their non-LGBT peers who experience less frequent or no harassment (grade-point average of 2.7 for frequently harassed students versus 3.1 for other students). (CDC, 2009d). U.S. Secretary Kathleen Sebelius of the U.S. Health and Human Services in her 2009 message to LGBT suggested the following to help overcome the negative aspects in the life of LGBT youth.

What Schools Can Do. Schools that have clear policies, procedures and activities designed to prevent bullying and have supportive staff and student organizations can be effective in reducing verbal and physical harassment. These kinds of positive school climates are associated with reduced suicide risk and better mental health among LGBT students. For youth to thrive in their schools and communities, they need to feel socially, emotionally, and physically safe. To help promote health and safety among LGBTQ youth, schools can implement the following:

- Prohibit bullying, harassment, and violence against all students;
- Identify "safe spaces," such as counselors' offices, designated classrooms, or student organizations, where LGBTQ youth can receive support from administrators, teachers, or other school staff;
- **Ensure that health curricula or educational materials include HIV, other STD, or pregnancy prevention information that is relevant to LGBTQ youth (such as ensuring that curricula or materials use inclusive language or terminology);**
- Encourage school district and school staff to develop and publicize trainings on how to create safe and supportive school environments for all students, regardless of sexual orientation or gender identity and encourage staff to attend

these trainings;

- Facilitate access to community-based providers who have experience providing health services, including HIV/STD testing and counseling, to LGBTQ youth; and
- Facilitate access to community-based providers who have experience in providing social and psychological services to LGBTQ youth.
  (CDC, 2009d)

California Laws Related to Lesbian, Gay, Transgender Students. All children should be treated with respect, regardless of their haircuts, makeup, body piercings, or manner of dress. It is imperative that teachers, even those with their own biases, or personal prejudices, must provide a **safe, nurturing and comfortable environment** for their students. The law throughout the nation is very specific to avoid discrimination, and the California Law below is very specific. The first section reads:

California Education Code 200. It is the policy of the State of California to afford all persons in public schools, regardless of their **disability, gender, nationality, race or ethnicity, religion, sexual orientation, or any other characteristic** that is contained in the definition of hate crimes set forth in Section 422.55 of the Penal Code, equal rights and opportunities in the educational institutions of the state. The purpose of this chapter is to prohibit acts that are contrary to that policy and to provide remedies therefore. (*EC 200-201*).

High Rate of Alcohol and Drug Abuse. The rate of alcoholism among gay youth is 50% higher than among straight youth and marijuana use among gay youth is three times higher than among straight youth, according to a 1995 study in *The Journal of School Health*. A 1991 study in *Pediatrics* also found that 85 percent of the gay youth that had attempted suicide had used illicit drugs. In 1993, the Gay and Lesbian Task Force concluded that 68% of young gay men and 83% of young lesbians between the ages of 12 and 20 had used alcohol and other drugs.

Suicide and Isolation. For decades research has shown that young adults who identify as gay, lesbian or bisexual are more likely to have suicidal thoughts than their heterosexual counterparts. (Krisberg, 2007). Lesbian, gay and bisexual youth represent 30% of all teen suicides and are two to six times more likely to attempt suicide than their heterosexual counterparts. (Marino, 1995). Suicide is the leading cause of death for gay and lesbian youth. (Gibson, 1989). Martin and Hedrik reported in 1988 that the social isolation of gay youth is evident because they are at risk of being thrown out of their families, expelled from their peer group, or lose their religious/social identity. The *Journal of School Health* in 1995 reported that 41% of gay and lesbian youth felt negative attitudes from family and friends. According to the 1995-96 Human Relations Commission's Report on Hate Crimes, gays and lesbians are the second largest targeted groups of hate crimes. Eighty percent of gay and lesbian youth are victims of insults. (Pilkington and D'Augelli, 1995).

Issues of Physical and Verbal Violence Facing Gay and Lesbian Youth. Forty percent of gay youth reported being threatened by physical attack. (Pilkington and D'Augelli,1995). Twenty-two percent of boys and twenty-nine percent of girls report being physically attacked by other students. Seven percent report being **physically hurt by the teacher**. (Pilkington and D'Augelli, 1995).

High Rate of Runaways and Homeless. The U.S. Department of Health and Human Services estimates that lesbian, gay, transgender and bisexual teens represents as much as 25% of all the homeless youth in the United States. (Thomas, Marino, 1995). Twenty-six percent of gays and lesbians are forced to leave home because of conflicts over their sexual orientation. (Gibson, 1989). Twenty-eight percent of gay and lesbian youth drop out of school because of discomfort in the school environment. Further analysis of the available research suggests that between 20 percent and 40 percent of all homeless youth identify as lesbian, gay, bisexual or transgender. (Ray, 2006). Schools do not adequately protect gay youth, rarely allow gay-straight alliance clubs or groups to meet, and many teachers are often reluctant to stop harassment or aggressively rebut numerous homophobic remarks. (Gibson,1989). Gay-Straight Alliance clubs in California have grown from 40 clubs in 1998 to more than 830 in 2011. (GSAN, 2011).

Special Considerations for Working with Gay and Lesbian Students

Teachers can be very influential to their students. It is very important to consider the following methods to improve relationships with gay and lesbian students: Be yourself. Be aware of your comfort level as well as your personal biases. Establish trust. Use the vocabulary that the student uses; i.e. if the student uses "gay or lesbian" to identify themselves, use that term. Show respect for the sensitivities of students. **Do not make assumptions** or attempt to generalize or label concerning a student's orientation. Students may be experiencing grief issues due to rejection from home, church, classmates, friends. Be aware that parents may or may not know about the student's sexual orientation. Know when and where to seek help. Locate resources in your community. Helping the student to build a support system is critical.

What might lesbians/gays be afraid of?

- Rejection, loss of relationships
- Harassment/abuse
- Being thrown out of the family/house
- Being forced to undergo psychotherapy
- Having their partner arrested
- Loss of financial support
- Losing their job
- Physical violence

Why might lesbians/gays want to come out?

- End the hiding game
- Live honestly
- Feel closer to family and friends
- Be able to feel "whole" around others
- Stop wasting energy by hiding all of the time
- Feel a sense of integrity
- Make a statement that "gay is O.K."

Useful Definitions Related to Gay and Lesbian Youth

Many teachers may have little or no known contact with gay or lesbian students and may feel uncomfortable having a conversation merely because of lack of knowledge of acceptable terminology related to homosexuality. Some teachers also may harbor homophobic attitudes about gay and lesbian students, but **it is critical that teachers strive to separate their personal biases and treat all students with the same amount of dignity and respect, regardless of their sexual orientation.** Some helpful terms are identified below.

Bisexuality: Sexual attraction to and/or behavior with both sexes. **Note:** Many gay youth may label themselves as bisexual to avoid any stigma of being gay.

Coming Out: The process of becoming aware of one's sexual orientation, accepting it and telling others about it. Coming out is a never-ending process. Many teens may not be advised to "come out" **unless issues addressing their safety are met.**

Gay: Men and women who accept their homosexual orientation and identify themselves as being gay. There are gay people in every sector of society and among every ethnic and racial group.

Homophobia: The irrational fear and intolerance of homosexuality, bisexuality, lesbian and gay men. Homophobia is the root of anti-gay violence.

Homosexuality: Sexual attraction to a person of the same sex. It is has no known cause, and is not considered a form of mental illness.

In the closet: Hiding about one's sexual orientation. This means having to avoid or elude the truth in order to protect oneself from discrimination and anti-gay violence.

Lesbian: Females who are attracted to other females. Most prefer the term "lesbian," because it gives gay women an identity independent from men.

Queer: This term once was considered historically a very derogatory word, but in recent years, it has been reclaimed by gay activists.

209

Transgender: This refers to a gay male and a lesbian female who are gender atypical. The man has a woman's gender identity, and the woman has a man's gender identity. Unlike many homosexual students, these students cannot pass for heterosexual; thus, they are victims of more harassment and hate crimes. They are more likely to be kicked out of their homes due to parents who can't accept an effeminate son or a masculine daughter. **A Transsexual** is a male or female that may also undergo body changes, such as surgical, and hormonal modifications to live as the chosen sex.

Transphobia: Hatred of individuals who deviate from the gender norm.

Gay and Lesbian Youth-Sensitivity and Acceptance

The California Department of Education published a booklet back in 1987 that served as a source for schools to deal with sensitive and controversial issues related to sexuality. This document, *Human Sexuality Guidelines,* was intended to assist teachers and school boards in developing methods, techniques and policies to help students with sexual concerns, and also to serve as a guide to assist teachers with curricula related to controversial topics dealing with sexual concerns. **Masturbation, homosexuality and bisexuality may be discussed in a school setting; but schools should have a specific written policy that will allow teachers to implement curricula.** Unfortunately, however, even as recently as 2010 a Mississippi school cancelled the prom because a lesbian couple wanted to attend. Many districts are very reluctant to include any discussion about homosexuality for fear of causing negative publicity.

Media messages about sexuality are powerful indeed. Schools, parents or clergy may help to assist students with their emerging sexual identity, but adults are faced with the fact that students are presented mixed messages every single day through radio, TV, video clips, movies and thousands of advertisements focusing on sex. These messages are designed to sell everything from nail polish, to laundry soap or toothpaste. The multitude of sexual images on the Internet makes the problem even more exasperating. During the time of adolescence, young people gain an increased awareness of their bodies and begin to ponder the sources, intensity and expression of their sexual feelings. During this time, they may ask questions surrounding homosexual and heterosexual orientations. School, religious or family teachings may be in direct conflict with contemporary popular messages. **This dissonance can generate frustration, concern and confusion in the minds of youth. Teachers should strive to maintain a neutral position and allow students to view both sides of the issues discussed in class.**

Experts estimate that in the 2000 U.S. census populations, about 5-10 percent were homosexual. Many students will have questions about their own sexual identity, but may find it extremely difficult to discuss their orientation, even with close friends. A teen girl may feel very close and even say "I love you," to a best friend. Boys too, may form very close relationships with friends, but may not vocalize their affection for their peers because of societal restrictions on male expression of feelings. Teachers have the duty to separate their own biases and reluctance to discuss sensitive topics, whether they deal with health education, social studies or language in English literature. Several prominent issues may arise for the teacher in dealing with homosexuality discussions.

How does the teacher deal with questions regarding the source of heterosexual or homosexual orientation? A continuous debate centers on the derivation of sexual orientation. Is it *nature* or *nurture*? Are people born gay or straight or do they develop their orientation through experiences and influences by family peers, etc.? These questions are difficult to answer, but teachers can explain that the current information remains inconclusive and unclear, but it appears that a combination of genetic and some behavioral influence both play a role in sexual orientation.

Love is not about gender...

How does the teacher discuss questions regarding propriety of sexual behavior and orientations? In discussing sexuality or HIV prevention, educators often refer to family cultural or religious beliefs. Such comments or references lie outside the scientific domain of sex and HIV education and the following guideline is recommended: **Personal, family, cultural and/or religious beliefs may be acknowledged, explored and compared; however, these beliefs must ultimately be referred back to the individual and their family or culture for final decision.**

Responsible sex education and HIV prevention does not encourage racism or sexism in any form, or the stereotyping of persons infected by HIV. The respect and value and integrity of *all individuals* should always be maintained. The use of "gender neutral," terminology can significantly help the educator discuss sensitive topics with students. Instead of referring to their "girlfriend" or "boyfriend," the teacher can use the term "partner" which includes homosexual, bisexual and heterosexual students.

How does the teacher respond to concerns and needs of gay and lesbian youth? It is likely that some students attending classes on family life education, STD education or HIV/AIDS prevention have had homosexual and bisexual, feelings or experiences. These students must feel that they are fully included during the lessons and discussions. Teachers should acknowledge that it is "okay" for students to have a range of sexual feelings for their peers. Some gay students will also have sexual experiences with peers. As teachers teach subject matter content, their students should be reminded about confidentiality and the "right to pass rule," to help avoid embarrassment and unwanted disclosure. Teachers can also use anonymous sources, such as the "question box," where students can ask personal questions without identifying themselves. For detailed sources and links do a **Google Search** under: Gay, Bi, Lesbian, and Transgender (GBLT) resources in California.

Kids with Gay, Lesbian or transgender Parents

In recent years there seems to be much less prejudice towards gay, lesbian and transgender people in the U.S. Nonetheless, there still are numerous individuals that harbor prejudices and some of that discrimination spills over from the parent to the child and is expressed in the school setting. When it comes to everyday activities in school, all children should be able to attend school in a safe and nurturing atmosphere without the fear of any discrimination. According to the American Academy of Child and Adolescent Psychiatry (AACAP), there may be millions of children in the United States that have lesbian, gay, bisexual and/or transgender (LGBT) parents. Some LGBT parents conceived their children in heterosexual marriages, and others may have adopted children or conceived using laboratory or donor pregnancies. A few states currently have laws supportive of LGBT couple adoption. What is the effect having LGBT parents? (AACAP, 2006).

Many people wonder if having a gay parent or two gay parents can make life difficult or even harmful to kids. Current research, however, reveals that kids with lesbian or gay parents or even transgender parents do not differ in their emotional development than kids from heterosexual parents. (AACAP, 2006). The key is the quality of parent and child relationship and not the parent's sexual orientation that will help youth develop healthy emotional lives and adjustments with peers. Contrary to popular belief children of LGBT parents:

- Are not more likely to be sexually abused;
- Are not more likely to be gay than children with heterosexual parents;
- Do not show differences in whether they think of themselves as male or female (gender identity); and
- Do not show differences in their male and female behaviors (gender role behavior).

Even thought research shows that children of gay and lesbian parents are well adjusted,

212

many of these kids still face additional challenges compared to straight kids. They may be teased, bullied by peers or even discriminated by school officials such as not allowing gay couples to attend school dances. Parents can help their kids deal with these pressures by allowing for regular open communication appropriate to the child's age and maturity level; preparing the child to answer questions or comments about their background and family life; developing a local support group of other families of LGBT parents, and considering living in a community more accepting to diversity. Sometimes, however, professional help may be necessary to help youth make family adjustments. School counselors, school nurses or school psychologists may serve to improve the daily life of kids living with LGBT parents. (AACAP, 2006).

Obesity and School Kids

The news about childhood obesity has been all over the news throughout the decade of 2000-2010, and unless you have been hiding in the mountains, you must have heard about the serious problem Americans face regarding obesity, especially obesity in children. The CDC has an excellent website that dramatically illustrates the serious trend in increased obesity for all Americans displaying a U.S. map indicating how obesity has increased from 1985-2009. Every middle school and high school in the U.S. should show the parents this slide show at a parent-teacher or back to school night meeting. The link is updated regularly and can be accessed at: http://www.cdc.gov/obesity/data/trends.html.

Why is Childhood Obesity a Problem?

The scientific community has documented the obesity problem and doctors, especially pediatricians, are very much concerned that obesity can lead to many health and mental problems in children. They include heart disease (caused by elevated cholesterol and/or high blood pressure), type 2 diabetes, asthma, sleep apnea and social discrimination. Obese children and teens have been found to have risk factors for cardiovascular disease (CVD), including high cholesterol levels, high blood pressure, and abnormal glucose tolerance. In a population-based sample of 5- to 17-year-olds, almost 60% of overweight children had at least one CVD risk factor while 25 percent of overweight children had two or more CVD risk factors. Additionally CDC reports indicated other less severe but very debilitating problems to include:

- Asthma is a disease of the lungs in which the airways become blocked or narrowed causing breathing difficulty. Studies have identified an association between childhood overweight and asthma;
- Hepatic steatosis or the fatty degeneration of the liver caused by a high concentration of liver enzymes. Weight reduction causes liver enzymes to normalize;

213

- Sleep apnea is a less common complication of overweight for children and adolescents. Sleep apnea is a sleep-associated breathing disorder defined as the cessation of breathing during sleep that lasts for at least 10 seconds. Sleep apnea is characterized by loud snoring and labored breathing. During sleep apnea, oxygen levels in the blood can fall dramatically. One study estimated that sleep apnea occurs in about 7% of overweight children;
- Type 2 diabetes is increasingly being reported among children and adolescents who are overweight;
- While diabetes and glucose intolerance, a precursor of diabetes, are common health effects of adult obesity, **only in recent years has Type 2 diabetes begun to emerge as a health-related problem among children and adolescents**. Onset of diabetes in children and adolescents can result in advanced complications such as CVD and kidney failure; and
- Studies have shown that obese children and teens are more likely to become obese as adults. (CDC, 2011d).

What Can Parents or Teachers do to Prevent Overweight and Obesity?

The list below has been stated and restated many times to Americans seeking to control their own weight; but it needs to be repeated again to help parents and school personnel strive to maintain healthy children. Many of these concepts have been suggested from the Surgeon General's first report on nutrition written in 1988. To help children develop better, healthier eating habits:

- Provide plenty of vegetables, fruits, and whole-grain products;
- Include low-fat or non-fat milk or dairy products;
- Choose lean meats, poultry, fish, lentils, and beans for protein;
- Serve reasonably-sized portions;
- Encourage your family to drink lots of water;
- Limit sugar-sweetened beverages; and
- Limit consumption of sugar and saturated fat.

Researchers Anderson and Whittaker of Ohio State recently simplified some of the easiest ways to help overcome obesity by listing **three simple solutions:**

1. *Students should participate in regular eating of meals with the family 5 times weekly.*
2. *Children should get adequate sleep, about 10.5 hours each night.*
3. *Parents should limit total "screen time" to 2 hours daily.*
   (Anderson, Whittaker, 2010). For information on First Lady Michelle Obama, and her program to prevent obesity in youth, Google: Let's Move.

Reduce Sedentary Time. Make kids move! There was a time in America when kids just went outside and played. This child play may have included playing tag, running, hide and seek or other 'creative type of fun games.' Today far too much time is spent in front of some type of electronic screen i.e., TV, video game, smart phone etc., and kids need to move around. Some communities may not provide a safe place for kids to play; but parents should try to get kids out of the house!   In addition to encouraging physical activity, help children avoid too much sedentary time. Although quiet time for reading and homework is fine, limit the time your children watch television, play video games, or surf the web to no more than 2 hours per day. Additionally, the American Academy of Pediatrics (AAP) does not recommend television viewing for children age 2 or younger. Instead, encourage kids to find fun activities to do with family members or on their own that simply involve more activity.

Obesity – Don't Blame it all on Video Images

By 2009, much has been said about the epidemic of obesity, and countless adults, barely in their thirties themselves, can't seem to understand why we have such a problem with child obesity. Just tell the kids to " go outside and play," seems to be the mantra by many adults. Going out to play has many different meanings to parents and their kids. During the summer, this author use to get on his bike as a young child, ride all day with friends and cousins, crawl down into the L.A. river sewer system to look for alligators, monsters and leeches with a flashlight! Today, some kids can't even go out to play because the neighborhood is too dangerous, or they can't be supervised by working parents. Worse yet, some kids go outside with their portable games and 'play with the video games.'

Ronald Sturm and colleagues reported interesting findings regarding the activities, and/or playtime of kids in 2005. Sturm found the following: (1), the free time of children has substantially declined due to increased time away from home, mostly in school or day care programs; (2) organized sports participation has increased; (3) unstructured playtime has decreased to allow time to get to organized sports; and (4) time spent in sedentary activities such as watching TV, having conversations, or other leisure activities also declined just as the obesity epidemic became a major problem. (Sturm, 2005). Common suggestions for the cause of the obesity epidemic among kids include reduced PE classes at school, increased homework assignments, vending machines on campus, TV, larger portion servings, fast food restaurants, video games and numerous other causes. Childhood obesity is a very complex problem, and while it may be difficult to overcome, some basic educational interventions can help.

Nutrition and Teenagers

Childhood obesity in the U.S. has more than tripled since the 1970s. In general, during the decade of 1995-2005 children and teens have reduced smoking rates, drug use, and rates of pregnancy. But all of those gains are now considered to be negated by the obesity epidemic. The *LA Times* stated, "The health risks of being fat far outweigh progress among U.S. children in birthrates, smoking and drug abuse. A report from Duke University and the Foundation for Child Development indicated the adolescent birthrate has dropped from 20 per 1,000 girls in 1992 to about 10 per 1000 in 2004. Binge drinking among high school seniors has also fallen from 36.9% in 1975 to about 29% in 2004. The number of youth offenders has also fallen since 1993. Young people age 12 to 17 that were victims of crime in 1994 were about 120 per 1,000. Crimes in that same group were estimated at about 45 per 1,000 in 2004. Professor Kenneth Land, a sociologist at Duke University, and developer of the report, said, "If you took away the huge declines in crime, violence and risky behaviors since the early 1990s, the picture for America's children would be bleak." (*LA Times*, 2005). **Poor diet, lack of exercise and excessive amount of screen time (games, TV, Internet, video's, etc.), are producing a population of kids that may not live as long as their parents.** (Klich, 2008).

School boards are taking notice and slowly taking action. In December 2004 *The National Association of State Boards of Education* ran a detailed article addressing childhood obesity. Some of the findings: more Latino and African-American youth are overweight than white youth; adolescents from poor families are twice as likely to be overweight as kids from families with higher income. What are the complications over time impacting obesity, especially in kids? **The Short-term Complications of Overweight Youth include:** high blood pressure, high blood cholesterol, lipid disorders, type 2 diabetes, insulin resistance, impaired glucose tolerance, metabolic syndrome (high triglycerides, high cholesterol, blood abnormalities), menstrual irregularities, accelerated growth, bowed legs, hip disorders, social discrimination, depression, low self-esteem, substance use, asthma and sleep apnea. Over time a complex series of long-term complications may arise. (NASBE, 2004). **The Long-term Complications of Overweight Youth include:** cancer of the breast, colon, gall bladder, kidney and prostate. Cardiovascular complications include high blood pressure, high blood cholesterol, cardiovascular disease and stroke. Orthopedic problems include osteoarthritis and musculoskeletal disorders. Females suffer gestational diabetes, increased cesarean section deliveries, toxemia, overdue births, induced labors and longer labors, menstrual irregularities, urinary infections and urinary incontinence. (NASBE, 2004; Dietz, 1998). Another excellent source dealing with school health and problems of obesity and lack of exercise in youth is:

216

www.healthinschools.org. Other national efforts regarding adolescent health are listed through the University of California at: **http://nahic.ucsf.edu/.**

Child Obesity Rate Hits Plateau? A Light at the End of the Tunnel.

On May 28, 2008, Cynthia Ogden and colleagues from the National Center for Health Statistics, reported in *JAMA* that, by measuring Body Mass Index (BMI) in a study of 8165 children and adolescents as part of the 2003-2004 and 2005-2006 National Health and Nutrition Examination Survey (NHANES), nationally representative surveys of the U.S. civilian, noninstitutionalized population. They concluded, **"The prevalence of high BMI for age among children and adolescents showed no significant changes between 2003-2004 and 2005-2006 and no significant trend variation between 1999 and 2006."** (Ogden, Carroll, Flegal, 2010). **This is exciting news!** Perhaps kids are as fat as they can get, and intervention methods in schools, promoting exercise and campaigns to get children to eat less junk food, may just be starting to work. Ogden stated that the levels of obesity are still too high, but these findings might result in some optimism. (Ogden, Carroll, Flegal, 2010). To read the details of this unique report, click on the URL: **http://jama.ama-assn.org/**, or Google Ogden , Whittaker and Obesity 2010.

By 2009, the CDC organized a very comprehensive solution posted on the Internet that can help school boards, teachers, administrators and parents review hundreds of attempts of schools around the nation to help overcome the obesity problem facing Americans. The website describes schools that promote ideas to improve cafeteria offerings, deal with vending machine contracts, promote staff wellness, and suggest various fund raising plans kids and teachers can utilize. A Google search for "Nutrition, Making it Happen," will provide details of these programs. The URL is: **http://apps.nccd.cdc.gov/MIH/MainPage.aspx.**

Nutrition 101: The Basics

Proper nutrition to prevent obesity and the subsequent health problems listed above, especially in the school setting, can play a critical role. **Nutrients** are any substances that are taken into the body to provide energy without any deleterious effects. **Macronutrients** include **carbohydrates, fats, proteins, and water**. These are the major foods needed daily by all individuals. **Micronutrients**, are the foods needed in very small proportions, they include **vitamins and minerals.** Proteins, carbohydrates, and fats are the nutrients that supply the body with fuel for energy. This energy is expressed in **Calories** (kilo calories), or the amount of energy found in food. Carbohydrates provide the body with bulk, and assists in many chemical reactions. Fats and other lipids are needed for insulation, energy storage, protection, transport of fat-soluble vitamins and serve as structural components of the body. Protein regulates body functions (especially enzymes) and helps to build cell and tissue structure.

Carbohydrates

Many individuals, especially students in school, do not understand the role of carbohydrate foods. Carbohydrates often have a reputation of empty caloric foods that cause

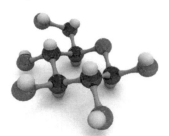 weight gain. Many people think that it is the sugar loaded foods that cause weight and health problems. This is not entirely true. In fact, some cultures such as in China, consume as high as 69% of their total food as **complex carbohydrate**, (fruits and vegetables) 10% protein and only 21% fat. Americans could dramatically improve their health if they were to add more complex carbohydrates, such as fruits and vegetables, to their daily food intake. **Many Americans consume greater than forty-five percent of food as fat!**

What exactly are carbohydrates? Most carbohydrates are made of sugars, starches and cellulose. All carbohydrates are organic molecules containing carbon, hydrogen and oxygen (CHO). They vary in size from simple sugars like **glucose, $C_6H_{12}O_6$** (pictured above, the sugar found in blood) to very large compounds called **polysaccharides.** Sugar sub-units are used to describe carbohydrates. They are either **monosaccharides,** (one sugar) **disaccharides** (two sugars) or **polysaccharides** (many sugars). This simply refers to the number of sugars within each molecule. **Complex carbohydrates** are a combination of starches and fibers. Carbohydrates are found in fruits, vegetables, breads, cereals, and grains and provide the major source of energy of life. Ultimately most food is digested and converted into simple glucose that provides energy for the cell, and for students to stay awake and read this book! Since 2000, however, millions of kids in China are now suffering with obesity as fast food companies sell their products in Asia.

Each gram of carbohydrate provides four calories of energy. The most important function of carbohydrates is to provide energy. The other two functions of carbohydrates are to provide water-insoluble fiber, which helps the large intestine move its contents faster, and the making of nonessential amino acids, fats and genetic materials such as structural components of DNA and RNA.

Carbohydrates and Health Problems

Too little fiber from complex carbohydrate (grains, beans, vegetables, legumes) can cause constipation, hemorrhoids and eventually lead to cancer of the colon. The body must eliminate solid wastes by the action of water-insoluble fibers in the large intestine that swell. This will cause the stool to move faster through the digestive tract. Individuals that consume large amounts of foods from plants usually have a much smoother elimination system and usually do not suffer constipation and hemorrhoids. (Klurfeld, 1987).

218

Colon cancer is a leading cause of cancer death in America. High fiber diets have been associated with the prevention of colon cancer. One theory suggests that if the feces move quickly through the digestive tract, there will be less time for exposure of the lining to any fecal carcinogens. Table sugar, honey and most simple sugars produce energy but provide little else required for balanced nutrition. This is why soda is often referred to as "junk food," or "empty calorie food." One should wonder if soda is even a food? Despite the multi-million dollar elaborate commercials, soda pop is nothing more than sugar, syrup and carbon dioxide. In addition to providing little, if any, real nutritional value, the bacteria that are found in plaque in the mouth react with sugar to form organic acids, and ultimately contribute to dental caries (cavities) in children and sometimes adults.

Fats (Lipids)

Fats, also known as lipids, are very large molecules composed of fatty acids and glycerin. They too are made of carbon, hydrogen and oxygen, **CHO,** molecules but in different configurations and proportions than carbohydrates. **Fats provide nine calories per gram** compared to only four from both carbohydrate and protein. Fats have six major functions in the body. (1) Fats provide energy in a concentrated form, (2) provide essential fatty acids (especially important for infants), (3) transport fat-soluble vitamins A, D, E and K, (4) build structural components of skin, hair and nerve endings, (5) control body temperature in adipose tissue, and (6) protect and cushion vital organs.

Fats and Health Problems

Fats cause major health problems to Americans. We eat too much in the form of oily foods, such as fat enriched cookies and red meats, (beef, pork and lamb). The major reason the body cannot burn fat as well as protein or carbohydrate is that lipids contain nine calories per gram (compared to only four calories for carbohydrates and proteins). Excessive intake of fats contributes to the following prominent American health problems:

(1) obesity ;
(2) cardiovascular disease occurs as fats begin clogging the coronary arteries and slowing down the transportation of oxygen and blood chemicals;
(3) increased risk of cardiovascular disease in diabetics; and
(4) cancer-the second leading cause of death in the U.S. High fat diets have been associated with cancer of the breast, colon, rectum, uterus and prostate.

Proteins

Proteins are the largest chemical compounds in living things. They are very complex molecules made of thousands of atoms. Like carbohydrates and fats the basic elements of proteins are also CHO, but the elements nitrogen (N), and Sulfur (S) are also included (**CHONS**). The building blocks of all proteins are called **amino acids**. These compounds provide a valuable diverse function for the body. The three major functions of proteins are to (1) provide structure in the form of bone, hair, skin tissue and most body organs (2) regulate body processes. This is done by the formation of enzymes, hormones, antibodies and other cells to aid metabolism (3) **produce energy, (4 calories per gram) like carbohydrates**. Examples of foods high in protein include meats, fowl, eggs, cheese, tofu, fish, nuts, and legumes (dried beans). Protein requirements actually are requirements for the essential amino acids. The human body can make 13 of the 22 amino acids of life. If a person consumes all nine essential amino acids, then it is possible to manufacture the other 13 amino acids.

Proteins and Health Problems

Low intake of protein is very rare in America, but many countries throughout the world do suffer from protein deficiency that can lead to several forms of starvation. Children from underdeveloped countries have suffered **marasmus** or **kwashiorkor**, the former is protein deficiency that leads to starvation by breaking down body protein; the latter is often found in children whose diets may or may not include enough calories. The victims' body may suffer abdominal distention and a wasting away appearance.

For many Americans the problem is **too much protein,** as well as **too much fat**, in the daily intake of foods. Protein from hot dogs, meats, cheeses and other food adds excess calories and can give rise to other problems. They include dehydration, calcium loss, high cholesterol and obesity. All of these conditions can increase the chances of **osteoporosis** (brittle bone disease), cancer, stroke or cardiovascular disease. These protein foods are often synonymously very high fat foods such as pork, beef or lamb meat products. During 2004, a popular documentary film, *"Supersize Me,"* was released reviewing the excessive intake and health problems resulting from fast foods eaten at Mc Donald's in the U.S. In 2005, the movie was nominated for an Academy Award. Teachers are encouraged to rent the movie to review the typical eating habits of many American children.

Americans have the healthiest toilets
in the world. This is because most of the
vitamins we purchase and use in excess
are water soluble and
are excreted in the urine.
...Nathan Matza

Vitamins and Minerals

Every year Americans spend billions of dollars on vitamins, minerals and other "exotic elixirs and supplements," with the idea that if they consume excess amounts, they will be healthier. This is not true and can be very dangerous. These micronutrients do not even supply energy. They serve to prevent deficiency diseases and maintain many specialized cells like, skin, hair and eye tissue.

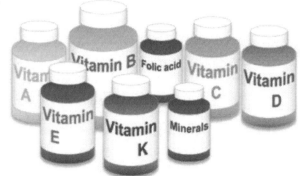

Vitamins are essential for life itself. Remember, vitamins do not supply energy but help carbohydrates, fats and proteins do their job as the macronutrients. The best source of vitamins and minerals can be obtained by eating a wide variety of complex carbohydrates, limited meats and dairy products with a heavy emphasis on fruits, whole grains and vegetables. Vitamins help regulate hormones, maintain healthy skin, mucus membranes, bones and teeth. They also assist the absorption of calcium and phosphorus, improve nerve function, help form hemoglobin in the red blood cells, prevent deficiency diseases (rare in America), and help build structural tissue such as cartilage and muscles.

Minerals are mostly salts derived from foods. The major nutritional minerals include calcium, phosphorus, magnesium, sodium, chloride and potassium. Minor elements include zinc, copper, iodine, selenium, and others. These chemicals help to form hard tissues such as bone and teeth, aid normal muscle and nerve function, and act as catalysts in enzyme systems that help to prevent diseases such as cancer. Even though minerals are ingested in small amounts, they play a very important role in many chemical reactions and biochemical processes. Teen girls, for example, need to include foods rich in calcium to prevent osteoporosis (brittle bones) and anemia (lack of iron in the blood) due to blood loss during menstruation. Instead of consumers ingesting a wide variety of supplements, they should **eat a wide variety of real foods**. It is ludicrous to think that a few overpriced supplements could replace the numerous micronutrients in many fruits, vegetables and whole grains. Foods such as mangoes, blueberries, pineapples, tomatoes and others are loaded with important nutrients.

Water

The human body contains more water than any other chemical. Water is a macronutrient, and, while life could continue for about four weeks without food, life would cease in less than seven days without water. You should drink up to 8 glasses of water a day to help provide for digestion and transport of nutrients, lubrication of joints and digestive muscles, maintenance of body temperature, and prevention of dehydration.

221

What About Milk: Is it for *Every* Body?

The singer Beyonce, a former spokeswoman for the milk campaign, and countless other actors, and celebrities say that milk has helped make them what they are today. The milk and dairy industry certainly wants to increase their sales with the focus of using calcium and other nutrients as an excellent source to build bones and improve bodily functions through good nutrition. The milk industry and health experts hope that many of these well known celebrities who don't mind being photographed with a milk mustache, can make milk fashionable again. Milk is a good source of calcium to help prevent **osteoporosis**, which affects 25 million Americans, mostly women, each year. While milk is a reasonably good food, it does come from animal tissues, is made of saturated fats, and causes **lactose intolerance** to millions of people around the world. David Paige, a researcher at Johns Hopkins University in Baltimore, says two-thirds of the world's adults have the problem of lactose intolerance, including many African-Americans, Hispanics, and Asians. Symptoms of lactose intolerance include gas, diarrhea and upset stomachs or **acute gastritis.** More than sixty percent of students in California represent people of color and many of these students may have adverse reactions to milk consumption. Solutions to overcome this problem include: drinking low-fat or non-fat milk, adding the enzyme lactase in milk, or using commercial products that have reduced or eliminated lactose sugar. (Halsey, 1997). Since the 2003 school year, many schools now offer soy products to students that cannot digest lactose in milk. For a very interesting perspective about milk and kids, read the book *Don't Drink Your Milk,* (1977) by pediatrician Frank Oski, MD, Former Director, Department of Pediatrics, Johns Hopkins University School of Medicine. Thus it is imperative that all teachers should be sensitive to different cultural issues, including nutrition to help students succeed in school.

California Child Nutrition Programs

In 1946 Congress passed the national School Lunch Act, the first of many child nutrition programs sponsored by the federal government. The Act was designed " ... as a measure of national security, to safeguard the health and well-being of the nation's children and to encourage the domestic consumption of nutritious agricultural commodities and other food, by assisting the states, through grants-in-aid and other means..." The United States Department of Agriculture (USDA) directs the Child Nutrition Program. In California the Department of Education/child Nutrition and Food Distribution division administers both the federal and state programs. The term *child nutrition* refers to both childcare and school-based programs. The list below explains the various programs available to assist youth by improving daily nutrition.

Federally Funded Programs.

The National School Lunch Program (NSLP) helps schools provide nutritious lunches to children at reasonable prices. Students receive meals free, at reduced cost, or at full cost, depending on the income level of a child's family.

The School Breakfast Program (SBP) helps schools and other agencies provide nutritious breakfasts to children at reasonable prices. **Recent studies have shown that children who eat a nutritious breakfast improve their learning and achievement at school; have longer attention spans, better behavior, and improved test scores.** Therefore, an increasing number of school districts are serving breakfast to children each morning.

The After School Care Snack Program (ASCSP) reimburses for snacks served to children through age 18 who participate in programs organized to provide after school care. The intent is to assist schools and public and private nonprofit organizations to operate organized programs of care that include educational enrichment activities known to prevent children's involvement in juvenile crime or other high risk behavior.

The Special Milk Program (SMP) ensures that, as a minimum, milk is provided to children. This program is available to children who do not have access to meal programs where milk is already a part of the meal pattern, such as with the NSLP.

The Nutrition Education and Training Program (NETP) uses federal, state and foundation funds to provide comprehensive nutrition information and education programs for children, teachers, child nutrition personnel, program administrators, and parents in schools and child care agencies. The focus of this program is to coordinate classroom instruction with consistent nutrition messages for healthy eating in the school lunch programs.

The Child Care Food Program (CCFP) is a federally and state funded program that helps licensed, nonprofit child care centers and child care homes provide nutritious, well-balanced meals to children age twelve and younger. Research has established that good eating habits developed in childhood can last a lifetime.

The Donated Food Program (DFP) is a federally funded program that makes available commodities to eligible public and private nonprofit agencies. The California Department of Education is the distributing agency. Available foods are those determined to be in excess supply or those purchased to improve the nutrition of school children nationwide.

The Summer Food Program (SFP) assists school districts and other local agencies with providing healthy meals to needy children 18 years of age and younger during periods when they are out of school for fifteen or more continuous school days.

State Funded Programs

The State-Mandated Child Nutrition Program (SMCNP) is a result of state legislation that requires public school districts to offer at least one nutritious meal to needy students every school day. This requirement applies even if a school does not participate in the NSLP or SBP. State funding is available for each free and reduced-price reimbursable breakfast and lunch served to children enrolled in the program.

The Pregnant and Lactating Students Meal Supplement Program (PAL) provides funds to school districts to serve additional food to pregnant or lactating students to help meet their extra nutritional needs. Any public school or private nonprofit agency that is participating in the NSLP or SBP is eligible to apply.

Hunger leads to anemia (lack of iron), obesity and significant risks of chronic disease. Studies have shown that dietary factors are associated with five of the ten leading causes of death in the United States including: heart disease, some cancers, stroke, diabetes, and atherosclerosis. Other prevalent health problems associated with food intake are growth retardation, iron-deficiency anemia, arthritis, and osteoporosis. In 2004, CDC Director Julie Gerberding, MD, and colleagues, reported **the total deaths in the U.S. from lack of exercise and obesity was greater than 350,000, and many researchers expect that deaths from obesity and lack of exercise will surpass the 430,000 annual deaths from tobacco in the U.S.** (Mokdad, Marks, Stroup et. al, 2004). In fact, in 2010 science experts reported that deaths from obesity and lack of regular exercise have now passed total tobacco deaths in the U.S. (Jia, Lubetkin, 2010). Since most food preferences and habits are developed very early in childhood, schools, parents and community leaders can provide powerful role models to enable youth to make positive choices, improve learning and realize much happier lives.

Adolescent Nutrition

For decades, nutritionists, health educators, physicians and researchers have recognized the need for youth to practice good sensible nutrition. While the Surgeon General's Report on Nutrition was last published in 1988; many Americans, and especially teens, still have not become aware, nor do they practice good nutrition. Healthful nutritional practices during childhood and adolescence, including consumption of a variety of fruits, vegetables and grains, accompanied with regular exercise, can serve to reduce morbidity and mortality rates in later years. Later in this chapter *The National Nutrition Objectives for the Year 2010,* are listed for review. These objectives focus on specific recommendations to improve the nutritional health of children and adolescents.

Growing Up

The Food Guide Pyramid (USDA) emphasizes such foods as carbohydrate-rich grain foods and fruits and vegetables necessary to supply vitamins, minerals, fiber and energy vital to good health. Adequate amounts of dairy products, lean meats, fish, poultry, eggs, dry beans and nuts also provide nutrients that contribute to proper growth and development. The pyramid was revised in 2004 and the new look or design was published in April, 2005. The new pyramid can be viewed with numerous interactive functions at mypyramid.gov. Unfortunately, expert nutritionist, Dr. Marion Nestle of a professor of nutrition, food studies and public health at New York University stated, "Obesity is concentrated among the poor — and they're people who don't have computers. Now not only do you have to have a computer, but you have to be computer savvy enough to use an extremely complicated Web site." (HIC, 2005). The graphic is listed at the end of this chapter. The major change from the 1992 version is the addition of a figure exercising and the addition of vertical food groups.

The U.S. Department of Agriculture (USDA) 'MyPyramid' illustrates:

- Personalization, demonstrated by the MyPyramid Web site. To find a personalized recommendation of the kinds and amounts of food to eat each day, go to MyPyramid.gov.
- Gradual improvement, encouraged by the slogan, "Steps to a Healthier You." It suggests that individuals can benefit from taking small steps to improve their diet and lifestyle each day.
- Physical activity, represented by the steps and the person climbing them, as a reminder of the importance of daily physical activity.
- Variety, symbolized by the six color bands representing the five food groups of MyPyramid and oils. Foods from all groups are needed each day for good health.
- Moderation, represented by the narrowing of each food group from bottom to top. The wider base stands for foods with little or no solid fats, added sugars, or caloric sweeteners. These should be selected more often to get the most nutrition from calories consumed.
- Proportionality, shown by the different widths of the food group bands. The widths suggest how much food a person should choose from each group. The widths are just a general guide, not exact proportions. **Check MyPyramid.gov for the amount that is right for you.**

The new food guidance system utilizes interactive technology found on MyPyramid.gov. MyPyramid contains interactive activities that make it easy for individuals to key in their age, gender and physical activity level so that they can get a more personalized recommendation on their daily calorie level based on the 2005 Dietary Guidelines for Americans. It also allows

225

individuals to find general food guidance and suggestions for making smart choices from each food group. Students are encouraged to go to MyPyramid.gov and use the numerous interactive tools to assess their nutritional and exercise programs. **For a detailed view of various other food pyramids, refer to the food guide pyramid chart at the end of this chapter and in the appendix.**

Children will usually grow about two inches per year and gain about four to seven pounds per year. Between the ages of six to twelve, children will usually grow an average of two feet and nearly double in weight. A decreased weight-for-height may indicate **acute under nutrition**. A decreased height-for-age may suggest **chronic under nutrition.** Failure to grow in this manner may be due to malnutrition, psychosocial deprivation, eating disorders, underlying chronic disease, infection or other factors. Every mother knows the difficulty of getting a child to eat certain kinds of foods, such as vegetables and fruits. Nutritionists recommend that parents encourage their kids to taste new foods in small quantities without forcing the issue. This should slowly teach the child how to accept and like new types of foods.

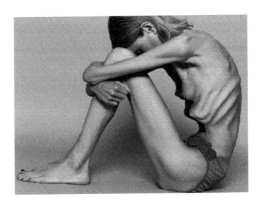

"I'm so tired of being fat! I'm going back to school weighing 119 pounds-I swear it. Three months in which to lose thirty pounds-but I'll do it, or die in the attempt."
...A 15-year-old American girl, circa 1926!

Teen Nutrition and Body Image

The previous quotation from 1926 illustrates how long young people, especially young girls have been obsessed with thinness. The adolescent growth spurt begins in girls at ages 10 or 11 and reaches its peak at age 12 and is completed at about 15 years of age. In boys, it begins at 12 or 13, peaks at 14 and ends about age 19. Adequate amounts of calcium and iron are particularly important to youngsters during this intensive growth period. From ages 11 to 24, both females and males should consume adequate amounts of foods high in these two elements.

Calcium intake over a lifetime will help prevent **osteoporosis**, a brittle bone disease of the elderly. The RDAs for calcium can be attained by eating at least three servings daily from the milk and cheese group, or eating foods such as green leafy vegetables, and seafood. Iron intake from some meats and fruits such as raisins, will help to prevent anemia.

Caloric needs vary among teenagers depending on their growth rate, genetics, and degree of maturation or body composition and activity level. Being overweight is one of the most serious nutritional problems of teens. The incidence of being overweight is particularly high among Hispanics, Native Americans and low-income African-Americans. Eating disorders are also common among many adolescents. According to the National Center for Health Statistics, one in 100 females between the ages of 12 and 18 have anorexia nervosa, a condition that causes people to severely limit their food intake. Both anorexia and bulimia, in which people binge and purge by vomiting or using laxatives, can lead to convulsions, kidney failure, irregular heartbeats, osteoporosis, amenorrhea and dental erosion.

Meal Patterns

Children and teens should eat at least three meals a day, beginning with breakfast, in order to meet energy needs throughout the day. Eating breakfast affects the body's cognitive and physical performance. If a child eats breakfast, they usually will be more alert in school and better able to learn and perform physical activities. Teenagers are notorious for having poor eating habits. Perhaps many of them feel it represents a badge of rebellion towards parental guidelines and recommendations. The following section describes the nutrition-related objectives, for students taken from the *National Nutrition Objectives for the Year 2010*. (Healthy People, 2010).

National Nutrition Objectives for the Year 2010
Related to the Health of Children, Adolescents and Young Adults

- Increase the proportion of people aged 2 years and older who consume at least two daily servings of fruit from 28 percent to 75 percent in 2010.
- Increase the proportion of people aged 2 years and older who consume at least three daily servings of vegetables, with at least one third being dark green or deep yellow vegetables, from 3 percent to 50 percent by 2010.
- Increase the proportion of people aged 2 years and older who consume at least six daily servings of grain products, with at least three being whole grains from 7 percent to 50 percent by 2010.
- Increase the proportion of people aged 2 years and older who consume less than 10 percent of calories from saturated fat from 36 percent to 75 percent in 2010.

- Increase the proportion of people aged 2 years and older who consume no more than 30 percent of calories from fat from 33 percent to 75 percent in 2010.
- Increase the proportion of people aged 2 years and older who consume 2,400 mg or less of sodium daily from 21 percent to 65 percent in 2010.
- Increase the proportion of people aged 2 years and older who meet dietary recommendations for calcium from 46 percent to 75 percent in 2010.
- Increase the proportion of children and adolescents aged 6 to 19 years whose intake of meals and snacks at schools contributes proportionally to good overall dietary quality.
- Increase the proportion of work sites that offer nutrition or weight management classes or counseling from 55 percent of work sites with 50 or more employees to 85 percent in 2010.
- Increase the proportion of physician office visits made by patients with a diagnosis of cardiovascular disease, diabetes or hyperlipidemia that include counseling or education related to diet and nutrition from 42 percent to 75 percent in 2010. **Source: For the complete report consult: Healthy People 2010: http://www.healthypeople.gov/.**

The Carnegie Council on Adolescent Development report, "Fateful Choices," addresses many issues and concerns about nutrition, such as malnutrition and eating disorders. The report states that, "Schools are the best place for preventive and remedial action because that is where most youngsters can be reached." The report stresses that nutrition education should begin at age six, and that health education needs to be delivered throughout all grade levels. The *Dietary Guidelines for Americans* emphasize qualitative dietary modifications to decrease risk of chronic disease. Students in school can be influenced by the models they see every day in the cafeteria and snack bar menus. The guidelines are modified from the original Surgeon General's Report on Nutrition published in 1988.

Health educators are all aware that it is extremely difficult to motivate teenagers to become interested in proper nutrition. As long as food "looks and tastes like French fries, it must be good"-seems to be the attitude of so many adolescents. Research has determined that teens do eat very poorly in general, and rarely eat significant amounts of fruits and vegetables that would approach the recommendations of the Food Guide Pyramid, and recommendations of the Surgeon General. Nutritionists examined 3 days of dietary data from respondents of the U.S. Department of Agriculture's "1989-1991 Continuing Survey of Food Intakes by Individuals." Students in the study totaled 3,148 children and adolescents aged 2 to 18 years. Foods were divided into major recognized categories of fruits, vegetables, grains, etc. and the researchers found:

"Nearly one quarter of all vegetables consumed by children and adolescents were French fries. Their intakes of all fruits and of dark green and/or deep yellow vegetables were very low compared with recommendations. Only one in five children consumed five or more servings of fruits and vegetables per day." (Krebs-Smith, Cook, & Subar, 1996). It is recommended that teens and younger children increase their intake of dark leafy green vegetables in order to supply the necessary vitamins, minerals and carbohydrates needed daily. At the same time they should reduce the total intake of saturated fats such as those that are often found in French fries and other oily, salty snack foods. The three most common vegetables consumed in the U.S. annually are, **iceberg lettuce, potato chips, and French fries!** (Nestle, 2002).

One medium popcorn & a soda combo is the same as three quarter pounders at MacDonald's + 12 pats of butter = 1600 Calories!...Nations Health, 2010.

The basic recommendations of The Surgeon General's report are:

- *Fats and cholesterol:* Reduce consumption of fat (especially saturated fat) and cholesterol. Choose foods relatively low in these substances such as vegetables, fruits, whole grain foods, fish, poultry, lean meats, and low-fat dairy products. Use food preparation methods that add little or no fat.
- *Energy and weight control:* Achieve and maintain a desirable body weight. To do so, choose a dietary pattern in which energy (caloric) intake is consistent with energy expenditure. To reduce energy intake, limit consumption of foods relatively high in calories, fats, and sugars, and minimize alcohol consumption. Increase energy expenditure through regular and sustained physical activity.

- *Complex carbohydrates and fiber:* Increase consumption of whole grain foods and cereal products, vegetables (including dried beans and peas), and fruits.
- *Sodium:* Reduce intake of sodium by choosing foods relatively low in sodium and limiting the amount of salt added in food preparation and at the table.
- *Alcohol:* To reduce the risk for chronic disease, take alcohol only in moderation (no more than two drinks a day), if at all. Avoid drinking any alcohol before or while driving, operating machinery, taking medications, or engaging in any other activity requiring judgment. Avoid drinking alcohol while pregnant.

Other Issues for Some People:

- *Fluoride:* Community water systems should contain fluoride at optimal levels for prevention of tooth decay. If such water is not available, use other appropriate sources of fluoride.
- *Sugars:* Those who are particularly vulnerable to dental caries (cavities), especially children, should limit their consumption and frequency of use of foods high in sugars.
- *Calcium:* Adolescent girls and adult women should increase consumption of foods high in calcium, including low-fat dairy products.
- *Iron:* Children, adolescents, and women of childbearing age should be sure to consume foods that are good sources of iron, such as lean meats, fish, certain beans, and iron-enriched cereals and whole grain products. This issue is of special concern for low-income families.

Source: *Surgeon General's Report on Nutrition*, 1988. USDHHS 88-50210.
The most recent guidelines, *Dietary Guidelines for Americans 2005 (USDA),* are listed at the end of this chapter.

In 1992, the U.S. Department of Agriculture released the **Food Guide Pyramid** which was a dramatic change from the "basic four" guidelines of good nutrition which have been in place for decades. This new pyramid guide, illustrated in the appendix, made dramatic changes in suggesting how Americans should eat. Many groups originally opposed the pyramid for political and economic reasons, because it limited the intake of milk products and meats. The pyramid suggests eating foods in **five major groups**, with the largest volume of nutrients at the base. Breads, cereals, rice and pasta serves as the large base of the pyramid. Next come vegetables and fruits. These two levels comprise the majority of food volume consumed in the form of complex carbohydrates. Milk, yogurt and cheese along with meat, poultry fish, dry beans and nuts form the top of the pyramid; but fats, oils and sweets appear at the apex, to be consumed in sparing amounts. Harvard researcher, Walter Willet, heads up a major nutritional study of a population of nurses and health professionals totaling nearly 300,000 people. As chair of the department of nutrition in the School of Public Health, Willett and his colleagues have been writing about the link between diet and disease. Willett has developed a modified pyramid food guide called the "Traditional Healthy Mediterranean Diet Pyramid." (See the appendix for diagrams of Willet). This diet was developed from traditional eating habits of residents of

230

southern Italy, and in Crete and Greece-regions with historically low chronic disease rates and high life expectancies.

This type of diet derives most of the fats from olive oil. One eats small portions of cheese or yogurt daily along with generous helpings of bread, grains, fruits, vegetables, beans and potatoes. It also includes modest amounts of poultry and fish. **Red meat is a very rare delicacy on this program.** (Mason, 1994). Experts such as Willet, recommend that people use the Mediterranean variation of the food guide pyramid to offer a wider choice of nutrients and decrease the total intake of meats and other saturated fat foods. Working with the World Health Organization, Willet developed **seven food groups**. Breads, fruits, and vegetables are still the major source of the daily complex carbohydrate; however, olive oil is added, some cheese and yogurt, followed by fish, eggs, and sweets, with red meat at the apex. Dr. Willet and his colleagues at Harvard School of Public Health have also published a new text promoting sensible health. See: Willett, et al., (2001). *Eat, Drink and Be Healthy.* Harvard University Press. See the appendix for Willett's pyramid charts. Google: The Oldways Preservation Exchange to view various pyramids.

Nutrition and Learning

Hunger and malnutrition impairs physical, mental and developmental activity, especially affecting the immune system. Over one third of families in California have serious problems getting enough food, and almost 40% of survey participants reported sending their children to bed hungry an average of five days each month. (Project Teach, 1993). Iron-deficiency anemia causes symptoms and behaviors often mistaken for learning disabilities or attention deficit disorders. Examples include listlessness, apathy, behavioral disturbances, poor attention span, irritability, and lower test scores. **While a major focus in schools has been to avoid drugs, more attention must be given to the daily diet of children and adolescents.**

Fitness and Learning

California children have poor levels of fitness. Only 16% of 5th graders, 20% of 7th graders and 26% of 9th graders were able to meet four or more fitness standards. Nationally, **children watch an average of 24 hours TV each week**; and TV viewing has been linked with decreased physical activity, increased serum cholesterol and increased prevalence of obesity. The most prevalent form of malnutrition is obesity, which leads to lower self-esteem and lower achievement scores. Over 25% of California's children are obese, and California's prevalence is higher than the national average. Other forms of eating disorders include anorexia, and adolescents and even pre-teens as young as ten years of age. Anorexic or bulimic females often are dancers, cheerleaders, and aerobic athletes. Anorexics feel that a normal or below normal weight is ideal, but continuously see themselves as "fat" even though they may be severely emaciated and facing death. **Symptoms of anorexia include:**

- refusal to maintain a normal body weight;
- an intense fear of gaining weight or becoming fat;
- ammenorrhea (absence of at least three menstrual periods); and
- a distorted body image, such that the person feels fat even when emaciated.

Bulimia differs from anorexia in that victims have recurrent episodes of binge eating followed by self-induced purging by vomiting or excessive use of laxatives. Bulimics rapidly consume several thousand calories a day and constantly resort to forcing themselves to vomit up the food. This vomiting serves as a relief of the guilt they feel from being out of control. In some cases, bulimics spend several hours a day gorging themselves and vomiting. **Symptoms of bulimia are similar to anorexia but also include:**

- recurring binge and purging of food;
- daily reliance on self-induced vomiting;
- constant use of laxatives, or diuretics (pills which induce water loss);
- extreme focus on exercise which may burn several thousand calories daily;
- damage to tooth enamel from stomach acids; and
- a minimum of 3 binge-purge episodes for a least 3 months.

Treatment for anorexia or bulimia needs to be provided by a therapist specializing in patients with addictive compulsive behaviors and eating disorders. This may include vitamin and nutrient supplementation and intense psychotherapy that focuses on self-esteem and family counseling. The victim may slowly start to recover; but it may take many months for the body to adjust to a normal pattern of eating and sensible exercise. Some psychiatrists have patients mold a model of their bodies through a process called **sculpting**. This is done with clay and the purpose is to help them talk through their feelings while building self-esteem. This work with clay may help young women develop the need to change the body from that of a little girl and slowly mold it into womanhood.

Bulimarexia is a disorder that includes both symptoms of anorexia and bulimia. It is estimated that 40 to 50% of anorexics also exhibit bulimic tendencies. It is important to remember that while 95% of people with eating disorders are women, about 5% are men. Male actors, dancers, wrestlers, and professional athletes, particularly low weight conscious groups such as jockeys, may be at high risk. (Science Daily, 2008).

The problem of eating disorders also transcends from the individual to society. As high fashion designers in salons of Paris and New York visualize a skinny woman being draped by the latest gowns and designs, young girls see this as the ultimate or epitome of sexiness and femininity to the point of psychological pathology. The average body shape of an American woman is not as skinny as a 'rail' (a funny looking duck-like bird), but that of a medium proportioned or even slightly overweight body. If parents, teachers, and designers would all recognize this fact, kids as young as 8-10 years of age wouldn't start worrying about getting fat, and hopefully the anorexic or bulimic victim may become a thing of the past.

Childhood Sex Abuse Linked To Bulimia

Eating disorders can have a devastating effect on the body of women and men as well. Recent studies have found a relationship between women suffering eating disorders and those who are victims of earlier sexual abuse. A national study found that women who were sexually abused as children are twice as likely to become bulimic as women who were not abused, according to Steven Wonderlich, associate chairman of the department of neuroscience at the University of North Dakota School of Medicine. "Child sexual abuse does not cause bulimia," according to Wonderlich, "but it may be a significant risk factor." Other research indicates that bulimia is a multifactor form of psychological dysfunction, but child abuse seems to be strongly related. (Christensen, 1996). The classroom teacher should be cognizant of this relationship when talking to kids about thinness, keeping in mind the that the youth may be a victim of sexual abuse.

Eating Disorders: Are You At Risk? Anorexia red flags to watch.

It may be hard to notice signs and symptoms of anorexia. People with anorexia often go to great lengths to disguise their thinness, eating habits or physical problems. How do you think about eating, dieting, and your body?

- A day rarely passes that I don't worry about how much I eat.
- I am embarrassed to be seen in a bathing suit.
- There are many foods that I always feel guilty about eating.
- I usually begin the day with a vow to diet.
- My thighs are too fat.
- I feel uncomfortable eating anything fattening in front of people.
- It makes me nervous if people can watch me from behind.
- After I eat a lot, I think about ways of getting rid of or burning up, calories.
- I hate seeing myself in a mirror.
- I feel terrible about myself if I don't do a lot of exercise every day.
- I find my naked body repulsive.
- If I eat too much, I sometimes vomit or take laxatives.
- My worst problem is the appearance of my body.

233

If you answered yes

2-4, you are typical and probably not at risk.

5-8, you are overly concerned with your weight. Watch your behaviors carefully.

9-14, you may be developing an eating disorder. Consider professional therapy.

Other Possible Red Flags Indicating Anorexia

1. Skipping meals
2. Making excuses for not eating
3. Eating only a few certain "safe" foods, usually those low in fat and calories
4. Adopting rigid meal or eating rituals, such as cutting food into tiny pieces or spitting food out after chewing
5. Weighing food
6. Cooking elaborate meals for others but refusing to eat
7. Repeated weighing of themselves
8. Frequent checking in the mirror for perceived flaws
9. Wearing baggy or layered clothing
10. Complaining about being fat
    (American Health, 1986), (Mayo, 2008), (NIMH, 2008).

Exercise and Weight Control: The Surgeon General's Report on Physical Activity

"The good news is -- you don't have to train like an Olympic athlete to enjoy the benefits of a healthy lifestyle," former Health and Human Services Secretary Shalala states. "Walking, bicycling, or even gardening for at least 30 minutes per day most days of the week are good for your health and good for your future." The first official report on Physical Activity and Health was released in 1996. The report confirmed the fact that moderate physical activity can substantially reduce the risk of death from heart disease, colon cancer, diabetes and high blood pressure. (USDHHS, 1996). During the 1950s, Americans emphasized team sports, during the 1970s, the focus was on aerobic workouts and today, the scientific research offers a new perspective on the importance of regular moderate physical activity for all Americans.

Moderate physical activity is defined as physical activity that uses 150 calories of energy per day, or 1,000 calories per week. Examples of moderate physical activity include walking briskly for 30 minutes, swimming laps for 20 minutes, washing and waxing a car for 45-60 minutes, and pushing a stroller 1 mile in 30 minutes. Regular exercise also appears to reduce the risk of depression and anxiety, improve mood, and enhance performance of daily tasks. Other findings include:

- More than 60 percent of adults do not achieve the recommended amount of physical activity, and 25 percent of adults are not physically active at all. Inactivity increases with age and is more common among women than men and among those with lower income and less education than among those with higher income or education;

- For people who are already moderately active, greater health benefits can be achieved by increasing the amount (duration, frequency, or intensity) of physical activity;
- Among young people aged 12-21, almost 50 percent are not vigorously active on a regular basis. Female adolescents are much less physically active than male adolescents. Physical activity declines dramatically with age during adolescence; and
- **High school students' enrollment in daily physical education classes dropped from 42 percent in 1991 to 25 percent in 1995. Only 19 percent of all high school students are physically active for 20 minutes or more in physical education classes every day during the school week.** (USDHHS, 1996).
  For current data from the Surgeon General's Report on Exercise and fitness, Google: Office of the Surgeon General.

Dietary Guidelines for Americans 2010 (USDA, HHS)

For many decades the food industry has continued to lobby, coerce, falsely advertise and use whatever means necessary to sell their products. While the industry often appears to *promote* good food, their ultimate goal is sales. The dietary guidelines below are now required to be reviewed every 5 years by The US Congress. **Most serious food scientists would routinely recommend that nearly all Americans eat less.** Look carefully at the 'verbs' included below and see if the **"eat less"** message is clear or ambiguous. (Nestle, 2002). In 2010, USDA and HHS together published the revised Guidelines for Americans. The research stressed three major points related to nutrition: **(1) Balance calories with physical activity to manage weight, (2) Consume more of certain foods and nutrients such as fruits, vegetables, whole grains, fat-free and low-fat dairy products, and seafood, (3) Consume fewer foods with sodium (salt), saturated fats, trans fats, cholesterol, added sugars, and refined grains.** Key recommendations for the General Population include all of the following:

- Prevent and/or reduce overweight and obesity through improved eating and physical activity behaviors;
- Control total calorie intake to manage body weight. For people who are overweight or obese, this will mean consuming fewer calories from foods and beverages;
- Increase physical activity and reduce time spent in sedentary behaviors;
- Maintain appropriate calorie balance during each stage of life-childhood, adolescence, adulthood, pregnancy and breastfeeding, and older age;
- Individuals should meet the following recommendations as part of a healthy eating pattern and while staying within their calorie needs;
- Increase vegetable and fruit intake;

- Eat a variety of vegetables, especially dark-green and red and orange vegetables and beans and peas;
- Consume at least half of all grains as whole grains. Increase whole-grain intake by replacing refined grains with whole grains;
- Increase intake of fat-free or low-fat milk and milk products, such as milk, yogurt, cheese, or fortified soy beverages;
- Choose a variety of protein foods, which include seafood, lean meat and poultry, eggs, beans and peas, soy products, and unsalted nuts and seeds;
- Increase the amount and variety of seafood consumed by choosing seafood in place of some meat and poultry;
- Replace protein foods that are higher in solid fats with choices that are lower in solid fats and calories and/or are sources of oils;
- Use oils to replace solid fats where possible;
- Choose foods that provide more potassium, dietary fiber, calcium, and vitamin D, which are nutrients of concern in American diets. These foods include vegetables, fruits, whole grains, and milk and milk products;
- Reduce daily sodium intake to less than 2,300 milligrams (mg) and further reduce intake to 1,500 mg among persons who are 51 and older and those of any age who are African American or have hypertension, diabetes, or chronic kidney disease. The 1,500 mg recommendation applies to about half of the U.S. population, including children, and the majority of adults;
- Consume less than 10 percent of calories from saturated fatty acids by replacing them with monounsaturated and polyunsaturated fatty acids;
- Consume less than 300 mg per day of dietary cholesterol;
- Keep trans fatty acid consumption as low as possible by limiting foods that contain synthetic sources of trans fats, such as partially hydrogenated oils, and by limiting other solid fats;
- Reduce the intake of calories from solid fats and added sugars;
- Limit the consumption of foods that contain refined grains, especially refined grain foods that contain solid fats, added sugars, and sodium;
- If alcohol is consumed, it should be consumed in moderation-up to one drink per day for women and two drinks per day for men-and only by adults of legal drinking age;
- Increase vegetable and fruit intake;
- Eat a variety of vegetables, especially dark-green and red and orange vegetables and beans and peas;
- Consume at least half of all grains as whole grains. Increase whole-grain intake by replacing refined grains with whole grains;
- Increase intake of fat-free or low-fat milk and milk products, such as milk, yogurt, cheese, or fortified soy beverages;

236

- Choose a variety of protein foods, which include seafood, lean meat and poultry, eggs, beans and peas, soy products, and unsalted nuts and seeds;
- Increase the amount and variety of seafood consumed by choosing seafood in place of some meat and poultry;
- Replace protein foods that are higher in solid fats with choices that are lower in solid fats and calories and/or are sources of oils;
- Use oils to replace solid fats where possible;
- Choose foods that provide more potassium, dietary fiber, calcium, and vitamin D, which are nutrients of concern in American diets. These foods include vegetables and fruits;
- Select an eating pattern that meets nutrient needs over time at an appropriate calorie level;
- Account for all foods and beverages consumed and assess how they fit within a total healthy eating pattern; and
- Follow food safety recommendations when preparing and eating foods to reduce the risk of foodborne illnesses. (USDA, HHS, 2010).

This excellent report is available on the Internet for free. The document is well written, addresses many special populations, colorful and very easy to understand. To obtain a copy, point your browser to: **www.dietaryguidelines.gov** for the complete report.

Matza's Tips for Good Nutrition

The official government guidelines above are very well prepared and comprehensive. This section includes some practical simple methods to stay healthy and avoid complications from obesity and lack of exercise. Many people spend thousands of dollars to promote weight loss. They over exercise, cause injuries, eat strange diets and try to "lose 99 pounds in 99 days with a 99% guarantee, by calling someplace in Connecticut and paying $99." These broadly stated, undocumented programs do not work to keep the weight off. Sensationalized TV talk show plans, do not a good diet make. Consult the following "how to" section for nutritional health, select the ones that work for you, exercise, and eat your way to nutritional health.

Provide an Adequate Diet for Your Baby

- Breast feed (exclude if medical problems arise);
- Delay other foods until the baby is 4-6 months old;
- Avoid adding salt or sugar to baby's food; and
- Babies should only be offered low fat foods after the age of two.

To Control Overeating

- Eat slowly, watch yourself in front of a mirror;
- Take smaller servings on smaller plates;
- Avoid "seconds;"
- Remove all food from the table immediately after eating;
- Keep snack foods away from the TV; and
- Avoid eating in front of the TV and mute the food commercials.

To Lose Weight

- Increase exercise;
- Eat a wide variety of foods low in calories and high in nutrients:
  --Eat more fruits, grains, and vegetables
  --Eat less fatty foods
  --Eat less sugar and sweets
  --Decrease alcohol and increase water intake; and
Do not weight yourself daily-take body measurements instead!

To Avoid Too Much Fat, Cholesterol and Saturated Fat

- Limit red meats (beef, pork and lamb) and trim the fat;
- Add more legumes, beans and soybean for meat protein;
- Broil , barbecue, boil or bake instead of frying food;
- Limit animal fats like butter, cream, and lard, as well as palm and coconut oil;
- Read food labels carefully for amounts and types of fats; and
- Eat more fish and lean chicken or turkey-**follow the food guide pyramid.**

To Eat More Starch and Fiber

- Eat more high fiber foods such as whole grains, dry beans, peas and cereals;
- Experiment with many vegetables like broccoli in the microwave oven;
- Keep fresh vegetables in the front part of the refrigerator for snacks; and
- Quickly stir-fry vegetables in peanut oil.

To Avoid too Much Sugar

- Choose less of all sugars: white, brown, raw, honey and syrups;
- Use sugar sweeteners (aspartame, saccharine) to replace sugars;

- Drink beverages and snacks that are sugar free;
- Eat fresh fruits at their peak of ripeness, the fructose is sweeter than table sugar;
- When selecting canned fruits, choose products without added sugars; and
- Experiment with unfamiliar fruits, whole pineapple, mango, kiwi, and cantaloupe.

To Avoid too Much Sodium

- Gradually switch to non-salted snacks;
- Cook without salt and avoid adding salt to foods;
- Replace sodium salt with salt substitutes (potassium);
- Flavor foods with a variety of unsalted spices, herbs, and lemon juice; and
- Limit your intake of chips, pretzels, condiments, (soy sauce, salsa, garlic salt).

2008 Physical Activity Guidelines for Americans Summary

The U.S. Department of Health and Human Services (HHS) releases regular reports on the physical activity for Americans. The 2008 edition complements the Dietary Guidelines for Americans as a joint effort of HHS and the U.S. Department of Agriculture (USDA). Even though TV adds and fat reducing books often promoted by world class elite athletes, try to sell Americans all types of diets, gadgets and gizmos; regular exercise is the real key to longevity. Rarely will any of us develop the sculpted bodies of these celebrated athletes. All we have to do is participate in some type of daily exercise to help our bodies stay fit and healthy. (USDHHS, 2008). The Guidelines suggest that all Americans aged 6 and older improve their health through appropriate physical activity. The *2008 Physical Activity Guidelines for Americans* describes the major research findings on the health benefits of physical activity:

- Regular physical activity reduces the risk of many adverse health outcomes.
- Some physical activity is better than none.
- For most health outcomes, additional benefits occur as the amount of physical activity increases through higher intensity, greater frequency, and/or longer duration.
- Most health benefits occur with at least 150 minutes (2 hours and 30 minutes) a week of moderate intensity physical activity, such as brisk walking. Additional benefits occur with more physical activity.
- Both aerobic (endurance) and muscle-strengthening (resistance) physical activity are beneficial.
- Health benefits occur for children and adolescents, young and middle-aged adults, older adults, and those in every studied racial and ethnic group.
- The health benefits of physical activity occur for people with disabilities.

- The benefits of physical activity far outweigh the possibility of adverse outcomes. USDHHS. (2008).

The Guidelines further suggests that children and adolescents should do about 60 minutes daily of physical activity. **Aerobic** (using much oxygen) exercise should be a least 3 days a week. **Muscle-strengthening**: As part of their 60 or more minutes of daily physical activity, children and adolescents should include muscle-strengthening physical activity on at least 3 days of the week. **Bone-strengthening**: As part of their 60 or more minutes of daily physical activity, children and adolescents should include bone-strengthening physical activity on at least 3 days of the week. They key is to encourage youth to do exercise that they enjoy, and offer variety. All adults should avoid inactivity. Some physical activity is better than none, and adults who participate in any amount of physical activity gain some health benefits.

- For substantial health benefits, adults should do at least 150 minutes (2 hours and 30 minutes) a week of moderate-intensity, or 75 minutes (1 hour and 15 minutes) a week of vigorous-intensity aerobic physical activity, or an equivalent combination of moderate- and vigorous intensity aerobic activity. Aerobic activity should be performed in episodes of at least 10 minutes, and preferably, it should be spread throughout the week.
- For additional and more extensive health benefits, adults should increase their aerobic physical activity to 300 minutes (5 hours) a week of moderate intensity, or 150 minutes a week of vigorous intensity aerobic physical activity, or an equivalent combination of moderate- and vigorous-intensity activity. Additional health benefits are gained by engaging in physical activity beyond this amount.
- Adults should also do muscle-strengthening activities that are moderate or high. USDHHS. (2008).
  For further reading on exercise related to older adults, pregnant women, and persons with disabilities, Google: *The 2008 Physical Activity Guidelines for Americans.*

Health Problems for Special Needs Students

During 1975 a landmark civil rights act was passed which dramatically changed the role of the school in helping handicapped children. Public Law 94-142, the Education for All Handicapped Children Act has allowed students with special needs to become part of the regular classroom setting; much as they should become part of the regular setting of real life. In 1990, the term "handicapped" was eliminated and the law renamed the **Individuals with Disabilities Education Act (IDEA) of 1990.** The law requires that children and youth be identified, evaluated in a multidisciplinary process using culturally appropriate instruments, and peers to the maximum extent possible. A special program or 'Individualized Education Plan' **(IEP),** must be developed and allow students to learn in the **'least restrictive' environment.**

240

Special educators are teachers that have extensive training and credentials in working with students at various levels of disability. They are very dedicated, spend much more time with individual students, and often are undervalued by their professional colleagues. It is beyond the scope of this text to delineate all of the special needs of this population of students; but teachers may wish to inquire about some basic questions within their school, or from the student's medical doctor. They include:

- Does the child's present condition require any specific physical restrictions?
- Can the child participate in PE or sports?
- Is there a need to shorten or modify the school day?
- Are there special emergency precautions that should be learned by school staff?
- Does the child need special protective equipment, helmets, etc.?
- Should the child have preferential seating?
- Does the child need physical, occupational, or speech therapy?
- Should the child have special counseling?
- Does the child require a modified diet?
- Does the child need assistance toileting?
- Does the child require special medication?
- Is there a special need for the wheelchair, or other medical equipment?
- Can the child talk freely about his or her disability?
- Will the parents approve?

The most important thing for educators to remember is that the special education, or special needs child, is like any other person, with health needs, desires, aspirations and dreams. These children and teenagers should be treated like any other person in the class, with dignity, respect and understanding. A simple private conversation with a student in a wheelchair to determine if they need special seating, lighting or other assistance in a caring and confidential manner, will dramatically influence student behavior, learning and acceptance by others.

Summary

This chapter discussed a very small sample of contemporary problems related to the health of teenagers. Suicide signs, unplanned pregnancy problems, adolescent nutritional requirements eating disorders, the obesity epidemic, homosexuality and practical concerns, were all discussed in order to assist the school teacher with the daily health needs of their students. It must be reiterated that while these problems seem overwhelming in scope and magnitude, most teachers will not deal nor address them on a daily or weekly basis. But, as many teachers gain the trust and confidence of their students, they should be ready to quickly respond and strive to guide the students to seek additional help and locate appropriate referral resources. Help should be suggested first from their own parents or caretakers, and secondly from the wide variety of school based or school linked professionals trained to respond on a regular basis.

MyPyramid (2005)

The revised pyramid 'MyPyramid' was published in April 2005. To view MyPyramid see: http://www.mypyramid.gov/.

MyPyramid Replaced (2011)

After nearly 20 years, the Food Guide Pyramid was replaced by the USDA in 2011. The new logo is now called **MyPlate**. (See Appendix for the **ChooseMyPlate** logo). The new logo was simplified to help consumers visually see the type of foods they should consume and includes the follow recommendations:

- *Balancing Calories:*
    - o Enjoy your food, but eat less
    - o Avoid oversized portions
- *Foods to Increase*
    - o Make half your plate fruits and vegetables.
    - o Make at least half your grains whole grains.
    - o Switch to fat-free or low-fat (1%) milk.
- *Foods to Reduce*
    - o Compare sodium in foods like soup, bread, and frozen meals-choose foods with lower numbers.
    - o Drink water instead of sugary drinks.

Chapter 9

Sexually Transmitted Disease (STDs)

*All human actions have one or
more of these seven causes:
chance, nature, compulsion,
habit, reason, passion
and desire.
...Aristotle*

Introduction to STDs

During the early 1970s, dozens of science teachers gathered in Sacramento California at the Department of Education to discuss the newly identified problem of 'venereal disease,' as it was impacting youth. The purpose of the meeting was to train secondary teachers (mostly science teachers) to identify the problems of syphilis, gonorrhea and a few other VDs as they were once called (from Venus, the goddess of love). Numerous lesson ideas and issues of confidentiality, and parental notification were discussed, and many of the teachers decided that this new problem would hopefully decrease in 10 or 15 years. Nothing at the time of course was know about HIV or the pandemic of AIDS that was about to unfold in the world during the early 1980s. Today venereal diseases are now called **sexually transmitted diseases,** or infections, i.e., **STDs or STIs,** and numerous curricula have been developed and implemented throughout the U.S. to assist teachers in dealing with these diseases that are sometimes considered the most common group of diseases in the U.S, next to the common cold.

Adolescents and STDs. In the United States, prevalence rates of many sexually acquired infections are highest among adolescents (Forhan, Gottlieb, 2009). For example, the reported rates of chlamydia and gonorrhea are highest among females aged 15–19 years, and many persons acquire HPV infection during their adolescent years. Research indicates that persons who initiate sex early in adolescence are at higher risk for STDs, along with persons residing in detention facilities, attending STD clinics, young men having sex with men (YMSM), and young people who use injection drugs. Some of the factors that bring about increased risk during adolescence include having multiple sexual partners concurrently, having sequential sexual partnerships of limited duration, failing to use barrier protection consistently and correctly. (Forhan, Gottlieb, 2009). While many parents may object to not being told about STD infection discovered in their kids, all 50 states and the District of Columbia explicitly allow minors to consent for their own health services for STDs; and with very few exceptions in unusual cases, no state requires parental consent for STD treatment for minors. (Forhan, Gottlieb, 2009). It is important to remember that despite the high rates of STD infection in adolescents, medical providers often do not inquire about sexual practices, or assess STD risks in their young patients. Parents and especially health care providers should have frank and appropriate discussions based upon the developmental level of maturity of youth to help young people get treated and prevent further infection. This open discussion with youth should also be aimed at identifying special risk behaviors such as unprotected oral, anal, or vaginal sex and drug-use behaviors. (Forhan, Gottlieb, Sternber, 2009; CDC, 2009e).

STDs in History

Arguments about the origins of STDs have been discussed perhaps as long as we have evidence of presence of these intimate infections, especially syphilis. Around 1530 many arguments debated the origin of this disease, once a very deadly plague before antibiotics were developed, by blaming others. The French called it the Italian disease and the Italians called it the French disease and the Dutch called it the Spanish disease. But other researchers suggest that evidence of syphilis existed in ancient times about 79 AD. Professor Mary Beard of Cambridge discovered remains of twins in Pompeii that clearly had evidence of congenital syphilis in the skeletal remains. (Beard, 2010). The history of many diseases in medicine provides interesting reading and teachers should encourage their students to investigate many of these topics to help eliminate many myths. It may not be that important to identify the exact origin of syphilis or other STDs, a question often asked by students; but it is important to help youth understand the risk of infection and methods to prevent the spread of these very common sexually transmitted diseases.

In the past, ideas about disease were based more on myth, mysticism and superstition than on scientific fact. People thought that diseases resulted from comets or the way stars and planets were aligned. Others believed diseases came from body fluids getting out of balance, from gods angered by human actions, or that diseases sprang from bad air in swamps. (malaria means *bad air*). Hippocrates recognized gonorrhea as early as 500 BC. (Note the adorable sketch of the famous Greek, father of western medicine). He described the manner of catching gonorrhea as "excesses" of the pleasures of Venus," (the goddess of love). The syphilis epidemic of the 1500s was blamed on a conjunction of Jupiter and Saturn on October 14, 1484! Others thought that "seed fermentation" took place in the vagina of a wanton women that had several sex partners. Martin Lister, a famous English physician (1638-1712), believed syphilis came from American sailors who had eaten large iguanas. Even the practice of masturbation, considered normal today by most experts, was called **self-pollution** during the 1800s. About 1890, D.S. Hutton said, "there are various names given to the unnatural and degrading vice of producing venereal excitement by the hand, or other means, generally resulting in a discharge of semen in the male and a corresponding emission in the female. Unfortunately it is a vice by no means uncommon among the youth of both sexes, and it frequently continued into the riper years." Finally, the true pathogen of syphilis was first discovered in 1905, and it wasn't until several decades later that antibiotics were developed to help destroy the syphilis bacteria. By 2004, syphilis became so rare in most U.S. populations that all but a handful of state public health departments no longer require a syphilis blood test for marriage. California eliminated the blood test for marriage in 1995.

During the 18th century medical sciences were not as advanced in scientific knowledge because the anatomy and physiology of the human body were still a mystery. European physicians still adhered to the dogmas of vitalists, iatrochemists, and iatrophysicists that focused on imbalance within the body. They believed it was the chemistry of the body that would heal. Each follower of these philosophies of medicine argued over which of their single causes explained all human health. European universities each had their own simplistic versions of the ills of the human body; and with various themes, thought that the ills of the human body were due to maladjustment of the bodies system. Doctors based their diagnosis of illness on the ancient beliefs of "humors," bodily "tension," or other cruder dogmas. The practice of "bleeding" with leeches to cure illness was common during the 18th century. In fact, the practice of medicine during that time, caused more harm than good since doctors did not sterilize their hands, or instruments. During the 17th and 18th century, doctors knew nothing of the Human Immunodeficiency Virus, which causes HIV disease or AIDS, new little about microscopic pathogens or genital warts, but many sexually transmitted diseases (STDs) were common during these times. Not surprisingly, in the 21st century, many people still cling to these old ideas and use all kinds of gadgets, potions, gizmos and elixirs: today we call them alternative medicine practices! Leeches, however, have made a comeback and are used again today by doctors. Not only do leeches suck out excess blood, but also leech saliva contains a powerful blood thinner (hirudin) that prevents coagulation. Doctors use leeches in reconstructive surgery because the little guys can suck blood for up to six hours. When they are full and finished feeding, they simply drop off the skin. Oh the wonder of these advanced annelid worms!

Today, sixteen-year-old high school students are infected with Chlamydia and genital warts have reached epidemic proportions. Young girls are getting diagnosed with pharyngeal gonorrhea infection from oral sex and have to explain their sore throats to their moms; while still claiming they are **technical virgins or TVs,** since they never had vaginal sex. While there has been a decline in some STDs, such as syphilis and chancroid, others such as genital warts caused by the human papillomavirus and genital herpes are infecting thousands of young people every year. The world is getting smaller with international travel and people are practicing their sexuality in many countries. Tragically, so are the STDs spreading to many countries. **The World Health Organization (WHO) estimates that 1 out of 100 sexually active people worldwide are HIV positive. Moreover, recent reports from the CDC indicate that 1 out of 22 African Americans, 1 out of 52 Hispanics, 1 out of 170 Whites and 1 out of 122 Asian Americans will**

be diagnosed with AIDS in their lifetime! Genital herpes still has no cure and millions of Americans contract one form of STD each year. (CDC, 1993; WHO, 2002; CDC, 2010e).

Transmission of STDs should be considered a result of risky sexual behavior, not a categorization of specific groups, as was once done with AIDS decades ago. Anyone that practices high-risk behavior is susceptible to STD. These behaviors include having unprotected sex, having multiple partners, sharing needles or other blood products, and injection drug abuse. The viruses and bacteria are totally blind to race, religion, ethnic origin, socioeconomic status, geography and sexual orientation. Yet, with all the media attention, and knowledge, people still contract STDs. Why is this? This chapter will explain and describe risky behaviors causing STD, explain modes of transmission, clarify myths related to STD and HIV, and offer solutions for prevention. The major focus will be on the impact on adolescent children.

During the 1990s, in every newspaper in the country, it was nearly impossible not to find an article related to HIV or AIDS. Since 2000, however, much less emphasis on HIV/AIDS has been published in the mainstream media. Perhaps this is due to the introduction of protease inhibitors in 1995, newer AIDS medicines (also called 'the cocktail'), which have extend life for AIDS patients; or perhaps the media is not as interested in HIV/AIDS much today because it is not as graphic, or newsworthy as in the past. Previous attention to this deadly disease, however, has overshadowed the 10 or so more common STDs. HIV and AIDS will be discussed, but remember that AIDS is only 1 of the commonly sexually transmitted diseases infecting greater than 5 million Americans, gay or straight, male or female, young or old, every year and passed from person to person mostly by sexual contact.

Throughout the twentieth century, no disease has attracted more attention than HIV. As recently as 1993, this fatal incurable disease was the number 1 killer of men and women ages 25-44, however, AIDS dropped down to number 5 in this age group by 2002. Death from HIV is still a major killer to Hispanics and African-Americans. **During the late 1980s, Former Surgeon General C. Everett Koop boldly made AIDS information readily available by mailing booklets discussing the basic information about AIDS to every home in the entire United States.** This open, honest and candid approach originally presented by Dr. Koop about AIDS should also be used in order to better inform the public about all forms of STDs.

Several possibilities exist to explain the explosive growth of STDs in America. To begin with, society in America has become much more accepting of premarital sex. Sexual messages are an integral part of many product advertisements. Ad agencies know that sex sells. Sex is the central theme, covertly or overtly promoted, to sell everything including tennis shoes, watches or gas guzzling cars. Oral contraceptives are readily available--even for minors, replacing condom use but offering no protection against STD; and the total number of sexually active people has increased. Newer injectable contraceptives used once every three months, and surgical implants that last for five years, have recently arrived on the scene to help women prevent pregnancy. A side affect of these excellent drugs is that many youth, especially teen girls, think that "everything is cool," after they get the shot and do not have to return to the clinic for three months. Perhaps it is "cool" that they can reduce pregnancy rates by 99%, but products such as Depo-Provera™ injection, or the four-periods-a-year Seasonale™ birth control pill, offer no protection against STD, including HIV. In 2008, the CDC reported that among girls and young women, one in four are infected with at least one of four common STDs: genital warts (HPV), *Chlamydia*, genital herpes and trichomoniasis. (Ventura, 2007).

Many young people fall prey to similarly absurd attitudes about sexual matters. Recent published articles have stated many teenage girls are now practicing anal and oral sex to insure that they will stay virgins and avoid pregnancy! Young people even coined a new term, **technical virgin (TV)** that refers to the fact that the female had no vaginal intercourse. This concept has been circulating throughout the literature since about 2000; however, current data may not support this idea. Lindberg and colleagues reported in the summer of 2008, that about 55% of 15-19 year-olds have engaged in heterosexual oral sex, 50% engaged in vaginal sex and 11% have had anal sex. In her research from the Guttmacher Institute, Lindberg stated, " The Oral Sex 'Epidemic' is not supported by facts." **And, "both oral and anal sex are much more common among teens who have already had vaginal intercourse than among those who have not, suggesting that teens initiate a range of sexual activities around the same time, rather than substitute one for another.** There is a widespread belief that teens engage in nonvaginal forms of sex, especially oral sex, as a way to be sexually active while still claiming that technically, they are virgins. **However, our research shows that this supposed substitution of oral sex for vaginal sex is largely a myth.** There is no good evidence that teens who have not had intercourse engage in oral sex with a series of partners." Thus, some teens may first have oral sex prior to vaginal sex, while others may initiate vaginal intercourse before having oral sex, incrementally. According to the Guttmacher report, by six months after first vaginal sex, more than four out of five adolescents (81%) have also engaged in oral sex, and by three years after first intercourse, nine in 10 (92%) have done so. (Lindberg, Jones, & Santelli, 2008). Oftentimes, certain gang rituals may require potential members to have unprotected sex with an HIV positive person just to *join the gang.* Sadly the rate of genital wart infection in youth is at all time high. Hopefully the new HPV vaccine, described below, may reduce or even eliminate most cervical cancers in the future. (Lindberg, Jones, Santelli, 2008).

In the 1980s, Herpes made the front cover of *Time* magazine; *Chlamydia* has been written about in dozens of popular magazines, and even latex condoms made the cover of *Newsweek*, on December 9, 1991. The cover title: "Safe Sex-What You and Your Children Should Know." By 2012, many of the online websites on dating and other social networking services were including links to STD prevention as well as referrals for HIV testing. Who would ever imagine that the STD problem would be so wide spread that rubbers would appear on the cover of major magazines, many of which are now easily accessible by smart phones and other electronic media devices. Studies reported in 2009 indicate that the 5 most common STDs in the US are: **Herpes Simplex Virus (HSV2), which causes genital herpes, Human Papilloma Virus (HPV) which causes genital warts, Trichomonas, *Chlamydia* and Hepatitis B virus.** (Table 9.1). After a decade of gradual decline, some bacterial STDs (gonorrhea and Chlamydia) are on the increase, especially among men having sex with men (MSM), and among some heterosexual 15-24 year old age groups. (CDC, 2002g; CDC, 2009e).

Racial disparities, however, are significant and show much higher rates of reported STDs among some racial or ethnic minority groups than among whites. Contributing factors of this disparity include poverty, lack of access to health care and an already high prevalence of STDs in many communities of color that could increase the risk with each sexual encounter. Regardless of race, or gender, however, data reveal that sexually active adolescents and young adults are still at increased risk to contract STDs when compared to older adults. Health consequences of untreated STDs can significantly impair one's life. Annually at least 24,000 women in the U.S. become infertile. Untreated syphilis can lead to long-term complications, including damages to the brain and cardiovascular system. People with gonorrhea, chlamydia or syphilis are also at increased risk for HIV as a result of lowering the immune system. Young black men are of special concern as the group whom the rate of syphilis is increasing. (CDC, 2009e).

STDs in the U.S.: An Overview

The most recent national data indicate that STDs still remain a major public health problem and many challenges exist to help bring about behavioral change in sexual practices, especially risk taking by youth. The 2009 STD Surveillance report from the CDC found that there are about **19 million new STD infections each year**, which cost the U.S. healthcare system greater than $16 billion annually. The cost of STD infection to individuals in terms of acute and long-term care is even more difficult to access. (CDC, 2009e). Nonetheless, some progress has been made as the CDC data show:

- Gonorrhea: The national gonorrhea rate is at the lowest level ever recorded.
- Chlamydia: Continuing increases in chlamydia diagnoses likely reflect expanded screening efforts, and not necessarily a true increase in disease burden; this means that more people are protecting their health by getting tested and being linked to treatment. This is critical, since chlamydia is one of the most widespread STDs in the United States.
- Syphilis: For the first time in five years, reported syphilis cases did not increase among women overall. Likewise, cases of congenital syphilis (transmitted from mother to infant) did not increase for the first time in four years. (CDC, 2009e).

Sexually transmitted diseases (STDs), once called venereal diseases after Venus the goddess of love, are among the most common diseases in the United States today. Greater than 20 different STDs have been identified, and they affect more than 13 million adult men and women and a substantial number of adolescents between 15 and 20 years of age. It is estimated that the comprehensive cost of STDs in the U.S. is well in excess of $16 billion annually. (CDC, 2009e). The first step towards prevention of STDs, (sometimes called STIs for sexually transmitted infections), is to understand the ways in which they are spread, their common symptoms and how they can be prevented and treated. The National Institute of Allergy and Infectious Diseases (NIAID), a part of the National Institutes of Health, catalogues data on communicable diseases, and the brief summary below will explain the current state of sexually transmitted disease (STD) in America.

STDs affect women and men of all backgrounds and socioeconomic status. STDs are most prevalent among teenagers and young adults. Nearly two-thirds of all STDs occur in people younger than 25 years of age. During the last few decades, the incidence of STDs has been rising because many young people become sexually active at earlier ages and are marrying later in life, or not marrying at all. Divorce is more common and the net result is that sexually active people today are more likely to have multiple sex partners during their lives. Having multiple sex partners, especially without protection, greatly increase the risk for STDs including HIV, the virus that causes AIDS.

Even Older Americans get HIV. Older people are at increasing risk for HIV/AIDS and other STDs. A growing number of older people now have HIV/AIDS. About 19 percent of all people with HIV/AIDS in the U.S. are age 50 and older. Because older people don't get tested for HIV/AIDS on a regular basis, there may be even more cases than currently known. Why is this? In general, older Americans know less about HIV/AIDS and STDs than younger age groups because the elderly have been neglected by those responsible for education and prevention messages. In addition, older people are less likely than younger people to talk about their sex lives or drug use with their doctors, and unfortunately, doctors often don't ask older patients about their drug use or sexual habits. Finally, older people often mistake the symptoms of HIV/AIDS for the aches and pains of normal aging, so they are less likely to get tested. (NPIN, 2004).

Women are particularly at risk since many STDs initially cause no symptoms. When symptoms do develop, the infected female may confuse the symptoms for other diseases. Women also are more asymptomatic because they may delay seeking treatment and are unaware of a urogenital infection because their urethral passage is separate from the vaginal passage. (See the female and male diagram on gonorrhea in the appendix). Some STDs such as genital warts (Human Papilloma Virus) can lead to cervical cancer and others such as gonorrhea and Chlamydia may lead to **pelvic inflammatory disease** (PID). While gonorrhea and Chlamydia can be easily cured, rarely, a baby may become permanently disabled or even die from a congenital STD infection such as herpes or syphilis. The data from CDC includes the incidence of the 19 million annual cases of STD infection and they are listed below in Table 9.1

Listen to your doctor!

Table 9.1 STD Morbidity in the U.S. (CDC, 2009e).

STD	Incidence*
Trichomoniasis	7,400,000
Genital Warts/Human Papillomavirus (HPV)	6,200,000
Chlamydia trachomatis	1,210,000
Herpes (HSV)	1,600,000
Gonorrhea	336,742
Hepatitis B	60,000
AIDS	45,000
HIV	40,000
Syphilis	13,500

*New individual cases of a given disease.

STD Update-Circumcision and STDs: Is there a connection? Women benefit the most. For many years arguments have taken place between medical doctors, political activists, religious leaders and others about circumcision and the transmission of STDs. Most of the data has been inconclusive until a recent report by an Italian scientist in 2002. It was uncertain if a relationship existed between men without circumcised penises and the risk of human papilloma virus (HPV) or genital warts. The data now seems much more conclusive. Castellsagué reported that men with circumcised penises have a lesser chance of becoming infected with HPV than men with uncircumcised penises. Monogamous women whose male partners had six or more sexual partners and were circumcised had a lower risk of cervical cancer than women whose partners were uncircumcised. This study included over 1,500 men in five separate countries. While fathers often choose to have their sons circumcised so the child looks the same as themselves, and/or families circumcise the boys for religious reasons, we now have evidence that there is a medical benefit, and not so much as a 'tradition' among pediatricians. (Castellsagué, 2002). Additionally, in 2008, the CDC published new reports related to STDs and circumcision. These studies relate to the anatomical differences in penile tissues and were conducted in numerous countries throughout the world, with special emphasis on Africa and AIDS. (CDC, 2008b). The inner mucosa of the foreskin has less keratinization (deposition of fibrous protein), compared with the dry external skin surface, a higher density of target cells for HIV infection, and is more susceptible to HIV infection than other penile tissue in laboratory studies. The foreskin may also have greater susceptibility to traumatic tears during intercourse, providing a portal of entry for pathogens, including HIV. In addition, the microenvironment in the tissues between the unretracted foreskin and the glans penis may be conducive to the sruvival of viruses. Finally, the higher rates of sexually transmitted genital ulcerative disease, such as syphilis, observed in uncircumcised men may also increase susceptibility to HIV infection. (CDC, 2008b).

Another report from Lancet in 2011 indicated among HIV-negative sexual partners, male circumcision helps prevent the transmission of human papillomavirus from men to women; however, circumcision offers only partial protection and partners must still practice safe sex, the researchers pointed out. This study analyzed data from two clinical trials in Uganda that followed HIV-negative men and their HIV-negative female partners between 2003 and 2006. The incidence of new high-risk HPV infection was 23 percent lower for women with circumcised partners than for those with uncircumcised partners, the investigators found. Drs. Aaron Tobian and Maria Wawer, of Johns Hopkins University in Baltimore concluded: "Along with previous trial results in men, these findings indicate that male circumcision should now be accepted as an efficacious intervention for reducing heterosexually acquired high-risk and low-risk HPV infections in men who do not have HIV and in their female partners. However, our results indicate that protection is only partial; the promotion of safe sex practices is also important." In another commentary about circumcision, Dr. Anna R. Giuliano of the H. Lee Moffitt Cancer Center in Tampa, Fla., and colleagues wrote: "Recent findings add important evidence for the promotion of male circumcision in countries without well-established programs for cervical screening. Additional interventions to reduce HPV infection, such as provision of vaccines for HPV prevention, will be essential to reduce invasive cervical cancer worldwide. Male circumcision is associated with slight reductions in high-risk HPV, while licensed HPV vaccines protect with high effectiveness against only a limited number of HPV types. Therefore, the two interventions are likely to have important synergistic effects." (Lancet, 2011).

Male circumcision and other health conditions. Lack of male circumcision has also been associated with sexually transmitted genital ulcer disease and chlamydia, infant urinary tract infections, penile cancer, and cervical cancer in female partners of uncircumcised men. The research analysis concluded that there was a significantly lower risk for syphilis and chancroid among circumcised men; however, the reduced risk of herpes simplex virus type 2 (HSV2) infection had a borderline statistical significance. (CDC, 2008b).

A major part of this explosion of STD is related to sexual activity in young people. During the 1970s and 1980s many studies found that about 50% of students were sexually active by the time they finished their senior year in high school. By the 1990s, however, that number was greater than 70% for many populations in the U.S. Table 9.2 lists reported sexual practices of high school students in California and possible risks for various infections. Only since 2000 has there been an appreciable decline in sexual activity, especially intercourse, by young people.

Table 9.2   **Infections Associated with Specific Sexual Practices**

Sexual Practice	Possible Infection
Sex in the mouth (Oral-genital Sex)	gonorrhea, Herpes 1 and 2, Chlamydia, HPV, syphilis, hepatitis A and B, non A/B, LGV*, chancroid, LGV, GI**, viruses of influenza, candida, scabies, molluscum, cytomegalovirus (CMV), nongonococcal pharyngitis or urethritis (NGU), HIV
Sex in the anus (analintercourse)	gonorrhea, HSV 1 and 3, NGU, Chlamydia, HPV, syphilis, hepatitis A and B, non A/B, LGV*, chancroid, HIV, candida, fungal infections, scabies, CMV, molluscum, Trichomoniasis, E. coli, corynebacterium
Sex in the mouth and anus (Oral-anal sex or anilinction)	gonorrhea, HSV 1 and 2, HPV, syphilis, hepatitis A and B, non A/B, LGV,* candida, HIV, Scabies, molluscum, Shigella, E histolytica, salmonella, Giardia, helmninthic parasites (worms), Enterobius vermicularis, Strongyloides stercoralis, other enteric infections, E. coli
Sex by the hand (fist/finger insertion)	HIV, E. coli, Shigella, Salmonella, other enteric infection, *Lymphogranuloma, **Gardnerella

Source: Holmes, et al., (1990, 1999).

STDs are the major cause of preventable sterility in America. They have tripled the cases of tubal pregnancies in women, and caused complications including miscarriage, premature delivery and uterine infections after delivery. Anyone can contract an STD. Age, gender, sexual preference, race, religion or other classification does not affect the invasion of the pathogens. Even HIV infection has been recognized as a disease of high-risk behavior. Former U.S. Surgeon General Doctor C.E. Koop stated it well, "It's not who you are, but what you do that counts." (Koop, 1991).

Who Has STD?

STDs are considered to be an epidemic in the U.S. today. The Centers for Disease Control (CDC) estimate that nearly 19 million Americans are infected each year. That converts to over 50,000 cases of STD every day, or 2100 cases per hour! By the time you finish reading this page, several new cases of STD will be contracted in the United States. If current trends continue, one out of every four individuals between 15 and 55 years of age will become infected with at least one STD within their lifetime. By 2008, one in four teens did get infected with an STD. Teenagers that are sexually active have a 45% chance of contracting Chlamydia. (Sroka, 1992; NPIN, 2004; Ventura, 2007).

One major factor in the spread of STDs is the influence of dynamically changing demographic and sociocultural forces on its distribution. In most industrialized countries the incidence of the classical forms of STD, syphilis and gonorrhea, have declined among educated middle and upper class groups. In 1995, California, and nearly all states, eliminated the blood test for syphilis as a requirement for the marriage license, since the number of syphilis cases identified were so rare; and by 2011, only Mississippi and Montana required a blood test for marriage.

Within selected groups, such as urban poor, and minorities, the rates have increased. This is especially true among adolescents and particularly adolescent females. Prostitution has been the multiplier of STD. Thus as sex is exchanged for drugs, so is the invasion of HIV disease. Over 80% of all STDs are found in individuals between 15 and 30 years of age. (Holmes, 1990, CDC, 1995).

Data on the frequency and distribution of STDs are limited in several ways. Not all STDs are reportable, and even reportable diseases do not get reported completely. HIV disease screening tests can be done anonymously and many individuals choose not to disclose that they are being tested in fear of losing jobs, or becoming stigmatized as a drug user or homosexual. By 2005, many states still did not require AIDS infected patients to be reported by name, only number in public health surveillance documents. Recently, home-testing kits for HIV became available which eliminates the need for an individual to consult directly with a counselor or health care professional. This may be convenient for the patient, but could cloud the data and perhaps leave an individual extremely vulnerable upon receiving the results by mail or over the telephone. Since 2004, OraSure®, an oral swab of the mouth can detect HIV antibodies without drawing blood.

How Do You Know If You Have STD?

The very nature of STDs is another reason for the current epidemic. The early signs and symptoms may be so mild that they are often overlooked. A person without any obvious signs or symptoms of disease is called **asymptomatic**. This is of particular concern to women since the genital organs are mostly internal, and they usually only find out about an infection by being notified, hopefully by their partners. Unlike measles or mumps, the body does not develop an immunity, and one can become infected over and over. A co-infected person can transmit one or more pathogens at the same time. Several STDs have no known cure. AIDS, genital herpes, hepatitis B and genital warts are rapidly spreading viral STDs that have no cures at the present time. Infected individuals with these diseases can continue to infect others for the rest of their lives. Genital herpes hides in the nerve ganglia and may reoccur due to stress. Most people with AIDS will die; hepatitis B has a vaccine but may go undetected for years and destroy the liver; and genital warts, once mostly curable, may reappear in the vagina, on the cervix or penis for many years after initial exposure.

General symptoms of a sexually transmitted disease should only be considered if a person is sexually active. Abstinent individuals, especially teens, with no sexual history (virgins) do not have to worry providing they do not share needles, participate in ritual or unprofessional tattooing or body piercing, or come in contact with blood. General symptoms of STDs include:

- a discharge in the morning from the penis, vagina or anus;
- a sore that appears on the vagina, labia, penis, or scrotum;
- an itchy feeling in the pubic hairs, or genital organs;
- a fever, or pain in the abdominal area;
- an eruption of blisters around the anus, or genitals;
- severe night sweats, weight loss, swollen glands, chronic cough, heavy white coating on the tongue;

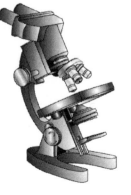

- small painless warts on the genitals; and
- a rash in patches on the back or genital area.

Each of these symptoms indicates that an individual may be infected, but only a doctor can specifically diagnose the correct disease and provide treatment. Sexually active women are at particular risk for all STDs because they often lack symptoms. The genital organs (vagina, cervix, uterus, and Fallopian tubes), are all internal and infection may not be noticed. **Females also have two distinct tubes, the urethra--for urination, and the vagina--for sexual activity**. This separation makes it difficult for women to notice any discharge that is the most common STD symptom. **Men, however, usually show symptoms within a couple of weeks because the urethra serves as a passage for both urine and sperm, i.e. only one tube.** For teenage women the risks of all forms of STD are even greater because teen girls have an underdeveloped genital mucosa. (See Appendix for female and male anatomy and the gonorrhea diagram).

Common STDs, Signs Symptoms, and Treatment

Each type of STD has a different pathogenic (disease causing) agent, mode of transmission, incubation period, and route of systemic transformation. Pathogens enter the mucus membranes that line the reproductive system, vagina, penis, anus and even the mouth. The pathogens hate light, cold and dryness. It is possible to catch several STDs at once. It is estimated that as many as 40% of people infected with STD are co-infected with a second sexually transmitted infection. (Holmes, 1990, 1999).

Chlamydia is currently the number one most common bacterial STD in the U.S. infecting nearly 3 million people annually. The pathogen is a bacterium, *Chlamydia trachomatis*. The disease is usually transmitted by sexual intercourse, but also can be transmitted by any contact of mucus membrane to mucus membrane, i.e., mouth to penis or vagina, anus or any combination in which genital mucus membranes come in contact. Symptoms are more common in males because, as stated above, the urethra is the single tube that passes both urine and sperm in men. Women, however, have two separate openings in the genital area, the vagina and the urethra. For this reason, it is estimated that as high as 75-80% of women are asymptomatic for both *Chlamydia* and gonorrhea. Men only have one opening, the urethra, which may become infected with the bacteria, and usually do show symptoms. Thus 75-80% of men usually are symptomatic, and will have painful urination, discharge or burning within days or a couple of weeks after exposure.

Symptoms of *Chlamydia* begin 7-21 days after infection. They include a discharge, (clear or milky), burning or pain while urinating, unusual vaginal bleeding, irregular periods, pelvic pain, irritation or itching, heavy feeling or swelling in the scrotum. Males usually are treated early because of noticeable symptoms; but females may not be aware of any infection. This could lead to a Pelvic Inflammatory Disease (PID) infection in the Fallopian tubes, and the bacteria may infect the bladder, or ovaries and could even lead to sterility. Asymptomatic women may have the disease and develop severe complications; thus it is critical that sexual partners communicate clearly and honestly about any possible infection.Treatment for *Chlamydia* is usually with antibiotics such as azithromycin, doxycycline and erythromycin. Treatment often only requires a single oral dose of antibiotics.

Gonorrhea infects more than 300,000 people each year. It is also caused by a bacteria, *Neisseria gonorrhea*, or "gonococcus." Symptoms can occur from 2-21 days and also includes a urethral discharge (usually more white or cloudy) from the penis, vagina or anus. Again, women are mostly asymptomatic, but may produce a little noticed, clear or sometimes white or green discharge. Chronic cases of gonorrhea in women can also lead to PID as described above. Treatment includes amoxicillin, ampicillin or injected ceftriaxone. Nongonococcal urethritis (NGU) refers to a sexually transmitted disease where the causative organism is difficult to determine. Symptoms are nearly the same as that for gonorrhea and the disease is usually caused by *Chlamydia* and *Ureaplasma* urealyticum and transmitted in coitus. Treatment is often only a single oral dose of doxycycline or tetracycline or erythromycin. (CDC, 2009e).

Syphilis has been around for thousands of years. It is believed that the "pestilence" in religious writings was probably syphilis. While syphilis is not usually fatal today, before World War One, and the development of antibiotics, many soldiers died from this bacterial disease. Syphilis is sometimes called the "great imitator" because the symptoms are similar to many other kinds of diseases. Symptoms may be a general tiredness, malaise, intestinal discomfort, skin rash or irritation, diarrhea or other very common symptoms such as the flu or common cold. Syphilis is caused by a spirochete bacteria, *Treponema pallidum* and is transmitted from open lesions during genital, oral, oral-genital or any combination of genital mucus membrane contact. The incubation period for syphilis is 1-12 weeks but could persist for years. The primary stage is characterized by a painless **chancre** (open sore) that appears at the site where the spirochete enters the body. The secondary stage occurs when the chancre disappears by itself, and a rash that can occur in patches, or all over the body. Latent syphilis or late stages may infect the heart, CNS or other body organ, and death can result if untreated. Death from syphilis is extremely rare with the wide range of antibiotics available today. Congenital syphilis may infect unborn children in utereo. Treatment is usually with penicillin, tetracycline or erythromycin. (CDC, 2009e).

Gardnerella vaginalis is a bacterial infection (often called bacterial vaginosis) primarily transmitted by intercourse. In women the symptoms include a fishy or musty smelling, thin discharge, like flour paste in consistency and usually gray in color. Most men are asymptomatic. Treatment is with metronidazole (Flagyl) ampicillin, or amoxicillin.

Moniliasis (Candidaisis) is a very common infection in women that is sometimes transmitted to men. The CDC estimates that nearly 75 percent of all women have had at least one genital **yeast infection** during their life. Women do not have to have intercourse to develop this condition. Sometimes referred to as a yeast infection, the fungus is caused by *Candida albicans* that may accelerate if a chemical change occurs in the vaginal mucosa. This frequently occurs with antibiotic treatment, or the wearing of tight pants, pantyhose, or non-cotton undergarments. Symptoms include a white milky or "cheesy" discharge and irritation of vaginal and vulvar tissue. Candida can also be transmitted to males through sexual intercourse. Treatment is usually with vaginal suppositories or creams such as Nystatin and miconazole.

One of the issues about STDs is that most females are asymptomatic and some do not get regular checkups from their gynocologist. During the 1980s several OTC products became available for women to purchase and treat common yeast infections, which often do not arise from sexual activity. The FDA approved these drugs for over-the-counter use, but this may cause serious problems for some women. One of the possible symptoms of HIV infection is a "recurrent vaginal yeast infection." The fungus occurs naturally in the vagina and other parts of the body; but if a woman continues to treat the infection by herself, without medical observation, she may be masking early symptoms of HIV disease. Thus, if a woman has a recurrent yeast infection, poorly manages her treatment and also is HIV positive, she may delay the time for specific diagnosis by a health care worker, and inhibit early treatment. For this reason some women may die sooner than men when they contract the virus that causes AIDS because they have no idea that they are infected.

Herpes simplex (HSV), genital herpes type 1 and 2 can be transmitted through sexual and close intimate bodily contact. CDC reported that results from a nationally representative study show that genital herpes infection is common in the United States. Nationwide, 16.2%, or about one out of six, people 14 to 49 years of age have genital HSV-2 infection. Over the past decade, the percentage of Americans with genital herpes infection in the U.S. has remained stable. (CDC, 2010g). The human body harbors hundreds of different kinds of organisms. Some are pathogenic, but the immune system keeps the numbers low and diseases do not usually occur. Herpes is caused by a virus. As with a common cold, viruses are very difficult to overcome. Several forms of herpes are known, such as Herpes Zoster (shingles) and Varicella (chickenpox). but only the two related to sexual activity are discussed in this book. HSV 1 is often called a "cold sore," and has symptoms that appear as watery blisters, and usually occur on the lips or around the mouth. Cold sores are very common in most people. Outbreaks of blisters arise because of stress, or possibly due to irritation from sunlight.

Genital Herpes (HSV2) sores are very infectious and can be passed from person to person, during the asymptomatic **prodromal period** (an early non-specific symptom, or set of symptoms), even without blisters being present. The blisters are painful, last about 7-10 days and eventually dry up. Once the sores are gone, the virus hides inside the body in the nerve ganglia. Blisters may reoccur at any time and there is no cure for herpes. Genital herpes (HSV 2) symptoms usually occur around the sex organs, the penis, vagina, anus, labia, scrotum or foreskin. The sores can be extremely painful and irritating, especially in females. They appear as red bumps or blisters (papules), and eventually rupture into open sores. Couples can still practice intercourse while having a herpes infection; but they must communicate openly and honestly about any infection and be extra careful. They need to communicate about the possibility of an outbreak, and use condoms for protection. Pregnant women with herpes sometimes have their children delivered by Cesarean section to prevent fetal infection. Doctors may make the determination for a Cesarean section based upon frequency and severity of previous herpes outbreaks before a pregnancy.

While there is no known cure for herpes, a variety of treatments may reduce symptoms. Treatment for herpes is with antiviral creams or pills of Acyclovir (Zovirax) Valacyclovir, or Famciclovir medications. Acyclovir may promote healing and suppress recurrent outbreaks and is sometimes used in cases of cold sores (HSV1). Valacyclovir uses acyclovir as its active ingredient but is better absorbed. The result is that valacyclovir gives symptomatic relief equal to acyclovir with less frequent dosing. Famciclovir is a relatively newer compound that works similarly to acyclovir, is better absorbed and is also being tested for use in first episodes and suppressive therapy. (ASHA, 1996). Call the Herpes Hotline at (919) 361-8488, for the latest updated information on HSV infection. Herpes 1 and 2 are interchangeable, and it is possible for individuals to have a cold sore, practice oral sex with a partner, and cause a genital herpes infection. It is estimated that nearly 50 % of genital herpes infections diagnosed today are type 1, and not type 2 as was thought in the recent past.

Hepatitis B is caused by a virus that can be transmitted with or without sexual contact. Blood, semen, vaginal secretions and saliva can transmit hepatitis B Virus. HBV is transmitted through activities that involve percutaneous (i.e., puncture through the skin) or mucosal contact with infectious blood or body fluids (e.g., semen, saliva), including injection drug use and sharing needles, syringes, or drug-preparation equipment, birth to an infected mother, contact with blood or open sores of an infected person, needle sticks or sharp instrument exposures, and sharing items such as razors or toothbrushes with an infected person. This pathogen may also transmitted by casual contact; but data about non-sexual transmission of hepatitis B is unclear at this time. Sexual transmission of Hepatitis B can occur by manual, oral or penile stimulation of the anus. This occurs as the mucus membranes come in contact with feces. Symptoms vary from nonexistent to mild, flu-like symptoms. However, HBV is not spread through food or water, sharing eating utensils, breastfeeding, hugging, kissing, hand holding, coughing, or sneezing. (CDC, 2009e).

Treatment: In 2005, the FDA approved a new Treatment for Chronic Hepatitis B. Baraclude (entecavir) tablets and oral solution for the treatment of chronic hepatitis B in adults. Treatment generally consists of bed rest and adequate fluid intake. A vaccine is now available for Hepatitis B and the American Academy of Pediatrics recommends routine vaccinations for infants, children and adolescents. Teachers, nurses and other school personnel that work in close proximity with students, such as special education or special-day students, should also be vaccinated against Hepatitis B. California law requires hepatitis B vaccinations for all entering 7th graders as of 1999.

Genital Warts (HPV): U.S. Congress Hears About Genital Warts. The dramatic increase of HPV infection in the U.S. was so significant that in 2004, the director of the CDC, Dr. Julie Gerberding, prepared a special report on this very common virus. The prevention strategies to Congress are listed below:

Report to Congress: Summary of Strategies to Prevent Genital HPV Infection

Based on currently available science, the following recommendations summarize the strategies most likely to be effective in preventing future infections with genital HPV infection and cervical cancer. Individual Strategies. The surest way to eliminate the risk for future genital HPV infections is to refrain from any genital contact with another infected individual. **For those who choose to be sexually active**, a long-term, mutually monogamous relationship with an uninfected partner is the strategy most likely to prevent future genital HPV infections. However, it is difficult to determine whether a partner who has been sexually active in the past is currently infected. **For those choosing to be sexually active and who are not in long-term mutually monogamous relationships,** reducing the number of sexual partners and choosing a partner less likely to be infected may reduce the risk of genital HPV infection. Partners less likely to be infected include those who have had no or few prior sex partners. ('less' likely is very difficult to determine!) While available scientific evidence suggests that the effect of condoms in preventing HPV infection is unknown, condom use has been associated with lower rates of the HPV-associated diseases of genital warts and cervical cancer. However, the available scientific evidence is not sufficient to recommend condoms as a primary prevention strategy for the prevention of genital HPV infection. There is evidence that indicates that the use of condoms may reduce the risk of cervical cancer. **Regular cervical cancer screening for all sexually active women and treatment of precancerous lesions remains the key strategy to prevent cervical cancer.** In the future, receiving a safe and effective HPV vaccine to help prevent genital HPV infection as well as the HPV-associated diseases of genital warts and cervical cancer would be an important prevention measure. However, an effective HPV vaccine would not replace other prevention strategies. (Gerberding, 2004).

It Took 30 Years. The First Vaccines Against an STD: Gardasil™ and Cervarix™

The 'future' vaccine was approved in 2006! It took almost 10 years from the discovery of an association between human papillomavirus (HPV) and cervical cancer to the finding of HPV type 16 in cervical cancer tissue. It took another 10 years to show that past infection with HPV16 increases the risk for subsequent development of invasive cervical cancer, and yet another 10 years before researchers could show that the seven most prevalent HPV types cause 87% of all cervical cancers. By comparison, the creation of HPV virus-like-particle (VLP) vaccines has been a rapid breakthrough. VLPs mimic the true structure of the virion and induce a striking antibody response after vaccination. Diane Harper and colleagues expanded this rapid development in a phase 2 trial in just over 1100 participants, a study that lasted 2.5 years. VLPs of the two most important oncogenic (tumor causing) HPV types, HPV16 and HPV18, were combined in a preventive vaccine. (Harper, Franco, Wheeler, et al., 2004).

In June 2006, the CDC Advisory Committee on Immunization Practices (ACIP) voted to recommend the first vaccine developed to prevent cervical cancer in females. This is exciting news since about 80% of sexually active people will get genital warts at some time in their lives. The new vaccine, Gardasil™, protects against four types of HPV that cause greater than 70% of cancers and 90% of genital warts. Gardasil™ is recommend for 11-12 year old girls, and can be given to girls as young as 9. Additionally, CDC recommends the vaccine for females from age 13-26 who have not yet received the vaccine. These recommendations stop at about age 26 for women, because it is assumed that a very small percentage of females will not have had sexual contact after 26. If a woman is sexually active, doctors still may recommend that they receive the vaccine; but the protection from the virus would be much less since these women may have already acquired HPV. Research is currently underway to determine the efficacy of the HPV vaccine for women older than 26, and the FDA may consider licensing the vaccine for this population of women. There are now two HPV vaccines, Gardasil and Cervarix, available to protect against the types of HPV that cause most cervical cancers.

The safety of the HPV vaccine was studied in clinical trials before it was licensed. For Gardasil, over 29,000 males and females participated in these trials. Cervarix was studied in over 30,000 females participating in several clinical trials performed all over the world. Cervarix has also been in use in other countries such as England and Europe prior to licensing from the Food and Drug Administration (FDA). (CDC, 2009f). As of February 14, 2011, approximately 33 million doses of Gardasil were distributed in the U.S. Since February 14, 2011, the Vaccine Adverse Event Reporting System (VAERS) received a total of 18,354 reports of adverse events following Gardasil vaccination in the U.S. (CDC, 2011e). Of these reports, 92% were reports of events considered to be non-serious, and 8% were reports of events considered serious. Based on all of the information we have today, CDC recommends HPV vaccination for the prevention of most types of cervical cancer. As with all approved vaccines, CDC and FDA will continue to closely monitor the safety of HPV vaccines. Any problems detected with these vaccines will be reported to health officials, healthcare providers, and the public and needed action will be taken to ensure the public's health and safety. (CDC, 2011e).

What about boys? Gardasil™ for boys or men was finally approved and the CDC reports that it is possible that vaccinating boys and males could prevent genital warts, and some rare penile and anal cancers. In September of 2009 the FDA approved recommendations of Gardasil™ for boys and men ages 9-26. While some parents of boys may object for various reasons, in the long run, when males are protected against genital warts, they could serve as an additional protection for their female partners against HPV and ultimately cancer of the cervix. Nonetheless, this vaccine will protect against about 70% of cervical cancers; but women must still get regular Pap tests to screen for other types of genital warts and cancers. The vaccine still will not protect women against about 10% of genital warts. (CDC, 2011e).

The Ethical Issue of HPV Vaccine Requirement. The summer of 2006 was, indeed, an historic date to help women in the U.S. and throughout the world prevent cervical cancer when the FDA licensed a vaccine against human papillomarvirus (HPV). By the summer of 2008 more than 40 states, including Michigan, Texas and Virginia have considered, or have written legislation requiring young girls to receive the HPV vaccine. All of the states included a parental exclusion option, as is also included in sexuality education curricula. The development of Gardasil™, Merck's HPV vaccine is of major public health importance and Gardasil™ was the very first vaccine that will prevent an STD known to cause a type of cancer. The prevention of cervical cancer in women should be a very exciting and easily accepted discovery; but due to political, religious and conservative objections, the vaccine has not been widely required for school attendance throughout most U.S. schools. More than 6 million people in the U.S. become infected with HPV annually, and nearly 10,000 women are diagnosed with cervical cancer, principally caused by HPV, the virus that causes genital warts. (Colgrove, 2006).

The Advisory Committee on Immunization Practices of the CDC recommended that the vaccine be given routinely to girls at 9 or 12 years of age and the vaccine is now approved for use in boys. Conservative groups initially objected to the requirement of the vaccine because, in their view, such a requirement would constitute an attempt by the secular state to force a girl or boy to receive a vaccine that would be irreconcilable with her family's religious values and beliefs. Additionally, many religious groups state that requiring the HPV vaccine would be much different than requiring routine vaccinations against "classic" childhood diseases such as polio, measles, and pertussis. One of the major arguments by some parents is that if a child is given the HPV vaccine they may become sexually permissive. Nonetheless, many practical pediatricians are simply telling the parents of young girls that they have to **get their shots to go to school-period.** And parents therefore will have no need to have detailed discussions on sexuality at an early age. (Colgrove, 2006).

Genital warts (HPV) now infect over 6 million people in the United States. Genital warts are caused by a virus, the human papilloma virus (HPV). The symptoms include raised "warty" appearing tumors on the genitals and also includes, raised, flesh colored lesions; genital lesions; genital sores (female); genital sores (male); anal warts; cauliflower-like appearing growths around the anus or female genitalia; increased dampness or moisture in the area of the growths; itching of the penis, scrotum, anal area, or a vulvar itch; increased vaginal discharge; and abnormal vaginal bleeding (not associated with a menstrual period) after sexual intercourse (post-coital).

Frequently no symptoms are noted from genital warts. Women may be completely asymptomatic with the warts hidden within the vaginal tract. Careful diagnosis by a STD specialist may uncover **vaginal asperities** (pre symptomatic genital warts), but women and some men may show no signs. Warts are easily transmitted from men to women through sexual intercourse. The warts are often difficult to see, even for a doctor, and have to be carefully removed. Removal is completed with liquid nitrogen, podophyllin, freezing or laser surgery. This can be painful, especially on the penis, vagina, or anus! Once the warts are removed, the doctor must use a chemical wash, examine the penis or vagina (colposcopy) carefully, and recommend patients use condoms until treatment is completed. Genital warts may reoccur for months or years after infection and has also been associated with cervical cancer in women. Other names for genital warts: Condylomata acuminata, penile warts, human papilloma virus (HPV), and venereal warts or condyloma.

Teenagers and young adults have the highest rate of STDs and are at risk not only because they practice dangerous behaviors, but also because of the actual nature of their genital tract and surrounding organs. HPV infection can ultimately lead to uterine or cervical cancer in women. Doctors Grace and Patrick report on HPV and the impact on the female adolescent genital mucosa:

> In adolescence, columnar epithelium extends from the endocervical canal into the vagina. This epithelium, not protected by cervical mucus, is the primary site of invasion by both Chlamydia and gonococcal pathogens. Until the squamocolumnar junction (transformation zone) has progressed to the endocervical canal, it is also biologically more susceptible to carcinogenic factors. This places younger patients at increased risk for cervical HPV infections, and subsequent cytological changes. (Grace, Patrick, 1992).

Pubic lice (pediculosis) are caused by an infestation of little "bugs," or insects that are usually transmitted by sexual intercourse. They live in the pubic areas, much like body lice in the head, and can cause itching and irritation. The causative organism, *Phthirus pubis,* may also be present on any hair of the body such as the face, beard, chest and even the eyelashes. This organism can also be transmitted non-sexually by sharing clothing, undergarments, or bedding. Treatment for lice can be obtained OTC by using a specially formulated insecticide in a shampoo or cream base. The chemical must be applied

carefully and all clothing, brushes, sheets, etc., must be washed at high temperatures to kill the eggs or "nits." Special fine-toothed combs are also provided with the medication to comb out any eggs after the adults are killed. In 2009, FDA approved benzyl alcohol (prescription only) to treat head lice. (Holmes, Mardh, Sparling et al., 1990, 1999; FDA, 2009). Students can receive treatment for lice at STD clinics, but must be vigilant for successful treatment that requires strict adherence to directions for application.

Chancroid is a very rare form of STD in the U.S., but found mostly in tropical or sub-tropical climates, and is caused by a bacterium, *Hemophilus ducreyi.* According to the CDC, since 1987, reported cases of chancroid declined steadily until 2001 when 38 cases were reported. In 2006, 33 cases of chancroid were reported in the United States. Only eight states reported one or more cases of chancroid in 2006. Although the overall decline in reported chancroid cases most likely reflects a decline in the incidence of this disease, these data should be interpreted with caution since *Hemophilus ducreyi* is difficult to culture and, as a result, this condition may be substantially under-diagnosed. Transmission is through sexual contact and also through mother to child during birth. Symptoms include genital ulcers, which are usually more noticeable in men, resulting in painful sores. Chancroid, along with herpes, and syphilis produce open sores that make individuals more susceptible to HIV infection because the virus that causes AIDS can enter open sores or lesions more readily. Diagnosis of Chancroid is difficult and special lab testing should be done for any type of genital ulcers. Chancroid is treated with the antibiotics Azithromycin, Ceftriaxone, Ciprofloxacin, or Erythromycin.

Trichomoniasis, now the most common STD, is caused by a protozoan parasite, *Trichomonas vaginalis,* and is usually passed by sexual contact with infected persons. The protozoan, sometimes called "trich," can actually live outside the body on external objects for as long 60-90 minutes, in urine for up to three hours, and in seminal fluid for six hours. Thus while it is possible, under very precise conditions, to contract trich by non-sexual contact, the chances, are extremely rare and most cases are from sexual activity. Symptoms of trichomonas are mostly found in women. Symptomatic women will produce a green foul-smelling discharge within 4 or 5 days after infection. The discharge also causes irritation to the vagina and vulva producing redness and pain. The organism has also been found under the foreskin of the penis without causing symptoms. Treatment for trich is simple, a microscopic exam of the discharge and treatment with metronidazole (Flagyl). Both partners should be treated to avoid re-infecting each other and to prevent spread of the disease. (CDC, 2011e).

Scabies is another form of STD. It is caused by a tiny mite, an arthropod related to a spider, that deposits eggs below the skin in the fingers, wrists, armpits or other creases in the body. The mite burrows into the skin, especially around the hands, feet, and male genitalia. It

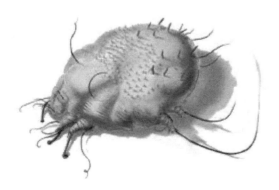

does not usually affect the neck and head, although it may occur in the neck of infants. The itching is due to an allergic reaction to the tiny mites, and is associated with a rash of red, raised spots. Transmission of scabies is by direct, prolonged, skin-to-skin contact with a person already infested with scabies. Contact generally must be prolonged (a quick handshake or hug will usually not spread infestation). Infestation is easily spread to sexual partners and household members. Infestation may also occur by sharing clothing, towels, and bedding. The diagnosis can be made difficult because the rash can look like other itchy conditions such as eczema. The itch is worse at night, and may often affect more than one family member. Scabies is easily spread by sexual contact and other close direct contact. Once the mite is identified, treatment can begin. This includes vigorous scrubbing of the infected areas, hot baths and treatment with Kwell lotion available by doctor's prescription. Since scabies may infect entire families, careful application should be done with adult supervision because Kwell lotion is especially toxic to children. For more information about the little inch mites (Scabies) Google CDC, Scabies.

Complications of STDs

Today most of the bacterial forms of STD are controllable and can be treated with a handful of antibiotics. Numerous complications, however, can develop and have severe consequences. A few of the many complications from bacterial STD infection include:

- Sterility-syphilis and Chlamydia;
- Stillbirth-syphilis, herpes;
- Permanent birth defects-herpes;
- Blindness-Chlamydia, gonorrhea syphilis, herpes;
- Aortic aneurysm-heart condition from syphilis;
- Meningitis-herpes, syphilis;
- Cervical cancer- genital warts;
- Ecotopic pregnancy (tubal pregnancy)-gonorrhea, Chlamydia;
- Arthritis-gonorrhea;
- Neonatal pneumonia-Chlamydia, gonorrhea;
- Neonatal ophthamalia-herpes in the brain;
- Liver cancer/failure-hepatitis B; and
- AIDS related opportunistic diseases- HIV (Ca. STD, 2002).

It is one of the joys of childhood that children think they will live forever. It is one of the curses of childhood in some of our meanest neighborhoods that children think they won't live to be much beyond 25 anyway. In a perverse way, both of those attitudes are contributing to the problem, because one group of our children think that they are at no risk because nothing can ever happen to them--they're bulletproof. Another group believes that no matter what they do, they don't have much of a future anyway. And they are bound together in a death spiral when it comes to this. This is crazy. We have got to find some way to tell them you must stop this.

President Clinton, December 6, 1995, to the White House Conference on HIV and AIDS.

More People Living with AIDS in the U.S.

The good news is that while it may be very difficult to manage with medications, a depressed immune system and considerable complacency about AIDS in the U.S. and other countries as well; more Americans are living many more years than expected with HIV. See the graph below to discover the increased lifespan of HIV patients.

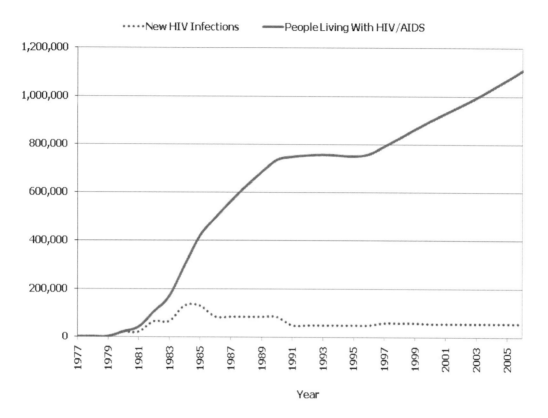

····New HIV Infections ──── People Living With HIV/AIDS

Year

Prevalence Estimates—United States, 2006. *MMWR* **2008;57(39):1073-76.**

Recent Trends in HIV

It has been more than three decades since HIV/AIDS was identified. In the 1980s it was merely considered a 'gay problem' and the virus was originally known with the acronym **GRID** (Gay Related Immune Deficiency Disease). It wasn't until 1986 that the virus was clearly identified as the Human Immunodeficiency Virus (HIV). The good news is that the number of people living with HIV in the U.S. (HIV prevalence) is higher than ever before. Some have been living with the virus for more than 20 years and could live another 20 or more years; others living with the disease for a number of years are taking 50 pills a day and suffering a myriad of side effects just to stay alive. CDC estimates that more than 1 million (1,106,400) adults and adolescents were living with HIV infection in the United States at the end of 2006, the most recent year for which national prevalence estimates are available. This represents an increase of approximately 11% from the previous estimate in 2003. The increase may be due to more people seeking care and antiretroviral treatment that can increase survival. While it is estimated that 1.7 million people in the U.S. have been infected with HIV, including about 600,000 who have already died; every 9 1/2 minutes someone in the U.S. is infected with HIV. And, the HIV/AIDS epidemic continues to have a disproportionate impact on certain populations, particularly racial and ethnic minorities and gay and bisexual men. (Kaiser, 2011).

Despite increases in the total number of people living with HIV, the annual number of new HIV infections (HIV incidence) has remained relatively stable. Furthermore, the great majority of persons with HIV do not transmit HIV to others. CDC estimates that during 2006 there were 5 transmissions per 100 persons living with HIV in the U.S. Is it possible that prevention efforts from schools and community agencies are finally taking hold on the general population? And finally, diagnoses of HIV infection reported to CDC have increased in recent years. In 2008, 41,269 persons were diagnosed with HIV infection in the 37 states with long term, confidential, name-based HIV infection reporting—an increase of 8% overall since 2005. The overall increase in diagnoses reported to CDC may be due to a increases in HIV testing, and uncertainty inherent in statistical estimates. (CDC, 2010d).

Even with many prevention and treatment successes, people are still dying from AIDS. HIV remains a significant cause of death for certain populations. For example, in 2006, HIV was the third leading cause of death for black males and black females aged 35-44 and the fourth leading cause of death for Hispanic/Latino males and females in the same age range. Overall, more than 576,000 persons with an AIDS diagnosis in the United States have died since the beginning of the epidemic through 2007 (the most recent year that death data are available). From 2005 through 2007, deaths of persons with a diagnosis of HIV infection have increased 17% and the estimated rate of deaths increased 14%. Many factors can make it difficult to interpret the data. For example

- the increases may be influenced by significant efforts that have been made to improve death reporting by state HIV surveillance programs;
- the number of people living with HIV infection has increased over time, so the number of deaths would also be expected to increase;
- the group of persons living with HIV infection is aging, which may result in an increased number of deaths from any cause, including those unrelated to HIV infection;
- there are uncertainties inherent in statistical estimates; and
- too many people are diagnosed with HIV late in the course of infection. Despite an increase in persons getting diagnosed with HIV earlier in the course of their infection, far too many continue to be diagnosed late. In 2008, about one-third (32%) of individuals with an HIV diagnosis reported to CDC received a diagnosis of AIDS within 12 months of their initial HIV diagnosis. (CDC, 2010d).

Additionally, AIDS disproportionately affects different parts of the country. HIV and AIDS have had a severe impact on all regions of the country. It remains mostly an urban disease, with the majority of individuals diagnosed with AIDS in 2008 residing in areas with more than 500,000 people. Areas hardest hit (by ranking of AIDS cases per 100,000 people) include Miami and Jacksonville, Florida; New Orleans and Baton Rouge, Louisiana; Baltimore, Maryland; and Washington D. C. (NCHHS, 2010).

HIV '101'

Common sense does not always take precedence when it comes to personal matters, or matters of the heart. This is especially true regarding sexual encounters. A talk radio psychiatrist was counseling a woman regarding her marital problems. She complained that her husband was flirting with another woman at work, and she was worried about his potential infidelity. She sounded as if she was in great pain because of a "possible sexual affair." The psychiatrist made a very simple recommendation. He told her, " Immediately after this talk, call your husband up at work and tell him to call you and tell you about his sexual activity, before he starts a sexual affair with the lady in marketing. Tell him, you can live with a broken heart, but you don't want to die of AIDS..." This little story illustrates the genuine seriousness regarding the deadly disease of AIDS. Since some patients live for many years with AIDS, the more accepted terms used to describe the virus is now HIV infection or HIV disease. This is because there is a growing population of infected and contagious HIV positive people that are living for many years without noticeable medical problems, but if they experience many sexual relations, they place their partners at risk. By 2007, many kids that were born HIV positive in the 1990s have grown up living with the virus. Some of these kids may have medical problems, but a good percentage nowadays may be able to live a relatively normal life. That means they are infectious already even though they may not have had sexual contact. Parents of children with HIV do not have to disclose any medical information to school officials unless they decide it may be in the best interest of their child. Some of these students, therefore may be in your class without your knowledge.

What is AIDS? The medical definition of AIDS is defined as a secondary or acquired immunodeficiency syndrome (AIDS) caused by the human immunodeficiency virus (HIV) and characterized by severe immune deficiency resulting in opportunistic infections, malignancies, and neurologic lesions in individuals without prior history of immunologic abnormality. It is usually fatal. Historically, the first case of AIDS was documented in 1959 in Manchester England. In 1968, the first death from AIDS was recorded in Saint Louis, and by the 1970s, many cases were occurring in New York City, but were not recognized. By July, 1981, there were a total of 30 AIDS cases reported in the U.S. It was then called the "gay disease" because most known cases were among gay white men, and, as stated above, the old acronym for the disease during this time was GRID, or Gay Related Immunodeficiency Disease. This term is no longer used since the disease has been found in all populations throughout the world. By the end of the decade of the 1980s, the total reported cases in the United States passed 100,000. By mid 1994 the number exceeded 350,000. By 1999 there were over 641, 000 cases, and by 2008 the estimate was between 900,000 to 980,000. Worldwide the 2009 estimate is about 40 million people living with AIDS. The World Health Organization (WHO), indicates that over 33 million AIDS cases worldwide are found in sub-Saharan Africa. (WHO, 2007).

One of the major problems of HIV disease is the long incubation period. Many people have been HIV positive for over 20 years and have had very little noticeable illness. Thus people diagnosed with the disease in 1980 were carrying the disease for many years before testing positive. It is estimated that there are over 1 million people in the U. S. that are HIV positive. This is very disturbing because they can infect millions of others without knowing about their own infection. Worse yet, while most people living with AIDS try their best to stay healthy, follow their doctors orders and practice safe sexual practices; a few are so angry that they choose not to tell anyone, including any potential sex partners that they are infected!

The CDC estimates that about 100,000 women in the United States are infected with HIV. The majority of these women are African-Americans. They comprise 11 percent of all AIDS cases, and the percentage increases each year. CDC estimated that by 2004, at least 125,000 children became orphans of this epidemic and needed to be cared for by family members, caring adults, or extended family members, or placed in foster care. This places a tremendous strain on the social welfare systems as both parents die leaving an orphaned child. (Novello, 1993) (CDC, 2004). The CDC now publishes detailed slide shows about HIV for public review. To view the most recent statistics on HIV, Google: CDC.gov/HIV.

HIV is the virus that causes AIDS, and it is HIV that is spread through the exchange of blood, semen, vaginal secretions, and breast milk. AIDS is a serious impairment in a person's natural immunity against disease, and the final stage of infection with HIV. A person infected with HIV is diagnosed as having AIDS if certain serious diseases or conditions develop. These conditions are known as opportunistic infections because they gain the "opportunity" to invade and infect the body when the immune system is depressed. Some examples are Kaposi's sarcoma, pneumocystis carinii pneumonia, and AIDS related dementia. In 1993, the CDC redefined the criteria for AIDS classification. One major change is that a patient is diagnosed with AIDS if the T-cell count is less than 200 cells/ml of blood and has history of an opportunistic infection. HIV is a retrovirus, which means that it carries its genetic information in the form of RNA, as opposed to DNA. Like other viruses, HIV cannot reproduce without the help of a host cell. One of the primary targets of the virus is the T-helper cell (T-Cell), a type of white blood cell that is a key part of the immune system's defense against diseases and infections.

At some point, the dormant, infected T-helper cells are triggered to start producing the virus. It is not yet known why the virus lies dormant longer in some people than others, or what triggers the cell to start producing the virus. As the T-helper cells produce more HIV and die, the immune system becomes aware of the infection and tries to fight back. The healthy T-helper cells signal the B-cells to fight the virus with antibodies. The attack against the virus is ineffective, however, and the final outcome of the battle is a decrease in T-helper cells and the spread of HIV infection. As the number of T-helper cells diminishes, the immune system becomes ineffective, and opportunistic diseases such as Kaposi sarcoma, pneumocystis carinii and numerous other infections overwhelm the body. Chronic infection from HIV disease leads to death.

"We grow up hating ourselves like society teaches us to.
If someone had been 'out' about their sexuality.
If the teachers hadn't been afraid to stop the 'fag' and 'dyke' jokes.
If my human sexuality class had even mentioned homosexuality.
If the school counselors would have been open to
a discussion of gay and lesbian issues.
If any of those possibilities had existed,
perhaps I would not have grown up hating what I was.
And, just perhaps, I wouldn't have caught
AIDS and attempted suicide."
--- Kyallee, 19

Gay and Bisexual Men and HIV

The CDC surveillance systems refer to gay and bisexual men as men who have sex with men (MSM). This group of all groups continue to be the risk group most severely affected by HIV. Additionally, this is the only risk group in the U.S. in which the annual number of new HIV infections is increasing. There is an urgent need to expand access to proven HIV prevention interventions for gay and bisexual men, as well as to develop new approaches to fight HIV in this population; however, it critical to understand that just because a person is gay, lesbian, transgender or bisexual (LGBT) does not mean they are more easily infected. It is not the group, but the behavior that will increase risk for HIV or any other STD as well. It is not 'who you are,' but 'what you do,' that matters the most. Many LGBT couples do practice safe sex and strive to be monogamous. The following data is an update from the CDC on gay and bisexual males (MSM):

- MSM account for nearly half of the more than one million people living with HIV in the U.S. (48%, or an estimated 532,000 total persons);
- MSM account for more than half of all new HIV infections in the U.S. each year (53%, or an estimated 28,700 infections);
- While CDC estimates that MSM account for just 4 percent of the U.S. male population aged 13 and older, the rate of new HIV diagnoses among MSM in the U.S. is more than 44 times that of other men (range: 522–989 per 100,000 MSM vs. 12 per 100,000 other men);
- MSM are the only risk group in the U.S. in which new HIV infections are increasing. While new infections have declined among both heterosexuals and injection drug users, the annual number of new HIV infections among MSM has been steadily increasing since the early 1990s;
- White MSM represent a greater number of new HIV infections than any other population, followed closely by black MSM (one of the dispropporionately affected subgroups in the U.S.);
- There are more new HIV infections among young black MSM aged 13-29 than among any other age and racial group of MSM;
- Most new infections among white MSM occur among those aged 30-39 followed by those aged 40-49; and
- Among Hispanic MSM, most new infections occur in the youngest age group 13-39, though a substantial number of new HIV infeceions also occur among those 30-39. (CDC, 2010 f).

AIDS continues to claim the lives of too many MSM. Since the beginning of the epidemic, more than 279,000 MSM with AIDS have died. Why does the disease affect this specific population? Many complex possibilities exist but CDC considers the following most significant: (1) high prevalence of HIV among gay and bisexual men means a greater risk of exposure, (2) lack of knowledge of HIV status since many individuals do not get tested regularly, (3) young black MSM that partner with older black men (among whom HIV prevalence is high) may increase risk, (4) complacency about risk among MSM (and many heterosexuals as well) about treatment of HIV with just a few drugs, (5) alcohol or other substance abuse, and (6) social or cultural discrimination where many may deny their sexual orientation or sexual practices. (CDC,

2010 f). It must be emphasized, however, that for all groups, gay, lesbian, bisexual, straight or transgender, or any combination therof, individuals should get the facts, get tested and continue regular specific, practical and intimate dialog about sexual practices with their partners in order to prevent HIV and other forms of sexually transmitted diseases.

High Risk Behaviors for HIV Infection. Teenagers are only at risk to contract HIV if they practice risky behaviors. Behaviors that place a teen, or anyone else include: anal sex, with or without a condom, unprotected sex with two or more partners, sharing needles and syringes to inject drugs, sex without a condom, sex with someone you don't know very well or with someone you know has several sex partners or any combination of the above!

How HIV is spread. AIDS is one of the most serious health problems to ever face the American public. Diseases like pneumocystis pneumonia, and Kaposi Sarcoma are now usually very rare, but HIV lowers the immunosuppression system, and is spread through sharing needles, or unprotected sexual activity. The main body fluid transmission of HIV is blood, semen, vaginal fluid and breast milk. The AIDS virus may live in the human body for years before actual symptoms appear. It primarily affects you by making you unable to fight other diseases. It is these opportunistic infections, and not HIV that can kill.

How Do You Get AIDS? It is very important to remember that it is not easy to contract AIDS. People have to actively practice a risk behavior to become infected with the virus. There are two main ways you can get AIDS. First, you can become infected with the virus that causes AIDS by having sex — oral, anal or vaginal — with someone who is infected with the AIDS virus. Second, you can be infected by sharing drug needles and syringes with an infected person. Babies of women who have been infected with the AIDS virus may be born with the infection because it can be transmitted from the mother to the baby before or during birth and through breast milk. In the U.S., however, the risk to a baby of an HIV infected mom has become very rare. See the box below about the near absence of pediatric AIDS in the U.S.

**AIDS and Newborn Babies: Risk Reduced to
Nearly Zero in the United States**

During 1992 it was estimated that 15-25 % of babies of HIV positive mothers became infected with the virus. By 1994 it was know that if a pregnant HIV positive woman was given AZT or other drugs, **early in the pregnancy**, her chance of infecting the baby with HIV can be reduced to as low as 8% or less. By 1999, Lindgren reported that the infection rate of perinatal AIDS cases could be reduced even lower, perhaps to as low 3%. Researchers also reported that if a woman is getting treatment with powerful AIDS-fighting drug regimens, the virus levels in the blood could be **reduced to less than 1%.** This low figure would make pediatric AIDS a thing of the past in the United States, but the pediatric AIDS cases worldwide are much higher and developing countries could also see a reduction if the cost of AZT was reduced. (Lindgren, Byers, Thomas, 1999).

Can You Become Infected? Yes, anyone can get infected with HIV if they engage in risky behavior. The male homosexual population was the first in this country to feel the effects of the disease. Worldwide, however, the predominant mode of transmission is by heterosexual contact (72% of cases). People who have died of AIDS in the U.S. have been male and female, rich and poor, white, African-American, Hispanic, Asian and American Indian.

What Are the Symptoms of AIDS? When a person is infected with HIV, the major problem is that the immune system will become depressed. This will allow a variety of diseases to attack the body and ultimately cause death. Let us compare the common cold as an example. If you catch a cold you may feel weak, have a running nose, congested lungs, etc., but eventually, after several days, you overcome the illness. In addition, your body has built up a resistance for that particular cold virus strain. HIV infection is different, the body cannot overcome the infection and severe problems, or opportunistic diseases result.

In the recent past the most common cause of death in AIDS patients was from the opportunistic infection (OI) called *Pneumocystis jirovecii* (formerly carinii) (PCP). PCP is a protozoal type of pneumonia that causes shortness of breath, a persistent dry cough, sharp chest pain, and difficulty in breathing. The second most common opportunistic infection seen in people with AIDS was Kaposi's sarcoma (KS), a rare form of cancer that produces brownish or purple blotches on the skin, in the mouth, nose and internal organs. The blotches are painless, but do not heal. HIV also causes unexplained dementia (mental deterioration) and meningitis (infection of the tissues covering the brain).

The following **opportunistic infections** are currently prevalent in most AIDS infected individuals: Candidiasis (Thrush) is a fungal infection of the mouth, throat, or vagina. CD4 cell range: can occur even with fairly high CD4 cells. Cytomegalovirus (CMV) is a viral infection that causes eye disease that can lead to blindness.CD4 cell range: under 50. Herpes simplex viruses can cause oral herpes (cold sores) or genital herpes. These are fairly common infections, but if you have HIV, the outbreaks can be much more frequent and more severe. They can occur at any CD4 cell count. Malaria is common in the developing world. It is more common and more severe in people with HIV infection. *Mycobacterium avium* complex (MAC or MAI) is a bacterial infection that can cause recurring fevers, general sick feelings, problems with digestion, and serious weight loss. CD4 cell range: under 75. Pneumocystis pneumonia (PCP) is a fungal infection that can cause a fatal pneumonia. CD4 cell range: under 200. Unfortunately this is still a fairly common OI in people who have not been tested or treated for HIV. Toxoplasmosis (Toxo) is a protozoal infection of the brain. T-cell range: under 100. Tuberculosis (TB) is a bacterial infection that attacks the lungs, and can cause meningitis. CD4 cell range: Everyone with HIV who tests positive for exposure to TB should be treated. (Kaiser, 2011).

In recent years, however, death from HIV infection was attributed to other causes. In a large study in New York City, non–HIV-related causes of death account for one fourth of all deaths of persons with AIDS. Cardiovascular disease, non–AIDS-defining cancer, and substance abuse account for most non–HIV-related deaths. Reducing deaths from these causes requires a shift in the health care model for persons with AIDS from a primary focus on managing HIV infection to providing care that addresses all aspects of physical and mental health. (Sackoff, Hanna, Pfeiffer, et al., 2006).

How Do You Get AIDS From Sex. The AIDS virus can be spread by sexual intercourse whether you are male or female, heterosexual, bisexual or homosexual. This happens because a person that is infected with the AIDS virus may have the virus in semen or vaginal fluids. The virus can enter the body through the vagina, penis, rectum or mouth. Anal intercourse, with or without a condom, is risky, compared to the thicker vaginal mucosa. The rectum is thin, and not biologically designed for penile penetration, filled with many blood vessels near the surface of the skin, and easily injured during anal intercourse.

World AIDS Day is December 1st

Remember, AIDS is sexually transmitted, and the AIDS virus is not the only infection that is passed through intimate sexual contact. Other sexually transmitted diseases, such as gonorrhea, hepatitis B, syphilis, herpes and Chlamydia, can also be contracted through oral, anal and vaginal intercourse. If you are infected with one of these diseases, especially those that produce open sores like syphilis, or herpes, and engage in risky behavior, you are at greater risk of getting AIDS.

Kissing. Social kissing or closed-mouth kissing is not a risk for transmission of HIV. Because there is a theoretical potential for contact with blood with "French" or open-mouth kissing, the CDC recommends against engaging in this activity with an infected person. Nonetheless, no carefully documented case of AIDS reported to the CDC can be attributed to transmission through any kind of kissing. Only one case, however, has ever been documented in the U.S. in 1996 where a couple transmitted HIV from one partner to the other by kissing. This case was the only documented case of HIV transmission via kissing in the mouth, and it was reported that the couple both had severe gum disease involving blood in the oral cavity. Individuals were suffering from gingivitis with inflamed and bleeding bums (CDC, 1997). To read the details of this extremely rare event related to kissing, Google HIV and kissing, 1996 or see: http://www.cdc.gov/mmwr/preview/mmwrhtml/00048364.htm. (CDC, 2010h).

Biting. A state department of health conducted an investigation involving an incident that suggested blood-to blood transmission of HIV by a human bite. There have been other reports in the medical literature in which HIV appeared to have been transmitted by a bite. Severe trauma with extensive tissue tearing and damage including the presence of blood were reported in each of these instances. Kids in school, especially elementary youth, may intentionally or unintentionally bite each other. Biting is not, however, considered a common way of transmitting HIV. Numerous reports have been recorded that did not result in transmission of HIV. (CDC, 1995b, CDC, 2010h).

Stop HIV... Stop STDs...
Start Talking...Now

You Won't Get AIDS From Insects — Or A Kiss

HIV, the virus that causes AIDS is difficult to contract and it is easily avoided. You won't just "catch" AIDS like a cold or flu because the virus is a different type. The AIDS virus is transmitted through sexual intercourse, the sharing of needles, or to babies of infected mothers before or during birth, and from breast milk.

You won't get the AIDS virus through everyday contact with the people around you in school, in the workplace, or stores. You won't get it by swimming in a pool, even if someone in the pool is infected with the AIDS virus. Students attending school with someone infected with the AIDS virus are not in danger from casual contact.

You won't get AIDS from a mosquito bite. The AIDS virus is not transmitted through a mosquito's salivary glands like other diseases such as malaria or yellow fever. You won't get it from bed bugs, lice, flies, or other insects, either.

You won't get AIDS from saliva, sweat, tears, urine or a bowel movement. HIV has been documented as present in saliva, but it would take 16 quarts of saliva to transmit a viral load to infect another person!

You won't get AIDS from a kiss. You won't get AIDS from clothes, a telephone, or from a toilet seat. It can't be passed by using a glass or eating utensils that someone else has used. You won't get the virus by being on a bus, train or crowded elevator with a person who is infected with the virus, or who has AIDS.

HIV is not transmitted by day-to-day contact in the workplace, schools, or social settings. HIV is not transmitted through shaking hands, hugging, or a casual kiss. You cannot become infected from a toilet seat, a drinking fountain, a doorknob, dishes, drinking glasses, food, or pets. HIV is not an airborne virus and the only way to contract the disease is to practice a risky behavior, such as unprotected sex, and sharing needles.

(CDC, 2009; CDC, 2010h).

Saliva, Tears and Sweat. HIV has been found in saliva and tears in very low quantities from some AIDS patients. It is important to understand that finding a small amount of virus in a specific body fluid does not mean that HIV can be transmitted by that body fluid. Contact with saliva, tears or sweat has never been shown to result in HIV transmission. During 1997, several methods were introduced to test for HIV with a swab in the mouth. This swab test, called OraSure, has been used extensively since 2000, and is an excellent test, especially for testing people in the community, such as drug users. This may easily confuse youth to think that if an AIDS test was done in the saliva, then HIV must be transmitted in the mouth. This is not the case. The swab tests for the antibodies of HIV, and not the virus of HIV in saliva. Contact with saliva has never been demonstrated as a method to transmit HIV (CDC, 1995b; CDC, 2010f). Exposure to saliva uncontaminated with blood is a rare mode of HIV transmission for at least five reasons; (1) saliva inhibits HIV infectivity; (2) HIV is infrequently isolated from saliva; (3) none of the approximately 800,000 cases of AIDS (as of 2008) reported to CDC have been attributed to exposure to saliva; (4) levels of HIV are low in the saliva of HIV-infected persons, even in the presence of periodontal disease; and (5) transmission of HIV in association with kissing has not been documented in students of nonsexual household contacts of HIV-infected persons. (CDC, 1997, Panlilio, 2005; CDC, 2010h).

Insects

Since the onset of the HIV epidemic, there has been concern about bloodsucking and biting insects transmitting the virus. Studies by the CDC and elsewhere have shown no evidence of HIV transmission through insects-even in areas where there are many cases of AIDS and large populations of insect vectors, such as mosquitoes. Experiments and observations indicate that

when an insect bites a person, it does not inject its own or a previously bitten person's or animal's blood into the next person bitten. The insect injects saliva, often including a lubricant or anticoagulant so the animal can feed more efficiently. Malaria and yellow fever are two well-known insect borne diseases. They are both transmitted by very specific kinds of mosquitoes, which have not been shown to transmit HIV infection. Some have been concerned that if an insect such as a mosquito has residual blood on their

mouthparts from a previous bite, that HIV can be transmitted. This is not true for two reasons. 1) infected people do not have constant, high levels of HIV in their bloodstream, and 2) insects such as mosquitoes "take a break," immediately after feeding i.e., they fly to a resting place to digest their food (CDC, 1995b; CDC, 2010h; CDC, 2010f).

HIV and People of Color

For a myriad of reasons, HIV has been a significant problem with two major groups of Americans, Hispanics and African Americans. The section below will describe some of the issues related to HIV/AIDS prevalence in these unique groups. Data on HIV/AIDS infection in Hispanics are summarized below from the most recent information reported by the CDC. The HIV/AIDS epidemic is a serious threat to the Hispanic community. In addition to being a population seriously affected by HIV, Hispanics continue to face challenges in accessing health care, prevention services, and HIV treatment. In 2005, HIV/AIDS was the fourth leading cause of death among Hispanic men and women aged 35 to 44. The CDC also reported:

- In 2008, Hispanics/Latinos accounted for more than 19% of the 42,439 new diagnoses of HIV infection in the 37 states and 5 US dependent areas with confidential name-based HIV infection reporting;

- For Hispanic men living with HIV/AIDS, the most common methods of HIV transmission were (in order) sexual contact with other men, injection drug use, and high-risk heterosexual contact;

- In 2006, the rate of chlamydial infection for Hispanics was about 3 times the rate for whites (not Hispanic/ Latino), and the rates of gonorrhea and syphilis for Hispanics were about twice the rates for whites;

- For Hispanic women living with HIV/AIDS, the most common methods of transmission were high-risk heterosexual contact and injection drug use;
- While Hispanic/Latino women represented a quarter (24%) of new infections among Hispanics/Latinos in 2006, their rate of HIV infection was nearly four

times that of white women (14.4/100,000 vs. 3.8/100,000);

- **At some point in life, 1 in 36 Hispanic/Latino men will be diagnosed with HIV, as will 1 in 106 Hispanic/Latina women.**

- In 2008, an estimated 7,864 Hispanics/ Latinos were diagnosed with AIDS in the U.S. and dependent areas, which has remained relatively stable since 2005; and

- By the end of 2007, an estimated 106,074 Hispanics/Latinos with an AIDS diagnosis had died in the U.S. and dependent areas. In 2007, HIV was the fifth leading cause of death among Hispanics/Latinos aged 35–44 and the sixth leading cause of death among Hispanics/Latinos aged 25–34 in the US. (CDC, 2008c; CDC, 2010i). (Google: CDC and HIV in Hispanics for current data).

Cultural Issues and HIV in Hispanics

The U.S. Hispanic community is a very diverse group of Americans. Each sub-group has specific traditions and cultural beliefs that may be quite different from the other. Risk factors for HIV infection differs by country of origin. Hispanics born in Puerto Rico, for example, are more likely to contract HIV as a result of injection drug use or high-risk heterosexual contact. By contrast, men having sex with men is the primary cause of infections among Hispanic men born in Central or South America, Cuba, Mexico or the U.S. Hispanic women and Hispanic men are most likely to be infected with HIV as a result of sex with men. Thus intervention programs need to be targeted to specific populations, i.e., injection drug use in Puerto Ricans and condom use to heterosexual couples. Additionally, issues of balance of power should be directed to Hispanic women.

Certain cultural beliefs can affect one's risk for HIV infection. For example, among men, machismo has positive implications for HIV prevention, such as strength and protection of the family; however, proving masculinity through power and dominance can lead both straight and gay Hispanic men to engage in risky sexual behavior. Greater acculturation into the U.S. culture has both negative (engaging in behaviors that increase the risk for HIV infection) and positive (communicating with partners about practicing safer sex) effects on the health behaviors of Hispanics. The migration patterns, social structure, language barriers, and lack of regular health care among transient Hispanic immigrants can affect awareness and hinder access to HIV/AIDS prevention and care. (CDC, 2008c).

HIV has become a major threat to Hispanic communities, many of which are disadvantaged even prior to the AIDS epidemic. Factors such as economic disparities, minority status, and language barriers all contribute to the disproportionate rates of AIDS in Hispanics. Hispanic children account for about 12% of the U.S. population under 13, but 24% of pediatric AIDS cases (CDC, 1994). Prevalence of HIV varies by region in Hispanic populations. In the Northeast many Hispanics are from Puerto Rico and the Dominican Republic, which reflects the geography of intra venous drug use (IVDU) in the U.S. Among Hispanics, Puerto Ricans have the highest prevalence of illegal drug use. This may be partially explained by the fact that most

Puerto Ricans in the U.S. live in New York City, New Jersey and Chicago, where poverty rates are much higher and illegal drugs more widely available. (De La Rosa, Khalsa & Rouse, 1990). Much lower prevalence rates are reported for Hispanics in the West and Southwest where many Hispanics are from Mexico and Central or South America. (Martin, 1995). Diaz researched the AIDS epidemic as it relates to the culture of Hispanics. Diaz summarizes the Hispanic AIDS problem well.

> Cultural influences such as machismo, familismo and homophobia may be internalized by Latino gay men and make safer sex practices difficult. Machismo dictates that intercourse is a way to prove masculinity. For gay Latinos, familismo can create conflict because families perceive homosexuality as sinful. Familial support is often achieved through silence about sexual preference, instilling low self-esteem and personal shame among Latino gay men. (Diaz, 1995).

HIV/AIDS and African Americans

According to the 2000 census, blacks make up approximately 13% of the US population. However, in 2005, blacks accounted for 18,121 (49%) of the estimated 37,331 new HIV/AIDS diagnoses in the United States in the 33 states with long-term, confidential name-based HIV reporting. Of all black men living with HIV/AIDS, the primary transmission category was sexual contact with other men, followed by injection drug use and high-risk heterosexual contact. Of all black women living with HIV/AIDS, the primary transmission category was high-risk heterosexual contact, followed by injection drug use. Of the estimated 141 infants perinatally infected with HIV, 91 (65%) were black. Of the estimated 18,849 people under the age of 25 whose diagnosis of HIV/AIDS was made during 2001–2004 in the 33 states with HIV reporting, 11,554 (61%) were black. HIV disproportionally affects blacks, and, of all racial and ethnic groups in the United States, HIV and AIDS have hit African Americans the hardest. The reasons are not directly related to race or ethnicity, but rather to some of the barriers faced by many African Americans. These barriers can include poverty, other sexually transmitted diseases, especially syphilis or Herpes, and stigma, (negative attitudes, beliefs, and actions directed at people living with HIV/AIDS) or directed at people who do things that might put them at risk for HIV. CDC reported that viewing HIV/AIDS by race and ethnicity, African Americans have: More illness. Even though blacks (including African-Americans) account for about 13% of the U.S. population, they account for about half (49%) of the people who get HIV and AIDS;

Shorter survival times. Blacks with AIDS often don't live as long as people of other races and ethnic groups with AIDS. This is due to the barriers mentioned above. More deaths. For African Americans and other blacks, HIV/AIDS is a leading cause of death. For black men, the most common ways of getting HIV are (in order) having unprotected sex with another man who has HIV, sharing injection drug works (like needles or syringes) with someone who has HIV, having unprotected sex with a woman who has HIV. For black women, the most common ways of getting HIV are (in order) having unprotected sex with a man who has HIV, sharing injection drug works (like needles or syringes) with someone who has HIV. Blacks at higher risk for HIV are those who are unaware of their partner's risk factors with other STDs (which affect more blacks than any other racial or ethnic group) who live in poverty (which is about one quarter of all blacks). (CDC, 2008c). Additional data related to blacks and HIV/AIDS include:

- In 2006, black men accounted for two-thirds of new infections (65%) among all blacks. The rate of new HIV infection for black men was 6 times as high as that of white men, nearly 3 times that of Hispanic/Latino men, and twice that of black women;

- In 2006, black men who have sex with men (MSM) represented 63% of new infections among all black men, and 35% among all MSM. HIV infection rates are higher among black MSM compared to other MSM. More new HIV infections occurred among young black MSM (aged 13–29) than among any other age and racial group of MSM;

- In 2006, the rate of new HIV infection for black women was nearly 15 times as high as that of white women and nearly 4 times that of Hispanic/Latina women;

- Although new HIV infections have remained fairly stable among blacks, from 2005–2008 estimated HIV diagnoses increased approximately 12%. This may be due to increased testing or diagnosis earlier in the course of HIV infection;

- **Atsome point in their lifetimes, 1 in 16 black men will be diagnosed with HIV infection, as will 1 in 32 black women;**

- From 2005–2008, the rate of HIV diagnoses among blacks increased from 68/100,000 persons to 74/100,000. This increase reflects the largest increase in rates of HIV diagnoses by race or ethnicity;

- By the end of 2007, an estimated 233,624 blacks with a diagnosis of AIDS had died in the U.S. and 5 dependent areas. In 2006, HIV was the ninth leading cause of death for all blacks and the third leading cause of death for both black men and black women aged 35–44. (CDC, 2010i).

Risk Factors: Race and ethnicity are not, themselves, risk factors for HIV infection. However, African Americans are more likely to face challenges associated with risk for HIV infection, including: Poverty. Nearly one in four African Americans lives in poverty. Studies have found a direct relationship between higher AIDS incidence and lower income. A variety of socioeconomic problems associated with poverty directly or indirectly increase HIV risks, including limited access to quality health care and HIV prevention education.

Denial: Although African Americans are responding to the HIV/AIDS crisis in their communities, many have been slow to join the effort. One reason is that some African- Americans are reluctant to acknowledge issues, such as homosexuality and drug use, that are associated with HIV infection. For example, studies show that a significant number of African American men who have sex with men identify themselves as heterosexual. As a result, they may not relate to prevention messages crafted for openly gay men. Without frank and open discussion of HIV risks, many African Americans will not get the information and support they need to protect them and their partners from HIV. (Amaro, 1995).

Partners at Risk: African American women are most likely to be infected with HIV as a result of sex with men. They may not be aware of their male partners' possible risks for HIV infection such as unprotected sex with multiple partners, bisexuality, or injection drug use. (Hader, 2001). Women who suspect that their partners are at risk for HIV infection may be reluctant to try to negotiate condom use. For example, some women may not insist on condom use out of fear that the man will leave them or withdraw financial support. (Amaro, 1995).

Substance Abuse: Injection drug use is the second leading cause of HIV infection for both African American men and women. But sharing needles is not the only HIV risk related to substance abuse. Both casual and chronic substance abusers are more likely to engage in high-risk behaviors, such as unprotected sex, when they are under the influence of drugs or alcohol.

Sexually Transmitted Disease (STD) Connection: For many of the reasons noted above, African Americans also have the highest STD rates in the nation. Compared to whites, African Americans are 24 times more likely to have gonorrhea and 8 times more likely to have syphilis. In part because of physical changes caused by STDs, including genital lesions that can serve as an entry point for HIV, the presence of certain STDs can increase the chances of contracting HIV by three- to five-fold. Similarly, because co-infection with HIV and another STD can cause increased HIV shedding, a person who is co-infected has a greater chance of spreading HIV to others. (Holmes, 1999).

HIV in African Americans and Hispanics

It cannot be emphasize enough that it is not race but risk behaviors that increase the chances of HIV infection in African Americans. It is not who you are but what you do that puts you at risk for HIV. While African-Americans are too often viewed as one minority group, they also have a very diverse makeup of people from many countries, cultures and religions. Populations of African Americans living in the U.S. are represented by Christian, Muslim, upper class, lower class, inner-city suburban, descendants of slaves, people from England and recent Caribbean immigrants. Current epidemiological surveillance does not record all the cultural, political economic and religious differences that may more accurately predict risk. (Moss, Krieger, 1995). Some African American and Latina women are at especially high risk for HIV infection, especially those from poorer neighborhoods. A study of disadvantaged out-of-school youth in the U.S. Job Corps found that young African American women had the highest rate of HIV infection, and that women 16-18 years old had 50% higher rates of infection than young men. Another study found that African-American and Hispanic adolescent females, and women with older boyfriends (3 years older or more) are at higher risk for HIV. (Valleroy, 1998; Miller, 1997).

Prevention with persons who are at very high risk for HIV infection

Persons who are HIV negative but at high risk for HIV must be continuously educated and supported at different phases of their lives. Since the beginning of the epidemic, new at-risk groups have emerged in addition to those that have been traditionally at highest risk, i.e., men who have sex with men and injection drug users. New populations increasingly at risk for HIV infection include racial and ethnic minorities, women, and adolescents. Each of these groups is the target of research and subsequent prevention interventions, including demonstration projects on using social networks for reaching persons at high risk for HIV infection in communities of color.

Encouraging people to know their HIV status.

Research shows that up to two-thirds of new infections are transmitted by people who don't know they are infected. Efforts to reach at-risk persons are enhanced by the availability of rapid HIV testing, which allows the results to be provided in minutes, rather than days; thus reducing the chance that persons may miss receiving their test results. Post-test counseling, including resources for managing HIV infection, is a part of this effort. Overall, CDC recommends that HIV testing become a routine part of medical care in high prevalence settings so that HIV infections are detected early and persons who test positive can quickly enter the medical care system for prevention and treatment services. For those who do not or cannot access typical medical facilities, CDC recommends HIV testing in nontraditional settings, such as correctional facilities or in areas where homeless youth congregate. Demonstration projects focusing on rapid HIV testing in these and other non-clinical settings are ongoing.

Common sense approach

Sometimes people just need to use common sense! But, many do not choose to do so when it comes to having sex. Numerous reports on individuals that have unprotected sex in reality means that they are having sex with all of the partners and the partners' partners' that had sex with everyone else! While it may be difficult, uncomfortable, or embarrassing for someone to address a potential sexual partner, they must speak out before they become intimate, or are influenced by alcohol or drugs. And, if either partner has been with numerous other partners, they should get tested for HIV and other STDs as well. Certainly, the best way would be for both partners, gay, straight, bisexual, or transgender, to get tested together-and then have protected sexual intimacy.

Preventing new infections: Only one pill for some

New treatments have helped HIV-positive people live longer with HIV before progressing to AIDS. Therefore, persons living with HIV are important partners in ongoing educational and prevention interventions to encourage safer sex and healthy behaviors over the course of their lifetimes and reduce their risk of transmitting HIV. In the summer of 2006, FDA approved a once-a-day, three-drugs-in-one combination drug called Atripla. These newer medications combine the active ingredients of three anti-retroviral drugs already in use to treat HIV/AIDS, Sustiva, Emtriva and Viread. These drugs have already been used together for some time as part of a "cocktail" therapy. This was a major step to help HIV/AIDS patients simplify their drug regimen, but many also must continue other drugs to deal with a myriad of side effects and to prevent numerous opportunistic infections. (FDA, 2006).

HIV in women-Are Women at Greater Risk? Risk Factors and Barriers to Prevention

For women of all races and ethnicities, the largest number of HIV/AIDS diagnoses during recent years was for women aged 15–39. From 2001 through 2004, the number of HIV/AIDS diagnoses for women aged 15–39 decreased for white, black, and Hispanic women. There was an increase in the number of HIV/AIDS diagnoses during this period for Asian and Pacific Islander women and for American Indian and Alaska Native women aged 15–39. (CDC, 2007c).

Biologic Vulnerability and Sexually Transmitted Diseases

Women are significantly more likely than men to contract HIV infection during vaginal intercourse. One reason is the body fluids (semen) passing from a man to a woman are greater in volume than body fluids (vaginal secretions) passing from a woman to a man. Additionally, the presence of some sexually transmitted diseases greatly increases the likelihood of acquiring or transmitting HIV infection because of lower immune response while infected. The rates of gonorrhea and syphilis are higher among women of color than among white women. These higher rates are especially marked at younger ages (15–24 years).

Substance Use

It is estimated that 1 in 5 new HIV diagnoses for women are related to injection drug use. Sharing needles and equipment contaminated with HIV is not the only risk associated with substance use. Women who use crack cocaine or other noninjection drugs may also be at high risk for the sexual transmission of HIV if they sell or trade sex for drugs. Also, both casual and chronic substance users are more likely to practice unprotected, or risky sex while under the influence of alcohol or other drugs. (CDC, 2007c).

Biological Differences Important

The rate of HIV infection, or for that matter any other STD infection in females can increase for several reasons. As previously stated, male to-female transmission of body fluids, rather than female to male, is a much more efficient and likely path to infect a woman with STD or HIV. One reason is that there are more men than women in the U.S. infected with HIV, and also the fact that the female genital tract has a larger surface area that may have small tears or lesions. Additionally, women may be victims of rape or sexual assault while under the influence of alcohol or other drugs. This could lead to tearing of the vaginal lining that would create a portal of entry for viral or bacterial invasion.

In women, the first signs of HIV infection may be any of the ones listed above or repeated recurrent yeast infections of the vagina. Vaginal yeast infections are common in women for many reasons other than HIV infection and can be treated with over-the-counter medications. Women with yeast infections that do not readily go away with treatment, however, or that occur over and over again, (recurrent) should be tested for HIV, especially if their behaviors place them at risk.

Women with HIV infection may also be at increased risk of cancer of the cervix, and other common conditions such as PID. In HIV-infected women, these conditions may be more severe or difficult to treat. All women practicing risky behaviors should get PAP smears at least once a year, and get tested for HIV at least every six months. (Ickovics, Rodin, 1992). Women can protect themselves from HIV infection in a number of ways. They should develop skills, attitudes and behaviors regarding condom use; and should routinely expect their partner to use condoms. This dual decision and sexual practice approach should bring about gender norms in all forms of sexual decision-making.

HIV and Youth

Young people in the U.S. are at persistent risk to contract HIV, if and only if, they practice risky behaviors. Not all kids use drugs, alcohol or take chances; but many youth experiment under the influence of peer pressure, etc. The HIV risk is especially notable in the minority community as described above for Hispanics and African Americans. Continual HIV prevention, and health education in general, including programs stressing abstinence and delaying sexual initiation can dramatically help young people. The following data from the CDC reflect HIV status to persons who are 13-24 years of age, for 2004: An estimated 4,883 young people received a diagnosis of HIV infection or AIDS, representing about 13% of the persons given a diagnosis during that year; HIV infection progressed to AIDS more slowly among young people than among all persons with a diagnosis of HIV infection.

On a global level over half of the 5.8 million new HIV infections in 1998 were among youth. Thus the highest incidence of HIV infection is among young people. Biological factors-including cervix development and greater efficiency of STD transmission from males to females-are partly responsible for heightened STD infection among young women. Other social factors include lack of access to health care and limited health education, especially related to prevention of STDs.

Teens are urged to remain abstinent while surrounded by images on television, movies and magazines of glamorous people having sex, smoking and drinking. Double standards still exist for girls-who are expected to remain virgins-and boys-who are pressured to prove their manhood through sexual activity and aggressiveness. Attitudes related to religion, culture and morality often deny teens the necessary sexuality education to help prevent all forms of STDs. HIV infection varies among different cultural groups of adolescents. (CDC, 2006). Google CDC and youth for the full report.

"If you're going to educate kids about AIDS,
you have to educate them about drugs as well.
If you're a youth, you're going to
experiment with drugs,
especially if you live in a metropolitan area.
Even though you get stupid with drugs,
you still think about things you don't want to do,
but you do it anyhow."
--- 16-year-old HIV positive youth from San Francisco

Does an Actual Case of STD Change Teen Behavior? Maybe not!

Every parent knows that sometimes, kids just don't listen! Even after students are given well prepared health education lessons related to the prevention of STDs and HIV/AIDS, they still may not change their risky behaviors. Researchers sought to examine sexual risk and condom use associated with perceived susceptibility to future STD infections among adolescents. The females were recently diagnosed with an incident of STD compared to those who were not diagnosed with an incident infection. Kershaw and colleagues at Yale University studied 308 adolescent females at two time intervals six months apart. In the study, 92 participants were diagnosed with an STD and 216 were not during this research. Kershaw and colleagues concluded. Kershaw stated, "Results indicated that adolescents did not significantly change their behaviors, attitudes, or perceptions following the diagnosis of an incident STD compared to those who were not diagnosed with an incident STD." The authors also wrote, "This suggests that an STD diagnosis alone is not sufficient to motivate adolescent females to reduce their sexual risk behavior and change their sexual risk attitudes and perceptions." (Kershaw, 2004). This seems much like the old adage: 'You can lead a horse to water, but you can't make it drink.' Different people seem to be motivated by many factors, and even an infection which could lead to reproductive sterility or possibly death from a virus may not change the behavior of some young people.

Do any Prevention Programs Bring About Change in Youth?

Yes, a variety of techniques and interventions can help students prevent HIV infection. Many school boards, parents and teachers often discuss the various programs to help prevent youth from becoming infected with the AIDS virus. Some support total abstinence education, others focus on meeting the needs of all students to include abstinence education, by using the "postponing sexual involvement approach," and still others may fully support issuing condoms in all secondary schools. Using the phrase "postponing sexual involvement" tells the student that sometime in one's life, they will have some kind of sexual relationship. The problem often debated by health educators and school leaders is, when is it OK? Several studies have shown that HIV education can bring about behavioral changes that will lower risk for young people. (Main, Iverson, McGloin, et al., 1994).

A group of 246 African American adolescents, separated by gender, attended 8 weekly sessions of a sexually explicit education program that included behavioral skills training. Most importantly in addition to basic factual data, students were also taught refusal skills, assertive communication, correct condom use, information provision, self-management, problem solving, and risk recognition. Findings from this study included:

- Of the sexually abstinent youth prior to the intervention, only 11.5% were sexually active one year later compared with 31% of the control group students;
- Among those sexually active prior to intervention, 42% of the control group remained so after one year versus only 27% of the intervention group;
- Youth who participated in the intervention were more likely to use condoms, and less likely to engage in unprotected vaginal or anal intercourse;

- The intervention group scored higher on the basic information than the controls; and
- Students in the intervention group were more skillful in handling pressures to engage in unprotected sex and provide information to peers than the control group. (St. Lawrence, Brasfield, Jefferson, et al., 1995).

State Mandated HIV/AIDS Prevention Instruction

The *California Education Code* (EC 51930-33) implemented the AIDS prevention instruction law in 1992. This law was specifically designed to help young people learn the dangers of HIV/AIDS and provided specific guidelines to schools in order to assist teachers in developing curricula. Governor Wilson signed amendments to the law during the summer of 1998. By January 2004 the entire sex education law was revised and simplified. A summary of this new law, The California Comprehensive Sex Education and HIV/AIDS Prevention Act, follows:

The California Comprehensive Sex Education and HIV/AIDS Prevention Act

Parent Notification: California Education Code requires the **district to notify parents** prior to HIV/AIDS instruction for student's grades 1-12. Some districts may require written consent of parent prior to AIDS instruction. [**Important**: Notification is not the same as Permission. **Parental permission for HIV/STD education is not required in California.**] The name of organizations and affiliation of guest speakers who present to students must be included in the notification. Parents must also have an opportunity to review any materials used in HIV/AIDS instruction. The **instruction** standard must be completed **at least once in junior high or middle school and once in high school.** Various school districts may choose exactly how and when to integrate the curricula, but *EC 51930-33* is very specific and states that **AIDS Prevention Instruction shall include**:

- Information on the nature of AIDS and its effects on the human body;
- Information on how HIV is and is not transmitted including information on activities that present the highest risk of HIV infection;
- Discussion of methods to reduce the risk of HIV infection;
- Emphasis on sexual abstinence, monogamy and the avoidance of multiple sexual partners;
- Emphasis on abstinence from IV drug use;
- **Statistics on the failure and success rates of condoms and other contraceptives in preventing HIV transmission;**
- Information on methods that may reduce the risk of HIV infection from IV drug use;
- Discussion of public health issues associated with AIDS;
- Information on local resources for HIV testing and medical care;
- **Development of refusal skills to assist pupils to overcome peer pressure and use effective decision making skill to avoid high risk activities;**

- Discussion about societal views on AIDS including stereotypes and myths regarding persons with AIDS;
- Emphasis on compassion for persons suffering from debilitating handicaps, and terminal diseases like AIDS;
- AIDS prevention instruction may not be conducted in a manner that advocates drug use, a particular sexual practice, or sexual activities;
- Materials should also be appropriate for use with pupils from a variety of backgrounds and special needs; and
- Instructional materials that are used to teach HIV/AIDS should use the latest statistics and information from the United States Surgeon General, Centers for Disease Control, the National Academy of Sciences, and peer reviewed scientific journals. (EC 51930-33).

Prevention Methods-Universal Precautions

School principals often are given curriculum materials, videos, lists of guest speakers, and even financial incentives to implement HIV instruction. While *EC 51930-33* requires secondary schools to implement AIDS education; many school leaders tend to avoid, delay or completely ignore the AIDS curriculum; especially in elementary schools where the *Education Code (EC)*, does not specify prevention education for HIV infection. Some administrators simply want to avoid controversy at all costs, unfortunately the cost **may be the life of a student.** Beyond the mere political and social implications, school managers should encourage all employees to practice **universal precautions** and not have to worry if a student, or employee has AIDS or not. Universal precautions also apply to other **blood-borne pathogens** such as Hepatitis B.

Blood borne pathogens (BBP) are disease-producing organisms present in human blood. They can be transmitted when infected blood, semen, vaginal secretions, or other body fluids that contain blood, come in contact with broken skin or mucus membranes of the eyes, nose, or mouth of an individual. Two of the most serious blood-borne pathogens are **Hepatitis B and HIV/AIDS.** The Hepatitis B virus is **100 times more infectious than HIV.**

What Exactly are Universal Precautions?

Universal Precautions are blood and body fluids infection control procedures used in all situations involving blood and body fluids, and are not limited to use with individuals known to be carrying a specific virus such as HIV or Hepatitis B. If a school principal were asked if a new student could be enrolled on their campus and that student is HIV positive or has AIDS, this should not be a problem. However, parents are not required to disclose any medical information about their child to the principal or school staff. The school administration must be certain that all employees are cautious to prevent infection to all students and other employees as well. This protection might include how a bus driver has to clean up vomit, how a coach might clean up blood from an injury, or how a cafeteria worker should protect students while handling food. Other examples of direct blood or body fluid contact that may occur at school and should be avoided are: bloody noses, bloody drainage from cuts and scrapes, blood caused by fights or sports injuries, accidents in shop or lab classes, contact with trash containing blood, bandages, or sharp objects, and soiled clothing by urine, feces or vomit. (CDE, 1999).

Universal precautions should be used on a routine basis for all persons whenever there is a **potential for exposure** to blood, body fluids, excretions, and tissues. Every school district should have a standardized procedure, in writing, to help protect all concerned. One simple, low cost technique, if funds are available, is to have plenty of latex gloves available for all employees working in situations where a potential exposure may result. All employees, especially school nurses, health workers, coaches, custodians, or food service workers should be protected. If a student is injured on the playground and blood is spilled, or some other fluid is spilled, an adult worker should quickly put on a pair of latex gloves and clean up the contaminated area.

Needles and sharp objects create the greatest risk of exposure to Hepatitis B and HIV through sticks and cuts with various sharp instruments. Never break, bend or re-cap a used needle or other instrument. Dispose of needles and sharp instruments in puncture-resistant containers designed for their disposal. Handle all sharp objects and broken glass with extreme caution. Immediately report any cut or needle stick to your supervisor. (CDE, 1999).

Hand washing is a very basic infection control procedure. Hands should always be washed before and after contact with each person. Wash hands with soap under a steady stream of water for at least 10 seconds. Teachers, administrators, and classified employees are often in contact with students either directly or indirectly, and can prevent the spread of dangerous pathogens of HIV and Hepatitis B as well as the common cold, and a plethora of other bacteria and viral microbes. Using a "cleansing wipe" or other hand wipe, especially if it is bactericidal, may significantly lower disease transmission.

Wear gloves. If a school employee is working with patients, or helping students with medical procedures they should wear gloves to avoid exposure to their blood, body fluids, secretions, excretions, tissues or mucus membranes. Wash hands before putting on gloves and after gloves have been removed and disposed. Gloves should be used when cleaning soiled instruments, surfaces, and when handling linens soiled with blood or body fluids, or when cleaning up spills of blood or body fluids. Most of this contact with a patient or student is usually uncommon for a classroom teacher; but if latex gloves are available for any contaminated materials, the infection chain can be broken.

Clean-up spills. Spilled or splattered blood should be cleaned up immediately. Using a daily fresh solution of household bleach and water (1:10 dilution) is adequate. The CDC only recommends a dilution of 1:99 of bleach and water; but most schools and other agencies are using the 1:10 ratio. The virus of AIDS and Hepatitis can easily be cleaned up with soap and water; so it is not necessary to remove all the color from a carpeted area to kill the pathogen. Many carpet cleaners have alcohol or other chemicals that will also kill infectious agents. (CDE, 1999).

Trash disposal. Any materials contaminated with blood or body fluids and requiring disposal should be sealed in a plastic bag and then put in the trash barrel. Never put sharp needles or objects in the plastic bag. Always dispose of sharp objects, glass, needles, etc., in puncture resistant containers clearly marked for disposal.

Casual contact. Casual contact with students or patients does not pose a risk of infection with HIV or Hepatitis B. Handshaking, touching, talking, visiting and other casual contact with people does not require any special infection control procedures since HIV and Hepatitis B are not spread through casual contact. A patient that has AIDS or is HIV positive has a much greater chance of contracting opportunistic infection agents by entering a room of non-infected people. This is because the patient may already have a compromised immune system. Nonetheless, regular hand washing or using microbicide gels can prevent many common infections. (CDE, 1999).

OSHA Worksite Regulations. Regulations became effective January 1993 requiring that employers comply with the federal and state Occupational Safety and Health Administration (OSHA) standards for the control of exposure to bloodborne pathogens at the worksite. Program components must include the identification of potential occupational exposure categories, environmental controls, exposure documentation procedures, employee education, and the provision of Hepatitis B vaccine and related medical care for exposed employees. Check with your district or agency's human resources department for complete details of the local policy. Always report to your immediate supervisor whenever you believe you may have been exposed to HIV or Hepatitis B through contact with a person's blood or body fluids. (CDE, 1999).

Prevention Methods-Condoms

Prevention is the most effective strategy for controlling the spread of infectious diseases. Prevention through avoiding exposure is the best strategy for controlling the spread of sexually transmitted disease (STD). Behavior that eliminates or reduces the risk of one STD will likely reduce the risk of all STDs; and the prevention of one case of STD can result in the prevention of many subsequent cases. **Abstinence** and sexual intercourse with one mutually faithful uninfected partner are the only totally effective prevention strategies. Proper use of condoms with each act of sexual intercourse can reduce, but not eliminate, risk of STD.

Condoms are the best preventive measure against AIDS besides not having sex and practicing safe behavior. But condoms are far from being foolproof. They have to be used properly. They have to be used every time you have sex, from start to finish. Many couples use condoms without any formal "training" or instruction. Most schools do not present detailed instructional condom use. The following guidelines are modified from the CDC.

- Use a condom with each act of intercourse;
- Use condoms made of latex rubber. Latex serves as a barrier to the virus;
- "Lambskin" or "natural membrane" condoms are not as good because of the pores in the material. Look for the word "latex" on the package;
- If the condom does not have a reservoir tip, pinch the tip enough to leave a half-inch space for semen to collect. Holding the tip, unroll the condom all the way to the base of the erect penis;
- After ejaculation and before the penis gets soft, grip the rim of the condom and carefully withdraw. Then gently pull the condom off the penis, making sure that semen doesn't spill out;
- Carefully handle the condom to avoid damaging it with fingernails, teeth, or other sharp objects;
- Ensure that no air is trapped in the tip of the condom;
- Ensure that adequate lubrication exists during intercourse, possibly requiring use of exogenous lubricants. Check the list of ingredients on the back of the lubricant package to make sure the lubricant is water-based. Do not use petroleum-based jelly, cold cream, baby oil or cooking shortening. These can weaken the condom and cause it to break;
- Do not use condoms with the spermicide Nonoxynol 9 (N-9) because studies show N-9 may increase the risk of infection from STDs;
- Condoms should not be stored in warm places, nor used beyond expiration dates;
- Read the expiration date carefully and discard outdated condoms;
- Condoms in damaged packages or those that show obvious signs of age (e.g., those that are brittle, sticky, or discolored) should not be used;
- The condom should be put on before any genital contact to prevent exposure to fluids that may contain infectious agents;
- If a condom breaks, it should be replaced immediately; and
- Condoms should never be reused. (CDC, 1993; CDC, 2002; Hiller, 2007).

Spermicides and STDs- Nonoxynol-9 and Sexually Transmitted Infections

As recently as 1999, the CDC recommended that spermicides such as Nonoxynol-9 offered good protection against STDs including HIV/AIDS. In the 1980s, it was discovered that nonoxynol-9 had the ability to inactivate, in vitro, several sexually transmitted infections, including gonorrhea, *Chlamydia*, trichomoniasis, herpes simplex virus, and HIV. Subsequent research sought to determine whether nonoxynol-9, used in various formulations, could also be used as a microbicide against these infections. The results of early studies were often conflicting, but overall mildly encouraging — a 1988 study found that the use of nonoxynol-9 gel slightly reduced the risk of women contracting *Chlamydia* and gonorrhea Similarly, a 1992 study involving female sex workers in Thailand found a 25 percent reduction in the incidence of cervical infection with nonoxynol-9 film (CDC, 2002f). **More recent studies have shown, however, that nonoxynol-9 (N-9) does not provide protection against sexually transmitted infections (STIs), and that in some cases, (N-9) may actually increase the risk of transmission by irritating the epithelium of the vagina and anus and creating a portal of**

entry for STD pathogens. (CDC, 2002f). Dr. Sharon Hiller, from the University of Pittsburgh

Using the Condom for Men

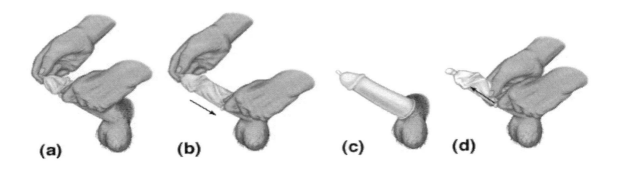

(a)   (b)   (c)   (d)

reported at the National STD Conference on December 3, 2007, that newer **microbicides**, that can be used to prevent STD may soon be available. FDA approval of drugs and other medicines often require several years before they are released to the public. Hiller states that these chemicals may be released by women using vaginal rings or other methods. Research trials for these products began development during 2008. (Hiller, 2007; AGI, 2005). As of 2011, several newer microbicides, including one brand called the "invisible condom," were in the testing stages in the U.S. and several other countries. Google microbicides for the latest research information and availability of these newer products.

A subsequent study of women with high STI risk who were not sex workers compared nonoxynol-9 gel and condom use against condom use alone for the prevention of gonorrhea and Chlamydia. The women who used the gel had a 20 percent higher incidence of gonorrhea or Chlamydia or both than women who only used condoms. Women had a 50 percent greater chance of acquiring gonorrhea if they used the gel than women who did not, but gel users had a comparable probability of acquiring Chlamydia (Roddy, et al., 2002). **Therefore it is not recommended that nonoxynol-9 be used to prevent STDs.** Currently there are numerous products being tested to replace N-9 and hopefully newer solutions, gels, etc., may also serve as a microbicide to protect from sexually transmitted diseases, including HIV/AIDS. (CDC, 2002f; AGI, 2005; Hiller, 2007).

Female condoms. Female condoms are made of polyurethane, have been FDA approved and available since 1993 in the U.S. as a protection against pregnancy and an option for the woman to take charge of her reproductive health. Chapter 10 will discuss the female condom and other forms of protection against pregnancy, but the CDC reports that female condoms can be somewhat reliable to protect against certain STDs. Laboratory studies indicate that the female condom (Reality™ and FC, FC2), which consists of a lubricated polyurethane sheath with a ring on each end that is inserted into the vagina, is an effective mechanical barrier to viruses, including HIV, and to semen. A limited number of clinical studies have evaluated the efficacy of female condoms in providing protection from STDs, including HIV. If used consistently and correctly, the female condom might substantially reduce the risk for STDs. When a male condom cannot be used properly, sex partners should consider using a female condom. Female condoms are costly compared with male condoms. The female condom also has been used for STD/HIV protection during receptive anal intercourse. Whereas it might provide some protection in this setting, its efficacy is undefined. It is important to remember, however, that couples should not use both a male condom and a female condom together since the friction of both surfaces could cause tearing. For details about the female condom, see: **http://www.femalehealth.com/.**

Female Condom

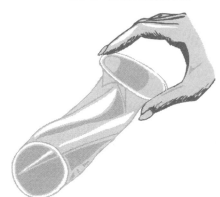

Vaginal spermicides, and diaphragms. Vaginal spermicides containing nonoxynol-9 (N-9) are not effective in preventing gonorrhea, chlamydia, or HIV infection. Additionally, frequent use of spermicides containing N-9 has been associated with disruption of the genital epithelium, which might be associated with an increased risk for HIV transmission. **Therefore, N-9 is not recommended for STD/HIV prevention.** On the basis of all available evidence, diaphragms should not be relied on as the sole source of protection against HIV infection. For some women diaphragm and spermicide use have been associated with an increased risk for bacterial urinary tract infections in women. (CDC, 2002f).

Why do condoms sometimes fail?

Condoms do not work 100% of the time. User failure, especially to inexperienced teens, includes failure to: 1) use a condom with each act of sexual intercourse, 2) put the condom on before any genital contact occurs, and 3) completely unroll the condom. Other user behaviors that may contribute to condom breakage include: inadequate lubrication, use of oil-based lubricants that weaken latex, and inadequate space at the tip of the condom. Product failure refers to condom breakage or leakage due to deterioration or poor manufacturing quality. Deterioration may result from age or improper post-manufacturing storage conditions. (MMWR, 1988).

Failure Rates of Condoms-Male and Female

In general, both female and male condoms have fairly low rates of breakage or slippage as users' experience with each method grows. Studies from the Guttmacher Institute report that in the southern U.S. from 1995-1998, only 3% of all female condoms slipped out of the woman's vagina. Also, only 3% of male condoms broke during use (7% among first-time users, compared with 2% among those that used male condoms 15 or more times). The slippage or breakage was close to the same even when the participants had more than one sexual partner. (Hollander, 2005).

Prevention Methods and HIV Testing--Should You Be Tested ?

Do you have the AIDS virus? If you have engaged in risky behavior, the only way to tell if you have the AIDS virus is by being tested. The U.S. Public Health Service recommends you should be counseled and tested if, since 1978, you have had any sexually transmitted disease or have shared needles for injecting drugs; if you are a man who has had sex with another man; or if you have had sex with a prostitute, male or female. You should also be tested if you have had **sex with anyone who you know, or suspect, has done any of these things.** Since this may be difficult to determine, **when in doubt, get tested.** If you are a woman who has been engaging in risky behavior and you plan to have a baby or are not using birth control, you should be tested. Your doctor may advise you to be tested if you have received a blood transfusion between 1978 and 1985. (USPHS, 1988). **Since 2006, the CDC recommends any sexually active person aged 13-64 be tested at least once for HIV even if that person is considered "low risk."** The questions below serve as a guide for people to ask themselves if they need to be testing for HIV/AIDS:

- Have you ever had "unprotected" sex (sex without a condom or other latex barrier)--oral, vaginal, or anal?
- Have you ever had sex with someone who was an IV drug user or had HIV?
- Have you ever had a sexually transmitted disease (STD) such as herpes, chlamydia, gonorrhea, trichomoniasis, or hepatitis?
- Have you ever had an unplanned pregnancy?
- Have you ever been sexually assaulted (raped, forced or talked into having sex when you didn't want to)?
- **Have you ever passed out or forgotten what happened after you were drinking or getting high?**
- Have you ever shared needles or other equipment to inject drugs or pierce the skin?
- Have you ever received a blood transfusion? (the risk is very low in the United States, but can vary in other countries)?
- Did your mother have HIV when you were born? (Bayer, Fairchild, 2006).

If you have been diagnosed with TB, your doctor may also advise you to be tested for the AIDS virus. If you test positive, and find you have been infected with the AIDS virus, you must take steps to protect your partner. More importantly, even though your test may be negative, you may still be infected with the AIDS virus and should take precautions not to transmit it to your partner. There are two types of AIDS tests that you might be given, depending on the situation. The ELISA test is the AIDS antibody test you usually hear about. ELISA, also called EIA, stands for Enzyme-Linked Immunosorbent Assay. It is the one used when you donate blood. It is also the first test used at clinics, hospitals, and counseling and testing centers. The ELISA test currently in use looks for the presence of antibodies that your body might have developed to fight the AIDS virus if it is present in your system. It does not test for the virus itself. A positive

ELISA test might not mean you're infected with the AIDS virus. However, it would be a sign that further testing is needed.

There are two kinds of tests that could be used if your blood shows a positive reaction to the ELISA test. One is called the Western Blot test and the other is called IFA. Either of these tests can be used to confirm a positive ELISA test. In 1996, a take home test became available to test for the AIDS virus. In the privacy of their homes, users extract a small amount of blood and send the specimen to a lab for HIV analysis. This is very convenient; but if a person is notified that they are HIV positive without any psychological or counseling support; they may resort to possible harm or suicide to themselves. Since 2002, **OraSure**, an oral antibody test has become available. Although OraSure is an oral test, it is not testing the saliva for the HIV virus. When our bodies become infected with a virus like HIV, our immune system creates antibodies to fight off the infection. **Like a blood test, the OraSure test is looking for antibodies to the HIV virus, not the actual virus itself.** These antibodies are found in the oral fluid found between the cheek and gum. This method was first used in the field on injection drug users, but now is available and well received by patients that wish to avoid needles. (CDC, 2010h).

A negative test is also not conclusive. If you have been infected with the virus recently, a negative test may mean that your body might not have had time to develop antibodies against the AIDS virus. Once you are infected, you will probably remain infected for life. It could take years for you to begin showing the symptoms of AIDS. If you are worried that you may have been infected, find out about the test. It can end a lot of needless worry on your part. It is often available free or at low cost. It is also recommended that you should be tested anonymously, if available. This will allow you to keep the test private and avoid possible political and social ramifications. But remember, **when in doubt, get tested.** (USPHS, 1988; CDC, 2010h).

The STD Hot Line

The CDC and the American Social Health Association sponsor an STD national hot line to provide information in a confidential setting. Volunteers staff the lines between 8 AM and 11 PM (Eastern time), Monday through Friday. Call them, they are very professional, caring and sensitive, and can direct you to a clinic in your area. Call the Hot line at **(800) 227-8922**. For AIDS information only call for help at (800) 342-AIDS. **http://www.ashastd.org/.**

For More Information About HIV

If you'd like to know more about AIDS or whether you should consider an AIDS test, talk to your local doctor, local health department, or hospital. In addition, you can get helpful, confidential information from the National AIDS Information line, **(800) 232-4636.** This center is open 24 hours a day.

STD Prevention

Some people will be sexually active without any regard for their health or the health of others. Most sensible people do not want to die or see their friends die. The following suggestions will help lower the risk of contracting STD and HIV disease in the adolescent population or any population of sexually active people exhibiting risky behaviors:

- Practice abstinence, it is 100 % protection against STD;
- Limit sexual partners;
- Practice monogamy, **talk to partners about sexual history**, multiple partner behaviors;
- Always use a condom, use it properly throughout the time of intercourse;
- Use only latex condoms, do not use oil base lubricants;
- Avoid sexual activity that could cause tears in the skin or tissues;
- Avoid contact of body fluids, blood, semen and breast milk in HIV mothers;
- Do not share needles, syringes or devices with blood;
- Use only sterile, disposable needles for tattoos;
- Sterilize any needles with bleach (this is not a guarantee);
- Look for any obvious signs, sores or symptoms of partner;
- Get tested for HIV every 6, months if sexually active;
- Read the latest information, become informed and tell others; and
- Talk to your doctor during regular physical exams, especially women.

So What is Explicit Safe Sex?

Oftentimes young people, and even adults with minimal sexual experiences get very confused, scared or frustrated when trying to decide what is and what is not safe regarding sexual intimacy. The following section, adapted from Dr. Hatcher's book *Contraceptive Technology,* should help clarify these issues for anyone thinking about sexual intimacy. The reader may find it silly or insulting reviewing some of these behaviors below; but sometimes there are those that need very specific guidelines While many of these details on sexual intimacy may be inappropriate to discuss with adolescents; teachers should be able to understand these risks if students were to inquire on specific practices.. The comments refer to risk behaviors associated with HIV infection, but apply to most other STDs as well. Have sex and stay safe:

Options during sexual intimacy and HIV/STD risk.

<u>Safe</u>

1. All **unprotected** sexual activities, when both partners are monogamous, trustworthy, and **known by testing** to be free of HIV and STDs
2. Sexual fantasies
3. Massage
4. Hugging
5. Body rubbing
6. Dry kissing
7. Solo masturbation without contact with a partner's semen, blood vaginal secretions, or broken skin
8. Erotic conversation, books, movies, videos, and electronic images
9. Erotic bathing and showering

10. Eroticizing feet, hands, hips, abdomen ears, and other body parts.

Low But Potential Risk

1. All sexual activities, when both partners are monogamous, trustworthy, but **have not been tested**
2. Wet kissing with no broken skin, cracked lips, or damaged mouth tissue
3. Hand-to-genital touching or mutual masturbation on healthy, intact skin or with a latex or plastic barrier
4. Vaginal or anal intercourse using latex or plastic condom correctly with adequate lubrication
5. Oral sex on a man using a latex or plastic condom
6. Oral sex on a woman using a latex or plastic barrier such as a female condom, dental dam, plastic wrap, or modified male condom (especially if the female does not have her period or vaginal discharge).

Unsafe in the absence of mutual monogamy, trust, and HIV/STD testing of both partners

1. Blood contact of any kind, including menstrual blood
2. Any vaginal or anal intercourse without a latex or plastic condom
3. Oral sex on a woman without a latex or plastic barrier such as a female condom, dental dam, plastic wrap, or modified condom (especially if the female does not have her period or vaginal discharge)
4. Oral sex on a man without a latex or plastic condom, especially if associated with semen in the mouth
5. Oral-anal contact
6. Shared sex toys or douching equipment
7. Any sex that causes tissue damage or bleeding, such as rough vaginal or anal intercourse or fisting (inserting the fist in the rectum). (Hatcher, 2004).

These guidelines were written with the intention of helping reproductive health care workers advise their patients on methods to prevent STDs including HIV/AIDS. **As specific as they may be, however, the guidelines could help anyone practice a safe and happy sex life.**

The charts on the following pages list a brief summary of common sexually transmitted diseases (STDs). Read them carefully and be able to briefly describe the typical signs, symptoms and treatments for most common STDs. Table 9.3 lists the type of test used for each specific STD. Google "Any Lab Test Now" for more consumer information.

Table 9. 3 Lab Testing Procedures for STDs

Disease	**Lab test**
Chlamydia	DNA, Urine
Gonorrhea	Urine
Hepatitis B (HBV)	Surface antigen
Herpes (HSV2)	Immunoglobulin IgG
HIV/AIDS	Western blot, ELISA
Syphilis	Antibody test, dark field
Genital Warts (HPV)	DNA, Pap test

(ALT, 2009).

The STD Summary Chart on the following pages is modified from CDC/STD. (http://www.cdc.gov/std, 2011).		
Disease	*Signs & Symptoms*	*Treatment & Complications*
Chlamydia	**Women:** Discharge, vaginal bleeding, bleeding between, periods, painful urination, fever, nausea, abdominal pain **Most Women Asymptomatic (without symptoms)** **Men:** Watery/white discharge from penis, burning/painful urination, signs occur 7-21 days **Cause: bacteria (*Chlamydia trachomatis*)**	**Treatment:** Antibiotics (azithromycin, doxycycline, sometimes only single dose **Complications:** Easily infect others, secondary infections, damage to reproductive organs esp. females, sterility, from pelvic inflammatory disease (PID), lowers immunity, greater risk for HIV, mother can infect newborn child *in utereo*
Genital Warts	Most people are asymptomatic, small bumpy, painless warts on genitals,(penis/vagina/scrotum/anus, labia) appear within weeks or months, warts may disappear, or increase in size, itching, burning around genitals after removal, varies and may stay for years, HPV can be passed on between straight and same-sex partners-even when the infected partner has no signs or symptoms **Cause: virus, human papilloma virus (HPV)**	**Treatment:** Minor surgery, burned off, liquid nitrogen, lasers **Complications:** Easily infect others, no complete cure, (virus clearance depends on immune response) may return/months or years later, high risk virus leads to cervical cancer, low risk virus strain = genital warts in women
Gonorrhea	**Women:** Discharge, vaginal bleeding, bleeding between periods, painful urination, fever, nausea, abdominal pain **Most Women Asymptomatic** **Men:** Mostly white discharge from penis, burning/painful urination, signs occur 7-21 days **Cause: bacteria (*Neisseria gonorrhea*)**	**Treatment:** Antibiotics, (often single dose) Ofloxacin, Cefixine, Ceftriaxine, shots/pills **Complications:** Easily infect others, secondary infections, damage to reproductive organs esp. females, sterility from pelvic inflammatory disease (PID), lowers immunity, greater risk for HIV mother can infect newborn child *in utereo*
Genital Herpes	Many people have no symptoms, from 1-30 days, flu-like symptoms, fever, small painful blisters on genitals, anus, or mouth (cold sores) itching before blisters erupt, blisters disappear but virus still present **Highly contagious** even before blisters erupt, (prodromal) cold sore in mouth can be transmitted to genitals **Cause: Virus (Herpes simplex virus, HSV2)**	**Treatment:** Antivirals/oral (**no cure, lifetime disease**) Acyclovir, famciclovir, valacyclovir May help some but blisters will reoccur, usually less severe **Complications:** Virus hides in nerve ganglion Can be fatal to newborns, caesarian section often recommended to HSV2 infected females (only if an active HSV2 outbreak)

Disease	Signs & Symptoms	Treatment & Complications
HIV/AIDS	Note: People infected with STDs 2-5 higher risk of HIV infection (lower immune system). N people may be asymptomatic for several years. Symptoms may appear months or years after infection, including unexplained weight loss, tiredness, white spots on mouth, flu-like symptoms, severe night sweats, swollen glands, chronic diarrhea, skin patches, headaches, shaking chills **In women:** recurrent yeast infection **Cause: Virus Human Immunodeficiency Virus (HIV)**	**Treatment:** Drugs will slow the replication of virus, protease inhibitors (cocktails) reduce viral load in many and extend life for many years, many patients take <u>40 drugs daily</u>, antifungals, antibiotics, antivirals treat symptoms of *opportunistic infections*. Fatal disease to most patients. Death from opportunistic infections **Complications:** Virus mutates, no cure, breast milk can infect infant, meds very expensive, unavailable for some drug/tobacco use, increases risk of infection HIV positive may be asymptomatic for years
Hepatitis B	**Transmission:** Birth (spread from an infected mother to baby during birth), sex with an infected partner, sharing needles, syringes, razors or toothbrushes with an infected person, direct contact with the blood or open sores of an infected person, flu-like symptoms, tiredness, jaundice (yellow skin, eyes), joint pain, dark urine, light color (clay) bowel movement **Cause: Virus, Hepatitis B Virus (HBV)**	**Treatment:** None, general rest, fluids **Complications:** Mother can pass virus to fetus, permanent damage to liver, easily transmitted via needle sharing, some recover, others no cure
Vaginitis	Some women asymptomatic, itching, burning, discharge in vagina, strong odor, color white, green, fishy odor, cheesy appearance Examples: trichomonas (protozoa),Yeast infection (fungi) Bacterial vaginosis (BV) (discharge) **Cause: bacteria, protozoa, fungi** Many vaginal infections are not caused by sexual contact (could be tight undergarments, pantyhose)	**Treatment:** Doctor may prescribe pills, creams, suppositories **Bacterial vaginosis.** metronidazole tablets Flagyl , MetroGel, Cleocin **Yeast infections.** Monistat, Gyne-Lotrimin, Vagistat, Diflucan **Trichomoniasis.** (Flagyl. tinidazole (Tindamax) tablets.
Syphilis	Reddish-brown painless sores (chancre) on penis, scrotum, vagina, labia (average 21 days) rash over body, flu-like symptoms, fever can attack any organ (systemic) Becoming rare in U.S., highest in men having sex with men **Cause: Bacteria (Treponema pallidum)**	**Treatment:** Antibiotics if treated early, (often single dose) problems if early treatment **Complications:** Systemic disease enters bloodstream, brain damage, heart disease, blindness, possible miscarriage, open sores, ulcers much higher risk for HIV infection.

Disease	Signs & Symptoms	Treatment & Complications
Pubic Lice (Crabs)	Itching, irritation in pubic hairs, external insect parasite symptoms like head lice, can also occur in facial hair **Cause: Crab louse (Phthirus pubis)**	Continued irritation transmitted to partners, may spread to any hair follicle **Treatment:** Lotions, ointments, shampoos, all available OTC, wash sheets, clothes, high, temperature Newer treatment = benzyl alcohol **Complications:** Can be transmitted without sexual contact of partner sharing clothing, underwear, etc. lice resistant to some medicines

Sexy Questions About STDs and Other Sexy Stuff

Most of the statements below were collected from high school students and several from graduate students in the teacher credential program.

Objective: Students will separate facts from myths related to common questions about sexually transmitted disease (STD), including HIV/AIDS. Think about how your students will respond.

Please read the following list of questions carefully **before class meets.** During class students will assemble in coed groups of 3-4 and read the questions aloud and decide if they are **true or false** and **DISCUSS WHY.** Remember to recognize the right of privacy of others. You have the right to pass at any time. Answers to questions are located at the end of this chapter.

1. If a man urinates immediately after sex, he can wash away most STD pathogens.
2. STD treatment is free and confidential to anyone in California over the age of 12.
3. Feminine hygiene products, sprays, deodorants, etc., will prevent STD infection.
4. Birth control pills will change the vaginal mucus in such a way that a STD infection may grow more readily.
5. Signs of gonorrhea and syphilis are usually obvious to most people.
6. Teenage females have an underdeveloped cervical/vaginal epithelium. This places them at even higher risk than adult women for STDs.
7. The new vaccines for HPV to prevent cervical cancer are now required for kids to enter public schools.
8. *Chlamydia* of the throat is possible through oral sexual activity.
9. Dental workers can easily transmit HIV even if they practice universal precautions.
10. Chancroid, herpes and syphilis infection increase the risk of HIV.
11. Usually a person will only have one form of STD at a time.
12. Today the risk of acquiring HIV infection from a blood transfusion in the U.S. is extremely low.
13. Birth control pills protect the body from most bacterial STDs, but not viral forms.
14. *Chlamydia*, syphilis and gonorrhea can be contracted from toilet seats or towels.
15. In 2007, researchers reported the possible risk of throat cancer from HPV infection acquired from oral sexual activity.
16. An infected female with STD will usually learn about her infection from another person.
17. African Americans and Hispanics are disproportionately infected with HIV.
18. Herpes 2 (HSV2) is caused by a protozoan, has no cure, and hides in the nerve ganglia.
19. Cold sores are referred to as Herpes 1 (HSV1) and only occur in the mouth area.
20. PID (pelvic inflammatory disease) rarely occurs in asymptomatic females suffering chronic cases of *Chlamydia.*
21. *Trichomonas* is caused by a protozoan, and symptoms include a genital discharge, mostly in women.
22. Candida is a very common infection in women, caused by a fungus and can be contracted without any sexual contact.
23. HIV is the virus that causes AIDS. It is this virus that is the usual cause of death.

24. The spermicide Nonoxynol-9 is no longer recommended as a microbicide for STDs.
25. California law requires a blood test before marriage for syphilis, gonorrhea, and HIV.
26. Any child care custodian, (teacher, counselor, police officer, etc.), can be sent to jail for revealing the HIV status of anyone over the age of 12, without written permission.
27. A guy will usually know when he has contracted most common forms of STD.
28. Symptoms of gonorrhea include a discharge, and burning sensation, mostly in males.
29. Medication for pubic lice can only be purchased with a doctor's prescription.
30. Antibiotics will cure gonorrhea, pubic lice and yeast infections.
31. Women can infect men with yeast infections without ever having sex with other partners.
32. Hepatitis B can be sexually transmitted, especially through anal sex.
33. Lesbian women cannot transmit STD if they are in a monogamous relationship.
34. Abreva® is a new type of antiviral OTC medicine used to treat genital herpes.
35. Genital herpes can cause painful blisters on the penis, vagina or vulva.
36. HPV is the virus that causes genital warts, and can be completely cured by a doctor with laser surgery or by burning or freezing the sores with chemicals.
37. A young woman of 19 could be infected with *Chlamydia*, be asymptomatic for the disease and become sterilized by infection in her Fallopian tubes.
38. Hepatitis B is caused by a virus and is much more easily transmitted than HIV.
39. Lambskin condoms are carefully checked by the FDA and offer the same protection against STD, as do latex condoms.
40. Deep kissing or "French Kissing" could cause small cuts in the mouth and easily transmit HIV or gonorrhea bacteria.
41. Oil based lubricants should not be used with latex condoms.
42. Gonorrhea, genital warts and genital herpes are curable forms of STD.
43. Infections of chancroid, syphilis and herpes sores will increase an individual's chance of contracting HIV.
44. *Phthirus pubis* is the organism that causes genital lice.
45. Gonorrhea is the most common STD in the U.S. today.
46. Female condoms made of polyurethane offer no protection against STDs.
47. Primary and secondary syphilis rates in the U.S. have dropped dramatically within the past few years.
48. Teenagers are at very high risk to contract STDs, especially HIV.
49. The actual documented cases of teenagers in the U.S. with HIV are very low and probably will remain low.
50. "*Trich*" *is* a common infection of the vagina, and not usually sexually transmitted.
51. A person infected with HIV could be asymptomatic and infectious for many years.
52. If a person is infected with herpes type 1 (HSV1) and has no blisters, they cannot infect another person.
53. It is much easier for a female to be infected with HIV than a male.
54. Sharing dildos can easily transmit AIDS.
55. Syphilis is a *systemic* disease and can attack any organ by traveling throughout the circulatory system.
56. Gonorrhea sometimes can infect joints and cause a form of arthritis.
57. When a pregnant woman is HIV positive, her baby will test positive for HIV antibodies.
58. A woman cannot be infected by genital herpes if a man does not ejaculate inside her vagina.

59. It is virtually impossible for two virgins to have sexual intercourse and transmit STD.
60. An HIV positive mother has a greater than 25% chance of infecting her baby.
61. If a person mutually masturbates another person, and then touches their own mucus membranes, they can easily become infected with STD from their partner.
62. A chancre is the most common symptom of *Chlamydia*.
63. Gay men and women have a much greater chance of being infected with STD.
64. Douching may help to prevent the growth of STD pathogens.
65. HIV, the virus that causes AIDS, will die if exposed to air.
66. Heavy, deep mouth, or "French kissing" is a high-risk behavior for HIV infection.
67. Ritual or "gang" tattooing increases the risk for HIV and Hepatitis B.
68. Circumcision of the penis may lower the risk of STD infection.
69. California law requires parental notification for teens to receive STD treatment or family planning services.
70. To be a virgin, a woman must have an intact hymen.
71. Spermicides, aerosols, condoms and diaphragms can be purchased by teenagers without seeing a medical doctor.
72. If a girl starts her period on May 1st, the "best" time for her to get pregnant is May 15th.
73. Pregnancy is actually possible without intercourse. (Excluding laboratory methods).
74. If a man removes his penis before ejaculation, a woman will not get pregnant.
75. A woman **cannot** get pregnant **before** her first menstrual period.
76. In California, unmarried minors under the age of 18 cannot legally have sexual intercourse.
77. Fraternal twins must be of the same sex.
78. Identical twins result from two sperms fertilizing one egg and then dividing.
79. Emergency contraception pills, if taken within 72 hours after unprotected intercourse, will limit the chances of pregnancy by 95%.
80. California law requires written parental notification for sex education. Teachers that do not obtain written parental notification may have their credentials revoked.

Answer Key for Student Questions in Chapters 9.

1. F	37. T	73. T
2. T	38. T	74. F
3. F	39. F	75. F
4. T	40. F	76. T
5. F	41. T	77. F
6. T	42. F	78. F
7. F	43. T	79. F
8. T	44. T	80. T
9. F	45. F	
10. T	46. F	
11. F	47. T	
12. T	48. F	
13. F	49. T	
14. F	50. F	
15. T	51. T	
16. T	52. F	
17. T	53. T	
18. F	54. F	
19. F	55. T	
20. F	56. T	
21. T	57. T	
22. T	58. F	
23. F	59. F	
24. T	60. F	
25. F	61. F	
26. T	62. F	
27. T	63. F	
28. T	64. F	
29. F	65. T	
30. F	66. F	
31. T	67. T	
32. T	68. T	
33. F	69. F	
34. F	70. F	
35. T	71. F	
36. F	72. T	

Chapter 10

Human Sexuality:
Focus on Teens

*Nothing helps people stay healthy
more than the power of
real knowledge about health.
...Dr. Roger Harms*

Magazines, TV programs, talk radio shows, movies and even bathing suit advertisements for little girls focus heavily on sex to catch the viewer's interest and sell everything from toothpaste to laundry soap. Oftentimes the messages are blatantly suggestive of sex. During the months of February, May and November, network TV stations run countless programs, stories, documentaries and many other forms of "entertainment" to sell products and gain rating points during "sweeps" month. The major emphasis of many programs, trailer messages and previews is sex used to solicit advertising. Teenagers experimenting with sex are constantly being exposed to this promotion of sexuality as a result of the powerful messages they read and view in the media, and hear from music lyrics and music videos. This plethora of sexual images frequently generates mixed messages for kids. Many parents, and educators tell them to wait and practice abstinence, but the electronic images say "have sex now." And numerous sexual messages are delivered to youth through music lyrics, and music videos. But, developing a healthy attitude toward personal sexuality is much more than media and messages. In most European countries, sexuality is taught very early as just another part of life and teens are often treated as young adults, given condoms and encouraged to practice safe sex.

Sexuality is more than the meshing of human bodies in various forms of intimate positions. **Human sexuality** is more than the attraction and physical consummation of two individuals, more than the lifelong goal of reaching mutual orgasm. Human sexuality refers to

300

you. How you feel about your gender identification, sexual preference, specific tastes, desires and experiences. Human sexuality is more of what happens between the ears than between the sheets!

The purpose of this chapter is to introduce students to human sexuality from a broad perspective with a special focus on adolescents. Topics discussed include gender identity, relationships, anatomy, physiology, family planning, sexual life cycles, sexual preference, sexual stimulation, sexual variety, sexual health, sexual assault, sex and society, and sexuality and the future. As you read the material and participate in discussions with friends, partners, spouses, students, lovers, family and classmates, remember to focus on **what is important to you and your partner.** Do not rely on talk shows or sensational tabloid media reports. Just because an opinion is **seen on TV** does not make it a fact. This "seen on TV" mentality frequently acts as a very powerful force that confuses kids, and many adults on all types of topics. And, always remember to keep in mind all of the implications of sexually transmitted diseases that were discussed in chapter nine.

Relationships

Someone once said happiness could be found if one has (1) someone to love (2) something to do, and (3) something to look forward to. Relationships are dynamic phases of our lives. Relationships of parents to children are constantly changing, even when the children become adults. Relationships between close school friends will grow, change, evolve or end. Psychologists indicate that one of the major tasks of early adulthood is to achieve intimacy with others. Just ask any typical high school student, especially the girls, about establishing intimacy. They will probably answer that they want a "boyfriend" or "girlfriend." Sending love notes, and gossip chatter among girls starts about the fourth grade and  never seems to end. **Intimacy** is the ability to open oneself to others in a way that permits mutual sharing and caring. Intimacy is a process of self-revelation, of exposing rather than hiding, of expressing rather than suppressing, of wanting to know another, and to be known by that other, as fully as possible. This starts with **verbal** communication and culminates with **physical** communication. Sometimes, the most powerful moment of intimacy takes place when two people touch each other ever so gently and look deeply into each other's eyes.

Intimacy is not a synonym for sex, but an intimate relationship often includes a sexual relationship, either heterosexual or homosexual. Intimacy represents a small part of the feelings people express with regard to each other. As relationships become more familiar, deeper in meaning and clearer in communication, most of us decide on one individual that is above all others and choose to share a life with that individual—this is what we call **love.** What is love? This topic would require another entire book to discuss, but humans have been talking about love for centuries. It starts in childhood and eventually matures and changes throughout adulthood.

Marriage

There was a time and place in the world where marriages were almost always arranged by a parent or a "matchmaker." This practice still takes place today in many places throughout the world. Most of the reasons involved for arranged marriages are either economic or political. In America, as new families are emigrating and bringing their own distinctive cultural beliefs such as arranged marriages, the U.S. population is starting to see arranged marriages occur as they did once before. This is especially true of Americans emigrated from the Middle East, Cambodia and India. Today, however, marital arrangements are quite different in the U.S. compared to many nations. Many American couples live together before marriage, others just live together and never marry, and, tragically, when teens marry because of an unplanned pregnancy, they only stay together for an average of 26 months. (Caparulo, 1992). Even though it is still controversial, many same sex couples have the same feelings and desires as heterosexual couples and wish to share their lives together without being ostracized or ridiculed for their personal beliefs. (Sternberg, 1988). And by 2011, even though it is a very controversial topic, several states were allowing or contemplating same sex marriages.

Why marry? For some young people it's just a convenience. Others take marriage seriously as a lifelong commitment to another person. Most people say they marry for love, yet one out every six brides is pregnant on her wedding day. Love is the best, perhaps the only, reason to marry. While love may lead to marriage, it takes many years for a mature love to develop from a marriage. The ultimate goal of each couple is to care as much about another person's happiness as they care about their own, perhaps even more than their own! Women and men look at qualities quite differently when they prepare their "laundry list" of traits for the ideal mate. Physical attractiveness is usually the most obvious quality, but psychologist Robert Sternberg of Yale University says that there are **5 crucial compatibilities for commitment**. They are: (1) shared values, (2) a willingness to change in response to each other, (3) a willingness to tolerate flaws, (4) a match in religious beliefs, and the ability to communicate effectively.

Relationships without Marriage

Leo, a man in his early 50s loves to live alone. Throughout his life he placed considerable energy into his work, starting his business and luckily earning considerable amounts of money. He is not a workaholic, but just a guy that works hard. He has had several relationships with women, traveled throughout the world and enjoyed many 'creature comforts,' such as fancy flat screen TVs, sports cars, and boats. Kids and a wife are not important to Leo. He is very happy and enjoys interacting with kids through nephews, nieces etc. the same argument could made for a women like Lina, although many would argue that women living alone is less common then men living alone. Is this a selfish way to live? Leo just says, "It works for me." **Living alone** is a perfectly acceptable arrangement for many people. There are over forty million single adults in

America. The quality of life for a single person today is significantly different than in the past. In the past, living alone was a transition stage for a person while they searched for a permanent life mate. Today, living alone is not only acceptable, but also preferred for many men and women. Being alone does not always mean being lonely. There are many ways a single person can be actively engaged in life without being lonely. **Some suggested ways to avoid loneliness include:** Develop a meaningful life of work and professional experiences. Build a social network of friends, and associates who care about you. Spend holidays with friends and families, or someone else's family. Open up to new experiences, new languages, different people and cultures. Go alone to special events, the movies or while traveling on vacation. Volunteer for community or civic affairs, religious or public events. Join a gym or SPA, work out and hang out with other exercise enthusiasts.

For many young adults **living with roommates** often starts with friends sharing expenses while working or attending school. Roommate relationships may improve, or abruptly end, but they can also last for many years. When the economy is unstable, people tend to join forces. This may develop into a form of **communal life.** One large house might be owned by a gay couple, 5 of the 6 bedrooms may house single college coeds, a married couple, and a retired railroad worker. Condominiums are often built with two master bedrooms and a shared common area, which may be owned by two couples. Communal life also includes biological families with many different generations living under the same roof. Many parents today find their 28-year-old child "returning to the nest" after "fledging" alone for ten years!

Whatever arrangement you choose, work on improving it and making it a meaningful part of your life. Most individuals will decide on one person as their life mate and should strive to keep communication open and flowing. Sending little notes, romantic e-mail messages, or just winking at your partner from across the room can be very powerful tools of romantic communication. Here are a few very simple guidelines adapted from a well known author, Gregory Godek, to help you keep your relationship working:

- Ask your partner about their feelings, interests. Never assume;
- Think of your partner as a complete person and not a sex object;
- Spend time everyday just focusing on your partner;
- Be a better lover. Pay attention to the small details;
- Build common interests;
- Don't play games, or manipulate your partner;
- Be polite, considerate and understanding;
- Give as much of yourself as you can, don't worry about what you should get;
- Give more and expect less; and
- Be patient. Patience is the *ultimate* virtue.
  (Godek, 1991, 1999, 2009).

Gender Identity

When a doctor delivers a new baby, the very first thing that is said to, or about that baby is its gender. "It's a girl," or "It's a boy." Gender and sex are not interchangeable terms. Gender includes the physical, psychological and sociological aspects, of being male or female. Sex only refers to the physical and genetic aspects. It is helpful to group gender determinants into three categories: prenatal factors, factors of infancy and childhood, and factors at puberty. **Prenatal factors** include the biological composition of the sperm and egg as they unite to form a **zygote** or newly fertilized egg. These factors are the **chromosomes**, 23 contributed from the mother and 23 from the father, totaling 46, the compliment of human beings. These microscopic cells develop gonads, penises, vaginas, testes and ovaries, fire up endocrine glands to produce cascades of hormones, and eventually become very active teenagers and sit in your classroom!

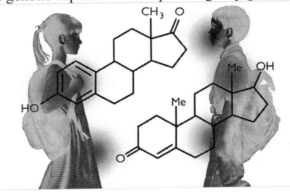

Factors of infancy and childhood start with the sex assignment at birth. Parents may spend countless hours researching the Internet to determine the name of the child, and planning on how to paint the nursery, and start to condition the child as a boy or girl. Girls are usually treated more softly, spoken to more quietly, and dressed with bows and ribbons. Boys, however, are treated more roughly, yelled at and taught to be tough and competitive in sports and school. **Factors at puberty** are the more familiar **secondary sex traits** that arise under the influence of hormones. They include: voice change, body and pubic hair growth, hormone secretion, breast development, muscle enlargement, hip widening, sweat gland excreting, and the initiation of the sex drive. During this time females start menstruating and males can ejaculate sperm.

Since the 1960s many of the factors listed above have been greatly influenced by **gender liberation,** or the process in which an individual can fulfill any job, hobby, or personal experience without being discriminated against because of gender. Women can work as truck drivers, return home at night to paint their nails and go out dancing. Men can choose nursing as a career, hang out with their friends and still ride motorcycles. Chapter eleven will address these topics in more detail from a legal perspective as they relate to youth.

Sexual Anatomy and Physiology

Many adults have a difficult time relating with their partner on a sexual level. Sometimes it has to do with emotional aspects related to communication and relating openly to another person. Many times, however, it is just lack of knowledge about basic reproductive anatomy. Couples often seek therapy for sexual problems because they do not know how to talk about sexuality. **Anatomy** is the study of structure or form, or "the parts," of the body of all living things, and **physiology** is the study of function, or "how these parts work." **Carefully review the reproduction diagrams in the appendix when reading and studying this section.**

"The Parts" (Anatomy)

Female Sex Organs. (See the appendix for detailed diagrams of the reproductive organs). Men and women have sexual organs that look quite a bit different, but they arise during the human embryonic condition from very similar primordial tissues. At about 7 weeks of embryonic development, both male and female genitalia are indeterminate, i.e., the tissue in the embryo looks female. Under the influence of X chromosomes, female organs (vagina, ovaries, Fallopian tubes) develop. Under the influence of the Y-chromosomes, male organs (penis, testis, scrotum) develop. This does not mean that all humans began as females, but merely that male and female genitalia had similar embryonic origins. (See diagram below). By 10-12 weeks the vagina and penis are distinctly present in baby girls and boys. They both have **gonads**, a general term referring to the sex cells. The external female sex organs include a pair of skin folds or **labia** (lips). Enclosed at the apex of the labia is the **clitoris** and its hood or **prepuce** (foreskin). The clitoris has many nerve endings and is a very sensitive organ stimulated during intercourse, much like the penis of a man. Just inside the labia are two openings, the **urethral opening** and the **vaginal opening.** The urethra leads into the urinary bladder that drains urine from the kidneys, and the vagina leads to the uterus, connected by the cervix. The vaginal opening is usually covered by a thin membrane at birth called the **hymen.** Despite the confusion of teens and some adults, **the presence or absence of the hymen at first intercourse is not a sign of virginity.** The hymen could easily tear from exercise, or by using a tampon.

Human Genital Developmental Embryology

During the eighth week of development in the embryo, the human genitals appear to be nearly the same. The undifferentiated gonads are present but cannot be identified distinctly as a penis or vagina. This fascinating process has been known for many years by embryologists and now can be observed in very clearly prepared high definition images. Search for 'embryo images online,' or go to the URL below to observe these remarkable images. The URL is: http://www.med.unc.edu/embryo_images/unit-genital/genital_htms/genital024.htm. The diagram below illustrates how the differentiation of the XX or XY chromosomal information unfolds as the penis of a boy or vagina of a girl. As stated earlier, this simply that males and females both have similar embryonic beginnings and by the fourth month the embryonic gender can be identified as a male or female.

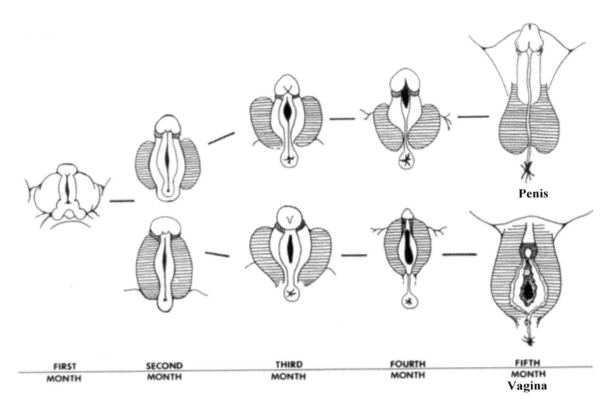

| FIRST MONTH | SECOND MONTH | THIRD MONTH | FOURTH MONTH | FIFTH MONTH |

Penis

Vagina

Indeterminate gonads

Human Genitalia Development

The size and shape of the vagina is analogous to a tube of toothpaste. It expands much in the same manner. The major function of the vagina is to receive the penis during intercourse and allow sperm to fertilize eggs that descend from the oviducts, or as they are called in humans, **Fallopian tubes**. At the end of the vaginal canal is the base of the **uterus**, also poetically known as the "womb" where the fetus will attach and grow. The **cervix** (neck of the uterus) is the narrow channel that leads into the uterus. A pair of **Fallopian tubes** lead out of the uterus toward a pair of **ovaries**. Inside the ovaries are hundreds of developing follicles that will release one ovum (egg) each month for about 38 years, until approximately age 45 to 50 for most American women. Near the age of fifty, most women reach menopause and stop menstruating.

Male Sex Organs. The genital organs of a man are mostly located outside the body. They include the **penis** and **scrotum**. The penis is made of a spongy tissue with many blood vessels inside. It becomes engorged and erect during sexual excitement. The **scrotum** is a pouch attached to the penis that contains a pair of testes. The **testes** are located outside the body in the scrotum to maintain optimal testicular temperature. The testes are about 5 °F less than the rest of the body temperature. The testes must be kept cooler than the internal body temperature or the sperm cells will not survive. Some men have low sperm counts because of wearing tight pants or "jockey type" underwear that may inhibit sperm development. Attached to each testis is the **epididymis,** a long coiled tube that stores and ripens sperm cells before ejaculation.

The rounded tip of the penis is the **glans**. It is the most sensitive part of the penis and is important during sexual arousal. The glans is partially covered by the foreskin, but over 80% of American born males have the foreskin removed during infancy. This process is called **circumcision**, and is sometimes performed for religious reasons. There is a controversy as to whether boys should be circumcised. Some doctors state that circumcision may prevent penile cancer or other infections. Cook investigated the relationship of STDs in 2,776 heterosexual men attending an STD clinic and did identify some evidence of medical problems. A positive relationship was observed between uncircumcised status with both syphilis and gonorrhea. A negative relationship was also found between warts and lack of circumcision, but no apparent relationship was noted between uncircumcised status and genital herpes, Chlamydia infection, or **nongonococcal urethritis (NGU).** (Cook, 1994). For some parents, circumcision is only a religious ritual. It can also be a matter of family tradition, personal hygiene or preventive health care. For others, however, the procedure seems unnecessary or disfiguring. In 1999, the American Academy of Pediatrics (AAP) issued a policy statement that says the benefits aren't strong enough to recommend routine circumcision for all male newborns. Today, the AAP leaves the decision up to parents — and supports use of pain relief for infants who have the procedure. Some of the advantages of circumcision are easier hygiene, (cleaning the penis is just as easy for uncircumcised males), lower risk of urinary track infections, decreased risk of penile cancer, and prevention of inflammation of the penis during retraction. **New data, however, does consider that the circumcised penis may decrease the chance of women becoming infected with HPV or HIV as discussed in chapter 9.** (Castellsagué, 2002; CDC, 2008b). While most Americans still circumcise boys, some for religious reasons, there is no overwhelming research to support medical circumcision in boys. Most of the time, fathers just want their boys to look like them, and pediatricians can add the cost of the surgical procedure to medical bills. While there is an ongoing debate on weather to circumcise or not circumcise a baby boy, many experts agree that there does not seem to be a major loss in sensitivity around the penis during sexual activities of circumcised men.

Inside the testes there are thousands of **seminiferous** (sperm bearing) **tubules** where sperm are produced. Two tubes lead from the testes to pass sperm cells. They are   called the **Vas Deferentia** (singular: vas deferens). Three accessory organs are located inside the abdominal cavity and work with the vas deferens. The **prostate gland** produces nutrients for the sperm cells. In addition, there is a pair of **seminal vesicles** that store sperm and produce liquid secretions that aids in this function. There are also the **Bulbo-urethral glands** (Cowper's), two small glands that produce a pre-ejaculatory fluid that may contain sperm cells. The sperm cells and the ejaculatory fluids are called **semen** and are released through the urethra, which passes fluid out of the penis. Since the pre-ejaculatory fluid may have a small amount of sperm cells present, it is not a good practice to remove the penis before ejaculation to prevent pregnancy. Data on conception from pre-ejaculated fluid is under investigation at this time, and it is not clear as to how large a risk of pregnancy may result from pre-ejaculated fluids. Nonetheless, many couples that rely on this **"withdrawal method"** have a special title, they are called parents! It is difficult to understand the human reproductive system by just reading text in a book. Try to study all diagrams carefully, observe the classroom presentations, video images etc., to clarify how the human reproductive system works. Now to the functions.

"The Works" (Physiology)

The discussion of sexual anatomy would be useless without a detailed description of sexual physiology. However, this book is not intended to replace a detailed discussion on human sexuality. Students may wish to enroll in a human sexuality course for more specific details. **Physiology** is the study of function of living things. Sexual function will be explained based upon structure. Keep in mind that simply knowledge of the body parts, and how they work do not a meaningful sex life make! Remember that **human sexuality is much more related to what goes on in between the ears, than what happens below the waist.** Understanding basic anatomy and physiology, however, can certainly help.

Sexual stimulation is related to a stimulus and response network. Erotic stimulation between two people leads to arousal (excitement) that eventually culminates in an intensely pleasurable sensation called **orgasm.** **Physical stimulation** occurs through the sense organs. All nerve sensitive cells are received in the brain through the sensory system. Couples are aroused by what they see, touch, smell, taste and feel. The most obvious physical stimulation involves touching. Sexual encounters begin with various forms of hugging, kissing of the face, hands, arms and kissing all over the skin. The skin, the largest organ in the human body, is an organ with a large surface area, and many people are stimulated at different places on the body called **erogenous zones.** Highly sensitive areas are the vaginal opening, penis, nipples, breasts, and inside the thighs.

Psychological stimulation includes fantasies, dreams, ideas and memories of past experiences. All of this can contribute to the particular "mood" which may or may not excite an individual. Many couples get turned on just by a mere suggestion, or whisper of a sexual encounter. Sometimes if one partner calls the other on the phone and speaks very few words with a powerful sensuous tone, it can readily excite the other partner, cause vaginal lubrication and penile erection, even without their presence. A few individuals can actual reach orgasm by just kissing or touching. **Sexual response** comes about from numerous methods in which a couple, or an individual, chooses to become aroused. It could be by masturbation, mutual masturbation, oral sexual stimulation or intercourse.

Most genital reactions can be explained buy two physiological mechanisms. These mechanisms are **vasocongestion** and **myotonia.** Vasocongestion is the engorgement of tissues that result when the individual is excited i.e., more blood flows to the area than away from the tissue area. The penis becomes engorged with blood during erection. Myotonia is increased muscular tension, which culminates in rhythmical muscular contractions during orgasm. The sexual response cycle is characterized by four stages: the **excitement phase,** the **plateau phase,** the **orgasmic phase,** and the **resolution phase.** First, the **excitement phase.** In women, the labia and vaginal walls become moist with vaginal fluid, the clitoris engorges with blood and the uterus elevates. While it is often controversial, many experts include the **G-spot,** a highly sensitive small area in the vagina that, when stimulated, gives extreme sexual pleasure, and even a female type of ejaculation of fluids. In men, the penis becomes erect, and the testes expand and are pulled upward toward the base of the penile shaft during this phase. The **plateau phase** is a continuation of the excitement phase. The lower region of the vagina swells and the upper region expands, and more vaginal lubrication is secreted. The penis and testes become harder and the Bulbourethral gland secretes a small amount of pre-ejaculatory semen. Next is the **orgasmic phase.** In women the lower portion of the vagina rhythmically contracts, and the rectal sphincter contracts. Men experience continued rapid rhythmic contractions of the penis, urethra, prostate gland, seminal vesicles and muscles of the pelvic and rectal regions. This last stage is the **resolution phase** that causes all of the changes that occurred in the excitement phase to reverse. Blood flow diminishes, muscles relax and genital organs return to the relaxed state.

While the four stages are occurring in the genital organs, a more generalized body change related to sexual arousal takes place. Nipples enlarge in both men and women, breasts swell in both sexes, a flush occurs in the skin of the chest, but most of these changes are much more pronounced in women. The heart rate doubles and breathing rate is increased. A cry or moaning may occur during orgasm. Finally, after intercourse the body will feel relaxed and a sense of warmth and release of tension will result.

Hormones (from the Greek *hormon,* to set into motion) are the key elements in sexual development and function. They set things in motion. The entire process of sexual development and maturation is under the influence of a series of **endocrine glands** that produce these hormones. Near the center of the brain is the **hypothalamus,** a section of neurons that releases the hormone **gonadotropin-releasing hormone (GnRH)** into the bloodstream. **GnRH** will intern stimulate the **pituitary gland** to produce secretions by the testes and ovaries. The testes produce sex hormones called **androgens** and the ovaries produce two hormones **estrogens** and **progestins** (especially progesterone). Additionally, the **adrenal cortex** located near the kidneys, produces androgens in both sexes.

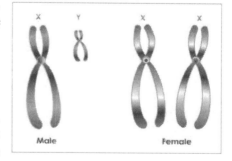

The Chromosomes of Sex

All cells of the body, except red blood cells, have **chromosomes**. Chromosomes contain the genetic blueprint of life, the genes and **DNA** that are responsible for the development of bodily traits, chemical reactions and sex determination. Humans have 46 chromosomes in their **somatic** (body) cells. Each sperm and egg cell has only 23 chromosomes. When a sperm meets and fertilizes an egg, the 46 chromosomes are reunited to form a human being. The 22 chromosomes in the sex cells are responsible for body traits (**autosomes**) and functions, but the remaining 23rd chromosome is called the **sex chromosome**. The sex chromosome determines gender, either male or female. The sex chromosome is said to be either **X-bearing** or **Y-bearing**. In sperm there are two types of sex chromosomes, X and Y, but in egg cells the sex chromosomes are all X bearing. When an X bearing sperm fertilizes an egg, the result is an **XX combination or a girl**. When a Y bearing sperm fertilizes an egg, the result is an **XY combination, or a boy.** Thus it is the male in humans that determines the sex of the offspring, and not the female.

During 2005, geneticists were surprised to learn that not only do females have the X chromosome that expresses the physical traits between males and females; but that the newly-cracked genetic code of the female X chromosome may help explain why women are so different from men. Drs. Ross and Sanger of the United Kingdom, and Dr. Laura Carrel, of Penn State, reported in *Nature*, April, 2005 that the X chromosome contains 1,100 genes, or about 5% of the human genome. They also discovered that females are far more variable than previously thought and, when it comes to genes, more complex than men. Dr. Ross stated, "The X chromosome is definitely the most extraordinary in the human genome in terms of its inheritance pattern, its unique biology... and in terms of its association with human disease." The research shows the Y chromosome is an eroded version of the X chromosome with only a few genes. The X chromosome is also bigger than the Y and because females have two copies, one X chromosome is largely switched off or inactivated. But not all of the genes on the silenced chromosome are inactivated, which could explain some of the differences between men and women. (Ross, Darren, Grafham, et. al, 2005). Does all this mean men are 'eroded' from female cells?

Sometimes **multiple births** come about during fertilization. This is because there may be two eggs ovulated. When two separate eggs are fertilized by two separate sperm, **fraternal twins** result, which can be of either sex. Or, the other possibility is when one newly fertilized egg may split and become two separate individuals. This is called **identical twins**. Genetic frequencies for multiple births vary among families and racial groups. The birthrate of identical or **monozygotic twins** (one sperm and egg that divides forming two embryos) is constant world wide (approximately 4 per 1000 births). Birth rates of **dizygotic** (two sperm plus two eggs forming two separate embryos) twins vary by race. The highest birth rate of dizygotic twinning occurs in African nations, and the lowest birth rate of dizygotic twinning occurs in Asia. The Yorubas of western Nigeria have a birth rate of 45 twins per 1000 live births, and approximately 90% are dizygotic. Globally, blacks produce the highest rate of multiple births while Asians have the lowest group to produce multiple births. (Fletcher, & Rosenkrantz, 2009). Since fraternal twins are derived from two separate eggs, they may be either the same sex, or of different sexes. When fraternal twins become adults, they look no more alike than other brothers and sisters in the same family. Identical twins, however, always are of the same sex because they came from the same egg that split by mitotic division. In summary, identical twins (monozygotic) result from one fertilized egg that splits into two cells creating exact copies, these twins must be the same sex. Fraternal twins (dizygotic) are from two separate egg cells fertilized by two separate sperm cells and can be of either sex.

Birth, Abortion and Birth Control in the U.S.

Various trends have developed during the past four decades related to adolescent reproductive health. The 1960s saw a much more liberal trend regarding sexuality in America which continued throughout the 70s and 80s. However, the epidemic of HIV, as discussed in Chapter   9, may have changed sexual behavior and contributed to the definite decline throughout the 2000s of teenage sexual risk taking. Schools with comprehensive sexuality education programs also have contributed to the decline. For example from 1985 until 2008 contraceptive use by adolescents has increased nearly 30% i.e., greater than 80% of teens reported using contraceptives during their first premarital sexual debut. (AGI, 2011). The following summary from the Guttmacher report below reflects the status of teen reproductive health as of 2011.

- Even though only 13% of teens have ever had vaginal sex by age 15, sexual activity is common by the late teen years; by age 19, seven in 10 teens of both sexes have had intercourse;
- Sexually active teens who do not use contraceptives have a 90% chance of becoming pregnant within a year;
- After substantial declines in the proportion of teens who had ever had sex between 1995 and 2002, the level did not change significantly from 2002 to 2006–2008;
- Teens in the United States and European teens have similar levels of sexual activity. However, European teens are more likely to use effective contraceptive methods; which result in substantially lower pregnancy rates;
- Most sexually experienced teens (79% of females and 87% of males) used contraceptives the first time they had sex;
- Contraceptive use at first premarital sex has been increasing. Fifty-six percent of women whose first premarital sex occurred before 1985 used a method, compared with 76% in 2000–2004 and 84% in 2005–2008;
- About 20% of female teens at risk of unintended pregnancy were not using any contraceptive method at last intercourse;
- Condom availability in schools is rare; in 2006, only 5% of American high schools made condoms available to students;
- The majority of the decline in teen pregnancy rates in the United States (86%) is due to teens' increasingly consistent contraceptive use; the rest is due to higher proportions of teens choosing to delay sexual activity;
- Despite the decline, the U.S. teen pregnancy rate continues to be one of the highest in the developed world—more than twice as high as rates in Canada (28 per 1,000 women aged 15–19 in 2006) and Sweden (31 per 1,000);
- During 2009 only Bulgaria surpassed pregnancy rate of U.S. teens;
- Teen childbearing is results in reduced educational attainment. Teen mothers are substantially less likely than women who delay childbearing to complete high

school or obtain a GED by age 22 (66% vs. 94%); and less than 2% of teens who have a baby before age 18 attain a college degree by age 30; and

- As of 2010, Laws in 36 states required that a minor seeking an abortion involve her parents in the decision. (AGI, 2011; Stobbe, 2010).

Minors' Consent and Reproductive Health

During the past 30 years, the legal liability of minors to consent to a wide range of sensitive health care services, especially reproductive health services, has undergone dramatic change throughout the U.S. Minors now have a much greater opportunity to receive health care for mental health, alcohol and drug treatment as well as many decisions related to their reproductive health. While many parents may object for their minor children to receive any health care without their expressed knowledge and consent, the new trend recognizes that many minors will not avail themselves to obtain health care if their parents are notified. As far back as 1971, California legislators approved the sale of condoms to anyone of any age with the intent of preventing STDs and not judging young people on their moral behaviors. Today, many states explicitly permit some or all minors to obtain prenatal care, and STD services. Conversely, however, abortion services do require parental notification of one kind or another for more than 35 states in the U.S. Some states may allow emancipated or married minors, to make decisions on abortions without parental notification.

Minors and Contraceptive Services. Twenty-six states and the District of Columbia allow all minors over the age of 12 to consent to contraceptive services. About 20 states allow only certain categories of minors to receive contraceptive services; and 4 states have no policy or case law. STD services for minors are allowed in all states and the District of Columbia. Eighteen of these states allow, but do not require, a doctor to inform a minor's parents that she or he is seeking or receiving STD services when the physician deems it in the minor's best interests. Most states allow minors to receive prenatal care. (AGI, 2011).

Minors and Abortion. The District of Columbia and 2 states explicitly allow all minors to consent to abortion services; 20 states require one parent consent and 12 states require prior notification of at least one parent. Four states require both notification of and consent from a parent prior to a minor's abortion; and 6 states have parental involvement laws that are temporarily or permanently enjoined. There are also 6 states that have no relevant policy or case law. (AGI, 2011).

Abortion Rates Declining

School systems frequently avoid any discussions related to abortion unless it is an integral part of the curriculum. Even then, many teachers hesitate to bring up controversial topics for fear of offending students or religious conservative parents. **A report from the Guttmacher Institute in January 2008 stated that the U.S. abortion rate continued a long-term decline, falling to the lowest level since 1974.** (AGI, 2008). The number of abortions declined to a total of 1.2 million in 2005, 25% below the all-time high of 1.6 million abortions in 1990. Sharon L.

Camp, president and CEO of the Guttmacher Institute stated, "Our policymakers at the state and federal levels need to understand that behind virtually every abortion is an unintended pregnancy, so we must redouble our efforts towards prevention, through better access to contraception." This reduction of surgical abortion has come about due to an increase of medication abortion, which allows women the opportunity to choose when to terminate the pregnancy and avoiding a surgical procedure. This data was presented at the Guttmacher Institute's 14th census of all known abortion providers in the United States. (AGI, 2008). Teachers need to remember that teenagers can avoid all of the conflict of abortions by practicing abstinence until they are ready for a permanent adult relationship (hopefully in marriage), use birth control if sexually active, and regularly talk about careers, friendships, intimacy issues with their partners and their parents.

What Do Teens Want to Know About Sexuality

Too often parents, teachers, administrators and school systems focus on information on preventing teen pregnancy and may even develop curricula to teach kids how to avoid sexual activity. However, sometimes it is simply a good idea to ask teens what they want to know or do about sex. The National Campaign to Prevent Teen and Unwanted Pregnancy has been asking what teens want adults to know about teen pregnancy from their perspective. For 15 years The National Campaign has asked teens from all over the country a fairly simple question: If you could give advice to your parents, teachers or other adults about teen pregnancy, what would you say? The most common responses from teens from the Campaign are: (1) *Show us why teen pregnancy is such a bad idea.* They want to hear directly from teen mothers and fathers about what it is like having a baby so young. (2) *Talk to us honestly about sex, love and relationships.* Teens state that just because they are young doesn't mean they can't fall in love or be deeply interested in sex. (3) *Telling us not to have sex is not enough.* Teens want to know *why* parents feel this way and want their conversations taken seriously. They also want to know how their parents felt about sex as a teen. (4) *Whether we are having sex or not, we need to be prepared.* They want to learn specific details about birth control and how to protect themselves from STDs. But they also want parents to know that their curiosity does not mean they will be sexually active. (5) *Pay attention to us before we get into trouble.* They also want encouragement, attention and support about sexual issues and don't want to be showered with attention only when there's a baby involved. (6) *Sometimes, all it takes not to have sex is not to have the opportunity.* If parents can't be  home with kids after school, they want something to do or to be able to talk to other adults comfortable with being around kids. Many times they have sex because there is nothing to do. They don't want parents to leave them alone so much. (7) ***We really care what you think, even if we don't always act like it.*** If we don't do exactly as you say, don't think you have failed us. (8) *Show us what good responsible relationships look like.* What you do to show love, affection and good communication is much more important than what you just say. (9) *Help us avoid*

313

unhealthy relationships. Teens want to be taught about early warning sounds such as pressure to have sex, jealously or constant text messages to keep us from spending time with friends and family. Help us understand stuff we read about in cyberspace. (10) *We hate "the talk" as much as you do.* Teens want parents to start the talk about sex and responsibility when they are very young and want the dialog to continue as they grow older. (National Campaign, 2011).

The U.S. spends more than $500 million annually to fund the abstinence only programs. Many school districts choose not to accept the federal funding because school boards want their youth to receive information about all types of contraception methods when they become adults. School health classes still emphasize abstinence as the only 100% way to prevent pregnancy and STDs; and health teachers always strive to encourage kids to postpone and wait until adulthood before participating in sex. What is quite troubling is that more than one in five adolescents (21% of females and 24% of males) received abstinence education without receiving instruction about birth control in 2002, compared with 8–9% in 1995. (AGI, 2007). Other recent facts related to teen reproductive trends:

- By 2002, one-third of teens had not received any formal instruction about contraception;
- One-quarter of sexually experienced teens **had not received** instruction about abstinence before first sex;
- Eighty-two percent of adults support comprehensive sex education that teaches students about both abstinence and other methods of preventing pregnancy and STIs;
- Only one-third of adults surveyed support abstinence only education, while half oppose the abstinence-only approach;
- Federal law establishes a stringent eight-point definition of "abstinence-only education" that requires programs to teach that sexual activity outside of marriage is wrong and harmful-for people of any age. The law also prohibits programs from advocating contraceptive use or discussing contraceptive methods except to emphasize their failure rates; and
- There is currently no federal program dedicated to supporting comprehensive sex education that teaches young people about both abstinence and contraception. (AGI, 2007).

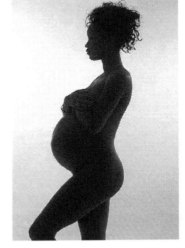

Puberty and the Reproductive Process

We all know that little boys become men and little girls become women. How this takes place, of course, is a complicated process under direct influence of hormones. **Puberty** is the development that occurs during adolescence. Although there is a distinct difference in boys and girls at birth and during childhood, the gonads are mostly quiescent and do not mature until they reach adolescence. This process is initiated by gonadotropic hormones (GnRH) produced in the hypothalamus in the brain. The pituitary gland is influenced by GnRH to produce two hormones. One is called **follicle-stimulation hormone (FSH)** that stimulates the ovary to produce eggs, and the testes to produce sperm. The other is **luteinizing hormone (LH)** that triggers ovulation and sperm production. When the hormones secrete their chemicals, bodily changes take place in boys and in girls. In the U.S. the development of females starts earlier than most other countries. In particular the **menarche** (first menstrual period), begins at about age 12.8 years. Females also begin a growth spurt that starts about age 9 or 10 and continues until age 14. Boys will develop sperm cells **spermarche** (first sperm ejaculation) about the same time, but the growth spurt will not occur until approximately age 14 or 15.

The **primary sexual traits** are those traits present at birth i.e., the presence of the male and female gonads: penis, vagina, testes and ovaries. **Secondary sex traits** unfold during the process of puberty. All of the familiar secondary sex traits are under the influence of hormones. **Examples of these secondary sex traits** include:

- hair growth under the armpit, on the face and pubic areas;
- breast development;
- uterus and vaginal enlargement;
- menarche, menstruation starting;
- body shape forms, fat deposition on the hips and rounding of the buttocks;
- body size increases;
- growth of the larynx increases, voice change lowering, in men and women;
- penis, testes and scrotum enlarge, spermarche, semen ejaculation begins;
- ovulation of eggs begins; and
- sweat glands enlarge, produce more fluids.

Teen Sexual Behavior Changed, by 2008

By every measure, the decade long decline in sexual activity among high school youth leveled off between 2001 and 2007, according to a CDC survey. (CDC, 2007d). And the rise in condom use reached a plateau in 2003. "The bottom line is: In all these areas, we don't seem to be making the progress we were making before," according to CDC/DASH director Howell Wechsler. The report did not identify the reasons for the changes, but experts said they could include: **the rising complacency about HIV/AIDS, changing attitudes about sex and pregnancy, shifts in ethnic diversity and the fact that some teens cannot be persuaded to wait to become sexually active.** Additionally, there is the ongoing array of movies, books, video games, advertising and cultural messages that glamorize sex. One merely has to look at a few contemporary TV ads and TV shows geared to youth to observe the overt sexual messages played before the eyes of youth. This study from the CDC was reported from the YRBS 2007 which polled 14,103 students representing 157 high schools nationwide. This report, again heated up the debate about abstinence-only education not meeting the needs of all kids, and reaffirmed the poor impact of abstinence only sex education without comprehensive sexuality education. (CDC, 2007d). (NPIN, 2008).

Intercourse, Menstruation and Pregnancy

The process of sexual intercourse culminates in pregnancy if a sperm cell fertilizes an egg cell. This will take place after a complex series of events including intercourse, sperm ejaculation, and ovulation, is completed. The menstrual (monthly) cycle is one of the major reproductive functions of the female body. The average length of the entire cycle is 28 days, but some women may have shorter or longer cycles. The first day of the cycle is the actual onset of bleeding. Since this is the easiest to notice, it is referred to as day one. There are four phases in the cycle-- the **menstrual phase, preovulatory phase, ovulation**, and the **postovulatory phase.** Students should review and carefully study the diagrams of the female menstrual cycle located in the appendix.

At day one, the lining of the uterus is sloughed off along with blood and uterine tissue. While this occurs, changes are taking place inside the ovary. The ovary has hundreds of specialized mammalian **Graafian follicles** inside, all maturing at different stages which ultimately release eggs at the rate of one each month. In baby girls, all eggs are present at birth, but don't get released until menarche around age 12; and a woman will produce about 400 eggs throughout her reproductive life. The innermost lining of the uterus, the **endometrium,** gradually increases in thickness from 1 to about 5 mm. (the thickness of a dime). By the 14th day the endometrium is nearly at its maximum thickness of approximately five millimeters. It is at this time that **ovulation (release of eggs)** will usually occur. Students should refer to the appendix for detailed human reproductive diagrams and also point browsers to course docs on the webpage nmatza.net, click on 'reprolesson' for detailed review.

If intercourse takes place while the egg is being ovulated, conception and pregnancy can occur. Human eggs are viable for approximately 24 hours. This means that "theoretically" a woman can only become **pregnant for one day** during the entire 28-day cycle. However, human sperm cells can live about 60-72 hours, and sometimes up to five days, which means that a pregnancy can occur for a period of several days. The problem arises when a couple, especially a teen couple, tries to "guess" or estimate which day is the "safe day." **There is no safe day!** The reason for this is that greater than 60-70% of women do not have an exact "textbook" menstrual cycle, which ovulates exactly every 28 days. Numerous factors may cause this menstrual irregularity. They include: illness, stress, weight gain, STDs, diet and exercise.

Therefore, couples should not rely on trying to determine when it is a *safe* day. Women have gotten pregnant on each of the 28 days, including before, during and after menstruation! A question often asked by teens, and some adults as well is: "When is it safe to have sex and not get pregnant?" **This answer must be repeated: there is not a safe day, to predict with 100% accuracy when a woman is ovulating. Many women have irregular periods as a result of stress, illness, weight loss or gain, or other medical complications.**

There is no safe day to have unprotected intercourse
and avoid a pregnancy.
This is because most women have irregular periods
...Nathan Matza.

Parents' Beliefs About Condoms and Oral Contraceptives

Parents should be the primary source for sexuality education for their kids. Many parents, however, do not feel comfortable discussing sensitive topics. In addition to embarrassment, a major problem with parents is simply lack of knowledge. Eisenberg and colleagues conducted telephone surveys using validated measures to provide data on beliefs about the effectiveness, safety and usability of condoms and the pill among 1,069 parents of 13-17-year-olds in Minnesota and Wisconsin in 2002. Various statistical tests were used to compare beliefs according to sex, age, race, religion, education, income and political orientation. Nearly 4 in 10 parents thought teens were using condoms correctly; almost four in 10 thought that most teenagers could use the pill correctly! Fathers had more accurate views about condoms than mothers, and mothers had a better understanding of the contraceptive pill. Whites were more likely than nonwhites to hold accurate beliefs about the pill's safety and effectiveness; and conservatives were less likely than liberals to hold accurate views about the effectiveness of condoms. **Thus, it is imperative that parents learn the facts and talk to their teens about sexuality, including STD prevention, life goals and the use of contraceptives in order to reinforce the values and mores of the home and accurate data regarding the safety and usability of condoms and the pill.** (Eisenberg, Bearinger, Sievint, et. al, 2004).

Sex Education Needs for Youth and Policies Since 2000

The following summary is adapted from a 2004 report from the Alan Guttmacher Institute: The teenage pregnancy rate is declining in the U.S., especially since about 2000. The proportion of high school students who use condoms has risen, yet U.S. teenagers still have the highest rates of pregnancy, birth and abortion than teenagers in most other developed countries. Nonetheless in the U.S. (1) More than 800,000 women younger than 20 become pregnant each year, (2) 80% of these pregnancies are unintended, (3) Nine million teenagers and young adults acquire an STD each year, and **(4) Two young people become infected with HIV every hour.** U.S. teens have higher rates of STDs and unintended pregnancy because they: are less likely to use contraceptives, have shorter relationships, and have more sexual partners. Other developed countries, especially western Europe, have lower rates of STDs and pregnancy because they have clear and unambiguous prevention messages, strong condemnation of teenage parenthood, societal supports for young people, much greater access to contraceptive and reproductive health services, and most importantly, comprehensive sex education. **Furthermore, many U.S. sex education teachers do not teach about contraception, may not be adequately trained to address sensitive topics, and frequently only spend time on key prevention topics such as HIV/AIDS education and basic anatomy and physiology of reproduction. (AGI, 2004).**

National Data on Teen Sexuality Education

Since 2001, The National Campaign to Prevent Teen and Unplanned Pregnancy has conducted numerous surveys related to teen sexuality behaviors dealing with decisions about relationships, sex, contraception and pregnancy. The 2010 edition *With One Voice* sought to update the recent attitudes and practices and opinions about adolescents including their attitudes and concerns about parents. A few of the findings include:

Parent Power

- Teens continue to say that parents (46%) most influence their decisions about sex. By comparison, just 20% say friends most influence their decisions;
- Hispanic teens (55%) are more likely than non-Hispanic black (50%) and non-Hispanic white (42%) teens to say that parents most influence their decisions about sex;
- Eight in ten teens (80%) say that it would be much easier for teens to delay sexual activity and avoid teen pregnancy if they were able to have more open, honest conversations about these topics with their parents;
- Six in ten teens (62%) wish they were able to talk more openly about relationships with their parents;
- Six in ten teens (63%) and adults (62%) agree that the primary reason teens don't use contraception is because they are afraid that their parents will find out; and
- Most parents say that if they learned that their teen was using contraception, they would be unhappy that they were having sex but happy that their daughter (63%) or son (69%) was using contraception. (National Campaign, 2011).

Knowledge and Fatalism

- Although 78% of teens say they have all the information they need to avoid an unplanned pregnancy: half of teens (49%) admit that they know "little or nothing" about condoms and how to use them, and one-third (34%) agree "it doesn't matter whether you use birth control or not, when it is your time to get pregnant, it will happen."

Abstinence and Contraception

- The overwhelming majority of teens (87%) and adults (93%) agree that it is important for teens to be given a strong message that they should not have sex until they are at least out of high school.; and
- Most teens (46%) and adults (73%) wish young people were getting information about both abstinence and contraception rather than either/or. (National Campaign, 2011).

Sex and regret

- Most teens (65% of girls and 57% of boys) who have had sex say they wish they had waited; and
- Teen girls (70%) are more likely than teen boys (50%) to believe it is very important than teens be encouraged to delay sex.

How Important is Preventing Pregnancy?

- About nine in ten teens (91% of girls and 87% of boys) and two-thirds of adults (66%) say that teen pregnancy is a "very important" problem in the United States;
- About nine in ten teens (95% of girls and 93% of boys) say it is important for them right now to avoid getting pregnant or causing a pregnancy; and

- When asked how they would react to getting pregnant/causing a pregnancy, 24% of girls and 22% of boys said "it would make my life a little more challenging, but I could manage." About seven in ten (69% of girls and 71% of boys) said "it would be a real challenge and I'm not sure how I would manage." (National Campaign, 2011).

Gender Differences
- Significant percentages of teens (63%) and adults (72%) agree that "teen boys often receive the message that they are expected to have sex."
- Most teens (71%) and adults (77%) also agree that "teen girls often receive the message that attracting boys and looking sexy is one of the most important things they can do." (National Campaign, 2011).

Sex or Steady
- Most teens (93% of girls and 88% of boys) say they would rather have a boyfriend/girlfriend and not have sex rather than have sex but not have a boyfriend or girlfriend. (National Campaign, 2011).

Media
- Most teens (79% of girls and 67% of boys) agree with the following statement: "When a TV show or character I like deals with teen pregnancy, it makes me think more about my own risk of becoming pregnant/causing a pregnancy and how to avoid it;"
- Three-quarters of teens (76%) and adults (75%) say that what they see in the media about sex, love, and relationships can be a good way to start conversations about these topics; and
- Among those teens who have watched MTV's 16 and Pregnant, 82% think the show helps teens better understand the challenges of teen pregnancy and parenthood and how to avoid it. (National Campaign, 2011).

Sexting
- Most teens (71%) and adults (81%) agree that sharing nude or semi-nude images of themselves or other teens electronically (through cell phones, websites, and/or social media networks) leads to more sex in real life. (National Campaign, 2011).

- **Teen Pregnancy and Education**
  About nine in ten teens (87%) and adults (90%) believe reducing teen pregnancy is a very effective way to reduce the high school dropout rate and improve academic achievement. (National Campaign, 2011).

Teen pregnancy and Religion
- Most teens (73%) and adults (70%) believe religious leaders and groups should be doing more to help prevent teen pregnancy.

320

The data from the National Campaign referenced above is truly outstanding. It is written very professionally and easy for the layperson to follow, and especially helpful for parents and teachers. The information is researched and scientifically prepared. Readers are encouraged to Google The National Campaign to read this carefully documented study. (National Campaign, 2011).

Teen Pregnancy Data for California Teens

Teenage pregnancy is a nationwide problem in the U.S. Most European countries are shocked when they hear about numbers approaching 1 million pregnancies each year by American teenagers. The pregnancy problem crosses all cultural, racial and socio-economic lines. However, the group with the highest percent of pregnancies is Hispanic teens. The most recent   analysis from the National Campaign to Prevent Teen Pregnancy shows that teen childbearing (teens 19 and younger) in California cost taxpayers (federal, state, and local) at least $896 million in 2004. (National Campaign, 2006; CDE, 2003).

- Of the total 2004 teen childbearing costs in California, 47% were federal costs and 53% were state and local costs;
- Most of the costs of teen childbearing are associated with negative consequences for the children of teen mothers;
- In California, in 2004, annual taxpayer costs associated with children born to teen mothers included: $227 million for public health care (Medicaid and SCHIP); $428 million for child welfare; $294 million for incarceration; and $342 million in lost tax revenue, due to decreased earnings and spending;
- The costs of childbearing are greatest for younger teens. In California, the average annual cost associated with a child born to a mother 17 and younger is $4,224;
- Between 1991 and 2004 there have been more than 855,900 teen births in California, costing taxpayers a total of $17.3 billion over that period;
- Nationally teen childbearing costs taxpayers at least $9.1 billion a year;
- In 1999, more than 57,000 babies were born to teenage mothers in California;
- The problem crosses all racial, cultural and socio-economic lines;
- In 1999, in California, one in three children is born out of wedlock. Among teenagers, this figure rises to two out of every three children;
- Slightly more than one in ten (12%) high school students had four or more sexual partners in their lifetime, with males being more likely to report having multiple partners than females;
- Nearly one-third of sexually active students reported that they drank alcohol or used drugs the last time they had sexual intercourse;
- The fact that national statistics have indicated that low-income and minority youth are less likely to use contraception the first time they have sexual intercourse has particular implications for California; and

321

Over the past two decades, teen childbearing trends in California have largely mirrored those across the United States. (National Campaign, 2006; CDE, 2003).

How does it affect the family, community and society?

- Teen births cost American taxpayers approximately $7 billion in state and federal money each year in public assistance services;
- Research shows that during the first 13 years of parenthood, the average adolescent mother receives AFDC and food stamps valued at more than $1,400 annually;
- Nearly 80 % of all unmarried teen mothers receive public assistance services within five years of the birth of their first child. In fact, some 55% of all mothers on public assistance were teenagers at the time their first child was born; and
- Each family that begins with a birth to a teenager is expected to cost the public an average of about $17,000 a year in some form of support over the next 20 years.

What are the health consequences for a teen mom and her baby?

- Teen mothers under age 15 are more at risk for pregnancy complications, such as premature or prolonged labor, anemia and high blood pressure;
- Low birth weight is more common among teenagers' babies than among those born to women in their twenties. Low birth weight babies are 40 times more likely to die within their first month of life;
- Each year, more than three million teens contract sexually transmitted infections, accounting for about one-fourth of the 12 million Americans infected annually; and
- One-fourth of all new human immunodeficiency virus (HIV) cases each year occur in people ages 13 to 21. Half are among people under age 25. A majority of these infections are transmitted sexually.

How are young parents affected?

- Teenage females who have children before completing high school are less likely to graduate from high school than a teenage female who does not have a child;
- About 64 % of teen mothers graduated from high school or earned a GED within two years after they would have graduated, compared to 94% of young women who did not give birth;
- Teen fathers are more likely to engage in delinquent behaviors and use alcohol routinely, deal drugs or quit school; and

322

- Teen parents are less likely to give their children proper nutrition, health care, cognitive and social stimulation and old-fashioned nurturing - the things all kids need to get a good start in life.

How are children affected?

- Children born to unmarried women who are under the age of 20 and have not completed high school are 10 times more likely to be poor than children born to married women who are 20 or older and have a high school diploma;
- Children born to teenage mothers are more likely to suffer severe health problems and are less likely to receive proper health care; and
- **Children born to teen mothers are more likely to drop out of high school. They have lower grade point averages, poor school attendance and are less likely to go to college. The sons of teen mothers are more likely to end up in jail.**

What do the parents of teens want for their kids?

Too often the multimedia messages regarding sex in America often grossly exaggerate or misrepresent many of the facts about human sexual behavior, mostly to gain the attention of readers of all ages. Sex sells and editors often use sexual headlines or feature stories with little regard to the actual data. Most American parents do want their kids to have a healthy sexual life and do, in fact, support most forms of sex education in schools. It is only a vocal minority, often with political agendas, that gets the attention of the media. Champlin reported that most parents (1) know little about what sex education is taught; (2) **want sex education to cover more;** (3) **want more information** on the basics of reproduction and abstinence; and (4) want more on negotiation skills, rape prevention and how to talk to partners about sex and birth. **Additionally, 80% of parents do want controversial topics, such as abortion and homosexuality, addressed as well. Most parents clearly understand that sex education is a public health issue and not a political issue.** (Champlin, 2002).

How can teachers, parents and schools help alleviate the problem?

- Support the Department of Health Services' programs, such as Family PACT, Community Challenge Grants, Male Involvement Program and Information and Education;
- Talk to youth about the importance of abstaining from sex or being responsible if sexually active;
- Show teens how to make responsible choices;
- Provide teens solid information about abstinence and how to prevent unplanned pregnancy;
- Serve as a role model by exemplifying the type of behavior we want our young people to exhibit;

323

- Show young men what it means to be sexually responsible and remind them that preventing teen pregnancy is an equal responsibility;
- Help youth, especially young men, understand how important it is to respect another person's decision to abstain from sex;
- Encourage teens to get involved in sports and other extracurricular activities;
- Listen to your children and their friends;
- Encourage other adults and parents to be a part of the solution;
- Volunteer in teen pregnancy prevention efforts;
- Provide support to local community organizations by working with teens;
- Encourage teens to seek help if they need it; and
- Discuss the issue with your churches, community organizations, etc. (Champlin, 2002).

Parental Monitoring-Check on your Kids Often!

As parents and families face difficult economic times for jobs, housing, etc., it becomes increasingly more difficult for them to monitor and keep an eye on their children, especially teens. Oftentimes there may only be a single parent, or both parents working which makes it very challenging to supervise kids. Many parents may think that teens are old enough to come home, do chores, start homework, walk the dog etc.; but they may forget that unsupervised kids for even a short time of 2-3 hours could result in risky sexual behavior leading to infection with STDs or pregnancy. Does this mean that teens should be recorded by hidden video cameras in the home, or other sophisticated means? Probably not. But ongoing communication is critical to prevent problems. Even the occasional or unannounced drop in grandparent, neighbor or other adult may help deter the youngster from not following the family rules.

What is parental monitoring?

Parental monitoring includes 1) the expectations parents have for their teen's behavior; 2) the actions parents take to keep track of their teen; and 3) the ways parents respond when their teen breaks the rules. Parents that are consistently checking on their children will do so when they ask questions like: Where will you be? Whom will you be with? What are the names of adults or parents present? When will you be home? Parents should also check with teens by phone (maybe even phone pictures), get to know and meet his or her friends and their parents, and talk with their child regarding making safe choices. Most importantly parents must set and enforce the rules clearly explaining the appropriate consequences. The rules and consequences, however, should evolve as the child matures. Remember that teens' desire for independence can bring opportunities for unhealthy or risky behavior. Research by Guilamo-Ramo and colleagues has shown that teens whose parents use effective monitoring are less likely to make poor decisions such as smoking, drinking, having sex, being physically aggressive or missing school. (Guilamo-Ramo, Jaccard, & Dittus, 2010). When the teens know the parents disapprove of risky behavior, they are less likely to practice these risks. While some parents may find it necessary to read their kids Facebook or other social network page every day; it may just be best to talk face

324

to face and ask their teen what is going on throughout their day. Parents should review, modify and implement many of the tips below, based upon their own family rules and mores to help monitor their teens and keep them safe:

- Talk with your teen about your rules and expectations, and explain consequences for breaking the rules;

- Talk and listen to your teen often about how he or she feels and what he or she is thinking;

- Know who your teen's friends are;

- Talk with your teen about the plans he or she has with friends, what he or she is doing after school, and where he or she will be going;

- Set expectations for when your teen will come home, and expect a call if he or she is going to be late;

- Ask whether an adult will be present when your teen is visiting a friend's home and talk to the adult to confirm;

- Get to know your teen's boyfriend or girlfriend and the parents of your teen's friends. Invite them in to your home;

- Talk with your relatives, your neighbors, your teen's teachers, and other adults who know your teen. Ask them to share what they observe about your teen's behaviors, moods, or friends;

- Monitor how your teen spends money;

- Keep track of how your teen spends time online, and talk about using the Internet safely. Explain that you want them only to 'friend' someone online if they know them in real life;

- Pay attention to your teen's mood and behavior at home, and discuss any concerns you might have;

- If your teen does break a rule, enforce the consequences fairly and consistently. Write the rules and post them on the refrigerator; and

- Make sure your teen knows how to contact you at all times. (Guilamo-Ramo, Jaccard, Dittus, 2010).

Sexual Development

Childhood sexuality is a distinct part of life. It is just another form of learning by a child about the body and the way people relate to one another. It even starts before birth. Clitoral erections, vaginal lubrication and penile erections have been documented even before a child is born. By age 3 or 4 children learn the differences between males and females. Children are curious about their genitals, the source of babies, breasts on their mothers and the penis and beard on their fathers. By age 8 or 9 the overt curiosity may diminish, but the interest still remains.

Adolescent sexuality is literally an explosion of organs, feelings and hormonal production. Teenagers examine their bodies very carefully, usually in private, and count each and every hair or increase in breast size almost on a daily basis. Of course, this is not true of all teenagers, many just let things develop when they are ready.

Puberty is a powerfully emotional time for adolescents. They are questioning authority, thinking about careers, and are often challenging everybody and everything. The values and beliefs they have learned from their families may also be challenged. They are very vulnerable at this time and assign great value on the influence of their peers. Many adolescents find this time very difficult, as they deal with acne, endure voice changes, and literally watch their body parts erupt. Parents also find this a difficult time to communicate with their kids. **Abstinence**, the absence of sexual activity, can be a genuine relief for the adolescent at this time.

Adult sexuality becomes much clearer during adulthood. Nonetheless, adults change in their practices, desires and sexual pleasures. Sexual intensity is highest in men at age 18 and in women at age 30 or beyond. This does not mean that the

best arrangement for a sexual and emotional relationship must include an 18-year-old high school senior boy and a 32-year-old woman! Everyone is an individual with his or her own needs, desires, sexual styles and tastes. Sexuality can continue throughout life. People in their 50s, 60s, 70s and 80s can continue to have a relationship including sex until death. The frequency, duration and type of activity must be discussed and developed as the years pass.

Sexual Preference

Psychiatrist Sigmund Freud argued that we all start off *bisexual*, or attracted to both sexes. As illustrated earlier in this chapter, even during the early stages of fetal development, the genitals are undifferentiated and will only change in appearance under the influence of either **X or Y**-chromosomes. **Sexual orientation** is the attraction to a particular sex. It involves physical, psychological and social factors.

Heterosexuality is the dominant form of sexual orientation in all cultures. Heterosexuality is attraction of the opposite sex. **Homosexuality** is attraction of the same sex. Many cultures have particular taboos related to homosexual relationships, but in reality there is a wide range of sexual preferences. As far back as 1948, Albert Kinsey proposed a **sexual preference continuum.** His continuum included:

- exclusively heterosexual with no homosexual preference;
- predominately heterosexual, only incidentally homosexual;
- predominately heterosexual but more than incidentally homosexual;
- equally homosexual and heterosexual;
- predominately homosexual but more than incidentally heterosexual;
- predominately homosexual but incidentally heterosexual; and
- exclusively homosexual with no heterosexual preference.
(Kinsey, Pomeroy, 1948).

Many researchers in human sexuality have argued where the numbers fall along the spectrum with only about 1-2 % of men and women identifying with the extreme ends of the continuum as exclusively heterosexual or homosexual. The main point is that there is a continuum. Unfortunately homosexuality is a very threatening, upsetting and politically charged topic for many people. Simply because homosexuals are viewed by some as different, does not mean that they are wrong or bad individuals. Many religious groups regard all homosexuality as a form of sin and do not accept it in any form. Yet, there are homosexual clergy, men and women working in all sorts of jobs, and living lives like any other individuals. Being gay is often very difficult since most of society is not. Researchers at the Kinsey Institute of Sex Research in Indiana have studied the origin of homosexuality for over 10 years. The evidence concerning homosexuality is still unclear. It does not come about because of social or psychological conditioning. In 1993, several reports stated that a biochemical explanation for homosexuality may be found within a range of about 100 genes. (Hamer, Copeland, 1995).

Most homosexuals do not fit the stereotypical "feminine-limp-wrist-male gay," or the butch and "dyke" female lesbian. There are gay football players, women models, judges, teachers, lawyers, doctors and rickshaw pullers. The happiest relationships in the gay population, which should not be a surprise, are those that maintain a long lasting, stable, close couple relationship, the equivalent to heterosexual marriages. As California and other states approve gay marriage, perhaps Americans will become less homophobic.

Sexual Variation

What is normal? A woman may choose to wear men's clothing, including a suit and tie. Is this normal? A man may wear a tailored skirt with a shirt and tie. Is this normal? If a woman kisses another woman, is it sexual? What about a man? Many cultures express very different cultural styles, and what is *normal* is very subjective indeed. If a person sees a man wearing a dress walking through a market, does that mean the man is gay? People are individuals and in a cursory glance followed by a judgment we may only see a small part of the individuality or sexual expression, without giving regard to the wholeness of the person being observed. Attraction to individuals of both sexes is called **bisexuality.** Little is known about bisexuals, but the fear of HIV infection has generated much interest. Women are particularly concerned with not knowing the sexual history of their partners in relation to HIV, gay or straight. Researchers believe that the largest groups of bisexuals are married men, rarely have sex with other women and keep their sexual encounters secret.

Transsexuality is the process of having an actual sex change. Most transsexuals are men with feelings and emotions that make them feel like women inside. With extensive counseling, and radical surgery, many men have made the transformation from male to female and are living happy lives. Similarly, women may undergo counseling and operations to transform to a male body and identity. Candidates need to be screened carefully by physicians and psychologists in order to obtain successful transformations. (Crooks, Baur, 1993). The American Psychiatric Association (APA) lists certain sexual practices as **sexual deviations.** They include the following:

- Fetishism-- Obtaining sexual pleasure from an inanimate object or part of the body;
- Pedophilia-- Sex between an adult and a child (a felony in all states);
- Transvestitism --Becoming sexually aroused by wearing clothes of the opposite sex;
- Exhibitionism--Exposing one's genitals to an unwilling observer;
- Voyeurism--Obtaining sexual gratification by observing people undressing or involved in sexual activity;
- Sadism--Becoming sexually aroused by inflicting physical or mental pain; and
- Masochism--Obtaining sexual gratification by suffering physical or mental pain.

Choices for Family Planning

The human body is programmed for reproduction. Everyone does not choose to have children, nor does everyone even decide to have sex! But there is the problem of unwanted pregnancy. Family planning has been going on for thousands of years. Cleopatra reportedly used crocodile dung as a contraceptive; others tried dung of other animals, rags soaked in toxic chemicals and other various herbs and exotic elixirs. **One birth control method described was for a woman to step over a grave at midnight and hold her breath.** (Perhaps this may have caused her to slip and miscarry the fetus)?

By the time a woman is 21 years of age, or if she is sexually active, it is recommended that she has a **gynecological exam (pelvic),** before using contraceptive devices. This usually includes: weight, height, and blood pressure readings. Women should also have a yearly breast exam to check for lumps or other signs of breast cancer. An external palpitation of the abdomen checking for any abnormalities, an internal pelvic exam, during which a Pap smear is taken to check for cervical cancer, and additional tests for pregnancy, or sexually transmitted diseases are performed, if necessary.

Choosing a form of birth control is a very personal decision for couples to make. The decision should be made based upon individual needs, medical problems, and preferences. Most importantly, couples should talk about the options. Are they ready to have a child now? Did they talk about risks for STDs and HIV disease. Do they plan on getting married first and having sexual relations after marriage i.e., practice abstinence until they are ready for a permanent relationship? Think about your own reproductive practices and take charge of your sexual health. Your contraceptive needs may change throughout your life. To decide which method to use now, consider how well each one will work for you:

1. How well will it fit into your lifestyle?
2. How effective will it be?
3. How safe will it be?
4. How affordable will it be?
5. How reversible will it be?
6. Will it help prevent sexually transmitted infections?

Family Planning and Contraceptive Use

Health educators have been teaching about birth control for decades, despite many political, and administrative barriers. Most health teachers go at great length to notify parents about the family life curriculum and lessons on contraceptive use. This allows parents the option of excusing their child without embarrassment. Contraceptive use among sexually active teenagers increased between 1995 and 2002, and teenagers chose more effective contraceptive methods. Perhaps the efforts of health teachers are getting through, at least to some youth. Among contraceptive methods most frequently used by teenagers, the injectable (Depo-Provera and oral contraceptive (the ''pill'') are the most reliable methods, with a failure rate of 0.3 percent with perfect use, followed by the male condom at 2 percent. Methods with higher failure rates with perfect use include periodic abstinence (1–9 percent) and withdrawal (4 percent) (Martinez, Mosher, Dawson, 2004). These numbers may vary, according to correctness of use.

In 2002, 83 percent of never-married female adolescents who had sexual intercourse in the past 3 months had used at least one method of contraception; and the most common methods were condoms and oral contraceptives. Nine percent of sexually experienced teenagers with recent intercourse used other hormonal methods. These methods include injectables (such as **Depo-Provera®** and **LunelleT®** injectables), skin implants (**Implanon®** replacing **Norplant®**) contraceptive patch, and emergency contraception (the use of high-dose oral contraceptives shortly after intercourse i.e., Plan B, progesterone only). Between 1995 and 2002, notable increases in some methods of contraception were observed. The percentage of adolescent women who had ever used the pill increased from 52 percent to 61 percent, and those who had ever used the very effective injectable methods increased from 10 percent to 21 percent over the time period. (Martinez, Mosher, Abma, et al., 2005).

When a couple decides to be sexually intimate, they must communicate about sexual health, emotional concern and contraception. Since most people will use a variety of contraceptive methods throughout their lives, they should become knowledgeable about various contraceptive methods. Most importantly, both partners should be able to talk openly, freely and

329

without embarrassment with their health care worker i.e., nurse, nurse practioner or medical doctor. Whatever method is chosen, it should be one that can be acceptable to both the woman and the man. A detailed reference of various contraceptive methods is the classic reference, *Contraceptive Technology* (2007), by Doctor Robert Hatcher and colleagues. This excellent resource is written for health care workers and health educators, and can be easily understood by the lay public as well. The following summary is adapted from Hatcher's book and his most recent text, *Choices*. (Hatcher, 2007; Hatcher, Rachael & Moynihan, 2010).

Adolescents and birth control methods. Teachers and health care providers that work with adolescents should be aware of several issues that relate specifically to adolescents. U.S. teenagers have the highest STDs of any population, especially ages 15-19; and Chlamydia infection and HPV infection are the most common STDs for adolescents.

Nearly all U.S. adolescents can consent to the confidential diagnosis and treatment of STDs. This can be done without parental consent or knowledge. Many states also allow adolescents to consent to HIV counseling and testing. All forms of birth control are available to minors providing they are over the age of 12. While many feel that it is not morally right for a young child in the 6th grade to receive birth control services, others support the concept that the child may obtain help, prevent a life impacting unplanned pregnancy, receive treatment or even are saved from the possibility of death from HIV. Selecting a method of birth control is a very personal decision for adult women and is even more embarrassing for teenage girls that may not have had a pelvic exam, or have very limited sexual experience. Each method has its risks and the user should read all materials, instructions and enclosures carefully before use. Some methods have side effects that are minor, others could be dangerous if the woman has a particular medical complication. In using various birth control methods it is important to remember that **the total risks to the health of a woman of all forms of birth control are much less than the total risks of a pregnancy!** While many clinics use nurse practitioners (highly trained advanced practice nurses), a medical doctor must be consulted for women and teenagers that may require special care or modifications for different types of birth control.

Margaret Sanger-Family Planning Pioneer

Margaret Sanger was a pioneering leader of the birth control movement in America during the early 1900s. Sanger's personal experience and work as a public health nurse convinced her to encourage people to have smaller families. In 1915, she was arrested for conducting a birth control clinic in Brooklyn, New York and **indicted for sending birth-control information through the mail.** Gradually, however, Sanger won support from the public courts. One New York City clinic, opened by Sanger in 1923, continued to function through the 1970s. In the 1920s, Sanger formed the first American and international birth control conferences, and the National Committee on Federal Legislation for Birth Control. Margaret Sanger gained worldwide renown, respect, and admiration for founding the American birth control movement and, later, the Planned Parenthood Federation of America. Sanger brought about the reversal of federal and state "Comstock laws" that prohibited publication and distribution of information about sex, sexuality, contraception, and human reproduction. Sanger simply wanted to encourage family planning efforts throughout the world. She was a visionary and established the following principles:

- Stated that a woman's right to control her body is the foundation of her human rights;
- Promoted that every person should be able to decide when or whether to have a child;
- Supported the idea that every child should be wanted and loved;
- **Advance the revolutionary idea that women are entitled to sexual pleasure and fulfillment;**
- Furthered the contemporary American model for the protection of civil rights through nonviolent civil disobedience;
- Created access to birth control for low income, minority, and immigrant women; and
- Expanded the American concept of volunteerism and grassroots organizing by setting up a network of volunteer-driven family planning centers across the U.S. (PPA, 2004).

Her books include *Woman and The New Race* (1920), *Happiness in Marriage* (1926), and an autobiography (1938). She was born in Corning, New York. For details on the life of Margaret Sanger see: **www.plannedparenthood.org/**

Family Planning Methods

Masturbation and Insanity?

Too often kids are told not to have sex. Some parents would be happy if their kids never had sex, and the comedian Billy Crystal use to say his daughters are not allowed to have sex until after he dies! Masturbation, or the act of stimulating ones sexual organs is very common in men, and probably very common in many women, although women are often too embarrassed to admit any masturbatory activity. Young adolescents boys; however, are often interested and will discuss it openly among friends, perhaps at the same time they measure penis size and boast about sexual conquest and other sophomoric topics. Masturbation does not cause palms to grow hair or make one become insane. In fact, masturbation can certainly be a great form of sexual relief for teens and adults as well; even though most adults may not admit their private intimate activity. Masturbation is certainly one of the best ways to prevent STDs because one is having sex with someone they 'truly trust!' In the 19th century much was said about the negative consequences of masturbation and the following interesting quote from Dr. Robertson paints the picture of sexual knowledge of the time, circa 1898.

Excerpts from The Transactions of the Medical Society of the State of California, 1898.
Relation existing between the sexual organs and insanity, with especial reference to masturbation by J.W. Robertson, M.D. Llivermore, California

"Of all sexual conditions complicating insanity, none occupy the importance either in the professional or lay mind that masturbation holds. It is a vice of most frequent occurrence amongst our sane population, and it is almost universally practiced by the insane. That masturbation alone, in the normal individual, produces insanity is certainly not true; for were this the fact, the accommodations of our asylums would have to be so increased as to hold at least 500,000 rather than the 5,000 insane credited to our State." "There should be a sharp distinction drawn between the masturbation of insanity and insanity produced by masturbation, or the so-called masturbational insanity. Even when masturbation is most persistent, there is no ground for positively claiming it as a causative factor; this we term the `masturbation of insanity." It is frequently merely the first symptom observed."

"Dr. Hoisholt, of Stockton, said that he heartily agreed with Dr. Robertson in what he had said as to the popular belief in masturbation being a cause of insanity, and also as to the many mutilations that had been made with the excuse of helping to remedy the condition of alienation by removing the ovaries, clitoris, etc. He was of the opinion that more education on the part of the general practitioner of medicine, as to the proper relation existing between insanity and the sexual organs, in the question of cause and effect, was certainly desirable. While, as stated by Dr. Robertson, we very commonly find masturbation accompanying insanity, we very rarely can say that the vice has been to any extent the cause of the insanity itself. It is more often the result than the cause, popular superstition to the contrary." (Robertson, 2001).

Masturbation History: Speaking the Truth in 1994

In the mid 1990s, Dr. Jocelyn Elders became the fifteenth Surgeon General and the first African American woman to be appointed by President Clinton as Surgeon General. Dr. Elders was a staunch advocate for the prevention of teenage pregnancy; but quickly ended her work for the President because of her comments on masturbation. In December of 1994 she answered a question during World AIDS Day in New York City. The question dealt with comprehensive sexuality education and the possibility of masturbation being included in the health education curricula. As quoted from White House transcripts, Dr. elders stated, "I think that is something that is a part of human sexuality and it's a part of something that perhaps should be taught." She did not indicate that teachers should deliver specific methods for masturbation, but simply wished to offer another outlet for youth to prevent pregnancy and STDs. She continued on that day saying, "But we've not even taught our children the very basics. And I feel that we have tried ignorance for a very long time, and it's time we try education." Today most reasonable parents would think of this as a possible way for their children to delay sexual debut and prevent pregnancy and disease; however for her courage and strength of character to say what was right and needed to be said, she was promptly fired by then president Bill Clinton. Her one year in office brought a tragic end to a public health leader sincerely focused on helping youth. (Jehl, 1994).

Abstinence

The percentages of effectiveness compiled in the following summary are calculated based upon 100 women using each method for a period of one year. Remember that **abstinence** is the only method that offers **(100%)** protection from pregnancy and STDs. The **advantages and disadvantages** of **abstinence** include:

Advantages of Abstinence

> ✓ Abstinence is free and available to all;
> ✓ Abstinence may boost an individual's self esteem;
> ✓ Abstinence can be started or returned to at any time in one's life
> ✓ Abstinence may increase the creativity in a relationship as partners express intimacy; and find new ways to express pleasure with each other;
> ✓ Abstinence is extremely effective in preventing pregnancy and STD infection;
> ✓ Abstinence has no medical side effects; and
> ✓ Abstinence is free. (Hatcher, 2007; Hatcher, Rachel, Moynihan, 2010).

Thus a major advantage of abstinence that a couple can still touch, hold each other, give and receive pleasure without intercourse. The percentages listed below about various methods of contraception refer to the number of women experiencing an unintended pregnancy during the first year of **typical use**. The percentages could vary depending upon if a couple used the method exactly the same each and every time- a rather rare occurrence.

Disadvantages of Abstinence

> ✓ Abstinence only education has been shown to be ineffective;
> ✓ Lack of sexual pleasure;
> ✓ Birth control may be unavailable if couples change their mind during a heated moment;
> ✓ Communication with a partner about abstinence may be very difficult;
> ✓ Some couples may become extremely frustrated by not having sex;
> ✓ Abstinence from penis/vagina contact only may increase the risk of STDs, such as anal, oral sex and mutual masturbation.
> ✓ Abstinence may increase the creativity in a relationship as partners find new ways to express intimacy;
> ✓ Abstinence is extremely effective in preventing pregnancy and STD infection;
> ✓ Abstinence has no medical side effects; and
> ✓ Abstinence is free. (Hatcher, 2007; Hatcher, Rachel, Moynihan, 2010).

Outercourse

Intercourse is the obvious direct connection between a couple of the penis and vagina. Outercourse, however, refers to numerous types of sexual intimacy between people that has many distinct advantages, especially to young people and teens. As there is no close contact of penis and vagina, outercourse is essentially almost 100% safe against pregnancy and STDs. Intimacy through outercourse can be accomplished by holding hands, mutual masturbation, kissing, petting above and below the belt. Many women may reach orgasm with only outercourse. If any oral-genital contact takes place, however, the risk of infection may increase. Advantages include no supplies needed, no fluid deposited, no medical complication, may increase closeness and fulfill specific cultural or religious beliefs. Disadvantages include extreme frustration by not having sexual contact, requires extreme willpower by both parties, and if vaginal sex does occur, partners may not have supplies for birth control or protection of STDs. (Hatcher, Rachel, Moynihan, 2010).

Female Sterilization

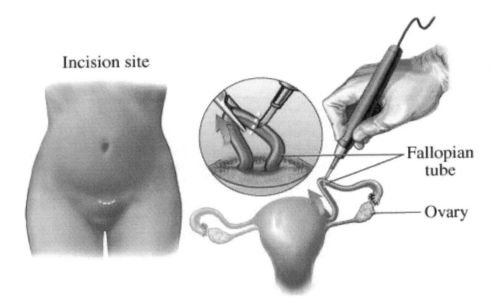

Tubal sterilization is **(99.5%)** effective. This method requires a minor surgical incision into the body by tying or occluding the Fallopian tubes. This procedure is often done after the birth of the last child. **Advantages:** permanent, no other device needed, minimal health risks. **Disadvantages:** reversal very uncommon, no protection against STDs, possible psychological impact of sterilization and its irreversibility.

Withdrawal (70-75% effective)

Withdrawal is the removal of the penis from the vagina during sex. This is an extremely difficult task for a man to control, especially a young adolescent who may have minimal experience with intercourse. When the penis is removed, the man may ejaculate sperm very near the vagina that could ultimately lead to a pregnancy. While this is not very common, it may happen to a teen couple. It is estimated that couples that use the withdrawal method have about a 27% chance of an accidental pregnancy in the first year. (Hatcher, 2010). Some advantages of this method include no fluid deposited into the vagina, no supplies needed, completely private and no use of chemicals, hormones or medications. The disadvantages include a very high risk of pregnancy at a time when a man is very excited and may not be able to remove the penis in time to prevent ejaculation. Additionally, a small amount of liquid present before ejaculation known as 'precum,' secreted from the **bulbourethral gland,** (formerly known as Cowper's gland) could contain sperm cells and result in conception, and this method offers little or no protection against STDs including HIV. (Hatcher, 2010).

Implants (99.5% effective) were introduced and approved by the FDA in 1990. The implants were the first major new type of technology for birth control in the U.S. for many years. Norplants® were 6 slender silicone rubber capsules, each about the size of a matchstick Norplants® were removed from the market in 2002. Today there are now three forms of these **long acting reversible contraceptives** (LARCs), **Implanon®, ParaGard®,** and **Mirena®** They contain the contraceptive steroid **levonorgestrol** and replaced by another product called Implanon®. Implanon® is a relatively new contraceptive technology that's injected underneath the skin of the upper arm by a health care provider. The Food and Drug Administration (FDA)

approved Implanon® in 2006. Implanon® is much like Norplant (which is no longer available in the United States), but with only one rod. The Implanon® rod (pictured above), slowly releases a progestogenic hormone called etonogestrel **over the course of three years.** Implanon® is inserted relatively painlessly into the underside of the arm, upper part. This is done under local anesthesia. The entire process only takes a few minutes to insert. A woman won't be able to see the rod in the skin, unless she is very thin. She can feel the rod with the hand. Insertion problems are rare; but some women may feel a slight swelling.

The rod is about the size of a matchstick (40 mm x 2 mm in diameter), and is made of a biodegradable material commonly used in artificial joints. **Once inserted the rod protects a woman against pregnancy for up to three years.** Women do not ovulate for about the first 30 months. This may be quite advantageous for the mature, responsible adult; for teens, however, it may be just <u>too</u> reliable. Teen girls may think 'everything is cool,' as was stated earlier for STD prevention. **But implants or most other birth control methods, like oral contraceptives, offer no protection against STDs.** (Hatcher, 2010).

How Does Implanon® Work? Implanon® releases a hormone — progestin. The progestin in Implanon® works by keeping a woman's ovaries from releasing eggs — ovulation. Pregnancy cannot happen if there is no egg to join with sperm. The hormone in the implant also prevents pregnancy by thickening a woman's cervical mucus. The mucus blocks sperm and keeps it from joining with an egg. Possible side effects of Implanon® include: Menstrual Changes-This is the most common side effect experienced. The amount of bleeding may vary from irregular or unpredictable spotting and light bleeding. The time in between periods may also vary. For most women, periods become fewer and lighter. **After one year, 1 out of 3 women who use** Implanon® **will stop having periods completely.** Since 1998, there have been more than 4.5 million Implanon® units sold worldwide. It is a progestin-only method of birth control and does not contain estrogen. Implanon® does not contain latex or silicone and will not dissolve. While Implanon® has been used in other countries since 1998, it is not yet widely available in the U.S. Women should check with their health care providers or call their gynecologist for availability. (Hatcher, 2007; Hatcher, Rachel, Moynihan, 2010).

Intrauterine Devices (IUDs) **(97-99% effectiveness)** were all removed from the market in 1986 because of lawsuits and several cases of PID in women. Since 2000 however, a resurgence  of IUDs in the U.S. has taken place for women that choose this method. Because of the problems two decades ago, many women are uninformed about IUDs. Two brands remain, the LNG-IUS® **Mirena IUD** pictured below, and The Copper T® **ParaGard IUD.** ParaGard can remain in the woman's uterus for 10 to 12 years or longer and has been shown to reduce the chances of pregnancy as an emergency contraceptive method to one in one thousand. The mechanism of the IUD works by preventing sperm from fertilizing the egg. They are inserted by a doctor and rest inside the uterus next to the cervix. It was once believed that the IUD inhibited implantation of the newly fertilized blastocyst. This is no longer believed true. **The IUD interferes with the movement of the sperm or inhibits fertilization. This is not a form of abortion, since the sperm never fertilizes the egg.** New research indicates that the risk of bacterial infection from IUD use is very rare. **Advantages:** IUDs are highly effective, protect against ectopic pregnancy, can be left in place for many years, no planning necessary, private, unnoticed and well liked by users. **Disadvantages:** no protection against STDs, possible expulsion unnoticed by some users after a couple of months, cramping, abnormal bleeding, and heavy menstrual flow. (Hatcher, 2007).

The following diagram is an illustration of the **ParaGard IUD** as it would be inserted into the uterus of a woman.

Transdermal Contraceptive Patch (OrthoEvra®) (93-94% effective). The Transdermal contraceptive patch (Ortho Evra) is a lightweight, water-thin, flexible patch that consists of three layers that sticks to a woman's skin (like a bandage) and delivers both estrogen and progestin which stops ovulation. The patch has a protective polyester layer, a

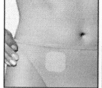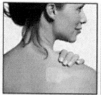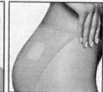

Wearing the Patch
The contraceptive patch can be worn on four places on your body.

Abdomen   Upper Outer Arm   Upper Torso (front or back, but not your breasts)   Buttocks

Source: Ortho-McNeil Pharmaceutical, 2001.

medicated adhesive layer, and a clear liner. Once the hormones are released into the system, they act the same as orally administered hormones to prevent pregnancy. Each patch lasts 7 days, women replace the patch for 3 weeks, then have a 7 day patch-free week, during which time they will start withdrawal bleeding. **Advantages:** The patch is safe, effective and rapidly reversible, may decrease acne and facial hair, does not require any pills or injections, may increase sexual pleasure in women because of lack of pregnancy fears. The patch can be used by women throughout their reproductive life. (Not recommended for smokers over age 35). **Disadvantages:** While the patch avoids the problem of taking a pill daily, and the patch has to be checked and changed weekly. It is also difficult to conceal which limits privacy. **The patch offers no protection against STDs.**

Vaginal Contraceptive Ring (NuvaRing) (99% effective). The NuvaRing (pictured below) is a flexible, soft clear plastic ring that is inserted inside the vagina. The woman places the ring high in the vagina once every 28 days and it is kept in place for 21 days, then removed for a 7-day ring-free period to permit withdrawal bleeding. Most women do not feel any different during intercourse with the NuvaRing in place and hormone levels are adjusted within the first day and contraceptive protection begins without delays, as seen in the Transdermal patch. **Advantages:** The ring is a once a month self-administered method which offers privacy and easy of use for most women. It is also relatively easy for a woman to confirm that the ring is in place. Fewer than 10% of women experience untimely spotting or bleeding. **Disadvantages:** Some women

may not feel comfortable touching their genitals to place the ring inside. The rings may be stored at room temperature, but it is preferred to keep the ring refrigerated to prolong their life. Very few women reported side effects such as headaches, nausea and tenderness of breasts. **The NuvaRing offers no protection against STDs.**

      Vasectomy (99.85% effective) is a method of surgical separation of the vas deferens to prevent sperm from passing out of the body. The procedure is also done with a local anesthetic in a doctor's office and should be considered permanent. Reversals can be performed with success rates of 50-80% reported. **Advantages:** permanent, no preparation needed, no fear of pregnancy. **Disadvantages:** no protection against STDs, possible psychological impact of sterilization and its irreversibility. (Hatcher, 2007; Hatcher, Rachel, Moynihan, 2010).

Birth control pills (97% effective) have been around since 1960. The current varieties of birth control pills available today are much safer than those of the recent past. They work by inhibiting ovulation. **Advantages:** reliable, easily used, reduces menstrual cramping, regulates menstrual cycle, suppresses endometriosis, lower incidence of breast and ovarian cysts, PID and ovarian cancer. **Disadvantages:** Doctors prescription required, irregular menstrual periods, bleeding between periods, nausea, weight gain, fluid retention, breast tenderness, no protection against STDs, risk of circulatory disease (especially for smokers).

FDA Approves Contraceptive With 'Almost' No Periods!

In 2007 the Food and Drug Administration (FDA) approved **Lybrel®**, the first continuous use drug product for prevention of pregnancy. The new contraceptive, Lybrel®, comes in a 28 day-pill pack with low-dose combination tablets that contain 90 micrograms of a progestin, levonorgestrel, and 20 micrograms of an estrogen, ethinyl estradiol, which are active ingredients available in other approved oral contraceptives. Continuous contraception works the same way as the 21 days on-seven days off cycle. It stops the body's monthly preparation for pregnancy by lowering the production of hormones that make pregnancy possible. Other contraceptive pill regimens have placebo or pill-free intervals lasting four to seven days that stimulate a menstrual cycle. Lybrel® is designed to be taken without the placebo or pill-free time interval. **Women who use Lybrel® would not have a scheduled menstrual period, but will most likely have unplanned, breakthrough, unscheduled bleeding or spotting.**

The safety and efficacy of Lybrel® as a contraceptive method were supported by two one-year clinical studies, enrolling more than 2,400 women, ages 18 to 49. Health care professionals and patients are advised that when considering the use of Lybrel®, the convenience of having no scheduled menstruation should be weighed against the inconvenience of unscheduled bleeding or spotting. The occurrence of unscheduled bleeding decreases over time in most women who continue to take Lybrel® for a full year. **In the primary clinical study, 59 percent of the women who took Lybrel® for one year had no bleeding or spotting during the last month of the study.** Like other available oral contraceptives, Lybrel® is effective for prevention of pregnancy when used as directed. The risks of using Lybrel® are similar to the risks of other conventional oral contraceptives and include an increased risk of blood clots, heart attacks, (especially from smokers) and strokes. And, as with other oral contraceptives, Lybrel® does not protect against STDs and HIV infection. (FDA, 2007b).

Depo-Provera® Injection Depo-Provera® may become one of the most popular and widely used methods of birth control in America. **Depo-Provera® (97-99% effectiveness)** is a reversible prescription method of birth control. It is a synthetic hormone that is injected into the buttock or arm every 12 weeks. The hormone is like the one produced by the body to regulate the menstrual cycle. Depo-Provera® hormone keeps the ovaries from releasing eggs. It also thickens the cervical mucus. This keeps sperm from joining with an egg. Depo-Provera® is one of the most effective reversible methods of birth control. Of every 1,000 women who use Depo-Provera®, only three will become pregnant during the first year. Depo-Provera® provides no protection against sexually transmitted infections. **Advantages** of Depo-Provera®: Depo-Provera® is very convenient, and it: prevents pregnancy for 12 weeks; can be used by women who cannot take estrogen; reduces menstrual cramps and anemia; protects against endometrial and ovarian cysts; can be used while breast feeding (six weeks after delivery); and does not need to be taken daily or put in place before vaginal intercourse.

Possible Problems While Using Depo-Provera®

Most women adjust to using Depo-Provera® with few or no problems. However, as with all medicines, there may be some side effects for some women. **It is important to consider that there is no way to stop the effects of Depo-Provera®. Side effects may continue until the shot wears off (12-14 weeks).** It takes an average of 10 months for women to get pregnant after their last injection. For some, it may take only 12 weeks after the last shot to get pregnant. For others, it may take up to 18 months. **Side Effects:** The most common side effect of Depo-Provera® is not serious. It is irregular bleeding. This may include: irregular intervals between periods; longer menstrual flow; spotting between periods; and no bleeding for months at a time. Less common side effects include: increased appetite and weight gain; headache; sore breasts; nausea; nervousness; dizziness; depression; skin rashes or spotty darkening of the skin; hair loss; increased hair on face or body; and, increased or decreased sex drive. These side effects, however, are more common in the first six to 12 months of use. The longer a woman uses Depo-Provera® the more likely that she will stop having menstrual periods. **More than half of Depo-Provera® users have no periods after one year of use.**

Important Concern For Teen Girls. Using an injection method, while an excellent protection against pregnancy, may just be too good of a method for young girls. If a teenager is taking a monthly shot, or using an implant, she may feel so protected as to take risks with her sexual behaviors, such as having multiple partners and placing herself at risk for STDs including HIV infection. These hormone-based products offer no protection against STDs including HIV/AIDS. Couples should continue to use male condoms to protect against pathogenic infection.

Condoms (88% effectiveness) are now readily available for anyone to purchase. No age limits are required for purchase. Condoms are made of latex sheaths that are placed over the penis before intercourse., or polyurethane (plastic) material. **Advantages:** readily available, inexpensive, protection against most STDs, the man takes responsibility, easy to carry and use, available to minors, may prolong ejaculation, available in different colors and sizes. **Disadvantages:** Breakage, storage problems, some people are allergic to latex, forgetting to leave pouch for semen, requires some practice, some men have difficulty keeping an erection wearing a condom, requires water-based

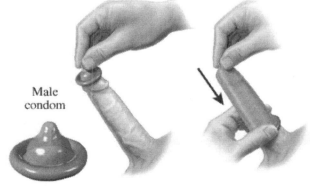

Male condom

lubricants, semen seepage, not placing condom on penis at beginning of intercourse. Sadly, theft has caused some retail stores in high crime areas to lock up condoms, both male and female types, which make it even more difficult or embarrassing especially for teenagers.

Condoms plus spermicidal foam (95% effectiveness) offer protection much greater than either method used alone. Both products are readily available without a prescription. **Advantages:** available OTC, inexpensive, dual responsibility of both partners, and minimal side effects. Easy accessibility and ready availability make this method excellent for teenagers. **Disadvantages:** spermicides offer no protection for STDs (see chapter 9), some allergic reactions to latex or foams, messy, some reduction in sensation. (Hatcher, 2007; Hatcher, Rachel, Moynihan, 2010).

Female condoms (88%, estimated effectiveness) The female condom has been available in Europe since 1992 and was approved by the (FDA) in 1993. It is available in many countries, at least in limited quantities, throughout the world. The female condom (sometimes called FC) is available under several brand names in different countries including Reality, Femidom, Dominique, Femy, Myfemy, Protectiv' and Care. The female condom is

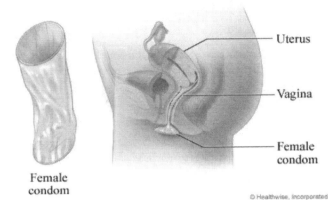

Female condom

Uterus

Vagina

Female condom

© Healthwise, Incorporated

a made of a **polyurethane or nitrile (FC2)** sheath or pouch about 6.5 inches in length. At each end there is a flexible ring. At the closed end of the sheath, the flexible ring is inserted into the vagina to hold the female condom in place. At the other open end of the sheath, the ring stays outside the vulva at the entrance to the vagina. This ring acts as a guide during penetration and it also prevents bunching of the sheath up inside the vagina. The female condom has a silicone-based lubricant on the inside of the condom, but additional lubrication can be used. The condom does not contain spermicide. In 2005 the makers of the female condom announced a new product called FC2. This has the same design as the original version but is made of nitrile, which may make it cheaper to produce. The FC2 began large-scale production in 2007. By 2009, the new female condom became available and approved by the FDA. This version is now made of nitrile, is less expensive and makes **less noise during intercourse**. Many women complained about the noise of previous polyurethane materials. The United Nations Population Fund (UNFPA) is already procuring the FC2. The United States Agency for International Development (USAID) plans to switch to the new product if it gains FDA approval.

The female condom has two rings, one that is closed and comes to rest next to the cervix. This method may be awkward for women. Some women find this approach just another form of female responsibility; but for others it can serve as a protection against STDs and pregnancy, with the woman being fully in charge of her reproductive health. **Advantages:** protects against

340

STDs, the external portion also covers the labia and may offer some additional protection against STDs, easily inserted (can be inserted up to 8 hours before intercourse), no medicines required, rarely breaks, doctor visit not required. **Disadvantage:** cost may be prohibitive for some couples (estimates $2-5 each) planning before intercourse, unacceptable aesthetically for some couples, not as effective against STDs as a male condom, and the outer ring must protrude outside the vulva. The polyethylene female condom also makes noise during penetration, and some couples find this disadvantage unacceptable. **Note: Couples should not use both a male and female condom together because friction of the two services can cause leakage or breakage.**

Cervical caps with spermicides (82% effectiveness) are latex rubber ringed devices that are placed inside the vagina near the cervix. The cervical cap looks like a large thimble with a tall dome. Cervical caps have been used in Europe for several years; but only were approved in the U.S. in 1988. They must be fitted by a doctor, and used with a spermicide. Cervical caps sometimes become dislodged and may scratch the vagina or cervix. **Advantages:** easy to use, left in place for hours, protection of STDs with spermicide, reusable. Can be kept in place for up to 48 hours even with continuous acts of intercourse. **Disadvantages:** Improper fitting, deterioration of latex with oil based medicines, allergic reaction to rubber, cervical abrasions, possible Toxic Shock Syndrome (TSS) if left in place for extended periods.

Diaphragms with spermicide, (82-85% effectiveness) work much the same as the cervical cap, but they are larger in size and must have spermicide added inside the ring of the cup shape, and reapplied if intercourse is repeated. A woman must be fitted for a diaphragm by a doctor and will have to change diaphragms if she has a weight change of 10 pounds or more. Diaphragms are reusable and will last for several years. **Advantages:** reusable, no hormones or medication required, side effects rare, inexpensive. **Disadvantages:** Many women do not like touching their vaginas, improper fitting can be removed too soon (within 6-8 hours after coitus), putting it on may interrupt sex, insufficient amount of spermicide used, leakage and slippage. (Hatcher, 2010).

Fertility Awareness (80% effectiveness) is done by estimating the exact date of a woman's ovulation day. This requires elaborate calendars, and body temperature measurements. Usually, the body temperature drops slightly just before ovulation. A variation of the fertility method is the mucus method where a woman checks the appearance and consistency of cervical mucus to determine ovulation. **Advantages:** accepted by the Catholic church, no medicine or devices needed, always available. **Disadvantages:** irregularity of periods, charting required, no intercourse during "unsafe days."

Spermicides: Foams, creams, suppositories and jellies (70-79% effectiveness) are various preparations of the spermicide **Nonoxynol-9** and are placed on or near the cervix, the opening of the uterus. The spermicide should be inserted less than 1 hour, but at least 15 minutes before intercourse. Spermicides come with **Nonoxynol-9**, which destroy sperm cells on contact. They are all available OTC. They must be inserted with an applicator, or the hand and must dissolve inside the vagina. **Advantages:** purchased OTC, minimal health risks, easy to carry and use, no need for partner involvement. **Disadvantages:** not enough used during intercourse, leaving spermicide in too long before intercourse, messy, poorly dispersed, douching within 6-8 hours after intercourse, allergic reactions. Couples that rely only on spermicides , even if used correctly have about an 18% chance of becoming pregnant. Thus it is recommended that couples use both spermicides and other methods such as   male condoms together. (Hatcher, 2007; Hatcher, Rachel, Moynihan, 2010). To read a very well illustrated source on all of the available contraceptive methods, consult Dr. Robert Hatcher's website by using a search engine such as Google: managingcontraception. Hatcher is an expert and author of the classic and easy to read and understand text, *Contraceptive Technology* now in its 19th edition

New Warning from FDA on Spermicides

In December of 2007, The U.S. Food and Drug Administration (FDA) issued a final rule that manufacturers of over-the-counter (OTC) stand-alone vaginal contraceptive and spermicidal products containing the chemical ingredient nonoxynol 9 (N9) include a warning that the **chemical N9 does not provide protection against infection from HIV (the virus that causes AIDS) or other sexually transmitted diseases (STDs).** These 'stand-alone' spermicides include gels, foams, films, or inserts containing N9 that are used by themselves for contraception. According to administrator Janet Woodcock of the FDA, "FDA is issuing this final rule to correct misconceptions that the chemical N9 in these widely available stand-alone contraceptive products protects against sexually transmitted diseases, including HIV infection." She added, "Clinical research has shown that N9 provides no protection against sexually transmitted diseases to the woman if her sexual partner is infected with an STD pathogen or HIV." Additionally, FDA is requiring that the labels warn consumers that the chemical N9 in stand-alone vaginal contraceptives and spermicides can irritate the vagina and rectum, which may increase the risk of contracting HIV/AIDS from an infected partner. FDA is requiring that labeling of OTC vaginal contraceptive/spermicidal products containing N9 bear the **following warnings**: For vaginal use only, Not for rectal (anal) use. **Sexually transmitted diseases (STDs) alert:** This product does not protect against HIV/AIDS or other STDs and may increase the risk of getting HIV from an infected partner. Do not use if you or your sex partner has HIV/AIDS. If you do not know if you or your sex partner is infected, choose another form of birth control. When using this product you may get vaginal irritation (burning, itching, or a rash). Stop use and ask a doctor if you or your partner get burning, itching, a rash or other irritation of the vagina or penis. You can use nonoxynol 9 for birth control with or without a diaphragm or condom if you have sex with only one partner who is not infected with HIV and who has no other sexual partners or HIV risk factors. When used correctly every time you have sex, latex condoms greatly reduce, but do not eliminate the risk of catching or spreading HIV, the virus that causes AIDS. Use a latex condom without nonoxynol 9 if you or your sex partner has HIV/AIDS, multiple sex partners, or other HIV risk factors. (FDA, 2007). The final rule is posted on the URL: **http://www.fda.gov/OHRMS/DOCKETS/98fr/07-6111.htm**. For an easy to use and easy to understand updated information source on all forms of family planning, consult the URL: **http://www.plannedparenthood.org/.**

The sponge returns. During April 2005, Allendale Pharmaceuticals announced the return of the contraceptive sponge. The sponge was made famous through a famous episode of Seinfield when the character Elaine decided if potential partners were 'spongeworthy.' In 2007

Synova took over the production of the sponge from Allendale and has marketed it again in the U.S. The sponge is a round, disposable device soaked with spermicide that is inserted into the vagina to block a woman's cervix. One sponge can be used for 24 hours through repeated acts of sexual intercourse. The sponge does not contain hormones, as birth control pills do, and is reported to be between 89-91% effective against pregnancy, but offers no protection for STDs.

Today, the need for protection against unwanted pregnancy and STDs is more important than any other time in history. With the introduction of HIV, the deadly virus that causes AIDS, all couples need to communicate about protection and the use of safe sex practices. But what if a man does not wish to cooperate? How can a young teenager communicate about her sexual feelings? Below is a list of related suggestions for condom use:

Condom Comebacks: What to say to your partner

"You won't catch anything from me."

If you love me, respect my health.
Condoms protect. Love doesn't.
It's so sexy when a man cares.
I forgot to take the pill.
No balloon, no party.

"Just this once."

Only kids make decisions like that.
I'm suddenly extremely sleepy.
It only takes once.
No way.

"It spoils the mood."

We could always go to a movie or the mall.
It puts me in the mood.
So does your attitude
Not if I help.

"It takes too long."

You'll be turning me on every second.
I love it when you take your time.
What's the rush?
I'll wait.

"Condoms taste terrible."

Lets try the new flavored ones.
Raspberry is my favorite.

"It doesn't feel good."

When I feel safer, I go wild.
AIDS feels worse.
I'd feel better.
Just wait.

**Or the classic condom comeback of all:
"Either suit up for the game or go play it by yourself!"**

It doesn't matter how you say it. Just find a way to use a condom with every partner, every time. Protect yourself and protect the ones you love.

Unintended Pregnancy: The Options

It is estimated that one in ten women aged 15-19 become pregnant in the U.S. each year, and 80% of those pregnancies are unintended. Pregnancy is the number one cause of high school dropout for girls. Teenagers often must go on welfare to pay for the expenses of the pregnancy and baby. This causes significant economic problems for young adult women and pregnancy and motherhood make them less able to compete in the job market.

Regardless of age or circumstances, an unintended pregnancy can create serious problems and profoundly affect the entire life of the developing fetus. The fathers of these unintended pregnancies also experience a great deal of conflict, and psychological distress. They may feel resentful and isolated, because the woman can make all decisions about her baby while the father is financially responsible for the child that he may not even be able to see or influence. Tragically, fathers concerns are often ignored. **Nonetheless, teachers should remember that the majority of males that inseminate teen girls are men over the age of twenty-one!** Choices for the pregnant female include (1) keeping the baby (2) adoption (3) termination of the pregnancy.

Keeping the baby generates a new set of choices. Should she take care of the child and become a single parent? If feasible, could she marry the father? Perhaps she could stay in her parent's home and use family members to serve as a support system. In many ethnic groups this is very common. Hispanics and African-Americans usually have a larger extended family than do white families. This will allow an aunt, uncle, grandmother or other family member to help with childcare. Often, many white families have their relatives living further away and even out of state making shared childcare difficult. Whatever arrangement is decided, there must be a clear commitment of the childcare provider to help the child develop, especially for the first 5-6 years.

Adoption is a viable choice under certain circumstances. Until about 1970 most women with unintended pregnancies placed their babies for adoption. Today that has changed dramatically. Only about 3-5 % of mothers relinquish their babies for adoption, i.e., **97% of teen girls that allow their pregnancy to go to term, will keep their babies.** Several forms of adoption exist and laws vary from state to state. Teachers should remember to refer to the parents of adopted children as "parents" or "adoptive parents." Such terms as "real parents," or "natural parents," are inappropriate and often confusing and demeaning for the child to understand.

Agency adoption usually involves the state, or local county office of social service that will help the **birth mother** locate adoptive parents. This may be a laborious task involving much documentation during the search. It is important that proper terminology is used to create a positive approach to adoption. **Birth mother** refers to the biological mother and **adoptive mother** refers to the mother receiving the child. Once again, be mindful that such terms as "real mom" or "real dad", or "natural" parents tend to place a negative veil over the adoptive process. If the "real mother" is the natural parent, then does that mean that the adoptive mother is the "unnatural parent?"

Private adoption differs from agency adoption in that it usually involves an attorney that acts as an intermediary to help create a match of the birth parents with the adoptive parents. While the private adoption process may be expensive, costing several thousand dollars, it can be very efficient if all the necessary preparations are completed in advance, and if both parties are continually advised of the progress. If a potential adoptive couple is willing to accept any baby of any race or medical condition, this process can locate a baby very quickly. However, when the couple demands a perfectly healthy, high IQ, beautiful baby, the process becomes difficult. As couples decide to accept a child regardless of racial or ethnic background, their chances will be increased, and most importantly, the child will be able to move into a loving family.

Termination of the pregnancy can occur either naturally by **miscarriage** or **spontaneous abortion.** (Chapter eight discussed the increase risk of health problems to teen mothers and their babies). Or, a woman may decide to terminate the pregnancy herself. This is viewed by many as a very controversial topic and some even consider any form of **induced abortion as murder.** Abortion foes often state that life begins at the moment of conception. Others feel that life begins only when the heart beats at about 5 weeks of gestation. Still others only consider the baby alive after the actual birth process when the infant takes its first breath of air. Legally, a child is not a "person" until after birth.

Abortion is done in several ways. Legally, an abortion can be performed up to the 24th week of pregnancy, but it is very rare that a doctor will perform an abortion past the 10-12 week period. The earlier it is done the simpler the procedure, and the lower the rate of risks to the woman. **Vacuum curettage** accounts for about 90% of abortions in the U.S., and most of these are done within the first trimester, or first 12 weeks of pregnancy. The cervix is opened, and a thin plastic tube is inserted which is connected to a suction pump. The uterine lining along with fetal and placental tissue, is then suctioned out. The entire process can be done in less than one hour.

Beyond the first trimester, the uterus is enlarged and its walls have become thinner. This makes it difficult for the contents to be removed. A doctor must perform a **dilation and curettage (D and C)** that is a safer method at this advanced stage. The D and C is done on a dilated cervix by scraping out the inner wall of the uterus with a metal curette to ensure that all fetal tissue is removed. The Supreme Court has struggled with the debate as well. The historic *Roe vs. Wade* decision in 1973, legalized a woman's right to obtain an abortion from a qualified doctor. In 1989 the Supreme Court again ruled on the issue of abortion. It did not overturn *Roe vs. Wade*, but the new ruling *(Webster vs. Reproductive Health Services)* did uphold a restrictive Missouri abortion law. This law basically allows states to decide on abortion as they see fit. It also restricted the use of taxpayer-supported facilities for abortion. In January of 1993, President Clinton signed an executive order that overruled these restrictions.

Pregnancy termination is a very complex issue. Pro-choice and anti-abortion groups have a very difficult time coming to any compromise. The best way to diffuse the problem is to avoid a pregnancy in the first place. Public schools, colleges and universities should improve educational programs related to sex education topics, including methods of contraception use. Many European countries have sex education taught throughout the entire school years, including discussions on birth control. Many countries such as the Netherlands, have very low rates of abortion and unplanned pregnancies. Americans need to look at other models and see why they work so well.

Psychological considerations may cause certain effects in women after having an abortion. She must live with this decision for her entire life. While serious emotional complications are rare for women that have had abortions, some women and their male partners may suffer depression, grief, regret or sense of loss.

Sexual assault

As sexual messages pervade society, many problems arise. The problems of STDs are epidemic, children are receiving mixed messages about sexuality at a very early age, and the mass media constantly reinforces sexuality through various avenues. Ultimately, problematic sexual behaviors occur. Four major problems that are of great relevance to the adolescent population are (1) child molestation, (2) incest, (3) sexual harassment, and (4) rape.

Child molestation is any sexual interaction forced upon a child, usually anyone under the age of 18. This includes inappropriate touching, fondling, exhibiting sexual organs, oral, anal, or vaginal intercourse. Even making suggestive, sexual remarks to a child is considered a form of molestation. Molesters are often referred to as **pedophiles**, people who perform sexual acts on children and develop a complete fixation on a child as a sexual person, usually with no interest in adult sexual activity. Most pedophiles are males and are often relatives, friends or someone close to the child, such as a minister, teacher or counselor. The stereotypical molester image of an old man, wearing a trench coat, attacking children in back alleys, is not true. That type of molestation only represents a very small percentage of child sexual abusers. In recent years graphic images of child abuse have appeared on the Internet. Teachers, administrators and parents should carefully monitor child exposure to these illegal websites. Most schools now use blocking filters to prevent explicit sexual content from being viewed on school computers; but many technology savvy youth can find ways around blocking filters, even during school!

Incest is sexual activity of any kind between family members. This includes biological relatives, adoptive relatives and **even live-in boyfriends or girlfriends**. Victims of incest suffer from intense psychological damage. Many never fully recover or move on to establish healthy adult sexual relationships. Often, the loss of trust is most pronounced for the victim, especially females; and they cannot relate or trust any male authority figures. This includes future dates, bosses, ushers, or even parking lot attendants that may resemble the perpetrator. There is help available for the victim. Schools and all child care custodians are required by law to file a "suspected child abuse" form for any child that they think may be sexually abused (*PC 11166*). Support groups also exist to help victims. Classes in schools teach children how to protect themselves, not to allow touching in intimate areas, and how to tell someone about the problem. Incest is a felony in most states and is punishable by severe prison sentences. Prosecution and sentencing of perpetrators is difficult because children have a fear of telling, don't remember many of the details, and allow many years to pass before a case even reaches the courtroom. Legal aspects of child abuse and sexual assault are discussed in chapter eleven, and several topics are reviewed as teacher references.

> **Megan's Law now online.** After years of debate and controversy, California law permitted publishing detailed information related to **convicted** sex offenders on the Internet. The website: **http://meganslaw.ca.gov/** now allows users to access names, photos, detailed criminal history and often exact addresses of convicted sex offenders. The website became available in the fall of 2004 and was quickly used by thousands of users. This website should be used with caution to protect the rights of others. It is also imperative for teachers, parents and others to remember that the maps displayed only represent **convicted offenders. Many others are still at large...**

Many times adults go years without discussing sexual abuse that occurred during childhood, and then never report because of statutes of limitation. California passed a new law in 1990 that allows any individual to open a case of child abuse **"at any time such that they can recall the details."** Adult victims are now prosecuting sexual abusers many years after the events occurred. While it may be difficult to prosecute such cases, victims may enjoy a sense of relief or closure when they follow up on specific cases. Since 1994 all public schools that teach human sexuality as part of the curriculum must include instruction on sexual assault and rape prevention. This law is fully explained in chapter 11 on legal aspects of health education.

Rape refers to any form of sex in which one person forces another person to participate. Many states require penetration of the penis into the vagina to establish rape, but in many cases, penile-vaginal contact never occurs. Other forms of sexual assault do occur, such as anal intercourse, oral sex, or penetration of the sex organs by fingers or objects. **Statutory rape** is sexual intercourse with a child. Laws in some states only specify a female as a victim, but California law now includes minor males as well. Teachers must exercise caution in determining the age of the sexual partners when discussing sexual activity with minors. While statutory rape laws are rarely enforced, the majority of male sexual partners of teen girls are over 21 years of age, and it is the relative "age difference" that a judge will take into account when considering prosecuting cases of statutory rape.

Age of consent for sex varies, but most states define the child as anyone under the age of 18. **Acquaintance rape** is the most common form of rape in the youth and young adult population, especially on high school and college campuses. It is forced sex with a friend, partner or other person that the victim knows. Even if a person has been sexually involved with a partner that partner cannot be excused from rape. The problem is that young women may have a difficult time sending messages, such as flirting, teasing and trying to attract a man, without becoming a rape victim. This can be confusing and men also need to be able to read the non-verbal messages that women send by asking women to clarify their intentions related to sexual activity. The American College Health Association suggests the following to **prevent acquaintance rape:**

Women

- Know your sexual desires and limits. If unsure, STOP and talk about it;
- Communicate your limits clearly. Speak firmly, take action;
- Be assertive. Passivity can be interpreted as permission;
- Be aware that your nonverbal actions send a message;
- Pay attention to what is happening around you. Drive your own car if possible;
- Trust your intuitions. If you feel that you are being pressured for unwanted sex, you probably are; and
- Avoid excessive use of alcohol or drugs. They interfere with clear thinking and decisions.

Men

- Know your sexual desires and limits. Communicate them clearly. It's OK not to "score;"
- Intimate relationships are not counted by "points;"
- Being turned down when you ask for sex is not a personal rejection;
- Accept the woman's decision. "No means No." Don't read other meanings into the answer;
- Don't assume that sexy clothes or flirtation means that a woman wants to have sex;
- Don't assume that previous sexual activity implies permission to the current situation; and
- Avoid excessive use of alcohol or drugs. They interfere with clear thinking and decisions.

Protection from sexual assault

Common sense is probably the best recommendation to prevent sexual abuse, however, the list below can be helpful to children and teens. Teens need to learn to practice behaviors that will reduce their risk to sexual assault situations. This information is especially helpful **for those with *limited* "common sense."**

1. Wear clothing that is non-restrictive and functional-it's difficult to run in heels.
2. Take a course in self-defense.
3. Keep emergency phone numbers handy.
4. Discuss safety techniques with friends, neighbors, children and baby sitters.
5. Keep change in your wallet for emergencies.
6. Walk in well-traveled, well-lighted areas.
7. Hold your keys between your fingers, they can become a weapon of defense.
8. Keep a grip on your purse. Use the shoulder strap.
9. If a driver asks directions, and you have fears, say "I don' t know."

10. Scream **FIRE, CALL POLICE**, instead of **help** in an emergency.
11. Always lock your car. Automatic door locks should be a must for all cars.
12. Keep your gas tank filled when driving.
13. Have your keys in your hand when returning to your car, avoid fumbling.
14. If followed, don't drive home, drive to a police station.
15. Don't pick up hitchhikers.
16. Set your auto alarm if equipped.
17. Ask for I.D and verify employment from repair workers.
18. Don't leave extra keys under the doormat.
19. Avoid leaving mail, or other information with your address in open view.
20. List your name on your mailbox with last name and first initials only.
21. Develop a buddy system. Have a friend or neighbor keep an eye out for you.
22. Install a peephole in your front door.
23. If sexually assaulted or raped, call the police and do not take a shower.
24. Request a female officer to take reports if you desire. It is required by law.
25. Keep your phone number and address private, and unlisted, carry a cell phone.
26. Limit any disclosure of personal information, especially on the Internet!

Sexuality and the Future

On June 15, 1989 Michael Harrison, a pediatric surgeon, performed an astonishing procedure on a 24-week-old fetus, **while in the uterus of the mother**. Doctor Harrison opened up the womb, corrected a diaphragmatic hernia, and returned the fetus to the uterus, re-supplied the amniotic fluid, and closed the wound. Seven weeks later--on August 5, 1989, in Ann Arbor Michigan--little Blake Schultz was born by cesarean section. This procedure was truly pioneering. Today there are many more events that are already happening related to sexuality and the birth of children. Some predict that during the 21st century, sexual intercourse, solely for the purpose of having babies, will become extinct. People will still have intercourse, **of course,** but methods of obtaining a child will be very different. Some of the cutting edge procedures include: (1) artificial insemination, (2) artificial inovulation (3) surrogate parenting (4) cloning. Since 2008, the CDC now refers to these methods as Assisted Reproductive Technology (ART).

What is Assisted Reproductive Technology (ART)? Although various definitions have been used for ART, the definition used by CDC is based on the 1992 Fertility Clinic Success Rate and Certification Act that requires CDC to publish the annual ART Success Rates Report. According to this definition, ART includes all fertility treatments in which both eggs and sperm are handled. In general, ART procedures involve surgically removing eggs from a woman's ovaries, combining them with sperm in the laboratory, and returning them to the woman's body or donating them to another woman. They do NOT include treatments in which only sperm are handled (i.e., intrauterine—or artificial—insemination) or procedures in which a woman takes medicine only to stimulate egg production without the intention of having eggs retrieved. (CDC, 2008d). ART has been used in the United States since 1981 to help women become pregnant, most commonly through the transfer of fertilized human eggs into a woman's uterus (in vitro fertilization). However, deciding whether to undergo this expensive and time-consuming treatment can be difficult. According to CDC's 2008 ART Success Rates Report, 148,055 ART cycles were performed at 436 reporting clinics in the United States during 2008, resulting in 46,326 live births (deliveries of one or more living infants) and 61,426 infants. Although the use of ART is still relatively rare as compared to the potential demand, its use has doubled over the past decade. Today, over 1% of all infants born in the United States every year are conceived using ART. Assisted Reproductive Technology can alleviate the burden of infertility on individuals and families, but it can also present challenges to public health, as evidenced by the high rates of multiple delivery, preterm delivery, and low birth-weight delivery experienced with ART. During the past ten years ART technologies have become very sophisticated and women often have to decide on issues related to multiple births; thus monitoring the outcomes of technologies that affect reproduction, such as contraception and ART, has become an important public health and social concern. (CDC, 2008d).

Artificial or assisted insemination is a process in which a doctor physically implants the semen of a man inside the uterus of the mother for fertilization. This practice has been available with animals for over 200 years, but did not become standard medical practice until the 1930s. Couples use this technique if the father is sterile, and often have the semen supplied by a "donor" father. Today, semen can be kept frozen in liquid nitrogen for several years, and when a couple decides to bear a child they can select sperm from a donor. Information about the health history, age, race, and even religion of the donor is given to the potential couple to choose the biological father of their child. Human eggs can now be stored and preserved for years by this method.

Artificial or assisted inovulation (in vitro fertilization, IVF) involves the placing of sperm and eggs in a sterile culture dish. Sometimes this method is called the creation of "test tube babies." Sperm can easily be obtained by ejaculation, but the eggs must be removed under sedation. A needle is attached to an internal ultrasound probe which is inserted virginally. The ultrasound helps locate the ovarian follicles. The needle then punctures each follicle and the fluid is suctioned to remove the eggs and fluid from the follicle. The two gametes are then **fertilized outside the body**, and an embryo will form and be reinserted into the mothers' uterus. Another option is to use a **surrogate** uterus by allowing another woman to bear the child. This surrogate mother will only be supplying the uterus for pregnancy. All the chromosomes, however, were supplied by the biological parents. Some states have banned this practice and refer to the procedure as a form of "prostitution!" Many variations of this technique have occurred since 1978, when Louise Joy Brown was the first child conceived *in vitro* and born in Oldham, England. Maternal grandmothers have been surrogates for their daughters, sisters have supplied the uterus, and single women have been inseminated by sperm donors, or became pregnant by artificial inovulation. Some states do not allow any form of surrogate mothering, and have made it illegal.

Cloning is by far the most radical approach to producing a baby. This process involves taking a somatic cell from the body of a woman and inserting the 46-chromosome compliment into her egg cell after her 23 chromosomes have been removed. An embryo will form and the

351

baby will be a carbon copy clone of the mother, much like taking a cutting from a plant and rooting it to form an entire tree! In 1968, J. B. Gurdon was able to clone frogs, and later it was done with rats and other mammals. In 1997, a sheep named "Dolly" was produced in the laboratory using cloning; but, many states, and the U.S. government has restricted research on cloning of human cells. Cloning may be possible for humans by using surrogates. While numerous news accounts throughout 2001 and 2002 mentioned the possibility of a human clone, no human cloning has occurred as of this writing and by 2010, 15 states have outlawed human cloning. The social and political implications of cloning procedures, however, are complex and mind-boggling. Who is to decide who will get a child? Should single people have less of a priority than couples to choose a child? Other issues involving determination of characteristics of offspring also emerge. Is it moral to only abort female babies? Infanticide to female babies is a common practice in China. Could a professional basketball team clone cells of Shaquille O'Neil to be used a latter date? These are only a few of the issues on the horizon. Many of these reproductive issues will continue to be debated for decades.

Numerous legal cases have been fought in court in recent years. The scientific procedures are developing at a much faster rate then the legal system can accommodate. Many questions need to be answered. Should a divorced female be allowed to use her ex-husband's frozen sperm to bear a child? Do frozen eggs in a lab container have legal rights to the estate of a wealthy deceased couple? Will an attorney decide to allow embryos to survive after the parents have died? Will a clergyperson make a decision on life or death of laboratory embryonic tissues? While many cases of innovative sexual procedures are fascinating in scope, the legal ramifications of these cutting edge procedures can create an endless and very expensive nightmare. For a very interesting and classic novel about cloning, read Nancy Freedman's book *Joshua Son of None* (1978) a story about the cloning of President John F. Kennedy. Copies are available in paperback through the Internet.

Summary

This chapter discussed human sexuality from a number of perspectives. The major focus for the classroom teacher was the impact of sexual topics on adolescents. Issues centering on relationships, marriage, gender identity and anatomy and physiology were explained and illustrated. The topics of teen pregnancy, abstinence, and sexual preference were also explored. Methods of family planning including surgical procedures used today and those procedures and reproductive methods planned for the future, were also identified and reviewed.

Chapter eleven will more fully address the legal implications of sexual assault, rape, child abuse and molestation prevention in such a way as to assist the teacher to act *in loco parentis,* and serve to assist all students in their charge. Human sexuality is much more than the physical act of intercourse, both for adults and children. Many "experts" may not agree as to the appropriate age for youth to become involved with sexuality, but it is undeniable that teens will continue to struggle with their emerging sexuality much the same as do adults.   If adolescents are given well-planned family life or sexuality education programs in school, they may be able to prolong abstinence, avoid STDs exploitation and grow up as happy, well-adjusted adults.

Chapter 11

Health Education: Legal Aspects

No one can safely expose himself to Danger. The man who has often Escaped is caught at last.
...Seneca

The *Commission for Teacher Preparation and Licensing shall privately admonish, publically reprove, revoke or suspend a credential for immoral or unprofessional conduct, for persistent defiance of and refusal to obey, the laws regulating the duties of persons serving in the public school system (EC44421).* The preceding message is offered primarily to help teachers prepare materials in a professional and legal manner when using any controversial health education curricula. The intent of the law is to provide for the help and protection of students and is not intended to find ways to dismiss teachers nor to prosecute them unnecessarily. However, if an educator does not follow procedures, the school board can recommend immediate suspension and or revocation of the certification credential! Teacher candidates are required to take courses that will certify they have not been convicted of a crime, including fingerprinting, specifically to help protect children. While it is rare, school boards have fired teachers for such driving under the influence (DUI), as well as serious offenses l such as; sexual crimes. **Always get written approval, of any topic, in any course that may be controversial and require review by school administrative staff or school board members.** Controversial topics do not always deal with sexuality, and could include such topics as religion, animal research, evolution, global warming, the pledge of allegiance and flag burning. One of the fundamental tenets of the "Code of Ethics of the Teaching Profession" is that **the teacher must protect the health and safety of**

students. This is more than a moral duty. It is also a legal duty as stated by the California Supreme Court. (See The Complete Code of Ethics of the Teaching Profession on page 431).

Warning: For The Protection Of Student's Rights of Privacy; Parental Notification; HIV/AIDS Education; and School Safety and Violence Prevention, Provisions of The California Education Code 51930-51939; 32228 and other mandates, Teachers Must Secure Written School Board Approval Before Discussing Controversial Topics.

Again it cannot be emphasized enough that the above statement is meant to remind teachers to be professional, follow school board policies and address lessons and teaching strategies carefully and cautiously. If a topic may be sensitive or controversial, be sure to discuss it with the administration and **get written approval** before addressing students. Obvious topics such as abortion, contraception, or suicide would normally be taught in a health class; but other subject area teachers may also be addressing controversial topics with their minor students. Examples of other sensitive topics include creationism, gun control, feminism, vampire cults, hate crimes and same sex marriage. While many of these topics are timely and current, and can teach students how to think about different viewpoints, teachers should always discuss these issues with the school administration, before delivering lessons. Many parents would be very unhappy if their child was exposed to topics that do not conform to their personal or religious beliefs. **The goals of this chapter are to help teachers identify laws and policies to protect students, clarify situations that may or may not result in litigation, and practice problem solving on legal and health issues related to the classroom.**

Students completing the health education for teachers' course often have a sense that they will be overwhelmed with significant health, medical and legal problems facing their students. It is not likely that new teachers will have their students attempt suicide, develop eating disorders, recover from drug abuse, explode fireworks, and discuss personal sexual abuse, all by the end of the first month of teaching! It is important, however, that teachers are fully prepared to recognize the problem, write necessary reports, and help the student find proper professional assistance, often by consulting district approved community health agencies. Sometimes this may require legal intervention or even immediate contact with police authorities. Thus while a math teacher may help students construct graphs; an English teacher may help her kids write a poem; or an art teacher may help students design a poster; the teacher should always be cognizant of any legal and or abusive problem that could be impacting the child.

The teacher is a **certificated employee** (some states use the term licensed employee) of the school district and authorized to perform professional duties in charge of minor children. All students are children until they reach age 18, and it is especially important for the secondary educator to remember that even though a few of the students may look like they are 23, they still are minor children! With few exceptions, California law requires children to attend school from age 6-18. It is also important for the educator to think how they would feel if their own children were under the direction of a teacher and the teacher did not carefully monitor, supervise and protect their child. Schoolteachers are public employees and, in addition to teaching subject matter, also serve as guardians of kids in their class. ***In loco parentis*** is the legal phrase that empowers teachers and other adults to **take the place of the parent** in the school setting. While many new, younger, teachers may not have children of their own, or have limited experience with working with youth, they **are required by state law to take charge and provide a reasonably safe and healthy environment for their students.** This may be a significant adjustment for many beginning teachers, and effective classroom management methods are imperative to maintain a positive learning environment. In most cases *in loco parentis* only applies to public schools. Private schools or religious schools still have to follow the law regarding child abuse prevention, etc., but they may set their own guidelines regarding students in their private school environment.

Schools, under the direction of teachers, are required to return students safely home each day hopefully with the same health status as when they left. Litigation may result against a school or teacher due to negligence, inadequate supervision or failure to render appropriate aid to the injured. In a court of law, the **reasonable person** concept is used by lawyers and judges. The words **"reasonable person" are the key terms.** The term **reasonable person** is a phrase used to denote a hypothetical person who exercises qualities of attention, knowledge, intelligence, and judgment that society requires of its members for the protection of their own interest and the interests of others. Try to think how an attorney would think and act in a court case, and use common sense in dealing with minor children under your supervision. Teachers must understand that in a court of law an attorney will use expressions like, "would a reasonable and prudent person allow this child to be endangered by...?" Or, "a reasonable person would never leave minor children unattended..." Every precaution must be taken to protect the student's health, safety and the welfare of other students in the class. As a result of highly publicized recent events of violence in Colorado, and Virginia and the September 11, 2001 tragedy in New York City, professional educators should become very familiar with the most recent laws related to kids and follow administrative guidelines especially from campus police and vice principals in charge of supervision. Since 2009, some schools in Texas now allow teachers to bring guns on campus! While that law may be extreme, teachers should exercise discretion, and strive to use common sense when dealing with students. In this chapter selected topics important to the health status of students to review will include, physical conditions, hazardous conditions, field trips, and a special emphasis on legal aspects for the prevention of child abuse and neglect.

Physical Conditions

America has become an extremely litigious society in recent years. The legal system is overloaded with many genuinely important cases to settle as well as a plethora of frivolous cases that are often thrown out by **"reasonable"** judges. What should seem like the most obvious situation related to the physical environment of students in school, may often be overlooked by the professional educator. Perhaps this is because teachers are so intent in doing their very best focusing on curricula in helping their students to learn, that they may not notice obvious dangers. Since 2000, literally hundreds of schools around the state, and the nation as well, have been undergoing reconstruction, upgrading (such as elevators), to meet the needs of disabled students, and even the building of a few brand new schools. Many of our schools are much older than 50 years. In California, the state has aided schools with funds for older schools; and this, coupled with local tax increases, has allowed schools to undergo great physical changes.

Many of the new changes in schools bring noisy machines, tractors, jackhammers, carpenters and many mounds of dirt on the campus. Teachers should be especially cautious as students move about the campus and may be attracted to dangerous or unsafe situations. A loose brick may look like fun for a child to toss to his or her friends, but could result in serious consequences. Keep watchful for these situations, especially near your classroom.

School boards, which are notoriously strapped for funds, realize that when a lawsuit is brought against them, difficult decisions must be made. School board members usually settle out of court due to lack of funding to pursue a given issue to its end. **A reasonable and prudent** person would ensure that the classroom represents a safe environment in which students can participate without danger to their physical, psychological or emotional well-being. There are many things to consider. Lighting should be regulated, colors cannot be "too bright," and the room temperature should range between 68 and 72 degrees Fahrenheit. Windows cannot open inward. The glass or protruding jagged edges would present a hazard to students working near the window area. Ventilation should be clean and free of particulate matter, dust or toxins such as asbestos, or other pollutants. Portable fans need to have school approval, or should be located out of reach of students.

Emergency systems including evacuation routes for fires, earthquakes or disasters need to be clearly posted, and explained to students. Recent earthquakes in California since the 1990s, and the devastating damage to Japan in 2011 attest to the importance of pre-planning and organization. Keep in mind that many students have arrived in the U.S. from Mexico, Japan, or China and may be extremely sensitive to impending disasters, such as earthquakes or floods that occurred in their native lands. Frequent fire drills and evacuation procedures are given periodically to assure student safety and help children feel safe and prepared in the event of a genuine emergency. Some kids and teachers died during the shootings at Columbine High School in Colorado in 1999, and at Virginia Tech University in 2007. Thus it is critical that teachers, staff and all adults in a school setting be especially watchful to protect all students and employees as well. With the presence of cell phones, text messaging and the Internet, a typical spat between a few kids could quickly escalate to a very dangerous situation in the school environment in only a few minutes. **Any accident that occurs in the classroom, or any suspicion of possible violence, etc., must be reported as soon as possible, in writing, to the appropriate administrator, or campus police.**

Electronic Aggression-The New Cyber Threat to Youth

For many decades, kids have been spreading rumors, writing silly notes in bathroom stalls, and gossiping in endless ways. Remember when you were in elementary or junior high school and kids (especially girls) would send notes around the room shaped like **little triangles** so they could shoot them around the room without the teacher seeing them? It is estimated nowadays that over 80% of adolescents own at least one type of media technology, e.g., cell phone, computer with Internet access, or personal data assistant devices (PDAs). While this explosion of technology has certainly produced many benefits for schoolwork, research, e-mail, etc., the technology can generate significant safety problems as well. Adolescents are using instant messages, e-mail, text messages, and often spend much time on social networking websites. Two major problems resulting are (1) it allows youth to talk to people worldwide, and (2) it allows youth to talk to people worldwide! The latter is not a typographical error. So many times, kids will mention all of the 'friends' that they allow to join their buddy lists, but they may not have ever met these 'friends,' in the real world. A good rule of thumb is that parents should only allow 'real' friends on their kids social network pages.

Kids may feel more comfortable communicating with family, friends, peers and may even develop stronger and safer connections. The opposite problem, however, is that for many youth, who do not interact with 'real live people in the real live world,' have difficulties adjusting to social relationships and reality. Some potential risks of using these new forms of media and ever-evolving technology are also starting to emerge. Many adolescents are becoming victims of **electronic aggression** perpetrated by peers with this new technology. Examples include adolescents creating Web sites or sending e-mail or text messages that are intended to embarrass or harass a peer and/or to threaten physical harm. This activity is gaining much attention, especially by schools, because of the possible risk to safety and possible harm to students. State and federal legislators and schools in Florida, South Carolina, Utah, and Oregon are creating new policies to deal with this new **cyberbullying**. New York City is now enforcing an existing law banning communication devices in school buildings, and Washington State recently passed a law requiring the inclusion of cyberbullying in school district harassment prevention policies. (Hertz, David-Ferdon, 2008). Teachers should be especially watchful and enforce the school rules on cell phones and other **electronic signaling devices**. Schools usually have acceptable usage policies (AUPs) for operating computers on campus, etc., but the portable devices students carry around can be difficult to monitor, and since  the research is new in this area, much more needs to be determined as to the dangers of video games, violent images, etc., and the behavior of young people. Most of the time the conflict, fistfight or other altercation takes place outside the school grounds; but the school is where the problem can start-all from the click of a mouse, or the touch of a button on an electronic device. (David-Ferdon, Feldman, 2007). In 2007, *The Journal of Adolescent Health* published an extensive series of articles dealing with this new **electronic aggression.** More research is currently underway. Click on the following URL for further details of this unique problem: **http://www.jahonline.org/content/suppl07.** Or Google: electronic aggression for numerous updated links.

Electronic Aggression is defined as any type of harassment or bullying (teasing, telling lies, making fun of someone, making rude or mean comments, spreading rumors, or making threatening or aggressive comments) that occurs through email, a chat room, instant messaging, a website (including blogs), or text messaging. (Hertz, David-Ferdon, 2008). Technology and adolescents seem destined for each other; both are young, fast paced, and ever changing. In previous generations teens readily embraced new technologies, such as record players, TVs, cassette players, computers, and VCRs, but the past two decades have witnessed a virtual explosion in new technology, including cell phones, iPods, iPads, MP-3s, DVDs, and PDAs (personal digital assistants) or electronic tablets. While the new technology has been eagerly embraced by adolescents and has led to an expanded vocabulary, including instant messaging ("IMing"), blogging, and text messaging; teachers must be able to respond with the technology in a safe and sometimes curricular manner. For example, while cell phones are often a distraction from learning when used in the classroom, many creative teachers are allowing their students to use their *smart* cell phones to access the Internet in class. Hence, thirty-five kids with cell phones could serve as a mini computer lab session, for free!

In response to this electronic explosion, many states and school districts have, for example, established policies about the use of cell phones on school grounds and developed policies to block access to certain websites on school computers. Many teachers and caregivers have taken action individually by spot-checking websites used by young people, such as Face book. It is important to remember that any kind of aggression is defined perpetrated through technology as any type of harassment or bullying (teasing, telling lies, making fun of someone, making rude or mean comments, sending nude photos electronically, spreading rumors, or making threatening or aggressive comments) that occurs through email, a chat room, instant messaging, a website (including blogs), or text messaging. (Hertz, David-Ferdon, 2008). Finally, teachers as busy workers, not only must prepare lessons and follow guidelines from their districts, they must also carefully monitor any electronic devices to protect all of their students.

Safe Schools Planning Checklist

The California Department of Education (CDE) provides a checklist that school managers, staff and teachers should use to be especially careful to protect kids. Share the list below with fellow colleagues and school leaders to keep your kids safe. Ask your principal if your school has:

1. **Comprehensive School Safety Plan.** A school safety plan has been established and updated annually for the school as required by *California Education Code* Section 32280 et seq. The "Safe Schools - A Planning Guide for Action (2002 Edition)" and the "Safe Schools - A Planning Guide for Action Workbook (2002 Edition)," are excellent resource materials for creating safe and effective schools.

2. **Discipline Policies and Practices.** Existing school-site discipline rules and procedures are regularly reviewed to ensure that they are being appropriately enforced and address student behavior problems and school safety issues. **Student handbooks are given to all students and parents that explain codes of conduct, unacceptable behavior, and disciplinary consequences.**

3. **Funding**. Available funding sources are being targeted to address school safety issues. Funding sources available to nearly every district include the School Safety and Violence Prevention Act funds (Assembly Bill 1113 funds) and Title IV Safe and Drug-Free Schools and Communities funds.

4. **Professional Development Activities**. All school personnel receive appropriate professional development that includes training on current laws affecting school safety, safe school strategies, implementation of science-based prevention curriculum, crisis response planning, consistent enforcement of school discipline policies, and child abuse reporting.

5. **Counseling and Guidance Services**. Effective counseling and guidance services are available to all students (e.g., psychological and social services; attendance improvement; dropout prevention and recovery, and appropriate referral systems).

6. **Collaborative Relationships**. Students, parents, community organizations, and law enforcement agencies are actively involved in activities that contribute to improving school safety.

7. **Safe School Programs and Strategies**. Effective prevention/intervention programs and strategies are being used consistently to create a safe and drug-free learning environment and to address school safety and violence prevention issues that frequently impact campuses such as: **bullying prevention, gang risk intervention, conflict management, classroom management, hate violence-motivated behavior, harassment, internet safety, youth development, student assistance program, or other intervention and referral system.**

8. **Campus Security.** Access to campuses has been appropriately restricted. The use of campus supervisors, security personnel, security equipment (e.g., communication systems, surveillance cameras and other detection devices, etc.), are appropriately utilized. (CDE, 2009).

It may be difficult or uncomfortable for new teachers to discuss the safety issues listed above; but a safe and stress free school is paramount for a healthy school environment. Talk to your principal and be sure that he or she is following the CDE guidelines.

Accurate documentation is extremely important in the event of any accident, fight, or other problem involving students. It is critical that teachers keep a logbook with notes, facts and other detailed information about incidents involving students, fights, and observations about suspected child abuse. Teachers should document specific details of events, and these notes may be subpoenaed in a court of law at a latter date. School boards have detailed policies relating to individual classrooms, the physical setting, and teacher responsibilities in each given district. Emergency beepers or telephones may be required in high crime schools for the protection of all the students and staff. The emergency 911-phone number can be the quickest source of help while teachers are notifying the building administrators. Most high schools employ campus police officers.

Field Trips

In the recent past school field trips were merely an extension of the class and a wonderful enrichment experience for most kids. Kids could visit an art museum, zoo, or participate in the business world during the school day. Keep in mind that many of your students that were born and raised in California and rarely left their own neighborhoods, have never been to the mountains, or have never even seen the Pacific Ocean! Today, however, increased concern about liability, and fuel costs has dramatically limited field trips, or has all but eliminated them for students in many schools. Principals do not want to take any chances that may place kids at risk or harm, and many teachers do not want to deal with the administrative and supervision problems that field trips entail. Cost is often a major factor for field trips, and sometimes the only practical way to obtain funds is by using fund raising volunteer activities such as car washes, or jog-a-thons, etc. Transportation and fuel costs, especially diesel fuel, are often so high that entire school athletic teams and bands have to provide their own transportation to attend athletic events, and field trips beyond 50 miles may be extremely costly and unavailable for students.

An approved field trip is an extension of the classroom experience and all of the school rules, and regulations apply. **From the time the student enters the bus until the time he or she exits, the teacher is in full charge and responsible for the welfare of all students.** It is recommended that teachers secure parental permission slips, with the signature, date and emergency phone numbers **before allowing students to attend any field trip.** While these documents are not legal in court (one cannot sign away the rights of minors), permission slips are an excellent idea to document **reasonable intent** of the teacher and administrative team. This is especially important at the secondary level where students often 'forge' their parent's signature. Students also need to be reminded that school activities come first and field trips are a privilege. Common courtesies, and most school rules, require students to also obtain permission from all the teachers of classes they will not attend.

Field trips cannot be made mandatory and students that remain at school cannot be penalized nor assigned more vigorous work while the class is on the trip. If students on the field trip are given an opportunity to earn "extra credit" by writing reports, etc., students that remain at school must be given the same opportunity. **Students may not be released to anyone on the field trip that is not the parent of the child, legal guardian, or other legally authorized person. Implied consent** is a term that describes a situation in which a teacher acts in a "wishy-washy" or indifferent manner to student requests. If the student wants to dash across the street during lunch on the field trip and the teacher says, "I know you would rather eat at Mac Donald's, but you ought to be here." Instead of, "We will all meet in the cafeteria at 11:45 AM, eat lunch together, and no one will be allowed to leave the area to go off the site." The latter approach, when heard and witnessed by students and others, indicates a more authoritative and specific leadership role of the teacher as the adult supervisor. Litigation could still come about, but the teacher did not 'imply' that students were allowed to run across the street to a restaurant.

Supervision of students is critical. Nowadays, school districts have complex, detailed manuals describing the procedures for field trips. In general, a teacher may need to have 1 adult for each 10 students to supervise students at all times during the trip. **Inadequate supervision** is one of the **most common charges** brought against a teacher in a lawsuit. It may seem complicated or even prohibitive to plan and organize a field trip, but if done with proper approvals, keeping within school guidelines, however, it can be a very rewarding experience for students. A field trip may open up a whole "New World" of knowledge and numerous opportunities, particularly for city kids.

Hazardous Conditions

Leaky faucets, damaged electrical outlets, loose tiles, broken windows, loose roofing materials, or chemical spills, are only a few of the common problems that present a danger to students in school. When a teacher is assigned a classroom, he or she must inspect and check for any problems before students enter. If a genuine hazard exists, mark the work order **emergency, hazardous condition,** and the maintenance staff may respond more quickly.

Simple precautions can be taken to avoid serious accidents or incidents in the classroom. Safety tests are now mandatory for science lab classes, shop classes or other situations that require dangerous equipment. A teacher should identify the electrical power source in the room; locate a switch or valve that may be used to turn off the gas jets in a lab. Many rooms are designed with master controls at the teacher's demonstration area to help avoid student pranks or dangerous activities. This is particularly helpful for substitute teachers. **Safety goggles are a must for any chemical use other than water.** Goggles must meet specific standards, and districts must supply them for all students and staff. Eye washes, chemical showers, and fire blankets should be operable, clearly marked and accessible.

As an additional safety measure, parental permission is required for any "unusual activity" at school. The activity might be a walk to the local mall to visit a business only two blocks from school, use of an electrical device not normally part of the curriculum, or consumption of some special food for a lab demonstration. **When in doubt, teachers should document these events** and keep copies of the paperwork at home.

Liability Insurance-Protect Yourself, Protect your Students

The school district holds insurance policies for employees that protect them against liability during the performance of their duties. As professionals, teachers should also have additional liability insurance to protect themselves while performing their professional duties. Professional organizations usually include liability insurance as part of the professional dues. The California Teachers Association (CTA) provides a $1 million liability insurance policy for its members; this coverage is above and beyond the school insurance liability.

Selected Education Code Sections Related to Health Education

California law requires parents to be notified to allow their child to be given instruction in family life, HIV/AIDS or sex education courses. Selected summaries of *The California Education Code* are reviewed **explained** in detail on the website **http://www.hkresources.org**, and students should thoroughly read *EC 51930–51939* to fully understand the details of these specific laws. A sample letter to parents is also included on page 366 for teachers to adapt for their particular school setting. This letter can be modified for many uses in other classes that may offer any "unusual activity." The laws discussed in the section below and on the Healthy Kids Resource Center website, are selected examples of laws pertaining to students in the public school setting. While the legal documentation on laws related to students is very comprehensive, the laws discussed below serve as a reference for teachers to help them understand the **intent of the law. The primary intent of California laws are designed to protect students, staff members and school personnel.** Sources are taken from the *California Education Code, The California Health* and *Safety Code* and from *The California Penal Code.* The entire collection of all laws in the state of California can be easily accessed on the Internet under California laws on the website **http://www.leginfo.ca.gov/calaw.html**

Most parents consider it very important to reinforce their family morals, values and beliefs as it relates to reproductive health and decisions about sexuality for their children. A small percentage of parents, however, may object to any discussion on sexuality education and may simply have their children excused from that portion of a course. This law does not, however, excuse the student from the entire health education instructional program. The 2004 revised HIV/AIDS mandate *EC 51930–51939* at a minimum, requires school boards to have basic information about prevention of HIV/AIDS, but parents can choose to excuse their child from AIDS prevention lessons as well. If a parent chooses to excuse their child, the child under 18 years of age should not be involved in the discussion and presentation of these topics, even if the child expresses the desire to attend "just because their friends are in class." The teacher should also be cautious and tactful so as not to embarrass the student in front of their classmates. California law requires **parental notification** when their child will be given instruction in family life or sex education courses. Notification is not the same as permission. **School boards may also choose to require written permission for various instruction, etc., but the law on health topics only requires parents to be notified.** The law states, "Whenever any part of the instruction in health, family life education, and sex education conflicts with the religious training and beliefs of the parent or guardian of any pupil, the pupil, upon written request of the parent or guardian, shall be excused from the part of the training which conflicts with such religious training and beliefs, as used in this section, **'religious beliefs' include personal moral convictions."**

Minors and Sexual Activity

Donovan, a social scientist, reported that **that at least half of all babies born to minor women are fathered by adult men.** In addition, there is a widespread perception that these young mothers account for the large increase in welfare caseloads over the last 25 years. A growing number of policy makers, legislators, and community members, have supported enforcing statutory rape laws as a means not only to reduce unwanted pregnancy in teen girls, but also as a way to lower welfare costs. Pregnancy rates can be lowered and welfare costs reduced if states more rigorously enforce statutory rape laws. It is estimated that **adult men over 21 years of age, cause greater than 60% of teen pregnancies** in California. (Donovan, 1997-1999).

Statutory rape

Statutory rape is prohibition of any sexual intercourse between adults and minors. Statutory rape laws are based on the premise that until a person reaches a certain age, that individual is legally incapable of consenting to sexual intercourse. Statutory rape was codified into English law more than 700 years ago, when it became illegal "to ravish," with or without her consent, a "maiden" under the age of 12. In 1576, the age of consent was lowered to 10. Statutory rape laws became part of the American legal system through English common law. Early lawmakers in this country adopted 10 as the age of consent. However, during the 19th century, states gradually raised the age of consent, in some cases to 12. Today, the age of consent ranges from 14 to 18 years of age, in **more than half of the states in the U.S.; the age of**

consent is 16. California age of consent is 18. **(See *California Penal Code* 261.5 for the complete law).**

Recently, statutory rape laws have been applied to males as well as females, and most laws are gender neutral. A few states also permit a defendant to claim that he or she mistakenly believed that the minor was older than was actually the case. Considerable variation exists throughout the states on statutory rape cases. District attorneys have difficulty with these cases because women are frequently reluctant to report rape cases and do not want to go into court and discuss sexual abuse. During the late 1990s, California began a concerted effort to use these laws as a means of reducing pregnancies and births among minor children. In the fall of 1995, Governor Wilson announced a plan allocating $2.4 million of the state's adolescent pregnancy prevention funds to support prosecution of statutory rape cases. The plan, known as **the Statutory Rape Vertical Prosecution Program**, provides funding to hire additional personnel to work exclusively on statutory rape cases.

From a cultural perspective, it is important for teachers to recognize that many other countries, and immigrants living in the U.S., have very different ideas related to age of consent. See the link: **http://www.avert.org/age-of-consent.htm** to view these laws around the world and specific states in the U.S. Each state law, however, will not recognize the laws of students from other countries and any adult having sexual relationships with minors can be prosecuted.

Several other states have also moved to identify and punish "male predators," the term often used by politicians and the media to describe adult men who have sex with minors. Delaware, for example, enacted the "Sexual Predator Act of 1996," which doubles the penalty for adults convicted of having sex with adolescents who are 10 or more years younger than themselves and increases the sentence for adults who have intercourse with minors younger than 14. California law can automatically add 8 years to a rape conviction sentence if the crime was committed using date rape drugs such as GHB, or Rohypnol. Other states like Georgia, Florida, Texas and Pennsylvania have rewritten the laws and raised the age of consent to discourage sexual activity between adults and minors. Most judges decide the merit of many cases based upon the **age difference between the minor and adult before allowing a case to continue.** (Donovan, 1997). In 2011 a very impressive presentation was broadcasted reviewing issues about sexual relations in America with an emphasis on the European approach. The show, "Let's Talk About Sex," was aired on The Learning Channel and is available for purchase. Google "Let's Talk About Sex, 2011" to locate a copy.

It is critical that teachers of all subjects follow the legal mandates to protect students. While 34 students in a class may wish to discuss adoption, pregnancy, vampires, devil worship etc., one child may be very embarrassed and reluctant to hear topics against his or her family teachings. That is why letters to notify parents are imperative. Not just to avoid litigation, but to protect all kids. The sample letter below can be adapted to any school setting.

Important Resource: See *Law in the School* (2000)**, only available online for free download from nmatza.net and click on course documents/laws.**

Sample Letter to Parents Regarding Family Life/Sex Education

Dear Parent:

In conformity with the *California Education Code* Sections **51930**-51939, 60650, 51890, and other mandates, your child will be given instruction in health education. This course includes materials on tobacco, alcohol and drug abuse; sexually transmitted disease education; HIV/AIDS prevention; human sexuality and prevention of sexual assault or rape. Some instruction will include materials, illustrations and discussion of human reproductive function and the prevention of disease.

If you **DO NOT WISH** your child to participate in this area of instruction, please sign and return the tear-off below to the teacher. Because the tear-off portion is small, it is sometimes lost in transit. To ensure that your wishes are known, we suggest that you call the assistant principal, at (123) 123-4567 only if you **DO NOT WISH** your child to receive instruction in the areas described above.

Sincerely,

_____   _____
Health Teacher   Administrator

-------------------------------------tear-off---
To: _____
     Teacher

My child **MAY NOT ATTEND** any classroom instruction dealing with human reproduction or be present when human reproduction organs are pictured or described, or participate in any discussion about HIV/AIDS.

_____   _____
Name of Student   Date

_____   _____
Parent/Guardian Signature   Phone

Major Legislative Changes on Sexuality Education, January 2004. (EC 51930-51939).

Effective January 1, 2004, the California Legislature rewrote, summarized and revised many of the mandates related to sexuality education for K-12 schools. After many debates and arguments, the law was finalized and went into effect on January 1, 2004. Schools may select certain topics to be taught in schools, **but when the law states "shall," instruction becomes mandatory.** Parents, however, do have the right to exclude students from portions of the instruction for personal or religious reasons by notifying the school principal.

The law is called: **The California Comprehensive Sexual Health and HIV/AIDS Prevention Education Act.** The original bill was called SB 71, and written by Senator Shelia Kuhel. The abridged text, **EC 51933,** is listed below. For a complete understanding of the new law, students should read the entire group of mandates, *EC 51930 – 51939.* These laws can be accessed from the California Law link: **http://www.leginfo.ca.gov/calaw.html.**

EC 51933. (a) School districts may provide comprehensive sexual health education, consisting of age-appropriate instruction, in any kindergarten to grade 12, inclusive, **using instructors trained in the appropriate courses.**

(b) A school district that elects to offer comprehensive sexual health education pursuant to subdivision (a), whether taught by school district personnel or outside consultants, **shall satisfy all of the following criteria:**

(1) Instruction and materials shall be age appropriate.

(2) All factual information presented shall be medically accurate and objective.

(3) Instruction shall be made available on an equal basis to a pupil who is an English learner, consistent with the existing curriculum and alternative options for an English learner pupil as otherwise provided in this code.

(4) Instruction and materials shall be appropriate for use with pupils of all races, genders, sexual orientations, ethnic and cultural backgrounds, and pupils with disabilities.

(5) Instruction and materials shall be accessible to pupils with disabilities, including, but not limited to, the provision of a modified curriculum, materials and instruction in alternative formats, and auxiliary aids.

(6) Instruction and materials shall encourage a pupil to communicate with his or her parents or guardians about human sexuality.

(7) **Instruction and materials shall teach respect for marriage and committed relationships.**

(8) Commencing in grade 7, instruction and materials shall teach that abstinence from sexual intercourse is the only certain way to prevent unintended pregnancy, teach that abstinence from sexual activity is the only certain way to prevent sexually transmitted diseases, and **provide information about the value of abstinence while also providing medically accurate information on other methods of preventing pregnancy and sexually transmitted diseases.**

(9) Commencing in grade 7, instruction and materials shall provide information about sexually transmitted diseases. This instruction shall include how sexually transmitted diseases are and are not transmitted, the effectiveness and safety of all federal Food and Drug

Administration (FDA) approved methods of reducing the risk of contracting sexually transmitted diseases, and information on local resources for testing and medical care for sexually transmitted diseases.

(10) **Commencing in grade 7, instruction and materials shall provide information about the effectiveness and safety of all FDA-approved contraceptive methods in preventing pregnancy, including, but not limited to, emergency contraception.**

(11) Commencing in grade 7, instruction and materials shall provide pupils with skills for making and implementing responsible decisions about sexuality.

(12) Commencing in grade 7, instruction and materials shall provide pupils with information on the law on surrendering physical custody of a minor child 72 hours or younger, pursuant to Section 1255.7 of the Health and Safety Code and Section 271.5 of the Penal Code.

(c) A school district that elects to offer comprehensive sexual health education pursuant to subdivision (a) earlier than grade 7 may provide age appropriate and medically accurate information on any of the general topics contained in paragraphs (8) to (12), inclusive, of subdivision (b). (d) If a school district elects to offer comprehensive sexual health education pursuant to subdivision (a), whether taught by school district personnel or outside consultants, the school district shall comply with the following:

(1) **Instruction and materials may not teach or promote religious doctrine.**

(2) Instruction and materials may not reflect or promote bias against any person on the basis of any category protected by Section 220.

Food Sales, Nutrition and Obesity Prevention (EC 49430-49431).

Earlier discussion in this text, and classroom presentations reviewed the major national epidemic of obesity in the U.S. During March of 2005, California Governor Arnold Schwarzenegger stated he wanted to ban all sales of junk food in California schools. "Vending machines in schools should be filled with fresh fruits, vegetables and milk," Schwarzenegger said during a question-and-answer session with fans on the final day of his Arnold Classic bodybuilding weekend. (Werner, 2005). The governor was concerned about the health of kids, but the legislature has already taken steps to assist schools to improve the nutritional health of youth, and hopefully reduce the major obesity problem. Legislation was introduced in the 2005-2006 session by Senator Martha Escutia, D-Norwalk, which would ban soft drink sales in public schools. Since 2002, many school districts have implemented various programs to improve nutrition. San Francisco, Los Angeles Unified, Santa Ana Unified and numerous other school districts have implemented specific guidelines aligned with the state mandates listed below which ban sales of junk foods. While these new laws only included grades K-8, many schools also included 9-12 graders. The legislators originally reacted to numerous special groups to exclude high school kids because "high school kids were mature enough to make proper nutrition decisions." Finally, on July 1, 2007, high school kids were also included as described in *EC 49431*. Still, many schools and teachers may not be in compliance and are still selling candy, or have vending machines selling soda for fund raising.

Teachers must remember how powerful they serve as role models to their students. It is not necessary to hide all junk foods consumed by teachers in front of students, but teachers should not reward students with candy or other poor nutritional foods. Some anecdotal data in 2005 have reported teachers not only selling candy within their classrooms, but some educators would sell sodas, etc., from the faculty lounge! As these newer laws are implemented, students, teachers, schools, and districts will adjust and hopefully become healthier. Kids and their schools should not become slaves to the soda marketing contracts used as fund raising programs. Readers are encouraged to read the entire group of new nutrition related mandates **EC 49430-49436.** Several laws are excerpted and listed below.

California Education Code Section 49430-49436

49431.   (a) At each elementary school, and in those schools participating in the pilot program created pursuant to Section 49433.7, the sale of all foods on school grounds shall be approved for compliance with the nutrition standards in this section by the person or persons responsible for implementing these provisions as designated by the school district.

(b) (1) At each elementary school, the only food that may be sold to a pupil during breakfast and lunch periods is food that is sold as a full meal. This paragraph does not prohibit the sale of fruit, nonfried vegetables, legumes, beverages, dairy products, or grain products as individual food items if they meet the requirements set forth in this subdivision.

(2) An individual food item sold to a pupil during morning or afternoon breaks at an elementary school shall meet all of the following standards: (A) Not more than 35 percent of its total calories shall be from fat. This subparagraph does not apply to the sale of nuts or seeds.

(B) Not more than 10 percent of its total calories shall be from saturated fat.

(C) **Not more than 35 percent of its total weight shall be composed of sugar**. This subparagraph does not apply to the sale of fruits or vegetables.

(c) An elementary school may permit the sale of food items that do not comply with subdivision (a) or (b) as part of a school fundraising event in any of the following circumstances:

(1) The items are sold by pupils of the school and the sale of those items takes place off of school premises.

(2) The items are sold by pupils of the school and the sale of those items takes place at least one-half hour after the end of the school day.

(d) Notwithstanding Article 3 (commencing with Section 33050) of Chapter 1 of Part 20, compliance with this section may not be waived.

49431.5. (a) **Commencing July 1, 2004, regardless of the time of day,** beverages, other than water, milk, 100 percent fruit juices, or fruit-based drinks that are composed of no less than 50 percent fruit juice and have no added sweeteners, may not be sold to a pupil at an elementary school.

(b) An elementary school may permit the sale of beverages that do not comply with subdivision (a) as part of a school fundraising event in any of the following circumstances:

(1) The items are sold by pupils of the school and the **sale of those items takes place off the premises of the school.**

(2) The items are sold by pupils of the school and the sale of those items **takes place one-half hour or more after the end of the school day.**

(c) Commencing July 1, 2004, from one-half hour before the start of the school day to one-half hour after the end of the school day, **only the following beverages may be sold to a pupil at a middle or junior high school:**

(1) Fruit-based drinks that are composed of no less than 50 percent fruit juice and have no added sweeteners.

(2) Drinking water.

(3) Milk, including, but not limited to, chocolate milk, soy milk, rice milk, and other similar dairy or nondairy milk.

(4) An electrolyte replacement beverage that contains no more than 42 grams of added sweetener per 20-ounce serving.

(d) A middle or junior high school may permit the sale of beverages that do not comply with subdivision (c) as part of a school event if the sale of those items meets all of the following criteria:

(1) The sale occurs during a school-sponsored event and takes place at the location of that event after the end of the school day.

(2) Vending machines, pupil stores, and cafeterias are not used no sooner than one-half hour after the end of the school day.

(e) This section does not prohibit an elementary, middle or junior high school from making available through a vending machine any beverage allowed under subdivision (a) or (c) at any time of day, or, in middle and junior high schools, any product that does not comply with subdivision (c) if the product only is available not later than one-half hour before the start of the school day and not sooner than one-half hour after the end of the school day.

(f) For the purposes of this section, "added sweetener" means any additive that enhances the sweetness of the beverage, including, but not limited to, added sugar, but does not include the natural sugar or sugars that are contained within the fruit juice which is a component of the beverage.

49431.2. (a) **Commencing July 1, 2007**, snacks sold to a pupil in middle, junior, or high school, except food served as part of a USDA meal program, shall meet all of the following standards:

(1) Not more than 35 percent of its total calories shall be from fat. This paragraph does not apply to the sale of nuts, nut butters, seeds, eggs, cheese packaged for individual sale, fruits, vegetables that have not been deep fried, or legumes.

(2) Not more than 10 percent of its total calories shall be from saturated fat. This subparagraph does not apply to eggs or cheese packaged for individual sale.

(3) Not more than 35 percent of its total weight shall be composed of sugar, including naturally occurring and added sugars. This paragraph does not apply to the sale of fruits or vegetables that have not been deep fried.

(4) No more than 250 calories per individual food item.

(b) Commencing July 1, 2007, entree items sold to a pupil in middle, junior, or high school, except food served as part of a USDA meal program, shall contain no more than 400 calories per entree, shall contain no more than 4 grams of fat per 100 calories contained in each entree, and shall be categorized as entree items in the School Breakfast Program or National School Lunch Program.

(c) A middle, junior, or high school may permit the sale of food items that do not comply with subdivision (a) or (b) in any of the following circumstances:

(1) The sale of those items takes place off of and away from school premises.

(2) The sale of those items takes place on school premises at least one-half hour after the end of the school day.

(3) The sale of those items occurs during a school-sponsored pupil activity after the end of the school day.

(d) It is the intent of the Legislature that the governing board of a school district annually review its compliance with the nutrition standards described in this section.

49432. By January 1, 2004, every public school may post a summary of nutrition and physical activity laws and regulations, and shall post the school district's nutrition and physical activity policies, in public view within all school cafeterias or other central eating areas. The State Department of Education shall develop the summary of state law and regulations.

For a detailed discussion of these new laws, point your browser to the California Law: **http://www.leginfo.ca.gov/calaw.html**

How To Lose Your Credential! *(EC 44421)*

The certification document of any person charged with the responsibility of making any instructional material available for inspection under this section or who is charged with the responsibility of notifying a parent or guardian of any class conduct within the purview of this section, and who knowingly and willfully fails to make such instructional material available for inspection or to notify such parent or guardian, may be revoked or suspended because of such act. The certification document of any person who knowingly and willfully requires a pupil to attend a class within the purview of this section when a request that the pupil not attend has been received from the parent or guardian may be revoked or suspended because of such act. *(EC 44421)*.

Preventing Violence and Gang Behavior is now considered a public health problem and not merely a police matter. Schools need to be prepared and proactive to protect students from violence. Gangs, violence and criminal behavior are all now classified as a public health issue because mortality and morbidity rates have profoundly impacted youth populations, especially among young black males. In 1994, an Orange County California high school took a proactive stance to prevent violence and developed emergency procedures beyond the classical problems of fires, and earthquakes. Teachers and administrators consulted local police authorities for expert information, and a detailed plan was researched, published and implemented for teachers and all staff members. Topics include:

- general emergency procedures-911 calls, who to call on campus;
- lock down instructions;
- bomb threats-"what to do and not do;"
- student safety;
- gunfire on campus, and drive-by shootings;
- hostage incidents;
- psychotic, narcotic, or suicidal student;
- riot or gang incident;
- violent student in class, armed and unarmed, and
- incident reports and witnesses.
  (Carr, Eliot, 1994, 2002).

The National Center for Mental Health Promotion and Youth Violence Prevention (NCMHP), provides technical assistance and training to 83 school districts and communities that receive grants from the Substance Abuse and Mental Health Services Administration (SAMHSA) of the U.S. Department of Health and Human Services. They offer many programs and services to schools and also make recommendations and key strategies to prevent violence from erupting. Some of the NCMHP suggestions include:

- Policies that control the availability of alcohol, tobacco, other drugs, and weapons through pricing, deterrence, and incentives for not using, and restrictions on availability;
- Price increases can also reduce alcohol-related problems, including motor vehicle crashes, driving while intoxicated, rape, robbery, suicide, and cancer death rates;
- Restricting the use of tobacco in public places and private workplaces because it lowers average daily cigarette consumption among adults and youth;
- Imposing severe penalties for carrying concealed handguns without a permit reduced firearm homicides and robberies;
- Prohibiting alcohol and tobacco billboards and other forms of outdoor advertising near schools and other locations where children are likely to be present;
- Limiting the number of alcohol and tobacco advertisements that can be placed in the windows of alcohol retail outlets;
- Publicizing efforts to limit alcohol, tobacco, and firearms advertising and industry sponsorships;
- Increasing the price of alcohol or tobacco through excise taxes is associated with effectively reducing consumption vehicle crashes, driving while intoxicated, rape, robbery, suicide, and cancer death rates;
- Setting the legal blood alcohol content limit to .00 or .02 for people under the age of 21 significantly reduces traffic deaths among young

372

people;

- Educate adults about keeping guns and other weapons out of reach of children;
- Increase local and state budgets for effective prevention programs, including community policing and high-risk youth programs; and
- Reclaim housing projects, parks, and other places where young people congregate to drink alcohol or to buy, sell, or abuse drugs. (NCMHP, 2004).

While most of the suggestions or key strategies listed above deal with alcohol, tobacco or weapons; it is important for the teacher to remember that those products may be influencing violence in many communities, especially when readily available to youth. The website for NCMHP is: **http://www.promoteprevent.org/**.

Many educators enter the teaching profession with much enthusiasm, excitement, and energy trying to do their best to meet the needs of their students. They read all the latest data related to their subject specialty and genuinely want to teach their students the most current facts. In their zeal, they may jump too quickly from reading relevant materials that can be shared with students to presenting that information without obtaining necessary board approval. This is true in all subject matter areas. Social studies teachers may wish to discuss the politics of abortion. English teachers may read from the poetry of Chaucer that may offend some parents in the community. Biology teachers might need special approval to discuss creationism, intelligent design and evolution. Even a math teacher could be admonished for using statistics of teen drug or pregnancy rates while giving a lesson on graphing. Health education addresses many topics that are socially and politically relevant and can generate controversy if materials are not prepared and implemented in a professional manner, with full approval of local parents through the governing school board. Family life education is one topic that needs to be carefully examined in such a way as to show students all sides or points of view.

The *Family Life-Sex Education Guidelines*, published by the California State Department of Education in 1987, was an attempt to help districts develop local procedures for instruction in human sexuality. The Guideline recommends a district wide Family Life Education Advisory Committee composed of educators, nurses, and a wide variety of community members. Districts need to decide how topics such as homosexuality, abortion, contraception, and masturbation will, or will not, be addressed. Parents should be informed of the district's position, and teachers should receive specific training in fulfilling the district's policy.

Some districts may avoid all instruction related to controversial topics. This approach may increase students' interest in controversial issues and does not provide students with information they need to make decisions. Other approaches vary from presenting limited information to directing students to examine all viewpoints. One approach is to prepare a statement, limit discussion to that statement, and then refer students to their families or religious leaders for a detailed follow up discussion.

Another approach is to lead students in an objective discussion that helps them analyze situations from many points of view. The teacher would neither support a partisan nor maintain a neutral position, but would help students examine various aspects of a given controversial topic. The topic of abortion, for example, can be discussed by students by considering implications of psychological and physical effects, emotional trauma and consequences of repeated abortions. The State Guidelines state, "The teacher, school, and material should avoid either advocating or censuring abortion." (CDE, 1987).

Child Abuse and Neglect

Sixteen year old Wanda came home from a date at 2 AM on a school night. Her father was waiting in the living room and went into a rage when she arrived. She was warned that she was to be home no later than 11 PM and he pushed Wanda very hard across the room and slammed her into a wall. Wanda bruised her knee and was very upset from his actions. Is this an example of child abuse? Maybe yes and maybe no. All parents reach a point where they "blow their cool" and overact. Wanda's dad may have a close relationship with her, but just went overboard in this one time **episodic event.** What then is child abuse? How does it affect the classroom teacher? And what does a professional educator have to do as a mandated reporter?

It is estimated that there are as many as three million children abused or neglected in America every year, including five thousand deaths due to child abuse. While this large number may be shocking to some, experts agree that this is only an estimate and probably under-represents the actual problem. (Johnson, 1992; Mead, 2006). Parents and others have been trying to discipline children for thousands of years. For many years it was a private matter and dealt with within the home or family setting. It wasn't until the twentieth century that children were considered property and parents could do as they wished with them regarding chores, punishment or abuse. Religious groups for centuries stated, "spare the rod and spoil the child." **It was only as recently as 1986 that corporal punishment was outlawed in public schools in California.** Nonetheless, as of 2008 the following states do allow some form of corporal punishment, i.e., **paddling of kids**: Alabama, Arizona, Arkansas, Colorado, Florida, Georgia, Idaho Indiana, Kansas, Kentucky, Louisiana, Mississippi, Missouri, New Mexico, North Carolina, Ohio, Oklahoma, South Carolina, Tennessee and Texas. There are several bills in Congress to encourage these states to reconsider and/or eliminate corporal punishment. For details about this issue, Google: U.S. states allowing corporal punishment. (CFED, 2011).

Why would anyone want to deliberately harm a child, especially his or her own flesh and blood? The scope and extent of the problem is overwhelming for most to comprehend, but the fact remains that child abuse does exist. Child abuse exists in all schools and at all socioeconomic levels. Child abuse prevention expert James Mead stated,

> Child abuse is a serious problem that dates back as far as recorded history. Over the centuries children have been killed, abandoned, neglected, and chastised with cruelty. Despite this, the maltreatment of children by their parents has aroused public concern only in recent times. The motives for killing and abusing children

are many. The practice of infanticide, which is the killing of newborn babies by drowning, suffocation, exposure to the elements, or throwing them away, recurs throughout history for many reasons. (Mead, Balch, Maggio, 1985).

Many studies show that 90% of convicted criminals were abused as children. There are numerous theories, ideas and opinions as to why an adult would abuse a child. Several of these ideas are listed below. Significant causative factors for abuse to date include:

Parent abused as a child. Of parents currently identified as abusers, 85 to 90 percent were abused themselves.

Unrealistic expectations. Too often parents see their own lives being replayed through their child. The father may want his son to be a football player because he played football; the mother may want her daughter to succeed in school, or become a beauty queen, because she was a beauty queen. Perhaps the parents want their children to succeed **because they did not succeed as children themselves.** A younger child may be expected to be toilet trained merely for the convenience of the parent, and not because the level of development of the child has moved at a rate that pleases the parent. Parents may see the lack of compliance as a form of disobedience.

Parental stress. Everyone has to deal with stress at work, at home or with friends. Some parents may have heavy involvement with alcoholism, drug addiction, prostitution, marital or financial problems, teen pregnancy, or illegal activities that can lead to abuse of the child.

Social isolation. So many families are disintegrated in the U.S. today. Social scientists see the decomposition of the nuclear family as a major factor related to crime and decreased child success in school. Less than 10% of American families have this **"nuclear family"** relationship, which includes both biological parents. Rare are the households of yesterday with dad going to work, mom at home taking care of the kids and the house, with a dog named Rusty! Families are separated and live in many places in this country. Quite often there is no significant adult for the child to come home to, this is especially true when both parents work.

Delay in maternal infant bonding. The process of maternal infant bonding begins when the parent makes first eye contact with the child. Common problems that inhibit this bonding are low birth weight, FAS, premature birth and Cesarean birth. Neonatal stress often results. Numerous problems to the new baby result and the infant is immediately taken to the neonatal intensive care unit. The longer the delay in bonding, the greater the risk to the child becomes.

Over punishment. All children act up in some fashion or another. Many parents lack the skill or knowledge to discipline them appropriately and overreact in certain family situations. The adult may gain emotional relief by punishing the child, but the child may suffer deep emotional scars as a result. Punishment may become more severe, more frequent and ultimately escalate to the level that can endanger the life of the child.

Lack of education. The role model a child sees when growing up will very likely be the model the child will use to raise their own children. Parents that fail to study techniques of child rearing allow their emotions to berate the child, or simply do not want to learn how to help their children. The child may develop more tolerance to abuse while living with a constant regimen of maltreatment.

Defining Abuse

Child abuse is defined as **"any non-accidental act of commission or omission that endangers a child's physical, mental or emotional well being."** (Mead, 1985). This may include assault, corporal punishment, neglect, inadequate supervision, sexual abuse or exploitation.

Signs and Symptoms of Abuse

Teachers are in a unique position to help observe, evaluate and report any possible situations related to child abuse. Those teachers that work with students in athletics, physical education, dance, or cheerleading, may observe students' arms, legs, etc., more often, and notice visible bruises or injuries.   A classroom teacher may notice injuries on the back of students' arms or legs simply by walking up and down the isles in class and observing very carefully. Others may notice a particular sensitivity or shyness from the student that does not seem characteristic of their personality. The important point to remember is that **teachers report suspicions and do not diagnose signs of abuse.** This problem may be very upsetting and emotional for an educator, but it is best for educators to follow the law, write the report, provide the student with emotional support, if feasible, and then **go back to work. Common signs and symptoms of child abuse include:**

- injuries to several body surfaces;
- bruises of different ages or colors;
- wrap around injuries (belt marks, cords, wires);
- imprint objects from buckles, rings or spoons;
- overly fearful child;
- parents unable to explain injury, or act nervously;
- burns, imprints, cigarette burns, hot liquid marks;
- difficulty in sitting in chair (sexual abuse, penetration);
- very self conscious about sex;
- nervous around adults, running away from home;
- extreme provocativeness at early age;
- STDs, oral, anal or rectal; genital or urethral trauma;
- phobias, avoidance behavior;
- excessive masturbation;
- withdrawal from social relationships;

- poor peer relationships;
- child is apathetic or pesters adults unreasonably;
- overly friendly, follows teachers around everywhere;
- inordinate attention to detail and repetitive rhythmic movements;
- arrives to school very early and stays very late;
- very private about an injury (such as a casted limb);
- promiscuity or prostitution, and
- substance abuse.
  (Mead, et al., 1985; Committee on Child Abuse, 1991; Attorney General, 1996, 2000).

 Each of these items alone may not seem to indicate child abuse, but observance of several items could be definite symptoms of abuse. Many times a teacher may not know the exact situation the student is experiencing, but when something at a "gut level" feeling appears to be occurring, it probably indicates some form of abuse. Teachers in school systems meet and interact with students every day. During the course of their workday, teachers may easily observe specific indicators that may lead them to suspect some form of abuse of their students. For example, **sleep disorders are often the number one sign of abuse.** Some indicators are more specific to younger children grades K-6, while others are more common in older children attending middle or high school classes. The following indicators can help teachers determine whether to suspect and file reports for abuse. **Teachers should be particularly watchful and consider filing reports if the child:**

Behavioral Indicators-In general

- is frightened of parents or caretakers, or at the other extreme, is overprotective of parents or caretakers;
- is excessively passive, overly compliant, apathetic, fearful or withdrawn, or at the other extreme, excessively aggressive, destructive or violent;
- or caretaker attempts to hide injuries, wears inappropriate clothing for hot weather, misses PE or refuses to change into gym attire;
- is frightened of going home;
- is apprehensive when other children cry;
- suffers from seizures or vomiting; and
- **as a teenager, exhibits depression, self-mutilation, suicide attempts, sleeping or eating disorders, or drug or alcohol abuse.**

Behavioral Indicators-Adolescents and Older Children

- withdrawal;
- chronic fatigue;

- clinical depression;
- overly compliant;
- poor hygiene or excessive bathing;
- poor peer relations and social skills/difficulty making friends;
- alcohol or drug abuse;
- prostitution or excessive promiscuity;
- academic failure or sudden drop in grades;
- refusal to dress for PE;
- fearful of restrooms or showers;
- arriving early to school or staying late;
- extraordinary fear of males (in cases of male perpetrator and female victim);
- setting fires; and
- crying without provocation.

As a **mandated reporter**, teachers should also be especially watchful of the parent or caretakers to protect the child and report any suspected problems. The parent or caretaker may simply dismiss any "unusual" behavior as a phase, or rare activity the child may be exhibiting. Teachers should observe if:

- the parents or caretakers place unreasonable demands or impossible expectations based upon the child's developmental capacity;
- the child is used as a "battleground" for custody or marital conflicts;
- the child is used to satisfy the parent's or caretakers own ego needs, and,
- the child is "objectified" by the perpetrator, e.g., the parent refers to the child as "it" ("it cried," "it died"). (Attorney General, 2000).

Excellent source for teachers: Megan's Law now online. After years of debate and controversy, California law permitted publishing information related to sex offenders on the Internet. The website: **http://meganslaw.ca.gov** now allows users to access names, photos, detailed criminal history and often exact addresses of convicted sex offenders. The website became available in the fall of 2004 and was quickly used by thousands of users. This website should be used with caution to protect the rights of others. It is also imperative for teachers, parents and others to remember that the maps displayed only represent **convicted offenders. Many others are still at large...**

When is it <u>Not</u> Child Abuse?

Students constantly play, push, shove and exhibit physical activity with each other. While this may be very annoying to the teacher; most of this activity is normal. Kids are growing, their hormone levels are changing, and adolescent bodies are growing "new stuff," all of which cause them to move and exhibit horseplay at times. Teachers should certainly maintain classroom control related to discipline, but teachers should always be very careful to observe a situation of potential abuse. **The following situations usually are not reportable as abuse:**

- Injuries caused by two children fighting during a push-shove, horseplay session;
- Injuries caused by a peace officer as a result of reasonable and necessary force of the officer acting within the course of their duty;
- Age-appropriate sex play or conduct between consenting minors is not, in and of itself sexual abuse. Sexual conduct between consenting teenagers (age14-17) is also not, in and of itself, reportable. **However, any sexual contact by anyone over the age of 14 with a child 13 and under, is reportable, even if the both parties consent**. Moreover, pregnancy of a minor does not, in and of itself, constitute the basis of reasonable suspicion of sexual abuse. However, other statements by the minor such as coercion, or a **significant age disparity** between the minor and her partner may lead to a reasonable suspicion of sexual abuse that must be reported. It is estimated that adult men in excess of 21 years of age inseminate 60-75% of teen girls that become pregnant. (California Attorney General, 1996, 2000).

Mandatory reporting

California law (*Penal Code 11166*) requires teachers and others that work with minor children to immediately report any suspicions of abuse within 36 hours, by telephone, and in writing, to the child protective agency in the county in which the alleged abuse took place. Ideally the teacher should call child protective services **before 3 PM.** This will allow child protective services or law enforcement officers to respond before the child may be subjected to additional abuse when the parent arrives home. It is critical for the educator to understand that teachers have the primary responsibility to report any suspicions and that **responsibility cannot be delegated.**
School boards have clearly defined policies and may require that the teacher report to the nurse, principal, counselor or other employee, but the teacher must also report to the child protective services. **Failure to report within the required timelines could result in 6 months in jail, a $1000 fine, possible criminal prosecution and revocation of the teaching credential!**

Since 1986, *The California Penal Code* Section 11166 has included not only teachers, but also any adults that work with minors as responsible for reporting any suspicion of child abuse. Prior to 1986 a long list of mandated reporters were named which included: doctors, counselors, clergy, judges, teachers, social workers, and many professionals. The law was amended to include "and others" to the list. A part-time coach or custodian working with children would be examples of "others" required to file a report.

When in Doubt, Report!

Oh What to Do. What to Do?

Teachers are required to report suspected child abuse <u>immediately</u> and in writing <u>within 36 hours</u> after given information about suspected child abuse. (*California Penal Code* 11166).

Where to go for help

It must be restated again that the classroom teacher is the person responsible for mandated reporting of suspected child abuse and this duty cannot be delegated to anyone else. Each town, city or county area has a specific agency responsible for collecting data, responding to calls and making reports to the district attorney or police for subsequent prosecution. California law requires that a suspected abuse report be filed in the **county in which the abuse took place.** The responsible agency may have several different names such as the following

- county welfare department;
- child protective services, children services;
- department of social services;
- health and human services;
- child abuse registry;
- county juvenile probation department;
- local police or sheriff; and
- local mental health department.

When a child enters this juvenile justice system there may seem to be an overwhelming amount of bureaucratic paperwork, administrative procedures and unnecessary red tape that will hinder the process of helping the child. Be patient. Teachers and others that file a child abuse report are often very frustrated because of the lack of information given to them. The public service agencies may or may not notify the reporting person as to the disposition of the child they are trying to help. More often than not, no information is given. However, **if a professional educator does not take the first step, nothing will be done.** This may be even more detrimental to the child for many years thereafter.

Recent changes during the 1980s and 1990s have made the child abuse problem more workable for the teacher and most importantly, more streamlined to help the child. There was a time when a child was interviewed 20-30 times by teachers, administrators, police officers, social workers and counselors. Today, many courts allow a videotaping of the child interview to be used as evidence in certain circumstances. Electronic filing by FAX machines are now allowed in some counties. DNA fingerprinting and the use of evidence from genetic materials of a suspect to match against the victim, has significantly improved the process of gathering and presenting evidence. **While electronic filing of reports (via FAX) is convenient and very rapid, teachers should also file hard copies and keep duplicate copies of all *Penal Code* 11166 forms.** *PC 11166* is also posted on nmatza.net under course documents/laws.

When cases are presented and completed in the court system, rarely does the perpetrator get convicted. Oftentimes, the child was traumatized by the abuse, can't remember exact details, or may fear the break up of a family, as in the case of incest. Keep in mind, however, that any adult of a couple not married could be tried for incest if they have sex with a minor living with them. The law considers this situation as the parent " acting in the role of the father or mother" and is therefore considered incest. Support groups such as Parents United, or Parents Anonymous have national networks that seek to help parents keep the family intact, and strive to save relationships and ultimately allow the child to heal. **Some experts feel that a child may never totally heal from being victimized...**

The teaching profession can be a very rewarding profession as teachers work with students to help them learn, develop self-esteem and overcome difficulties. Nonetheless, it requires adequate preparation for safety, prevention of accidents and injury and carefully documented records of any unusual events such as field trips. The following suggestions can prevent problems and avoid injury:

- plan for safety, inspect equipment regularly;
- know the health status of students;
- consider the readiness of the student for the activity;
- teach proper techniques or procedures;
- use safety tests and equipment such as goggles and gloves;
- provide for proper ventilation, especially in labs or shops;
- keep updated with CPR and safety certification;
- notify the administrator in writing of any problems/keep copies of documents;

- call the parent immediately if the student commits any dangerous act, or acts inappropriately;
- report incidents as soon as possible and keep accurate records;
- do not use personal vehicles to transport students;
- **do not leave students unsupervised without a certificated employee present;**
- secure written parental permission when necessary;
- carefully read all board policies and procedures, and,
- **if litigation results, seek a qualified attorney! (CTA will provide 1-2 hours of free legal advice for members).**

The legal system is not designed to have teachers lose their credentials and their jobs. **The primary intent of the law is to protect the student, i.e., minor child, while in the school setting.** The key issues in a court of law include that a "reasonable and prudent person take precaution, plan for safety, inspect regularly and provide a properly supervised place for students to learn." If the teacher remembers this basic concept, communicates problems to the school officials and carefully documents the necessary facts, few problems will develop. It is only when a teacher is careless, does not follow standard school procedures or board policies or neglects to document the facts that litigation may develop. The laws are merely designed to protect the children and offer them help and guidance to a healthy, happy life.

Since 1996, the state of California has developed an on-line comprehensive listing of all of the laws in California. Teachers are invited to access this database to review current laws and amendments that arise. Consult the website for school laws in the Education Code on the Internet. Point your browser to: **http://www.ca.gov/calaw.html**. Student teachers enrolled in HSc 411B are required to use the Internet to solve legal problems as they relate to their students in the public school setting. All of the data listed below can be accessed and reviewed at the Healthy Kids Resource Center **http://www.hkresources.org**.

Summary

This chapter presented numerous laws, guidelines and issues related to health and the legal implications encountered by the classroom teacher. Specific data reviewed the current laws related to sexuality education and HIV/AIDS as now required in California schools since 2004. Students are now able to apply numerous concepts using the problem-solving approach on legal issues that they may face when the begin teaching. Keep in mind the importance of reporting any suspicions related to child abuse to protect your students. Kids do have numerous problems, and sometimes it is just the classroom teacher that will be there everyday to help them. That classroom teacher could very well be you. Remember, **if not you, then who? If not now, then when?** We must protect our youth! You help build the future of our youth. Read what Dr. Frank Trujillo said about teaching and how important the role of the teacher builds the builders.

Who Builds the Builders?

"There are so many things you could do with your life. You could decide to build houses. Or sell cars. Or you could determine to build bridges. Or grow crops. Or design tall buildings. Or write books. Or act out parts on the stage…It's true. There are many, many things you could do with your life. You could decide to do any of these things. And more. Or, you could decide to teach…Perhaps you could teach. You could perhaps teach the people who build these things and do these things. And more. It is teachers who build the people who build these things. And more. Much, much more. They build the builders."

… Francis Xavier Trujillo, EdD.

Student Assignment: School Health and Legal Aspects

Objective: Teacher candidates will research and solve health related problems using California laws on the Internet.

Procedures: Read the assignment below, answer all questions and use a cooperative group team to discuss the issues and legal ramifications involved.

Read the Healthy Kids Resource Center (HKRC) website on school health laws. (www.hkresources.org). The Healthy Kids Resource Center (HKRC) has condensed the most important laws related to youth and health education. Knowledge of these laws can significantly help teachers with their daily classroom routines, and will help teachers make relevant decisions for the protection of their students. These laws may also have profound legal implications on their professional performance. **Note:** The laws have been edited for clarity and brevity. In the conduct of professional educational policy or practice, consult **http://www.ca.gov/calaw.html** for any complete legal text. Send e-mail to Professor Matza for questions: **nmatza@csulb.edu.**

Students are to click on www.hkresources.org and carefully read the sections below that summarize health education laws related to youth. Students may wish to copy all the files on health laws in the HKRC to a disk using the university high-speed access, send the laws to their e-mail account, or print a hard copy for later reading and study. All these sites are available on any computer with Internet access, either at home or many places on earth! Class discussion will follow after students complete the legal search and review. Click on "Laws Related to School Health." Use the search tool and you can search by (a) law number, (b) key word, or (c) categories. Review all of the following laws:

California Education Code (EC)

200-202, 35183, 35294, 49426, 49430-49436, 51220, 49423, 44645, 49530-36, 51890-91, 44810-11, 60041, 33041, 48907, 51510-51513, 51240, 48900-26, 49000-01, 49330-34, 44049, 51260-69, 51202, 51280, 35294, 48908, 60044, 44808.5, 51913, 51937-39.

California Penal Code (PC) 260-262, (esp. 261.5), 422.6, 11166

California Health and Safety Code (HSC) 120975-121125, 11605, 22961, 104350-104485, 120230, 22961, 104350.

The Grassley Amendment-Federal Statue, on the next page.

Federal Statutes and Health-The Grassley Amendment

The Grassley Amendment: Sec/ 1017. Protection of Pupil Rights.
Section 439 of the General Education Provisions Act (20 U.S.C. 1232g) is amended to read as follows:
"(a) All instructional materials, including teacher's manuals, films, tapes or other supplementary material which will be used in connection with any survey, analysis, or evaluation as part of any applicable program shall be available for inspection by the parents or guardians of the children."

"(b) No student shall be required, as part of any applicable program, to submit to a survey, analysis, or evaluation that reveals information concerning:

1.   political affiliations;
2.   mental and psychological problems potentially embarrassing to the student or his family;
3.   sex behavior and attitudes;
4.   illegal, anti-social, self-incriminating and demeaning behavior;
5.   critical appraisals of other individuals with whom respondents have close family relationships;
6.   legally recognized privileged or analogous relationships, such as those of lawyers, physicians, and ministers; or
7.   income (other than that required by law to determine eligibility for participation in a program or for receiving financial assistance under such program), without the prior consent of the student (if the student is an adult or emancipated minor), or in the case of an unemancipated minor, without the prior written consent of the parents."

"c) Educational agencies and institutions shall give parents and students effective notice of their rights under this section."

"(d) ENFORCEMENT.--The secretary shall take such action as the Secretary determines appropriate to enforce this section, except that action to terminated assistance provided under an applicable program shall be taken only if the Secretary determines that--

(1) there has been a failure to comply with such section; and

(2) compliance with such section cannot be secured by voluntary means."

"(e) OFFICE AND REVIEW BOARD--The Secretary shall establish or designate an office and review board within the Department of Education to investigate, process, review, and adjudicate violations of the rights established under this section."

Project 3 required for all students. You may wish to read the laws first and then answer the questions below, or try to read each question and search the HKRC laws related to school health **before the class discussion** and you complete the final written report. *Health Education for Teachers: Laws Related to School Health.*

Using the California Health Kids Resource Center website **www.hkresources.org**

(A)   Briefly (in a few sentences) describe the appropriate professional course of action and/or considerations in the following situations.

(B)   Cite the legal reference(s) i.e., title and number of the law(s), that supports the action. E.g. "Child Abuse Reporting Law" (PC 11166).

1.   Iris, a high school freshman, comes to the class to tell her teacher Mr. Kasawa that she was HIV positive. Iris tells Mr. K that she hasn't told anyone else, not even her parents. Your principal, Dr. East, told his staff that he must be notified of all HIV positive students.

2.   Health teachers at your school want to plan a health program intervention as a result of the high teenage pregnancy in your city. They plan on asking students questions regarding their attitudes about sex, drug use and nutritional habits.

3.   Leroy Garcia-Hong came to school walking with a limp and wearing a tee shirt that read "Fuck off and Die." He later removed his artificial leg in your period six class and acted up with other students.

4.   Itumi is a very large 7th grader and one day got so angry that she punched Miss Sweets in the jaw.

5.   Several of your 10th grade girls came to class with the latest cell phone clutched in their hands. They also liked to take photos of classmates and you.

6.   Seymour continued to listen to his i-Pod (with headphones), even after Mr. Lockjaw told him to turn off the power. Can a teacher   legally remove an object from a student's possession?

7.   The school nurse recently suspended 35 of the 7th grade students for not having evidence of Whooping Cough vaccination booster (DTaP), even though all their other shots were up to date.

8.   You are a member of the district textbook committee. Is any content prohibited in instructional materials used in California schools?

9.   Sally Dimples is a new rookie assistant principal and has to present a report to the school board next Tuesday. She asked you if schools are required to teach health.

10.   Willie is in your homeroom and asked if he could run to his locker to get a report for first period Spanish class. You said OK but did not issue a hall pass. He was later caught at the local mini-market selling marijuana.

11.   Ms. Jackson-Lee is planning to teach human reproduction and sexual responsibility to her 7th grade science class this year. Is there legally specified content or requirements?

12.   Rocko is in your 6th period Chinese class and never seems to sit still. One day he confided in you that a teacher on campus was touching his sexual parts. You immediately told the principal who told you he would file a child abuse report.

13.   Three boys in your math class are making strange hand signals and talking to others at the door in your class. You think they may be using gang signs.

14.   You are teaching an aerobics class in PE and notice different colored bruises on the leg of one of your senior girls, Tomeeka. When approached, Tomeeka said she fell off her bike.

15.   Bonnie constantly talks in your history class, and one day you got so angry that you told her to leave the room and that you are suspending her from your class.

16.   A new teacher was recently hired to teach health. He is an openly gay man and decided to discuss homosexuality in the family life education unit.

17.   You invited an HIV positive speaker from the American Red Cross to your class, and your principal said that the board policy requires written permission from parents.

18.   You are the faculty advisor for the junior class and the class president purchased candy at a wholesale grocers to sell on campus as a fundraiser. She issued a case to each officer and expected him or her to sell candy during periods 2-6.

19.   Cyberbullying is a new concern in schools. Lena is in your homeroom and was showing her boyfriend a photo taken with Lena's smart phone camera. The photo was of Martha (your student aide) taken in the girl's locker room showing Martha's breasts. Several kids were laughing because the photo was posted on the Internet. This all happened between 8 AM and 10 AM today! What will you do?

Chapter 12

Common Health Problems in the School Setting

We make a living by what we get,
we make a life by what we give.
...Sir Winston Churchill

Introduction

Previous chapters of this text described specific issues related to classroom management, drugs, alcohol and tobacco use and topics dealing with sexuality, STDs and legal issues, to help guide the classroom teacher in a practical everyday useful manner. After teaching health science for teachers for twenty-five years, this author had requests from readers to include a section addressing common health problems of kids. The topics below do not attempt to review all of the problems in the classroom; but to cover a wide range of health problems, diseases, and issues facing the teacher and provide the educator with recommendations for management. Children with chronic health conditions spend most of their day in the school system; and the complexity of their illness management can alter their daily school experience. Research has found that educators and other school professionals have positive attitudes with these students, but concerns about specific diseases, especially chronic diseases such as asthma do exist. Thus, health care workers can assist these professionals by providing appropriate information about the risk and functional impact of child chronic health conditions. (Olson, Seidler, Goodman, 2004). **It is imperative that teachers remember to always respect the privacy of students and their parents by not revealing or discussing medical or psychological issues in front of others, especially classmates.** Numerous sources were consulted while writing this chapter and teachers may find the *Manual of School Health,* a text written for school nurses of particular value. The text is clearly written by professional nurses. (Lewis, Bear, 2009).

For specific details on common health problems, teachers are also strongly encouraged to consult the various Internet websites referenced at the end of each section to obtain current information on health problems of youth.

Teachers should strive to avoid sending students out of class unnecessarily. Some kids are always looking for a reason to leave class, to meander throughout the campus or sleep in the nurse's office. Practice regular universal precautions, and remind students, and all staff members, to wash their hands regularly. Keep tissues, sanitary wipes and antibacterial gels readily available to allow students to clean up and hence avoid sending them to the front office.

An example of a public health problem in schools is the outbreak of whooping cough during 2010. According to the California Department of Public Health (CDPH), by June of 2010 California recorded 910 cases of Whooping Cough (Pertussis) which was a four fold increase from 2009 when only 219 cases were documented, and by the end of 2010 about 12 infants died. Pertussis is a highly contagious disease, and unimmunized young infants are particularly vulnerable. While this epidemic generated much concern with school principals, the school nurse present, serving as a public health role, was able to educate the staff, local families and promote proper immunizations. The new pertussis immunizations requirement affects all students – current, new, and transfers – in public and private schools. The law has two phases: During the 2011-12 school year, all students entering into grades 7, 8, 9, 10, 11, or 12 need proof of a whooping cough booster (Tdap) shot before starting school and for 2012-13 and future school years, all students entering into grade 7 will need proof of a Tdap shot before starting school. (CDPH, 2010).

It is important to remember that neither vaccination nor illness from pertussis provides lifetime immunity. Pregnant women may be vaccinated against pertussis before pregnancy, during pregnancy or after giving birth. Fathers may be vaccinated at any time, but preferably before the birth of their baby. CDPH encourages birthing hospitals to implement policies to vaccinate new mothers and fathers before sending newborns home. CDPH is providing vaccine free of charge to hospitals. Others who may have contact with infants, including family members, healthcare workers, and childcare workers, should also be vaccinated. A typical case of pertussis in children and adults starts with a cough and runny nose for one-to-two weeks, followed by weeks to months of rapid coughing fits that sometimes end with a whooping sound. Fever is rare.

Help the School Nurse

With so many budgetary constraints facing school boards, it is often the school nursing services that get cut from the budget. Many schools do not have full time nurses and some have very few or only use licensed nurses aides. Critical to the educational experience of kids in school is seat time. Understanding medical issues is helpful to teachers so that they may be able to make better decisions about keeping the child or adolescent in class rather than sending them to the heath office or school nurse. Consultation with the school nurse is critical when a teacher sees trends in absenteeism or chronic medical problems that interfere with the learning process. School nurses frequently assess to see if children are actually ill or are dealing with somatic symptoms reflecting deeper emotional issues. School nurses are oftentimes educating and informing parents and administrators on what is manageable at school or must be handled in a more restrictive manner (such as home-hospital, or independent-study). **Teachers should always strive to keep kids in school unless there is a genuine, significant and persistent medical condition that should be managed at home.** Periodic staff workshops with the certificated school nurse are helpful in reinforcing attendance and quality attention in the classroom.

Terminology associated with diseases and common school health problems

Many of the topics below are described from a medical perspective with the ultimate goal of providing teachers with an understanding to help them assist their students in the classrooms. Below is a vocabulary list to assist the reader with these terms.

Infectious Agent-Microorganisms that cause a disease. E.g., bacteria, viruses, fungi, protozoa, other parasites and aberrant proteins known as prions.

Reservoir of Infection-The organism, animal, person, plant, water, or food that allows the infectious agent (pathogen) to live.

Portal of Entry-The route a pathogen takes to enter a host. Examples include mucus membranes, skin, respiratory system, and gastrointestinal tract.

Portal of Exit-The route a pathogen takes out of an infected host. Examples include insect bites, hypodermic needles, and bleeding, or sexual contact.

Means of Transmission-The route followed by the expelled pathogen into the new host. Examples include the eyes, mouth, mucus membranes, or the skin.

Direct Contact-Person to person uninterrupted contact from kissing, touching, or sexual contact.

Indirect Contact-Transfer of the infectious agent from some other substance to the host. Examples include breathing, kissing, sexual contact, coughing or contact with food.

Host-An organism that harbors or nourishes another organism (the parasite). Examples include humans as hosts of head lice, strep throat bacteria or intestinal worms.

Immunity-Resistance or security against a given disease or infectious agent.

Antibodies-Protein substances produced in the body to fight against infectious disease or other pathogens.

Antigens-Proteins or polysaccharides in the body that stimulate an immune response against foreign substances or pathogens, and aid in producing antibodies.

Pathogen-Any disease-causing organism.

Epidemic-A classification of a disease that appears as a new case within a given population during a specific time period.

Pandemic-A classification of a disease that spreads through human populations across a wide range or region, such as a continent or worldwide.

Fomite-A fomite is any inanimate object such as a cup, eating utensil, article of clothing, capable of carrying infectious pathogens and transferring them from one individual to another. A dish sponge, or rag could serve as a fomite to transmit infection.

Health Problems, Diseases Common in Kids

Most health issues of students involve some element of universal precautions. For example, nosebleeds, pink eye or impetigo can be transmitted solely by touch; so hand washing should be emphasized for all students and staff as well. Minor first aid problems could also be handled by the classroom teacher. This should eliminate unnecessary trips to the health office and allow the student to continue with instruction.

Epistaxis (nosebleed)

While a child having a nosebleed in class may not be a major problem, teachers should be prepared to help them overcome discomfort and embarrassment. It is not the intention of this chapter to include numerous problems related to first aid, but a bleeding nose is often very common and the teacher could easily help with this problem. Follow these simple steps.

1. Students should sit with head erect, lean forward to avoid drainage into the throat.
2. Have the student apply firm but gentle pressure over the bleeding nostril for up to 10 minutes. If the teacher needs to help, schools should provide disposable gloves.
3. Apply a cold compress.
4. Notify parents or guardians if bleeding does not stop within about 15 minutes to get further medical care and remind the student not to blow or pick the nose.

Conjunctivitis "Pink Eye"

Description: Pink eye (conjunctivitis) is an inflammation or infection of the transparent membrane (conjunctiva) that lines the eyelid and is a very common health problem associated with the school age child. Teachers should be vigilant to protect all students by reporting and referring this potentially contagious problem to the school nurse.

Etiology: Conjunctivitis is caused by bacteria (*H. influenzae, S. pneumoniae*) viruses (adenovirus, herpes virus), sunlight, wind, contaminated eye drops, allergy and other irritants.

Transmission: When infectious, pink eye is transmitted by direct contact of infected tissues or transmitted by the fingers, clothing, or other fomite. Children are often in close contact and may touch the eyes, pencils, pens, or other object during the class activities.

Conjunctivitis

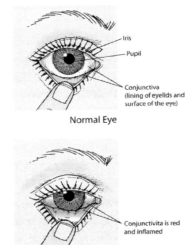

Normal Eye

Eye with Conjunctivitis

Signs/Symptoms: Incubation period is 24 to 72 hours and the pathogens can be transmitted at any time during the course of active infection. Symptoms include pink sclera of the eye, eyelid in one or both eyes. This may be followed by mild to severe inflammation, blurred vision and a purulent discharge. Tearing may or may not be profuse depending upon if the infection is bacterial or viral. Allergic symptoms may include itching, erythema (reddening) of the conjunctiva especially after exposure to seasonal allergens, i.e., pollen, wind, etc.

Diagnosis: Health care providers will conduct a visual examination and may obtain an eye culture to determine the exact nature of infection.

Treatment: Physicians will treat pink eye with antibiotics, or other eye drops if the diagnosis is bacterial. Cool or warm compresses may be applied, and **hand washing must always be emphasized.**

Educational Considerations: Students should be excused from school during the acute phase and should be allowed to return after initial treatment and upon physician recommendation. Students with allergic conjunctivitis should not be excused from school. All children should be reminded of regular hand washing with warm water and soap throughout the day.

Prognosis: Conjunctivitis can recur with or without medical treatment and may be managed with proper care. Hand washing should always be emphasized.

Website References: www.aoa.org. The American Optometric Association.

Impetigo

Description: A superficial bacterial infection of the skin most common among children 2-6 years of age but also common with people that play contact sports such as football, wrestling, etc., regardless of age.

Etiology: Impetigo is caused by a streptococcus (*S. pyogenes*) bacteria that also causes strep throat. Recent reports from the American Academy of Family Physicians indicate that both types of impetigo (bullous and nonbullous/blister and nonblister) are caused by the same pathogen, *S. pyogenes.*

Transmission: Impetigo infection is spread by direct contact with nasal carriers or lesions.

Signs/Symptoms: Incubation period is 2 to 5 days but the communicability lasts until the lesions are dry. Lesions are most commonly found on the face and extremities. Lesions of one or more will appear on the skin with surrounding reddened tissues. Pustules may rupture producing sticky honey-colored crust. Airborne dried streptococci are not infectious to intact skin.

Diagnosis: Visual examination by health care provider.

Treatment: Antibiotic applied locally or systemically under doctor's treatment. Good hand washing and a clean dressing to prevent exposure to others are recommended.

Educational Considerations: Students should not return to school until lesions are dry, and younger children must be excluded for 24 hours. Secondary students should also be encouraged to wash hands and avoid direct contact with others.

Prognosis: With rare exceptions, most students will be able to return to class quickly. Sometimes the medical doctor may order oral antibiotics treatment for an extended time.

Website References: www.kidshealth.org/parent/infections/skin/impetigo.html

Sty (Hordeolum)

Description: A sty (also spelled stye) is a localized infection or abscess of the sebaceous gland near the root of eyelashes and generally is on the lower eyelid.

Etiology: The most common cause is a staphylococcus infection, *S. aureus.*

Transmission: Direct contact from the hand or other object.

Signs/Symptoms: Redness, swelling and pain in the localized area of the eye. There may also be an external nodule or internal growth near the eyelash margins. Slight blurred vision may also occur. The sty may often resemble a pimple within 2 to 3 days of infection.

Diagnosis: Examination by a health care worker, nurse, or medical doctor.

Treatment: Many stys may drain on their own, but a folded clean, warm, damp cloth, as a compress could facilitate the drainage. It is not recommended to squeeze the stye, but to allow the drainage to occur after compression.

Educational Considerations: Parents should be contacted and checked to see if medical treatment has started. Good hand washing is important and students should be told not to squeeze the eye or touch it to prevent further infection. If compresses do not reduce the sty within a few days, students may need to receive prescriptions for oral or topical antibiotics from medical staff.

Prognosis: Most students should be able to return to class within a day or so upon treatment.

Website References: www.medicinenet.com/sty/article.htm

Asthma

Description: Asthma is the most common respiratory ailment in children. Asthma is characterized by a chronic inflammation disorder of the airways (bronchi) characterized by recurring episodes of breathlessness, and wheezing. Asthma often co-exists with allergies and may be exacerbated by exposure to allergens or other triggers. Allergic asthma is the most common type of asthma; but kids and many adults may also suffer non-allergic asthma.

Etiology: Numerous factors may bring about an asthma attack. These include allergic reactions to pollen, feathers, dust mites, pet dander, and second hand smoke from tobacco or environmental chemicals and particulates. Non-allergic asthma may result from stress, anxiety, exercise, cold or viral particles in the air. Asthma is a complex disorder involving biological, immunological, infectious, endocrine, and psychological factors. These factors may appear in varying degrees with both children and adults.

Transmission: Asthma is not a communicable disease.

Signs/Symptoms: Common symptoms include continuous coughing, frequent and irregular breathing, wheezing, flared nostrils, fever, stomach and chest pain, unusual sweating, hunched-over (tripoding) posture and unusual fatigue.

Diagnosis: Family doctors, pediatricians or allergy specialists will conduct a complete physical exam with an emphasis on breathing, inhalation and exhalation and seek to identify recurrent wheezing, coughing, trouble breathing, chest tightness and symptoms that occur or worsen at night.

Treatment: When an asthma attack occurs, the student should calm down, drink fluids and take the prescribed medication, often via an inhaler, or nebulizer, and rest. Inhalers including the bronchodilator *Albuterol* may be prescribed by the doctor and made available at the school site preferably locked in the office. School nurses may also have the doctor provide a backup inhaler for students to use in the classroom during a particularly difficult episode. Secondary students, that are capable of managing their asthma, are allowed to 'self carry' asthma medications, such as inhalers as described per district protocols.

Educational Considerations: Teachers should be informed of any specific allergies the student may have, the type of reaction that may result and how to handle any problems during the school day.

Prognosis: As with most health problems, the student should try to stay in school and participate in daily activities. Kids with allergic or non-allergic asthma can be treated with medications and return to normal activities as soon as possible. Many famous individuals such as President John F. Kennedy, comedian Bob Hope and Olympian Jackie Joiner-Kersey have lived productive lives and have been very successful while suffering asthma.

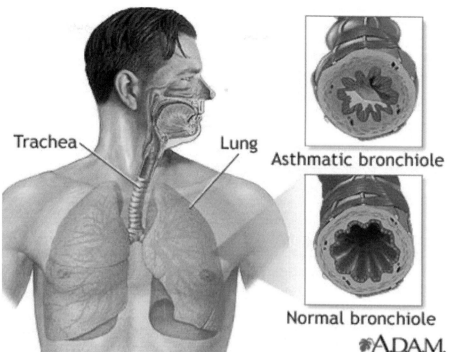

Trachea

Lung

Asthmatic bronchiole

Normal bronchiole

ADAM.

Website References: www.aafa.org, Asthma and Allergy Foundation of America, **www.lungusa.org. The American Lung Association.**

Diabetes

Description: Diabetes is a disease in which the body does not produce or utilize the hormone insulin. Insulin converts sugar, starches and other food nutrients into energy for daily life. The disease is associated with both environmental and behavioral factors such as obesity and lack of exercise. Greater than 20 million adults and kids in the U.S., or 7% of the population suffer from diabetes. It is estimated that nearly 15 million have been diagnosed with diabetes, but more than 6 million adults and kid. There are two major types of diabetes, called type 1 and type 2. **Type 1 diabetes was also called insulin dependent diabetes mellitus (IDDM).** In type 1 diabetes, the pancreas undergoes an autoimmune attack by the body itself, and is rendered incapable of making insulin. Of all the patients with diabetes, about 10% of the patients have type 1 diabetes and the remaining 90% have type 2 diabetes. Children with type 1 can live a normal life and have usually have little interaction with the school health staff. **Type 2diabetes** was also referred to **as non-insulin dependent diabetes mellitus** (NIDDM), or adult onset diabetes mellitus (AODM). In type 2 diabetes, patients can still produce insulin, but do so relatively inadequately for their body's needs, particularly in the face of insulin resistance. In many cases this actually means the pancreas produces larger than normal quantities of insulin. Type 2 diabetes was once diagnosed mostly in individuals over 30 years old and the incidence increases with age. In recent years, however, there have been an alarming number of patients with type 2 diabetes who are

barely in their teen years. **In fact, for the first time in the history of humans, type 2 diabetes is now more common than type 1 diabetes in childhood. Most of these cases are a direct result of poor eating habits, higher body weight, and lack of exercise.**
Etiology: Lack of insulin production from the pancreas, or inadequate utilization of insulin in the bloodstream. **Signs/Symptoms: In type 1 diabetes,** students may exhibit excessive eating, drinking or urination. Weakness, irritability nausea, vomiting or weight loss. This may be accompanied by dry skin, skin infections, blurred vision, constipation, fruity breath odor and abdominal pain.

Diagnosis: Health care workers run blood tests to examine sugar level present in the blood or urine.

Treatment: The primary goal is to help the patient manage sugar in the blood or urine to normal levels. For children, this may mean regular insulin injections, or insulin delivery using an insulin pump. The school nurse can assist the student following doctor's orders and school protocols regarding medication at school. Diet, regular exercise and weight management must also be promoted and followed for students with type 2 diabetes.

Educational Considerations: Students will need attention if they have low (**hypoglycemia**) or high (**hyperglycemia**) blood sugar. School nurses consult with parents and doctors to help the child be aware of signs and symptoms, and to regulate proper food intake and/or receive insulin injections or manage insulin with a diabetic pump. Children in the school setting with the insulin pump now can participate in nearly all-regular school activities, including exercise, running and playing. Since the secondary aged child (grades 7-12) may experience rapid growth, sudden stress, illness, or sporadic eating patterns, the teacher should be particularly observant of any changes described above.

Prognosis: With modern day medications, regular exercise, weight management and continuous monitoring of blood sugar, kids with diabetes can live a normal life. The ultimate research goal will be a cure for diabetes.

Website References: http://www.diabetes.org/about-diabetes.jsp. The American Diabetes Association, **http://www.cdc.gov/diabetes**. The CDC Chronic Disease Prevention and Health Promotion, **http://www.jdrf.org/index.cfm?page_id=100686**. The Juvenile Diabetes Research Foundation International, **http://www2.niddk.nih.gov/**. The National Institutes of Diabetes and Digestive Diseases and Kidney Diseases.

Epilepsy/Seizure Disorder

Description: Epilepsy is a neurological condition that produces disturbances in the normal electrical functions of the brain. Normal brain function occurs by millions of tiny electrical charges passing between neurons and to all parts of the body. Patients have epilepsy when the normal pattern of nerve functions may be interrupted by intermittent bursts of electrical energy more intense than usual. This could affect consciousness, bodily movements or other sensations.

The child with these symptoms may only have it occur for a short period of time.

Etiology: Epilepsy is commonly referred to as a **seizure disorder**. People may have a seizure and not be epileptic. The epileptic may have unusual bursts of energy in only one area of the brain (partial seizure), or it may affect numerous nerve cells throughout the brain (generalized seizure). When electrical bursts subside, normal brain function will return. People with epilepsy may have the condition since birth, or it could develop from exposure to toxic agents, infections or structural abnormalities, or for reasons not totally understood. Epilepsy affects people of all ages, races, and nationalities.

Signs/Symptoms: Children or adults may have convulsion with or without a fever, short periods of blackout or confused memory, occasional "fainting spells" in which bladder or bowel control is lost, followed by extreme fatigue, **episodes of blank staring, brief periods of no response to questions or instructions (very important for the observant teacher),** sudden stiffening or falls for no apparent reason, episodes of blinking or chewing at inappropriate times, repeated movements that look out of place or unnatural, muscle jerks of arms, legs or body, and sudden fear, anger or panic for no reason. Or, odd changes in the way things look, sound, smell or feel. Clusters of swift jerking movements may occur in babies.

Diagnosis: The major tool in diagnosing epilepsy by a physician, usually a neurologist, is a careful medical history by collecting data on any possible seizures. An electroencephalograph (EEG) may also be used to record brain waves. Additionally, other imaging tools such as CT (computerized tomography) MRI (magnetic resonance imaging) or PET scans (positron emission tomography), can help the doctor pinpoint exact areas of the brain undergoing seizures.

Treatment: After a doctor has diagnosed epilepsy, the next step is to select treatment. Sometimes an underling condition, such as a tumor can be surgically removed to correct the problem. Surgery is an alternative for some people whose seizures cannot be controlled by medications. Surgery for epilepsy has been used for more than a century, but its use dramatically increased in the 1980s and 1990s, reflecting its effectiveness as an alternative to seizure medicines.

The benefits of surgery should be weighed carefully against its risks, however, because there is no guarantee that it will be successful in controlling seizures. Generally the seizures will not return after surgery. Anticonvulsants, and more than twenty medications are available to treat epilepsy. Other surgical methods include stimulation of the vagus nerve, or special diets. It is possible for the patient with a seizure disorder, such as epilepsy, to lead a relatively normal life. Alexander the Great, Julius Cesar, Vincent Van Gogh, actor Danny Glover, the Russian writer Dostoyevsky and many other very famous people suffered from epilepsy.

Educational Considerations: Teachers should be notified by parents or nursing staff if a student suffers loss of consciousness, fainting, or seizures. Safety and avoidance of embarrassment should be major considerations when helping students. Stay calm and watch carefully for falling students that may hit objects, chairs, tables etc. Once the seizure has subsided, talk calmly, gently turn the student to the side and loosen any tight clothing around the neck. Do not restrain the student, and if available, place a pillow or soft object under the head. Do not allow other classmates to crowd the student. Give them some space and privacy if possible. **State law requires the inclusion of specific triggers for seizures in the student emergency health plan (EHP), or Individual Health Plan (IHP).**

Prognosis: Most people can live a normal life with epilepsy and children should be able to participate in all recreational, educational and vocational activities.

Website References: http://www.epilepsyfoundation.org/about/faq. Or consult The Epilepsy Foundation, **http://www.aesnet.org/.** The American Epilepsy Society.

Allergies

Description: An allergy is an overreaction of the body's defense system to some substance, or allergen. The mast cells in the blood release the enzyme **histamine** that give rise to a myriad of allergic symptoms. Numerous triggers cause allergies to begin. Common triggers include pollen, animal hair, or dander, house dust, feathers, drugs, insect bites or stings, and various foods such as shellfish, milk, or peanuts.

Signs/Symptoms: Typically a person may develop a rash, or hives, bumps on the skin, nasal congestion, wheezing, hay fever, bronchitis, sneezing, intestinal upset, and swollen, dry or itchy eyes. Sometimes allergic reactions increase rapidly or when exposed to heat, cold, sunlight, or emotional stress.

Diagnosis: Doctors can diagnose different types of allergies using various skin tests. Doctors have used skin tests for decades to determine if the symptoms relate to a specific allergen, or other agent. Physicians may also use blood tests to identify specific biochemical reactions or additional medical conditions. Blood tests may be indicated for those patients that cannot be diagnosed with skin tests due to other dermatologic conditions.

Treatment: Most allergic reactions are treated with antihistaminic drugs, and many are available over the counter. There are several types of medications used to treat and prevent allergy symptoms. Medications are available in pill and liquid forms, nasal sprays, eye drops and skin creams. These medicines include corticosteroids, decongestants, leukotriene modifiers (prevent inflammation from immune system), and cromolyn sodium that prevent the release of histamine during an allergic reaction.

Educational Considerations: Teachers should be informed of the specific allergy, the type of allergic reaction that is likely to occur and any specific instructions or medications that the student must use throughout the school day. An emergency care plan should also be in place.

Prognosis: Most allergic reactions are annoying, but rarely debilitating.

Special Allergy: Peanuts. With the recent obesity epidemic facing America, it is very important to avoid any kind of high fat foods, or candy etc., as rewards for learning. In fact food should not be used in the classroom since many children could have unknown allergies and neither the parents nor the child would be aware of any potential reaction. Educators should be especially cautious when peanuts are in the classroom. Some schools do not allow peanut products, or do not serve peanut butter because a few students may suffer severe, or **life threatening anaphylactic reactions**. Approximately 1.5 million people in the U.S. suffer from peanut allergies. **Peanut allergies comprise the most common cause of life-threatening allergic reactions,** including 80 percent of fatal or near-fatal reactions annually. Teachers should avoid using peanuts as a treat, for some kids may have reactions just by opening up a sandwich or a bag of peanuts present in the room. Allergists can test to diagnose peanut allergies to prevent risks to kids and adults as well. Peanut allergies may begin within a few minutes of exposure. Be observant to watch out for the following: itching, redness, swelling, shortness of breath, wheezing, nausea, abdominal pain, lightheadedness or **loss of consciousness, (anaphylaxis)**. The chemicals in peanuts can cause hives to develop on the areas of the skin that have come in contact with peanuts or traces of peanuts. Hives may spread to the rest of the body.

Website References: http://www.acaai.org. American College of Allergy, Asthma and Immunology (ACAAI).

Scoliosis

Description: Scoliosis is a medical condition characterized by the vertebral column (spine) curved from side to side. The spine may also be rotated. The condition occurs more commonly in females than males and usually develops during periods of active growth (10-16 years).

Etiology: On an x-ray, the spine of an individual with a typical scoliosis may look more like an "S" or a "C" than a straight line. Scoliosis is caused by anomalies of the vertebra at birth (congenital), or as infantile, juvenile, adolescent, or adult (idiopathic) scoliosis according to when the anomaly occurred. Sometimes, however a secondary symptom may result from other conditions such as cerebral palsy or spinal muscular atrophy. **If a family history of scoliosis exists, the risk is seven times greater.**

Signs/Symptoms, Diagnosis: Signs or symptoms may develop slowly and be painless. Parents may not notice symptoms of a child because individuals dress themselves and may be modest. The school nurse is required to screen for scoliosis and may observe the following: unequally elevated shoulder, scapula (shoulder blade) prominence or elevation, unilateral fullness of waist or extra folds, elevation of the iliac crest (hip bone), lumbar or thoracic prominence while bending, unequal rib prominence and hair tufts, dimples, or discoloration at end of the spine. The photograph on this page illustrates an irregular curvature of the spine. Referrals to doctors are made by the school nurse when the curvature is greater than seven degrees. **Treatment:** Sate law requires **screening**, during the **7th grade for girls and 8th grade for boys.** Doctors may order special braces to be worn day and night for 2-4 years for moderate scoliosis, but more severe cases with curvatures greater than 40 degrees may require corrective surgery.

Educational Considerations: As always, teachers should provide a nurturing, safe and comfortable environment for all students. Physical activity may have to be limited and socialization issues could cause problems of low self-esteem with some kids. Doctors frequently employ a **"watchful waiting"** approach to closely monitor any changes during the teen years. A teenage girl or boy may be embarrassed wearing a brace, or may have to have special seating arrangements; but he or she should be able to participate with other students as in the regular classroom.

Prognosis: Some experts in orthopedics suggest not using bracing as treatment, depending on the age and severity of the curvature; but most children should be able to function normally as adults. The American Academy of Orthopedic Surgeons has written extensively on pros and cons of scoliosis treatment.

Website References: National Scoliosis Foundation, **www.scoliosis.org.** The American Academy of Orthopedic Surgeons, **http://www.aaos.org/.**

Summary

Teachers should remember that many of the common health problems reviewed above may or may not be disclosed to the school nurse, teacher or administrative staff. Schools have parents fill out various forms to elicit this health information from parents to protect the child, avoid accidents, or embarrassment, etc.; but parents are not required to reveal medical information to others. Strive to be watchful for any unusual behavior, medical symptom, or awkward movement that you observe and ask the child if they are doing well. Follow up your observations with contacts with the credentialed school nurse.

Hopefully after reading the details of numerous health problems, issues and situations that young people must face today, teachers can be more knowledgeable and better prepared to enter the classroom to deliver their specific content lessons. While many of the topics addressed can be difficult to manage, such as classroom management and dealing with sensitive topics like reporting child abuse; educators now have the resources and can quickly find new information to allow them to recognize specific problems with their students, counsel or advise them as necessary, find appropriate resources and simply go back to work.

About the Author

Academic Summary
Nathan Matza, MA, DrPH(c), CHES
nmatza@csulb.edu

Nathan Matza has worked for more than four decades as a full time high school teacher, health science teacher and professor, and currently, is a lecturer in the Department of Health Science at California State University, Long Beach. He holds a Bachelor of Science and Master of Arts Degree, (California State University, Long Beach) and postgraduate research for a Doctorate of Public Health, (DrPH), (Loma Linda University). He also holds credentials as a Nationally Certified Health Education Specialist (CHES), and life credentials, in secondary teaching (health science & biological science), standard supervision (administrative), and Specially Designed Academic Instruction in English (SDAIE) from the state of California. He also holds a certificate in computer technology from Boise State University.

Teaching Experience

As a high school teacher Matza taught: physiology, biology, field biology, life sciences, integrated science, health science, computer skills and health science for English Language Learners (ELL) students. His major focus of teaching has been health science education since 1977. As a university professor he taught: HSc 411b, Health Science for Teachers since 1983, and EDSS 300, 450, credential classes and methods for teaching health education for health majors. He also taught HSc 210, Introduction to Health Science, and supervised student teachers as a master teacher and university supervisor at middle and high schools in LA and Orange County.

Writing and Volunteering Experience

Professor Matza was a contributing author of The *Health Framework for California Public Schools: Kindergarten Through Grade Twelve*, (1994). **He has also written:** *A Curriculum Guide For Health Education* (1989, 1995), *Contemporary Health Education,* (1995, 1998), contributing author of *Project Teach Health Pre-service Resource Manual for University Instructors of Health Education* (1993, 1999), *Tobacco Use Prevention, in, The Comprehensive School Health Challenge,* Cortese, Middelton, eds. (1994, ETR Associates), and two college textbooks for secondary educators, ***Health Science for Teachers*** (1998, Revised edition 2004, 3rd ed., 2007, 4th ed., 2010, 5th ed., 2013), and *Creative Health Science Lessons* (1998). Matza also served as a contributing author to the *Los Angeles Times*. He has been a member of the executive board of the California Association of School Health Educators (CASHE) since 1980, and has published articles in The California Association of Health, Physical, Education,

Recreation and Dance Journal (CAHPERD) and the CASHE Newsletter. Additionally, Professor Matza:

- Publishes a comprehensive list of Health Education Internet Websites at nmatza.net;
- Served as a policy board member of the statewide California Physical Education-Health Subject Matter Project (CPE-HP) (1998-2003);
- Served and as a member of peer nominated, statewide Leadership Enhancement and Development in Health Forum (LEAD) at the California State Department of Education. (2000-2002);
- Served on the Subject matter curriculum project (2001-2003);
- Delivered numerous workshops at the California Health Framework Conferences (1999-2002);
- Volunteered for Career Day at Bret Harte Middle School, LAUSD (2008-2011);
- Volunteered for the California Department of Education Health Education Assessment Project (HEAP) (2008-2009);
- Attended the University of Southern California Keck School of Medicine Childhood Obesity Conference, Los Angeles CA (2008, 2009, 2010);
- Volunteered as a technical consultant for the National Association of Hispanic Nurses and the California School Nurses Association (2005-2009);
- Presented a workshop on Health Education at The School Nurses Organization (SNOA) of Arizona, Phoenix AZ (2010);
- Delivered numerous workshops, lectures on health education and technology;
- Has written many curriculum materials, including a summary of the State Health Framework for the Orange County Department of Education;
- Served on numerous district, county and statewide committees on health education, and has taken a leadership role for the advocacy of health education of all students; and
- Addressed school boards of education in Los Angeles, Huntington Beach, and the California State Board of Education on health standards, and curricula issues.

Nathan Matza also served as a consultant for the:

- California State Department of Education
- Los Angeles County Department of Education
- Los Angeles Unified School District
- Orange County Department of Education
- Huntington Beach Union High School District
- Buena Park School District
- San Diego City Schools
- San Diego County office of Education
- California State University Fullerton
- Paramount Unified Schools
- California Maritime Academy (CASHE Conference)

- Alameda County Department of Education
- National Association of Hispanic Nurses (NAHN)

- California School Nurses Association (CSNO) and;
- The California State Board of Education on health standards.

Academic Summary

- Nathan Matza has been recognized as an expert in health education teaching;
- Served a six-year assignment as a district level Mentor Teacher for health teachers;
- Advised college graduate students;
- Matza was have been selected as a Teacher of the year and a finalist for the President's Award for Excellence in Teaching;
- Professor Matza has been a teacher for over 40 years and;
- At age 17 he earned the Eagle Scout Medal, Boy Scouts of America.

Contact Information: nmatza@csulb.edu.

References

The following references are cited throughout this text, but numerous other citations are also included to guide the reader to a multitude of resources related to adolescent health. Readers should be aware that Internet Websites offered as citations and/or sources for further information may have changed or disappeared between the time this was written and when it was read. To locate the exact citation, Google the title and author where indicated to quickly locate the latest source of information on relevant health topics and issues.

ABC NEWS, Interactive Videodisk. (1997). Drugs and Substance Abuse. New York. American Broadcasting Company.

African American Profile. Author. (2011). Office of Minority Health. Retrieved January 6, 2011: http://minorityhealth.hhs.gov/templates/browse.aspx?lvl=2&lvlid=51.

Alan Guttmacher Institute (AGI). (1994). *Sex and America's Teenagers*. New York. NY: Planned Parenthood. Retrieved: March 10, 2005: http://www.ppacca.org/site/pp.asp?c=kuJYJeO4F&b=139496.

Alan Guttmacher Institute (AGI). (2004). Sex Education: Needs, Programs and Policies. Retrieved May 10, 2005: http://www.guttmacher.org/presentations/ed_slides.html.

Alan Guttmacher Institute (AGI). (2005). Condoms, Contraceptives and Nonoxynol-9: Complex Issues Obscured by Ideology. Retrieved June 2, 2011: http://www.guttmacher.org/pubs/tgr/08/2/gr080204.html.

Alan Guttmacher Institute (AGI). (2006a). Get In the Know: 20 Questions About Pregnancy, Contraception, and Abortion. Retrieved: March 28, 2008: http://www.guttmacher.org/in-the-know/index.html.

Alan Guttmacher Institute (AGI). (2006b). Facts on American Teens' Sexual and Reproductive Health. Retrieved: May 5, 2008 http://www.guttmacher.org/pubs/fb_ATSRH.html.

Alan Guttmacher Institute (AGI). (2007). Retrieved: June 4, 2008: Facts on American Teens' Sexual and Reproductive Health http://www.guttmacher.org/pubs/fb_ATSRH.pdf.

Alan Guttmacher Institute (AGI). (2008). U.S. Abortion Continues Long-Term Decline. Retrieved: June 4, 2008: http://www.guttmacher.org/media/nr/2008/01/17/index.html

Alan Guttmacher Institute (AGI). (2011). Facts on American Teens' Sexual and Reproductive Health. Retrieved March 12, 2011: http://www.guttmacher.org/pubs/FB-ATSRH.html.

Alcohol and Alcoholism: Alcohol Alert. (1999). National Institute on Alcohol Abuse and Alcoholism. (NIAAA). Retrieved January 11, 2009: http://pubs.niaaa.nih.gov/publications/aa46.htm.

Alcohol and Alcoholism: Alcohol Alert. (2007). National Institute on Alcohol Abuse and Alcoholism. (NIAAA). Retrieved June 11, 2008: http://pubs.niaaa.nih.gov/publications/AA67/AA67.htm.

Alcohol and Alcoholism: Alcohol Alert. (2008). What You Don't Know Can Harm You. Retrieved June 18, 2008: http://ncadi.samhsa.gov/govpubs/ph326x/.

American Academy of Child and Adolescent Psychiatry (AACAP). (2006). Children with Lesbian, Gay, Bisexual and Transgender Parents. Facts for Families #92.

American Health. (1986). To Be Sure You're Not At Risk. October, p. 72.

American Lung Association (ALA). (2010) On First Anniversary of Tobacco Regulation Law, FDA Cracks Down on Tobacco Marketing. Retrieved February 8, 2010: http://www.lungusa.org/press-room/press-releases/tobacco-regulation-anniversary.html.

Anderson, S., Cohen, P., Naumova, E., et al. (2007). Adolescent Obesity And Risk For Subsequent Major Depressive Disorder and Anxiety Disorder: Prospective Evidence. *Psychosomatic Medicine*, 69(8), 740-747.

Anderson, S., Whitaker, R. (2010). Household Routines and Obesity in US Preschool-Aged Children. Pediatrics:125/3, 420-428.

Any Lab Test (ALT). (2009). STD Tests. Retrieved April 1, 2011: http://seattlelabtest.com/lab-tests/product/chlamydia-dna-urine/.

AIDS in the Third World. (1999). *Economist, 350:81*: Author.

Alcohol And Tobacco Lobbies Are Big Spenders. (1992). Prevention File, Summer: Alcohol, Tobacco and Other Drugs. University of California, San Diego, p 6-8. Author.

Allensworth, D., Lawson, E., Nicholson L., et al., Eds. (1997*), Schools and Health: Our Nation's Investment*. Institute of Medicine. Washington, DC: National Academy Press.

Altman, D., Lolly-Rasenick-Doss, L. (1991). Sustained Effects on an Educational Program to Reduce Sales of Cigarettes to Minors. *American Journal of Public Health*, 81:891-893.

Amaro, H. (1995). Love, Sex, and Power: Considering Women's Realities in HIV Prevention. *American Journal of Psychology,* 50(6): 437-447.

American Cancer Society (ACS). (2007). The Joint Committee on National Health Education Standards. National Health Education Standards: Achieving Excellence (2nd Edition). Atlanta: American Cancer Society.

American Heart Association (AHA). News Release. (1991). November.

American Heart Association (AHA). (2005). *Heart Disease and Stroke: 2005 Update.*

American Lung Association (ALA). (2005). American Lung Association Links Socio-Economic Factors to Environmental Health Hazards. Retrieved: March 14, 2005. http://www.lungusa.org/site/pp.asp?c=dvLUK9O0E&b=22542.

American School Health Association (ASHA). (1996). Questions and Answers About Herpes. Research Triangle Park, North Carolina.

American Social Health Association. (1998). Sexually Transmitted Diseases in America: How Many Cases and at What Cost? Menlo Park, CA: Kaiser Family Foundation.

American Public Health Association (APHA). (2011). I Frank, S. "Excessive Texting, Social Networking Linked to Health Risks for Teenagers*."* *In Nations Health.* January , 2011. Annual Meeting of The American Public Health Association. November, 2010.Denver, Colorado.

Austin, G., Skager, R., (2004). *10th Biennial California Student Survey: Drug, Alcohol and Tobacco Use.* California Attorney General's Office, California Department of Education.

Austin, S., Melly, S., Sanchez, B., et al. (2005). Clustering Of Fast Food Restaurants Around Schools: A Novel Application of Spatial Statistics to The Study of Food Environments. *American Journal of Public Health*, 95(9), 1575-1581.

Austin, S., Kim, J., Wiecha, J., et al., (2007). School-Based Overweight Preventive Intervention Lowers Incidence of Disordered Weight-Control Behaviors in Early Adolescent Girls. *Archives of Pediatrics & Adolescent Medicine*, 161 (9), 865-869.

Banks, D., (2000). To Your Health: Red Wine? *The Green Line*. University of Illinois Extension. Retrieved: July 5, 2004: www.urbanext.uiuc.edu/greenline.

Barrett, S., Jarvis, W., Kroger, M., London, W. (2008). *Consumer Health*. McGraw-Hill. New York, NY.

Bauman, V., (2008). ABC NEWS. (2008). N.Y Cigarette Tax Climbs to Nation's Highest New York's Cigarette Tax Climbs Past New Jersey's to Become Highest in The Nation. Retrieved July 15, 2008: http://abcnews.go.com/print?id=4985448.

Bayer, R., Fairchild, A., (2006). Changing the Paradigm for HIV Testing -The End of Exceptionalism. *New England Journal of Medicine,* 355;(7) 647-649.

Beard, M. (2010). BBC News. Pompeii Skeletons Reveal Secrets of Roman Family Life. Retrieved May 2, 2011: http://www.bbc.co.uk/news/world-europe-11952322.

Behman, R., Kliegman, R., Arvin, M., editors. (1996). *Nelson Textbook of Pediatrics*. 15th ed. Philadelphia, PA: W. B. Saunders Company. 1996.

Berglas, N., Brindis, C., Cohen, J. (2003). *Adolescent Pregnancy and Childbearing in California*. California Resource Bureau.

Beloc N., Breslow L., (1972). Relationship of Health Status and Health Practices. *Preventive Medicine,* 1:409-421.

Black S., Markides K., (1993). Acculturation and Alcohol Consumption in Puerto Rican, Cuban-American and Mexican-American Females In The Unites States. *American Journal of Public Health,* 83:890-893.

Blum A. (1991). The Marlboro Grand Prix: Circumvention Of The Television Ban On Tobacco Advertising. *New England Journal of Medicine*, 324:913-917.

Blum, R., Rhinehart, P., (1998). *Reducing the Risk: Connections That Make a Difference in the Lives of Youth*. Minneapolis MN: University of Minnesota.

Boreland, R. (1992). More than Two Million California Non-Smokers Exposed to Second-hand Smoke in the Workplace in 1990. American Medical Association News Release, August 11, 1992.

Bottom Line/Personal, (1992). August 15, p. 7.

Brainard J. (1996). *Cultural Diversity in the Health Classroom,* New York: Glenco.

Brody, A., Mandelkern, M., London, E., Childress, A. et al. (2002). Brain Metabolic Changes During Cigarette Craving. *Archives of General Psychiatry*. 59:1162-1172.

California Attorney General's Office. (1996). *Child Abuse*. California Department of Justice, Office of the Attorney General, Doc D1-7020. Sacramento, CA.

California Attorney General's Office (2000). *Law in the School*. California Department of Justice, Office of the Attorney General. Sacramento, CA. Retrieved May 1, 2008: http://www.safestate.org/shop/index.cfm? cat=2&navid=107&action=list.

407

California Attorney General's Office Department of Justice. (2007). *Child Abuse: Educator's Responsibility.* Attorney General's Office. Retrieved August 7, 30, 2008: http://www.safestate.org/shop/index.cfm? cat=2&navid=107&action=list.

California Department of Public Health (CDPH). (2010). Whooping Cough May be Worst Epidemic in 50 Years. Retrieved May 1, 2011: http://www.cdph.ca.gov/Pages/NR10-041.aspx.

California Department of Education (CDE). (1987). *Family Life/Sex Education Guidelines*, Sacramento, CA.

California Department of Education (CDE). (1991). *Not Schools Alone: Guidelines for Schools and Communities to Prevent the Use of Tobacco, Alcohol and Other Drugs Among Children and Youth.* Office of Health Kids, Healthy Schools. California. Sacramento, CA.

California Department of Education (CDE). (1994, 2003). *Health Framework for California Public Schools: Kindergarten Through Grade Twelve,* Sacramento. CA.

California Department of Education (CDE). (1997). California Youth Risk Behavior Survey. Sacramento, CA.

California Department of Education (CDE). (1999). Science Safety Handbook for California Public Schools. Retrieved: May 2, 2011: http://www.cde.ca.gov/pd/ca/sc/documents/scisafebk.pdf.

California Department of Education (CDE). (2008). Health Education Standards. Retrieved June 9, 2008: http://www.cde.ca.gov/ci/he/.

California Department of Education (CDE). (2009). The Adolescent Brain and Substance Use. Retrieved January 12, 2011: http://www.gettingresults.org/Pages/articles/Results-Issue12.pdf.

California STD HIV Prevention Training Center. (CA.STD). (2002). STD Overview for Non-Clinicians. Anaheim, CA. March 1, 2002.

California Adult Tobacco Survey (CATS). (2006). Reducing Exposure to Secondhand Smoke Retrieved June 15, 2008: http://www.tobaccofreeca.com/secondhand_smoke.html.

Campaign for Tobacco Free Kids. (CTFK). (2008). Cigarette Taxes Reduces Smoking, Especially Among Kids. Retrieved May 14, 2008:http://www.tobaccofreekids.org/research/factsheets/pdf/0146.pdf.

Campaign for Tobacco Free Kids. (CTFK). (2009). The Rise of Cigars and Cigar-Smoking Harms. Retrieved February 8, 2011: http://www.cdc.gov/tobacco/data_statistics/fact_sheets/tobacco _industry/cigars/index.htm#overview.

Campaign for Tobacco Free Kids. (CTFK). (2010). FDA Authority Over Tobacco. Retrieved May 2, 2011. http://www.tobaccofreekids.org/campaign/federal/.

Campbell, K., Crawford, D., Salmon, J., et al. (2007). Associations Between the Home Food Environment and Obesity-Promoting Eating Behaviors in Adolescence. *Obesity,* 15(3), 719-730.

Center on Alcohol Marketing and Youth (CAMY). (2007a). Alcohol Advertising and Youth. Retrieved May 22, 2008: http://camy.org/factsheets/print.php?FactsheetID=1.

Center on Alcohol Marketing and Youth (CAMY). (2010b). Youth Exposure to Alcohol Advertising on Television, 2001-2009. Retrieved January 11, 2012: http://www.camy.org/research/Youth_Exposure_to_Alcohol_ Ads_on_TV_Growing_Faster_Than_Adults/index.html.

Caprolo, F. (1992). *Human Sexuality-Teachers Edition.* Lexington KY: D.C. Heath.

Carmona, R. (2004). The Health Consequences of Smoking: A Report of The Surgeon General 2004. Retrieved March 14, 2005: http://www.cdc.gov/tobacco/sgr/sgr_2004/pressrelease.htm.

Carmona, R. (2005). U.S. Surgeon General Releases Advisory on Alcohol Use in Pregnancy. Surgeon General 2004. Retrieved July 22, 2008: http://www.hhs.gov/surgeongeneral/pressreleases/sg02222005.html.

Carmona, R. (2006). The Health Consequences of Smoking A Report of The Surgeon General 2006. Retrieved May 19, 2008: http://www.surgeongeneral.gov/library/secondhandsmoke/report/executivesummary.pdf.

Castellsagué, X., Bosch, X., Muñoz N., et al. (2002). Male Circumcision, Penile Human Papillomavirus Infection, and Cervical Cancer in Female Partners. *New England Journal of Medicine*, 346:1105-1112.

Carr K., Elliot J., Carson A., et al. (2002). Emergency Procedures for Criminal Acts. Westminster High School. Westminster, California. Unpublished.

Centers For Disease Control and Prevention (CDC). (1991). Premarital Sexual Experience Among Adolescent Women- United States, 1970-1988. *MMWR* 39:929-932.

Centers For Disease Control and Prevention (CDC). (1992). Update: Acquired Immunodeficiency Syndrome-United States, 1991. *MMWR* 41:463-468.

Centers For Disease Control and Prevention. (CDC). (1993a). Sexually Transmitted Disease Guidelines. Retrieved September 5, 2008: http://www.cdc.gov/std/treatment/.

Centers for Disease Control and Prevention (CDC). (1993b). HIV AIDS Surveillance Report. 5: 1-30.

Centers For Disease Control and Prevention (CDC). (1994a). HIV AIDS Surveillance Report. 5: 1-12.

Centers For Disease Control and Prevention (CDC). (1994b). HIV/AIDS Surveillance Report, Vol. 6., No. 2, Summary of Findings.

Centers For Disease Control and Prevention (CDC). (1994c). HIV/AIDS Prevention, Facts About: Adolescents and HIV/AIDS. December.

Centers For Disease Control and Prevention (CDC). (1995a). HIV/AIDS Prevention. Fact Sheet Adolescents and HIV/AIDS. USDHHS.

Centers For Disease Control and Prevention (CDC). (1995b). The Human Immunodeficiency Virus and its Transmission. USDHHS.

Centers For Disease Control and Prevention (CDC). (1996a). HIV/AIDS Prevention Fact Sheet, HIV Prevention Community Planning. USDHHS.

Centers For Disease Control and Prevention (CDC). (1996b). HIV/AIDS Prevention Fact Sheet, Surveillance of Health Care Workers with HIV/AIDS. USDHHS.

Centers For Disease Control and Prevention (CDC). (1996c). HIV/AIDS Prevention Fact Sheet, Condoms and Their Use in Preventing HIV Infection and Other STDs. USDHHS.

Centers for Disease Control and Prevention (CDC). (1997a). Summary of Notifiable Diseases in The United States, 1996. *MMWR* 45:1-103.

Centers for Disease Control and Prevention (CDC). (1997b). Transmission of HIV Possibly Associated With Exposure of Mucous Membranes to Contaminated Blood. *MMWR* 46:620-623.

Centers for Disease Control and Prevention (CDC). (1998). Trends in Sexual Risk Behaviors Among High School Students-United States, 1991-1997. MMWR 47:749-752.

Centers for Disease Control and Prevention (CDC). (1999). GHB Use in New York and Texas. *MMWR* 46:281-283.

Centers for Disease Control and Prevention (CDC). (2000). Adolescent Population Characteristics: Statistics and Trends a Brief Summary. Health, United States, Adolescent Health Chartbook.

Centers for Disease Control and Prevention (CDC). (2002a). Youth Risk Behavior Surveillance United States, 2001. *MMWR* 51(SS04); 1-64.

Centers for Disease Control and Prevention (CDC). (2002b). Trends in Cigarette Smoking Among High School Students-United States, 1991-2001. 51(19);409-412.

Centers for Disease Control and Prevention (CDC). (2002c). CDC HIV/STD/TB Prevention News Update, June 17, 2002.

Centers for Disease Control and Prevention (CDC). (2002d). HIV/ AIDS Surveillance report 2002;14.

Centers for Disease Control and Prevention (CDC). (2002e). National Center for Health Statistics. National Vital Statistics Report. 50(16).

Centers for Disease Control and Prevention (CDC). (2002f). Obesity Trends Among U.S. Adults.

Centers for Disease Control and Prevention (CDC). (2002g). Sexually Transmitted Diseases Treatment Guidelines. 51 RR6. Retrieved September 22, 2008: http://www.cdc.gov/std/treatment.

Centers for Disease Control and Prevention (CDC). (2003). Trends in Reportable Sexually Transmitted Diseases in the United States, 2003 National Data on Chlamydia, Gonorrhea and Syphilis.

Centers for Disease Control and Prevention (CDC). (2003). Youth Risk Behavior Surveillance -United States, 2003. MMWR May 21, 2004 / 53(SS02);1-96. Retrieved May 2, 2005: http://www.cdc.gov/mmwr/preview/mmwrhtml/ss5302a1.htm.

Centers for Disease Control and Prevention. (CDC). (2004). New U.S. data show fewer Americans Have Herpes but rates of other sexually transmitted diseases still high. Retrieved April. 12, 2005: http://www.cdc.gov/std/2004STDConf/MediaRelease/Trends.htm.

Centers for Disease Control and Prevention (CDC). CDC/ HIV/AIDS (2004). Centers for Disease Control, HIV/AIDS Surveillance Report 2003 (2004), Vol. 15, Table 11, page 21.

Centers for Disease Control and Prevention. (CDC). (2005). Coordinated School Health Programs. Retrieved February 14, 2005: http://www.cdc.gov/HealthyYouth/CSHP/index.htm.

Centers for Disease Control and Prevention. (CDC). (2006a). National Center for Chronic Disease Prevention and Health Promotion, Youth Risk Behavior Survey. Unpublished analysis.

Centers for Disease Control and Prevention. (CDC). (2006b). HIV/AIDS Among Youth. Retrieved June 22, 2008: http://www.cdc.gov/hiv/resources/factsheets/youth.htm.

Centers for Disease Control and Prevention (CDC). (2007a). Department of Health and Human Services. Surgeon General's call to action to prevent and reduce underage drinking Retrieved June 15, 2008: http://www.surgeongeneral.gov/topics/underagedrinking/about.html.

Centers for Disease Control and Prevention (CDC). (2007b). CDC, National Center for Injury Prevention and Control. Youth Suicide. Retrieved August 27, 2008: www.cdc.gov/ncipc/dvp/Suicide/youthsuicide.htm.

Centers for Disease Control and Prevention (CDC). (2007c). HIV/AIDS Among Women. Retrieved June 4, 2008: http://www.cdc.gov/hiv/topics/women/resources/factsheets/women.htm

Centers for Disease Control and Prevention (CDC). (2007d). Youth Risk Behavior Surveillance -United States, 2007. Retrieved June 4, 2008: http://www.cdc.gov/HealthyYouth/yrbs/index.htm.

Centers for Disease Control and Prevention (CDC). (2007e). Adolescent Health in the United States, 2007. (2008). Retrieved January 12, 2011: http://www.cdc.gov/nchs/data/misc/adolescent2007.pdf.

Centers for Disease Control and Prevention (CDC). (2008a). Tobacco Use and Pregnancy. Retrieved June 15, 2008: http://www.cdc.gov/reproductivehealth/tobaccousepregnancy/index.htm.

Centers for Disease Control and Prevention (CDC). (2008b). Male Circumcision and Risk for HIV Transmission: Implications for the United States. Retrieved June 28, 2008: http://www.cdc.gov/hiv/resources/factsheets/circumcision.htm.

Centers for Disease Control and Prevention. (CDC). (2008c). What's New HIV/AIDS. Retrieved: May 28, 2008: http://www.cdc.gov/hiv/whatsnew.htm.

Centers for Disease Control and Prevention. (CDC). (2008d). Assisted Reproductive Technology(ART). Retrieved April 22, 2011: http://www.cdc.gov/art/ART2008/index.htm.

Centers for Disease Control and Prevention (CDC). (2009a). U.S. Obesity Trends 1985-2009. Retrieved Jan 5, 2010: http://www.cdc.gov/obesity/data/trends.html.

Centers for Disease Control and Prevention (CDC). (2009b). Healthy Youth: Making it Happen! Nutrition Success Stories. Retrieved January 5, 2009: http://apps.nccd.cdc.gov/MIH/MainPage.aspx.

Centers for Disease Control and Prevention (CDC). (2009c). Alcohol and Public Health. Retrieved: March 1, 2011: http://www.cdc.gov/alcohol/fact-sheets/underage-drinking.htm.

Centers for Disease Control and Prevention (CDC). (2009d). Lesbian, Gay, Bisexual and Transgender Health. Retrieved March 14, 2011: http://www.cdc.gov/lgbthealth/youth.htm.

Centers for Disease Control and Prevention (CDC). (2009e). Sexually Transmitted Disease Surveillance, 2008. Atlanta, GA: US Department of Health and Human Services.

Centers for Disease Control and Prevention (CDC). (2009f). Genital HPF Infection Fact Sheet. Retrieved April 1, 2011: http://www.cdc.gov/std/HPV/STDFact-HPV.htm.

Centers for Disease Control and Prevention (CDC). (2010a). YRBSS: Youth Risk Behavior Surveillance System. Retrieved from: http://www.cdc.gov/HealthyYouth/yrbs/index.htm

Centers for Disease Control and Prevention (CDC). (2010b). Cigarette Use Among High School Students --- United States, 1991—2009. Retrieved January 22, 2011: http://www.cdc.gov/mmwr/preview/mmwrhtml/mm5926a1.htm.

Centers for Disease Control and Prevention (CDC) (2010c). HIV/AIDS Among Gay and Bisexual Men. Retrieved January 15, 2011: http://www.cdc.gov/nchhstp/newsroom/docs/FastFacts-MSM-FINAL508COMP.pdf.

Centers for Disease Control and Prevention (CDC) (2010d). Health, United States, 2010. Retrieved May 15, 2011: http://www.cdc.gov/search.do?q=suicide+rates+15-24+year+2010&spell=1&ie=UTF-8.

Centers for Disease Control and Prevention (CDC) (2010 e). Morbidity mortality Weekly Report (MMWR).
        Estimated Lifetime Risk for Diagnosis of HIV Infection Among Hispanics/Latinos-37 States and Puerto Rico.

Centers for Disease Control and Prevention (CDC) (2010 f). HIV and AIDS Among Gay and
        Bisexual Men. Retrieved March 22, 2011:
        http://www.cdc.gov/nchhstp/newsroom/docs/FastFacts-MSM-FINAL508COMP.pdf.

Centers for Disease Control and Prevention (CDC) (2010g). Genital Herpes - CDC Fact Sheet. Retrieved April 1,
        2011: http://www.cdc.gov/std/herpes/STDFact-Herpes.htm.

Centers for Disease Control and Prevention (CDC) (2010 h). HIV Transmission. Retrieved June 1, 2011:
        http://www.cdc.gov/hiv/resources/qa/transmission.htm.

Centers for Disease Control and Prevention (CDC) (2010 i). HIV Among Hispanics/Latinos. Retrieved May 6, 2011:
        http://www.cdc.gov/hiv/hispanics/index.htm.

Centers for Disease Control and Prevention (CDC). (2011a). Sex History Doesn't Always Match STD Status.
        Retrieved January 9, 2011: http://www.thebody.com/content/art60114.html?wn.

Centers for Disease Control and Prevention (CDC). (2011b). Fetal Alcohol Spectrum Disorders (FASDs).
        Retrieved March 5, 2011: http://www.cdc.gov/ncbddd/fasd/facts.html.

Centers for Disease Control and Prevention (CDC). (2011c). Alcohol and Public Health. Retrieved March 22, 2011:
        http://www.cdc.gov/alcohol/fact-sheets/alcohol-use.htm.

Centers for Disease Control and Prevention (CDC). (20111d). Healthy Weight - it's not a diet, it's
        a lifestyle! Retrieved March 22, 2011: http://www.cdc.gov/healthyweight/children/.

Champlin S. (2002). Are Kids from Mars? Parents from Venus? What Each Wants from Sex Education. Paper
        Presented at Healthy Schools, Healthy People VIII. Los Angeles, California Jan 16-18, 2002.

Centers for Disease Control and Prevention (CDC). (20111e). Reports of Health Concerns Following HPV
        Vaccination. Retrieved: March 23, 2011: http://www.cdc.gov/vaccinesafety/vaccines/hpv/gardasil.html.

Center for Effective Discipline (CFED). (2011). Discipline at Schools. Retrieved April 18, 2011:
        http://www.stophitting.com/index.php?page=statesbanning.

Chasnoff, I., Burns, W., Schnoll, S. & Burns, K. (1985). Cocaine in Pregnancy. New England Journal of
        Medicine; 313:666-669.

Chau M., Kalyani T., Wright, V. (2010). National Center for Children in Poverty (NCCP). Basic Facts About
        Low-income Children, 2009 Children Aged 12 through 17 , 2009- Children Aged 12 through 17.
        Retrieved January 11, 2011: http://www.nccp.org/publications/pub_974.html.

Children of Alcoholics: Are They Different? (1990). USDHHS Alcohol Alert. National Institute On Alcohol Abuse
        and Alcoholism, No. 9 PH 288, 76:746-752. 84: 543-547.

Christensen D. (1996). Medical Tribune News Service, August 20.

Christopher S., Roosa M. (1990a). An Evaluation of Adolescent Pregnancy Prevention Program: Is' Just Say NO'
        Enough? *Family Relations*, 39:68-72.

Christopher S., Roosa M. (1990b). Evaluation of an Abstinence Only Adolescent Pregnancy Prevention Program:
        A Replication. *Family Relations,* 39:363-67.

Clarren S., Sampson, P., Laarsen, J., et al. (1987). Facial Effects of Fetal Alcohol Exposure: Assessment by Photographs and Morphometric Analysis. *American Journal of Medical Genetics,* 26:651-666.

Coates T., Makadon H. (1995). *HIV Prevention: Looking Back, Looking Ahead,* University of California, San Francisco.

Colgrove, J., (2006). The Ethics and Politics of Compulsory HPV Vaccination. *New England Journal of Medicine.* 355:2389-2391.

Committee on Child Abuse and Neglect: Guidelines for the Evaluation of Child Sexual Abuse. (1991). *Pediatrics,* 87:254-260.

Committee on Nutrition. (2003). Prevention of Pediatric Overweight and Obesity. *Pediatrics,* 112(2), 424-430.

Connelly, J., Duaso, M., & Butler, G. (2007). A Systematic Review of Controlled Trials of Interventions to Prevent Childhood Obesity and Overweight: A Realistic Synthesis of the Evidence. *Public Health,* 121(7), 510-517.

Connolly G., Alpert, H., Ferris, W. et al. (2007). Trends in Smoke Nicotine Yield and Relationship to Design Characteristics Among Popular U.S. Cigarette Brands, 1997-2005. A Report of the Tobacco Research Program Division of Public Health Practice. Harvard School of Public Health.

Cook S., Koutsky, L., King, K. (1994). Circumcision and Sexually Transmitted Diseases. *American Journal of Public Health,* 84: 197-201.

Crooks R., Baur K. (1993). *Our Sexuality.* Benjamin Cummings. New York, NY. p. 606-624.

Cross C. (2004). Genes and Alcoholism. The Human Genome, Genes and the Body. Retrieved April 1, 2005: http://www.wellcome.ac.uk/en/genome/genesandbody/hg06f013.html.

Cooper, D. (2004) Obesity and Diabetes. National Association of Hispanic Nurses, Dia de los Muertos Conference, University of California, Irvine Medical Center. May 1, 2004.

Daniel, E. (1997). *Jump Start with WebLinks,* Englewood, CO: Morton Publishing.

Dare to Be More. (2011). We Dare to Be. Retrieved February 1, 2011: http://www.dare.com/home/documents/2008AnnualReport.pdf.

David-Ferdon, C., Feldman, M. (2007). Electronic Media, Violence, and Adolescents: An Emerging Public Health Problem. *Journal of Adolescent Health.* 41: 6, S1-S5.

DefinitionofWelness, (2011). Definition of Health Education. Retrieved January 5, 2011: http://www.definitionofwellness.com/dictionary/health-education.html

De La Rosa M., Khalsa J., Rouse B. (1990). Hispanics and Illicit Drug Use: A Review of Recent Findings. *International Journal of Addiction,* 25:665-691.

Dietz W. (1998). Health Consequences Of Obesity In Youth: Childhood Predictors Of Adult Disease. *Supplement of Pediatrics,* 3 (101):518-525.

DiClemente, R., Durbin, M., Siegel, D., et al. (1992). Determinants of Condom Use Among Junior High School Students In A Minority, Inner-City School District. *Pediatrics,* 89:197-201.

DiClemente R., Hansen W., Ponton L. (1996). *Handbook of Adolescent Risk Behavior.* New York, NY: Plenum. p1.

DiClemente R., Santelli J., Crosby, R. (Eds.). (2009). *Adolescent Health: Understanding and Preventing Risk Behaviors and Adverse Health Outcomes.* Jossey-Bass/John Wiley & Sons, Hoboken, NJ.

Diaz, T., Buehler, J., Castro, K., et al. (1993). AIDS Trends Among Hispanics in the United States. *American Journal of Public Health,* 83:504-509.

Diaz, R. (1995). Latino Gay Men and The Psycho-Cultural Barriers to AIDS Prevention. In Levine M., Gagnon J., Narde P., eds. *A Plague of Our Own: The Impact of the AIDS Epidemic on Gay Men and Lesbians.* Chicago: University of Chicago Press.

DOC News and Views. (1992). *The Journal of Medical Activism.* Spring, 7:2-6.

Donovan, P. (1997). Can Statutory Rape Laws be Effective in Preventing Adolescent Pregnancy? *Family Planning Perspectives,* 29:30-34.

Drug Free Workplace Act (DFWA). (1988). 41 USC CHAPTER 10 - DRUG-FREE WORKPLACE Retrieved: March 22, 2011: http://uscode.house.gov/download/pls/41C10.txt.

Dryfoos, J. (1985). A Time for New Thinking About Teenage Pregnancy. *American Journal of Public Health.* 75:13-14.

Dryfoos J., (1990). Adolescents at Risk: Prevalence and Prevention. New York, NY: Oxford.

Dufour, M., Archer L., Gordis E. (1992). Alcohol and the Elderly, Clinic in Geriatric Medicine. *Health Promotion and Disease Prevention,* 8:134-135. University Press.

Duncan, G., Brooks-Gunn. J., (eds). (1997). *Consequences of Growing Up Poor.* New York, NY: Russell Sage Press.

Edell D. (1999). *Eat, Drink and Be Merry.* HarperCollins. New York, N.Y.

Edell, D. (2004). *Life, Liberty, and the Pursuit of Healthiness: Dr. Deans Commonsense Guide for Anything That Ails You.* HarperCollins. New York, NY.

Eisenberg M., Bearinger T., Sieving R., et al. (2004). Parents Beliefs About Condoms and Oral Contraceptives: Are They Medically Accurate? *Perspectives on Sexual and Reproductive Health.* 36:2. 50-57. Retrieved May 1, 2005: www.guttmacher.org/pubs/journals/3605004.html

Eisenberg M., Bernat, D., Bearinger L., et al. (2008). Support for Comprehensive Sexuality Education: Perspectives from Parents of School-Age Youth. *Journal of Adolescent Health,* 42:4, 352-359.

Elders J. (1994a). *Alcohol.* ABC Interactive Video Disk. American Broadcasting Company.

Elders J., Perry C., Eriksen M., et al. (1994b). The Report of the Surgeon General: Preventing Tobacco Use among Young People. *American Journal of Public Health,* 84:543-547.

Elizabeth, D., Baur, L. (2007). Adolescent Obesity: Making a Difference to the Epidemic. *International Journal of Adolescent Medicine and Health,* 19(3), 235-243.

Evans, D. (2009). Top 25 Technology Predictions. Chief Futurist, Cisco IBSG Innovations Practice. Retrieved December 14, 2010: http://www.cisco.com/web/about/ac79/docs/Top_25_Predictions_121409rev.pdf.

Farrelly, M., Davis. C., Lyndon H., et al. (2005). Evidence of a Dose—Response Relationship Between "Truth" Antismoking Ads and Youth Smoking Prevalence. *American Journal of Public Health,* 95 (3):425-431.

Farrelly, M., Davis, K., Haviland, L., Messeri, P., Healton, C. (2009). Antismoking Ads and Youth Smoking Prevalence *American Journal of Preventive Medicine*. 36:5. 379-384.

Food and Drug Administration (FDA). (2009). FDA Approves Benzoyl Lotion for the Treatment of Head Lice. Retrieved May 14, 2011: http://www.fda.gov/newsevents/newsroom/pressannouncements/ucm149562.htm.

Feighery, E., Altman, D. (1991). The Effects of Combining Education and Enforcement to Reduce Tobacco Sales to Minors. *Journal of the American Medical Association,* 266:3159-61.

Fetro, J. (1991). Step-*by-Step to Substance Use Prevention: The Planning Guide for School- Based Programs,* Santa Cruz, CA: ETR Associates.

Fiore, M., Croyle R., Curry S, et al. (2004). Preventing 3 Million Premature Deaths and Helping 5 Million Smokers Quit: A National Action Plan For Smoking Cessation. *American Journal of Public Health,* 94:205–229.

Fischer, P., Schwartz, M. (1991). Brand Logo Recognition by Children Aged 3 to 6 Years. *Journal of the American Medical Association,* 266:3145-48.

Fisher, C. (1999). The Status of Health Education in California's Public School Districts: A Comparison to State and National Recommendations and Status Reports. Unpublished Doctoral Dissertation, University of Southern California. Personal Communication.

Fletcher, G., Rosenkrantz, T. (2009). Multiple Births. Retrieved April 11, 2011: http://emedicine.medscape.com/article/977234-overview#showall.

Flegal, K., Carroll, M., Ogden, C., Curtin, L. (2010). Prevalence and Trends in Obesity among US Adults, 1999-2008. *Journal of the American Medical Association.* 20; 303(3):235-41.

Food and Drug Administration (FDA). (2006). FDA Approves the First Once-a-Day Three-Drug Combination Tablet for Treatment of HIV-1. *FDA News.* PO6-96. July 12, 2006.

Food and Drug Administration (FDA). (2007a). FDA Mandates New Warning for Nonoxynol 9 OTC Contraceptive Products Label Must Warn Consumers Products Do Not Protect Against STDs and HIV/AIDS. *FDA News.* Retrieved June 4, 2008: http://www.fda.gov/bbs/topics/NEWS/2007/NEW01758.html.

Food and Drug Administration (FDA). (2007b). FDA Approves Contraceptive for Continuous Use. Retrieved June 22, 2008: http://www.fda.gov/bbs/topics/NEWS/2007/NEW01637.html.

Forney P., Forney M., Ripley, W. (1988). Alcohol And Adolescents: Knowledge, Attitudes, and Behavior. *Journal Of Adolescent Health Care,* 9:194-202.

Fowler S., (1996). Second Hand Smoke Wide Spread. CDC Fact Sheet. Retrieved March 15, 2005: http://www.cdc.gov/od/oc/media/pressrel/second1.htm.

French, S., & Story, M. (2006). Obesity prevention in schools. In M. Goran, & M. Sothern (Ed.), *Handbook of Pediatric Obesity* (pp. 291-310.). Boca Raton, FL: Taylor & Francis.

Forhan, S., Gottlieb, S., Sternberg, M., et al. (2009). Prevalence of Sexually Transmitted Infections Among Female Adolescents Aged 14 to 19 in the United States. *Pediatrics*;124:1505–12.

Federal Trade Commission (FTC). (1999). Self-Regulation in the Alcohol Industry: A Review of Industry Efforts to Avoid Promoting Alcohol to Underage Consumers (Washington, DC: Federal Trade Commission.

Gallegos, S. (2007). Are We Still Winning Against Tobacco? A Presentation at the California Association of School Health Educators (CASHE), Annual Conference, 2007. UCLA Conference Center, Lake Arrowhead, CA.

Gambrell, A., Haffner, D. (1993). *Unfinished Business: A SIECUS Assessment of State Sexuality Education Programs.* New York: Sex Information and Education Council of the U.S.18.

Gay, Straight Alliance Network. (GSAN). (2011). Retrieved May, 2011: http://gsanetwork.org/.

Gerberding, J. (2004). Report to Congress: Prevention of Genital Human Papillomavirus Infection. Centers for Disease Control and Prevention (CDC). January, 2004.

Godek, G. (1991). *1001 Ways to be Romantic*, and (1999), Naperville, Illinois. Sourcebook Casablanca.

Godek, G. (1999). *10,000 Ways to be Romantic.* Naperville, Illinois. Sourcebook Casablanca.

Godek, G. (2009). *10,000 Ways to Say I Love You.* (2009). Naperville, Illinois. Sourcebook Casablanca.

Gold M., (1989). *Drugs of Abuse: A Comprehensive Series for Clinicians-Marijuana.* New York, NY, Plenum Book Publishers.

Gold M., (1991). *Drugs of Abuse: A Comprehensive Series for Clinician -Alcohol.* New York, NY, Plenum Book Publishers.

Gold M., (1993). *Drugs of Abuse: A Comprehensive Series for Clinicians-Cocaine.* New York, NY, Plenum Book Publishers.

Gold M., (1995). *Drugs of Abuse: A Comprehensive Series for Clinicians-Tobacco.* New York, NY, Plenum Book Publishers.

Goldberg, I., Mosca, L., Piano, M., et al. (2001). Wine and Your Heart A Science Advisory for Healthcare Professionals From the Nutrition Committee, Council on Epidemiology and Prevention, and Council on Cardiovascular Nursing of the American Heart Association. *Circulation*, 103:472-475.

Goldstein, A. *Addiction From Biology to Drug Policy.* (2001). New York, NY: Oxford University Press.

Gomez, C., Marin B. (1996). Gender, Culture and Power: Barriers to HIV Prevention Strategies For Women. *Journal of Sex Research*, 33(4): 355-62.

Gordon, T. (1973, 2001). *Teacher Effectiveness Training (TET).* Gordon Training International.

Gordon, T. (1973, 2006). *Leadership Effectiveness Training (LET).* Gordon Training International.

Glantz, S. (1987). Achieving a Smoke free Society. *Circulation* 83 (1):1-12.

Glantz, S. (1992, 1998). *Tobacco, Biology and Politics*, Waco, TX Health EDCO.

Glantz, S., Slade, J., Bero, L., et al. (1998) *Cigarette Papers.* University of California Press: Berkeley.

Glantz, S., Charlesworth, A. (1999). Tourism and Hotel Revenues Before and After Passage of Smoke-Free Restaurant Ordinances. *Journal of the American Medical Association.* 281:1911-1918.

Glantz, S., Parmley, W. (2001). Even a Little Secondhand Smoke is Dangerous. *Journal of the American Medical Association*, 286: 462-463.

Guilamo-Ramos V., Jaccard , J., Dittus P. (2010). *Parental Monitoring of Adolescents: Current Perspectives for Researchers and Practitioners.* New York: Columbia University Press.

Gyurcsik, N., Spink, K., Bray, R., et al. (2006). An Ecologically Based Examination of Barriers to Physical Activity In Students From Grade Seven Through First-Year University. *Journal of Adolescent Health*, 38, 704-711.

Hader, S., Smith D., Moore J, et al. (2001). HIV infection in women in the United States: Status at the millennium. *Journal of the American Medical Association,* 285(9):1186-1192.

Hanson, R., Venturelli, P., Fleckenstein, A. (2002). *Drugs and Society, 7th ed.* Jones and Bartlett. Sudburry, Massachusetts.

Ibid, p. 4.

Ibid, p. 26.

Ibid, p. 28.

Hamer, D., Copeland, P. (1995). The Science of Desire: The Search for the Gay Gene and the Biology of Behavior. *New England Journal of Medicine,* 332 (19):1311-1312.

Hanson, R. (2005). Alcohol Problems and Solutions: Facts and Fiction. Retrieved March 29, 2005: http://www2.potsdam.edu/alcohol-info/AlcoholFactsAndFiction.html.

Harper, D., Franco, L., Wheeler, D. (2004). Efficacy Of A Bivalent L1 Virus-Like Particle Vaccine In Prevention of Infection With Human Papillomavirus Types 16 and 18 in Young Women: a Randomized Controlled Trial. *Lancet.* 364: 1757-65.

Hashibe M, Morgenstern H, Cui Y, et al. (2006). Marijuana Use and the Risk of Lung and Upper Aerodigestive Tract Cancers: Results of a Population-based Case-control Study. Cancer Epidemiology Biomarkers Prevention, 15(10):1829–1834.

Healthy Children (2010). Alcohol: The Most Popular Choice. Retrieved March 3, 2011: http://www.healthychildren.org/English/ages-stages/teen/substance.

Healthy People 2020. (2011). Adolescent Health. Retrieved January 17, 2011: http://www.healthypeople.gov/2020/topicsobjectives2020/overview.aspx?topicid=2.

Hertz M., David-Ferdon, C. (2008). Electronic Media and Youth Violence: A CDC Issue Brief for Educators and Caregivers. Retrieved April 6, 2011: http://www.cdc.gov/ncipc/dvp/YVP/electronic_agression_brief_for_parents.pdf.

Holistic Internet Community (HIC). (2005). Critics Point Out drawbacks to 'MyPyramid.' Retrieved May 3, 2011: http://www.holistic.com/holistic/learning.nsf/ed8732a8bed2f2a4872569060015ca74/589bd61e97 49978c87256ff6005c532b!OpenDocument.

Hollander, D. (2005). Failure Rates of Male and Female Condoms Fall with Use. *International Family Planning Perspectives.* 31, 2. Retrieved May 28, 2008: http://www.guttmacher.org/pubs/journals/3109405.html.

Hurd, Y., Wang, X., Anderson, V., et al. (2006). Effects of Marijuana Exposure on the Human Fetal Brain: Molecular Imaging Studies. *Neurotoxicology and Teratology*, 28:386–402.

Institute of Medicine. (1997). Committee on Prevention and Control of Sexually Transmitted Diseases. The Hidden Epidemic: Confronting Sexually Transmitted Diseases. Eng TR and Butler WT, eds. Washington, DC: National Academy Press.

417

Health Central. (2001). *Experts Downplay the Benefits of Wine.* Retrieved March 15, 2005:
    http://www.healthcentral.com/PrintFormat/PrintFullText.cfm?id=47478

Hatcher R., Stewart, S., Trussell, J. et al. (1998). *Contraceptive Technology 17ᵗʰ Edition,* New York NY:
    Irvington Press.

Hatcher R., Stewart, S., Trussell, J. et al. (2007). *Contraceptive Technology 19ʰ Edition,* New York NY:
    Irvington Press.

Hatcher, R., Rachel, S. , Moynihan, A., (2010). *Choices.* Tiger GA. Bridging the Gap Foundation.

Hawkins, D. (2002). Elementary School Program Reduces Pregnancy, STDs, in Young Adults. *Archives of Pediatrics
    & Adolescent Medicine,* 156:438-47.

Hawkins, D., Lishner, D., and Catalano, R. (1985). Childhood Predictors of Adolescent Substance Abuse, Etiology
    of Drug Abuse: Implications for Prevention. Washington, D.C. USDHHS.

Hawkins, D., Lishner, D., and Catalano, R. (2000). Developmental Risk Factors for Youth Violence. *Journal of
    Adolescent Health.* 26:3:176-186.

Halsey, E. (1997). Is milk really good for you? Not for everyone. Correspondent Cable News Network, January 9.

Hiller, S. (2007). Microbicide Overview. CDC HIV Prevention Conference, Atlanta, GA. December 3, 2007.

Hirsch, D. (2011). Suicide Prevention Center. L.A. Suicide Prevention Center. Didi Hirsh Mental
    Health Services. Retrieved July 3, 2011: http://www.didihirsch.org/services/emergency/spc.

Hollingworth, W., Ebel, B., et al. (2006). Prevention of Deaths From Harmful Drinking in the United States:
    The Potential Effects of Tax Increases and Advertising Bans on Young Drinkers. *Journal of Studies on
    Alcohol,* 67:300-308.

Holmes, K., Mardh, P., Sparling, P., et al. (eds). (1999). *Sexually Transmitted Diseases.* New York, NY:
    McGraw Hill.

Huntington Beach Community Clinic. (HBCC). (2002). Huntington Beach, CA. Classroom presentation.
    Personal communication.

Jellinek, M. (2010). *The Disease Concept of Alcoholism.* Eastford CT: Martino Publishing.

Ickovics J., Rodin J. (1992). Women and AIDS in the United States: Epidemiology, Natural History, and Mediating
    Mechanisms. *Health Psychology,* 11:1-16.

Inspector General. (1992). U.S. Department Of Health And Human Services. Youth and Alcohol: Dangerous
    and Deadly Consequences: Report to the Surgeon General, April.

International Association for K-12 Online Learning (iNACOL). (2010). iNACOL National Standards of Quality for
    Online Courses. Retrieved March 3, 2011:http://www.inacol.org/research/nationalstandards/index.php.

Iribarren C., Tekawa I., Sidney S., et al. (1999). Effect of Cigar Smoking on the Risk of Cardiovascular Disease,
    Chronic Obstructive Pulmonary Disease, and Cancer in Men. *The New England Journal of Medicine,*
    340:1773-1780.

Jacobs, E. (1990). Clinical Professor of Medicine, USC School of Medicine. Marijuana and Tobacco Update.
    Presented At The Annual Conference Of California Association Of School Health Educators (CASHE).
    November 18, 1990. Pacific Palisades, CA.

Jasuja, G., Chou, C., Riggs, N., et al. (2008). Early Cigarette use and Psychological Distress as Predictors of Obesity Risk in Adulthood. *Nicotine & Tobacco Research*, 10(2), 325-335.

Jehl, D. (1994). Surgeon General Forced to Resign by White House. *New York Times.* December 9, 1994.

Jia, H., Lubetkin, E., (2010). *Science Daily.* Obesity-Related Quality-Adjusted Life Years Lost in the U.S. from 1993 to 2008. Retrieved Jan 5, 2011: http://www.sciencedaily.com/releases/2010/08/100803072934.htm.

Jorgensen R., Potts V., Camp B. (1993). Project Taking Charge: Six-Month Follow-Up of a Pregnancy Prevention Program for Early Adolescents. *Family Relations,* 42: 401-06.

Jemmott, J., Jemmot L., Fong, G. (1992). Reductions In HIV Risk-Associated Sexual Behaviors Among Black Male Adolescents: Effects Of An AIDS Prevention Intervention. *American Journal of Public Health,* 82: 372-377.

Johnson, B. (1992). *For Their Sake.* P. 5-6. Martinsville, IN: For Kids Sake.

Jones, F. (1987). *Positive Classroom Discipline.* New York NY: Mc Graw Hill.

Jones, F. (2008). *Tools for Teaching.* New York NY: Mc Graw-Hill. Retrieved May 7, 2008: http://www.fredjones.com/.

Jones K., Smith D. (1973). Recognition of the Fetal Alcohol Syndrome in Early Infancy. *Lancet* 2: 999-1001.

Journal of the American Medical Association. (1996). Medical News & Perspectives April 24. Author.

Kaiser Family Foundation. (2000). Fact Sheet on Teen Sexual Activity. Retrieved May 7, 2008: www.kff.org.

Kaiser Family Foundation. (2011). The HIV Epidemic in the United States. Retrieved April 22, 2011: http://www.kff.org/hivaids/upload/3029-12.pdf.

Kershaw T., Lewis, J., Nicolla, J, et al. (2004). Sexual Risk Following a Sexually Transmitted Disease Diagnosis: The More Things Change the More they Stay the Same. *Journal of Behavioral Medicine*, 27(5):445-461.

KidsHealth. (2008). How TV affects your child. Retrieved May 10, 2008: http://www.kidshealth.org/parent/positive/family/tv_affects_child.html.

Kidsnet (1997). Kidsnet Clearinghouse for Children's Television. 6856 Eastern Ave, NW, Suite208, Washington, DC 20012. Retrieved May 22, 2008: http://www.kidsnet.org.

Kipke, M., Iverson, E., Moore, et al. (2007). Food And Park Environments: Neighborhood-Level Risks For Childhood Obesity In East Los Angeles. *Journal of Adolescent Health*, 40(4), 325-333.

Kirby D., Barth R., Leland, et al. (1991). Reducing the Risk: Impact of a New Curriculum on Sexual Risk-Taking. *Family Planning Perspectives*, 23: 253-263.

Kirby D. (1994). School-based Programs to Reduce Sexual Risk Behaviors: A Review of Effectiveness, *Public Health Reports*, 109: 339-60.

Kirby D. (1997). *No Easy Answers: Research Findings on Programs to Reduce Teen Pregnancy.* Washington, DC: The National Campaign to Prevent Teen Pregnancy.

Kirby D. (2007). *Emerging Answers: Research Findings on Programs to Reduce Teen Pregnancy and Sexually Transmitted Diseases.* National Campaign to Prevent Teen and Unplanned Pregnancy. Washington, D.C.

Kirby D., Haffner, D. (1992). The Need For School-Based Sexuality Education. *Principles and Practices of Student Health,* Wallace (ed.). Oakland, CA: Third Party Press.

Kirby D., Short, L., Collins J., et al. (1994). School-Based Programs to Reduce Sexual Risk Behaviors: A Review of Effectiveness. *Public Health Reports,* 109: 339-360.

Kinsey A., Pomeroy, W. (1948). *Sexual Behavior in the Human Male.* Philadelphia, PA Saunders.

Klich, W. (2008). American Academy of Pediatrics. Baylor University School of Medicine.

Klurfeld D. (1987). The Role Of Dietary Fiber In Gastrointestinal Disease. *Journal of the American Dietetic Association,* 87 :1172-1177.

Koblinsky M., Timyan, J., and Gay J., eds. (1993). *The Health of Women: A Global Perspective.* San Francisco, CA: Westview Press.

Kohler P., Manhart L., Lafferty E. (2008). Abstinence-Only Comprehensive Sex Education and the Initiation of Sexual Activity and Teen Pregnancy. *Journal of Adolescent Health.* 42(4): 344-351.

Koop C. (1989). Smoking: Everything You and Your Family Need to Know. Home Box Office Productions.

Koop C., Ibid. p. 188.

Koop C. (1991). Koop, *Memoirs of America's Family Doctor.* New York, NY: Random House, p.164-184.

Krebs-Smith S., Cook A., Subar A., et al. (1996). Fruit and Vegetable Intakes of Children and Adolescents in the United States. *Archives of Pediatrics and Adolescent Medicine,* 150:81-86.

Krisberg, K., (2007). Suicide Risk Higher Among Gays, Lesbians. *The Nations Health.* Dec, 1.

Krugman R. (1992). Abuse: Nature and significance of the problem. *Principles and Practices of Student Health,* Wallace (ed.) Oakland, CA: Third Party Press.

Lavin A., Shapiro G., Weill K. (1992). *Creating an Agenda for School- Based Health Promotion: A Review of Selected Reports.* Harvard School Health Education Project, Department of Health and Social Behavior, Harvard School of Public Health.

Lancet, (2011). Author. Circumcision Helps Cut HPV Transmission Rate, Study Finds. *The Lancet, News release,* Jan. 6, 2011.

Lewis K., Bear B. (2009). *Manual of School Health.* New York, NY: Saunders.

Lindberg, L., Jones, R., Santelli, J. (2008). Perception That Teens Frequently Substitute Oral Sex for Intercourse a Myth. *Journal of Adolescent Health.* 43(1).

Lindgren, M., Byers, R., Thomas, T. (1999). Trends in Perinatal Transmission of HIV/AIDS in The United States. *Journal of the American Medica l Association.* 282:531-538.

Livingston A. (2006). The Condition Of Education 2006 In Brief. Washington, DC: U.S. Department of Education, National Center for Education Statistics.

Lender M., Kirby J. (1982). *Drinking in America.* New York, NY: Saunders.

Los Angeles Times. (1997). March 21, Page 1.

Los Angeles Times. (1997). May 1, Page 1.

Los Angeles Times. (1998). March 8, Page 1.

Los Angeles Times. (2002). June 21, Page 1.

Los Angeles Times. (2005). March 31, Page A9.

Lovato, C., Allensworth O., Chan M. (1989). *School Health in America: An Assessment of State Policies to Protect and Improve the Health of Students. (5th Edition).* American School Health Association, Kent, OH.

Lowry, R., Wechsler, H., Galuska, D.A., Fulton, J.E., & Kann, L. (2002). Television Viewing and its Associations with Overweight, Sedentary Lifestyle, and Insufficient Consumption of Fruits and Vegetables Among US High School Students: Differences by Race, Ethnicity, and Gender. *Journal of School Health,* 72(10), 413-421.

Loya R. (Unpublished Research) (1993). Personal Communication, February 14, 1993.

Lucia, S. (1963). *A History of Wine as Therapy.* Philadelphia, PA: J. B. Lippincott.

McCarthy A. (2000). *Healthy Teens: Facing the Challenges of Young Lives.* Bridge Communications. Birmingham, Michigan.

MacKay A., Duran, C. (2007). *Adolescent Health in the United States, 2007.* National Center for Health Statistics. 2007. Retrieved May 1, 2008:http://www.cdc.gov/nchs/data/misc/adolescent2007.pdf.

Madden P., Grube J. (1994). The Frequency and Nature of Alcohol and Tobacco Advertising in Televised Sports, 1990 through 1992. *American Journal of Public Health,* 84:297-299.

Mamsen, L., Lutterodt1, M., Andersen, E., Skouby, S., Sorensen, K., Andersen, C. and Byskov A. (2010). Cigarette Smoking During Early Pregnancy Reduces the Number of Embryonic Germ and Somatic Cells. *Human Reproduction.* 00:00-1-7.

Martinez, C., Mosher, G., Abma, J., et al. (2005). Fertility, Family Planning, and Reproductive Health of U.S. Women: Data from the 2002 National Survey of Family Growth. National Center for Health Statistics. Vital Health Stat 23(25).

Martinez, C., Mosher, G., Dawson, D., (2004). Teenagers In The United States: Sexual Activity, Contraceptive Use, and Childbearing, 2002. National Center for Health Statistics. Vital Health Stat 23 (24).

Main D., Iverson, D., McGloin J., et al. (1994). Preventing HIV Infection Among Adolescents: Evaluation of a School-Based Education Program. *Preventive Medicine,* 23:409-417.

Males, M. (1993). School-age pregnancy: Why Hasn't Prevention Worked? *Journal of School Health,* 63: 429-432.

Males, M. (2002). *Los Angeles Times.* February 17, 2002.

McNeely, C., Blanchard, J. (2010). *The Teen Years Explained: A Guide to Healthy Adolescent Development.* Johns Hopkins Bloomberg School of Public Health.

Mayo Clinic Newsletter. (2004). Secondhand Smoke: Protect Yourself from the Dangers. Retrieved March 14, 2005: http://www.mayoclinic.com/invoke.cfm?id=CC00023&si=2424.

Mayo Clinic Mental Health. (2008). Anorexia Nervosa. (Mayo, 2008). Retrieved July 10, 2008: http://www.mayoclinic.com/health/anorexia/DS00606/DSECTION=2.

Mann, J. (1999). Wanted: A Realistic Attitude Toward Teen Sex. *Washington Post.* Jan 20, 1999, p. C14.

Marin, B. (1995). Analysis of AIDS Prevention among African Americans and Latinos in the United States. Report Prepared for the Office of Technology Assessment.

Marin, B., Gomez, C., Hearst, N. (1993). Multiple Heterosexual Partners and Condom Use among Hispanics and Non-Hispanic Whites. *Family Planning Perspectives,* 25:170-174.

Marin, B. (2003). HIV Prevention in the Hispanic Community: Sex, Culture, and Empowerment. *Journal of Transcultural Nursing,* 14(3). 186-192).

Mason, M, (1994). The Man Who Has A Beef with Your Diet. *Health.* May/June.

Matza N., English J., Lovato C., et al. (1993). *Project Teach: Health Education Preservice Resource Manual.* California Department of Education, Sacramento, CA.

Matza, N. (1994). Tobacco Use Prevention. In *The Comprehensive School Challenge.* Cortese P., Middleton K., (ed.). Santa Cruz, CA: ETR Associates.

Matza, N. (1994-2003). Adolescent Survey Of Health Problems In A Multicultural, Multiethnic High School. Unpublished.

Matza, N. (1998). *Creative Health Science Lessons.* Copy Pro, Long Beach, CA.

Matza, N. (2004). *Health Science for Teachers Revised Edition.* Copy Pro, Long Beach, CA.

Matza, N. (2007). *Health Science for Teachers, 3rd Edition.* Copy Pro, Long Beach, CA.

Matza, N. (2010). *Health Science for Teachers, 4th Edition.* Copy Pro, Long Beach, CA.

Marx, E., Wooley, S., Northrop, D. (1998). *Health is Academic.* Columbia University. New York, NY: Teachers College Press.

Mead, J., Balch, G., Maggio, E. (1985). *Investigating Child Abuse.* Brea, CA: For Kids Sake Press.

Mead, J. (1999, 2006, 2007). Personal communication.

Medical News & Perspectives. (1996). April 24 *Journal of the American Medical Association.*

Metropolitan Life Insurance. (1985). *Statistical Bulletin,* 66: 20-23.

Metropolitan Life Foundation. (1988). An Evaluation of Comprehensive Health Education in American Public Schools. New York.

Miller, K., Clark, L., Moore, J. (1997). Sexual Initiation with Older Male Partners and Subsequent HIV Risk Behavior Among Female Adolescents. *Family Planning Perspectives,* 29:212-214.

Mittleman M., Lewis R,. Maclure M., Sherwood J., Muller J. (2001). Triggering Myocardial Infarction by Marijuana. Circulation 103(23): 2805–2809.

Mokdad, A. (2003). Prevalence of Obesity, Diabetes, and Obesity-Related Health Risk Factors, 2001. *Journal of the American Medical Association,* 289:76-79.

Mokdad, A., Marks J., Stroup D, et al. (2004). Actual Causes of Death in The United States, 2000. *Journal of the American Medical Association,* 291:1238-1245.

Molnar, B., Gortmaker, S., Bull, F., et al. (2004). Unsafe to Play? Neighborhood Disorder and Lack of Safety Predict Reduced Physical Activity among Urban Children and Adolescents. *American Journal of Health Promotion,* 18(5), 378-386.

Montgomery, S., Ekbom, A. (2002) in BMJ, Enheten för Klinisk Epidemiologi, Karolinska Sjukhuset L1:00, SE-171 76, Stockholm, Sweden.

Morbidity and Mortality Weekly Report. (MMWR). (1988). 37,133-137.

Morbidity and Mortality Weekly Report. (MMWR). (1993). 42 (RR-14).

Morbidity and Mortality Weekly Report. (MMWR). (1996). Youth Risk Behavior Surveillance- United States, 1995. 45 (SS-4).

Morbidity and Mortality Weekly Report. (MMWR). (2006). Youth Risk Behavior Surveillance- United States, 2005. 55-(SS-4).

Morbidity and Mortality Weekly Report. (MMWR). (2010). 59 (43);1400-1406. State-Specific Prevalence of Cigarette Smoking and Smokeless Tobacco Use Among Adults-United States, 2009.

Morrison S., Rogers P., Thomas M. (1995). Alcohol and Adolescents. *Pediatric Clinics Of North America,* 42:371-387.

Morrison, M., Krugman, D., Park, P. (2007) Under the Radar: Smokeless Tobacco Advertising in Magazines with Substantial Youth Readership *American Journal of Public Health,* 98(3): 543-548.

Moss N., Krieger N. (1995). Measuring Social Inequalities In Health: Report on the Conference of the National Institutes of Health. *Public Health Reports,* 110:302-305.

Murkamal, K., (2008). The Effects of Smoking and Drinking on Cardiovascular Disease and Risk Factors. NIAAA. Retrieved June, 22, 2008: http://pubs.niaaa.nih.gov/publications/arh293/199-202.htm.

National Association of State Boards of Education. (1998). *Policy Update: The Role of Education in Teen Pregnancy Prevention.* Alexandria, VA: Policy Information Clearinghouse.

National Association of State Boards of Education. (2004). Childhood Overweight: The Current Scope of the Problem. The National Association of State Boards of Education. December, 2004. 15-18.

National Adolescent Student Health Survey. (NASHS) (1988). *Health Education,* 19:4-8.

National Center for HIV/AIDS, Hepatitis, STD & Prevention. (NCHHS). (2010). HIV in the United States: An Overview. Retrieved July 4, 2011: http://www.cdc.gov/hiv/topics/surveillance/resources/factsheets/us_overview.htm.

National Campaign to Prevent Teen and Unplanned Pregnancy. (2006). By the Numbers: The Public Cost of Teen Childbearing in California. Retrieved April 22, 2011: http://www.thenationalcampaign.org/costs/pdf/states/california/onepager.pdf

National Campaign to Prevent Teen and Unplanned Pregnancy. (2011) What Teens Want Adults to Know About Teen Pregnancy. Retrieved January 11, 2011: http://www.thenationalcampaign.org/resources/pdf/pubs/talking_back.pdf

National Cancer Institute (2010). 7:24. Retrieved December 14, 2010: http://www.cancer.gov/ncicancerbulletin/121410/page2.

National Institute on Alcohol Abuse and Alcoholism. (2008). Alcohol: A Women' Health Issue. Retrieved March 8, 2011: http://pubs.niaaa.nih.gov/publications/brochurewomen/women.htm#problem.

National Prevention Information Network (NPIN). (2004). STDs Today. Retrieved May 25, 2008: http://www.cdcnpin.org/scripts/std/std.asp#19.

National Prevention Information Network (NPIN). (2008). Decline in Teen Sex Levels Off, Survey Shows. Retrieved July 2, 2008: http://www.cdcnpin.org/scripts/display/NewsDisplay.asp?NewsNbr=51007.

National Institute on Drug Abuse (NIDA). News Release. (2002). Significant Deficits in Mental Skills Observed in Toddlers Exposed to Cocaine Before Birth. Retrieved July,9, 2008: http://www.drugabuse.gov/DrugPages/Cocaine.html.

National Institute on Drug Abuse (NIDA) (2003). Preventing Drug Use Among Children and Adolescents, Second Edition. Retrieved: March 8, 2011: http://www.nida.nih.gov/pdf/prevention/RedBook.pdf.

National Institute on Drug Abuse (NIDA). (2006). NIDA Info, Marijuana Facts. Retrieved June 22, 2008: http://www.nida.nih.gov/infofacts/marijuana.html.

National Institute on Drug Abuse (NIDA). (2007). Cocaine. Retrieved August 22, 2008: http://www.nida.nih.gov/drugpages/cocaine.html.

National Institute on Drug Abuse (NIDA) (2010a). Commonly Abused Drugs. Retrieved January 23, 2011: http://www.nida.nih.gov/DrugPages/DrugsofAbuse.html.

National Institute on Drug Abuse (2010b). NIDA Info Facts: Marijuana. Retrieved April 9, 2011: http://www.nida.nih.gov/infofacts/marijuana.html.

National Institute of Mental Health (NIMH). (2008). Eating Disorders. Retrieved July 1, 2008: http://www.nimh.nih.gov/health/publications/eating-disorders/summary.shtml.

National Cancer Institute (NCI) (2001). Risks Associated with Smoking Cigarettes with Low Machine-Measured Yields of Tar and Nicotine. Smoking and Tobacco Control Monograph 13.

National Center for Mental Health Promotion and Youth Violence Prevention. (NCMHP). (2004) Retrieved May 15, 2008: http://www.promoteprevent.org/publications/center- briefs/prevention_brief_key_strategies3.pdf.

National Center for Health Statistics (NCHS) (2004). Teens Delaying Sexual Activity: Using Contraception More Effectively. Retrieved February 5, 2005: http://www.cdc.gov/nchs/pressroom/04news/teens.htm.

National Education Association. (1997a). What's a Teacher to Do. *NEA Today.* Feb., p.25.

National Education Association. (1997b). *NEA Today.* Getting Tough on Gun Violence. April p.22.

National Guidelines Task Force (1991). Guidelines For Comprehensive Sexuality Education: Kindergarten-12th Grade. New York: Sex Information And Education Council Of The U.S.

National Household Survey on Drug Abuse, (NASDA). (2001).

National Survey on Drug Use and Health (NSDUH). (2007). Patterns and Trends in Inhalant Use by Adolescent Males and Females: 2002-2005. Retrieved April 1, 2011: http://www.drugabuse.gov/NIDA_notes/NNvol21N4/BBoard.html#Adolescent.

National Vital Statistics Report (NVSR) (2010). Births, Marriages, Divorces, and Deaths: Provisional Data for 2009. Retrieved January 5, 2010: http://www.cdc.gov/nchs/data/nvsr/nvsr58/nvsr58_25.htm.

Nazario, S. (1999). Heavy Drinking by Mexican American Men. *Los Angeles Times,* March 21.

NCHS (1996). Health, United States. Report, with Special Profile of Women's Health, HHS# 017-022-01339-8 (June 18, 1996).

Nestle, M. (2002). *Food Politics.* Berkeley, CA: University of California Press.

Nestle, M. (2006). *What to Eat.* New York, NY: North Point Press.

New York Times. (1997). March 21, Page 1.

Nguyen-Michel, S., Unger, J., Spruijut-Metz, D. (2007). Dietary Correlates of Emotional Eating in Adolescence. *Appetite*, 49(2), 494-499.

Nonsmoker's Bill of Rights. (1992). National Interagency Council on Smoking and Health, 419 Park Avenue, New York, New York. 10016.

Novello, A. (1993). Surgeon General's Report to the American Public on HIV Infection and AIDS. Centers for Disease Control and Prevention (CDC). Retrieved May 5, 2011: http://wonder.cdc.gov/wonder/sci_data/misc/type_txt/sgrpt.asp.

Nutrition and Your Health: Dietary Guidelines for Americans. (2000). U.S. Department of Agriculture and Health and Human Services. Washington, DC.

O' Carrol, P., Saltzman L., Smith, J. (1992). Suicide. Principles and Practices of Student Health, Wallace (ed.) Oakland, CA. Third Party Press.

Office of Safe and Drug Free Schools. (OSDFS). (2011). Title IV, SDFSCA of the Improving America's Schools Act of 1994.

Ogden, C., Carroll, M., Flegal, K., (2008). High Body Mass Index for Age Among U.S. Children and Adolescents, 2003-2006. *Journal of the American Medical Association,* 299(20): 2401-2405.

Olson, A., Seidler, B., Goodman, D., et al. (2004). School Professionals' Perceptions About the Impact of Chronic Illness in the Classroom. *Archives of Pediatrics and Adolescent Medicine.* 158:53-58.

Panlilio, A., Cardo, D., Grohskopf, L., et al. (2005). Updated U.S. Public Health Service Guidelines for the Management of Occupational Exposures to HIV and Recommendations for Postexposure Prophylaxis. *Morbidity, Mortality Weekly Report* (MMWR), 54(RR09);1-17.

Park, M., Mulye, T., Adams, S, Brindis, C. Irwin, C. (2006). The Health Status of Young Adults in the U.S. *American Journal of Adolescent Health,* 29, 305-317.

Patrick, C. (1953 *Alcohol, Culture, and Society.* Durham, NC: Duke University Press. Reprint Edition by AMS Press, New York, 1970.

Pease, A. (2004). *Signals.* New York, NY: Bantam Books.

Pease, A. , Pease, B. (2006). *The Definitive Book of Body Language.* New York, NY: Bantam Books.

Peck, M. (1987). In Youth Suicide: The Role of School Consultation, *Adolescent Psychiatry*, S. Feinstein (ed.). Vol. 14.

Pechmann, L. Levine, et al., (2005). Impulsive and Self-Conscious: Adolescents' Vulnerability to Advertising and Promotion, *Journal of Public Policy and Marketing.* 24: 202-221.

Pentz, M., Jasuja, G., Rohrbach, L., et al. (2006). Translation in Tobacco and Drug Abuse Prevention/Cessation Research. *Evaluation and the Health Professions*, 29(2), 246-271.

Parascandola, M. (2001). Parascandola Responds. *American Journal of Public Health* 91: 1345-1345.

Perspectives on Sexual and Reproductive Health. (2004), 36(2): 50-57. Author.

Peterson, J., Catania J., Dolcini M, et al. (1993). Data from the National AIDS Behavioral Surveys III. Multiple Sexual Partners Among Blacks In High-Risk Cities. *Family Planning Perspectives*, 25:263-267.

Peterson, J. (1995). AIDS Related Risks And Same-Sex Behaviors Among African American Men. In *AIDS, Identity And Community*. Herk G., Green B., Eds. Thousand Oaks, CA: Sage Publications. p. 85-104.

Peterson, K., Fox, M. (2007). Addressing The Epidemic Of Childhood Obesity Through School-Based Interventions: What Has Been Done And Where Do We Go From Here? *The Journal of Law, Medicine, & Ethics*, 35(1), 113-130.

Peterson-Portis, M., Burhansstipanov, L. (1986). *What the Teacher Should Know About Student Health Problems,* 2nd ed. Edina, MN: Bellwether Press.

Pew Hispanic Center. (2011). Demographic Profiles of Hispanics in California. Retrieved Feb 1, 2011: http://pewhispanic.org/reports/report.php?ReportID=117.

Polen M., Sidney S, Tekawa I., Sadler M, & Friedman G. (1993). Health Care Use by Frequent Marijuana Smokers Who do not Smoke Tobacco. Western Journal of Medicine 158(6):596–601.

Psychiatric News. (2011). NIDA Director Warns Against Complacency on Marijuana Use. Retrieved April 22, 2011: http://pn.psychiatryonline.org/content/46/3/10.1.full.

Protect the Truth. The Truth Campaign. (2010). Author. Retrieved February 1, 2011: http://www.protectthetruth.org/truthcampaign.htm.

Ray, N., (2006). *Lesbian, Gay, Bisexual And Transgender Youth an Epidemic of Homelessness*. The National Gay and Lesbian Task Force Policy Institute. Retrieved June 19, 2008: http://graphics8.nytimes.com/packages/pdf/national/20070307HomelessYouth.pdf.

Reuters News Service (1996). Majenie, P. April 2, 1996. The Male Contraceptive.

Rivera (Matza), M. (2005). *Pride and Prejudice: The Effects of Hispanic Culture on School Health.* California School Nurses Organization (CSNO) Project. CSNO Conference Feb. 6, 2005. Hollywood, CA.

Robertosn, J. (2001). Excerpts from The Transactions of the Medical Society of the State of California, 1898. Relation Existing Between the Sexual Organs and Insanity, with Especial Reference to Masturbation. *Western Journal of Medicine.* 175 (1).

Robins, C., Kaplan, H., Martin, S. (1985). Antecedents of Pregnancy Among Unmarried Adolescents. *Journal of Marriage and the Family.* 47: 567-83.

Rogers, P., Adger, H., (1993). Alcohol And Adolescents State Of The Art Reviews. *Adolescent Medicine* 4:295-304.

Roosa, M., Christopher, F. (1990). Evaluation Of An Abstinence-Only Adolescent Pregnancy Program: A Replication. *Family Relations,* 39: 363-367.

Roper, S. (1994). *Teens Talk about Sex: Adolescent Sexuality in the 90s.* New York, NY: Starch Worldwide.

Ross, M., Darren V., Grafham D., et al. (2005). The DNA sequence of the human X Chromosome. *Nature, 434*, 325 – 337.

Sabogal, F., Faigeles, B., Catania, J. (1993). Multiple Sex Partners Among Hispanics in the United States: The National AIDS Behavioral Surveys. *Family Planning Perspectives,* 25:257-262.

Sackoff, J., Hanna, D., Pfeiffer, M., et al. (2006). Causes of Death among Persons with AIDS in the Era of Highly Active Antiretroviral Therapy: New York City. *Annals of Internal Medicine,* 145; 6, 397-406.

Saksvig, B., Catellier, D., Pfeiffer, K, et al. (2007). Travel by Walking Before and After School and Physical Activity Among Adolescent Girls. *Archives of Pediatrics & Adolescent Medicine,* 161(2), 153-158.

Samber, S. (1997). Researchers Are on Their Way to Understanding Genetic Role in Alcoholism. *NCADI Reporter.*

Sargent, D., Wills, T., Stoolmiller, M. et al. (2006). Alcohol Use in Motion Pictures and Its Relation with Early-Onset Teen Drinking. *Journal of Studies on Alcohol* 67:54-65.

Sawhill, I. (1998). Teen Pregnancy Prevention: Welfare Reform's Missing Component. Washington, DC: The Brookings Institution. Policy brief 38:1–8.

Science Daily. (2008). Author. Three Out of Four Women Have Disordered Eating. Retrieved April, 3, 2011: http://www.sciencedaily.com/releases/2008/04/080422202514.htm.

Sharma, M. (2007). International School-Based Interventions For Preventing Obesity In Children. *Obesity Review,* 8(2), 155-167.

Shetty, A., Maldonado, Y. (2001) HIV Transmission Prevention Of Perinatal HIV-1 Transmission In The United States. *Neonatal Reviews.* 2001; 2:E83-E93, American Academy of Pediatrics.

Siegel, M., Albers, A., Cheng, M., et al. (2008). Local Restaurant Smoking Regulations and the Adolescent Smoking Initiation Process. *Archives of Pediatrics and Adolescent Medicine,* 162(5) 399.

Siegel, R. (1989, 2005). *Intoxication: The Universal Drive for Mind Altering Substances.* Park Street Press. Rochester, Vermont.

Snyder, L., Milici, F., Slater, M., et al. (2006). Effects of Alcohol Advertising Exposure on Drinking Among Youth. *Archives of Pediatrics and Adolescent Medicine,* 160:18-24.

Squires, S. (1986). America's Drugs of Abuse. *Washington Post Health,* November 4, 1986.

Sroka, S. (1992, 1997, 2004). STD Update. Lectures given at the California Association of School Health Educators (CASHE), Annual Conference, Pacific Palisades, Lake Arrowhead CA.

Sroka, S. (2008, 2009). Personal Communication.

Sternberg, R. Barnes., M. (1988). *The Psychology of Love.* New Haven: Yale University Press.

Stobbe, M. (2010). US teen birth rate still far higher than W. Europe. Retrieved August, 22, 2011: http://www.physorg.com/news/2010-12-teen-birth-higher-europe.html.

Strunin, L., Hingson R. (1994). Alcohol Use And Risk For HIV Infection. Alcohol And Health Research World, Vol. 17, No. 1, National Institute On Alcohol Abuse and Alcoholism.

Sieving, R., Resnick M., Bearinger L, et al., (1997). Cognitive and Behavioral Predictors Of Sexually Transmitted Disease Risk Behavior Among Sexually Active Adolescents. *Archives of Pediatric Adolescent Medicine,* 151:243-251.

Smith, D., Wesson D., Calhoun S. (1997). Newsletter, Haight Ashbury Free Clinics San Francisco, CA, 94118.

Sorahan, B. (1997). Marijuana and Youth. *British Journal of Cancer.* (Jan.) 2:76.

St. Lawerence, J., Brasfield T., Jefferson K., et al., (1995). Cognitive-Behavioral Intervention to Reduce African American Adolescents' Risk for HIV Infection. *Journal Of Consulting and Clinical Psychology,* 63: 221-237.

Sturm, R. (2005). Childhood Obesity-What We Can Learn from Existing Data on Societal Trends. *Preventing Chronic Disease.* Retrieved May 21, 2008: http://www.cdc.gov/pcd/issues/2005/jan/04_0038.htm.

Tannen, D. (2001). *You Just Don't Understand.* New York, NY: Harper Collins.

The National Campaign to Prevent Teen Pregnancy. (1997). *Whatever Happened to Childhood?* The Problem of Teen Pregnancy in the United States. Washington, DC: Author.

The National Campaign to Prevent Teen Pregnancy. (2008). *Teen Population by Race and Ethnicity.* The Problem of Teen and Unplanned Pregnancy in the United States. Washington, DC: Author.

Tobacco Free Kids. (2010). FDA Authority Over Tobacco. Retrieved: January 31, 2011: http://www.tobaccofreekids.org/reports/fda/.

Tucker, L. (1987). Alcohol and Adolescents: Who Drinks and Who Doesn't. *Pediatrician,* 14:32-38.

U.S. Bureau of the Census. (2007). Foreign-Born Population Of The United States: Current Population Survey— March 2004. Detailed Tables (PPL-176). Retrieved: June 1, 2008: www.census.gov/population/www/socdemo/foreign/ppl-176.html.

U.S. Department of Education (1994). *Growing Up Drug Free: A Parent's Guide to Prevention* National Clearinghouse for Alcohol and drug Information Retrieved: June 22, 2008: http://www.health.org.

U.S. Public Health Service. (1990). Model Sale of Tobacco Products to Minors Act. Washington, DC: U.S. Department of Health and Human Services, Public Health Service.

U.S. Department of Health and Human Services (USDHHS), (1986). The Health Consequences of Involuntary Smoking: A Report of the Surgeon General. (CDC). 87-8398.

USDHHS. (1988). The Health Consequences of Smoking: A Report of the Surgeon General. DHHS Publication (CDC) 88-8046.

USDHHS. (1989). Centers for Disease Control, Office on Smoking and Health, Smoking Tobacco and Health: A Fact Book, P. 11

USDHHS. (1990). Public Health Service: *Healthy People 2000: National Health Promotion and Disease Prevention Objectives.* Washington, DC, U.S. Government Printing Office.

USDHHS. (1991,1992). National Center for Health Statistics, United States and Prevention Profile: Health, p. 170.

USDHHS. (1993a). National Institute on Drug Abuse, National Household Survey on Drug Abuse: Population Estimates. pp. 83, 89, 29, 35, 41, 53.

USDHHS. (1993b). National Institute on Alcohol Abuse and Alcoholism, Eighth Special Report to the U.S. Congress on Alcohol and Health, P. 245.

USDHHS. (1993c). National Institute on Drug Abuse, Alcohol Use and Alcohol Problems in Women: Epidemiological Trends and Problems Of Drug Dependence 1992. Research Monograph 132, P. 30.

USDHHS. (1995). Centers for Disease Control and Prevention, *MMWR*, 44:5.

USDHHS. (2008). Public Health Service: *Healthy People 2010.* Retrieved May 22, 2008: http://www.healthypeople.gov/.

USDHHS. (2008). 2008 Physical Activity Guidelines for Americans Summary. Retrieved April 23, 2011: http://www.health.gov/paguidelines/guidelines/summary.aspx.

USDHHS. (2010a). Public Health Service. Office of the Surgeon General. A Report of the Surgeon General: How Tobacco Smoke Causes Disease The Biology and Behavioral Basis for Smoking-Attributable Disease. Retrieved December 14, 2010: http://www.surgeongeneral.gov/library/tobaccosmoke/report/index.html.

USDHHS. (2010b). Public Health Service. (2010. Women's Health, 2010. Retrieved February 1, 2011: http://mchb.hrsa.gov/whusa10/pdfs/w10.pdf.

USPHS (1988). *America Responds to AIDS.* Centers for Disease Control. Pamphlet.

USPHS (1988). *Vital Statistics of the United States: Vol. 1 Natality.* Washington, DC: U.S. Department of Health and Human Services, Tables 1-6, 1-32, 1-59.

U.S. Department of Justice. (1994). Bureau Of Justice Statistics Special Report, Murder In Families, P. 3.

Varnes, J. (1994). Preservice Education: Providing Health Knowledge for All Teachers, in *The Comprehensive School Health Challenge,* Middleton K., Cortese P., (ed.), Santa Cruz, CA: ETR Associates.

Valleroy, L. MacKellar, D., Karon J., et al. (1998). HIV Infection in Disadvantaged Out-Of- School Youth: Prevalence for U.S. Job Corps Entrants, 1990 Through 1996. *Journal Of Acquired Immune Deficiency Syndromes And Human Retrovirilology,* 19:67-73.

Ventura, S. Albert, B. (2007) U.S. Centers for Disease Control and Prevention, National Campaign to Prevent Teen and Unplanned Pregnancy, Washington, CDC report, Births: Preliminary Data for 2006.

Vinciullo, F., Bradley, B. (2009). A Correlational Study of the Relationship of a Coordinated School Health Program and School Achievement: A Case for School Health. *Journal of School Nursing.* 25:453.

Volkow, N., (2004). MDMA, Ecstasy Abuse. Retrieved: April 12, 2005: http://www.drugabuse.gov/ResearchReports/MDMA/.

Volkow, N. (2003). *Preventing Drug Use Among Children and Adolescents A Research Based Guide for Parents and Educators.* National Institute of Health, National Institute on Drug Abuse. 2nd ed. NIH Publication No. 04-4212(A).

Wardle, J., Brodersen, N., Boniface, D. (2007). School-Based Physical Activity and Changes in Adiposity. *International Journal Of Obesity*, 31(9), 1464-1468.

Waxman, H., (2004). The Content Of Federally Funded Abstinence-Only Education Programs United States. House of Representatives Committee on Government Reform Minority Staff Special Investigations Division, December, 2004.

Webster, W., Brown-Woodman, P., (2005) Cocaine as a Cause of Congenital Malformations of Vascular Origin: Experimental Evidence in the Rat. Wiley, New York.

Women's Health. (2007). HRSA's. Women's Health USA 2007 Reports Sharp Drop In HIV- Positive Newborns, USA. Retrieved July 2, 2008: http://mchb.hrsa.gov/whusa_07/.

Women's Sports Foundation. (1998). *The Women's Sports Foundation Report: Sport and Teen Pregnancy.* East Meadow, NY: Author.

Wetzstein, C. (1999). Europe's Take on Teen-Age Sexuality Hit, Despite Pluses. *Washington Times,* January 27, 1999. P. A18.

Werner, E. (2005). Governor Proposes Banning Junk Food at Schools: Fruits, Vegetables and Milk Offered as Healthy options. *Associated Press.* Retrieved: March 12, 2005.

White House at Work. (1998). www.white-house.gov.

Wind, R., (2008). Perception that Teens Frequently Substitute Oral Sex for Intercourse a Myth. Guttmacher Institute News Release. Retrieved: January 5, 2011:http://www.guttmacher.org/media/nr/2008/05/20/index.html.

Wire, S. (2008). Federal Funding of Abstinence-Only Sex Education Programs Debated. *Los Angeles Times,* April 24, 2008, P 1.

World Bank. (2003). *Adolescent Health.* Retrieved: May 8, 2008: http://siteresources.worldbank.org/HEALTHNUTRITIONANDPOPULATION/Resources/281627-1095698140167/Rosen-AHDFinal.pdf.

World Health Organization (WHO), (1991). World No Tobacco Day, May, 1991.

World Health Organization (WHO), (2005). Global Strategy on Diet, Physical Activity and Health. Retrieved March 19, 2005: http://www.who.int/dietphysicalactivity/publications/facts/obesity/en/.

World Health Organization (WHO). (2008). *WHO Report On The Global Tobacco Epidemic*, 2008. Retrieved May 15, 2008.

Yurgelun-Todd H., Pope H. (1996). The Residual Cognitive Effects of Heavy Marijuana Use in College Students. *Journal Of The American Medical Association,* 275:521-527.

Zabin, L. (1992). Teenage Pregnancy. *Principles and Practices of Student Health,* Wallace (ed.) Oakland, CA: Third Party Press.

Zabin, L., Hirsh M, Smith E, et al. (1986). Evaluation Of a Pregnancy Prevention Program for Urban Teenagers. *Family Planning Perspectives,* 3:119-126.

Code of Ethics of the Education Profession

Preamble

The educator, believing in the worth and dignity of each human being, recognizes the supreme importance of the pursuit of truth, devotion to excellence, and the nurture of the democratic principles. Essential to these goals is the protection of freedom to learn and to teach and the guarantee of equal educational opportunity for all. The educator accepts the responsibility to adhere to the highest ethical standards.

The educator recognizes the magnitude of the responsibility inherent in the teaching process. The desire for the respect and confidence of one's colleagues, of students, of parents, and of the members of the community provides the incentive to attain and maintain the highest possible degree of ethical conduct. The Code of Ethics of the Education Profession indicates the aspiration of all educators and provides standards by which to judge conduct.

The remedies specified by the NEA and/or its affiliates for the violation of any provision of this Code shall be exclusive and no such provision shall be enforceable in any form other than the one specifically designated by the NEA or its affiliates.

PRINCIPLE I

Commitment to the Student

The educator strives to help each student realize his or her potential as a worthy and effective member of society. The educator therefore works to stimulate the spirit of inquiry, the acquisition of knowledge and understanding, and the thoughtful formulation of worthy goals.

In fulfillment of the obligation to the student, the educator--

- Shall not unreasonably restrain the student from independent action in the pursuit of learning.
- Shall not unreasonably deny the student's access to varying points of view.
- Shall not deliberately suppress or distort subject matter relevant to the student's progress.
- **Shall make reasonable effort to protect the student from conditions harmful to learning or to health and safety.**
- Shall not intentionally expose the student to embarrassment or disparagement.
- Shall not on the basis of race, color, creed, sex, national origin, marital status, political or religious beliefs, family, social or cultural background, or sexual orientation, unfairly--
  a. Exclude any student from participation in any program b. Deny benefits to any student c. Grant any advantage to any student
- Shall not use professional relationships with students for private advantage.
- Shall not disclose information about students obtained in the course of professional service unless disclosure serves a compelling professional purpose or is required by law.

PRINCIPLE II

Commitment to the Profession

The education profession is vested by the public with a trust and responsibility requiring the highest ideals of professional service.

In the belief that the quality of the services of the education profession directly influences the nation and its citizens, the educator shall exert every effort to raise professional standards, to promote a climate that encourages the exercise of professional judgment, to achieve conditions that attract persons worthy of the trust to careers in education, and to assist in preventing the practice of the profession by unqualified persons. In fulfillment of the obligation to the profession, the educator--

- Shall not in an application for a professional position deliberately make a false statement or fail to disclose a material fact related to competency and qualifications.
- Shall not misrepresent his/her professional qualifications.
- Shall not assist any entry into the profession of a person known to be unqualified in respect to character, education, or other relevant attribute.
- Shall not knowingly make a false statement concerning the qualifications of a candidate for a professional position.
- Shall not assist a noneducator in the unauthorized practice of teaching.
- Shall not disclose information about colleagues obtained in the course of professional service unless disclosure serves a compelling professional purpose or is required by law.
- Shall not knowingly make false or malicious statements about a colleague.
- Shall not accept any gratuity, gift, or favor that might impair or appear to influence professional decisions or action.
  Adopted by the NEA 1975 Representative Assembly.

APPENDIX

Health Problem Solving/Application and Synthesis

Read the problems carefully and be prepared for a class discussion.

Diagrams, Charts

1. Health Problem Solving.

2. Diagrams of the female and male reproductive systems should be correlated with the readings in chapters 9 and 10.

3. Review the chart on gonorrhea for class discussion on STDs.

4. Pyramid diagrams illustrate both the 1992 and 2005 version of the Food Guide Pyramid, the new **MyPlate Icon (2011),** and the Mediterranean pyramid version.

Health Problem Solving: Application & Synthesis

REMEMBER: Teachers do not diagnose health problems; they only report observations.

OBJECTIVE: Students will discuss health related problems in the classroom and suggest practical solutions.

Instructions

It is now about the third week of the semester and the following situations came about in your class. You are a first year probationary teacher. Assemble into coed groups of three or four. Read the following scenarios in your groups and solve the student health problem. Be prepared to review your group discussion with the class.

1.   Julio is one of your students from El Salvador. He came to talk to you about his dad and uncle who have been offering him cigarettes while they go fishing. His dad speaks only limited English and works for the school district as a custodian. Julio hates smoking and he does not want to offend his family. He is 14 and likes to play soccer. **Offer him some help.**

2.   While traveling to the county museum, Mary was talking to you about her boyfriend Leroy. He wants to have sex with her on prom night and has promised that he is still a virgin. Leroy wants to do this on Prom night. They met in church and are very much in love. Mary is 17 and feels that it is finally about time to do it! All of her girlfriends have been bugging her to *ditch the virgin thing.* Hannah is her best friend and said that she only has anal intercourse with Bobby so she can still be a virgin! She really trusts you as her teacher and would never talk to her parents. They are too religious. **What will you do? What should you do?**

3.   One morning in your first period class, Rosie was touched on the buttocks by a very quiet conservative boy named Leo. This happened just as class was dismissed and you witness the entire process. You told Leo to apologize and yet sensed that Rosie was very embarrassed. **What will you do? What should you do?**

4.   Oscar is captain of the varsity cheer leading team. He is a very popular student and works hard to keep the team in shape and have them prevent injuries at games. Two of the sophomore girls, Myra and Cynthia are very attractive and each weighs about one hundred pounds. They both earn straight A's. Myra and Cynthia like to run 5-8 miles everyday after two hours of cheer leading practice. **What can Oscar do? What health problem do you suspect? What should you do?**

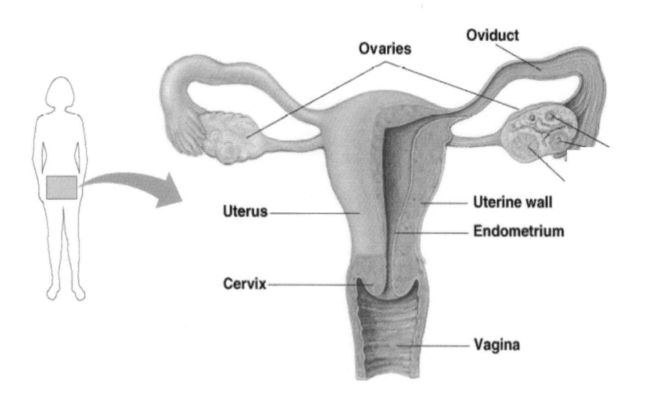

Female Reproductive System (Frontal View)

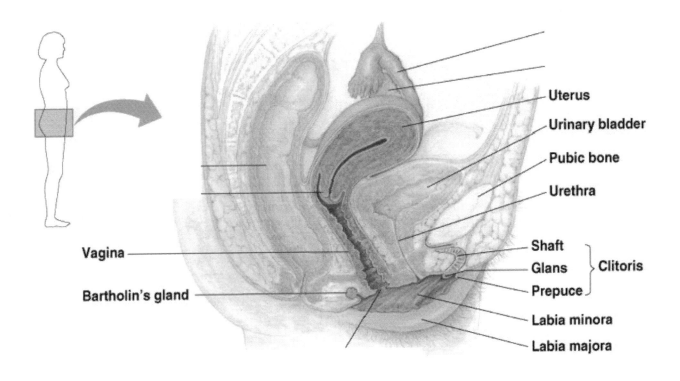

Vagina

Bartholin's gland

Uterus

Urinary bladder

Pubic bone

Urethra

Shaft ⎤
Glans ⎬ Clitoris
Prepuce ⎦

Labia minora

Labia majora

Female Reproductive System (Side View)

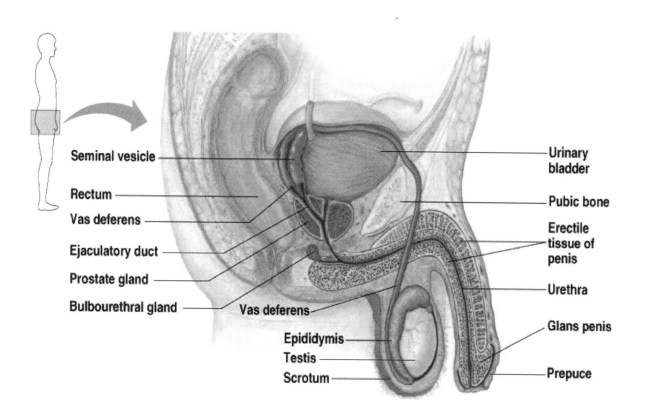

Male Reproductive System (side view)

Female Menstrual/Ovarian Cycle

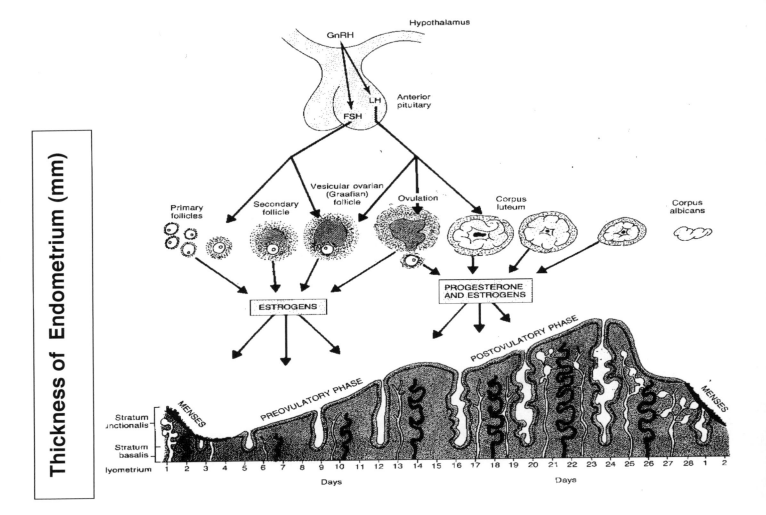

Thickness of Endometrium (mm)

Stratum
functionalis

Stratum
basalis

Myometrium

MENSES

PREOVULATORY PHASE

POSTOVULATORY PHASE

MENSES

Days 1 2 3 4 5 6 7 8 9 10 11 12 13 14 15 16 17 18 19 20 21 22 23 24 25 26 27 28 1 2

Days

Days

**Time (days)
When is it Safe?**

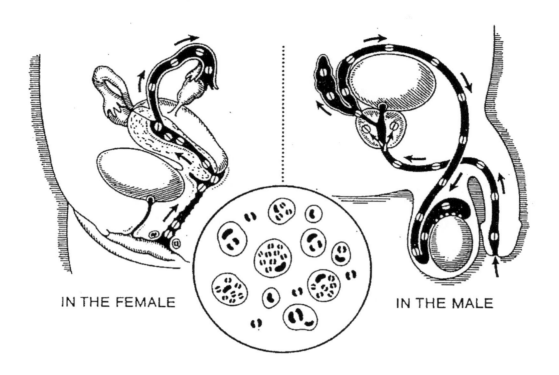

IN THE FEMALE   IN THE MALE

<u>Diagram illustrating pelvic infection of an STD (gonorrhea).</u> What differences do you notice related to the route of infection of the male vs. the female anatomy? Why are most females asymptomatic? Label the following <u>during</u> the classroom lecture:

<u>Male</u>   **<u>Female</u>**

penis   vagina
urethra   urethra
vas deferens   bladder
gonorrhea bacteria   uterus
testis   Fallopian tube
bladder
gonorrhea bacteria

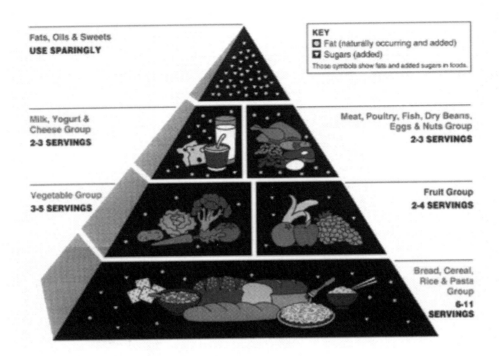

Food Guide Pyramid (USDA, 1992)

Food Guide Pyramid (USDA, 2005)

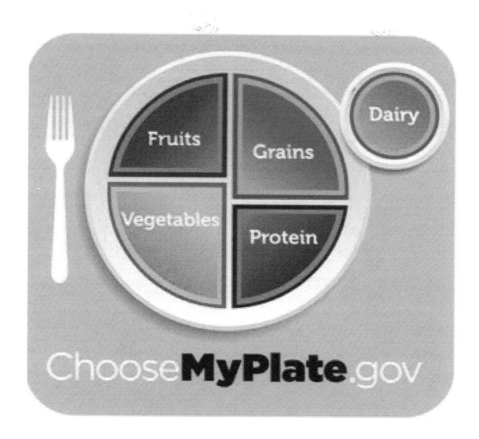

ChooseMyPlate Logo (2011)

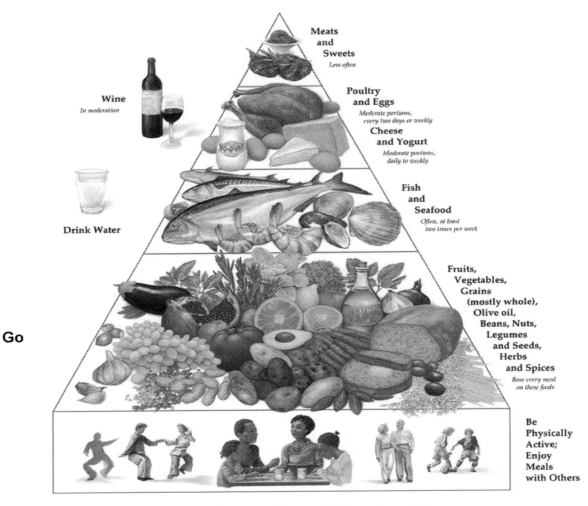

Mediterranean Pyramid for additional variations.

44348318R00250